The Edinburgh Companion to Modernism and Technology

Edinburgh Companions to Literature and the Humanities

Recent volumes in the series
The Edinburgh Companion to Animal Studies
Edited by Lynn Turner, Undine Sellbach and Ron Broglio

The Edinburgh Companion to Contemporary Narrative Theories
Edited by Zara Dinnen and Robyn Warhol

The Edinburgh Companion to Ezra Pound and the Arts
Edited by Roxana Preda

The Edinburgh Companion to Elizabeth Bishop
Edited by Jonathan Ellis

The Edinburgh Companion to Gothic and the Arts
Edited by David Punter

The Edinburgh Companion to Literature and Music
Edited by Delia da Sousa Correa

The Edinburgh Companion to D. H. Lawrence and the Arts
Catherine Brown and Susan Reid

The Edinburgh Companion to the Prose Poem
Mary Ann Caws and Michel Delville

The Edinburgh Companion to Nonsense
Anna Barton and James Williams

The Edinburgh Companion to Virginia Woolf and Contemporary Global Literature
Edited by Jeanne Dubino, Catherine W. Hollis, Paulina Pajak, Celise Lypka and Vara Neverow

The Edinburgh Companion to Irish Modernism
Maud Ellmann, Sian White and Vicki Mahaffey

The Edinburgh Companion to the Essay
Mario Aquilina, Nicole B. Wallack and Bob Cowser Jnr.

The Edinburgh Companion to Vegan Literary Studies
Laura Wright and Emelia Quinn

The Edinburgh Companion to Modernism and Technology
Alex Goody and Ian Whittington

The Edinburgh Companion to Jane Austen and the Arts
Joe Bray and Hannah Moss

The Edinburgh Companion to Modernism in Contemporary Theatre
Adrian Curtin, Nicholas Johnson, Naomi Paxton and Claire Warden

The Edinburgh Companion to Women in Publishing, 1900–2000
Nicola Wilson, Elizabeth Gordon Willson, Alice Staveley, Helen Southworth, Daniela La Penna, Sophie Heywood and Claire Battershill

The Edinburgh Companion to British Colonial Periodicals
Caroline Davis, David Finkelstein and David Johnson

The Edinburgh Companion to First World War Periodicals
Marysa Demoor, Cedric van Dijck and Birgit Van Puymbroeck

The Edinburgh Companion to Don DeLillo and the Arts
Catherine Gander

The Edinburgh Companion to Literature and Sound Studies
Helen Groth and Julian Murphet

The Edinburgh Companion to Modernism, Myth and Religion
Suzanne Hobson and Andrew D. Radford

The Edinburgh Companion to the Eighteenth-Century British Novel and the Arts
Jakub Lipski and M-C. Newbould

The Edinburgh Companion to Curatorial Futures
Bridget Crone and Bassam El Baroni

Please see our website for a complete list of titles in the series
https://edinburghuniversitypress.com/series/ecl

Forthcoming
The Edinburgh Companion to Charles Dickens and the Arts
Edited by Juliet John and Claire Wood

The Edinburgh Companion to the Brontës and the Arts
Amber Regis and Deborah Wynne

The Edinburgh Companion to Science Fiction and the Medical Humanities
Gavin Miller, Anna McFarlane and Donna McCormack

The Edinburgh Companion to W. B. Yeats and the Arts
Tom Walker, Adrian Paterson and Charles Armstrong

The Edinburgh Companion to Modernism and Technology

Edited by Alex Goody and Ian Whittington

EDINBURGH
University Press

Edinburgh University Press is one of the leading university presses in the UK. We publish academic books and journals in our selected subject areas across the humanities and social sciences, combining cutting-edge scholarship with high editorial and production values to produce academic works of lasting importance. For more information visit our website: edinburghuniversitypress.com

© editorial matter and organisation, Alex Goody and Ian Whittington 2022, 2025
© the chapters their several authors 2022, 2025

Edinburgh University Press Ltd
13 Infirmary Street
Edinburgh EH1 1LT

First published in hardback by Edinburgh University Press 2022

Typeset in 10/12 Adobe Sabon by
IDSUK (DataConnection) Ltd

A CIP record for this book is available from the British Library

ISBN 978 1 4744 6054 5 (hardback)
ISBN 978 1 3995 5709 2 (paperback)
ISBN 978 1 4744 6055 2 (webready PDF)
ISBN 978 1 4744 6056 9 (epub)

The right of Alex Goody and Ian Whittington to be identified as the editor of this work has been asserted in accordance with the Copyright, Designs and Patents Act 1988, and the Copyright and Related Rights Regulations 2003 (SI No. 2498).

Contents

List of Figures — viii
Acknowledgements — xi

Introduction: Modernist Technology Studies — 1
Alex Goody and Ian Whittington

Part I. Machines

1. Electricity: Technologies and Aesthetics — 23
   Laura Ludtke

2. Clocks: Modernist Heterochrony and the Contemporary Big Clock — 36
   Charles Tung

3. Print: Anaïs Nin's Embodied Encounters with Print Technology — 51
   Jennifer Sorensen

4. Subways: Underground Networks Through Modernist Poetry and Prose — 63
   Sunny Stalter-Pace

5. Automobiles: The Modernist Gaze and Speed's Visual Limit-field — 78
   Enda Duffy

6. Aeroplanes: Rethinking Aeriality in a Long 1930s — 91
   Leo Mellor

7. Robots: Gendered Machines and Anxious Technophilia — 105
   Katherine Shingler

Part II. Media

8. Materials: Glass, Iron and Ghostly Fabric — 125
   David Trotter

CONTENTS

9. Advertising: Magazine Ads and the Creation of Femininity in Early Twentieth-century America   138
   Einav Rabinovitch-Fox

10. Photography: Gertrude Käsebier and the Maternal Line of Sight   155
    Alix Beeston

11. X-rays: Technological Revelation and its Cultural Receptions   175
    Tom Slevin

12. Cinema: Notes on Germaine Dulac's 'Integral Cinema', Form and Spirit   192
    Felicity Gee

13. Radio: Blindness, Disability and Technology   212
    Emily Bloom

14. Music: Modernist Remediation and Technologies of Listening   226
    Josh Epstein

15. Performance: Machine Dances and the Avant-garde's Technological Imaginary   243
    Emilie Morin

16. Amplification: At Home with *Marlene Dietrich Overseas*   257
    Damien Keane

Part III. Bodies

17. Sex: Hypnosis, Hormones, Birth Control and the Modernist Body   273
    Jana Funke

18. Race: Fordism, Factories and the Mechanical Reproduction of Racial Identity   286
    Joshua Lam

19. Technics: Education and Pharmakon in Lawrence, Simondon and Stiegler   300
    Jeff Wallace

20. Germs: The Shocks, Politics and Aesthetics of Microbial Modernism   314
    Maebh Long

21. Noise: Labour, Industry and Embodiment in Interwar Factory Fiction   328
    Anna Snaith

Part IV. Systems

22. Nation: GPO Documentaries and Infrastructures of the Nation-state   345
    Janice Ho

23. Infrastructure: Women Writers Confront Large Technological Systems   362
    Jennifer L. Lieberman

24. Paperwork: Atomic Age Bureaucracy in C. P. Snow's *Strangers and Brothers*   376
    Caroline Z. Krzakowski

25. Information: Literature and Knowledge in the Age of Bradshaw
    and Baedeker   390
    James Purdon

26. Computation: The Work of Calculation Between Human and Mechanism   404
    Andrew Pilsch

27. Networks: Modernism in Circulation, 1920–2020   417
    Shawna Ross

28. War: Modernism in Camouflage, Strategic Fantasy and the
    Technological Sublime   432
    Patrick Deer

Notes on Contributors   447

Index   451

Figures

Figure 2.1	The Time Traveller's mantel clocks in George Pal's *The Time Machine*, 1960, and Doc Brown's dresser clocks in Robert Zemeckis's *Back to the Future*, 1985.	43
Figure 2.2	The Doomsday Clock on the cover of the *Bulletin of Atomic Scientists*, 1947, and the staircase inside the Clock of the Long Now, 2011.	44
Figure 2.3	Edward Curtis's 'In a Piegan Lodge', 1910, and the architectural design for a US Post Office building with clock tower in the *Annual Report of the Supervising Architect of the Treasury Department*, 1888, reprinted in Lois Craig's *The Federal Presence*, 1984.	46
Figure 7.1	Marcel Duchamp, *Mariée (Bride)*, 1912. Philadelphia Museum of Art, The Louise and Walter Arensberg Collection, 1950. © Photo SCALA, Florence. © Succession Marcel Duchamp / ADAGP, Paris and DACS, London 2021. / © Jacques Villon / ADAGP, Paris and DACS, London.	110
Figure 7.2	Marcel Duchamp, *La Mariée mise à nu par ses célibataires, même (The Large Glass)*, 1915–23. Philadelphia Museum of Art, bequest of Katherine S. Dreier, 1952. © Photo SCALA, Florence. © Association Marcel Duchamp / ADAGP, Paris and DACS, London 2021.	112
Figure 7.3	Francis Picabia, *Jeune fille américaine dans l'état de nudité*, *291*, 5–6 (July–August 1915), p. 4. © ADAGP, Paris and DACS, London 2021.	113
Figure 7.4	Francis Picabia, *Fille née sans mère*, *291*, 4 (June 1915), p. 2. © ADAGP, Paris and DACS, London 2021.	114
Figure 7.5	Francis Picabia, *Voilà ELLE*, *291*, 9 (November 1915), p. 3. © ADAGP, Paris and DACS, London 2021.	115
Figure 7.6	Marius de Zayas, 'Elle', *291*, 9 (November 1915), p. 2.	116
Figure 9.1	Cannon Towels advertisement, *Vogue*, 1 October 1931. Image published with permission of ProQuest LLC. Further reproduction is prohibited without permission.	142
Figure 9.2	Ford advertisement, *Vogue*, 1 April 1924. Image published with permission of ProQuest LLC. Further reproduction is prohibited without permission.	144

Figure 9.3	'The Suffrage and the Switch', General Electric advertisement, *The Independent*, 18 August 1923.	146
Figure 9.4	'This Beauty Every Girl Can Have', Palmolive advertisement, *The Ladies' Home Journal*, January 1922. Image published with permission of ProQuest LLC. Further reproduction is prohibited without permission.	150
Figure 10.1	Gertrude Käsebier, 'Lollipops', ca. 1910. Digital positive from the original gelatin silver negative. Library of Congress, Gift of Mina Turner, 2006684252.	156
Figure 10.2	Gertrude Käsebier, 'Blessed Art Thou among Women', 1899. Photogravure. Brooklyn Museum, Gift of Mr and Mrs Miguel LaSalle and Peter Sinclair, 83.263.	158
Figure 10.3	Gertrude Käsebier, 'The Manger (Ideal Motherhood)', 1899. Platinum print. J. Paul Getty Museum, 84.XM.160.1.	159
Figure10.4	Gertrude Käsebier, Hermine Turner photographing Mason and Mina Turner on the roof of Käsebier's studio at 315 Fifth Avenue (variant of prize-winning photograph in Kodak advertising contest), ca. 1909. Platinum print. George Eastman Museum, Gift of Hermine Turner. Courtesy of the George Eastman Museum.	164
Figure 10.5	Kodak catalogue cover, ca. 1900s. Image courtesy of the Martha Cooper Collection.	165
Figure 10.6	Gertrude Käsebier's Photographic Workroom, ca. 1915. Special Collections, University of Delaware Libraries, Gift of William I. Homer.	166
Figure 10.7	Gertrude Käsebier, 'Real Motherhood', 1900. Platinum on tissue. Museums Collections, Special Collections and Museums, University of Delaware, Gift of Philip and Laura T. Shevlin, 1994.07.003.	169
Figure 11.1	Wilhelm Röntgen, X-ray photograph of Anne Berthe Röntgen, 22 December 1895.	176
Figure 11.2	'Variations sur les rayons X', *La Nature*, May 1896.	177
Figure 11.3	'An X-ray shadow picture', *Popular Electricity in Plain English* magazine, May 1909.	180
Figure 11.4	Illustration from *Life* magazine, February 1896.	180
Figure 11.5	Umberto Boccioni, *Development of a Bottle in Space*, 1912. Metropolitan Museum of Art, Bequest of Lydia Winston Malbin, 1989.	185
Figure 11.6	Umberto Boccioni, *Table + Bottle + House*, 1912. Pencil on paper. Civico Gabinetto dei Desegni, Castello Sforzesco, Milan.	186
Figure 11.7	Marcel Duchamp, *Nude Descending a Staircase, No. 2*, 1912. Philadelphia Museum of Art. The Louise and Walter Arensberg Collection. © Association Marcel Duchamp / ADAGP, Paris and DACS, London 2021.	189
Figure 12.1	*Arabesques*, Germaine Dulac, 1929.	195
Figure 12.2	*Arabesques*, Germaine Dulac, 1929.	196
Figure 12.3	Intertitle, *La Coquille et le clergyman*, Germaine Dulac, 1927.	202

LIST OF ILLUSTRATIONS

Figure 12.4	*Thèmes et variations*, Germaine Dulac, 1928.	205
Figure 12.5	*Thèmes et variations*, Germaine Dulac, 1928.	206
Figure 13.1	'Blind listener, Mr Oransby (right), listening to his Crystal Radio Set with headphones, December 1929'. Reproduced with permission from the BBC Photo Library.	220
Figure 14.1	BBC Engineer, in *BBC: The Voice of Britain*, dir. Stuart Legg (BFI).	233
Figure 14.2	Sir Adrian Boult conducting the BBC Symphony Orchestra in a performance of Beethoven's Fifth Symphony, in *BBC: The Voice of Britain*.	233
Figure 14.3	Sir Adrian Boult's baton giving a downbeat, in *BBC: The Voice of Britain*.	233
Figure 14.4	Hand of a BBC engineer during Beethoven performance, in *BBC: The Voice of Britain*.	234
Figure 14.5	Schoolyard round game, in *Listen to Britain*, dir. Humphrey Jennings and ed. Stewart McAllister (BFI).	236
Figure 14.6	Factory loudspeaker, in *Listen to Britain*.	236
Figure 14.7	Women singing to *Music While You Work*, in *Listen to Britain*.	236
Figure 14.8	Final frame of *Listen to Britain*.	238
Figure 15.1	Copy print: Members of the Bauhaus Stage Workshop on the Roof of the Studio Building, 1927 (printed ca. 1948), Harvard Art Museums/Busch-Reisinger Museum, Gift of Herbert Bayer, © President and Fellows of Harvard College, © T. Lux Feininger, © Estate of T. Lux Feininger, BR48.121.	253
Figure 22.1	Railway tracks, *Night Mail*. BFI National Archive; COI / Crown ©.	349
Figure 22.2	Railway switch levers, *Night Mail*. BFI National Archive; COI / Crown ©.	349
Figure 22.3	Telegraph wires, *Night Mail*. BFI National Archive; COI / Crown ©.	349
Figure 22.4	Pigeonholes, *Night Mail*. BFI National Archive; COI / Crown ©.	350
Figure 22.5	The ocular power of the expert, *The Coming of the Dial*. BFI National Archive; COI / Crown ©.	352
Figure 22.6	Post office staff working together, *6:30 Collection*. BFI National Archive; COI / Crown ©.	353
Figure 22.7	'Gutted GPO Dublin'. The Postal Museum ©.	356
Figure 22.8	Dudley Buxton, 'Automatic Suffragette Exterminating Pillar-Box (Patent NOT Applied For) Postcard'. The Postal Museum ©.	358
Figure 27.1	Network graph of Virginia Woolf's *Mrs Dalloway*. © Samuel Alexander. Reproduced with permission.	418
Figure 27.2	Network graph of John Dos Passos's *USA*. © Samuel Alexander. Reproduced with permission.	419

Acknowledgements

THE EDITORS WOULD like to thank Edinburgh University Press, and particularly Jackie Jones, for the opportunity to edit this volume. We would also like to thank Susannah Butler, whose patience and editorial good judgement were both much appreciated, and all of our authors, who have managed to produce such brilliance in the midst of a global pandemic. We thank them for their goodwill, their fortitude and their intellectual generosity. Special thanks go to Felicity Gee for stepping in at the eleventh hour to provide an excellent chapter on 'Cinema' for this volume. Our gratitude also goes to our anonymous readers for their kind and useful feedback on our proposal, and to all our colleagues who gave advice and support as we worked on this volume.

Alex's personal thanks go to the School of English and Modern Languages at Oxford Brookes University, who supported her work on the volume; in particular she would like to thank Antonia Mackay and Andrea Macrae for their sheer brilliance. She is also grateful to the wider modernist studies community in the UK, who have made it a sustaining environment in which to do academic research. Finally, she would like to thank all the Willoughby-Goodys (and Cooks and Ashworths) for their love and care, with special thanks to Jasmine.

Ian's personal thanks go to his colleagues at the University of Mississippi, whose flexibility and compassion allowed him the time to focus on shepherding this volume through a pandemic and new parenthood. In particular, he is grateful to Ivo Kamps, Caroline Wigginton, Dan Stout, Matt Bondurant and Ally Nick. Most importantly, he would like to thank Claire Byrne, for making it all worth it, and young Torin Byrne, for making it all new.

Introduction:
Modernist Technology Studies

Alex Goody and Ian Whittington

IN THE SPRING of 2020, almost a century after his final novel was published, E. M. Forster was suddenly current. On social media, on the BBC website and in web publications like *The Nautilus*, commentators hemmed in by the global Covid-19 pandemic found in Forster an unlikely prophet of their newly isolated and richly mediated existence (Perkowitz 2020; Gompertz 2020). Confined to their homes, wrapped in a machinic embrace, lulled by the hum of electronics and gorging on information whose circulation they were themselves sustaining, readers across the globe might be forgiven for identifying with the protagonists, not of Forster's Edwardian novels of class and interpersonal relations, but of his 1909 novella 'The Machine Stops'. One of the earliest descriptions of a total media system as the twentieth century would come to know it, 'The Machine Stops' imagines humankind ensconced in honeycomb-like cells underground, with music, books and information available at the touch of a button. Travel, though once common, has become an anxious experience, as residents of an earth altered by unspecified ecological devastation resist the urge to journey by airship merely to see the interior of another human residence. Presiding above it all – until its titular arrest – is the Machine, a substitute God in the form of an all-surrounding technological envelope whose continued smooth functioning has become its own justification. As the character Vashti tells her son, Kuno, 'You mustn't say anything against the Machine' (Forster 1928: 4).

Forster, attentive as he was to the nuances of embodied human connection, saw in his own time the first whispers of a technologised future in which humans risked a terrible corporeal attenuation: 'Men seldom moved their bodies,' the narrator tells us; 'all unrest was concentrated in the soul' (10). Kuno, who emerges as the doomed hero of the tale, struggles against the perceptual effects of the technological cocoon. Kuno's attempts to convince his mother of the Machine's dehumanising effects ground Forster's tale in the language of its *fin-de-siècle* media ecosystem: 'We say "space is annihilated," but we have annihilated not space, but the sense thereof. We have lost a part of ourselves' (17). Better, in Kuno's mind, to return to an unmediated, direct bodily experience of the world in which 'Man is the measure' (18).

Forster's prediction may have been overly dire, but what stands out – and what binds our historical moment to his, modernist, one – is his ability to envision a global system of linked technologies whose contours and relations we have inherited. 'The Machine Stops' imagines a metastasised version of the socially and historically specific media system whose early twentieth-century emergence, as Julian Murphet has argued, was crucial to the radical reshaping of the arts that we know today under the name of modernism (Murphet 2009: 10–15). Since the turn of the millennium, modernist scholars have seized on the central significance of technology in newly interdisciplinary readings of the period that have emerged under the auspices of the 'new modernist studies' first described by Douglas Mao and Rebecca Walkowitz in their 2008 *PMLA* report on the state of the field. Mao and Walkowitz argue that critical attention to the proliferation of technologies in the modernist era – particularly the role that mass communications play in promoting global and transnational ways of thinking and writing – represents a vibrant new direction in modernist studies (742–5). This *Edinburgh Companion to Modernism and Technology* fully realises the vibrancy of this new direction and captures how modernist technology studies have developed, and continue to develop, in the twenty-first century. By focusing on the historical relationship between modernist practices and technologies of production, consumption, distribution and representation, the manner in which writers and artists have explored the human impact of new technologies, and the literary and artistic questions raised by new technologies, this volume presents modernism, modernity and technology as mutually defining, conceptually intertwined categories that demand to be considered together.

Of course, the turn to technology in modernist studies pre-dates the 'new' modernist expansion of the field: the foundational text of American studies, Leo Marx's *The Machine in the Garden*, had placed technology at the centre of American culture back in 1964, reading *The Great Gatsby* as a modern fable of the archetypal 'protean conflict figured by the machine's increasing dominance of the visible world' (364). In the same period, erstwhile literary scholar Marshall McLuhan was using William Shakespeare, Ezra Pound and James Joyce to spark his theories about the constitutive function of mediation in *The Gutenberg Galaxy* (1962) and *Understanding Media* (1964). In *The Mechanic Muse* (1987), Hugh Kenner – a student of McLuhan's in the 1940s – made significant claims about the impact of the technological environment of the early twentieth century on the aesthetics of modernism in Pound, Joyce, T. S. Eliot and Samuel Beckett. Cecelia Tichi's *Shifting Gears*, from the same year, deployed the 'gear and girder technology' of American modernity as a direct analogy for Ernest Hemingway, John Dos Passos and William Carlos Williams's 'radically new conception [. . .] of the written word' (1987: 16). Stephen Kern's *The Culture of Time and Space 1880–1918* (1983) and Martha Banta's *Taylored Lives: Narrative Productions in the Age of Taylor, Veblen and Ford* (1993) are significant volumes in the development of modernist technology studies, exploring how radical shifts in the human conception and experience of the world derive from changes in technology and culture, but are not restricted to a single technological innovation or sphere of life. As these foundational works make plain, and the chapters of this volume corroborate, modernists themselves were keenly aware of the machines and media that helped to configure their lives and work.

Recent years have seen a surge of historically inflected and theoretically aware scholarly engagement with the diverse machinery of modernity; it is such newly vital currents in modernist studies that inform the chapters in this volume. Modernist technology studies does not limit itself to the isolated consideration of a particular author's response to technology (Eliot, Virginia Woolf, Pound), nor to the way a particular movement (Futurism or Bauhaus, for example) engages with the second industrial revolution. Rather, it seeks to understand the early twentieth century as what David Trotter has called the 'first media age' (Trotter 2013). In this broader view, the technological is comprehended as a mode of realising, utilising and being in the world, as well as the tools, perspectives, innovations and topographies generated by technological and scientific processes. For most of our contributors, this composite understanding of 'the technological' is mediated in and through language, a position which implicitly aligns with the more overt stance taken by modernist scholars working within the emerging field of technography. Exemplified by the Open Humanities Press series *Technographies*, this approach seeks to bridge the gulf between literary analyses that privilege a humanist, anthropocentric textuality and those that focus on media and technologies through a materialist, posthuman lens. It does so by focusing on writing as 'the form of mediation through which human reality and technical reality are most readily understood to be mutually articulative' (Purdon 2017: 6). As James Purdon frames it, contemporary work in modernism and other fields of the cultural humanities needs to appreciate not only how 'writing is technological, through and through', but also how the technical is itself discursive and so 'the converse is also true: technology is written, through and through' (Purdon 2017: 8). Sean Pryor and David Trotter point out in their introduction to the first volume in the *Technographies* series that there are historical and etymological reasons for doing so: the Greek τεχνολογία (*technología*) originally described not a material device, object or system, but rather a specialist discourse (Pryor and Trotter 2016: 15–16; see also Purdon 2017: 5–6). The technological, then, was first a craft – a *technē* – of the written word. And yet, while literary studies has accustomed itself to thinking of writing as a technologised practice (whether of stylus, pen, type or electrons), scholars have tended to gloss over the ways that technologies both are articulated through discursive practices, and articulate themselves through patterns and forms that can be called rhetorical insofar as they are expressive, even persuasive, in ways legible to their users (Pryor and Trotter 2016: 15–16). Attending properly to the ways that 'writing mediates technology', Pryor and Trotter argue, might help us to 'recuperate some of the strangeness [. . .] of the idea of "technology"' (2016: 10, 15).

For modernists themselves the technologies of the early twentieth century were indeed often strange, even if much of the strangeness lay in the speed with which the extraordinary became assimilated into the fabric of ordinary life, something Steven Connor has noted of the technologies of vocal disembodiment that flourished around the turn of the twentieth century (2000: 410). Nor did modernists hold themselves aloof from these assimilations: the period can be characterised, as it is by Mark Morrisson, as a period of 'rampant boundary crossing' in which science, technology and literature are mutually informing paradigms in an era of innovation and change (Morrisson 2016: 44). Contemporary studies of modernism and technology serve to rework, if not entirely debunk, the pervasive mid-twentieth-century assumption of a fundamental opposition between modernism (understood in its canonical formulations as an elite artistic practice) and technologies of mass communication, transportation and consumption.[1] Instead, these studies illustrate how modernism, as an expression of modernity, is inescapably technological, even when particular facets of technology provide the focus for modernists' aesthetic, political or social critique. One key aim of modernist technology studies is thus to parse modernist aesthetics in order to perceive, in Mark Goble's words, 'all the ways in which they gratify and indulge their mediums and materialities of communication', and to grasp 'the way that modernist expression wants to wire bodies into circuits with all manner of machines' (Goble 2010: 8, 12).

As outdated critical divisions between media and between 'brows' (high, low and middle) have waned, work on modernism and media has flourished. The field of modernist studies is now rich with work on modernism and cinema, which has opened up the discourses around visual media, and work on modernism's engagement with radio, sound technologies and communication technologies.[2] That the reach of the technological extends beyond these familiar media is demonstrated in recent modernist studies criticism; Victoria Rosner's *Machines for Living: Modernism and Domestic Life* (2020), for example, unearths a 'modernization of domesticity' (25) that moved far beyond the concrete introduction of domestic and media technologies into the home, while Adrienne Brown's *The Black Skyscraper* (2017) apprehends the modernist cityscape as not only a technologically enabled environment serviced by ultramodern lifts and built of steel and concrete and glass, but one with profound repercussions for the cultural formation of race in the USA. Modernist technology studies now intertwines with other fields such as critical disability studies, critical race studies and animal studies, resulting in intersectional work, some of which is showcased in this volume, that exceeds the normative canons and assumptions of previous generations. In other modes, scholars are exploring modernist art, literature and culture through the frames of twenty-first-century technology, using theoretical concepts and contemporary formal innovations to rethink modernist aesthetics, and the tools of digital humanities to generate new topographies of modernism, modernist texts and modernist objects.[3]

The diversity of approaches and topics in modernist technology studies reflects our own distance from, and connection to, the modernist era. We live in a society pervaded by technology that has its origins in the early twentieth century, but are also able to deploy digital technologies and the methodological tools that derive from them, distinguishing us from the writers and artists of modernism. We are also acutely aware of the role that we, as humans, have played in creating the technological systems of the Anthropocene and, thus, of the apocalyptic repercussions of the technosphere that was emerging at the beginning of the twentieth century. This is perhaps the most salient conclusion of Forster's 'The Machine Stops' today: that the apparent spatial annihilation and userly disembodiment associated with modernist technologies are false flags by which those technologies mask their pronounced material effects on the world shared by human and non-human actors. At our own moment of drastically elevated stakes, the chapters in this volume look back on the effects, causes and theories of technology that preoccupied the writers and artists of the early twentieth century, and explore how our current conceptualisations of technology refract new understandings of modernist practice.

Technology in Theory

The early decades of the twentieth century saw the rise of new forms of technologically attuned cultural criticism articulated to the machine aesthetic and machine fears of modernism. This writing inaugurated an understanding of technology as central to the modernist era in ways unprecedented in previous generations, and it was often closely imbricated with the tumultuous political upheavals of the times. The chapters in this *Companion* draw on this long and complex history of theoretical engagements with technology. In surveying the major developments in twentieth-century theories of technology as it relates to cultural production, this Introduction seeks to provide readers, especially those new to the field, with a common understanding of the intellectual foundations on which the chapters in this volume are built.

It is perhaps their understanding of the tight interweaving of politics with technologies of representation and transmission that has granted the thinkers associated with the Frankfurt School the most influential and enduring positions in the study of culture and technology. Walter Benjamin, whose 'The Work of Art in the Age of its Technological Reproducibility' became a foundational text for critical and cultural theory, took his own life fleeing the Nazis in 1940. Benjamin's work, as evidenced by the contributions to this volume, resonates through modernist technology studies, foregrounding a central tension in the cultures of modern technology: Benjamin identifies, on the one hand, a link between a certain kind of technological mass culture and fascism, and on the other the liberating potential in technology's decentring of bourgeois-humanist notions of art, subjectivity and the individual. For Benjamin, 'technical reproducibility' transforms art, destroying elitism and generating 'new productive forces' and new modes of perception (Benjamin 2008: 27). In Benjamin's vision, technology offers revolutionary and creative possibilities for an alternate collective existence, rather than the inevitable production of a commodified experience and a domination of the natural world. 'The mastery of nature, so the imperialists teach, is the purpose of all technology,' he notes; however, 'technology is not the mastery of nature but of the relation between man and nature [. . .] In technology a *physis* is being organized through which mankind's contact with the cosmos takes a new and different form' (Benjamin 1979: 104).

Other theorists associated with the Frankfurt School – including Max Horkheimer and Theodor Adorno – were also victims of fascism, leaving Germany for the USA after Hitler's rise to power. Their critiques bear the mark of that history, and are fundamentally a response to the totalitarianism that inevitably results from the 'technological rationality' that arose during the early twentieth century (Adorno and Horkheimer 2002: 121). Herbert Marcuse had been Martin Heidegger's assistant in Freiberg in the early 1930s but he too left Nazi Germany and eventually settled in the USA. In his *One-Dimensional Man* Marcuse describes a 'technological process of mechanization and standardization' (1964: 3) that, despite an original intention to produce freedom from want and to liberate the individual, actually demands conformity and the erosion of independence of thought and autonomy. Rather than celebrating the liberation from bourgeois traditions of privilege and authority as Benjamin did, Adorno and Horkheimer, and Marcuse after them, feared that the levelling effected by technical reproduction erased the freedom and integrity of the human individual.

In *Dialectic of Enlightenment* Adorno and Horkheimer argue that modern culture is an exhaustive technological mediation, wherein everything appears ontologically similar:

> technological rationality effects an equalizing quantification, bringing everything in line with itself, rubbing out the non-identical and so paving the way for its own superfluousness . . . Thinking reifies itself into a self-running, automatic process striving to be like the machine which it itself produces so that ultimately the machine can replace it. (25)

For Adorno and Horkheimer, 'standardization and serial production' lie at the core of the Culture Industry – their term for the mass culture produced by and in the service of modern technological capitalist consumerism – which 'has sacrificed that which made the logic of the work different from that of the social system' (121). Further, they argue that mass leisure itself always functions under the conditions of industrial production because '[a]musement under late capitalism is the prolongation of work' and 'the fabrication of amusement commodities . . . is determined so fundamentally [by the technologies of fabrication] that people during their time off can experience nothing other than the afterimage of the work process itself' (137). This sense that the Taylorite factory, with its seamless integration of human bodies with mechanical capitalist production, is the shape of all culture is echoed by other German critics of the time. Benjamin saw 'the Fun Fair with its Dodgem cars and other similar amusements [as] nothing but a taste of the drill to which the unskilled labourer is subjected in the factory' (2007 [1939]: 176) and Siegfried Kracauer, in 'The Mass Ornament', understood the synchronised dancing of the Tiller Girls as an industrial assembly line process in which 'the hands in the factory correspond to the legs of the Tiller Girls' (1995 [1927]: 79).

Though such anthropocentric approaches dominated, the relationship between humankind, technology and non-human nature concerned many early and mid-twentieth-century thinkers in ways that presage contemporary analyses. In Heidegger's 'The Question Concerning Technology' (1954), for example, the ontological view of modern technology that takes the world as a 'standing reserve' (*Bestand*) to be utilised is inevitably one which annihilates human freedom as it destroys nature. Indeed, a productive coupling of critical technology studies and environmental awareness emerged from the modernist era, illustrated by the work of Lewis Mumford. Fundamentally concerned with the relationship between technology, agency and power, Mumford's social histories of technology emphasise the place of technology within a wider concept of technics that exceeds functional or utilitarian applications. In his later works this concern is focused on the contemporary emergence of powerful technological systems or 'megatechnics'. In *Technics and Human Development*, the first of two volumes that make up *The Myth of the Machine*, Mumford describes 'megatechnics' as 'a uniform, all-enveloping, super-planetary structure, designed for automatic operation', within which 'man will become a passive, purposeless, machine-conditioned animal whose proper functions [. . .] will either be fed into the machine or strictly limited and controlled for the benefit of de-personalized, collective organizations' (1967: 3). In contrast to megatechnics Mumford proposed the concept of 'biotechnics', a form of post-industrial system that limits its negative effects on the ecology and the organism (1970: 395); this concept was a significant influence on subsequent American environmental thinking and its key theorists, such as Murray Bookchin.[4]

That the 'question' of technology also extended beyond the material process of resourcing, inventing and producing and into the information and publicity systems of modern capitalism is evident in the work of Edward Bernays and Walter Lippmann. For Bernays the technological modern world and its mass media raised particular queries about, and opportunities for, the manufacture of public approval. The titles of his books track a subtle change in the framing of that manufacture: what he once comfortably termed *Propaganda* (1928) became, in 1945, the new field of *Public Relations* (both fields concerned, in the words of Bernays's oft-quoted dictum, with 'the engineering of consent'; 1947: 113). Walter Lippmann, whose background was likewise in propaganda, was more concerned with exposing the flaws in the information system than deploying the power of the mass media technosphere. In *Public Opinion* (1922), which Mark Wollaeger describes as 'one of the founding books of modern media studies' (2006: 25), Lippmann's focus is on the mediated nature of modern existence, in which the informational environment produced by technology is 'too big, too complex' and therefore impossible for the individual to comprehend. Instead, the modern individual inhabits a subjective image of the world, a 'pseudo-environment' in which the 'connection between reality and human response [is] [. . .] indirect and inferred' (Lippmann 1991 [1922]: 15–16, 27). This prescient conception of a technologically mediated world, which sounds very much like the simulacra of postmodernism, appeared in the 'high modernist' year of 1922.

The political implications of the mass media Culture Industry, the dangers and possibilities of powerful technological systems and the subservience of the human to technology all concerned mid-century critics. As the century drew on, critics assessed the continued imbrication of technology with cultural production, integrating new media – satellite communications, computers and television among them – into their understanding of modernity and using those technologies to redefine the borders and texture of modernism as an aesthetic practice. Marshall McLuhan was the iconic theorist of the new media of the Sixties generation, identifying a shift from a mechanical age to an electric age, an era of speed and simultaneity in which technology effects a physical evolution of the human being. Jessica Pressman positions McLuhan, who began his career as a professor of English, as the 'midpoint between modernism and digital modernism' (Pressman 2014: 47–52, 54). McLuhan's invocation of Pound (with whom he corresponded) and Joyce to underpin his media theory signalled his investment in the theoretical dimension of all creative arts: 'It's always been the artist who perceives the alterations in man caused by a new medium, who recognizes that the future is the present, and uses his work to prepare the ground for it,' he told one interviewer (McLuhan and Norden 1969: 56). It is possible to see, in the multimodal, collage form of some of his work – *The Medium is the Massage* was accompanied by a Columbia Records album, for example – a blending of modernist experimentation with radical media theory:

> **All**
> **media**
> **are**
> **extensions**
> **of**
> **some**
> **human**
> **faculty—**
> **psychic**
> **or**
> **physical.** (McLuhan and Fiore 1967: 26)

McLuhan's conception of media as an 'extension' of the self, an 'outering' and altering of 'sense ratios or patterns of perception', responds to the technological developments of his era; he was writing at the dawn of the computer age, of the 'television generation' and of 'information war[s] [. . .] fought by subtle electric informational media' (1967: 127, 138). His famous adage, 'the medium is the message', is not concerned with the content of technological innovations and mass media; rather, it identifies how meaning inheres in the changes 'of scale or pace or pattern' of communication and interpersonal connection that a new medium generates (2001 [1964]: 8). Further, McLuhan's contention that the 'content of any medium is always another medium' (2001 [1964]: 8) prefigured the conception of 'remediation' that was taken up at the century's end by Jay Bolter and David Grusin (2000), enabling new accounts of modernist cultural forms and their relationship to contemporary and digital media.

McLuhan's celebratory vision of a world transformed into a 'global village' in which '"space" has vanished', a 'simultaneous happening' where '[i]nformation pours upon us, instantaneously and continuously' (McLuhan and Fiore 1967: 63), is at odds with Mumford's warnings about the destructive effects of systems of 'megatechnics' in *The Pentagon of Power* (1970). But the major rival to Mumford's thinking at the mid-century was not so much McLuhan as Jacques Ellul. Ellul postulates that the 'technical milieu absorbs the natural' and replaces nature (1964: 79), and that technology has become a self-augmenting force, imposing unprecedented adaptations on the human. He criticises Mumford for what he sees as his narrow focus on modern technology (1964: 98); Ellul's *The Technological Society* offers a conception of 'technique' that is much wider than Mumford's technics, arguing that technique 'integrates the machine into society', facilitating a takeover under the guise of human technological adeptness (5). The impact on the human is fundamental, penetrating 'the deepest recesses of the human being' (325), so that as 'technique enters every area of life, including the human, it ceases to be external to man and becomes his very substance' (6). Ellul identifies 'standardization', 'rationalization' and 'impersonality' (11–12) as the key elements of the contemporary technological society and posits that 'nothing at all escapes technique today' (22). Technology for Ellul is purposeless, unpredictable, morally indifferent, non-ideological, and has become autonomous and universal. *The Technological Society* ultimately offers a bleak vision of a 'monolithic technical world' that cannot 'be checked or guided' (428).

Raymond Williams, possibly the central figure in the emergence of cultural and media studies in the UK academy, was unpersuaded by Ellul's chilling vision of society, politics, economics and the human absorbed into the self-augmenting process of the technical, a vision Williams described as a 'fatalistic' and 'extreme formulation' hampered by 'distortions' (1972: 57, 59). Williams's own, much more sanguine, writing on communication technologies testifies to his affirmative interest in the practices and cultures of everyday life. Williams rejects technological determinism, technophilia and indeed technophobia, foregrounding the politics and social contexts of technological development, which he reads as a contingent rather than determined process. This put Williams in direct conflict with McLuhan's ideas: for McLuhan, Williams claimed, 'all media operations are in fact desocialised; they are simply physical events in an abstracted sensorium' (1974: 127). In contrast, Williams argues that 'technology is always, in a full sense, social' and is 'necessarily in a complex and variable connection with other social relations and institutions' (1981: 227). Williams points to the development of broadcasting, for example, as an extensive period of technological development and experimentation that was crucially linked to complex social milieus and changing definitions of public and private. He also saw a correlation between technological innovation and modernism, noting that '[p]hotography, cinema, radio, television, reproduction and recording all make their decisive advances during the period identified as Modernist' (Williams 1989: 50). Williams's influence is hard to overstate: his is one of the early but enduring voices to fuse literary analysis, Marxist theory and the study of technology.

While McLuhan and Williams might be held up as exemplars of technological determinism and of the social construction of technology, respectively, recent decades have seen the emergence of what might be called a 'soft determinist' school of thinking about media. Cultural historian Lisa Gitelman represents an influential voice within that school, and her description of media captures a view that animates many of the contributions to this volume: media are, she argues in *Always Already New*, 'socially realized structures of communication, where structures include both technological forms and their associated protocols, and where communication is a cultural practice' (Gitelman 2006: 7). This flexible approach acknowledges the constitutive function that technological systems can exert on the human communities of which they are a part, without ignoring the range of behaviours that shape the evolving form and function of those systems. Machines barely determine themselves, let alone us: phonographs were once business machines; radio broadcasts were, in their earliest days, sometimes transmitted via telephone lines; microwave ovens were developed from the magnetron tubes used to generate short-wave military radar. An accurate genealogy of modernist technologies recognises the role played in their development by contingency, institutional pressures and socially embedded practices of uptake, modification and repurposing.

Beginning in the last decades of the twentieth century, a flurry of new approaches to the study of technology began to emerge, which can be loosely assembled under the question of what comes after or alongside the human. Many such posthumanisms scramble the question of determinism by radically reshaping the category of agency itself: for example, the Actor-Network Theory (ANT) developed by Bruno Latour, Michel Callon, John Law and others imagines technological devices as agents in an essentially non-hierarchical network of relations with other agents (whether human or non-human, organic or inorganic, simple or complex). Crucial to ANT analyses of these networks is the distinction between 'intermediaries' – those components of the network that transmit the force or effect of some other agent essentially unchanged – and 'mediators', which exert their own effects on the forces that move through them (Latour 2005: 105). In Latour's statement of the 'principle of irreduction' that serves as an essential starting point for ANT methodology, the implications for media studies are clear even if Latour's aims are broader: 'a concatenation of mediators does not trace the same connections and does not require the same type of explanations as a retinue of intermediaries transporting a cause' (2005: 107). Technological media translate the forces that pass through them; only a close and careful analysis of the relations between technologies, human users and other agents – one that does not presuppose a greater agentic power reserved for humans – can accurately describe the play of forces in a network.

Even before Actor Network Theory, Donna Haraway's germinal 'Cyborg Manifesto' (1985; revised 1991) was troubling the human/machine boundary. The essay offers a revolutionary account of the 'theorized and fabricated hybrids of machine and organism' that constitute the cyborg figuration, 'fusions' formed from the 'leaky distinction' between humans and their technologies, and in the process raises pointed questions about agency, autonomy and ethics (1991: 150, 175, 152). Since Haraway, other forms of posthuman thinking that dethrone the humanist subject have flourished. Rosi Braidotti argues for 'the need to rethink subjectivity as a collective assemblage that encompasses human and nonhuman actors, technological mediation, animals, plants, and the planet as a whole' (Braidotti 2017: 9). Jane Bennett, in *Vibrant Matter: A Political Ecology of Things* (2010), offers a similarly anti-hierarchical and pointedly ethical argument about the 'public value' in reassessing 'nonhuman, thingly power, the material agency of natural bodies and technological artifacts' (2010: xiii). Such a reassessment is urgently needed, given the ecological and political crises of the twenty-first century. As Bennett argues,

> If human culture is inextricably enmeshed with vibrant, nonhuman agencies, and if human intentionality can be agentic only if accompanied by a vast entourage of nonhumans, then it seems that the appropriate unit of analysis for democratic theory is neither the individual human nor an exclusively human collective but the (ontologically heterogeneous) 'public' coalescing around a problem,

a public that includes non-human (and technological) actants (2010: 108). N. Katherine Hayles, meanwhile, highlights the 'entanglements and interpenetrations of human and technical cognitive systems' (2017: 40) which have decentred the thinking human subject and which demonstrate that the 'search for meaning [. . .] [is] a pervasive activity among humans, animals, and technical devices, with many different kinds of agents contributing to a rich ecology of collaborating, reinforcing, contesting, and conflicting interpretations' (2017: 212).

The posthumanist recognition of human–technical assemblages and the 'vibrant matter' (both technological and organic) of the non-human world is of particular relevance to modernism. Joyce himself uses the term 'posthuman' to describe his characterisation of Molly Bloom in *Ulysses* (Joyce 1957: 180), and explorations of posthuman modernisms have found in Joyce's work a ready resource for rethinking the humanist subject and its relation to the mechanics of language in a technical world (Borg 2007), or for considering non-human ethics (Ebury 2017). For Jeff Wallace it is the work of D. H. Lawrence, and his engagement with scientific writing and discourse, that offer a principal site for exploring the animal–human–machine nexus in modernism (Wallace 2005), whilst Virginia Woolf remains a touchstone for Braidotti's critical theory (see Braidotti 2008 and 2014; Braidotti and Regan 2017). Posthuman theory is also mobilised in recent work that moves on from a single-author focus. Erin Edwards ranges over different modernists and modernist sites to examine the corpse as 'post*humanist*, representing a significant reconfiguration of the humanist discourses that define the human's hierarchical relation to natural and technological worlds' (Edwards 2018: 5). In her exploration of the modernist corpse Edwards examines its technological mediation and presentation, and in doing so, reads literary modernism as 'actively engaged in material assemblages with other technical media forms, such as photography, film, and sound recording' (Edwards 2018: 15). Ruben Borg takes 'posthuman theory to be a *product* of modernism, a mythology or a conceptual grammar by which modernism thinks through some of the contradictions inherent in its historical moment', and goes on to look through the 'cybernetic eye' of Woolf, Conrad, Hitchcock, Pirandello, Beckett and others (Borg 2019: 6, 13). This new work in modernist studies illustrates that the convergence of posthuman and postanthropocentric discourses in contemporary critical thought have reoriented critical attention to how modernist artist and writers explored different understandings of materiality, engaged with virtual and cyborg bodies or non-human subjectivities, and deconstructed the border between bodies and things.

The relationship between bodies and things, or more accurately between humans and technical objects, has been the concern of media archaeology, much of which attends to the media ecology of the early twentieth century and has roots in early film history. Though all varieties of media archaeology are fundamentally concerned with the material culture of media technology there are, nevertheless, stark differences between how the relation between the human and the technical is conceived. Where Gitelman (as discussed above) is interested in the interplay of social and technological forces in forming 'media' as we know them, Friedrich Kittler, who has been enormously influential in the field, is most usually read as a techno-determinist, as evidenced by his oft-quoted dictum that 'media determine our situation' (Kittler 1999: xxxix).[5] In his work from the 1980s and 1990s Kittler firmly distances himself from a subject-centred approach, occluding the human in his exploration of the discourse networks of the nineteenth and twentieth centuries (in which he links physical, technological, discursive and social systems), and in his account of the advent of the inscription machines (gramophones, film and typewriters) that reduced linguistic signs and the symbolic to bare 'materiality and technicity' (1999: 15). Thus, for Kittler, the advent of mechanical storage 'designates the turning point at which communications technologies can no longer be related back to humans. Instead the former have formed the latter' (211). Kittler identifies the cusp of the twentieth century as a point of rupture and, as Stephen Sale and Laura Salisbury point out, he became a 'key reference point' for modernist scholars exploring 'the materiality of media in transition in the [...] period described in the second half of *Discourse Networks* when literature's monopoly came to an end with media differentiation' (2015: xxix).

Other theorists of media and technology who have been taken up in modernist studies in recent years include Vilém Flusser and Gilbert Simondon,[6] both of whom propose a more complex understanding of the interrelationship between the human and the technical. Flusser rejects technological determinism, and proposes a paradigm of the 'apparatus–operator complex' – which he sees as 'the motivating force behind all contemporary social and technological change' (Ströhl 2002: xii) – to get inside the 'black box' of technology (Flusser 2000: 16). Flusser is concerned to demystify the 'magical' power of this black box and undo the ontological alienation and programmed behaviour it generates. In *Towards a Philosophy of Photography* Flusser articulates his ideas of the 'apparatus', which is his term for non-human (technical) agency; he describes 'the photographic universe as the product of cameras and distribution apparatuses [...] industrial apparatuses, advertising apparatuses, political, economic management apparatuses' and thus 'the whole complex of apparatuses is therefore a super-black-box made up of black boxes' (Flusser 2000: 71). The 'complex' Flusser proposes of 'apparatus–operator' signals the interdependent functioning of human and machine, each of which exists only through its relationship with the other. Flusser is crucially interested in the humanistic, in the possibility of 'playing against' the apparatus and programmed behaviour (Flusser 2000: 80), and speculates about the possibility of a future 'telematic society' where, 'although mass media are being used almost exclusively for discourse, they could be changed in a way that would allow for dialogue as well' (Flusser 2002: 170, 19).

Simondon also takes on the black box of technology and rejects the assumption that 'technical objects do not contain a human reality within them' (2017 [1958]: 15). Rather than reducing technical objects to their utilitarian function, Simondon offers a dynamic theory of technology in which a 'technical ensemble', infused with social as well as machinic potential, enacts its effects amid a 'milieu' and in 'relation' to other objects and forces. The technical ensemble, that is, involves more than particular tools or machines; it also involves the relations amongst technical objects (tools and machines), the relations between them and the humans who use them, and the relations between them and their environments. The human is with(in) this ensemble and not alienated from or threatened by it: 'man [sic] functions as permanent inventor and coordinator of the machines around him. He [sic] is *among* the machines that work with him [sic]' (2017 [1958]: 18). Both Flusser and Simondon are interested in the assemblage of agential subject and technicity, pointing to the human reality that pertains in any technological ensemble.

By diffusing agency throughout a system of organic and inorganic actants capable of producing effects, these posthumanist theories at once free humans from the grip of a maniacal technological determinism and puncture any notion of the uniqueness of human effectuality. If we remain, as Simondon says, 'permanent inventors and coordinators' of our technological envelope, we also surrender the sense of a unique human autonomy that many modernists struggled to sustain in the face of an accelerating world. A century past modernism's heyday, faced with a range of existential threats both novel (anthropogenic climate change) and oddly echoic (global pandemic), the challenge has never been so stark: to see ourselves clearly in relation to the technologies that shape us as we shape them; to act as part of immense and complex systems we only partially understand; to delight in technological possibility even as we learn to curb the excesses that threaten to stop the machine entirely.

Chapter Overview

This volume is organised into four parts which reflect but also seek to generate the taxonomies of technology in modernist studies, in which technology can be variously conceived as apparatus, medium, process or system. Our concrete and quotidian experience of technology most often manifests, as it did for those living in the early twentieth century, in the form of machinery and equipment, in the things produced through the application of scientific and technical knowledge. It is in encounters with these things that the entanglement of human life processes and machine processes becomes most apparent; the opening section of the volume, **Machines**, therefore examines a series of crucial early innovations and inventions that altered the way individuals lived, worked and moved. The chapters explore different vectors of the modernist human–machine assemblage and consider the relations between forms of artistic production and the advances or apparatuses that remade daily life, from the organisation of time under modern cultures of efficiency to the sense of distances suddenly abridged thanks to new modes of transportation. But, as with our current Internet of Things, the machines of modernism were embedded in complex networks of association and configuration and so, as the chapters here and in subsequent parts of this volume articulate, these machines can never be experienced as discrete objects without an attendant awareness of the systems within which they operate.

In the contribution on 'Electricity', Laura Ludtke points to the undecidability of electricity, from its essence to its dubious modernity, and analyses how electric lights were deployed in early modernist poetry. In the next chapter, 'Clocks', Charles Tung reads in modernism's many timepieces not only the assertion of personal, subjective time in resistance to public, ordered temporalities, but also a 'new heterochronic order' whose disjunctive temporal scales and rates urge a new, anti-triumphalist perspective across the first century of the Anthropocene and beyond. Following this, Jennifer Sorensen offers an account of modernist 'Print' that focuses on modernist writers' embodied, physical engagement with print cultures, exploring the direct encounters with printing technologies that Anaïs Nin records in her diaries. In subsequent chapters Sunny Stalter-Pace, Enda Duffy and Leo Mellor consider transport technologies that, in contrasting ways, shape human perception and modernist writing. Stalter-Pace argues that the 'Subways' of modern cities across the world (London, New York, Paris, Buenos Aires) generated different forms of 'underground connection' that meant city space could be ordered in new ways. The subway experience of liminality, segmentation and disruption (of distances, and of the distinction between the local and the global) can, she argues, be read as 'literal enactments' of the meanings and strategies of modernist texts. Enda Duffy's 'Automobiles' postulates that the entirely new 'speed gaze' demanded of drivers by their cars engendered effects, not only in the cinematic arts whose hectic field of representation mirrors the windscreen, but also in the modernist techniques of stream of consciousness whose unfolding perspective places readers, as it were, in the driver's seat. In the chapter on 'Aeroplanes' Leo Mellor explores 'aeriality' in writing of the long 1930s and identifies an, often unsettling, aerial vista that reveals both literal and cultural patterns and is accompanied and interleaved with disconcerting bodily sensations. The paranoia and unease that characterise the individual response to this aerial vista manifest textually, Mellor argues, at the level of both language and structure. Finally, in this part of the book, Katherine Shingler considers humanoid technology in the form of 'Robots', tracing versions of the machine-woman across a transnational avant-garde and arguing that the *fin-de-siècle* ambivalence towards the machine takes a particular turn with the 'disruptions to sex and gender threatened by the imagined figure of the robot'.

If human life became increasingly entangled with new machines over the course of the late nineteenth and early twentieth centuries, it was also increasingly experienced through new representational means – in other words, new **Media**. 'Medium' is a capacious term whose resonances (as John Guillory (2010) has demonstrated) extend from divine intercession and spiritual channelling to the tools of the *beaux-arts* and the electro-mechanical technologies that joined their ranks, beginning in the nineteenth century. But as David Trotter outlines, in his chapter on 'Materials', modernist media included 'useful matter' like the iron and glass that shaped much of the built environment, and that became substances of concern for many modernist authors. These materials, Trotter argues, 'created a context for literary experiment', and their effect on the literary text cannot be accounted for entirely through cultural materialist approaches.

The most common contemporary usage of the word 'medium' relates to technological mediation, the transmission of information and cultural representations by electronic signals or other means, and the centrality of this usage reflects a modernist ascendancy that has never been challenged or reversed. Central to this ascendancy, as Einav Rabinovitch-Fox demonstrates in 'Advertising', was the rapid and widespread circulation of consumer advertising fuelled by improved print technology and increased discretionary spending among the middle classes. Women were particular targets for this newly visual advertising regime, as corporate entities sought to appeal to changing notions of (predominantly white, middle-class) femininity in ways that celebrated and secured new freedoms without appearing too radical. Much as women's agency has been written out of the narrative of modernist advertising, their vital role in the cultural history of photography has been effaced. In the chapter on 'Photography', Alix Beeston argues for renewed attention to the œuvre of Gertrude Käsebier, who was not only influential in the development of modernist photography as a whole but emerges as emblematic of the vernacular and feminised aspects that have been pushed out of narratives of modernism more generally, to the detriment of our understanding of the period. Tom Slevin's chapter, meanwhile, shows how X-rays, like other visual media, fundamentally transformed the relationship of modern subjects to their bodies, as they began to perceive the human form as newly legible and permeable. Felicity Gee's exploration of Germaine Dulac's 'Integral Cinema' in the chapter on 'Cinema', like Beeston on Käsebier, also thinks through feminised and indeed feminist aspects of this modernist technology. Gee's analysis moves across Dulac's avant-garde cinematography and film-philosophy, highlighting how this work reflects on and also generates an affective encounter between the human sensorium and the cinematic apparatus.

Rounding out this section are a quartet of chapters that remind us that mediation can be an auditory and immersive experience, and not only a two-dimensional visual one. Emily Bloom unpacks the connections between broadcasting and disability in 'Radio', pointing out that the casual metaphors of 'blindness' that attached themselves to the medium, though generative, rarely involved any serious engagement with blind listeners. Josh Epstein's chapter on 'Music' positions non-verbal sound in the intermedial context of interwar and Second World War film, as a way of demonstrating that composers saw their music as deeply technological and woven into the larger media matrix of modernity. For Emilie Morin, a kindred intermediality manifests itself throughout the corpus of avant-garde performance by artists affiliated with Dada and Bauhaus, affording new visions of the human body-as-mechanism in their theatrical and dance productions. Damien Keane, in 'Amplification', explores the acoustic and informational feedback loops that connect the Second World War propaganda contributions of Marlene Dietrich to the intelligence files the FBI used to document her movements and those of other émigrés; fidelity and intimacy are watchwords that obtain as much in the culture of hi-fi and that of the security state, both of which emerged from the technological matrix of the Second World War.

The subsequent part of the book offers specific focus on **Bodies** and mechanisms. From the late 1990s, following Tim Armstrong's landmark volume *Modernism, Technology and the Body* (1998), modernist technology studies have paid close attention to the embodiment of technology and to its various affects and effects on the human form. Armstrong himself considers technologies of prosthesis, consumption and rejuvenation in his account of the role modernist technologies of the body had in generating an artistic avant-garde. In *The Senses of Modernism* (2002), Sara Danius examined how the senses have become technologically mediated in modernity, seeing a progressive internalisation of the technological modes of phonography, telephony, motoring and cinematography in key modernist writers and artists. This topic has remained an insistent area of study for scholars, refracted now through emergent interests in prosthetics, virology, haptics and the modernist posthuman. If technologies are, as McLuhan theorises, extensions of ourselves, they are also extensions *on to* and *into* the self of that which is normally understood to be outside the self. Thus, the contributions to the third part of this book on *Bodies* assert the primacy of the body as a locus of techno-cultural interaction and mediation. Jana Funke begins with a focus on hypnosis, hormones and birth control, illustrating how modernist texts negotiate the production of desires and sexed bodies through these modern technologies of 'Sex'. Joshua Lam's examination of 'Race' takes as its focal point the Fordist factory as a site in which regimes of industrialised management produced the very categories of racialised bodies that they disciplined. In the account of 'Technics' Jeff Wallace reads D. H. Lawrence's education essays through Simondon and Stiegler, and thus, instead of discovering resonances with the pseudo-science of eugenics, locates a progressive technics in Lawrence, one which celebrates a 'life-equality with the world of things' and gestures towards a corporeal technical ensemble that might enable 'participatory modes of knowledge, education and politics'. In the chapter on 'Germs' Maebh Long explores the contagious world of modernity, discovering a fragmented and flattened modernist body and an attendant aesthetic 'invested in the shock of the microscopic and the threat of the dimly perceived'. In 'Noise' Anna Snaith focuses on interwar British writing that depicts industrial racket to explore the role that literature played in 'the shaping, staging and resisting of definitions of noise'. Snaith argues for the importance of attending to the impact of noise on the body in working-class industrial fiction and examining the 'complex and competing narratives about the symbolism and semiotics of noise' this writing offers.

The final part of the volume considers *Systems*: those technological assemblages whose connectivity enables the flow of information, resources and people. In 'Nation,' Janice Ho considers the constitutive function of state agencies in forming the nation, taking as her key example the General Post Office (GPO) in the UK, which at various points mediated the country's mail, telecommunications, documentary film output and many financial services. The centralised infrastructural role of the GPO might be contrasted with the more diffuse and asymmetrical large-scale systems Jennifer Lieberman analyses in 'Infrastructure'. By focusing on how the meanings of infrastructure emerge in gendered and racialised contexts through the work of Charlotte Perkins Gilman and Pauline Hopkins, Lieberman maps a plurality of responses to the networks emerging in the early twentieth century. Caroline Krzakowski, in 'Paperwork', tackles the technology of the nation-state from another perspective: the bureaucratic protocols and documents of the British Civil Service in the atomic age. Through close readings of C. P. Snow's novels *The New Men* and *Corridors of Power*, Krzakowski demonstrates how mid-century realist fiction could structure itself around the very paperwork which undergirds the nuclear state as a technologised system, thereby attesting to the real, if attenuated, power of information workers within the government. 'Information', as James Purdon argues in the chapter of the same name, was everywhere in the modernist era, even if 'information technology' as we know it was still some decades away. Instead, 'information' named a set of genres of writing built around discontinuous units of information largely stripped of narrative – a set of genres that became the textual other through which modernism came to know itself.

Though the computer age would not begin in earnest until after the Second World War, Andrew Pilsch demonstrates in his chapter on 'Computation' that modernists, including Gertrude Stein and André Breton, developed compositional practices that bore an uncanny resemblance to the algorithmic methods under development in interwar mathematics. Moving the discussion into the twenty-first century, Shawna Ross links up the 'Networks' of modernism with present-day tools of mapping and analysis, reading in the nascent webs of affiliation between modernist artists a model of collaborative and decentred agency that presages the network imaginary of our own moment. Like the networks that structure our informational lives, the technological roots of 'War' as it is experienced today reach back to the modernist moment of crisis, as Patrick Deer argues in the closing chapter of the volume. Deeply ambivalent about the mingled menace and fascination of mechanised combat, modernists often found themselves mobilised in relation to war, whether as official artists and shapers of coherent national narratives or as critics of what Deer calls the 'technological sublime' of modern warfare.

Between the promise of illumination and the threat of the total annihilation of human time, the chapters in this *Companion* encompass the heterogeneous and often conflicting ways that technology shaped modernism and vice versa. If the dominant narrative of technology in the twentieth century is that it served as a prosthetic extension of the human body and its abilities, the texts surveyed herein indicate that artists and intellectuals of the era understood a deeper level of imbrication: of modern technologies with modern bodies, of means of representation with the object represented, and of technological and infrastructural systems with the human networks they sustain.

Notes

1. Influential formulations of this position can be found in Greenberg (1939), Huyssen (1986) and Carey (1992).
2. For accounts of the relationship between modernism and visual technologies including photography and cinema, see Marcus (2007), North (2005 and 2009), Trotter (2007) and Beeston (2018), among many others. For the relationship of radio and other sound media to modernism, see Avery (2006), Cohen et al. (2009), Keane (2014), Dinsman (2015), Bloom (2017), Mansell (2017), Napolin (2020), and Lodhi and Wrigley (2020).
3. For overviews of modernist digital humanities scholarship, see Shawna Ross (2016 and 2018), Gabriel Hankins (2018), and Stephen Ross and Jentery Sayers (2014). See also the 'Manifesto of Modernist Digital Humanities' by Christie et al. (2014).
4. For a recent collection surveying the intersection of technology and the environment in modern Britain, see Agar and Ward (2018).
5. For other versions of media archaeology see, for example, Parikka (2012), Ernst (2003, 2005) and Elsaesser (2004).
6. For recent work on Flusser and modernism see Aaron Jaffe et al. (2021). For recent work in modernist studies that draws on Simondon see Eric White (2020); see also Jeff Wallace's chapter on 'Technics' in this volume.

Works Cited

Adorno, Theodor and Max Horkheimer (2002 [1947]), *Dialectic of Enlightenment*, trans. Edmund Jephcott. Stanford, CA: Stanford University Press.
Agar, Jon and Jacob Ward, eds (2018), *Histories of Technology, the Environment and Modern Britain*. London: UCL Press.
Armstrong, Tim (1998), *Modernism, Technology, and the Body*. Cambridge: Cambridge University Press.
Avery, Todd (2006), *Radio Modernism: Literature, Ethics, and the BBC, 1922–1938*. Burlington, VT: Ashgate.
Banta, Martha (1993), *Taylored Lives: Narrative Productions in the Age of Taylor, Veblen and Ford*. Chicago: University of Chicago Press.
Beeston, Alix (2018), *In and Out of Sight: Modernist Writing and the Photographic Unseen*. Oxford: Oxford University Press.
Benjamin, Walter (1979 [1928]), 'One-Way Street', in *One-Way Street and Other Writings*, trans. Edmund Jephcott. London: New Left Books, pp. 45–104.
Benjamin, Walter (2007 [1939]), 'On Some Motifs in Baudelaire', in *Illuminations: Essays and Reflections*, trans. Harry Zohn, ed. Hannah Arendt. New York: Shocken Books, pp. 155–200.
Benjamin, Walter (2008 [1935–6]), 'The Work of Art in the Age of Its Technological Reproducibility' (second version), trans. Edmund Jephcott and Harry Zohn, in *The Work of Art in the Age of Its Technological Reproducibility and Other Writings on Media*, ed. Michael W. Jennings, Brigid Doherty and Thomas Y. Levin. Cambridge, MA: Harvard University Press, pp. 19–55.
Bennett, Jane (2010), *Vibrant Matter: A Political Ecology of Things*. Durham, NC: Duke University Press.
Bernays, Edward R. (1928), *Propaganda*. New York: Horace Liveright.
Bernays, Edward R. (1945), *Public Relations*. Boston: Bellman.
Bernays, Edward R. (1947), 'The Engineering of Consent', *Annals of the American Academy of Political and Social Science*, 250 (March), pp. 113–20.
Bloom, Emily (2017), *The Wireless Past: Anglo-Irish Writers and the BBC, 1931–1968*. Oxford: Oxford University Press.
Bolter, Jay David and Richard Grusin (2000), *Remediation: Understanding New Media*. Cambridge, MA: MIT Press.
Borg, Ruben (2007), *The Measureless Time of Joyce, Deleuze and Derrida*. London: Continuum.
Borg, Ruben (2019), *Fantasies of Self-Mourning: Modernism, the Posthuman and the Finite*. Amsterdam: Brill.
Braidotti, Rosi (2008), 'Intensive Genre and the Demise of Gender', *Angelaki*, 13: 2, pp. 45–57.
Braidotti, Rosi (2014), 'Writing as a Nomadic Subject', *Comparative Critical Studies*, 11: 2–3, pp. 163–84.
Braidotti, Rosi (2017), 'Posthuman Critical Theory', *Journal of Posthuman Studies*, 1: 1, pp. 9–25.
Braidotti, Rosi and Lisa Regan (2017), 'Our Times Are Always Out of Joint: Feminist Relational Ethics in and of the World Today: An Interview with Rosi Braidotti', *Women: A Cultural Review*, 28: 2, pp. 171–92.
Brown, Adrienne (2017), *The Black Skyscraper: Architecture and the Perception of Race*. Baltimore: Johns Hopkins University Press.
Carey, John (1992), *The Intellectuals and the Masses: Pride and Prejudice Among the Literary Intelligentsia, 1880–1939*. London: Faber & Faber.
Christie, Alex, Andrew Pilsch, Shawna Ross and Katie Tanagawa (2014), 'Manifesto of Modernist Digital Humanities' (online publication), <http://dx.doi.org/10.17613/M6824T> (last accessed 29 July 2021).
Cohen, Debra Rae, Michael Coyle and Jane Lewty, eds (2009), *Broadcasting Modernism*. Gainesville: University of Florida Press.

Connor, Steven (2000), *Dumbstruck: A Cultural History of Ventriloquism*. Oxford: Oxford University Press.
Danius, Sara (2002), *The Senses of Modernism: Technology, Perception, and Aesthetics*. Ithaca, NY: Cornell University Press.
Dinsman, Melissa (2015), *Modernism at the Microphone: Radio, Propaganda, and Literary Aesthetics During World War II*. London: Bloomsbury.
Ebury, Katherine, ed. (2017), *Joyce, Animals and the Nonhuman, Humanities* journal, Special Issue, 6: 3 (September).
Edwards, Erin (2018), *The Modernist Corpse: Posthumanism and the Posthumous*. Minneapolis: University of Minnesota Press.
Ellul, Jacques (1964), *The Technological Society*, trans. John Wilkinson. New York: Random House.
Elsaesser, Thomas (2004), 'The New Film History as Media Archaeology', *CINéMAS*, 14: 2–3, pp. 71–117.
Ernst, Wolfgang (2003), 'Telling versus Counting? A Media Archaeological Point of View', *Intermédialités*, 2 (Autumn), pp. 31–44.
Ernst, Wolfgang (2005), 'Let There Be Irony: Cultural History and Media Archaeology in Parallel Lines', *Art History*, 28: 5 (November), pp. 582–603.
Flusser, Vilém (2000), *Towards a Philosophy of Photography*, trans Anthony Matthews. London: Reaktion Books.
Flusser, Vilém (2002), *Writings*, trans. Erik Eisel, ed. Andreas Ströhl. Minneapolis: University of Minnesota Press.
Forster, E. M. (1928), 'The Machine Stops', *The Eternal Moment and Other Stories*. New York: Harcourt Brace Jovanovich.
Gitelman, Lisa (2006), *Always Already New: Media, History and the Data of Culture*. Cambridge, MA: MIT Press.
Goble, Mark (2010), *Beautiful Circuits: Modernism and the Mediated Life*. New York: Columbia University Press.
Gompertz, Will (2020), 'The Machine Stops: Will Gompertz Reviews E. M. Forster's Work', *BBC News*, 30 May, <https://www.bbc.com/news/entertainment-arts-52821993> (last accessed 28 July 2020).
Greenberg, Clement (1939), 'Avant-Garde and Kitsch', *Partisan Review*, 6, pp. 34–49.
Guillory, John (2010), 'Genesis of the Media Concept', *Critical Inquiry*, 36 (Winter), pp. 321–62.
Hankins, Gabriel (2018), 'We Are All Digital Modernists Now', *Modernism/modernity Print Plus*, 3, Cycle 2 (August 7), <https://doi.org/10.26597/mod.0054> (last accessed 17 January 2022).
Haraway, Donna (1991), 'A Cyborg Manifesto: Science, Technology and Socialist-Feminism in the Late Twentieth Century', in *Simians, Cyborgs, and Women: The Reinvention of Nature*. London: Routledge, pp. 149–81.
Hayles, N. Katherine (2017), *Unthought: The Power of the Cognitive Unconscious*. Chicago: University of Chicago Press.
Heidegger, Martin (1977 [1954]), 'The Question Concerning Technology', in *Basic Writings*, ed. David Farrell Krell. New York: Harper & Row.
Huyssen, Andreas (1986), *After the Great Divide: Modernism, Mass Culture, Postmodernism*. Bloomington: Indiana University Press.
Jaffe, Aaron, Michael F. Miller and Rodrigo Martini (2021), *Understanding Flusser, Understanding Modernism*. London: Bloomsbury.
Joyce, James (1957), *Letters of James Joyce*, vol. 1, ed. Stuart Gilbert. New York: Viking.
Keane, Damien (2014), *Ireland and the Problem of Information: Irish Writing, Radio, Late Modernist Communication*, University Park: Pennsylvania State University Press.

Kenner, Hugh (1987), *The Mechanic Muse*. Oxford: Oxford University Press.
Kern, Stephen (1983), *The Culture of Time and Space, 1880–1918*. Cambridge, MA: Harvard University Press.
Kittler, Friedrich (1999), *Gramophone, Film, Typewriter*, trans. Geoffrey Winthrop-Young and Michael Wutz. Stanford, CA: Stanford University Press.
Kracauer, Siegfried (1995 [1927]), 'The Mass Ornament', in *The Mass Ornament: Weimar Essays*. Cambridge, MA: Harvard University Press, pp. 75–88.
Latour, Bruno (2005), *Reassembling the Social: An Introduction to Actor-Network-Theory*. Oxford: Oxford University Press.
Lippmann, Walter (1991 [1922]), *Public Opinion*. New Brunswick, NJ: Transaction.
Lodhi, Aasiya and Amanda Wrigley (2020), *Radio Modernisms: Features, Cultures and the BBC*. London: Routledge.
McLuhan, Marshall (1962), *The Gutenberg Galaxy: The Making of Typographic Man*. Toronto: University of Toronto Press.
McLuhan, Marshall (2001 [1964]), *Understanding Media: The Extensions of Man*. New York: Routledge.
McLuhan, Marshall and Quentin Fiore (1967), *The Medium is the Massage: An Inventory of Effects*. New York: Bantam Books.
McLuhan, Marshall and Eric Norden (1969), 'Playboy Interview: Marshall McLuhan: A Candid Conversation with the High Priest of Popcult and Metaphysician of Media', *Playboy*, 16: 3 (March), pp. 53–74, 158.
Mansell, James (2017), *The Age of Noise in Britain: Hearing Modernity*. Champaign: University of Illinois Press.
Mao, Douglas and Rebecca Walkowitz (2008), 'The New Modernist Studies', *PMLA*, 123: 3 (May), pp. 737–48.
Marcus, Laura (2007), *The Tenth Muse: Writing about Cinema in the Modernist Period*. Oxford: Oxford University Press.
Marcuse, Herbert (1964), *One-Dimensional Man: Studies in the Ideology of Advanced Industrial Society*. Boston: Beacon.
Marx, Leo (1964), *The Machine in the Garden: Technology and the Pastoral Ideal in America*. Oxford: Oxford University Press.
Morrisson, Mark (2016), *Modernism, Science and Technology*. London: Bloomsbury.
Mumford, Lewis (1967), *Technics and Human Development: The Myth of the Machine, Vol. 1*. New York: Harcourt, Brace, Jovanovich.
Mumford, Lewis (1970), *The Pentagon of Power: The Myth of the Machine, Vol. 2*. New York: Harcourt, Brace, Jovanovitch.
Murphet, Julian (2009), *Multimedia Modernism: Literature and the Anglo-American Avant-Garde*. Cambridge: Cambridge University Press.
Napolin, Julie Beth (2020), *The Fact of Resonance: Modernist Acoustics and Narrative Form*. New York: Fordham University Press.
North, Michael (2005), *Camera Works: Photography and the Twentieth-Century Word*. Oxford: Oxford University Press.
North, Michael (2009), *Machine-Age Comedy*. Oxford: Oxford University Press.
Parikka, Jussi (2012), *What is Media Archaeology?*. London: Polity Press.
Perkowitz, Sidney (2020), 'Only Disconnect! A Pandemic Reading of E. M. Forster', *The Nautilus*, 83 (26 March), <http://nautil.us/issue/83/intelligence/only-disconnect-a-pandemic-reading-of-em-forster> (last accessed 28 July 2020).
Pressman, Jessica (2014), *Digital Modernism: Making It New in New Media*. Oxford: Oxford University Press.
Pryor, Sean and David Trotter (2016), *Writing, Medium, Machine: Modern Technographies*. London: Open Humanities Press.

Purdon, James (2017), 'Literature—Technology—Media: Towards a new Technography', *Literature Compass*, 15: 1, pp. 1–9.
Rosner, Victoria (2020), *Machines for Living: Modernism and Domestic Life*. Oxford: Oxford University Press.
Ross, Shawna (2016), 'Introduction', in *Reading Modernism with Machines*, ed. Shawna Ross and James O'Sullivan. Houndmills: Palgrave Macmillan, pp. 1–13.
Ross, Shawna (2018), 'From Practice to Theory: A Forum on the Future of Modernist Digital Humanities', *Modernism/modernity Print Plus*, 3, Cycle 2 (7 August), <https://doi.org/10.26597/mod.0053> (last accessed 17 January 2022).
Ross, Stephen and Jentery Sayers (2014), 'Modernism Meets Digital Humanities', *Literature Compass*, 11: 9, pp. 625–33.
Sale, Stephen and Laura Salisbury (2015), *Kittler Now: Current Perspectives in Kittler Studies*. Cambridge: Polity Press.
Simondon, Gilbert (2017 [1958]), *On the Mode of Existence of Technical Objects*, trans. Cecile Malaspian and John Rogove. Minneapolis: Univocal.
Ströhl, Andreas (2002), 'Introduction', in Vilém Flusser, *Writings*, trans. Erik Eisel, ed. Andreas Ströhl. Minneapolis: University of Minnesota Press, pp. ix–xxxvii.
Tichi, Cecelia (1987), *Shifting Gears: Technology, Literature, Culture in Modernist America*. Chapel Hill: University of North Carolina Press.
Trotter, David (2007), *Cinema and Modernism*. Oxford: Wiley-Blackwell.
Trotter, David (2013), *Literature in the First Media Age: Britain Between the Wars*. Cambridge, MA: Harvard University Press.
Wallace, Jeff (2005), *D. H. Lawrence, Science, and the Posthuman*. Houndmills: Palgrave Macmillan.
White, Eric (2020), *Reading Machines in the Modernist Transatlantic: Avant-Gardes, Technology and the Everyday*. Edinburgh: Edinburgh University Press.
Williams, Raymond (1972), 'The Technological Society and British Politics', *Government and Opposition*, 7: 1 (Winter), pp. 56–84.
Williams, Raymond (1974), *Television: Technology and Cultural Form*. London: Fontana.
Williams, Raymond (1981), 'Communication Technologies and Social Institutions', in *Contact: Human Communication and Its History*, ed. Raymond Williams. London: Thames and Hudson, pp. 226–38.
Williams, Raymond (1989), 'When Was Modernism?', *New Left Review*, 175 (May–June), pp. 48–52.
Wollaeger, Mark (2006), *Modernism, Media, and Propaganda: British Narrative from 1900 to 1945*. Princeton, NJ: Princeton University Press.

Part I

Machines

1

Electricity: Technologies and Aesthetics

Laura Ludtke

In the first movement of *Orlando*, Virginia Woolf's 1928 gender- and genre-bending novel set in Elizabethan England, night is marked by an absence of light.[1] For Woolf, darkness was the predominant experience of night in the seventeenth century; instances of nocturnal illumination only demonstrate the inherent fallibility of light. The introduction of the electric light does not occur in the novel at the time of its advent in the late 1870s, but in 1928, the moment in which the novel's final movement is set. Woolf employs electric lights to signal the close of a very long nineteenth century and herald the belated beginning of the twentieth century. Orlando is astonished by the convenience of the instantaneous illumination of 'a whole room', of 'hundreds of rooms' at 'a touch'. Not only was 'the sky [. . .] bright all night long' but so too were 'the pavements' (Woolf 2008: 283). This proliferation of artificial illumination across the city distinguishes 'the present moment' from that preceding it. Orlando's new world appears more vibrant and vital; '[t]here was something definite and distinct about the age', something modern (Woolf 2008: 284). Following Woolf's example, we take for granted that the electric light was an accepted object and, indeed, symbol of modernity. But was this still the case, fifty years after the first commercially viable electric lights were introduced in London's streets?

As one of electricity's most prominent and prevalent technologies, the electric light is entangled with an elision of technology and modernity and of modernity with modernisation. But electricity, electric lights and modernity are not interchangeable. Graeme Gooday challenges the presumption that 'electrification and modernization are integral features of the same phenomenon, and thus that electricity is synonymous with modernity' (Gooday 2008: 14–15). The orthogonal processes of domestication and modernisation were neither assured nor easily accomplished; before the electric light could become an object of modernity and, in turn, a modernist object, it needed first to be romanticised 'as both an upper-class luxury and a mysterious magical force' and anthropomorphised 'as benign fairy, goddess, wizard or imp' (Gooday 2008: 19).

In Britain, this process was hampered by overt literary resistance to the electric light. Robert Louis Stevenson exemplifies this resistance in his 1878 essay 'A Plea for Gas Lamps', in which he decried the 'new sort of urban star now shin[ing] out nightly, horrible, unearthly, obnoxious to the human eye' (Stevenson 1928: 231). But it is also evident in Hilaire Belloc's satirical 'Newdigate Poem' from 1894–96, which used rote-seeming heroic couplets and a belaboured iambic pentameter to subvert the so-called 'benefits of the electric light' by rendering them in bathetic terms (Belloc 1910). Works embracing the electric light, such as H. G. Wells's 1899 novel *The Sleeper Awakes* or Richard Marsh's 1897 novel *The Beetle*, tend to be popular and genre fiction rather than literary (Ludtke 2020; Dobson 2017). In modernist fiction, this resistance manifests in Woolf's depiction of electric lights in her novels *Night and Day* (1919) and *Mrs Dalloway* (1925). In *Night and Day*, the intimate drawing room in the prominent Hilbery family's home in Chelsea is contrasted with the small Bloomsbury flat of the suffragist Mary Datchet. While the drawing room is distinguished by its romantic, sociable illumination, 'all silver where the candles were grouped on the tea-table, and ruddy again in the firelight', in Datchet's flat, '[t]he unshaded electric light shining upon the table covered with papers' renders the 'small room [. . .] extremely concentrated and bright' (Woolf 2009: 4, 83). Of the numerous instances of artificial lights in *Mrs Dalloway*, set in post-war London, only the lights in the kitchen, where Mrs Walker frantically prepares the supper for Clarissa's party, are explicitly electric, distinguished by their excessive glare. In keeping with the Dalloways' social status and class conventions, the formal rooms in which the party takes place are lit with 'candlesticks', while the back garden is festooned with 'fairy lamps' (Woolf 2000: 140; 145, 162). In both novels, the electric light delineates existing divisions between generations and social classes.

Of course, not all modernist writers were averse to or resisted depicting the electric light. In Dorothy Richardson's *The Tunnel*, published in 1919 but set in the early 1890s, Miriam Henderson's work in the dentists' practice is illuminated by a 'single five candle-power bulb, drawn low and screened by a green glass shade' (Richardson 1979: 72). Richardson frequently uses artificial light across her *Pilgrimage* novel sequence to establish (or transgress) boundaries between personal and shared or public spaces. In E. M. Forster's 1910 novel *Howards End*, while Aunt Munt suggests the intrusion of electric light from a neighbour's unshaded window will bring about destruction of privacy (and propriety), Margaret sees the 'electric-light globes blossoming in triplets' in Mr Wilcox's offices at the Imperial and West African Rubber Company as a sign of his family's corporate values and their attraction to modernity for modernity's sake (Forster 2000: 51, 157). Electric lights abound in John Cournos's 1922 novel *Babel* and establish a stark contrast between pre-war London and New York. In London, electric lights are 'dingy' and 'tired', and in Soho, known for its nightlife, they are used alongside gas lamps to mitigate the city's distinctive fog, whereas in New York, Broadway is 'the Milky Way of man-created universe': everything is electrified – from a cat playing with yarn on a sewing machine to a lady brushing her teeth in her boudoir – and, thus, commodified (Cournos 1922: 99, 133, 368). In Aldous Huxley's 1923 novel *Antic Hay*, Theodore Gumbril recalls with melancholy the lighting restrictions of the Great War imposed to protect Londoners from zeppelin raids, when 'the electric moons above the roadway were in almost total eclipse' (Huxley 2004: 74). The great variety of electric illumination represented in modernist fiction, of which these are only a few examples, is a testament to the fact that electrification and modernisation were protracted and asymmetrical processes.

This chapter explores these connections between electricity, its technologies and aesthetics in early modernism. While its primary focus is a period spanning from 1910 to 1922, it draws connections between this time and the last two decades of the nineteenth century to demonstrate that the relationship of electricity and modernism is as much one of discontinuity as it is of continuity. By challenging the 'revolutionary' status of electrical technologies in what is ostensibly an 'age of electricity' we can begin to disentangle the association of modernity with electricity and its technologies.

This chapter examines three different examples of this interconnection: the first traces the sense of vagueness inherent to the electrical analogies Ezra Pound and Wyndham Lewis use to establish Vorticism as a literary and artistic movement back to the electrical debates of the late nineteenth century; the second relocates T. S. Eliot and Mina Loy's deliberate eschewal of the electric light in their early poetry in the context of the tropes of urban observation of that same period; and the third reconsiders the status of Giacomo Balla's painting *The Street Lamp* and Loy's lampshade designs in the materialist electrical aesthetics established by Italian Futurists Umberto Boccioni and F. T. Marinetti in their manifestos.

An 'Age of Electricity'

Electricity, as well as its many associated technologies, is frequently conceived of as being paradigm-breaking. In his influential study *The Culture of Time and Space, 1880–1918*, Stephen Kern refers to the period of cultural and technological change with which he is concerned as an 'age of electricity'.[2] Electrical technologies – the telegraph, electric light, telephone and radio – seemed instantaneous and allowed users to feel as though they were transcending space and time (Kern 1983: 15; 114). Kern asserts that the electric light, in particular, 'challenged' the accepted belief that time was both linear and constant because it was singularly responsible for 'a blurring of the division of day and night' (Kern 1983: 29). However, it is more accurate to suggest that electricity represented a form of technological continuity rather than of discontinuity. As Carolyn Marvin contends, electricity was accorded a revolutionary status only in comparisons made between its advent and that of the steam engine in the eighteenth century. In such comparisons, 'the work of electricity was presented as continuing the work of the past', effectively 'revers[ing] the usual meaning of *revolution* as a decisive break with the past' (Marvin 1988: 206).

Where electric lighting is concerned, its introduction into cities such as London tended to reproduce the networks of illumination and systems of distribution already in place for gas lighting and heat. The process of electrification was as much about converting users to adjacent and similar technologies as it was about convincing them to adopt new, unparalleled ones. Moreover, the critical tendency to single the electric light out as a revolutionary technology arises from a flattening of such technological nuances and chronology. In attending to the electric light, it is important to recall that the technologies available in the early 1880s (arc and filament lamps) differ greatly from those of the 1890s (incandescent lamps), let alone those of the 1910s (neon tube and glow lamps), the 1920s (electric automobile headlamps) and the 1930s (floodlighting).

While we tend to locate the 'age of electricity' as spanning the last two decades of the nineteenth century and the first two decades of the twentieth, it is a much longer history, beginning with initial experiments with arc lighting in the 1840s and extending to the establishment of regional utilities and transmission systems – the National Grid in Great Britain (1926–46), the 'Shannon Scheme' in Ireland (1929) or the Tennessee Valley Authority in the United States (1933–9) – in the 1930s and 1940s. These initiatives are often seen as belated projects of modernisation (Hughes 1983: 352–62, 294–8; ESB 2020), but it was not until the early 1930s, when these projects facilitated the 'mass consumption of electricity', that electrification could finally be conceived in terms of modernity (Gooday 2008: 16). Electricity and its technologies, therefore, are neither 'ephemeral' nor 'eternal' in the Baudelairean sense (Baudelaire 1964: 13), nor do they align with the Benjaminian conception of the modern as what is 'new in connection with that which has always already been there' (Benjamin 1999: 1010 (G, 8)). If anything, the electrical revolution of the late nineteenth and early twentieth centuries was a conceptual not a technological paradigm shift.

Despite the prevalence of electricity and its technologies in the late nineteenth century, there was still widespread uncertainty about electricity's nature in technological as well as theoretical terms. For Gooday, the 'recurrent positing of the question "what is electricity?"' is not linked to 'a mass outbreak of metaphysics' in the general public, but is due to the successive introductions of 'new kinds of electrical technology' over a period of forty years (Gooday 2008: 59). Electrical technologies developed and introduced in the 1840s (telegraphy), 1850s (electrotherapy), the late 1870s (early arc and incandescent electric lighting) and the late 1880s (electric heat and power from a central supply) represented a series of conceptual disruptions for the general public that resulted in a recurrent uncertainty. In this context, while 'the work of electricity' was far from novel, as Marvin asserts, the *workings* of electricity certainly were.

Electric Matters

In his 1913 essay 'The Serious Artist', Ezra Pound describes poetic inspiration as 'a sort of energy, something more or less like electricity or radioactivity' (Pound 1954: 49). This simile is replete with the language of inexactitude and suggests a lack of knowledge about the topic. But Pound had a sophisticated understanding of electricity, energy and the ether, and knowingly incorporated scientific language into his poetry and criticism (Nänny 1973; Bell 1981; Kayman 1986; Kenner 1987). His conception of energy, for instance, was shaped by Hudson Maxim's popular treatment of the conservation of energy in *The Science of Poetry and the Philosophy of Language*, which he reviewed in 1912. And, when developing the central concept of Vorticism, he drew on Helmholtz's vortex theory as also popularised by Maxim (Bell 1981: 27, 161, 160–1). Pound's familiarity with contemporary electrical science – or at least popular iterations of it – indicates an awareness with one of the field's major unresolved concerns: the question of what, precisely, electricity was. Appreciating the power behind this uncertainty, Pound and Lewis harnessed the indefinite and indeterminate nature of electricity as analogies, similes and metaphors conveying a conception of creative potential and influence that distinguished them from their predecessors and avant-garde competitors.

Determining the nature of electricity dominated many avenues of scientific and technological enquiry in the nineteenth century (Gooday 2008: 37–59; Marvin 1988: 10–11, 56–62; Nye 1990: 138–84). With the discovery of electro-magnetic waves, the electron, X-rays; the development of wireless telegraphy, the induction motor and other electrical technologies; and the performance of experiments relating to the luminiferous ether and the speed of light, electrical science was at the centre of scientific innovation in the 1890s and early 1900s (Daly 2010: 283). Debates took place across many registers and between different factions, involving scientists, mathematicians, electrical engineers, electrical promoters, popularisers of science, historians of science and, indeed, lay persons. There was little agreement as to whether electricity was an energy, a force or some kind of matter, but the divisions were most pronounced between those who were interested in conducting experiments to discover the properties and behaviour of electricity and those who wanted to exploit electricity (and its applications) as a commodity (Gooday 2008: 38). All parties were united in their desire to know, in their respective fields, whether electricity was material or immaterial. For potential providers and consumers, whether electricity was a 'material commodity' or an 'ethereal mystery' mattered because it determined whether and how it could be measured, distributed and priced (Gooday 2008: 38). At the highest register, physicists and engineers contested the existence of the ether, an 'imponderable medium' first conceived as a conceptual aid to understanding how invisible substances, effects or forces (such as light, heat, electricity and magnetism) travelled across distances in space (Luckhurst 2002: 85–91). The debates of the late nineteenth century did not decisively conclude in the early twentieth century and, in the mind of the general public, the desire to know the precise nature of electricity was supplanted by biddable vagueness of great potential.

Wyndham Lewis drew on this indeterminacy in his essay 'A Review of Contemporary Art', which opens with a forceful comparison between French Cubism, Italian Futurism and English Vorticism. While Futurist art was 'swarming, exploding, burgeoning with life', Vorticist painting was 'electric with a more mastered, vivid vitality' (Lewis 1981: 38). It is not immediately evident what it means to be 'electric' or to have 'a more mastered, vivid vitality', only that these concepts are important to the Vorticist aesthetics he establishes. Instead of clarifying, he offers another divisive, scientific analogy that compares contemporary European painting with 'the laboratory of an anatomist', where subjects are continually examined and dissected, setting it at odds with the true 'objective' of painting, which should be to capture life and to 'profess [. . .] some kind of energy' (Lewis 1981: 39). As with Pound's 'sort of energy' in 'The Serious Artist', the abstractness of Lewis's 'some kind of energy' is an effective if oblique analogy because of its indefiniteness. Lewis's essay was first published in the July 1915 issue of the Vorticist magazine *Blast* (also known as *Blast 2* or the 'War Number') alongside Pound's poem 'A Dogmatic Statement on the Game and Play of Chess', which enacts some of the ideas about energy and poetic creativity Pound articulates in his critical writing. When read in this context, Lewis's use of terms like 'electric' and 'energy' need not be understood as abstract but as contributing to the magazine's larger strategy to define Vorticism as distinct from contemporary avant-garde movements (Hatherley 2010; Klein 2013). At the same time, Pound's verse lines, which have the effect of a massing vortex (Logemann 2013: 86), respond to Lewis's call for art to consist of 'lines and masses' that 'imply force and action' (Lewis 1981: 44).

Patricia Rae connects Pound's use of energy in the poem more explicitly with his critical discussion of poems as '"sources" of energy' in general and, in particular, with his establishment of a 'scientific poetics'. Vorticist poets aspire, she explains, 'to represent a cluster of associated percepts [sic], ideas, and emotions whose origins remain unknown'. They achieve this representation through the 'Image', Pound's term for the poetic technique more often associated with Imagism, but which Rae here identifies as a 'second use of the term' to mean 'the interpretive or absolute metaphor' (Rae 1997: 94, 95). This 'Image' – a metaphor of the vortex and its tumultuous energy – distinguished the Vorticists in both their insistence on linguistic and metaphoric unconventionality and their experiments in form (Whitworth 2010: 190, 146). If, as the electrical debates of the late nineteenth century established, the nature of electricity was unknowable or, at least, indefinite, then electricity and its related topics are a powerful source upon which the Vorticist 'Image' can draw.

Light Verse

Also published in the second issue of *Blast*, T. S. Eliot's iconic city poem 'Rhapsody on a Windy Night' depicts one of the most prominent and memorable lights in modernist verse (Eliot 1963: 16–18). To convey the lamplight's aural resonance in the streetscape of his memory, Eliot introduces a synaesthetic analogy in which each street lamp's 'beats' are like 'a fatalistic drum'. Given the electric and energetic analogies Pound and Lewis deploy in their contributions to this issue, we might expect Eliot to do the same, particularly in his depiction of the street lamp. Yet the lamp's anthropomorphic attributes – it 'sputtered', 'muttered' and 'hummed' – evoke gas, not electric lighting. When considered alongside other representations of the city in *Blast 2* – woodcuts such as Frederick Etchells's 'Hyde Park' and Helen Saunders's 'Atlantic City' or travelogues like Jessica Dismorr's 'London Notes' and Lewis's longer 'The Crowd Master' – 'Rhapsody' fits less obviously in the magazine's Vorticist programme. Indeed, Eliot's depiction of urban illumination and the nocturnal street scene disrupts our expectations about what forms of lighting are depicted in early modernist verse and how.

Writing to John Hayward on 9 September 1942, Eliot explicates the linguistic origin of his synaesthetic analogy, indicating that 'any reference to the reverberes [. . .] wd. take the mind directly to *pre-war* London' (Eliot 2015: 1:420).[3] Here, 'reverberes' refers both to the poem's lamps and to their beats, since the French noun *réverbère* (from the Latin *verbere*, 'to beat') obliquely alludes to a style of reflector common to late nineteenth-century gas lamps. But the connection Eliot makes with pre-war London in this contextual paratext effectively (mis)directs readers away from the earlier French origins of the term.

Although electric lights were becoming increasingly common, gas lighting remained the predominant form of street lighting in pre-war London (Inwood 2005: 292; Hughes 1983: 227–61). Reflectors were used with gas street lamps and pre-date the advent of electric lighting, but in the early twentieth century were more commonly associated with electric lights because they could mitigate the effects of glare produced by electric lights, especially arc lamps (Bowers 1998: 195–200; Otter 2008: 224). However, the pre-history of the reflector coincides with early public illumination initiatives in late eighteenth-century Paris and antecedes the introduction of gas street lighting in early nineteenth-century London.[4] Introduced in the late 1780s, *réverbères* were a form of 'oil-powered reflector [lamp]' hung intermittently above the city streets (Conlin 2013: 180–7). The reflectors diffused a more 'generalized illumination' (Otter 2008: 194). But, as well as making city more visible and 'expos[ing] actions to public vision, legibility, recognition, or shame' (Otter 2008: 194), this form of early public illumination enabled artists and authors to begin capturing the city at night (Conlin 2013: 185, 187).

With its beat-like exhortations to look ('regard') and to notice ('remark') punctuating the three images around which the speaker's memory of the nocturnal perambulations are structured – the woman, the cat and the moon – Eliot's street lamp connects with a tradition preceding Baudelaire's figure of the urban observer: the *flâneur* (Baudelaire 1964: 9). Relocating Eliot's lamp-beats in their historical context foregrounds the rich illuminary past underpinning the linguistic and allusive innovation of his analogy. But it also destabilises the poem's proximity to the Vorticists' concern with pre-war and wartime London. Indeed, the poem's disjunction with the tenets of Vorticism becomes more apparent when it is placed in conversation with Mina Loy's chronically overlooked poem 'Café du Néant'. Soaked in morbid, Symbolist imagery (disembodied eyes, the ephemeral flame of a candle, 'decomposing' fruit), 'Café du Néant' offers an alternative treatment of the belatedly decadent Paris Eliot portrays in 'Rhapsody' ('a dead geranium', 'the 'twisted branch upon the beach', an eroded skeleton) (Loy 1997: 16–17; Eliot 1963: 16–18). First published in *The International* in August 1913, the poem recalls the café scene in Montmartre, where Loy lived from 1903 to 1907 (Bozhkova 2019: paras 4–5; Prescott 2017: paras 6–14; Burke 1996: 177, 185–6). Whereas Eliot's lamps give a sense of the vastness of the desolate streets, Loy's 'Little tapers leaning lighted diagonally' and 'leaning to the breath of baited bodies' seated at the macabre café's 'coffin tables' render its claustrophobic atmosphere even more funebrial. Eliot's street lamp instructs the speaker to '"Regard that woman / Who hesitates toward you in the light of the door / Which opens on her like a grin."' Both speaker and reader in Eliot's poem become complicit in the lamp's glaring gaze, which reduces the exposed woman to her perceived bodily imperfections: we note '"the border of her dress [. . . is] torn / and stained with sand"' and how '"the corner of her eye / Twists like a crooked pin"'. Loy juxtaposes the 'harmonious' and (implicitly) gradual decay of the 'brandy cherries / In winking glasses' with the sudden and utter 'putrefaction' of a cabaret performer, caught up in the intensity of the stage's 'concentric lighting', which has been 'focussed precisely on her'. In a moment of precipitous disenchantment, the lights lay bare life's literal and metaphorical transience (Prescott 2017: 13–14). Here, Loy's lights do not just reveal the tawdry and unforgiving physicality of life; they destroy it.

The decision not to portray the electric light as the subject or, indeed, object of their respective poems is not symptomatic of a modernist eschewal of electric light. Rather, because electric lights proved exceedingly resistant to the process of romanticisation, they were not suited to Loy's and Eliot's respective poetic strategies to ironise the nocturnal lightscape – in 'Café du Néant' the candle becomes a 'Synthetic symbol LIFE' and in 'Rhapsody' the street is 'Held in lunar synthesis'. Moreover, the melancholic and moribund lightscapes depicted in each poem – defiantly not 'profess[ing . . .] some kind of energy' but a sort of entropy – are antithetical to the Vorticist (and Futurist) aesthetics.

Electrical Aesthetics

Bursting with life and light, Giacomo Balla's iconic painting *The Street Lamp* exemplifies the aesthetics of the electric light established by the Italian Futurists in the second decade of the twentieth century. The painting marked a shift in Balla's style and attention towards the Futurists' interest in concepts of speed, technology, violence, the industrial city and energy. But how much did it represent a break from the agricultural and crafts-focused work he exhibited at the Rome Esposizione Internazionale in the autumn of 1911? For, despite its association with Umberto Boccioni's *The City Rises* (1910), which depicts workers renovating the central power plant in Milan, the painting remains closely connected with Balla's earlier work, *The Worker's Day* (1904–7), through a continuity of subject-matter: urban illumination (Rainey et al. 2009: 309; Poggi 2009: 117). The painting bears the date 1909, although Balla probably painted it between 1910 and 1911, with the majority of the work being undertaken in late 1911, bringing into question its position in the early chronology of the Futurist movement. And, while it was listed in the catalogue for the Exhibition of Futurist Paintings at the Bernheim-Jeune Gallery in Paris in 1912, it was not actually among the works on display (Poggi 2009: 117). Indeed, Balla was only loosely affiliated with the Futurists proper at the time: he was a signatory to Boccioni's 'Technical Manifesto: Futurist Painting' in 1910, but remained more closely associated with Divisionism when working on the painting in 1911. The painting's exaltation of light – electric light – as a dynamic manifestation of both speed and technology proved irresistible to the Futurists, who eagerly and anachronistically implicated him in their movement. But, as these inconsistencies reveal, Balla and his painting had an ambivalent relationship with early Italian Futurism – an ambivalence that arises from their unique understanding and representation of light as both a visual phenomenon and a technology.

The Futurists championed electric light as a form of poetic and ideological iconoclasm which sought to destroy sentimental lunar aesthetics and symbology, evident in F. T. Marinetti's exhortation to 'murder the moon-light' in the prose poem accompanying 'The Founding and Manifesto of Futurism', as well as Boccioni's reverence for 'the glare of electric lamps' in the 'Technical Manifesto'. In their 'repudiation' of 'Passéist Venice', Marinetti, Boccioni, Carlo Carrà and Luigi Russolo call for 'the reign of divine Electric Light [to] finally come to liberate Venice from its venal moonlight' (Marinetti et al. 2009: 68). In place of the moon, they wanted 'electric lamps with a thousand rays of light that can brutally stab and strangle the mysterious shadows' (Marinetti et al. 2009: 68). Reflecting on the painting's significance in 1954, when it was acquired by the Museum of Modern Art in New York, Balla explains that he obtained 'the dazzle of the light [. . .] by means of the combination of pure colours'. He feels its originality was due to the 'scientific' techniques he applied 'to represent the light by separating the colors that composed it' (Chessa and Russolo 2012: 36). By emphasising the aesthetics of the light over the aesthetics of the lamp as technology, Balla aligns his work with the Futurists' interest in the quality of the electric light.

From a strictly technological perspective, the Futurists' attraction to the destructive intensity of this light is intriguing because it suggests an interest in a particular form of electric light: the arc lamp, which was one of the first commercially viable forms of electric lighting and was known for the power and absoluteness of its illumination. But, by 1911, while its glaring aesthetics were instantaneously recognisable, arc lighting was no longer a novel technology. Although its original Italian title, *Lampada ad Arco* ('the arc lamp'), has been simplified in translation as *The Street Lamp* or *Street Light*, Balla's painting explicitly portrays these aesthetics, locating it in a particular historical moment. The more generic translations efface the technological specificity of Balla's original title and suggest a uniformity in street lighting that did not exist during that period. Arguably, the electric arc lamp is less disruptive as a technology than the techniques Balla uses to represent it visually – techniques he deploys to translate the contemporary uncertainty about the nature of electricity into an electrical aesthetics. Attending to such nuances unsettles the intimacy between technology and modernity often implied by Futurist aesthetics to reveal an ambivalence greater than that exposed by this rereading of Balla's *Lampada ad Arco*. The aesthetics of the electric arc lamp also offer a point of intersection between Balla's painting and Futurism worth troubling a little further so that we can draw out their illuminary nuances.

Up until this point, we have not really addressed the issue of distinguishing the electric light as a technology from electric light as a visual phenomenon, nor acknowledged the extent to which these two concepts have been elided culturally as well as linguistically. This elision is not the result of an aversion to representing technology; rather, it reveals an imbrication of technology and a phenomenon unique to electric light facilitated by the light's singular lack of flame. The elision is evident in Balla's *Lampada ad Arco*, but culminates in Pablo Picasso's 1937 oil painting *Guernica*, where the light that emanates from the shade covering the iconic eye-shaded incandescent bulb is depicted like rays from the sun and is contrasted with the purely symbolic kerosene lamp brandished by the woman protruding through an open window.[5] Picasso simultaneously fractures the relationship between perception and perspective, and destabilises the relationship between the technology of light and its illumination. Here, the electric light has superseded even the sun – an extreme step for even Balla and the Futurists, who wanted only to challenge our sentimental attachment to the moon.

In its depiction of electric light outshining the moon (the putative triumph of technology over nature), Balla's painting can be seen as a visual analogue for Marinetti's 1909 prose poem 'Let's Murder the Moonlight', wherein the 'three hundred electric moons', powered hydroelectrically, 'cancel' out 'the ancient green queen of love' (Marinetti 2009: 59). The viewer struggles to separate out the flecks of light curving away from the lamp's globe from the surrounding matter in a manner similar to the visual effect described by Boccioni, wherein 'a street pavement that has been soaked by rain beneath the glare of the electric lamps can be an abyss gaping into the very center of the earth' (Boccioni et al. 2009: 65). He thought it possible for the light to annihilate not only the moonlight, but space as well. The Futurists' aesthetics were such that they preferred a dominating and destructive light that 'exceed[ed] the data of vision' (Rainey et al. 2009: 309). But Mina Loy, who was more of a Futurist outsider than a Futurist proper, saw another way to elide technology and visual phenomenon in her take on early modernist electrical aesthetics: the lampshade.

When Loy arrived in New York from Florence in late 1916 as an enigmatic figure of the avant-garde, she began to fashion lampshades, not to function as a supplement to her poetry and art, but to sustain her. She had long been interested in the decorative arts and was fascinated by the German *Jugendstil* lamps and glass she saw at the Secession shows while living in Munich in the 1890s (Burke 1996: 56). For Loy, as for Baudelaire, the boundaries between fashion and art were permeable: thus, glare was not problematic, but a possibility.

Loy's early lampshade designs featured 'old-fashioned sailing ships' and projected images on to surfaces like 'a magic lantern show' (Burke 1996: 224). Far from being 'modern', Loy's lampshades from this period evoke the visual tropes of the late nineteenth century (Potter 2018: 47–68). In their construction, however, using Cellophane and other ephemeral materials, her shades exceeded the innovation of their Victorian antecedents, which were often made of patterned silk, a material preferred for its durability, elegance and convenience (Gordon 1891: 36, 46). Making lampshades was an activity traditionally undertaken by women, but the status of Loy's shades as *objets d'art* (Burke 1996: 227; Hayden 2018: 73) contravenes the gendered binary underpinning Alice Gordon's bourgeois expectation that the (mostly) female readers of her 1891 manual, *Decorative Electricity*, 'divide [their] electric lights into two classes, the practical and the decorative' (Gordon 1891: 16).

Loy returned to making lampshades in Paris in the mid-1920s, assembling whole lamps from flea market finds in 'every conceivable shape' (Burke 1996: 340–1). This time her efforts were more conventionally commercial: she had a wealthy if unpredictable business partner and a small shop on the rue du Colisée on the city's expensive Right Bank. One of her most popular designs, 'L'Ombre féerique' (magical or fairy shadows), gestures not just to the enchantment of the magic lantern show, but also to representations of electric light as fairies or *fées* in the early 1900s. Following the success of the shop's first season, Loy's designs proved a hot commodity; in 1928, they were imitated, mass produced and sold by competitors who wished to capitalise on her originality. And yet, although her designs were reproduced and proliferated, few of Loy's original shades survive, only further confirming their ephemerality as modernist objects.

The aesthetics of Loy's lampshades rely on the layering of transparent, semi-transparent and opaque materials, as well as on the interplay of light against the materials – or, indeed, if we conceive of light as a form of matter as Boccioni did, through the materials and permeating the surrounding matter. In an article in the *Daily Telegraph* from October 1929, Loy is credited with inventing a 'substitute' for glass –*'verrovoile'* – that produced a 'new lighting effect'. This discovery is billed as 'revolutionising [. . .] the artificial flower and lamp-shade industry' (White 2020; Expert 1929).[6] While the material 'diffuses light perfectly' and could be used to create lampshades, its more unique property was its plasticity: before it solidified it was pliable and could be shaped into any form. Unlike the light radiating freely from Balla's unshaded arc lamp, Loy's *'verrovoile'* shades could harness light's creative potential, transforming, shaping and enveloping the light cast through them. As a 'new medium' that could be moulded into old or familiar shapes, *'verrovoile'* subverted the electrical aesthetics established by the Futurists. Crudely translated as glass-silk, Loy's own term for her innovative 'artificial glass', *'verrovoile'*, conveys a sense of delicacy and softness but also frangibility – a counterpoint to the violent masculinity associated with Italian Futurism and an important contribution to the electrical aesthetics of early modernism.

In an 'age of electricity', it is unsurprising that early modernist writers and artists engaged imaginatively with its ideas and terminology, its analogies and aesthetics. Electricity represented the greatest potential, through its many applications and proliferation, to transform modern life. As this chapter demonstrates, despite critical tendencies to treat of electricity and its technologies as inherently *modern, transformative* and *shocking*, the early modernists were less invested in electricity's status as 'new' or 'revolutionary' than their predecessors. And, while the precise nature of electricity is not readily knowable (even in the twenty-first century), at the beginning of the twentieth century, early modernists understood and exploited this indefiniteness for their own ideological and aesthetic purposes. Vorticists like Pound and Lewis drew on electrical analogies in their critical and poetic work to articulate their conception of creativity and to differentiate their avant-garde movement from their competitors. Futurists like Balla, Boccioni and Marinetti advanced material theories of energy and electricity in their manifestos, poetry and paintings. Those adjacent to the avant-garde or at its extremities, figures such as Eliot and Loy, further troubled the already contentious relationship of electricity and modernity by revisiting, repeating and revising the illuminary tropes and innovations of the late nineteenth century and, indeed, in the case of Eliot's *réverbères*, even the late eighteenth century. Loy's lampshades, however, are the most interesting modernist object to consider because of their many contradictions. For, while her 'fairy shades' were romanticising, not modernising, figures and, in that respect, continued the romantic history of the electric light, her use of innovative materials enabled her to shape and manipulate the electric light's most transient aspect: its light.

Notes

1. This book chapter would not have been possible without the support and encouragement of Rachel Crossland, Michael Whitworth, Shelley King, Alexander Lewis and this volume's incisive editors: Alex Goody and Ian Whittington. The chapter is also the work of a precarious scholar who has, over the course of its composition and publication, had four different institutional affiliations and two periods of under- and unemployment (one of which was during a global pandemic).
2. Before Kern used the phrase 'age of electricity' in *The Culture of Time and Space*, it was the title of a series of articles by the engineer William Preece, published in *Time* in 1882, as well as of Park Benjamin's 1886 popular monograph on electricity.
3. These sorts of interventions were common practice in Eliot's private correspondence (Dickey 2020).
4. There were no similar initiatives in London until the early nineteenth century.
5. E. Luanne McKinnon provides an extended analysis of Picasso's use of light in this painting in her dissertation (2015).
6. I am grateful to Alex Goody for drawing my attention to this particular source.

Works Cited

Baudelaire, Charles (1964), *The Painter of Modern Life and Other Essays*, trans. Jonathan Mayne. London: Phaidon Press.
Bell, Ian F. A. (1981), *Critic as Scientist: The Modernist Poetics of Ezra Pound*. London and New York: Methuen.
Belloc, Hilaire (1910), 'Newdigate Poem', in *Sonnets and Verse*. London: Duckworth, pp. 94–8.
Benjamin, Walter (1999), *The Arcades Project*, trans. Howard Eiland and Kevin McLaughlin. Cambridge, MA, and London: Belknap Press of Harvard University Press.
Boccioni, Umberto, Carlo Carrà, Luigi Russolo, Giacomo Balla and Gino Severini (2009), 'Technical Manifesto: Futurist Painting', in *Futurism: An Anthology*, ed. Lawrence S Rainey, Christine Poggi and Laura Wittman. New Haven, CT, and London: Yale University Press, pp. 64–5.
Bowers, Brian (1998), *Lengthening the Day: A History of Lighting Technology*. Oxford and New York: Oxford University Press.
Bozhkova, Yasna (2019), 'Cross-Cultural Baedeker: Mina Loy's Cosmopolitan Modernism', *E-Rea*, 16 (16.2), <https://doi.org/10.4000/erea.7368> (last accessed 3 March 2022).
Burke, Carolyn (1996), *Becoming Modern: The Life of Mina Loy*. New York: Farrar, Straus, and Giroux.
Chessa, Luciano and Luigi Russolo (2012), *Luigi Russolo, Futurist: Noise, Visual Arts, and the Occult*. Berkeley: University of California Press.
Conlin, Jonathan (2013), *Tales of Two Cities: Paris, London and the Birth of the Modern City*. London: Atlantic Books.
Cournos, John (1922), *Babel*. New York: Boni and Liverlight.
Daly, Nicholas (2010), 'The Machine Age', in *The Oxford Handbook of Modernisms*, ed. Peter Brooker, Andrzej Gąsiorek, Deborah Longworth and Andrew Thacker. Oxford: Oxford University Press, pp. 283–99.

Dickey, Frances (2020), 'Reports from the Emily Hale Archive', International T. S. Eliot Society, <https://tseliotsociety.wildapricot.org/news> (last accessed 18 January 2022).

Dobson, Eleanor (2017), 'Gods and Ghost-Light: Ancient Egypt, Electricity, and X-Rays', *Victorian Literature and Culture*, 45: 1, pp. 119–35.

Eliot, T. S. (1963), *Collected Poems 1909–1962*. London: Faber and Faber.

Eliot, T. S. (2015), *The Poems of T. S. Eliot*, ed. Christopher Ricks and Jim McCue, Vol. 1. Baltimore: Johns Hopkins University Press.

ESB (2020), 'Electrifying Ireland, 1927–1978', Electricity Supply Board Archives, <https://esbarchives.ie> (last accessed 18 January 2022).

Expert, Our Paris Fashion (1929), 'Novel Floral Decorations that Light up Modern Interiors', *Daily Telegraph*, 11 October, p. 7.

Forster, E. M. (2000), *Howards End*. New York: Penguin Classics.

Gooday, Graeme (2008), *Domesticating Electricity: Technology, Uncertainty and Gender, 1880–1914*. London: Pickering & Chatto.

Gordon, J. E. H. (Mrs) (1891), *Decorative Electricity*. London: Sampson Low, Marston, Searle, & Rivington.

Hatherley, Owen (2010), 'Casting Spells: The Vortex and the Absence of a British Avant-Garde', *The Journal of Wyndham Lewis Studies*, 1: 1, pp. 1–18, 168.

Hayden, Sarah (2018), *Curious Disciplines: Mina Loy and Avant-Garde Artisthood*, Recencies. Albuquerque: University of New Mexico Press.

Hughes, Thomas Parke (1983), *Networks of Power: Electrification in Western Society, 1880–1930*. Baltimore and London: Johns Hopkins University Press.

Huxley, Aldous (2003), *Antic Hay*. London: Vintage.

Inwood, Stephen (2005), *City of Cities: The Birth of Modern London*. London: Macmillan.

Kayman, Martin A. (1986), *The Modernism of Ezra Pound: The Science of Poetry*. London: Macmillan.

Kenner, Hugh (1987), *The Mechanic Muse*. New York and Oxford: Oxford University Press.

Kern, Stephen (1983), *The Culture of Time and Space, 1880–1918*. Cambridge, MA: Harvard University Press.

Klein, Scott W. (2013), 'How German Is It: Vorticism, Nationalism, and the Paradox of Aesthetic Self-Definition', in *Vorticism: New Perspectives*, ed. Mark Antliff and Scott W. Klein. Oxford: Oxford University Press, pp. 51–67.

Lewis, Wyndham (1981), 'A Review of Contemporary Art', in *Blast 2*, ed. Wyndham Lewis. Santa Barbara, CA: Black Sparrow Press, pp. 38–47.

Logemann, Andrew (2013), 'Physics as Narrative: Lewis, Pound and the London Vortex', in *Vibratory Modernism*, ed. Anthony Enns and Shelley Trower. London: Palgrave Macmillan, pp. 80–95.

Loy, Mina (1997), *The Lost Lunar Baedeker: Poems of Mina Loy*, ed. Roger L. Conover. New York: Farrar, Straus, Giroux.

Luckhurst, Roger (2002), *The Invention of Telepathy, 1870–1901*. Oxford: Oxford University Press.

Ludtke, Laura (2020), 'Sleep, Disruption and the "Nightmare of Total Illumination" in Late Nineteenth and Early Twentieth-Century Dystopian Fiction', *Interface Focus*, 10: 3, <https://doi.org/https://doi.org/10.1098/rsfs.2019.0130> (last accessed 18 January 2022).

McKinnon, E. Luanne (2015), *Picasso's Guernica and the Shadow of Incandescence*, unpublished PhD Thesis, University of Virginia.

Marinetti, F. T. (2009), 'The Founding and Manifesto of Futurism', in *Futurism: An Anthology*, ed. Lawrence S. Rainey, Christine; Poggi and Laura Wittman. New Haven, CT: Yale University Press, pp. 51–9.

Marinetti, F. T., Umberto Boccioni, Carlo Carrà and Luigi Russolo (2009), 'Against Passéist Venice', in *Futurism: An Anthology*, ed. Lawrence S. Rainey, Christine Poggi and Laura Wittman. New Haven, CT: Yale University Press, pp. 67–70.

Marvin, Carolyn (1988), *When Old Technologies Were New: Thinking About Electric Communication in the Late Nineteenth Century*. Oxford: Oxford University Press.
Nänny, Max (1973), *Ezra Pound: Poetics for an Electric Age*, Bern: Francke.
Nye, David (1990), *Electrifying America: Social Meanings of a New Technology, 1880–1940*. Cambridge, MA: MIT Press.
Otter, Chris (2008), *The Victorian Eye: A Political History of Light and Vision in Britain, 1800–1910*. Chicago: University of Chicago Press.
Poggi, Christine (2009), *Inventing Futurism: The Art and Politics of Artificial Optimism*. Princeton, NJ: Princeton University Press.
Potter, Jonathan (2018), *Discourses of Vision in Nineteenth-Century Britain: Seeing, Thinking, Writing*, Palgrave Studies in Nineteenth-Century Writing and Culture. Cham, Switzerland: Palgrave Macmillan.
Pound, Ezra (1954), 'The Serious Artist', in *Literary Essays of Ezra Pound*, ed. T. S. Eliot. London: Faber and Faber, pp. 41–57.
Prescott, Tara (2017), *Poetic Salvage: Reading Mina Loy*. Lewisburg, PA: Bucknell University Press.
Rae, Patricia (1997), *The Practical Muse: Pragmatist Poetics in Hulme, Pound, and Stevens*. Lewisburg, PA: Bucknell University Press.
Rainey, Lawrence S., Christine Poggi and Laura Wittman, eds (2009), *Futurism: An Anthology*. New Haven, CT, and London: Yale University Press.
Richardson, Dorothy M. (1979), 'The Tunnel', in *Pilgrimage II*. London: Virago, pp. 9–288.
Stevenson, Robert Louis (1928 [1878]), 'A Plea for Gas Lamps', in *Virginibus Puerisque: and Later Essays*. London and Glasgow: Collins' Clear-Type Press, pp. 226–34.
White, Eric (2020), *Reading Machines in the Modernist Transatlantic*. Edinburgh: Edinburgh University Press.
Whitworth, Michael H. (2010), *Reading Modernist Poetry*. Reading Poetry. Chichester: Wiley-Blackwell.
Woolf, Virginia (2000), *Mrs Dalloway*, new edition, Oxford World's Classics. Oxford: Oxford University Press.
Woolf, Virginia (2008), *Orlando: A Biography*, Oxford World's Classics. Oxford: Oxford University Press.
Woolf, Virginia (2009), *Night and Day*, Oxford World's Classics. Oxford: Oxford University Press.

2

Clocks: Modernist Heterochrony and the Contemporary Big Clock

Charles Tung

Modernist Clockwork

LIKE THE CYBERDYNE Systems model 101 cyborg in James Cameron's *The Terminator* who suddenly materialises in a crackling time-displacement sphere in 1984 Los Angeles, the machine-human entity in E. V. Odle's *The Clockwork Man* appears abruptly in the middle of a cricket match in an English village, having time-travelled to 1923 from 8,000 years in the future. In Odle's text, which Brian Stableford and David Langford call 'the earliest major cyborg novel', this future human is 'capable of going not only someplace but also somewhen', because a special kind of clock has been implanted in his brain (Stableford and Langford 2018; Odle 1923: 90). By means of this internal 'mechanical contrivance', the clockwork man is not locked in the world of mechanistic linearity but freed from it – the clock allows him to access 'a multiform world . . . a world of many dimensions' (Odle 1923: 180, 146–7). While the novel's anxieties about the cyborg's loss of humanity tilt the narrative's sympathies toward the 'Makers' rather than their clockwork, toward humanist finitude and freedom over slavish mechanism, *The Clockwork Man* also seizes 'upon the clock as the possible symbol of a new counterpoint in human affairs', a device for thinking beyond the usual conception of historicity and its limitations, the 'old problems of Time and Space' (Odle 1923: 80). Odle's character Gregg, who considers the clock as an element in the final stages of human development, remarks that the 'clock, perhaps, was the index of a new and enlarged order of things', a symbol of speculative insights beyond what 'his limited faculties could perceive' (Odle 1923: 110, 111).

As an index of the order of things, the clock appears so frequently in early twentieth-century cultural production that, as Michael Levenson has said of the trope's encompassing theme of temporality, 'it can be taken as a cultural signature' (Levenson 2004: 197). However one calculates the exact bookends of canonical modernism, the period's time obsession lands squarely within what the historian Alexis McCrossen claims was 'the height of the public clock era in the United States and indeed throughout the world' (McCrossen 2013: 6). As her book, *Marking Modern Times: A History of Clocks, Watches, and Other Timekeepers in American Life*, demonstrates, this apex of public time occurred from the 1870s to the 1930s, during which an estimated 15,000 new public clocks were erected across the US, with countless extensions of official order appearing on walls, desks and mantelpieces. Paul Glennie and Nigel Thrift focus on an earlier span (1300–1800) in their history of timekeeping in England and Wales, in order to track the slow rise of the late medieval public clock and the historically specific complex of practices constituting public time. While they contest narratives of clock time that posit a technologically determined monolithic entity, their work in *Shaping the Day* underlines how the dominant account of clock time is tied to late nineteenth- and early twentieth-century industry and capitalist production, imperial control and urbanisation (Glennie and Thrift 2009: 42–53). During this period, according to E. P. Thompson's foundational account, the transition in England 'to mature industrial society' placed the clock at the centre of new manufacturing techniques and practices of supervising labour, ways of creating efficient 'time routines', and an experiential and cultural 'time-sense' produced by 'technological conditioning' (Thompson 1967: 79–80). Citing the 'deadly statistical clock' of Charles Dickens's *Hard Times* – the 'emblem of Thomas Gradgrind . . . "which measured every second with a beat like a rap upon a coffin-lid"' – Thompson cast the clock as the figure of a 'rationalism [that] has grown new sociological dimensions since Gradgrind's time' (Thompson 1967: 96).

Thus, rather than signifying 'a new and enlarged order of things', the clock has most frequently come to stand for the opposite – a strict and homogeneous order, a narrowing and regimenting world of quantification, regulation and uniformity. The dominant critical narrative surrounding the clock in modernist texts centres so much on their subjectivist antipathy to these devices that we could easily designate the early twentieth century in literature as the height of the private anti-clock era. As Theodore Ziolkowski once put it,

> in virtually every case . . . the clock is summoned forth as a negative symbol by the subjective consciousness of an individual who wishes to assert his own private time against the claims of public life. Clocks in modern literature seem to exist only to be ignored, dropped, shattered, deformed. (Ziolkowski 1969: 188)

While Randall Stevenson's more recent study almost fifty years later makes space for 'modernist temporalities . . . beyond mind altogether', modernism remains largely under the rubric of 'time in the mind': although writers move 'along a spectrum of possibilities' between the two poles of subjective time and 'time on the clock', they nevertheless 'shifted their priorities – towards mind rather than machine . . . . "Time on the clock", after all, inevitably remains a "time in the mind" itself . . . impossible to expunge completely from consciousness' (Stevenson 2018: 122). Even with Stevenson's deft flexibility in his comprehensive account of imaginative engagements with regimented public time, his account gravitates toward what Virginia Woolf's *Orlando* (1928) called 'the queer element of the human spirit . . . the timepiece of the mind' (Woolf 2006: 72). Woolf's novel has served, as David Leon Higdon points out, as 'the twentieth-century *locus classicus*' for the idea that, ultimately, 'public-mechanic-objective-clock time merits less attention than private-subjective-organic-psychological time' (Higdon 1976: 52).

While I do not wish to dismiss or downplay the critical strengths and affective power of the dominant reading of the clock, the figure of the timepiece – in modernist literature and in the strain of contemporary culture which extends rhizomatically from it – also suggests a new heterochronic order. In this enlarged order of things, one clock implies the existence of others marking different histories and governing varying scales. In this way, the device of the clock – literary and literal – functions to remind us that, as Glennie and Thrift remark, 'clocks are not a general instrument. Instead clocks operate in many networks of practices at once . . . [and] are assemblages of signs and things' (Glennie and Thrift 2009: 73–4). Indeed, as they argue, 'what we call time is an ungainly mixture of times – unfolding at different speeds in different spaces – which intersect and interact in all manner of ways' (66). In this chapter, I would like to argue likewise that clocks are not (only) a general symbol. Rather, across the long twentieth century, clocks have in many cases functioned as a symbolic technology that makes explicit the assemblages of cultural machines into which the image of the timepiece is plugged. As the operation of this image comes more frequently to serve the theme of planetary disaster, the machinic character of big clocks in cultural discourse, such as the Doomsday Clock and the Clock of the Long Now, tells time in ways that James Purdon would call 'technographic' – a mode that 'seeks to bring to consciousness the technicity of text and the textuality of technics' (Purdon 2018: 7). In the zone of 'the mutual mediation of technology and literature', the big clocks that emerge from the proliferation of clocks from modernism to the present become part of a counter-infrastructure supporting the production of temporal defamiliarisation and historiographic estrangement (Purdon 2018: 7). In this sense, big clocks are clockpunk machines, which, from the perspective of Jussi Parikka's media archaeology, unearth anti-teleological possibilities buried in obsolescence, and which help to generate alternative histories and historical alternatives (Parikka 2017).

The Machine of Modernity, the Machinic Assemblage of Clocks

Representations of timepieces in canonical modernism are famous for their hostility toward modernity, of which the clock is not only the master symbol but also the central instrument in its technological infrastructure. Consider Joseph Conrad's *The Secret Agent* (1907), based on the actual anarchist plan in 1894 to blow up the prime meridian and the Royal Observatory in Greenwich, whose operations had come to stand for the coordination of modern life at a distance (the synchronisation of clocks on ships and in train stations). A decade earlier, at the 1884 International Meridian Conference, the machinery and clockwork of Greenwich had successfully helped to establish the universal day based on the mean solar time in a borough of Britain's capital city, London. In James Joyce's *Ulysses* (1922), a novel organised around, among other things, different kinds of timing, Leopold Bloom observes that Dublin's 'timeball on the ballast office' is tied to Greenwich (invented by the Royal Navy to synchronise marine chronometers, timeballs usually dropped from observatory towers, where ships off shore could see them). Bloom's chain of inferences suggestively connect his observation that Dublin's 'clock is worked by an electric wire from Dunsink [Observatory]' to the techno-political idea that the city and the format of its citizens' lives are plugged directly into the larger nets and networks controlled by London. The parallactic temporal distance between Dublin and London was twenty-five minutes up until the Easter Rising in 1916 (Joyce 1986: 137).

Following these well-known literary representations, equally famous critical accounts of timepieces likewise foreground this humanist antipathy to the clock's symbolic and material–infrastructural functions. Starting with the most recent, John Durham Peters's account of clocks and 'sky media' asserts that 'the watch is the prime symbol of modernity, a time bomb marking our Faustian mortgage of ourselves' (Peters 2015: 225). As Jimena Canales points out, whereas clocks once 'were symbols of a universal order maintained and set in motion by God himself', modern clocks had begun to produce and literally mark a new, homogeneous, inhospitable temporality that had significant 'human costs in terms of lived time' (Canales 2016: 115, 114, 123). Those costs measured the distance between a humanist valorisation of lived experience and the dehumanising machinery of modernity. Lewis Mumford's oft-quoted passage from *Technics and Civilization* that claims that the 'clock, not the steam engine, is the key-machine of the modern industrial age' reaches back to earlier analyses of the unnatural construction of clock-time units in the historical circumstances underlying the West's progressive vision of itself (Mumford 1934: 14–15). In 1847, Karl Marx's *The Poverty of Philosophy* had figured 'the pendulum of the clock' as a measure of value that effaces the human, such that 'Time is everything' and a human being becomes 'nothing . . . no more than the carcase of time' (Marx 1910: 57). In 1923, citing this particular indictment of 'the subordination of man to the machine' (57), Georg Lukács's *History and Class Consciousness* described the capitalist 'process of labour' in factories as 'rational mechanisation extend[ing] right into the worker's soul' – a process in which the clock 'freezes' and 'fragments' the 'qualitative, variable, flowing nature' of human temporality 'into abstract, exactly measurable, physical space' (Lukács 1972: 88, 90).

In modernist studies, scholars have tended to anchor opposition to the clock in their commitment to the particular temporal textures of subjective life. Against such particularity and uniqueness were the large-scale changes generated by new technologies of transport, communication and coordination, which depended on clock time as 'the most ubiquitous of modern technical infrastructures . . . deeply embedded in scientific, cultural, institutional, economic, and military realities' (Mackenzie 2001: 236). Clocks were necessary to plan the efficient movements of bodies, messages and products – on the factory floor, in urban spaces, in military operations, over telegraph and wireless networks, on marine trade routes, across passenger and commercial train tracks. If modernity entailed these efforts to eliminate lag and waste through precise timing and synchronisation, then much of the art and thinking that falls under the banner of modernism provides a poignant contrast in which duration is the major counter-term to the clock, a *durée* not defined quantitatively as a span or length, but rather as a qualitative, dynamic, vitalist flux. While late nineteenth-century engineers like Sanford Fleming had successfully advocated for the standardisation of time based on a single prime meridian – a universal 'civil time' that, as Adam Barrows puts it, transformed 'the earth itself into a perfect cosmopolitan clock' – the dominant account of modernism has usually located cultural resistance to this clock-time world in Henri Bergson's redefinition of time as interior states of consciousness that 'melt into and permeate one another' (Barrows 2011: 32; Bergson 1913: 104).

For Bergson, the clock was precisely the wrong symbol for time, since its operations were essentially spatial and therefore negations of the temporal. As he wrote in 1889, 'the pendulum of the clock cuts up into distinct fragments and spreads out, so to speak, lengthwise the dynamic and undivided tension of the spring' in exactly the same way that the frozen 'simultaneities of physical phenomena' – of things that exist in space as opposed to processes unfolding – chop up our 'inner life in which succession implies interpenetration' (Bergson 1913: 228). While true duration for Bergson is 'nothing else but the melting of states into one another', clock time comprises the detemporalised subdivisions of *durée* into spatialised, homogeneous points: 'When I follow with my eyes on the dial of a clock the movement of the hand which corresponds to the oscillations of the pendulum,' he argued, 'I do not measure duration . . . I merely count simultaneities' (Bergson 1913: 107–8). His valorisation of vital duration with its repudiation of the clock seems to inform many, if not all, of the scenes and styles of melting, flowing, fragmentation and spreading out in modernist literature. The ambiguity of modernism's representations of the clock have long been seen in modernist studies as expressing the twentieth century's larger ambivalence toward the technological culture of modernity – a tension marked by the retreat to organic subjectivity or the Futurist celebration of 'the extension of human powers in the machine', on the one hand, and the critique of 'the totality of industrial civilization . . . as depersonalised and empty', on the other (Armstrong 2003: 165).

No doubt literary modernism engaged this ambivalence between the 'mechanical, monotonous clock-face of time' and the vital fluctuations of human life and subjectivity (Lawrence 1998: 483), but it also explored another ambivalence: on the one hand, 'the clock' conceived rightly as the symbol of modernity and its technical infrastructure for imperial and capitalist coordination based on a singular time, and on the other hand, the rise of many clocks, understood as the symbol of non-subjective temporal multiplicity. Bergson's public debate with Albert Einstein in 1922 made this second ambivalence clear. In Einstein's twin paradox, one twin on earth and one twin travelling at high speeds would discover upon their reunion that the earthbound twin had aged much more. In countering Einstein's special relativity, Bergson's understanding of simultaneities had refused to give up the correspondence between the clock and the subject, whereas Einstein's understanding of the now in which one checks the clock corresponded not to the subject but to frames of reference. For Bergson, '"to know what time it is" consists in finding a correspondence, not between one clock and another one, but between one clock and the present moment, the event which just passed' for the person checking the time (Bergson 1972: 1344).[1] By contrast, as the astrophysicist Adam Frank puts it, 'under the physics of relativity, all measures of simultaneity are frame-dependent': Einstein destroyed 'the intuitive idea – hardwired into our brains' – not only that the now is defined in relation to subjective becoming, but that 'only one "now" exists' (Frank 2011: 146). 'There can be no universally recognised, simultaneous present, no "now" for all creation', because different clocks tick at different rates in different reference frames (Frank 2011: 136). As Einstein wrote in 1905, in his famous paper 'On the Electrodynamics of Moving Bodies',

> we cannot attach any absolute signification to the concept of simultaneity . . . two events which, viewed from a system of co-ordinates, are simultaneous, can no longer be looked upon as simultaneous events when envisaged from a system which is in motion relatively to that system. (Einstein et al. 1923: 42–3)

In *Relativity: The Special and General Theory*, Einstein demonstrated that 'as a consequence of its motion the clock goes more slowly than when at rest' and that a second ticked off on one clock does not equal one second on another – if a 'clock is moving with the velocity v', then 'the time which elapses between two strokes of the clock is not one second, but seconds, *i.e.*, a somewhat larger time' (Einstein 1920: 44). As Peter Galison argues, Einstein's work in the patent office in Bern shows up clearly in his theory of special relativity, which made use of 'some of the most symbolised mechanisms of modernity' – trains, wires, synchronisation devices – to work through the problem of non-simultaneity with respect to clocks at a distance, 'precisely the practical, technological issue that had been racking North America and Europe for the last thirty years' (Galison 2003: 255, 256). While practical adjustments could be made for the time of signal transmission necessary for the correspondence determining simultaneity, the 'new enlarged order of things' that Odle attributes to 'a multiform world' is an order with no 'single overarching Newtonian cosmic time' (Frank 2011: 133). What remains, as Frank describes it, is only 'a relativistic patchwork of times, each measured by observers moving relative to one another' (Frank 2011: 134).

The Enlarged Order of Heterochrony

Thus, the symbolic value and material operations of the clock that I wish to underscore here link the clock not to Time (with a capital T and in the singular) but to other clocks, to the profusion of clocks in twentieth-century cultural production and beyond, to a non-subjective, non-humanist network of temporal multiplicity that we might call heterochrony. The hostility toward modernity inscribed in the cultural presence of the clock, in other words, is not anchored solely in subjectivist concerns to protect humanist visions of unquantifiable temporality, but also, and with equal importance, in the political–historiographic objection to modernity's aggressive institutionalisation of a single clock. On the very first page of *Einstein's Clocks, Poincare's Maps*, Galison provides what I think is one of the clearest descriptions of Odle's new order of 'the clock as the possible symbol of a new counterpoint':

> In Einstein's electrotechnical world, there was no place for such a 'universally audible tick-tock' that we can call time, no way to define time meaningfully except in reference to a definite system of linked clocks. Time flows at different rates for one clock-system in motion with respect to another . . . .. 'Times' replace 'time'. (Galison 2003: 13)

Another way of reading the clock in this period, then, is as a symbol and synecdoche for clocks in the plural, for a situation in which 'we can very well imagine as many clocks as we like' (Einstein and Infeld 1938: 190).

Heterochrony is a useful name for this pluralisation of times, because it captures the coexistence of unsynchronised difference as well as the otherness of entire reference frames beyond individuals. In 'Of Other Spaces', Michel Foucault briefly used this term to describe the way heterotopias' archival temporal collocation functioned as an 'absolute break . . . with traditional time', the way certain sites seem to 'enclose in one place all times, all epochs, all forms, all tastes' in defiance of Newtonian time's assignment of elapsed events to a definite position in the past (Foucault 1986: 26). But the better angle on this term comes from its original use by Ernst Haeckel in 1875 in the context of evolutionary developmental biology: here heterochrony signified deviations from the fiction of a master ontogenetic clock, which was thought to have governed the unilinear progress of embryonic development wherein every adult stage of a species' evolution is replayed in the individual organism. The fiction that ontogeny recapitulates phylogeny in this way was destroyed by the aberrations Haeckel himself observed, and such deviations in the rate of embryonic processes are now seen as the engines of evolutionary variation itself. Thus, heterochrony is not the figure for the exception that proves the rule of unilinear development, which Haeckel believed was the case, but is rather the signifier of the machinic assemblage of desynchronised timings of organ development that alter the morphological unity of the present.

Many clocks in modernism are heterochronic in that 'the time' or the present they reference is a tissue of disjunctive timings and anachronistic phenomena, a clash of time-telling devices and times. Woolf's *Orlando* investigates temporal relativity not simply because of the multiple selves that occupy any seemingly individual person, but also because her work's 'difficult business – this time-keeping' acknowledges the 'sixty or seventy different times which beat simultaneously in every normal human system', which scales up to different times within any seemingly non-subjective present (Woolf 2006: 223). *Mrs Dalloway* makes it clear that Woolf's London is a space in which multiple clocks and very different histories are not in step with each other. The clocks that preside over the novel's action – Big Ben, St Margaret's, Rigby and Lowndes, Harley Street's – might appear to signify exclusively the unification of all the characters' lives within the regular and regularising pulse of empire, nation, commerce and medicine, but they also point to the divergence of a number of different social, economic and political histories, represented primarily by Clarissa Dalloway and Septimus Warren Smith, but also arguably by Doris Kilman's position, Elizabeth Dalloway's access to new futures and Mr Bentley's daydream in Greenwich of Einstein and the desire to get outside one's reference frame. In Faulkner's *The Sound and the Fury*, while the Compsons' pocket watch and broken kitchen clock relentlessly keep the time that measures the family members' failures to keep pace with different trajectories of development (sexual, existential, social, economic), the clocks also point to a range of different coordinate systems in which time is elapsing differently. The clocks in the jeweller's shop epitomise this heterochrony: the eldest brother, Quentin Compson, sees in the shop window 'a dozen watches' showing 'a dozen different hours' (Faulkner 1994: 54). The shop's loud, contradictory ticking underlines, even where there is overlap and intersection, the stark differences and lag among the histories evoked by the African American characters on mules and streetcars, Southerners on trains and in cars, North-to-South telegrams and the New York stock market.

Heterochronic clock images – from modernism to the mantelpieces in George Pal's *The Time Machine* (1960) and Robert Zemeckis's *Back to the Future* (1985) – and the aspiration to the condition of weird time-telling draw on the tendency of the clock to become or imply many clocks (Figure 2.1). Even without Einstein, the mechanical clock worked to reveal the time's number, rates and scales as often as it symbolised the coercive regularity of a monolithic modernity. Against the consolidation of a single metric for the coordination of empire and the quantification of capitalism, the heterochronic clock revealed the irregularity of planetary rotation, the imperfection of regimenting mechanisms and the historicity of the isotopic and isochronic space-time fictions that tried to conjure nature to their schemes. Even as the synchronisation network expanded across steam pipes, telegraph wires, mobile phone masts and fibre-optic cables, as well as commercial, scientific and cultural institutions, many clocks continued to produce and reveal heterochronic difference. These disparities of multiple clocks were and are not primarily about playful, dialectic-destroying difference, but about the disjunctive tensions among different timescales that reconfigure the site of politics and historical intervention.

Figure 2.1 The Time Traveller's mantel clocks in George Pal's *The Time Machine*, 1960, and Doc Brown's dresser clocks in Robert Zemeckis's *Back to the Future*, 1985.

Big Clocks

The planetary clock is a trope and a device that is often understood to tell an ultimate time, to assert the most basic horizon for all other forms of time-telling, and to reduce the discordance and disjunctiveness of multiple clocks and timescales to the one inexorable line for reckoning environmental morbidity and species mortality. In this respect, the ticking of the clock of first modernity, which governed the short-term coordination and distribution of goods, is absorbed into the ticking of the big clock of second modernity, which, as Ulrich Beck theorised, is concerned to manage the long-term and large-scale 'hazards and insecurities induced and introduced by modernisation itself' (Beck 1992: 21). The big clock of ecological risk is the mechanism for thinking forward to the arrival of dangers set in motion by the history and networks that had produced the 'one, true, "cosmopolitan" time of modernity' (Barrows 2011: 102). For instance, the Doomsday Clock, which was invented at the end of the Second World War by the *Bulletin of Atomic Scientists*, functioned to register our proximity to a midnight or zero hour of nuclear extinction (Figure 2.2). In the age of nuclear criticism, the culmination of techno-scientific development in nuclear war was a clock narrative that produced a negative universality in which, as Molly Wallace points out, all were asked to imagine 'the future's nonexistence': the Doomsday Clock was the figure for 'the possibility that there would be no future', for the fact that time itself would be annihilated (Wallace 2016: 6, 4). Similarly, the Clock of the Long Now, a massive clock designed to last 10,000 years, is meant to shift all of humanity's short-term focus to the ultimate timeline of extinction and species death. Since 'ten thousand years is about the

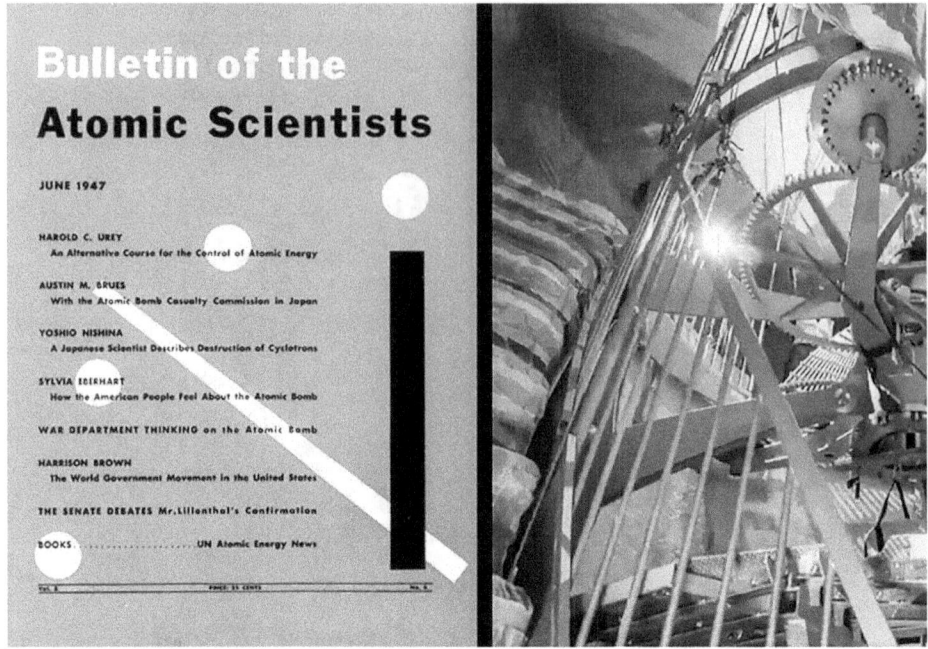

Figure 2.2 The Doomsday Clock on the cover of the *Bulletin of Atomic Scientists*, 1947, and the staircase inside the Clock of the Long Now, 2011.

age of civilization', the clock's technical–symbolic function is to 'measure out a future of civilization equal to its past' (Long Now Foundation n.d.). The history that begins with the invention of agriculture is thus only half-way done, and human civilisation finds itself at a crossroads, faced with the choice of an alternative to 'the short-horizon perspective that goes with burgeoning market economies (next quarter) and the spread of democracy (next election)': since '*Now* is the period in which people feel they live and act and have responsibility . . . we need things that give people a sense of the long now' (Brand 1999: 133).

However, in both cases, the Doomsday and Long Now clocks reveal not only the tendency to collapse different social rhythms into the one true time of the planet, but also the presence of multiple temporal orders that must be reckoned with (rather than abandoned), if the course of planetary history is to be altered. With respect to the misleading aspects of the Doomsday Clock, Wallace points to the difficulty of reading 'its face . . . [which now ought to measure] different scales of the temporality (and, indeed, spatiality) of risk' (Wallace 2016: 17). She argues that the 'Clock might better be conceived, then, not only as a countdown to some potential future annihilation, but also as . . . .. syncopating a present that contains multiple catastrophes, historical and to come, simultaneously' (17). Similarly, while the Clock of the Long Now attempts to synchronise human efforts with the survivalist measures that have tuned out all non-essential rhythms, its operation will reveal heterochronic disjunction amid its well-crafted, theme-park historicising. When the Clock's projected visitors walk through the attraction's giant internal 'clock mechanics', ranging from fastest ('tick[ing] once per day') to slowest (measuring 'the equinoxes, a 25,784-year cycle'), the journey through the gears raises questions about the variety of timescales that overlap but refuse to nest fully within what Srinivas Aravamudan calls catachronism – the unification of time in which the entirety of the line until now becomes the simplistic causal track headed toward 'a future proclaimed as determinate' (Aravamudan 2013: 8). As a self-congratulatory project that will have led to human survival, the Clock's ties to Disney historicism (Hillis's work at Disney Imagineering) and to Amazon.com (Jeff Bezos is now helping to fund the project) reveal how the catachronic theme-park thrills of short-term delivery systems for goods and texts function as a giant distraction. What they distract from are the necessary engagements with the disjunctive historicity in which the operations of capitalist temporal horizons do not simply disappear in the zoom-out to a planetary timeline of human civilisation.

Big clocks – clocks that may or may not be physically large but whose symbolic scope or infrastructural connections are mammoth – have a history that attests to this kind of zooming out in which all times are nested within one time. Thomas Allen argues that monumental clocks in the nineteenth century projected 'grand temporal visions inspired by problems of population, by the need for narrative structures to manage the movement of people as populations across historical time' (Allen 2015: para. 4). Such visions informed the aesthetic refocusings from the domestic time-spaces of liberal subjectivity to the collective destiny of human populations. It is for this reason that the clock that Edward Curtis famously removed from his 1910 photograph 'In a Piegan Lodge' can be seen as a big clock. In this staging of indigeneity, the presence of the clock is both a synecdoche and a metaphor for the time-telling of human civilisation in which indigenous peoples were actively 'disappeared' from history. The image from the original glass negative reveals what Curtis felt was the intrusive presence of the clock between the two seated figures, which disrupted the 'Indianness' of the picture's constructed present (Gidley 2001: 51). In a later photograph included in Volume 6 of *The North American Indian*, Curtis had manipulated the image in the photogravure process, retouching the clock out of existence, in some sense a guilty erasure of the evidence of the violent settler-colonial presence in the histories of indigenous peoples, specifically that of the Blackfoot Tribe. However, 'clocks were relatively common among the Blackfeet once the tribe had become settled on reservations', as Shamoon Zamir writes, and by eliminating all signs of the violence of deculturation, Curtis presents a historiographically seamless moment of 'the Indian' and 'the premodern' that simultaneously affirms the existence of the big clock operating elsewhere, and preserves the unitary conception and monolithic nature of US, world and human history from which 'the Indian' is excluded (Zamir 2014: 56).

Starting with Johannes Fabian's *Time and the Other* (1983), the critique of the disappearance of smaller clocks into the largest, or their exclusion from the universal timeline of human development, tends to repudiate allochronism, the 'denial of coevalness' of 'others', the refusal of the simultaneity of non-Western peoples in the ethnographic present of white anthropology (Fabian 2014: 33). In her reading of Curtis's denial of the clock, McCrossen discusses in general 'the extent to which federal buildings and timepieces were meant to . . . reinforce racial hierarchies' and mentions a late nineteenth-century architectural design for a US Post Office building and clock tower (McCrossen 2013: 150). On the outside of the official government building and the clock tower, as Lois Craig notes, stands 'a parade of ethnic stereotypes', who 'marvel at the splendour of the federal presence' (Craig 1984: 166). Here, as in Curtis's segregation of a romanticised indigeneity from the time of civilisation and history, McCrossen articulates very clearly the standard reading:

> Anglo-Americans came to believe that other peoples lacked a sense of time, or if they had one, that it was a 'primitive' time sense. . . . Without clock time various states of savagery were certain. Living in time was an indicator of civilization, so much so that photographers and other ethnographers of 'primitive' peoples sometimes removed evidence of watch and clock ownership from their records. (McCrossen 2013: 150)

The big clock of 'the human' relegates all others' histories to the position of exteriority or anteriority.

Today, the ambition to be included in the one true time of history and human civilisation can be seen as a capitulation to the self-serving and aggrandising imperial/settler fantasy of a singular timeline. Stuart Brand's book on the Clock of the Long Now argues for the scaling up of the present by pointing out that

> *Now* is the period in which people feel they live and act and have responsibility. For most of us *now* is about a week, sometimes a year. For some traditional tribes in the American northeast and Australia *now* is seven generations back and forward (175 years each direction).

Figure 2.3 Edward Curtis's 'In a Piegan Lodge', 1910, and the architectural design for a US Post Office building with clock tower in the *Annual Report of the Supervising Architect of the Treasury Department*, 1888, reprinted in Lois Craig's *The Federal Presence*, 1984.

However, the Long Now that supersedes and subsumes these nows is the ultimate timeframe necessary to save the species and the planet, on which his and Hillis's Clock is mean to refocus our attention (Brand 1999: 133). While the need for rescaling the present is not wrong, the conception that there is really only one time that matters, and that this time is a neutral big tent for the coeval dwelling of times themselves, reasserts 'the apocalyptic understanding of time underlying Western modernity', 'the traditional apocalyptic temporality' that Diletta de Cristofaro ascribes to the Doomsday Clock. For de Cristofaro, this big clock locks time into dystopian or utopian teleological schemes rather than fostering the 'critical temporalities' that reveal the function of such apocalyptic revelations (de Cristofaro 2018: 2; 2020: 6–7). Zamir's reading of Curtis's erasure of the clock, which was owned by the Blackfeet subjects themselves (Little Plume and Yellow Kidney), is that the photographer's gesture 'violates not only the two Native Americans' agency but also the imperative of documentary verity on which the ethnographic project rests'; that the original picture containing the clock documents is 'a deep and multiple temporality . . .. The lodge exists within or, better, contains within itself, at least two distinct regimes of time, the time of a non-Native American modernity and the time of Piegan culture' (Zamir 2014: 60).

Zamir's reading of the Piegan lodge as an almost science-fictional space striated by different times speaks to the way in which the present is being retheorised as the site of many other clocks, the clocks of others. For instance, in *Beyond Settler Time: Temporal Sovereignty and Indigenous Self-Determination*, Mark Rifkin argues that the effort to revise our accounts of history and the present – to be more inclusive and to offer 'temporal recognition' – upholds the settler-colonial fantasy of a neutral, unified history and ubiquitous modernity, the 'singular temporal formation that itself marks the sole possibility for moving toward the future' (Rifkin 2017: 15). What has appeared as a critical gesture to 'always historicise' has never been neutral because it presumes that 'the dominant coordinates of Euramerican sociality and governance still provide the basis through which to register processes of becoming' (10). Indeed, Rifkin makes use of Einstein and clock systems in order to emphasise non-subjective reference frames whose 'material existence and efficacy . . . are not reducible to a single, ostensibly neutral vision of time as universal succession. The concept of frames of reference', he argues, 'provides a way of breaking up this presumed timeline by challenging the possibility of definitively determining simultaneity while still holding onto the potential for thinking about collective experiences of time' and sovereign temporal formations (20). Contemporary work on indigenous times and futures is crucial for rethinking the relations among the multiplicity of clocks – figured variously and relatively in size and shape – and for reconceptualising the new and the alternative in a context governed by the urgency of ultimate clocks. In this context, we must reconfigure alternativity not simply as the product of an explosive event within history, in which a radical break ushers in the absolutely new, but as a function and calculation of differently paced, non-synchronous but often intersecting lines.

Time in modernism is not defined solely by the big fateful clock nor by the myriad subjective temporal registers found everywhere in twentieth-century literature, but also by the multiplication of clocks, by the vitality, sovereignty, vampiric dependence and zombie-like persistence of many times. The strain of heterochronic modernism that connects to certain kinds of big clock and to contemporary critiques of settler imaginaries of the end of civilisation shifts from objects and ruins of the past to different pasts and timelines themselves. As in 'media anarchaeology', where 'technological dead ends, lost histories, circuitous routes, and alternative conceptions' reveal singular time to be a variantological medium comprising different times (Apperley and Parikka 2018: 352), the presence of the heterochronic clock from modernism to the twenty-first century signals not just the motley fabric of pastiche but the science-fictional scenario of coeval times and histories running through the texture of the present, various timepaths that parallel and intersect with big history without being reduced to it. In the register of postcolonial theory, the image of the heterochronic clock radicalises the nature of anachronism from chronological discrepancy to discrepant chronologies that reveal the present as a transverse construction in which, as Aravamudan puts it, we engage 'the multiple futures that exist in the now', rather than yield to 'the tyranny of a totalised now that purportedly leads to a singular future' (Aravamudan 2001: 351).

When powered by modernist clockwork, the big clock of human civilisation and the time of the planet – the clock that seems to preside over scenes of an ultimate fate, an absolute break and temporal reset, and even over omega-point fantasies of the death of time itself – ticks in a most peculiar way. The enlarged order of modernism's clocks reveals not only that time is elapsing differently in different reference frames, but also that the present and the experience afforded by it are shot through unevenly with a variety of temporal rates and scales. Ian Baucom describes this enlarged order as 'History 4°', a 'fourth order of history' that, in the face of the catastrophes generated by a 4°C increase in temperature, does not collapse the 'multitemporal ontology of the present' into apocalyptic unilinearity (Baucom 2014: 142, 123). Building on Dipesh Chakrabarty's historiographic scaling up from the 'History 1' of European modernity and 'History 2' of others' disruptive, out-of-joint historicity, Baucom sees 'History 3' as Chakrabarty's more recent attempts to theorise the disjunctive relationship of these histories to the Anthropocene, which requires the historian to rescale the human to the species and its collective ontological intertwinement with the non-human (Chakrabarty 2000; Baucom 2014: 140). These new challenges for historical narrative – the species protagonist, the phenomenological unavailability of the experience of hyperobjects, the disjunctive politics – require History 4°'s scalar historical method that recognises the 'multiple scales, orders, and classes of time' and fosters the 'multiple corresponding orientations to the possibility of the (just) future fashioning of those times' (Baucom 2014: 142). As a way of understanding the 'braided order of time' interweaving Histories 1, 2 and 3 together, History 4° comprises methodological insights in which one can hear the discordant ticking of modernism's clocks. This type of big historiographic clock does not drown out or silence through unification the sound of multiple clocks; rather, it makes them audible as they resonate across what may now be a much longer modernity than we bargained for, and through a network of heterochronic timepieces in which we might discern the 'pluridirectional' politics, side-shadowed possibilities and heterogeneous futures of times themselves.

Note

1. I am grateful to Judith Roof and her students, especially Andrew Battaglia and Brooke Clark, in the Mellon graduate research seminar on temporalities at the Humanities Research Center at Rice University, for an excellent conversation on big and small clocks. Canales quotes this passage from Bergson (2011: 188). See also her *The Physicist and the Philosopher* (2015).

Works Cited

Allen, Thomas (2015), 'Toward Endless Life: Population, Machinery, and Monumental Time', *Transatlantica: Revue d'études américaines*, 1, <http://journals.openedition.org/transatlantica/7379> (last accessed 18 January 2022).
Apperley, Thomas and Jussi Parikka (2018), 'Platform Studies' Epistemic Threshold', *Games and Culture*, 13: 4, pp. 349–69.
Aravamudan, Srinivas (2001), 'The Return of Anachronism', *MLQ: Modern Language Quarterly*, 62: 4, pp. 331–53.
Aravamudan, Srinivas (2013), 'The Catachronism of Climate Change', *Diacritics*, 41: 3, pp. 6–30.
Armstrong, Tim (2003), 'Technology: "Multiplied Man"', in *A Concise Companion to Modernism*, ed. D. Bradshaw. Oxford: Blackwell.
Barrows, Adam (2011), *The Cosmic Time of Empire: Modern Britain and World Literature*. Berkeley: University of California Press.
Baucom, Ian (2014), 'History 4°: Postcolonial Method and Anthropocene Time', *Cambridge Journal of Postcolonial Literary Inquiry*, 1: 1, pp. 123–42.
Beck, Ulrich (1992), *Risk Society: Towards a New Modernity*. London: Sage.
Bergson, Henri (1913 [1889]), *Time and Free Will: An Essay on the Immediate Data of Consciousness*. London: G. Allen.
Bergson, Henri (1972), 'Discussion avec Einstein', in *Mélanges*. Paris: Presses Universitaires de France, pp. 1340–7.
Brand, Stewart (1999), *The Clock of the Long Now: Time and Responsibility*. New York: Basic Books.
Canales, Jimena (2011), *A Tenth of a Second: A History*. Chicago: University of Chicago Press.
Canales, Jimena (2015), *The Physicist and the Philosopher: Einstein and Bergson and the Debate that Changed Our Understanding of Time*. Princeton, NJ: Princeton University Press.
Canales, Jimena (2016), 'Clock/Lived', in *Time: A Vocabulary of the Present*, ed. J. Burges and A. J. Elias. New York: New York University Press.
Chakrabarty, Dipesh (2000), *Provincializing Europe: Postcolonial Thought and Historical Difference*. Princeton, NJ: Princeton University Press.
Craig, Lois A. (1984), *The Federal Presence: Architecture, Politics, and National Design*. Cambridge, MA: MIT Press.
de Cristofaro, Diletta (2018), 'Critical Temporalities: Station Eleven and the Contemporary Post-Apocalyptic Novel', *Open Library of Humanities*, 4: 2, pp. 1–26.
de Cristofaro, Diletta (2020), *The Contemporary Post-Apocalyptic Novel: Critical Temporalities and the End Times*. London: Bloomsbury Academic.
Einstein, Albert (1920), *Relativity: The Special and General Theory*. New York: H. Holt.
Einstein, Albert and Leopold Infeld (1938), *The Evolution of Physics: The Growth of Ideas from Early Concepts to Relativity and Quanta*. New York: Simon and Schuster.
Einstein, Albert, Hermann Minkowski, Hermann Weyl and H. A. Lorentz (1923), *The Principle of Relativity: A Collection of Original Memoirs on the Special and General Theory of Relativity*. London: Methuen & Company.
Fabian, Johannes (2014 [1983]), *Time and the Other: How Anthropology Makes Its Object*, repr. New York: Columbia University Press.
Faulkner, William (1994), *The Sound and the Fury: Norton Critical Edition*, 2nd edn, ed. D. Minter. New York: W. W. Norton.
Foucault, Michel (1986), 'Of Other Spaces', *Diacritics*, 16: 1, pp. 22–7.
Frank, Adam (2011), *About Time: Cosmology and Culture at the Twilight of the Big Bang*. New York: Simon and Schuster.
Galison, Peter (2003), *Einstein's Clocks and Poincaré's Maps: Empires of Time*. New York: W. W. Norton.

Gidley, Mick (2001), 'Ways of Seeing the Curtis Project on the Plains', in *The Plains Indian Photographs of Edward S. Curtis*. Lincoln: University of Nebraska Press, pp. 39–66.
Glennie, Paul and Nigel Thrift (2009), *Shaping the Day: A History of Timekeeping in England and Wales, 1300–1800*. Oxford: Oxford University Press.
Higdon, David Leon (1976), 'A Poetics of Fictional "Time Shapes"', *Bucknell Review: A Scholarly Journal of Letters, Arts and Sciences*, 22: 2, pp. 50–68.
Joyce, James (1986), *Ulysses*, ed. H. W. Gabler. New York: Vintage Books.
Lawrence, D. H. (1998), *Women in Love*, ed. D. Bradshaw. Oxford: Oxford University Press.
Levenson, Michael (2004), 'The Time-Mind of the Twenties', in *The Cambridge History of Twentieth-Century English Literature*, ed. L. Marcus and P. Nicholls. Cambridge: Cambridge University Press, pp. 197–217.
Long Now Foundation (n.d.), 'Introduction – 10,000 Year Clock', <http://longnow.org/clock/> (last accessed 12 April 2020).
Lukács, Georg (1972 [1923]), *History and Class Consciousness: Studies in Marxist Dialectics*. Cambridge, MA: MIT Press.
McCrossen, Alexis (2013), *Marking Modern Times: A History of Clocks, Watches, and Other Timekeepers in American Life*. Chicago: University of Chicago Press.
Mackenzie, Adrian (2001), 'The Technicity of Time: From 1.00 Oscillations/Sec to 9,192,631,770 Hz', *Time & Society*, 10: 2–3, pp. 235–57.
Marx, Karl (1910 [1847]), *The Poverty of Philosophy: Being a Translation of the Misère de la philosophie (a Reply to 'La Philosophie de la misère' of M. Proudhon)*. Chicago: C. H. Kerr & Company.
Mumford, Lewis (1934), *Technics and Civilization*. New York: Harcourt, Brace & Co.
Odle, E. V. (1923), *The Clockwork Man*. London: Heinemann.
Parikka, Jussi (2017), 'Deep Times and Media Mines: A Descent into Ecological Materiality of Technology', in *General Ecology: The New Ecological Paradigm*, ed. E. Hörl and J. Burton. London: Bloomsbury, pp. 169–91.
Peters, John Durham (2015), *The Marvelous Clouds: Toward a Philosophy of Elemental Media*. Chicago: University of Chicago Press.
Purdon, James (2018), 'Literature – Technology – Media: Towards a New Technography', *Literature Compass*, 15: 1, e12432, pp. 1–9.
Rifkin, Mark (2017), *Beyond Settler Time: Temporal Sovereignty and Indigenous Self-Determination*. Durham, NC: Duke University Press.
Stableford, Brian M. and David Langford (2018), 'Cyborgs', in *The Encyclopedia of Science Fiction*, ed. John Clute, David Langford, Peter Nicholls and Graham Sleight. London: Gollancz, updated September 2021. <https://sf-encyclopedia.com/entry/cyborgs> (last accessed 16 February 2022).
Stevenson, Randall (2018), *Reading the Times: Temporality and History in Twentieth-Century Fiction*. Edinburgh: Edinburgh University Press.
Thompson, E. P. (1967), 'Time, Work-Discipline, and Industrial Capitalism', *Past and Present*, 38, pp. 56–97.
Wallace, Molly (2016), *Risk Criticism: Reading in an Age of Manufactured Uncertainties*. Ann Arbor: University of Michigan Press.
Woolf, Virginia (2006), *Orlando: A Biography (Annotated)*, ed. M. DiBattista. Orlando, FL: Harvest.
Zamir, Shamoon (2014), *The Gift of the Face: Portraiture and Time in Edward S. Curtis's The North American Indian*. Chapel Hill: University of North Carolina Press.
Ziolkowski, Theodore (1969), *Dimensions of the Modern Novel: German Texts and European Contexts*. Princeton, NJ: Princeton University Press.

3

PRINT: ANAÏS NIN'S EMBODIED ENCOUNTERS WITH PRINT TECHNOLOGY

Jennifer Sorensen

THE MODERNIST PERIOD witnessed an explosion of print technologies in terms of the variety of venues for publication, the vast circulation figures and the quantity of print forums. Faye Hammill and Mark Hussey provide a useful history of the burgeoning field in *Modernism's Print Cultures* and begin by explaining how this print expansion was enabled by technological innovations (2016: 15–16). Critical conversations about the intersections between modernist literature and the print marketplace have developed as a major discourse in the 'new modernist studies'. Building on the important work of Jerome McGann's *Black Riders* (1993), Jayne E. Marek's *Women Editing Modernism* (1995) and George Bornstein's *Material Modernism* (2001), scholarship has grown, especially in periodical studies focused on modernist little magazines and in work on Virginia and Leonard Woolf's Hogarth Press (see Brooker and Thacker 2009, Keyser 2010, Green 2017, Marcus 1996, McTaggart 2010, Southworth 2010, Battershill 2019a, 2019b, Willson 2009, Staveley 2009, 2018). Extending the field beyond modernist little magazines and the Hogarth Press, Lise Jaillant's *Publishing Modernist Fiction and Poetry* (2019) collects research analysing a large range of publishers and their roles in modernist print cultures. The theoretical approaches deployed within modernist print culture studies have become more central to the larger field, thanks to ambitious work by Ann Ardis and Patrick Collier in their edited collection *Transatlantic Print Culture, 1880–1940* and in Ardis's special issue of *Modernism/modernity* (September 2012). These collections of scholarship speak to recent moves in the field away from more narrow divisions between disciplines and toward 'convergences of periodical studies, book history, media history, and material culture studies that are enriching our understanding of modernism's complex relationship to the media ecologies of modernity' (Ardis 2012: v). This scholarship demonstrates how modernist print culture studies have embraced 'the transnational turn' in modernist studies and have expanded to consider global dimensions of modernist print cultures and to attend to intersections of race, gender and empire in the modernist print public sphere.

Despite this growing field of scholarship on modernist print culture, there has been less work focused on the 'technology' of modernist print and on how that technology required, mediated and transformed modernist bodies. More work needs to be done, particularly in connecting modernist print cultures to the rich fields of African American print culture studies and to theories of embodiment that incorporate intersections of race, gender, ability and class. While there has been a recent explosion of field-defining work on race and print culture, most of this work has been focused on earlier histories.[1] Recent contributions have expanded our knowledge about the production, marketing and aesthetics of African American modernist print cultures, including M. Genevieve West's *Zora Neale Hurston & American Literary Culture* (2005), John K. Young's *Black Writers, White Publishers* (2006), Caroline Goeser's *Picturing the New Negro* (2007) and the collection *Publishing Blackness* (2013), edited by George Hutchinson and John K. Young. This work speaks to a much-needed development to diversify the texts, authors and print venues that animate the field of modernist print culture studies. Indeed, modernist print culture studies needs to do more work to attend to how race intersected with the print marketplace to respond to urgent work like Urmila Seshagiri's *Race and the Modernist Imagination*. Seshagiri persuasively argues that as critics we must work to 'restore the long-obscured role of race in each writer's explicitly modern aesthetic, and, more broadly, reveal that modernism's worship of artistic form is inseparable from its investment in the forms of race' (2010: 12).

Modernists persistently portrayed print publication through embodied language. Virginia Woolf described working with her Hogarth Press as 'worse than 6 children at breast simultaneously', whilst Jean Rhys feared that the censorship of *Voyage in the Dark*'s ending would render it 'mutilated', and Jean Toomer figured the anthology publications of *Cane* as having 'dismembered' his book (Woolf 1977b: 55–66; Rhys 1984: 25; Toomer 1993: 102). These evocative descriptions hint at the intensity of authors' and publishers' conceptions of print publication as a visceral endeavour that was both vital and potentially violating. Print technology inflects modernist embodiment on several levels: print transforms the authorial body, produces bookish bodies and lends an embodied presence to typographical features. Modernists conceived and reconceived their work through physical and sometimes painful entanglements with print cultures.

The critical conversations on modernism and bodies developed by Tim Armstrong and Sara Danius focus largely on non-print modern technologies. Danius challenges the perceived 'anti-technological bias' in modernist literature through her analyses of what she calls 'technologies of perception' (2002: 5). Armstrong argues for the centrality of bodies to the experience of modernity and to the aesthetics of literary modernism, arguing that modernity 'offers the body as lack, at the same time as it offers technological compensation' (1999: 3). Mark Goble (2010) has enriched the field of modernist embodiment by bringing a more explicit focus on media theory and focusing on the telegraph, the telephone and photography as communicative media. Yet for Goble, Danius and Armstrong, modernist experiences with print technologies are mostly left out of their narratives. More recent critical work on modernism's bodies by Maren Tova Linett (2016), Rebecca Sanchez (2015) and Anne Anlin Cheng (2013, 2019) has largely focused on urgent questions of disability and race. Here, I will argue that attending to how print technologies reshaped modernist understandings of bodies can allow us to consider how, for many modernists, the act of printing and being printed was a profoundly embodied experience that could be either compensatory or fragmenting. Print offered ways to subvert or to engage with the capitalist marketplace. Print was not just one of many technologies that mediated how modernists experienced their daily lives – it was *the* technological mediator between their writing and their public.

Virginia Woolf is the modernist writer most famous for her engagement with the technologies of print, but less critical attention has been paid to her persistently physical descriptions of her embodied labours at the Hogarth Press. In the fuller version of the letter to Barbara Bagenal quoted above, Woolf describes the bodily strain of typesetting through a metaphoric comparison to the exhausting imagined act of nursing six children before stressing the tangible costs of her labours in her damaged handwriting: 'I have just finished setting up the whole of Mr Eliots [sic] poem with my own hands: You see how my hand trembles. Don't blame your eyes. It is my writing' (1977b: 55–6). As David Porter has demonstrated, Woolf was actively involved in 'virtually every aspect of production, from typesetting and proofreading to finding, stitching, and sewing the covers' (2000: 285). Indeed, the physical involvement of Woolf's body was one of the primary motivations for acquiring the press, according to Leonard Woolf, who wrote that, 'it would be a good thing if Virginia had a manual occupation of this kind which [. . .] would take her mind completely off her work' (L. Woolf 1964: 233). As he imagined, the manual labour of operating the press, setting and resetting the type, stitching and gluing the covers, was very intense – with their first small hand press (set up in the Woolfs' dining room) they could print only one page at a time. Donna Rhein has documented the physically demanding, slow, mechanical operation of the Woolfs' first hand press (1985: 4–5). Bringing the handle down to make the impression (often called 'machining') required force, and Leonard and often an assistant would handle that exertion as Virginia worked to set the type in the chase. As the quotation from Virginia about her shaking hands underscores, the physical taxation of setting a page of type is quite extreme: the painstaking and arduous process involves selecting each letter or piece of type individually, placing it on the composing stick, completing each word, punctuating and spacing each line, managing the leading between the lines, maintaining pressure to avoid any accidents or spills, carefully transferring the lines to the chase, locking up the chase and finally making sure the chase is securely mounted inside the press. Rhein draws attention to the many steps required to print on paper with such a small table-top machine – a process that involved both Woolfs (and later assistants) physically bending over the machine and working in concert to produce each page. Quite soon, they acquired a larger machine to speed up the process (5).

Yet even with the larger Minerva model, the Hogarth Press's success depended on the physical effort of Leonard and Virginia. Virginia makes this embodied side of the press work palpable in a letter to Roger Fry, explaining that they 'have been in a welter of Hogarth Press affairs, & my fingers are like cauliflowers from addressing envelopes'.[2] Even Woolf's famous statement of freedom through self-publishing is embedded in a diary entry that describes her press labours and her freedom in intensely embodied language:

> How my writing goes downhill! Another sacrifice to the Hogarth Press. Yet what I owe the Hogarth Press is barely paid for by the whole of my handwriting. Haven't I just written to Herbert Fisher refusing to do a book for the Home University Series on Post Victoria – knowing that I can write a book, a better book, a book off my own bat, for the Press if I wish! To think of being battened down in the hold of those University dons fairly makes my blood run cold. Yet I'm the only woman in England free to write what I like. (1977a: 42–3)

Woolf shifts from recounting the bodily sacrifice of her handwriting to using evocatively sensory language as she celebrates her escape from 'being battened down in the hold' of those 'dons', even the thought of which 'makes [her] blood run cold'. Woolf figures the press as a freedom that unfetters both mind and body. Her language of commerce to denote how the physical toll of presswork has 'barely paid for' all that she 'owes' to the machine, and her multiple exclamations underscore how the freedoms she exults in cannot fully be calculated through metaphors of economic exchange.

Woolf's experiences with hand printing, typesetting, binding and running her own press emphasise the materiality of modernist print technologies and stress the embodied labours that they required. Print technology insists on messy materiality and thus resists the kinds of disembodiment or fantasies of perfect embodiment that other modern media can encourage. Emily Apter and Elaine Freedgood have emphasised how material textual approaches could achieve a critical balance between micro and macro analyses by focusing on both the material details of a text and the larger networks, markets and institutions that produce it to allow for '"readings" of the text [that] are both distant and close' (2009: 140). These approaches will allow us to enrich research on print cultures, media histories of the period and theories of modernist embodiment, which have traditionally centred literature written by a small group of white men. Focusing on modernist print technology allows us to centre work by women writers and especially women writers of colour who often struggled to maintain space and control in an unwelcome print marketplace, including marginalised figures like Una Marson (editor of the journals *The Keys* and *The Cosmopolitan Monthly Magazine*) and Jessie Redmon Fauset (editor of *The Crisis*) (see Snaith 2014; Donnell 2003; Zackodnik 2012). In this chapter, I offer a reading of Anaïs Nin's experiences self-publishing her *Winter of Artifice* in 1942. Nin remains a relatively understudied figure in modernist literature and, while there has been a small amount of criticism focused on her diaries, very little critical attention has been paid to her letterpress printing experiences. Sally Dennison offers the most sustained account of Nin's letterpress printing experiences (1984) whilst Emily Larned provides the most thorough analysis of the aesthetics of the material forms of Nin's handprinted books (2016). In focusing on Nin I argue here for the value of attending to how women – particularly less frequently studied women – articulated their embodied experiences with print technology and with the modernist print marketplace.[3]

Anaïs Nin and Letterpress Exultation

Anaïs Nin served as an inspiration for self-publishers and earns the prime position of the first essay (ahead of the Woolfs' reflections on the Hogarth Press) in *The Publish It Yourself Handbook* (Nin 1973). Editor Bill Henderson frames her essay with the note that 'Anaïs Nin's printing and publishing experiences have inspired self-publishers and small-press people for years [. . .] This *Handbook* exists largely because of her early inspiration and support' (26). Sally Dennison has shown how, after several attempts to have her work published and widely circulated, Nin embraced the idea of publishing her work herself, starting with two failed attempts in 1935 and 1937. In December 1941, Anaïs Nin wrote in her diary about her disappointments trying to enter the print marketplace via traditional avenues. After listing a series of experiences that seemed encouraging of her work, but which ultimately left her without any publications that allowed it to circulate widely, Nin laments: 'One year lost. [. . .] There is no protection for the writer. Anyone can come and say he will publish it, keep it in a drawer for a year, and then return it' (175). Nin stresses her vulnerability and the sense of betrayal by agents and publishers who do not have the resources or desire to help her while also constraining her from publishing elsewhere: 'Meanwhile I am bound not to show it to anyone' (175). When articulating her unfulfilling experiences with trying to find a publisher, Nin describes the tension between the kind of work that she wants to write and the work that the market seems to demand. Nin articulates the demand that she sees for more traditional realist texts akin to Theodore Dreiser's 'old-fashioned stuffing' and contrasts that stodgy hyperdetailed realism with her own sense of 'modern tempo' and the potential appetite for something 'decant[ed]', 'compressed', into a 'meal' (176). She converts unnecessary stuffing to essential air and food – arguing for her art as both more natural and more exciting. Nin describes using a 'roller to squeeze out all superfluous matter' as an agent in her creative process (176). Rollers are used to ink up the platen in letterpress printing and, thus, this image suggests that her understanding of her work was mediated by her experiments with print technology.

Nin wants to imagine a market for her new style of writing and she describes the current print marketplace system as stultifying. Later in the same diary entry, Nin articulates her vision of the intellectual ruin wrought by the factory-like uniformity demanded by editors by describing 'how to murder a writer' (176). Unlike Woolf's description of the Press as like '6 children at the breast simultaneously', Nin figures her writer figure as male and describes the demands of the print marketplace as causing 'impoten[ce]' that 'sterilizes' through 'falsity' and 'forced books' (176). For Nin, both the market's demands that writers conform to 'order[s]' like 'the last best seller' and the financial rewards of such 'false situations' prove fatal to a previously 'spontaneous' writer (176).

Written during the Second World War, these diary entries describing her frustrations with the print marketplace are frequently interrupted by bulletins that emphasise the violent context of her writing. She follows the previous statement about how print markets murder writers with: 'JAPAN OPENS WAR ON THE UNITED STATES. FIRST AIR RAID OVER NEW YORK. FALSE ALARM. SHOCK' (1969: 176). Throughout her diary entries in the early 1940s, Nin connects her work and the materiality of her writing with the context of writing in wartime. Even her typewriter becomes a weapon of resistance against the violence of the world:

> Imperturbably I get my typewriter cleaned for more work because to me that means if the world loves war and destruction I won't go along with it. I will go on loving and writing until the bomb falls. I am not going to quit, abdicate, and play its game of death and power. (1969: 177)

The technology of her typewriter was not quite enough to get her work circulating to more readers; rather, it is described more as a private act of persistence. Soon after this entry, Nin moved to the technology of the letterpress as her mode of resistance to war and as a way to continue her creative labours.

In January 1942, Nin writes of the press's delivery and how she and Gonzalo More 'borrowed a book from the library on how to print' (1969: 181). Her description of their early attempts emphasises the painstaking effort: 'It took me an hour and half to typeset half a page' (1969: 181). Nin writes of the presswork as a passion project and even as 'a marvelous cure' that operates through 'creation' and 'independence' and that allows Nin to escape from the harsh world of the print marketplaces with 'publishers', 'rejections' and 'ignorance' (1969: 181). Like Woolf, Nin also found that her experiences working at manually setting type influenced her style and literary aesthetics: 'Typesetting slowly makes me analyze each phrase and tighten the style' (1969: 182). Throughout her diary entries describing her work with the press, Nin echoes Woolf's descriptions of the presswork as simultaneously physically exhausting, full of technical difficulties, and yet immensely rewarding and exciting.

Nin emphasises how her body is transformed through her contact with the machine: 'You are related bodily to a solid block of metal letters, to the weight of the trays, to the adroitness of the spacing, to the tempo and temper of the machine' (1969: 185–6). She exults in her bodily connections to the 'weight and solidity of metal' and describes her possession of 'the strength and power of the machine' as a 'conquest by the body, fingers, muscles' (1969: 186). She describes how the technology of printing transforms her body, almost prosthetically, into something both more powerful and more 'adroit' and 'deft' (1969: 185, 186). This diary entry is one of many where Nin imagines the fusion of her body with the materiality of the metal type and the strength of the machine.

Nin's language of bodily transformation and mastery is implicitly poised against the unmanageable historical context of the war and her lack of control with conventional publishers. In contrast to the 'frustrations' and 'anger' provoked by the publishers who have ignored, rejected or buried her work, the printing press offers 'concrete, definable, touchable' 'victories' (1969: 186). The physicality of printing – 'You can touch the page you wrote' – is matched, for Nin, by a productive 'energy' (1969: 186). The 'technical, mechanical problems' of the press and its processes thus allow Nin to achieve practicable, embodied 'solutions' that contrast with the 'void' generated by publishing institutions. Nin describes how she 'exult[s]' in both 'mastery' and 'discovery' in her presswork and she uses italics to stress her excitement at conquering problems '*[w]hich can be solved*' (1969: 186).

Throughout her diary entries in 1942, Nin writes about the material conditions of printing – repeatedly describing early errors, listing makeshift equipment and describing her tangible experiences working with the technology. Nin theorises how engaging with hand printing makes her more attentive to the materiality of language:

> If I pay no attention, then I do not lock the tray properly, and when I start printing the whole tray of letters falls into the machine. The words which first appeared in my head, out of the air, take body. Each letter has a weight. I can weigh each word again, to see if it is the right one. (1969: 186)

Nin describes her reconsideration of the 'weight' of 'each word' and 'each letter' moving between the technical mishap of the word avalanche caused by improper tray locking and the more mystical process by which the words from her 'head' 'take body'. Nin's conceptions of her own writing are transformed through this handling of the technological materiality of print. Language becomes more embodied for her as her own body becomes more and more engaged with the physical labours of operating the press.

In her detailed descriptions in the diary, Nin attempts to make the working materials of her craft tangible: 'I use soap boxes as shelves, to hold tools, paper, inks. [. . .] We study type faces while eating' (1969: 186). Nin describes the studio as a place full of makeshift objects, where the routines of the body become absorbed into her engagement with the press: 'We dreamt, ate, talked, slept with the press' (1969: 185). She repeatedly describes how the presswork absorbs all of her energies and how the ink permeates her body: 'We ate sandwiches with the taste of ink, got ink in our hair and inside our nails' (1969: 185). Her fascination with the presswork reverberates throughout the diary entries as she repeatedly emphasises her exultation in the materiality of the processes and production: 'The press mobilized our energies, and is a delight. At the end of the day you can see your work, weigh it. It is done. It exists' (186). The language here contrasts dramatically with her earlier statements about the sterilising and desiccating atmosphere of traditional print publication. Nin describes the materiality of the finished work in direct contrast to her earlier experiences with the print marketplace when her work disappeared into a drawer and seemed like a 'hoax' that was estranged from her control through others who condemned her work to non-circulation, non-tangibility (176).

In April 1942, Nin describes her process of setting type and printing, and again emphasises how her engagement with print technology has improved her craft as a writer. Nin's minute breaking down of the manual processes of setting type and page counting invite the reader into the kinds of intense attention to small material objects that she values:

> Take the letter O out of the box, place it next to the T, then a comma, then a space, and so on. Count page 1, 2, 3, and so on. Select the good ones while Gonzalo runs the machine. Day after day [. . .] The writing is often improved by the fact that I live so many hours with a page that I am able to scrutinize it, to question the essential words [. . .] The discipline of typesetting and printing is good for the writer. (1969: 192)

Here, print becomes a salutary 'discipline' that allows the physical processes of selecting type to enrich the writer's quest for the 'essential words'. The slowness of the time it takes to produce the page manually trains the writer's abilities to 'scrutinize'. Yet while the methodical process allows for greater discernment of her own work, Nin makes it clear that presswork is not a complete escape from the outside world; her entries vividly show the intersections between her press labours and her thoughts about her relationships and the events transpiring 'out in the world'. Nin describes these other thoughts as an 'undercurrent' that one might desire to 'annihilate' and notes that

> While I typeset, the radio plays one of my father's songs, and I am slowly, word by word, erecting the last monument to his failure as a father. To all the music from Russia, Germany, France, Spain, America, I weave the pattern of letters of metal. (1969: 192)

Nin's language casts her labours as 'weav[ing]' the letters and describes her actions as 'proclaiming that the most important of all achievements is to be a human being', which seems to conflate her labours in printing the book with the aesthetic projects expressed in it (1969: 192). Through the image of weaving, Nin casts her process of typesetting as intimately tied to her writerly productivity, her femininity and her memories.

For Nin, her modernist aesthetics are crucially bound up with her experiences with technologies of printing. Nin continually interweaves her ideas about literary texts with the processes of the machine. She enmeshes her theory of the novel as a genre within a passage that concludes with her typesetting and watching the press's pulse:

> This is what makes me rebel against the novel, which can only reveal a static fragment, freeze it, when the truth is not in that particular fragment but in continuous change. The novel arbitrarily chooses a moment in time, a segment. Frames it. Binds it. A fragment does not give us that continuously changing truth. Perhaps we cannot bear a continuously changing truth. Perhaps we have to believe there is a TOTAL truth once reached and thereafter permanent, fixed. TOTAL. The capital T on the right-hand side of the box. The regular rhythm of the machine. It is heavy for the old floor, and I see the floor curving slightly under its weight, I hear the huge pulse, and hear the creaking. (1969: 194)

Nin moves from her rebellion against the novel genre as being too arbitrarily restrictive, to imagining a 'permanent, fixed' 'TOTAL truth.' Her play with the small capital typeface draws the reader's attention to the material page of her diary entry as she draws us back into the technology of the letterpress and into the box sorting out a 'capital T'. She moves from abstractions in her theory of the novel into the material components of printing and finally figures the 'machine' as strangely embodied with a 'huge pulse'.

Nin writes of her inspirations for *Winter of Artifice* in diary entries that are interlaced with her responses to the violence of modernity and her bodily engagement with print technologies. In the same April 1942 entry that begins with taking type sorts out of the box, Nin refers to her artistic labours and her work at the press as transformative acts of resistance to the outer world: 'I am writing with a sensitivity which our modern world is intent on destroying, not knowing that this is the only antenna we have to our psychic nature' (1969: 194). Nin positions herself as 'an instrument of perception which must not allow itself to be destroyed by great violence, deafened by machine guns, calloused by harshness, though it is quite possible that I may not survive life in America' (1969: 194). Nin's language insistently fuses the corporeal and the mechanical: she describes herself as possessing an 'antenna' – which evokes an insect-like hypersensitive perceptive appendage and an inhuman technological apparatus of a radio or television antenna – and embodies an 'instrument' that refuses to be 'deafened' and 'calloused'. Throughout the entry Nin theorises her body as at once machine-like and as embodied and vulnerable.

After reflecting on the ways that she tries to resist these bodily and psychic traumas, Nin describes her bodily sacrifice to the presswork: 'I have not spared my hands. My nails are broken. I have not spared my book. I have slashed into its imperfections. It is shorter, better focused' (1969: 194). Again Nin emphasises the ways in which her embodied exertion at the press resonates with her intellectual labours revising her book. Her broken nails echo the passage cited earlier about Virginia Woolf's cauliflower fingers and emblematise how letterpress technology and presswork transform the bodies of these writer–printers and mediate their relationships to their writing.

Anaïs Nin provides an instructive example of a modernist writer who experienced both sides of the print marketplace – the position of empowerment and embodied labour as letterpress self-publisher and the state of vulnerability and lack of control in her dealings with mainstream presses. Later in her career, in her essay 'The Story of My

Printing Press', Nin reflects back on her experiences with self-publishing and emphasises how her letterpress printing was an act of defiance in the face of an unsympathetic print marketplace: 'In the 1940s, two of my books, *Winter of Artifice* and *Under a Glass Bell*, were rejected by American publishers [. . .] Both books were considered uncommercial. I did not accept the verdict and decided to print my own books' (1998: 29). Nin explains that the bodily demands of presswork forced her eventually to cede control to mainstream publishers:

> [T]he physical work was so overwhelming that it interfered with my writing. This is the only reason I accepted the offer of a commercial publisher and surrendered the press. Otherwise I would have liked to continue with my own press, controlling both the content and the design of the books. (1998: 31)

Nin's language stresses her sense of loss of complete creative 'control' over her work as an unfortunate 'surrender'. Nin echoes the kinds of trauma-invoking language that other modernists like Toomer, Rhys and Woolf used to describe their experiences with circulating in print in ways that escaped their control.

Nin assesses the fundamental struggle for many modernist writers endeavouring to publish work that challenged traditions and conventional expectations. She critiques traditional publishers for their fiscal attitudes toward books that reduce art to commerce (1998: 31). Nin faults the commercial publishers for having too much power in the marketplace and for 'disguis[ing]' their biases and 'impos[ing]' their choices on readers (1998: 31). She challenges publishers' reliance on vague (and implicitly sexist) categories of value as invalid, noting that 'The universal quality in good writing which publishers claim to recognize is impossible to define' (1998: 32). In contrast, Nin argues that '[her] books, which were not supposed to have this universal quality, were nevertheless bought and read by all kinds of people' (1998: 32). Thirty years later, Nin casts her rejection by those publishers as leading to her transformative work with the press: 'Today, instead of feeling embittered by the opposition of publishers, I am happy they opposed me, for the press had given me independence and confidence. I felt in direct contact with my public, and it was enough to sustain me through the following years' (1998: 32). Her hands-on experiences with print technology allowed her to feel connected to her art and to her readers. Despite the 'overwhelming' physical labour, Nin ultimately treasured her engagement with printing. Nin's experiences show how print as a technology can lead not to a greater sense of disembodiment or alienation from the work of art – but rather to a more 'direct', embodied and tangible connection between an author and her work and between the text and its readers. For Nin, Woolf and many other modernists, encounters with print technology required bodily sacrifices and exertion, but enabled creative freedoms, control over how their texts circulated, sustaining engagement with the production of their words, and new ways to theorise their art.

Notes

1. The 2010s have seen robust scholarly conversations about Black politics and 'Black print' with *Early African American Print Culture* (ed. Lara Langer Cohen and Jordan Alexander Stein, 2012), Eric Gardner's *Black Print Unbound* (2015), the *MELUS* Fall 2015 'Special

Issue: African American Print Cultures', edited by Joycelyn Moody and Howard Ramsby II, and Derrick Spires's *The Practice of Citizenship* (2019).
2. U of Sussex, SxMs18 Monks House Papers Letters III: Virginia Woolf, Farrell-Lubbock labelled box 72, Folder Fry, Roger. The Minerva was a larger treadle press that the Woolfs moved into the basement, allowing for more space to operate – a larger machine and chase allowed the Woolfs to print more pages at a time. Leonard Woolf biographer Victoria Glendenning documents how laborious treadling the larger machine was, citing Leonard's reflection that, after machining for several hours, he felt 'as though he had taken a great deal of exercise' (2006: 209).
3. I would like to thank Claire Battershill for introducing me to Nin's writing about letterpress through her MSA 2019 paper and for her generosity in sharing sources and in pointing me to the most relevant moments in the diary concerning Nin's embodied experiences with letterpress printing.

Works Cited

Apter, Emily and Elaine Freedgood (2009), 'Afterword', *Representations*, Special Issue on 'The Way We Read Now', 108: 1 (Fall), pp. 139–46.

Ardis, Ann, ed. (2012), 'Mediamorphosis: Print Culture and Transatlantic/Transnational Public Sphere(s)', *Modernism/modernity*, Special Issue, 19: 3 (September), pp. v–vii.

Ardis, Ann and Patrick Collier, eds (2008), *Transatlantic Print Culture, 1880–1940: Emerging Media, Emerging Modernisms*. Basingstoke: Palgrave Macmillan.

Armstrong, Tim (1999), *Modernism, Technology and the Body: A Cultural Study*. Cambridge: Cambridge University Press.

Battershill, Claire (2019a), *Modernist Lives: Biography and Autobiography at Leonard and Virginia Woolfs' Hogarth Press*. London: Bloomsbury Academic.

Battershill, Claire (2019b), '"Each Letter Has a Weight": Letterpress, Literary Composition, and Women Author-Printers', unpublished conference paper, *Modernist Studies Association Conference: Upheaval and Reconstruction*. Toronto, Canada (19 October).

Bornstein, George (2001), *Material Modernism: The Politics of the Page*. Cambridge: Cambridge University Press.

Brooker, Peter and Andrew Thacker, eds (2009), *The Oxford Critical and Cultural History of Modernist Magazines: Volume I Britain 1880–1955*. Oxford: Oxford University Press.

Brooker, Peter and Andrew Thacker, eds (2012), *The Oxford Critical and Cultural History of Modernist Magazines: Volume II North America 1894–1960*. Oxford: Oxford University Press.

Cheng, Anne Anlin (2013), *Second Skin: Josephine Baker and the Modern Surface*. Oxford: Oxford University Press.

Cheng, Anne Anlin (2019), *Ornamentalism*. Oxford: Oxford University Press.

Cohen, Lara Langer, and Stein, Jordan Alexander, eds (2012), *Early African American Print Culture*. Philadelphia: University of Pennsylvania Press.

Danius, Sara (2002), *The Senses of Modernism: Technology, Perception, and Aesthetics*. Ithaca, NY: Cornell University Press.

Dennison, Sally (1984), *Alternative Literary Publishing: Five Modern Histories*. Iowa City: University of Iowa Press.

Donnell, Alison (2003), 'Una Marson: Feminism, Anti-Colonialism and a Forgotten Fight for Freedom', in *West Indian Intellectuals in Britain*, ed. Bill Schwarz. Manchester: Manchester University Press, pp. 114–31.

Gardner, Eric (2015), *Black Print Unbound: The Christian Recorder, African American Literature, and Periodical Culture*. Oxford: Oxford University Press.

Glendenning, Victoria (2006), *Leonard Woolf: A Biography*. Cambridge: Free Press.

Goble, Mark (2010), *Beautiful Circuits: Modernism and the Mediated Life*. New York: Columbia University Press.

Goeser, Caroline (2007), *Picturing the New Negro: Harlem Renaissance Print Culture and Modern Black Identity*. Lawrence: University Press of Kansas.

Green, Barbara (2017), *Feminist Periodicals and Daily Life: Women and Modernity in British Culture*. Houndmills: Palgrave.

Hammill, Faye and Mark Hussey, eds (2016), *Modernism's Print Cultures*. London: Bloomsbury.

Hutchinson, George and John K. Young, eds (2013), *Publishing Blackness: Textual Constructions of Race since 1850*. Ann Arbor: University of Michigan Press.

Jaillant, Lise, ed. (2019), *Publishing Modernist Fiction and Poetry*. Edinburgh: Edinburgh University Press.

Keyser, Catherine (2010), *Playing Smart: New York Women Writers and Modern Magazine Culture*. New Brunswick, NJ: Rutgers University Press.

Larned, Emily (2016), 'The Intimate Books of Anaïs Nin: Diarist as Letterpress Printer', *Openings: Studies in Book Art*, 2: 1. Chicago: Temporary Services.

Linett, Maren Tova (2016), *Bodies of Modernism: Physical Disability in Transatlantic Modernist Literature*. Ann Arbor: University of Michigan Press.

McGann, Jerome (1993), *Black Riders: The Visible Language of Modernism*. Princeton, NJ: Princeton University Press.

McTaggart, Ursula (2010), '"Opening the Door": The Hogarth Press as Virginia Woolf's Outsider Society', *Tulsa Studies in Women's Literature*, 29: 1, pp. 63–81.

Marcus, Laura (1996), 'Virginia Woolf and the Hogarth Press', in *Modernist Writers and the Marketplace*, ed. Ian Willison, Warwick Gould and Warren Chernaik. New York: Macmillan Press, pp. 124–50.

Marek, Jayne E. (1995), *Women Editing Modernism: 'Little' Magazines and Literary History*. Lawrence: University Press of Kentucky.

Moody, Joycelyn and Howard Ramsby II, eds (2015), 'Special Issue: African American Print Cultures', *MELUS*, 40: 3 (Fall).

Nin, Anaïs (1969), *The Diary of Anaïs Nin, Volume III 1939–1944*, ed. Gunther Stuhlmann. New York, Sydney and London: Harcourt Brace Jovanovich.

Nin, Anaïs (1998), 'The Story of My Printing Press', in *The Publish It Yourself Handbook*, ed. Bill Henderson. Wainscott, NY: Pushcart Press, pp. 27–32.

Porter, David H. (2000), '"We All Sit on the Edge of Stools and Crack Jokes": Virginia Woolf and the Hogarth Press', in *Book Illustrated: Text, Image, and Culture, 1770–1930*, ed. Catherine J. Golden. New Castle, DE: Oak Knoll Press, pp. 277–309.

Rhein, Donna (1985), *The Handprinted Books of Leonard and Virginia Woolf at the Hogarth Press, 1917–1932*. Ann Arbor, MI: UMI Research Press.

Rhys, Jean (1984), *Jean Rhys Letters: 1931–1966*. London: Andre Deutsch.

Sanchez, Rebecca (2015), *Deafening Modernism: Embodied Language and Visual Poetics in American Literature*. New York: New York University Press.

Seshagiri, Urmila (2010), *Race and the Modernist Imagination*. Ithaca, NY: Cornell University Press.

Snaith, Anna (2014), *Modernist Voyages: Colonial Women Writers in London, 1890–1945*. Cambridge: Cambridge University Press.

Southworth, Helen, ed. (2010), *Leonard and Virginia Woolf: The Hogarth Press and the Networks of Modernism*. Edinburgh: Edinburgh University Press.

Spires, Derrick (2019), *The Practice of Citizenship: Black Politics and Print Culture in the Early United States*. Philadelphia: University of Pennsylvania Press.

Staveley, Alice (2009), 'Marketing Virginia Woolf: Women, War, and Public Relations in "Three Guineas"', *Book History*, 12, pp. 295–339.

Staveley, Alice (2018), 'Bibliographic Parturition in *Orlando*: Books, Babies, Freedom and Fame', in *Sentencing Orlando: Virginia Woolf and the Morphology of the Sentence*, ed. Elsa Högberg and Amy Bromley. Edinburgh: Edinburgh University Press, pp. 116–27.

Toomer, Jean (1993), *The Jean Toomer Reader: Selected Unpublished Writings*, ed. Frederik L. Rusch. Oxford: Oxford University Press.

U of Sussex, SxMs18 Monks House Papers Letters III: Virginia Woolf, Farrell-Lubbock labelled box 72, Folder Fry, Roger.

West, M. Genevieve (2005), *Zora Neale Hurston & American Literary Culture*. Gainsville: University of Press of Florida.

Willson, Elizabeth Gordon (2009), *Woolf's Head Publishing: The Highlights and New Lights of the Hogarth Press*. Edmonton: University of Alberta Press.

Woolf, Leonard (1964), *Beginning Again: An Autobiography of the Years 1911–1918*. London: Harcourt Brace Jovanovich.

Woolf, Virginia (1977a), *The Diary of Virginia Woolf, Volume III, 1925–1930*, ed. Anne Olivier Bell. London: Harcourt Brace Jovanovich.

Woolf, Virginia (1977b), *The Letters of Virginia Woolf: Volume III: 1923–1928*, ed. Nigel Nicolson and Joanne Trautman. London: Harcourt Brace Jovanovitch.

Young, John K. (2006), *Black Writers, White Publishers: Marketplace Politics in Twentieth-Century African American Literature*. Jackson: University Press of Mississippi.

Zackodnik, Teresa (2012), 'Recirculation and Feminist Black Internationalism in Jessie Fauset's "The Looking Glass" and Amy Jacques Garvey's "Our Women and What They Think"', *Modernism/modernity*, 19: 3 (September), pp. 437–59.

4

SUBWAYS: UNDERGROUND NETWORKS THROUGH MODERNIST POETRY AND PROSE

Sunny Stalter-Pace

Entering the System

SCHOLARS OF MODERNISM are accustomed to thinking about how technologies reorganise perception of time and space.[1] Subway systems built from the mid-nineteenth century to the early twentieth transformed passengers' perceptions of city space in modernist metropoles such as New York, London and Paris. Through their spatial organisation and the behaviours they encourage, modern subways model a new kind of movement that is at once physical and imaginative. Though these subways differ based on local geography, track layout and the like, they share a key structure: they connect distant points within city space without showing passengers the intervening sights and so ask the passengers to construct a kind of flexible, telescoping mental image of the city. The art and literature of the subway produced in this period reflects this modern experience formally and thematically through its unexpected short-circuits and transfers between seemingly distant places and registers of language. In *The Difficulties of Modernism*, Leonard Diepeveen identifies the many ways that modernist writing has been characterised by its compression (2013: 57). From posters to poems, the cultural production of this period argues for the parallels between the spatial compression of the subway and the rhetorical and narrative compressions of modernist literature. Both ask us to navigate underground connections.

Following Wiebe Bijker, I investigate in this chapter how the early twentieth-century subway fits together as a 'sociotechnical ensemble' comprising mechanical, cultural, social and behavioural components (Bijker 1997: 274), an ensemble in which shared spatial and mechanical traits interact in complex ways with the particularities of urban space and history. Self-consciously experimental writing of the period, especially poetry, illustrates and explores the ways that the subway builds up a sense of place. In the sections that follow, I consider the ways that modern poets use the subway to represent new forms of mobility and perception, new attitudes toward the crowd and new citational practices, among other changes. Where conventional forms of wayfinding have failed, both subway riding and subway writing model new forms of orientation.

To start with a definition of terms: in order to understand the subway's relation to modernism, it is helpful to understand what is meant precisely by a subway. Some historians of technology and literature have considered the subway as one instance of underground city-space construed more broadly (Mumford 1961: 478–80; Williams

1990: 73–81; Pike 2005: 20–68). For them, the subway operates in symbolic ways similar to those of the mine tunnel, the underground bunker, the sewer and the catacomb. These comparisons prove instructive for limning the importance of subterranean space to urban modernity. Other critics, particularly in the emerging field of mobility studies, discuss the theory and practice of subway mobility within the larger category of the railroad or the urban railway (Spalding 2014: 42–8). My understanding of the subway lies at the intersection of these two categories: an urban railway that mostly runs underground, across a networked system. I position myself at the intersection of these two conversations in order to gain a critical understanding of the subway as a technology that facilitated movement through the city while functioning frequently as a metonym for the city itself. For the modernist subject, accelerated mobility through subterranean space differed both from commuting on other modes of public transit and from making use of other underground spaces. The subway journey creates a distinct experience of liminal movement through a system whose logic cannot be immediately reconciled to that of the broader city.

Subway systems connect distant points within city space through a complex network of routes, which distinguishes them from underground railway tunnels like the Channel Tunnel. Mobility studies scholars have discussed the ways that all 'transport is itself an order-building intermediary' (Divall and Revill 2005: 105); a subway network is additionally a complexity-building intermediary, increasing the number of potential pathways through the city. These pathways are not limitless: they are fixed by the possible entrances, exits and transfer points within the system. But they do create new ways of ordering city space, as well as new modes of representing it.

This imaginative expansion may have even outpaced the expansion of infrastructure. The subway was a dominant setting and image in British mass culture, David Welsh notes, even in the pre-war era when the London Underground was 'little more than a patchwork of self-contained lines' (Welsh 2010: 8). The increase in possible pathways through the city and the potential for unexpected connections were reflected in a more experimental and free-associative style of subway writing. Acknowledging the influence of avant-garde movements such as Futurism upon British modernists, Welsh dubs this work 'Tubism' (2010: 8). 'Tubist' writers like Virginia Woolf use their writing to expand on the imagined potential changes in perception that were wrought by this new technology.

From their earliest incarnation, subways de-emphasised visual perception. Subway networks could transport their passengers from one point to another without showing them the intervening sights. Art historian Lynda Nead describes the changes in London after 'the world's first underground railway' opened in 1863:

> Now, instead of traversing space by following the logic of streets and other identifiable features, people could travel below the ground, on routes that obeyed the logic of their own lines and expediency. They could descend at one point in the city and emerge at another, with little sense of the spaces between, or the meaning of the time taken to make the journey. (Nead 2000: 36)

A joke in a musical comedy fifty years later makes the same point: 'Real Parisians know nothing of Paris. They ride underground in the Metro and never see anything' ('Broadway to Paris' 1913: 24). Riders on a crowded bus or drivers passing through a tunnel may temporarily lose their ability to orient themselves visually within city space; subway passengers forgo the possibility altogether. The modern subway is embedded in city life and city literature through its role as an underground connector, a networked space offering transfer points between wildly disparate places and times. And it is this underground connection, I argue, that should be understood as a central shared feature of the modernist subway.

I intend the concept of underground connection – both the literal transfer between subway lines and the more figurative mode of piecing together fragmented images of urban space – to be sufficiently capacious to allow comparison across modern subway systems. In his review essay 'Towards a Cultural History of Underground Railways,' Dhan Zunino Singh calls for a comparative history of the subway, one that acknowledges the structures shared across systems of subterranean urban transit as well as the local differences among them (Singh 2013: 112). For the purposes of this chapter, I consider the London Underground (first opened in 1863, electrified in 1890), the Paris Métro (1900) and the New York City Subway (1904). When relevant to the discussion, I also bring in the Berlin U-Bahn (1902), the Buenos Aires Subte, short for Subterráneo (1913), and the Moscow Metro (1935). Notably, their names emphasise either their urban location or their subterranean locale. These early systems were literally cut into the streets. Subway tunnels in the late nineteenth and early twentieth centuries were constructed in similar ways: some were ground-level railways relocated below the grade of the street; shallow tunnels were dug from street level and covered over when complete, and some of the deepest ones were blasted through unforgiving strata of solid rock.

Subways share cultural histories as well as modes of construction. David Pike points out that the subway was the first subterranean space used by all classes of city-dwellers in London, Paris, New York and Buenos Aires (2007: 56). The subway ride was a cross-class and cross-cultural badge of urban identity. But in his account of the Subte's early history, Singh informs us that even the images shared across urban cultures – like the subway as an underworld or cemetery – resonate differently, depending on local factors. 'The oddity of dwelling in the place of the dead was represented differently [in Buenos Aires] from the typical hellish representations of underground railways in other cities,' he writes, noting that 'Those representations were more related to the smoke-laden tunnel (London), the hot atmosphere (New York) or tragic accidents (Paris, after [the] 1903 Métro fire)' (Singh 2014: 99). Even when metaphors were shared across urban centres, these shared metaphors arose from different experiences of subway space. While the Buenos Aires subway entrances may have been funereal in their design, the movement of passengers through the system was perceived as swift and efficient compared to their previous experience navigating the street-level traffic. As such local details about subway experiences exemplify, expanding the comparative scope of modernism gives scholars a much more nuanced understanding of technology's use and meaning.

Early in his anthropological analysis of the contemporary Paris Métro, Marc Augé notes parenthetically that subway stations 'where several lines intersect' are called *correspondances* in French and *coincidenze* – coincidences – in Italian (Augé 2002: 7). The following sections of this chapter serve as transfer points for thinking about subways across modernist cities and literary traditions, emphasising the correspondences and coincidences that hint at underlying connections. I discuss some of the ways that a focus on the comparative experience of underground connection modifies current understanding of the modern subway, especially as the rider's experience is articulated through modernist writing. To find two trains going different directions is a coincidence of different possible pathways in the same space. It also opens up subway narratives by bringing together different people within them. Points of connection and crossing evoke the magnitude of the system for riders unable to perceive it in its totality.

Segmentation

The railway and the subway draw distant locations together, but they do so in ways that have different perceptual consequences for their riders. The railroad was perceived in the early nineteenth century as a technology that compressed – and even 'annihilated' – space and time (Schivelbusch 1987). Time and space were seen as compressed when travelling at the speed allowed by the railroad: a railway journey could be made faster than one by carriage, which shortened the time spent in transit and thus the perceived distance between places. Subway commutes also compressed space within the city, bringing distant neighbourhoods into far closer proximity with one another. But these two forms of rail travel differ dramatically in terms of their organisation of the intervening landscape. The railway produced what Schivelbusch terms 'panoramic perception', where the outside world seen through glass windows lost its dimension of depth and instead seemed more like an unrolling landscape of images to be consumed (1987: 60–4). In contrast, the images seen outside the subway window lack this continuity. Instead, the visible subway stations are punctuated by spaces of blankness, with occasional glimpses of passing trains or other elements of the infrastructure. Indeed, Niamh Sweeney notes that the Paris Métro creates an 'anti-panoramic' vision of Paris, one that operates in striking contrast to the continuity of the city as seen from the Eiffel Tower (2011: 36). The smooth unfurling of the landscape by train becomes segmented underground – a slideshow, not a film.

Even reading on the train changes when transferred to the subway. The subway reader is constantly aware of time passing on their commute, made visible by the successive names of subway stations and waves of fellow commuters entering and exiting the train. Schivelbusch understands the practice of reading on the train as creating an interior landscape that unfurls, uninterrupted, in parallel to the panoramic exterior landscape (1987: 65). When writing about subway reading, however, most essays emphasise the constant interruption of stops and starts, as well as the physical contact made by other passengers. A 1929 *New York Times* article discusses the necessary attributes that a subway commuter must have in order to read in transit. These include 'physical agility at times approaching acrobatics', along with patience, grit and an even temper ('Those Who Read in the Subway' 1929: SM9). Any semblance of placid absorption is hard won.

Subways shape the perception of the modern city in myriad ways. One of the most identifiable changes that can be seen across different urban centres is the newly salient feeling of segmentation that subway systems introduce within the mental maps of residents. Russian Symbolist Andrei Bely says in his memoirs, 'everyone lives in one of several Parises, and you could spend your life in the space that separates them, flying underground from *quartier* to *quartier* in the Métro' (qtd in Fabre 2002: 40). Paris becomes fragmented into smaller and smaller versions of itself, which the subway both separates and connects. Urban planner Kevin Lynch points to this modern experience of urban perception in his discussion of the ways that the Boston subway shapes residents' understanding of the city. 'The subway stations, strung along their invisible path systems,' Lynch writes, 'are strategic junction nodes' (1960: 74). Subway stations provide a concentrated burst of information – possible entrances and exits, additional information in the form of station names and advertisements – which shuts off when the doors close and the train pulls away. Where the 'panoramic perception' made possible by the railway gives travellers a consistent if flattened sense of the landscape between stations, the segmented perception of the subway emphasises the disconnected quality of stations.

This technological shift manifests itself stylistically in the fragmentation present in modern poetry, where the subway plays an important role as the setting. Here we might think of the first version of 'In a Station of the Metro', formatted as it appeared in the April 1913 issue *Poetry*:

The apparition   of these faces   in the crowd :
Petals   on a wet, black   bough . (Pound 1913: 12)

The parallelism between the first line and the second – faces in a crowd are like petals on a bough – is undercut by the unconventional spacing of words. Each phrase operates as a stand-alone perceptual unit; even the punctuation marks stand apart. In its first version, the poem embodies the segmented perception of its location. The poem suggests how the discreteness of perception in the subway becomes mirrored and extended by the segmented perceptions of its passengers. Even when they are observing aesthetically, subway passengers see the world in ways shaped by their movement through underground space.

Emphasis on the discreteness of individual perceptions pervades the poetry of the 1910s. It is one component of what Tim Conley calls 'a language born of the common experience of mass transit' which 'bespeak[s] an international community' (2014: 98). Critics discussing the subway as a setting in modern poetry have paid close attention to Richard Aldington's 'In the Tube', which was included in the 'Imagist Number' of little magazine *The Egoist* (see, for example, Morrisson 2001: 96–9; Thacker 2003: 193; Welsh 2010: 164). As the speaker scans his surroundings, the second stanza moves pitilessly through a series of segmented elements of the train's interior:

A row of advertisements,
A row of windows,
Set in brown woodwork pitted with brass nails
A row of hard faces,
Immobile,
In the swaying train,
Rush across the flickering background of fluted dingy tunnel;
A row of eyes,
Eyes of greed, of pitiful blankness, of plethoric complacency,
Immobile,
Gaze, stare at one point,
At my eyes.
                    (Aldington 1915: 74)

The eyes all stare at the same point, and they render the same judgement. Though the eyes of the passengers might reveal different emotional states, they are nevertheless 'immobile', fixed in their evaluative attitudes. This renders them even less flexible than the train's windows, which at least reveal the 'flickering background' of the exterior tunnels. We might anticipate that the speaker's 'immediate antipathy' toward the crowd would set him apart, an individual among the masses. But the speaker recognises his fellow passengers' hostility mirroring his own: 'I surprise the same thought/ In the brasslike eyes://*What right have you to live?*' (1915: 74). His sense of separation from the crowd is what enables him to identify with the passengers, who, like him, feel defensive and alone together.

Reading across cultural hierarchies, we can find this common language of isolation put toward different ends. In mass-circulation magazines published around the same time, American middlebrow poets also segmented the subway crowd, though more often into urban types inspired by local colour fiction and newspaper sketches (Zurier 2006: 100). Joyce Kilmer, for instance, describes 'Tired clerks, pale girls, street cleaners, business men,/Boys, priests and harlots, drunkards, students, thieves' (1910: 467). His sonnet looks away from the subway crowd and sees in the flickers of light and dark outside the carriage a hint of the overall structure through which they are moving, which, for this observant Catholic author, was that of God's goodness and love. Kilmer was one of many poets at the time who wrote subway verse to explore the sense of unity hinted at through the flashes of insight (Stalter-Pace 2013: 64–5). The segmented crowd does not always suggest shared alienation; it often evokes a sense of the sublime.

Station Names

By moving passengers beneath the landscape, the subway renders large sections of the city invisible. Abstract knowledge of the city substitutes for its more direct equivalent. Critics have discussed the importance of abstraction in Harry Beck's 1931 Underground map (Pike 2005: 21; Schwetman 2014: 90). Through its strategies of visual simplification and distortion, which Beck likened to looking at the city through a convex lens, this map emphasises the self-contained logic of the system (Hadlaw 2003: 32). Subway movement no longer needed to be imagined in a way that maintained a mimetic correspondence with the above-ground geography of London. The commute took place through an underground space that was not parallel to the reality of the surface city, but rather analogous to it.

Modernist writers describe the ways that station names function in this set-apart landscape, standing in metonymically for the surrounding neighbourhood that the subway passenger might otherwise never see. One passage in *Jacob's Room* begins by describing an accountant working in the City, then moves on to commuters donning their overcoats and leaving at the end of their working day (Woolf 1922: 109). The narration meditates on the stations that these commuters encounter while going home:

> 'Marble Arch – Shepherd's Bush' – to the majority the Arch and the Bush are eternally white letters upon a blue ground. Only at one point – it may be Acton, Holloway, Kensal Rise, Caledonian Road – does the name mean shops where you buy things, and houses, in one of which, down to the right, where the pollard trees

grow out of the paving stones, there is a square curtained window, and a bedroom. (1922: 109–10)

Taken together, these station names map a city whose everyday reality is experienced unequally, one that is often glimpsed through the subway commute alone. Marble Arch and Shepherd's Bush are part of the London Underground's Central line, and so would be encountered regularly on the journey between the west London suburbs and a workplace in central London. While Acton can be found near the western end of the Central line, the other stations mentioned are in different boroughs: Holloway and Caledonian Road in North London, and Kensal Rise in the Northwest. Though the locales may differ, residents of each neighbourhood have similarly detailed knowledge of their starting- and ending-points, supplemented by lower-definition information of the neighbourhoods between home and work. Knowledge of the city is a relative, lived experience whose myriad permutations cannot be represented on a transit map.[2]

Since they are not tied to the street-level grid, subway stations take on an outsized importance in cognitive maps of the underground city. In his *Arcades Project* section on 'Ancient Paris, Catacombs, Demolitions, the Decline of Paris', Walter Benjamin describes the ways that Parisian station names come to stand on their own:

> at dusk glowing red lights point the way into an underworld of names, Combat, Elysée, Georges V, Etienne Marcel, Solférino, Invalides, Vaugirard – they have all thrown off the humiliating fetters of street or square [. . .] Here, underground, nothing more of the collision, the intersection of names – that which aboveground forms the linguistic network of the city. Here each name dwells alone. (2002: 84)

These names become mythic, part of an 'underworld of names' because they detach themselves from the mapped, surface-level city. Station names operate as self-referential units. This existence promises a kind of separation of the urban subject from the crowd, across a threshold and into a quasi-mythical space of self-determination.

As Benjamin evocatively suggests, subway station names operate as sites of linguistic and geographic condensation. Hope Mirrlees begins her 1919 poem *Paris* with the utterance 'I want a holophrase' – that is, a single word that young children can use to stand in for a more complex request (Mirrlees 1919: 3). In this disjointed and imagistic poem, subway station names show how fragmentary and evocative language pervades the life of the city dweller. We might understand the names of subway stops along the Nord–Sud line as poetic holophrasis, both standing in for the subway journey and marking the speaker's trajectory through the city. The poem moves from 'RUE DU BAC' to 'SOLFERINO' to 'CHAMBRE DES DEPUTES' and finally, after a slow trip under the Seine, to 'CONCORDE' (Mirrlees 1919: 3). Critics discussing the poem have emphasised the historical and mythological references in the subway station names and how they operate in dialogue with other references in the poem (Pryor 2019: 44; Briggs 2005: 33). 'Rue du Bac', for example, refers to a sixteenth-century ferry at the end of that street, Solférino to a nineteenth-century battle. Attending to these proper names thus strengthens and gives additional specificity to Megan Beech's reading of *Paris*, where she argues that the poem's typography and spacing 'emulates and creates the multi-sensory nature of urban experience and perception' (Beech 2018: 72). A characteristic experience of the Métro is to understand the names of subway stations as simultaneously densely referential and completely everyday (Augé 2002: 19–23). Meditating on the histories of station names as one journeys through the subway system epitomises the experience of underground connection, where even a straightforward commute can move through stations whose referents branch wildly through space and time. Subway rides, then, become literal enactments of the meaning-making that takes place while reading a densely allusive modernist text.

Advertisements

Discussions of the visual character of subways in the early twentieth century have frequently concentrated on the iconic design of infrastructural elements. Along with Harry Beck's Tube map, one might think of Hector Guimard's Art Nouveau Métro entrances, for instance, or the vivid posters commissioned by Frank Pick (Bobrick 1994: 154–5; Saler 1999: 100–1). More prevalent across cities at the time was the everyday advertisement. Ads proliferated in the modern city, and by the turn of the twentieth century they had become bolder in appearance and placement (Zurier 2006: 56–7). Designers of the New York City Subway thought that the visual landscape of the platform would be reserved for station names and maps alone, but that belief was torn to shreds when subway builder August Belmont had holes drilled in station walls for advertising posters the day after the subway opened to the public (Brooks 1997: 69). Some systems saw even more visual clutter: David Welsh describes early photos of London subway stations where ads covered platform walls and parts of the tracks (2010: 62). Lynne Kirby understands the subway station in American silent film as 'a condensed version of the commercial chaos of city streets and marketplaces' (Kirby 1997: 135). In both cases, the chaos is more condensed because it is underground, not mitigated by the natural world or the unembellished parts of the built environment that might be marked 'Post No Bills'. The unavoidable prominence of advertisements as part of the underground landscape makes them an important element in the perception of urban life, one that is explored in much modern writing.

Sometimes advertisements appear in modernist literature as icons – a brand name, the flash of an image – while in other cases commercial slogans added to the jargon of the city. But in every case, advertising language is recognisably different from other forms of speech. Mirrlees's *Paris* creates a subway ride where brand names stand shoulder to shoulder with the names of subway stations:

> RUE DU BAC (DUBONNET)
> SOLFERINO (DUBONNET)
> CHAMBRES DES DEPUTES
> Brekekekek coax coax we are passing under the Seine
> DUBONNET
> (Mirrlees 1919:3)

It is a rare description of the Métro that fails to mention Dubonnet, an aperitif widely advertised in early twentieth-century France. Walter Benjamin, for instance, calls the brand name one of the 'guardians of the threshold' in his discussion of the Métro as underworld (2002: 84). Notably, the company's advertising strategy included posting placards in the Métro tunnels so they would flicker into view between stations (Ungar

2018: 52). I suspect that the parenthetical repetitions of Dubonnet in Mirrlees's poem are meant to mimic that specific placement. At the same time, brand names also seem to function in *Paris* as ghostly echoes of station names, suggesting the ways that commuting and consumption are intertwined.

Rather than focusing on the iconic, visual elements of advertising, as the Imagists did, artists and writers influenced by Dadaism were inclined to use the language of advertisements and public service announcements as a part of their poetry. This citational strategy creates a verbal collage, one where the private language of lyric and the public language of modernity clash. In his 'Subway Poem', Kurt Schwitters juxtaposes the dazzling visual effect of the bright subway station and the dark tunnels with the snatches of public speech read by passengers: '(super shoeshines)'; '(physician tested)'; and the final line, '(In case of crowds step to the center aisle)' (Schwitters 1920: 156). These slogans and prompts function in a similar way to the bus tickets and newspaper headlines pasted into Schwitters's visual art collages; they are set apart as specimens of everyday life in the modern city.

Baroness Elsa Von Freytag-Loringhoven wrote a similarly bricolaged poem, 'Subjoyride'. The poem, which 'takes the reader on an underworld journey past advertisement slogans along New York City's subway tunnels' (Gammel 2003: 278), fragments the advertising slogans of the subway and reconstitutes them into a comic pastiche (Conley 2014: 97). It also demonstrates the wit necessary to arrange that onrush of information into a semi-coherent message:

> Dear Mary – the mint with
> The hole – oh lifebuoy!
> Adheres well – delights
> Your taste – continuous
> Germicidal action.
>   (Von Freytag-Loringhoven 1920/2: 411)

These short, enjambed lines with dashes as caesurae emphasise the segmentation and discreteness of subway perception twice over. The poem moves associatively from Lifesavers candies to Lifebuoy soap, and then to the slogan of a product that combines properties of the two, Formamint throat tablets, whose 'continuous germicidal action' came from formaldehyde. By juxtaposing advertisements, the poem reveals their shared traits and their common underlying absurdity.

Much of the poem documents modern fears about health and hygiene (Goody 2019: 70). It ends, however, by asking readers to consider the subway as an aesthetic space, and does so in an imperative mood. 'Wake up your passengers –', enjoins a line almost midway through the final stanza (1920/2: 413):

> Don't envy Aunt Jemima's
> Self raising Cracker Jack
> Laxative knitted chemise
> With that chocolaty
> Taste – use Pickles in Pattern
> Follow Green Lions.
>   (Von Freytag-Loringhoven 1920/2: 413)

To recklessly enjoy a ride on the subway, the poem imagines, one must take up new habits and ways of seeing. Instead of the jealous attitude that might make a passenger responsive to these sales pitches, the poem suggests a defamiliarising frame of mind. The pickles in the penultimate line may be Heinz – 'Pickles in Patterns' was a slogan of theirs in the early 1920s – but by avoiding the brand name and emphasising their patterning, the poem moves into the realm of design.[3] Similarly, Green Lion may be a tobacco company, but it is also an alchemical symbol. 'Subjoyride' argues that the subway does not necessarily have to function as a technology of capitalism. It is a space that can be reimagined and transformed.

Is a Subway Local or Global?

Geographical boundaries are among the features reimagined – and occasionally reinforced – by advertising. In subway poetry, advertisements often seem to articulate the local and national identity being traced by the journey: to return to the 'Subjoyride', few brands represent the United States as forcefully as Aunt Jemima and Cracker Jack. But even in the early twentieth century, brands were transnational presences. The chubby baby that advertised the American brand Cadum Soap, for example, was 'the dominant advertising character' in France circa 1919 ('Is France the Advertising Man's Promised Land?' 1919: 130). Early twentieth-century advertisers bridged national borders through marketing as well as supply chains, creating a modern space that disrupted the distinction between otherwise distant locales.

On one of his visits to France, Russian Symbolist writer Andrei Bely re-encountered unexpected elements of home: 'Dubonnet was my first encounter in Paris; my relative Alexandre Benois my first encounter with a person. This caused sudden geographical confusion: is this Paris or Petersburg?' (qtd in Fabre 2002: 40). The subway system serves as a similar space of disorientation. The underground connections and crossovers particular to subway systems make them particularly apt spaces for modernist writers to engage in imaginative, border-crossing transfers. Brand names encroach upon everyday routines throughout modernist literature: we can think of the plane skywriting 'Glaxo' or 'Kreemo' during Clarissa's walk in *Mrs Dalloway* as one characteristic example. But the predominance of brand names in subway systems reveals something about the way that technological networks function in space as well. For Bely, brand names, like encounters with relatives, are signs of continuity between modernist cities rather than disruption between them.

In *We Have Never Been Modern*, Bruno Latour asks if the railway should be understood as a local or global network and then shows how it works at both scales:

> It is local at all points, since you always find sleepers and railroad workers, and you have stations and automatic ticket machines scattered along the way. Yet it is global, since it takes you from Madrid to Berlin or from Brest to Vladivostok. (Latour 2012: 117)

Modern subway systems, similarly, are local systems suffused with global meaning at levels both systemic and individual. The local reality of the subway system is thus constituted through the global.

Histories of modern subways can sometimes reveal the tension between national and international forces in the making of technological systems. Andrew Jenks's history of the Moscow Metro's construction discusses how newspapers announced 'The Entire Country Built the Metro', detailing the regions that had provided different raw materials for its construction (2000: 703). While these components were celebrated, Soviet engineers 'scrutinized the Berlin subway'; Jenks notes that the system's escalators 'bore a remarkable resemblance' to those in the London Tube stations (2000: 704). Even when subways were built as grand, unifying nationalistic projects, they contained within them the traces of other cities and other systems.

While subway design might suppress the traces of other cities' engineering, it often highlights the extractive relationship between the metropole and the colony. Mobility studies scholars discuss how transportation systems define a culture's sense of spatial scale (Divall and Revill 2005: 106). Modern subway posters compress and distort the scale of colonialism by eliding distances and emphasising the local accessibility of products from the colonies. British painter Ernest Michael Dinkel's poster from 1933, for example, invites passengers to 'Visit the Empire by London's Underground'. At the centre of the poster, a partial world map picks out British colonial holdings in red. The map is ringed by illustrations that represent 'The Wealth, Romance, and Beauty of the Empire'; beneath them is an image of a subway carriage and five roundels marking stations where this 'romance and beauty' can be experienced within London city limits.

These forces can be represented through commercial posters as well as nationalistic ones. To return to the beginning of Hope Mirrlees's poem *Paris* is to plunge into a stream of brand names with colonialist associations:

> I want a holophrase
> NORD-SUD
> ZIG-ZAG
> LION NOIR
> CACAO BLOOKER
> Black-figured vases in Etruscan tombs.
>   (Mirrlees 1919: 3)

The poem's third line, 'ZIG-ZAG', refers to a brand of rolling papers represented by the *Zouave* soldier associated with imperialism in North Africa (Briggs 2005: 33). Although it is unclear if she is referencing the specific image, 'Cacao Blooker' (Mirrlees 1919: 3) was also represented in at least one poster campaign of that era by a Ludwig Hohlwein image of a bare-chested African man with some cacao pods. These brand names contain within them a condensed way of seeing the world, one that implicitly embraces colonial conscription in North Africa and resource extraction in West Africa. By comparing the posters to ancient artefacts that might also be found underground, Mirrlees's poem denaturalises their ideological content.

Subway travellers, too, can represent the forces of empire, diaspora and travel central to the identities of modern cities. Marc Augé imagines the 'irruption of global history in our daily rides' when he notes contemporary subway passengers in Paris going to ethnic markets or tourist sites (2002: 14). In poetry of the 1920s, the subway often served as a liminal space, one that evoked the speaker's home as much as it did the alienated modern city. Russian poet Vladimir Mayakovsky imagines a 'revolt of the rails' where the Métro would defect from Paris and join him (and the Eiffel Tower) in a more egalitarian Moscow (1923: 109–10). In the same period, Russian exiles in Paris formed their own transnational literary community centred around the neighbourhood of Montparnasse (Rubins 2015). Artists located in both Moscow and Paris articulated the underground linkages that they saw, or hoped to see, between these two centres of culture.

New York subway poetry in the same period appealed to immigrant writers, perhaps because the in-between space it depicted could connect to diverse backgrounds and experiences. The subway car was a standard setting in Yiddish-language poetry written about the American Jewish experience of city life (Levinson 2012: 74). Poets Moyshe-Leyb Halpern and Yehoash both use the image of swaying on the subway car to connect the image of a commuter in transit to that of a faithful Jew in the midst of a prayer (Levinson 2012: 79; Yehoash 1919: 180). In his poem 'Subway Wind', Claude McKay uses the breeze from a lowered window to move imaginatively between a subway carriage in New York City and the West Indian home from which many people (McKay included) have emigrated (Posmentier 2017: 38). Where the subway of empire brings the fruits of the colonies to the urban centre in order to sell them, the diasporic subway offers a syncretic alternative where traditions and unresolved histories fuse with the habits of technological modernity.

Terminus

The sense of the modern subway system that coalesced in the early twentieth century transformed into a different kind of socio-technical ensemble in the middle decades of the century. Once Londoners sheltered in Tube stations to avoid bombings during the Blitz, it was difficult to imagine the Underground as a 'space of abstract circulation – the archetypal non-place' (Ashford 2013: 115). With the post-war dominance of the automobile in the US, the panoramic perception felt while travelling by train returned, this time experienced individually rather than collectively. New patterns of migration in the post-war era had a major influence on the subway's makeup and its reception as well (Anyinefa 2003; Brooks 1997; McLeod 2006). While the subway may have been the first subterranean space used by rich and poor alike, it came to be increasingly associated with the working classes and with minoritised racial groups. The subway remains a public space, but one that is shared unevenly.

The modern subway nevertheless echoes in contemporary journeys. Passengers today still move through abstracted landscapes that are informed by global and local pressures. And contemporary poetry continues to reckon with modern subway poetry and the ways it mapped underground connections.[4] Poet Jacques Jouet of the Oulipo group has transformed the segmentation of the subway commute into a literary constraint called the 'Metro-Poem', which is meant to be composed and written on the subway ride. The first stanza of 'Metro Poems', separately titled 'What is a metro poem?', defines the rules one must follow to write it: compose a line between the first station and the second, write it down when stopped at the second station, and so on; if you transfer to a new Underground line within the system, you may begin a new stanza. 'The poem's last line', Jouet writes, 'is written down on the platform of the last station' (Jouet and Monk 2001: 4). The later, numbered stanzas of 'Metro Poems' are just as time- and place-bound as those of early twentieth-century subway poets. But

Jouet begins with a structure that generates meaning across different subway systems, helping poets to think as they move through city space. I hope this essay serves the same function to scholars of modern technologies. Today's subways may cover the same territory, but riders and writers continue to develop new maps.

Notes

1. One of the foundational works in this area is Stephen Kern's *The Culture of Time and Space, 1880–1918* (1983). More recent critical engagements with this technological framework include Enda Duffy's *The Speed Handbook* (2009) and the collection *Moving Modernisms* (2016), edited by David Bradshaw, Laura Marcus and Rebecca Roach.
2. British artist Helen Scalway explored the private mappings of contemporary London subway space with her project 'Travelling Blind', where she asked commuters to draw a map of their London Underground. Some tried to replicate the official Tube diagram; others mapped their usual route with more or less success. See Charlotte Brunsdon, 'The Elsewhere of the London Underground', in *Electronic Elsewheres: Media, Technology, and the Experience of Social Space* (2010).
3. I have found reference to Heinz advertisements with the slogan 'Pickles in Patterns' only in publications from 1923 or later. Perhaps these ads were placed in subway stations before they appeared in print magazines.
4. The dominance of male authors in this tradition, for instance, shaped the narrative and citational form of Alice Notley's book-length poem from 1996, *The Descent of Alette*. See Julia Bloch, 'Alice Notley's Descent' (2012).

Works Cited

Aldington, Richard (1915), 'In the Tube', *The Egoist*, 1 May, p. 74.
Anyinefa, Koffi (2003), 'Le Métro parisien: figure de l'exotisme postcolonial', *French Forum*, 28: 2, pp. 77–98.
Ashford, David (2013), *London Underground: A Cultural Geography*. Liverpool: Liverpool University Press.
Augé, Marc (2002), *In the Metro*, trans. Tom Conley. Minneapolis: University of Minnesota Press.
Beech, Megan (2018), 'Obscure, Indecent and Brilliant', in *Virginia Woolf and the World of Books*, ed. Nicola Wilson and Claire Battershill. Liverpool: Liverpool University Press, pp. 70–5.
Benjamin, Walter (2002), *The Arcades Project*. Cambridge, MA: Belknap Press of Harvard University Press.
Bijker, Wiebe E. (1997), *Of Bicycles, Bakelites, and Bulbs: Toward a Theory of Sociotechnical Change*. Cambridge, MA: MIT Press.
Bloch, Julia (2012), 'Alice Notley's Descent: Modernist Genealogies and Gendered Literary Inheritance', *Journal of Modern Literature*, 35: 3, pp. 1–24.
Bobrick, Benson (1994), *Labyrinths of Iron: Subways in History, Myth, Art, Technology, and War*. New York: Henry Holt & Co.
Bradshaw, David, Laura Marcus and Rebecca Roach, eds (2016), *Moving Modernisms: Motion, Technology, and Modernity*. Oxford: Oxford University Press.
Briggs, Julia (2005), '"Printing Hope": Virginia Woolf, Hope Mirrlees, and the Iconic Imagery of Paris', in *Woolf in the Real World*, ed. Karen V. Kukil. Clemson, SC: Clemson University Press, pp. 31–6.
'Broadway to Paris' script (1913), Ole Olsen Collection, Ned Wayburn material Box 1, Folder 58, University of Southern California Cinematic Arts Library.

Brooks, Michael W. (1997), *Subway City: Riding the Trains, Reading New York*. New Brunswick, NJ: Rutgers University Press.
Brunsdon, Charlotte (2010), 'The Elsewhere of the London Underground', in *Electronic Elsewheres: Media, Technology, and the Experience of Social Space*, ed. and intro. Chris Berry, Soyoung Kim and Lynn Spigel. Minneapolis: University of Minnesota Press, pp. 197–233.
Conley, Tim (2014), 'City Transit Gloria: Mass Movements and Metropolitan Poetics', *Journal of Modern Literature*, 37: 4, pp. 91–108.
Diepeveen, Leonard (2013), *The Difficulties of Modernism*. New York: Routledge.
Dinkel, Ernest Michael (1933), *Poster; Visit the Empire, by Ernest Michael Dinkel, 1933*, Poster. Acton Depot, London Transport Museum, <https://www.ltmuseum.co.uk/collections/collections-online/posters/item/1983-4-3555> (last accessed 19 January 2022).
Divall, Colin and George Revill (2005), 'Cultures of Transport', *Journal of Transport History*, 26: 1, pp. 99–111.
Duffy, Enda (2009), *The Speed Handbook: Velocity, Pleasure, Modernism*. Durham, NC: Duke University Press.
Fabre, Gladys (2002), 'Paris: The Arts and the "Internationale de l'esprit"', in *Paris: Capital of the Arts, 1900–1968*, ed. Sarah Wilson and Eric De Chassey. London: Royal Academy of Arts, pp. 40–53.
Freytag-Loringhoven, Elsa Von (2012 [1920/2]), 'Subjoyride', in *Burning City: Poems of Metropolitan Modernity*, ed. Jed Rasula and Tim Conley. Notre Dame, IN: Action Books, pp. 411–13.
Gammel, Irene (2003), *Baroness Elsa: Gender, Dada, and Everyday Modernity – A Cultural Biography*. Cambridge, MA: MIT Press.
Goody, Alex (2019), *Modernist Poetry, Gender and Leisure Technologies: Machine Amusements*. New York: Palgrave Macmillan.
Hadlaw, Janin (2003), 'The London Underground Map: Imagining Modern Time and Space', *Design Issues*, 19: 1, pp. 25–35.
'Is France the Advertising Man's Promised Land?' (1919), *Printer's Ink*, 29 May.
Jenks, Andrew L. (2000), 'A Metro on the Mount: The Underground as a Church of Soviet Civilization', *Technology and Culture*, 41: 4 (1 October), pp. 697–724.
Jouet, Jacques and Ian Monk (2001), 'Metro Poems', *AA Files*, 45/6, pp. 4–14.
Kern, Stephen (1983), *The Culture of Time and Space, 1880–1918*. Cambridge, MA: Harvard University Press.
Kilmer, Joyce (1910), 'The Subway (96th Street to 137th Street)', *The Independent*, 1 September.
Kirby, Lynne (1997), *Parallel Tracks: The Railroad and Silent Cinema*. Durham, NC: Duke University Press.
Latour, Bruno (2012), *We Have Never Been Modern*, trans. Catherine Porter. Cambridge, MA: Harvard University Press.
Levinson, Julian (2012), 'On Some Motifs in Moyshe-Leyb Halpern: A Benjaminian Meditation on Yiddish Modernism', *Prooftexts: A Journal of Jewish Literary History*, 32: 1, pp. 63–88.
Lynch, Kevin (1960), *The Image of the City*. Cambridge, MA: MIT Press.
McLeod, John (2006), 'Orphia in the Underground: Postcolonial London Transport', in *Transport(s) in the British Empire and the Commonwealth/Transport(s) dans l'empire britannique et le Commonwealth*, ed. Michèle Lurdos and Judith Misrahi-Barak. Montpellier, France: Université Paul Valéry, pp. 389–405.
Mayakovsky, Vladimir (2012 [1923]), 'Paris (Chatting with the Eiffel Tower)', in *Burning City: Poems of Metropolitan Modernity*, ed. Jed Rasula and Tim Conley. Notre Dame, IN: Action Books, pp. 108–11.
Mirrlees, Hope (1919). *Paris: A Poem*, Richmond. London: Hogarth Press.
Morrisson, Mark S. (2001), *The Public Face of Modernism: Little Magazines, Audiences, and Reception, 1905–1920*. Madison: University of Wisconsin Press.

Mumford, Lewis (1961), *The City in History: Its Origins, Its Transformations, and Its Prospects*. New York: Houghton Mifflin Harcourt.
Nead, Lynda (2000), *Victorian Babylon: People, Streets, and Images in Nineteenth-Century London*. New Haven, CT: Yale University Press.
Pike, David Lawrence (2005), *Subterranean Cities: The World Beneath Paris and London, 1800–1945*. Ithaca, NY: Cornell University Press.
Pike, David Lawrence (2007), *Metropolis on the Styx: The Underworlds of Modern Urban Culture, 1800–2001*. Ithaca, NY: Cornell University Press.
Posmentier, Sonya (2017), *Cultivation and Catastrophe: The Lyric Ecology of Modern Black Literature*. Baltimore: Johns Hopkins University Press.
Pound, Ezra (1913), 'In a Station of the Metro', *Poetry: A Magazine of Verse*, 2: 1, p. 12.
Pryor, Sean (2019), 'A Poetics of Occasion in Hope Mirrlees's *Paris*', *Critical Quarterly*, 61: 1, pp. 37–53.
Rubins, Maria (2015), *Russian Montparnasse: Transnational Writing in Interwar Paris*, Palgrave Studies in Modern European Literature. Houndmills: Palgrave Macmillan.
Saler, Michael T. (1999), *The Avant-Garde in Interwar England: Medieval Modernism and the London Underground*. New York: Oxford University Press.
Schivelbusch, Wolfgang (1987), *The Railway Journey: The Industrialization of Time and Space in the Nineteenth Century*. Berkeley: University of California Press.
Schwetman, John D. (2014), 'Harry Beck's London Underground Map: A Convex Lens for the Global City', *Transfers*, 4: 2 (1 June), pp. 86–103.
Schwitters, Kurt (2012 [1920]), 'Subway Poem', in *Burning City: Poems of Metropolitan Modernity*, ed. Jed Rasula and Tim Conley, Notre Dame, IN: Action Books, p. 156.
Singh, Dhan Zunino (2013), 'Towards a Cultural History of Underground Railways', *Mobility in History*, 4: 1, pp. 106–12.
Singh, Dhan Zunino (2014), 'Meaningful Mobilities: The Experience of Underground Travel in the Buenos Aires Subte, 1913–1944', *The Journal of Transport History*, 35: 1, pp. 97–113.
Spalding, Steven D. (2014), 'Rail Networks, Mobility, and the Cultures of Cities: Introduction to the Special Section', *Transfers*, 4: 2, pp. 42–8.
Stalter-Pace, Sunny (2013), *Underground Movements: Modern Culture on the New York City Subway*. Amherst: University of Massachusetts Press.
Sweeney, Niamh (2011), 'Tour Eiffel/Paris Metro: Symbolic Associations and the Question of Scale in Representations of Simultaneity', *Irish Journal of French Studies*, 11, pp. 21–45.
Thacker, Andrew (2003), *Moving Through Modernity: Space and Geography in Modernism*. Manchester: Manchester University Press.
'Those Who Read in the Subway' (1929), *New York Times*, 30 June, SM9.
Ungar, Steven (2018), *Critical Mass: Social Documentary in France from the Silent Era to the New Wave*. Minneapolis: University of Minnesota Press.
Welsh, David (2010), *Underground Writing: The London Tube from George Gissing to Virginia Woolf*. Liverpool: Liverpool University Press.
Williams, Rosalind (2008 [1990]), *Notes on the Underground: An Essay on Technology, Society, and the Imagination*. Cambridge, MA: MIT Press.
Woolf, Virginia (1971 [1922]), *Jacob's Room*. London: Hogarth Press.
Yehoash (1919), 'Subway', in *Burning City: Poems of Metropolitan Modernity*, ed. Jed Rasula and Tim Conley. Notre Dame, IN: Action Books, p. 180.
Zurier, Rebecca (2006), *Picturing the City: Urban Vision and the Ashcan School*. Berkeley: University of California Press.

5

Automobiles: The Modernist Gaze and Speed's Visual Limit-field

Enda Duffy

'The rupture of metal and safety glass and the deliberate destruction of deliberately engineered artefacts, had left me lightheaded' (Ballard 1985: 125). In literature, the swirling buildup of the first phase of appalled fascination at what the automobile had wrought converged on one notorious text, J. G. Ballard's *Crash*. The automobile's promise of the thrilling experience of unprecedented personal speed, and the pushing of its driver's sensations to their limits, had made it a new kind of commodity: one which not only granted the usual pleasures of consumerism and status, but demanded new, extreme, use of one's senses, and which induced, in that very use, pleasurable stress. For Ballard, at the end of this era, it was only at the moment of the crash that the full implications of this new model of what it meant to be human in interaction with technology could be mapped in fascinated horror. Before him, many artists had experimented with elucidating the joys of car speeds: from Marinetti's pro-car oratorio in the 1909 'Futurist Manifesto' to the car chases of the first Hollywood films and the Jaguar spills of James Bond; the admiration for drivers and driving in Proust's *La Recherche* and the excitements of driving joyously delineated in Woolf's *Orlando*; the windscreen painting of Manet and the speeding-car photos of Jacques-Henri Lartigue. They had all been willing to celebrate the car as commodity, but with an undercurrent of concern about what is unleashed in the driver-subject. The experimental strategies of the various modernisms were excellent for plumbing the limits and the possible new intensities – of attentiveness, endurance, adrenaline rush and stress – that this new technology incited in its users. Delineating these stresses in turn drove various modernisms to their own limits of representation. This chapter will first consider the two poles of consumer celebration and terror which greeted the arrival of the automobile; we will then examine representations of the first sense stressed by the experience of driving at speed, that of sight. Seeing at speed became a modernist topic and a spur to new kinds of modernist representations and genres, which in turn prompted engineers to develop still newer technologies of seeing. Capturing the speed gaze became *the* task of the moving image; it also fostered a telegraphic, cinematic turn in literature and art.

The Automobile as Limit Commodity

In middlebrow fiction after 1900, the automobile, first produced in its modern form around 1896, appeared as the novel commodity, a further enhancement to established hierarchies of gender and class. Published at the very end of the long 'era of the horse', the historical stage when the speed of the fastest pack animal had set the limit to the land speed of humans and goods (the train, before the motorcar, had presaged its end), books such as E. Œ Somerville and Martin Ross's *Some Experiences of an Irish R.M.*[1] feature the automobile as a new wonder and rich man's toy. Like other comedies of manners of the era, Somerville and Ross's writing can be read as a farewell salute to horse lore, and to the ancient idea that speed was the outcome of a well-arranged conjunction of human and animal life. Published between 1899 and 1915, these stories are awash in horse-riding, judging and racing, at a time when the speed of a galloping horse was considered (except for the train) the fastest land speed. The *fin de siècle* saw a last hurrah of these cults of horse speeds. *Black Beauty: The Autobiography of a Horse*, by Anna Sewell, was published in 1877; the Ascot Gold Cup (won by Throwaway in 1904) is cited in *Ulysses* (1922); and the world of grooms, jockeys and betting is the setting of George Moore's naturalist masterpiece *Esther Waters* (1894). The key 1878 commission of the pioneering photographer of movement Eadweard Muybridge showed Leland Stanford's galloping horse. A quarter-century after Muybridge united horse speed, technology and the possibilities of seeing, in the rural lanes of the *Irish R.M.* stories the motorcar makes its daunting, speedful appearance.

It would be all too easy to read the car in these 'sketches' as a mere Edwardian accoutrement, an ornament on a par with tennis whites, motor-yachts, elaborate hats and bicycles – all of which also feature. The guileless Major Yeates is never more self-satisfied as when he dispenses with his stableboy–coachman, to take the wheel of his new automobile himself. However, once the automobile, half-way through the series, insinuates itself into almost every tale, the new machine's power to cover large distances at speed impinges upon and alters the outcome of almost every story. The car, stolen by the children of a nouveau-riche family, symbolically crashes into their shrubbery; faster than galloping hunt horses, it carries Lady Knox triumphantly to the scene of an eviction she prevents;[2] a car allows Major Yeates's guest to find the fox before the hunting party. The train, with its 'Bradshaw' timetables (Somerville and Ross 1984: 336), still tethers remote Shreelane to the British Empire, but in one of the best set-pieces the train is ridiculed for its slowness, and it is the Major's vast new automobile, symbol of the embrace of modernity, the masculine mastery of mechanics, upper-class family values, even of assured prosperity, that becomes the plot-changer (Somerville and Ross 1984: 273–86), and the necessary catalyst for many of the chronicled adventures.

The automobile, launched upon the Western upper-class scene, was the jewel in the crown of the early twentieth-century consumer universe. At the height of this first long stage of consumerism in the West, it was to be expected that the automobile, as the most glamourous commodity of all, would be the one that embodied the most profound effect. Comedies of Edwardian manners such as Somerville and Ross's *Irish R.M.* and even such innocent-seeming works as Kenneth Grahame's *The Wind in the Willows* (1908), in which Toad's car mania, and its 'spills' and 'speed thrills', are described in relishing detail, therefore function as advertising for the new invention. They also, however, imply a mass enthusiasm for this novel object, an enthusiasm awakened because here was not simply another inert consumer bauble, however streamlined, fashionable and opulent; rather, the car promised nothing less than access to a superhuman power – the power of speed. 'Rapid motion through space elates one,' wrote James Joyce in his short story about motor-racing, 'After the Race',[3] set during the running of the Gordon Bennett Cup race in the environs of Dublin in 1903

(Joyce 1967: 35–42). Yet, while this new, consumer-accessed experience elated, it also traumatised: here was a consumer good that held out a new promise, the allure of elation, of a thrill, but one sharpened by the low-level terror of constant, mortal danger.

To grasp how the pleasure of speed was sharpened by terror, and how this was represented in literature, consider the two fictional texts that may be said to bookend the automobile era. The first, prefiguring the automobile, is a terror text of train travel: Zola's *La Bête humaine* (*The Human Beast*) of 1890; the second, marking the end of the 'romance' of automobile travel eighty-three years later, is Ballard's *Crash* of 1973.[4] These two novels about the horrific *jouissance*, first, of train speed, then of car speed, both culminate in accounts of horrific crashes. In each, the propulsion of subjective desire, and even the progress of their romance plots, hinge on its culminating, gory crash. In each, the intimate defers to the technological, and technology's brutality, made manifest in the crash outcome, renders the intimate perverse. Each equates masculinity and driving the train or automobile: in each novel's logic, humans and technology undergird each other's power, and women are denied access. Each text's plot concerns the human trying to catch up to the machine's tremendous power. Their similarities, however, belie a crucial difference: Zola's train speed is experienced in part by its passengers, and by its observers from without, as a passive experience, whereas in Ballard's *Crash* speeds are experienced primarily by drivers. The personalisation of speed, represented by the move from the passenger experience in the train to the interaction of driver and automobile, is a function of the commodification of technologies. The automobile rendered technological speed subjective: each citizen as a driver got to embody, and participate in, the potential power of velocity. (In *La Bête humaine*, driving the train was labour, the task of an employee; in *Crash*, it is leisure.) Ballard's dystopian text lays bare the potential horror of this new consumer machine. In *Crash*'s *danse macabre*, Vaughan's schemes to crash into the cars of celebrities short-circuits the dream of any new versions of a more alert or energised subject born of this latest collaboration of humans and technology. Possibly the most shocking post-war British novel, *Crash* makes explicit the stakes in the new stage of techno-consumerism represented by the automobile.

The automobile offered all of the rewards of consumerism; it also brought closer to the surface the exploitative end-game underlying all power relations, including the commodity one – the ability to take life, to be killed, or to kill. Between these two poles, between the car in Somerville and Ross and the car in J. G. Ballard, there was the machine's demand that its users engage each of their senses, pay attention and take control more acutely. This new kind of commodity flaunted all of the glamour of previous commodities, but it also made intense demands of its users. It demanded an effort of attention, of using one's reflexes, of control, that was thrilling, and which, like other new thrills of the era, from such new sports as skiing to the rides at seaside fairgrounds, promised new realms of heightened sensation, new excitements, new somatic intensities. The car, its utilitarian task to increase the ease of transport, was offered within the logic of the commodity to each individual who could afford to be not simply a passive passenger, but a driver, so that the modern subject-consumer was granted access to a new sensation – the sensation of unprecedented speeds. It gave to people whose lives were increasingly governed by the society of the spectacle something quite contrary: it granted them a sense of power by allowing them each to access this new embodied sensation.

Most of the various modernisms, when the car entered their field of vision, were themselves either thrilled or terrified, or both – and deployed their own experiments to a maximum to delineate the new experiences that could be enabled by this novel and personalised technological speed. Representing the automobile and its speed promise pushed modernist forms to their limits in the same way that the new technology demanded increased use of their senses from its user–consumers. The remainder of this chapter will explore how one of the senses was twisted and reimagined by the new speed experience: that of sight. Sight, as we shall explore, was put under intense pressure by the simple requirement of a different gaze through the car windscreen, done at speed. The speeding car demanded of its driver a new kind of modern looking: a modernist gaze. This fast gaze, moreover, in the century increasingly given over to Debordian spectacles and Baudrillardian simulation, worked as the commodity's guarantee that it could still provide access to nothing less than actual sensation and real experience. If speed was a signature achievement of modernity, enabled by technology, then the automobile, which granted access to it for its users, allowed them to feel this modernity in their bones.

Sightlines: Post-Perspectival Modernism

Driving and looking, driving and the ferociously alert gaze, the hectic glance in the rear-view mirror, the intense attention to everything in front, the effect of seeing other objects zoom by out of 'the corner of one's eye', the blur with which the camera freezes movement in an instant: speeding and seeing have always had a tumultuous, intense and uneasy relationship. In 1917, Henri Matisse painted 'The Windshield, On the Road to Villacoublay',[5] showing a stretch of French road seen through a car windscreen. Despite the resolutely conventional scene, the frame of the metal pillars and roof rail – a techno-frame inside the picture's own ornate one – makes the work a thoroughly unconventional treatment of a standard Impressionist subject. Matisse, through his complex framing of a pastoral scene, makes clear that the possibilities of his observation post, the result of a new technology, are his true subject. The painting asks the viewer what one can see, and how one sees it, through a car window. The little steering wheel, the covers wrapping the posts and bars: these underline the fact that the artist must now make the automobile his studio, or rather, his *camera obscura*. The machine, made for movement, posits a new view, or a new symphony of simultaneous sight-lines, since the views seen here on each side, beyond the posts, make this a triptych for the age of speed technology, while the split windscreen (early cars used two sheets of glass) introduces a new bifocal horizon line, putting in question the rules of perspective in place since Masaccio. The covered car became, in effect, a giant camera apparatus, with the painter within it. In this painting of the artist's fascination with what can be seen from an automobile, the complex multiview effect – the doubled front- and two-side views, the extra view propped near the steering-wheel of a conventional painting of the scene, within the already complex painting – implies that nature can be framed by technology, but cannot be contained by it. It is as if mobility, or even its possibility, at some rate of speed, rapidly multiplies what can be seen. Nature can no longer be stilled in order to see it whole. The sloped scenes on each side, for example, suggest unframable infinities.

Matisse's complex juxtaposition of multiple perspectives of the same scene also highlights a fundamental uncanniness in 'The Windshield, On the Road to Villacoublay'.

This is underlined by the smaller painting-within-the painting, since it rests against the steering-wheel. With that placing, we are signalled that the car's driver is missing from the scene. The driver, in effect, is replaced by the painter; the car, given the driver's absence, cannot be moving. The mobility which excited the painter in its viewing possibilities is the very element that has to be denied, to allow painterly creation; it is as if his frustration at realising this is the very impetus that energises the work, and makes the bland landscape, literally, arresting. Driving *or* painting: Matisse records here something like the end of the 'arrested', still, 'contemplative' perspectival gaze before the onslaught of a post-perspectivism demanded by the gaze from the moving automobile. The painting confronts a venerable genre, the painterly view, with the sensory overload enabled by a new technology that demands a new kind of looking. In order to paint the work, the mobile viewing post, whose possibilities are the real subject of the painting, had to be stilled. The artwork, straining to suggest the multiplicity of new perspectives, with its doubled-horizon line, its slipping long views on each side, its painting-within-the painting propped where the driver should be driving – in sum, its mirror-box effect – all imply a limit-gaze, the limit instance of still viewing. (Omitted is a rear-view mirror scene: this piece of looking technology was only patented in 1921). Its uncanny stillness incites us to consider how a scene of movement, seen at speed, might appear.

The car, with its leather straps and glass, celebrated in Matisse's painting as in the first fictional accounts of the car as status symbol and in car advertising, was the supreme commodity. It also marks a new development in the history of reification. Replete even by 1917 with its glass and chrome curves, the car was a glamorous status symbol, but one which offered to overcome the very commodity inertia which ensured that the commodity's fascination could be read as superficial. Marx had defined reification as the manner in which, in modernity, real relations between people are invariably mediated by commodities; in this scenario, the commodity's inertia was the index of the *anomie* that registers as the subject's apprehension of reification's failed promise. The speeding automobile promised to overcome the stasis by which the commodity betrayed itself. In a formula that would be employed by other machines-as-commodities since, such as the personal computer, it offered not merely to perform a task faster, but instead, to provide the experience of that speed to the user–consumer. For the first drivers, the car offered more than status and the pleasure of a shiny commodity. It offered the experience of a new sensory overload, a forced new mobilisation of sensory perceptiveness, a stressful, exhilarating rush, of new sensations: the thrill of speed.

The young Joyce's 1904 story 'After the Race' toyed with the new allegiances and mis-alliances that would upend standard narratives as an after-effect of this new stimulant. It anticipated by four years the hyperbolic celebration of the speeding, crashing car that opens Filippo Marinetti's 'Manifesto of Futurism' of 1908, which appeared in *Le Figaro* in February 1909. Subsequent treatments, from Matisse's 1917 painting to passages in Proust and Woolf, show that the high arts, following on from the excited car chases of early films (from 'Runaway Match' of 1903, all the way to the forty-five-minute car chase in H. B. Halicki's 'Gone in Sixty Seconds' of 1974), were eager to atomise the new visual sensation. In volume 4 of *A la recherche de temps perdu*, published in 1922, Proust writes of how seeing from a car offers 'the perspective which sets a castle dancing about with a hill, a church and the sea, while one draws nearer to it however much it tries to huddle beneath its age-old foliage' (Proust 2003 [1922]: Vol. 4, 550). Summing up her astounded descriptions of the driver's lines of sight from the motorcar in *Orlando* (1928), Virginia Woolf could write 'While the motor car shot, swung, squeezed and slid for she was an expert driver, down Regent Street, down Haymarket . . . Nothing could be seen or read from start to finish' (Woolf 1956: 306–7; see also Woolf 1966).[6] Each makes clear that, at least from the moment that car cabs were enclosed, by 1910, and drivers allowed to drive at speed,[7] it was the disruption of any fixed and static seeing, experienced through the windscreen of a moving car, that registered the initial incredible speed experience. Disrupted seeing was the first index of the automobile speed's stress and elation. The various modernisms' windscreen teletopologies took the impress of the modern reckoning with this technoaesthetic: they register the sense of shock experienced by these first car drivers. This was enabled by high art's scope for a more flexible and scrupulous mimeticism, its ability to acknowledge the exciting shock at the demands imposed by the new technology. Since the commodity-machines are also proficient at making their users adapt, this is a shock now lost to us, and the gaze at speed that shocked at first has become mundane.

The sensory overload arriving through the car windscreen, with scene after scene flying to meet the viewer, signalled a new phase of prosthetic modernity in which the technology pushed its users towards their perceptual limits even as they felt the excitement with which they could be perceived by the speeding eye. Yet the mechanical speed-up worked simply. Through the windscreen of a speeding car the viewer is presented with an unprecedented succession and variety of scenes: a massive sensory overload of roads, nature, signs, structures, people, traffic. With all this flashing before her, the viewer shoulders the task of rapid editing, choosing moment by moment what is important, ignoring the rest, restitching discordant scenes into an improvised narrative. This fluid narrative, in turn, with its intensities and sights semi-seen, must then make sense of the mass of scenes which continue to appear at each moment. The relatively easy rhythm of the *flâneur*'s gaze, timed to the jaunt of the figure's gait, had in literary modernism helped launch experimental accounts of this disjointed, streamed looking; the automobile gaze sped it up. It was radically different to the contemplative gaze enabled by a more leisurely culture, one in which the fixing of observation points enabled more legible perspectives. The anxious driver, for example, focuses on a perspectival point, but one that must constantly move, on the road ahead, so that surrounding details are edited out: they become mere blur.[8] This blur then constitutes the sign of the limit of the visible in speed viewing. Italian Futurists such as Giacamo Balla were the modernists who experimented most urgently with representing the blur effect. Joyce's telegraphese used in representing Bloom's stream of consciousness in *Ulysses* (Joyce 1985: 150), or the avalanche of sights recorded in seconds in Woolf's description of the experience of seeing from the car driver's viewpoint in *Orlando* (Woolf 1956: 306–7), are close to blur textualities, modernist writing on looking that took its cue in part from attempts to describe the new experience of looking from the speeding automobile. Blur as a visual phenomenon is that excess scene that is excluded by the viewer–sampler, but which intrudes and still declares its presence, remaining at the edge of vision as a persistent shadowland that hints at the unconscious, the ghostly, the existence of the repressed or ignored. Blur's presence also implies that to observe at speed is to run the risk that scenes, and certainties about them, are liable to be decomposed and frayed. In this way, the look from the moving automobile, and the attempt to translate into text the result of what one saw at speed, form one basis of the representational and textual obscurity of much modernist writing.

The other new invention, the movie camera, may be considered the technological answer to the problems posed by the speed gaze. In early popular film, however, in contrast to early twentieth-century experimental textuality, new kinds of movement-image, such as the tracking shot – in which the movie camera, on a track, rapidly shot successive images as it moved (see Duffy and Boscagli 2021) – the closeup, and new ways to narrate the resultant spectacle such as fast editing, remained legible to viewers, and therefore appeared 'natural' to them, because of the match between the new medium and its spectacle. The moving camera could match its speed to the moving scene – for example, in scenes of the car chase: 'Car chase films represent the fusion of mind and machine, in which the will becomes manifest through mechanization,' as film historian Harvey O'Brien puts it (2012: 34).[9] The movie camera, in other words, was comfortable with seeing at speed in a way that literary forms (Proust, Woolf) and art forms (Matisse, Balla), rapidly adapting though they were, could never be. Yet this discomfort with describing the new sensation of speed, and in adapting their prose to the pulse of the new speeded-up technosphere, meant that text, painting and sculpture could best capture the shock of this particular new. It could also, possibly, better consider its implications.

To the scenic overload of seeing through a car windscreen was added a further uncertainty: the suspicion, fostered by the blur at the edge of vision and suggested by the presence of the intervening, transparent windscreen, that what is beyond it may have no material existence at all. The scene outside, whizzing by, might merely be a virtuality. One might think that constant exposure to new scenes, bearing in for their split-second closeup, could make what was seen in this way and at this rate more tangible. Seen from within the closed car, however, from inside a cinema looking at a screen or simply from behind a camera, the screen-frame invites the viewer to entertain the visible in the first place as a representation. What is seen through the windscreen is constantly othered in an heterotopising[10] look.

The apparently mundane gaze of the driver through a car windscreen, therefore, turns out to be a radically bifurcated experience, and the epitome of a contradiction at the heart of modernism.[11] Everything seen through the 'pare-brise' flies up close, only to be cast aside in a blur, and, at the same time, everything appears as on a screen, a simulation. These contrasting tendencies neatly partake of the two contrasting, most often used accounts of what it means to live, to see and to sense in modernity. On the one hand, the mass-of-onrushing-scenes scenario is one of the best examples in the modernist era of the shocking, overstimulating, hyperfatiguing modernist urban experience described by early sociologists such as Georg Simmel in 'Metropolis and Mental Life'. Simmel speaks of 'the intensification of nervous stimulation – the sharp discontinuity in the grasp of a single glance, the unexpectedness of onrushing impressions' (1950: 410). On the other hand, the suspicion that the scene seen through the windscreen is merely that – an image – evokes the persistent counter-description of modern existence as narcoticised, *anomie*-riven *flânerie* in a dreamscape of consumerist images, a keynote of the urban milieu delineated by Benjamin (Benjamin 2002) and theorised by Adorno (Adorno and Horkheimer 2002). The question posed by our simple example of what was, around 1900, a newly possible action – of looking through the windscreen of a speeding car – is this: how can these two accounts of modernist experience exist in tandem? For the contemporary reader, this question persists: how do readings that stress spectacle as the logical conclusion of Marx's account of modernity as mass reification jibe with those more excited readings of the modernist experience as one about getting up close to 'the shock of the new'?

Critiques of modernism have largely subsumed the reading of modernist obscurity as evidence of shocking sensory overload into another, which considers this obscurity to result from the text's registering of the blasé-riven blandness of modern reified culture. The modernist artwork's value gets cast as a quiet revolution: it subverts. Fredric Jameson gifted critics of modernism with the critical tools to grasp how every experimental work, despite itself, exemplified ideological self-incrimination: the more obscure a work, the more its aesthetic task could be understood as revealing that the culture from which it arose was 'a document of barbarism'.[12] Readings in his wake tend to cast the modernist artwork as a fragment that emerges from a Simmelean modernist urban milieu of shock, which then uses that shock, heightened aesthetically, as a weapon against the complacency of the consumerist dreamland. One issue with this critical view, when it meets the test of material history, is that for an early twentieth-century Western bourgeois subject, the actual shock, impossible to avoid, that came from engaging with the new technologies of the day was much greater than the presumed shock posed by the aesthetic obscurities employed to represent it. The shock of experiencing unprecedented speeds, and looking while doing so, was greater than the shock of reading about it in avant-garde prose. This suggests why critics should offer some space to that maligned construct, technological determinism. Post-Adornian defences of the highest culture, if they uncritically fetishise shock as merely an artistic uber-gesture, need to be coupled with a grasp of the effects of material changes brought about by science and technology. A fully materialist reading of the effects of new technologies of the modernist moment, from the telephone to the automobile to mass electrification, would read actual shock in all its varieties, as an experienced, sensational stimulus and event, which itself incited modernist experiment.[13]

What exactly happens when we are shocked? The newly agitated gaze through the car windscreen – a modernist *pare-brise* teletopology – reminds us that shock implies physiological disruption, prior to any cognitive or quasi-mystical change. Shock involves not just a bolt of aesthetic force that leads to a moment of (re)cognition. To describe shock simply in terms of the gaining of insight is to read modernist art as merely conceptual. More, such readings tempt us to underestimate the disruptive effects of other kinds of innovation, to imply that culture has a monopoly on shock. Reacting to new technologies, for example, shock-effects are registered by users as a perceptual, sensory, visceral limit, one which, first, begs to be described in all its complex details. Only in the second place might it alter the subject's 'field of vision', after it achieves a resetting of the set of perceptual and sensory possibilities that would determine the scope of any new insight. Consider the driver's gaze through the windscreen of an automobile round 1900, and its sensory overload of shocked seeing: undermined is the subject's sense of space, her place in it. For the nearest account of how this unfolded, and to begin to grasp its implications, we must turn briefly to the work of the great modern philosopher of memory-images, Henri Bergson.

Bergson's *Matter and Memory*, published in 1896 almost simultaneously with the first viable motorcars and the first films, is a meditation on moving images. It outlines a theory of how mental images are accessed by memory, and it describes how this must recast the ways we conceptualise both space and time. Aptly for any account of seeing at speed, Bergson's whole system is based upon an analysis of what the moving subject perceives. As his foremost explicator, Gilles Deleuze, explains, movement for Bergson is not reducible to mapped instances in conventionally conceptualised, that is, static, spaces. (Likewise, he does not think of images as 'filed away,' ready for retrieval.) Bergson's image, Deleuze proves, is rather always in transit or in flow; as Deleuze notes, 'It will always occur in the interval between the two [fixed points], in other words behind your back' (1986: 104). This is Deleuze's definition of Bergson's *durée* and it is the flowing space in which, he claims, change occurs. Bergson, in other words, reimagines space as an entity dynamically produced through motion, rather than an abstraction that must always be thought to precede motion. Space, in his term, is an unfolding. Since this unfolding must be perceived, Bergson's account is derived from examinations of subjective experience.

This stress, on the one hand, on what is experienced – subjectively, through the senses, beginning with sight – and on the other, on what occurs between any two hypothetical fixed points, that is, 'behind one's back', might appear to correspond to the dialectic we posited earlier in readings of modernist representations, between the reading that privileges the barrage of sensory experience and the alternative reading which begins with the suspicion that what is perceived is a mere representation, a spectacle. Since Bergson's formulation privileges a *durée* which invariably occurs exactly when one is not quite looking, that is, 'behind one's back', it always threatens to slide into a metaphysics. Bergson's metaphysical tendencies, despite the materialist basis for his speculations – like both William James and Sigmund Freud, he grounded his theory in what he had himself observed – help account for the enormous interest in his work in his day, and the relative obscurity into which it has fallen since. If, however, we look at the artistic productions influenced by Bergson, we discover artists fascinated by the promise of technologically enabled velocity, but trapped at his departure point: the belief that what matters is the perception of the moving subject. Take, for example, much of the painterly work of the Italian Futurists. For Balla and Bocconi, despite the manifestos, art experiments in representing speed often resolve around a fixed point, turning on a single subject or crowd, whether human or animal. Speed, in Futurist painting, tends to be represented as a vortex, rather than a blur. One example of many is the horses of Corrado Forlin's painting of the Palio, 'Splendore simultaneo del Palio di Siena', of 1937.[14] The effect of Futurist images and sculptures of racers, athletes, horses and birds, therefore, is to recast the Bergsonian flux into a glorification of a Nietzschean (or, at least, d'Annunzian) will to power – power achievable, the message becomes, by harnessing new technologies of personal speed. Similarly, the innovative photographer of speeding cars, Jacques-Henri Lartigue (see Baring 2020), nevertheless centres almost every image on a still point which comes to signify the racing-car driver's will, so that the images work in the final instance as glorifications of latter-day heroes.

How can modernist art both be subjective and, at the same time, describe what happens 'behind one's back', especially in relation to new ways of how to see? If we survey the whole early twentieth-century art field of 'car art', from the sketches in early car magazines to the streamline *moderne* of Tamara de Lempicka's 'Self Portrait in the Green Bugatti' of 1925, what one finds is image after image which celebrates the driver as privileged hero, one now posed seated, but accruing the force of the commodity, the car itself, and the propulsion engine that is new in it. The old heroic seated pose had placed the hero atop a horse; the new car seats tended lower, lower even than the cyclists celebrated in another genre of speed images such as Jean Metzinger's

'Au vélodrome' (1912).[15] Their Nietzschean determination[16] had to be represented by intimations of their intensity.

Yet one also on occasion comes across another view: attempts to show what the driver saw through the car windscreen. We are back, then, to Matisse's 'The Windshield, On the Road to Villacoublay', to photos, film shots and paintings, works which show ostensibly empty cars, where the viewer is supposed to put herself in the place of the non-existent driver. This is by no means the 'death of the subject', but rather, a stratagem to force one into complete subjective identification – a call for the viewer to situate her subjectivity in place of the missing one at the wheel. It is not, then, a case of the subject being erased by the speed of technology. Rather, it is a challenge to the viewer to call up, for herself, a more complex notion of the relation of new intensities of sensing, particularly of seeing, to a sense of self. In Deleuze's terms, this would be the modernist achievement of a body without organs.

This is precisely where literature – which, despite its professed desire, at its most intense moments in post-Romantic mode, to conjure 'images' (which, in fact, can tell only of what is beneath the scrim of text) – scores over actual images, such as paintings, photographs, even film scenes. This occurs, on the one hand, when the writer him- or herself takes the wheel: in autobiographies of early racing-car drivers, and later, tales built around car journeys, such as Flannery O'Connor's 'A Good Man is Hard to Find' (1955) and passages from the long line of road novels, from Evelyn Waugh's account of his Abyssinian travels (1937) to Jack Kerouac's *On the Road* (1957). In them, one can map how the act of seeing at speed never really ceased to shock, even as it became normalised. More significant, however, is the manner in which this newly feverish looking demanded of the automobile driver by the new technology came to influence accounts of seeing and the seen heavily, even when the writing in question has nothing overtly to do with speed movement and automobiles. Take the most characteristic new strategy of modernist prose, 'stream of consciousness'. Far from being a careful annotation of all that Clarissa Dalloway, Leopold Bloom or J. Alfred Prufrock thinks moment by moment, it functions, rather, very much as does Matisse's image of the driverless car. Just as that image forces us to project ourselves inside the car as inside a giant movie camera, and imagine what we see out of it, so too 'stream of consciousness' forces readers into the unprecedented task of, as it were, climbing into the very body of the character described and seeing, hearing and so on out of that character's senses. Not even the movies, modernism's own new art form and the medium which brought the new technology of the movie camera to the task of looking at speed, could quite equal this. Despite its experiments, such as the extreme closeup, it persisted in presenting to the viewer the seen as heterotopic spectacle: it still derived its logic from the idea of the seen as a view. 'Stream of consciousness', like film, offers an unfolding view but it sets itself a single rule: the stream-view, the flow-view, must always be through the character's own eyes, never the imagined view from without. With it, we as reader–viewers, coerced into complicity with a subjectivity so total that it does not allow us to heroicise its seeing subject, can only map a scene not as a 'scene', but as an 'unfolding', as Bergson understood space as seen. This unfolding, moreover, is not a matter of a series of 'insights' – a term with its origins in metaphysics – since that procedure would enable us to map once again the empty, static space we want to imagine the character inhabits. (The critic, like the detective-story reader searching for 'clues', can only do that with 'hindsight', a retrospective look.) Rather, the 'stream of consciousness' maps an adrenaline-fuelled, neurasthenic series of reactions to stimuli, a fraught and continuously improvised series of nervous reactions which, as we read, we are forced to experience *in lieu* of the character in the text which is prompting us to do so. The achievement of this new readerly self-projection even at the level of the reader's bodily sensation is, for the reader of modernist prose, truly new and shock-inducing. To grasp this, and to track it, as a seismograph measures tremors, would be to give modernist shock the detailed respect it is due, and to register how new technologies have rendered possible the sensation of this continuous and visceral kind of shock-effect. It would give tremulous modern bodies, which, in most Futurist paintings, are cast as in competition with the new machines, the kind of attention that registers their tremors and considers their significance. It would allow us to acknowledge forthrightly how, in many modernisms of speed and otherwise, imperialist–racist mindsets, the objectification of women, the snobbish approval of status and wealth, were unchanged or even heightened. It would also open a space, however, to understand the real change in human perception that was being ushered in by the technological prosthesis, and thereby to grasp its utopian potential. It would allow us to map the potential for future positive change propelled and empowered by speed.

Notes

1. The 'Irish R.M.' stories were collected as *Some Experiences of an Irish R.M.* (1899), *Further Experiences of an Irish R.M.* (1908) and *In Mr. Knox's Country* (1915).
2. On gender and the modernist automobile, see Thacker (2006: 175–89).
3. See Owens (2013).
4. On speed and masculinity in *La Bête humaine*, see Boscagli (1996: 78–80).
5. This painting is now in the Cleveland Museum of Art. Under the heading 'The Aesthetics of the Windshield', Sara Danius writes about it as 'a complicated play of frames'; she gives as its title 'La Pare-brise: sur la route de Villacoublay (The Windshield)'. See Danius (1995: 136). Danius notes that the painting was 'conceived during a motoring trip in southern France in 1916'; Villacoublay, as the online notes for the painting on the Cleveland Museum website states, is outside Paris. The airbase there, to which the car is apparently being driven, was established in 1911 and is still in use: it was from there that the remains of Princess Diana, who died in one of the most notorious car crashes of modern times, were flown back to Britain.
6. Hilary Clark sees Woolf's piece as a female riposte to the male *flâneur* of many modernist works, and speaks of 'epiphany as rape' (2004: 5) in this account of how fluid, gendered perception at speed brings feelings to a crisis.
7. The limit was set at twenty miles per hour in Britain in 1903, all limits were abolished in 1930, and a 30 mph speed limit in 'built-up areas' was reintroduced in 1935.
8. This is an extension of the argument I have made in Duffy (2009).
9. O'Brien cites *Bullitt* (1968, USA, directed by Peter Yates) and *Week-end* (1967, France, directed by Jean-Luc Godard).
10. See Foucault (1986).
11. For a somewhat different account of how the modernist automobile intervenes in early twenty-first-century critiques of modernism, see Leonard (2009: 221–41).
12. The phrase, from Walter Benjamin, is quoted as the epigram to Chapter 6, 'Conclusion: The Dialectics of Utopia and Ideology', by Fredric Jameson (1981: 281). In full: 'There has never been a document of culture which was not at one and the same time a document of barbarism.'

13. For rich readings of the scope and implications of modernism, dynamism and the kinetic, see Bradshaw et al. (2016).
14. Corrado Forlin's painting is reproduced in Tylus (2015: Fig. 2, p. 9). Oil on canvas. Private collection, Venice. Photograph by Matteo Chinellato.
15. Jean Metzinger, 'Au vélodrome', 1912, Peggy Guggenheim Museum, Venice. See *Cycling, Cubo-Futurism and the Fourth Dimension*, Erasmus Weddigen, curator, The Guggenheim Foundation, New York, Guggenheim Collection, Venice, 9 June–16 September 2012 (exhibition catalogue).
16. 'Everything I see is in principle within my reach, at least within reach of my sight, marked by the map of "I Can".' Paul Virilio attributes this quote, which sums up the critique of the Futurist representations of speed, to Merleau-Ponty. See Virilio (1994: 7).

Works Cited

Adorno, Theodor and Max Horkheimer (2002 [1944]), 'The Culture Industry: Enlightenment as Mass Deception', in *Dialectic of Enlightenment: Philosophical Fragments*, trans. Edmund Jephcott, ed. Gunzelin Schmid Noerr. Stanford, CA: Stanford University Press, 2002.
Ballard, J. G. (1985 [1973]), *Crash*. New York: Vintage.
Baring, Louise (2020), *Lartigue: The Boy and the Belle Époque*. London: Thames & Hudson.
Benjamin, Walter (2002), *The Arcades Project*, trans. Howard Eiland and Kevin McLaughlin, ed. Rolf Tiedemann. Cambridge, MA: Belknap Press of Harvard University Press.
Boscagli. Maurizia (1996), *The Eye on the Flesh: Fashions of Masculinity in the Early 20th Century*. Boulder, CO: Westview/Harper Collins.
Bradshaw, David, Laura Marcus and Rebecca Roach, eds (2016), *Moving Modernisms: Motion, Technology, and Modernity*. Oxford: Oxford University Press.
Clark, Hilary (2004), 'The Travelling Self in Virginia Woolf's "Evening Over Sussex: Reflections in a Motor Car"', *Virginia Woolf Miscellany* (Fall/Winter), pp. 6–8.
Danius, Sara (1995), *The Senses of Modernism: Technology, Perception and Aesthetics*. Ithaca, NY: Cornell University Press.
Deleuze, Gilles (1986), *Cinema I: The Movement Image*, trans. Hugh Tomlinson and Barbara Habberjam. Minneapolis: University of Minnesota Press.
Duffy, Enda (2009), 'Blur: Rapid Eye Movement and the Visuality of Speed', in *The Speed Handbook: Velocity, Pleasure, Modernism*. Durham, NC: Duke University Press, pp. 157–98.
Duffy, Enda and Maurizia Boscagli (2021), 'Cabiria', in *A Modernist Cinema*, ed. Michael Valdez Moses and Scott Klein. Oxford: Oxford University Press.
Foucault, Michel (1986), 'Of Other Spaces', *Diacritics*, 16 (Spring), pp. 22–7.
Jameson Fredric (1981), *The Political Unconscious: Narrative as a Socially Symbolic Act*. Ithaca, NY: Cornell University Press.
Joyce, James (1967 [1914]), 'After the Race', *Dubliners*. Harmondsworth: Penguin, pp. 35–42.
Joyce, James (1985), *Ulysses*, ed. Hans Gabler. New York: Vintage.
Kerouac, Jack (1957), *On the Road*. New York: Viking Press.
Leonard, Garry (2009), '"The Famished Roar of Automobiles": Modernity, the Internal Combustion Engine, and Modernism', in *Disciplining Modernism*, ed. Pamela Caughie. London: Palgrave Macmillan, pp. 221–41.
Moore, George (1894), *Esther Waters*. London: Walter Scott.
O'Brien, Harvey (2012), *Action Movies: The Cinema of Striking Back*. New York: Short Cuts, Wallflower Books/Columbia University Press.
O'Connor, Flannery (1955), *'A Good Man is Hard to Find' and Other Stories*. New York: Harcourt Brace.
Owens, Colin (2013), *Before Daybreak: 'After the Race' and the Origins of Joyce's Art*. Gainsville: University of Florida Press.

Proust, Marcel (2003), *In Search of Lost Time*, trans. Scott Moncrieff, Terence Kilmartin and Andreas Major, revised J. D. Enright. New York: Modern Library.
Sewell, Anna (1877), *Black Beauty: The Autobiography of a Horse*. London: Jarrold and Sons.
Simmel, Georg (1950 [1903]), 'The Metropolis and Mental Life', *The Sociology of Georg Simmel*, trans. and ed. K. H. Wolff. New York: Free Press, pp. 409–24.
Somerville E. Œ and Martin Ross (1984 [1899–1915]), *The Irish R.M.* Harmondsworth: Penguin.
Thacker, Andrew (2006), 'Traffic, Gender, Modernism', *The Sociological Review*, 54: 1 (October), pp. 175–89.
Tylus, Jane (2015), *Siena, City of Secrets*. Chicago: University of Chicago Press.
Virilio, Paul (1994), *The Vision Machine*, trans. Julie Rose. London and Bloomington, IN: British Film Institute.
Waugh, Evelyn (2010 [1931]), *Remote People: A Report from Ethiopia & British Africa 1930–31*. Harmondsworth: Penguin.
Woolf, Virginia (1956 [1928]), *Orlando*. New York: Harcourt Brace.
Woolf, Virginia (1966), 'Evening over Sussex: Reflections in a Motor Car', in *Collected Essays, Vol. 2*. London: Hogarth Press, pp. 290–2.
Zola, Emile (1977 [1890]), *La Bête humaine*, trans. Leonard Tancock. London: Penguin.

6

Aeroplanes: Rethinking Aeriality in a Long 1930s

Leo Mellor

The virtuosic opening of W. H. Auden's 'Poem XXX' from March 1930 – with its aircraft, pilots and aerial views – has proved enticingly talismanic for many accounts of interwar literature:

> Consider this and in our time
> As the hawk sees it or the helmeted airman:
> The clouds rift suddenly – look there
> At cigarette-end smouldering on a border
> At the first garden party of the year.
>   (Auden 1977: 46)

Our dependency on Auden's observer is established in these first lines; and then the omnipotence of his view, with its ability to target or focus on details, carries the line of sight into the, as yet, peaceful garden party. Later in the poem he has moved much further on, and (with his wirelesses and dance bands and interconnectivity) he negotiates technology and agency, imperative urgency and the possibilities of recounting sensations. These processes mean both trying to delineate where the human stops and where the machine begins, and trying to find a language for the strange sensations the machine enforces upon the human subject. Many have read this poem as overdetermined by its opening, which reveals Auden's totalitarian desires for allying his poetic viewpoint with the kestrel/bomber, and shows contempt for the little lives below which could be snuffed out at will (Cunningham 1988: 192).

But there is a much better example from Auden's writing for thinking about the multiple facets of aeriality. It is formally inventive and wildly unsatisfying, as well as being full of jokes that are never quite jokes and (nearly) entirely hawkless: it is 'The Journal of an Airman', the central section of *The Orators* (1932). This journal of a flyer, engaged in both introspection and fomenting an uprising, oscillates between registers of sub-Buchanesque bluff bravado and *fin-de-siècle* poised camp. It is a bricolage of prose epigrams, sestinas, doggerel, alphabets, genetic diagrams and telegraphese, as well as accomplished descriptions of aircraft maintenance, introspective diary-keeping, wished-for genealogies, letters to wounds, nightmares and fantasias of totalising attacks. But it is also manically elusive, 'endlessly hinting at a secret narrative the reader is duty bound to track down' (Smith 1994: 313). The clues come thick and fast – whether scraps of information from apparent spies, the list of possible airbases at 'Stubba, Smirirndale, Hamar and Sullom' (1977: 76) or the very idea of reconnaissance. There is mordant humour and horrific images but, then, calm and perspective: 'dawn, 13,000 feet. Shadows of struts falling across the cockpit. Perfect calm, light, strength. Yesterday positively the last time. Hands to remember please, always' (1977: 84). Even the final climactic sequence contains the airman's chivalric attempt to purify himself before his fate:

> Read Mifflin on Air Currents.
> A complete course for the commercial flying licence.
> The life of Count Zeppelin (obtainable in Air and Airways Library).
> Remember to pay Bryden's Bill.
> To answer C's letter.
> The £100 for Tom's holiday.
> Destroy all letters, snapshots, lockets, etc., of E.
> Further purification.
> Deep breathing exercises instead of smoking.
> A clean shirt, collar and handkerchief each morning till the end.
> (Auden 1977: 94)

'The Journal of an Airman' matters as it illustrates two interlocking tendencies concerning aeriality in writing of the period, tendencies which have been obscured or elided by the literary-critical focus on the hawk-like and death-bringing aerial view. These more interesting tendencies are potent as they can be seen in more expansive (and more comprehensible) length in much writing across many genres and authors. The tendencies are these: first, that the view from the plane offers a connective way of seeing patterns and shapes, both those literally spread out below *and* those implicit within culture and society; unsurprisingly such a vision is often strange, paranoiac and revelatory.[1] Second, such vistas and sights affect the body doing the perceiving when airborne, giving rise to a panoply of new (again, often paranoiac) corporeal sensations, from excitement to estrangement. The desire-for-destruction-from-above is still there, but it is part of a weirder and wilder cultural firmament: one which looks outward to the totality of the horizon and inward to nausea, euphoria and mania, with both scales cross-hatched together like overlapping vapour trails on a summer's day.[2]

Thus, this chapter shows why British writers of a 'long 1930s' or mid-century, stretching from approximately 1926 to 1951, used the aesthetic possibilities offered by flight to describe the violent and tumultuous world around them – and to test how language might capture the extreme sensations of pleasure, conflict and fear. The extended time period is deliberate, as it stress-tests some of these ideas by seeing how they were altered by the actualities of aeriality and bombardment during the Second World War.[3]

There are multiple contexts for how these texts were received when first published, but one of the most important was the growing aerial literacy, or 'airmindedness' as it were, of readers – or rather of spectators,[4] for as well as popular accounts of heroic extended flights, and the live air-pageants staged by the Royal Air Force every year, there was the increasingly common and powerful effect of actual images brought back from above or created within a studio to give the simulacrum of flight. All of the writers under consideration here owe something to the paradigms created by the visual treatment of aeriality, as both cultural fear and easily accessible route to the sublime. The works of Antoine de Saint-Exupéry, especially *Southern Mail* (1929) and *Night Flight* (1931), and their 1930s film adaptations, offer templates. But so too do detective thrillers such as Freeman Wills Crofts's *The 12.30 from Croydon* (1934), as do, inevitably, the science-fiction novels which, immediately after the First World War, had offered varieties of extrapolation from real biplanes and primitive navigation into imagined armadas of airships and totalising destruction, such as in Anderson Graham's *The Collapse of Homo Sapiens* (1923).[5] Such future fears lie outside the scope of this chapter, but their origins most certainly belong in the paranoia and unease of the awkwardly aerial body and in the glimpses of new vistas.

Uses of Nausea

Graham Greene's novella *The Bear Fell Free* (1935) is now sadly almost completely elided from his œuvre. It is a highly-wrought work in both senses: deeply mannered and near hysterical. This is a text about loyalty and deception which plays with the iconography of aircraft – and the airmen who cling to their totemic toys – in a non-linear stream of consciousness: one that awkwardly weaves together a performative masculinity with guilty and traumatised memories of the First World War. The plot is basic: a man goes on a flying expedition, leaving behind a party in the English countryside, and yet the expected narrative/flight arc is punctured by fragments of memory and dialogue – until his plane crashes and the alluring lights of New York go unvisited. The take-off, however, seems initially all about new perspectives:

> Heavy wheel, steel polished struts, lay on the swelling air, pressed it down towards the tents, the landladies, the fathers sleeping under handkerchiefs, the child sick behind the breakwater, the wooden spade rotting behind a rock, the Daily Mail reporter inspecting serial couples; they lay over life, the pool, the rocks, the yellow crawling tide; at the height one should have made some pertinent elder-statesman pronouncement, something serious and sad about suffering humanity, but all one felt was this growing fear, this conviction that there had been a mistake. (Greene 1935: n.p.)

A gap is visible here between what the pilot expects, that the view will allow him a sonorous 'pronouncement' over all those objects with their Audenesque definite articles, and what he actually 'felt', a growing inarticulate dread (with added nausea). Nowhere in the novella is this dread elucidated, but at the final moment of impact into the Atlantic waves, the mascot and signifier of dandyism – the teddy bear – falls free. A body of sorts thus gets to survive, but it is only the nostalgic comfort toy. Thus aviator masculinity in Greene is spelled out bleakly: it is the sense that while the accident, like so many in the interwar period, was due to a 'mistake', life itself might well now be mistaken and unviable – a sickness unto death.

Evelyn Waugh was another author who relished the teddy bear as a mascot and signifier of dandyism in *Brideshead Revisited*, but it is in his *Vile Bodies* (1930) that aeriality matters most. At the close of the novel, Ginger and Nina (ill matched and ill prepared for both flight and marriage) take off on their honeymoon. The exchange that follows shows how sensations (of how the world is perceived) can lead directly to sensations (within the body), but also how such a link deflates aerial romanticism. Ginger attempts to quote some Shakespeare at Nina – but what she actually sees is not the 'sceptr'd isle' he has been claiming such a vantage point allows. Rather:

> Nina looked down and saw inclined at an odd angle a horizon of straggling red suburb; arterial roads dotted with little cars; factories, some of them working, others empty and decaying; a disused canal; some distant hills sown with bungalows; wireless masts and overhead power cables; men and women were indiscernible except as tiny spots; they were marrying and shopping and making money and having children. The scene lurched and tilted again as the aeroplane struck a current of air.
> 'I think I'm going to be sick,' said Nina.
> 'Poor little girl,' said Ginger. 'That's what the paper bags are for.' (Waugh 2000: 168)

Here, brutally combined, come the (mixed, complex) sensations of matter and melancholia elicited by the iteration of the scene, all sickeningly sliding together in a paratactical blur of verbs despite the distance; and then, directly afterwards, the authentic corporeal sensations of the body – and the bathos of the sick-bag. Purgative repugnance is one response to 'reading' the ground from above, but there were other uses in feeling very sick at 10,000 feet – and one of them was detection.

Christopher St John Spriggs, better known by his pseudonym, Christopher Caudwell, combined theory and praxis in his twenty-nine years before being killed in the Spanish Civil War. His essays, posthumously collected as *Illusion and Reality* (1937) and *Studies in a Dying Culture* (1938), have remained a touchstone for any genealogy of British Marxist thought; yet in his formative years he was mainly known as a writer of successful thrillers and studies of aviation, such as *The Airship: Its Design, History, Operation and Future* (1931). His novel, *Death of an Airman* (1934), shows how sensations, and the apprehension of the strange sensations of aeriality, could be utilised as part of a schematic structure – whether of detection or political theory. Even the long debates that his theorising provoked after his death culminated in a magisterial judgement by E. P. Thompson which took the theorist back, for one last time, to the air: 'it is not difficult to see Caudwell as a phenomenon – as an extraordinary shooting-star crossing England's empirical night – as a premonitory sign of a more sophisticated Marxism' (Thompson 1995: 306). In *Death of an Airman* what matters is how the amateur detective, a Bishop from Australia who is learning to fly at a rundown aerodrome – staffed with clichés of flappers and hard-bitten pilots – uses the fact that, unlike everyone else, he is a novice and thus can still trust the feelings of acute internal discomfort aircraft give him:

> The Bishop clutched the side of his seat. Surely they were going to hit the ground! His inner being oozed away as the machine stood on its tail, flicked over on one wing tip, both wings vertical, and rotated round the tip in a turn that for the first time made the Bishop realise what a high-speed manoeuvre on an aeroplane was like. (Caudwell 2015: 107)

His systematic unease makes him a bad pilot but a good detective. He uncovers how the intricacies of capitalism allow a network of pan-European drug-smuggling, one where the ever-changing patterns of fog, exchange rates and airmail newspaper distribution are all germane – to both the intricacies of a genre-based plot and a hidden ideological structure.

Patterns

Some patterns (commercial, technological) shaped interwar aviation, while some others were revealed by the newly available viewpoints, with archaeology being a classic case (Hauser 2007). Another set of patterns were also, fundamentally, political – aircraft showed how connectivity mattered, as well as themselves being part of the connection (Trotter 2013). Malcolm Lowry's vast early novel, *In Ballast to the White Sea*, written in the early 1930s and supposed lost until recent years, is obsessed with interrelation. The opening pages show air as the key conduit of information:

> The two undergraduates looked down from Castle Hill on the old English town. [. . .] A brawling wind carried from the railway station, which never slumbered, the racket of the acceleration of engines, shunting the drowsy carriages [. . .] [T]he brothers inclined their ears to the cheering at a football match, now to the jaunty music – loud, loud – of the hurdy-gurdies on Midsummer Common: but again these clusters of sound, each of them a hail and farewell from separate worlds of objectivity, would die away almost in the swelling, as the groan of aeroplane engines quickly vanishes to a sigh in the gale. (Lowry 2014: 3)

There is – amazingly – no *actual* aircraft in this scene, but rather it is the *idea* of the aircraft that is indexical to knowing a soundscape, and so feeling the connections between such 'separate worlds of objectivity'. Later in the novel such ideas of connections are made urgent – and carried via a fully physically realised plane with a pensive pilot bringing news:

> '[a] lone airman, that wintry Easter, was flying over the Irish Sea. He was following the line of the old telegraph stations to Liverpool: Holyhead, Cefn Du, Point Lynas, Puffin Island, Great Ormes Head. [. . .] Like a needle his machine threaded cloud and cloud. (184)

The plane follows a past line of communication but now with extraordinary speed. And yet this vision of modernity-as-progress is then faced with a terrifying view:

> From the air it seemed like part of a country of the future, which had spread horizontally rather than vertically, but of a stupendous greatness [. . .] a continual, raving flux, beginning at one end of the world and ending at the other [. . .] The industrial revolution! Lancashire, thought the pilot, was certainly the county where that age had driven down its roots. Glass, factories, and cotton mills, weaving sheds, puddling furnaces, docks and dynamos, railways running on three levels . . . and intertwining them, a green, windblown countryside, thundering with horses' hooves, jagged with colour, groaning with crowds at the racetrack and at rugby matches, and the whole cabled and flexed with steel rivers and canals. It was marvellous but where was it going to all lead? (185)

Where indeed? The passage above – where free indirect discourse channels the airman's thoughts – leaves readers as nauseous eavesdroppers in the cockpit: excited by the futurist patterns of industry from above, but also haunted by the thought that this version of the sublime is filled with ominous potential, both of collective madness – the 'raving flux' – and of looming war.

John Sommerfeld also used aeriality as diagnostic, seeing pattern and potential in the view from above. His *May Day* (1936) presents London as a city ripe for revolution by seeing it as a complexly woven mesh, even down to repeated spider's-web metaphors, but with the repeated injunction that 'a big change' is needed (Sommerfield 2010: 41, 241). Yet his mode itself is also a critique: he contends that previous attempts at city narrative have failed because they lacked a point of view which could encompass both the directionlessness of individual lives and the potential of the working class. *May Day*, however, opens with a view, both vertiginous and totalising, which shows how interconnectivity *is* modern urban existence:

> there are shining tarred roads, glistening shop windows, arc lamps nightly flowering into electric buds, geometries of telephone wires and tramlines, traffic lights flinging continuous coloured fireworks in the air, a hundred thousand motorcars and buses [. . .] Railways writhe like worms under the clay, tangled with spider's webs and mazes of electric cables, drains and gaspipes. Then there are eight or nine million people. [. . .] In this whirlpool of matter-in-motion forces are at work creating history. These fragile shreds of flesh are protagonists in a battle. (25–6)

Another marker of *May Day*'s complexity is the way it is ready to indict capitalism, but it is also not naïve about the glamour that the oppressive city can project. It links spectacle with vulnerability and fear, through a return to aeriality:

> The red-hot worms of neon bulbs squirmed and wriggled. Searchlights, big guns bombarding the air with rays of absinthe green and rose-pink projected the names of automobiles and film stars onto a moving screen of clouds. The whole sky glowed with a dull red heat from the violence of the electric blows that were showered upon it. Ten thousand feet above, a flock of aeroplanes scattered themselves. This was a week of aerial night manoeuvres, raids were being staged to find the weak points in a barbed-wire fence of searchlights that laced the sky around London. These had got through. (189)

These 'worms [. . .] wriggling' might just have come all the way from Woolf's essay 'The Cinema' (1926), with its blot on the frame of *The Cabinet of Dr Caligari*, but as part of the web of explosive neon hieroglyphs of London they are more familiar from novels such as Gerald Kersh's *Night and the City* (1938). Yet this passage is rather different from either Woolf or Kersh: the illuminatory 'bombardment' upwards from the signs reverses the practice run of the bombers which look down on them as an ersatz aiming point. This is rehearsal: the implied next step in the causal chain would surely be a real attack. But before that comes there is the insurrectionary hope of May Day. A vast demonstration, whose scale cannot be fully comprehended from any earth-bound perspective, goes ahead, and yet it is understood as a portent through surveillance from a primitive helicopter:

A thousand feet above the contingents a police gyrocopter, its windmill sails flickering lazily in the blue air. The observer, looking down, saw the marchers, a long black snake, a slow-moving black river winding along the channels of the streets [. . .] [T]he dark mass flows through the streets, meanders like some caterpillar crawling across a map of London, its head a mile away from its tail, its red spots the colours of banners. (210–11)

This flickering vision below the eye-in-the-sky is that of a cityscape not reduced to abstraction but rather one animalistically animated by a mass of workers, as it is seen 'crawling' across London to be born.

Networks and Fears

Patterns can mean many things in culture – and an aerial view stimulated many other artists and writers, from Anni Albers to Gertrude Stein.[6] But seeing not a pattern but rather a network – with connective energies flowing between nodes – allows for a rather different aesthetic. Elizabeth Bowen's novel *To the North* (1932) is a study of the inadequacy of language and the capriciousness of desire, even in conditions of economic privilege. But it is also a piece of what can be understood as 'transit literature' – in that it investigates how movement corrals language and action, but also forces them into new and deliberate patterns (Trotter 2013: 218–63). The protagonists of the novel are nonchalant Cecilia, who flirts and reads at will, and Emmeline, who runs a travel agency and whose movements are preordained by knowledge of routes and connections, until she 'fuses with the "shadowy nets" of transportation: the railways, airlines, and shipping routes whose schedules she knows by heart' (Ellmann 2003: 109). Her entanglements throughout the novel culminate in a litany of human agency as movement on a grand scale: 'an immense idea of departure – expresses getting steam up and crashing from termini, liners clearing the docks, the shadows of planes rising, caravans winding out into the first dip of the desert – possessed her spirit' (Bowen 1987: 244). Thus thinking about this novel as one of selfhood shaped by the material conditions of modernity, whether by telephones or express trains, reveals much about why technology might change whatever we might recognise as character in a novel. But aircraft, and what aircraft do to the changing selfhood of characters, might also test the limits of narration and mutuality. Bowen stages a London–Paris flight at a key point in *To the North*, one that is both liberatory and subject-altering to her ambiguous protagonists. Emmeline and the appalling Markie (Mark Drinkwater) fly together from Croydon, and Markie notices as the aircraft climbs that

> Surrey and Kent looked flatter and like something with which one has ceased to have any relationship, noticeably less interesting – he had never liked either much. The grass, lawns and meadows, poorer in texture than he expected, looked like a rubbed billiard cloth. (136)

His ability to render bathetic tedium from a vista guards him against the manic wonder which overtakes Emmeline: 'the serrated gold coast-line and creeping line of the sea were verifying the atlas. An intenser green blue, opaque with its own colour, showed far down in the sparkling glassiness their tiny cruciform shadow' (137). Such a view cannot last – and arrival is heralded with both familiarity and dread: 'blood roared in ears as the plane with engines shut off, with a frightening cessation of sound plunged downwards in that arrival that always appears disastrous' (139). The familiarity in the journey does not negate the dread, and the shared nature of the trip does not mean shared understanding; the narrator had intoned that while in mid-air they 'both felt something gained or lost, though neither, perhaps, knew which' (136). Both Markie and Emmeline are part of networks – and travel within networks – but what they see, and what they feel about what they see, are very different indeed, presaging the *Liebestod* death-drive at the close of the novel (Trotter 2013: 245).

Graham Greene's *England Made Me* (1935), on the other hand, constructs a narrative that pays homage both to the melancholia of transience and to ephemeral spaces: it does not want a network to enable mutuality or comprehension. It is a bleak fairy tale of twins, brother Anthony and sister Kate, and their entanglements with Krogh, Kate's lover and boss, a seemingly all-powerful Swedish financier. But it is a novel that works through a rewriting of expectations on both personal and geographical scales, and to do this it relies on the allure of aircraft. For aircraft are a way to be modern, if not overtly modernist. A telling moment comes when a shot duck – a memory from Krogh's youth – is compared to a broken aeroplane, the artificial form of flight having now become the measure against which the natural is measured (Greene 1970: 39). In the main, though, the aircraft of this novel are non-metaphorical and active. As Fred Hall, Krogh's thuggish enforcer, travels across the Continent, he is sufficiently blasé about air travel to be lulled into a reverie:

> He closed his eyes again; he was no longer interested by the flight from Amsterdam; he knew the airports of Europe as well as he had once known stations on the Brighton line – shabby Le Bourget; the great scarlet rectangle of the Tempelhof as one came in from London in the dark, the headlamps lighting up the asphalt way; the white sand blowing up around the shed at Tallinn; Riga, where the Berlin to Leningrad plane came down and bright pink mineral waters were sold in a tinroofed shed. (161)

This is Europe remade spatially, with the replacement of national borders by nodes of significance and confident associations – directly analogous to the new model of fraudulent capitalism that Krogh himself practises. Yet this form of modernity itself unsettles the characters: Hall finds aerial commutes 'a comfortable dull way of travelling', compared to the tactile pleasures of the past: 'the weekend jaunt, the whisky and splash, the peroxide blonde' (161), which he could encounter in the more grounded journeys, with 'the racing tips from strangers in the Brighton Pullman' (162), and which did not require a vertiginous visual leap. The thing that seems to unsettle Hall the most is the abstraction that is forced upon him by being up in the air. The 'great scarlet rectangle' of Berlin's Tempelhof airport that he sees below is part of a sequence of patterns and shapes that means the view from above does not reveal objects beneath but rather shows a world of abstracted transience. This is part of Greene's engagement with something that could be termed the 'high-sublime', an idea within the more aerially intoxicated parts of aesthetic modernism that dates back at least to Yeats's 'An Irish Airman Foresees His Death' (1918). It is a concept filled with fragile connections and observable gnomic shapes, such as those in Virginia Woolf's essay 'Flying over London', written in the mid-1930s but not published until after the war, where the patterns noted by an aestheticising observer allow her to say: 'we fell into fleeciness, substance and colour; all the colours of pounded plums and dolphins and blankets and seas and rain clouds crushed together' (Woolf 2008: 210). Toward the end of the essay an attempt is made to fix a point of focus, but the view of London now looks more like an artistic composition than an actual city, and this only acts to destabilise the position of the narrator/observer/pattern-maker.

With Greene the aestheticising aspect of this destabilisation wrought by the aerial view is kept in tension with the linguistic: the shapes that the skywriting planes keep writing, in both *England Made Me* and his *The Confidential Agent* (1939), begin as puzzling abstractions but eventually resolve into words. Moreover, in the commentary Greene wrote for *The Future's in the Air* (1937), a documentary film celebrating the Empire Airmail service, the voiceover dwells on the patterns, 'draughtboards of fields' and shadows on water and land, but then resolves into a lyrical hymn of exotic but scribal interconnections: 'Letters to Indian Civil Servants; letter to the government in New Delhi [. . .], letters to Chinese scouts, letters to men in rickshaws' (Greene 2007: 503). The purpose of the aircraft becomes clear – it can (only) connect a mesh – and the purpose – airmail – is always set against the abstraction of what it has to fly over. The publicity department of Imperial Airways commissioned numerous other films along these lines, utilising a rhetoric of network as a way to perceive through technology the bonds holding a more restive empire together (Anthony 2011: 301–21).

War and the Body

This chapter has offered alternate modes for thinking about the importance of aeriality in literature if the hawk-bomber paradigm is recontextualised or even temporarily elided in some writings of the 1930s. This manœuvre becomes, obviously, harder to continue in the years of the Second World War itself.[7] One route would be to think through the implications of vulnerability and dread that the aircraft brought about for writers on the ground, ranging from the famous, Woolf's 'Thoughts on Peace in an Air-raid' (1941), through to those such as Arthur Gwynn-Browne's *FSP* (1942). On 27 May 1940 Gwynn-Browne – counter-intelligence officer, motorcyclist and singular stylist – was lying in the sand dunes at Dunkirk. Under bombing, his fears seem almost scripted by Gertrude Stein, a writer whom Gwynn-Browne had long admired. Her patterning of the lived perception of time was now used to recount his predicament:

> We lay with our faces in the earth sweating [. . .] I remembered thinking I did not feel fear and then wondering if my sweating was not after all just fear. Was it. I was thinking strongly. Time seemed suspended to be standing still. I thought, I will not be killed I will not be killed I will most certainly not be killed like an animal like this in a hole and like this. I said I will not be killed, I will not be killed I have things to do I will not be killed I will not be killed like this I have things to do like this I will not be killed like this I will not be killed like this. (Gwynn-Browne 2002: 120)

The vulnerable body under attack, with an asymmetry of power, is a staple of Second World War literature – and can occur in predictable and unpredictable places. Richard Hillary's celebrated memoir, *The Last Enemy* (1943), is an account of his pre-war upper-class life and his career as a Spitfire pilot – and, post-crash, his agonising burns and extensive hospital treatment. It is part of a genre which situates the body of the fighter-pilot, high above the sludge of the trenches and the industrialised warfare, as the inheritor of a chivalric tradition – notably in the best-selling memoir of Cecil Lewis, *Sagittarius Rising* (1936), which lauded the pilot, who existed in 'the only sphere in modern warfare where a man saw his adversary and faced him in mortal combat, the only sphere where there was still chivalry and honour' (Lewis 2014: 46). Hillary's version of this credo comes when he explains why he wants to fly:

> In a fighter plane, I believe, we have found a way to return to war as it ought to be, war which is individual combat between two people in which one either kills or is killed. It's exciting, it's individual, and it's disinterested. I shan't be sitting behind a long-range gun working out how to kill people sixty miles away. I shan't get maimed: either I get killed or I shall get a few pleasant putty medals and enjoy being stared at in a night club. (Hillary 1956: 21)

Yet, ironically, he did survive, albeit horribly maimed. The 'proem' to his book describes the sensations of baling out of his burning aircraft, the smell of burnt flesh and his drifting while waiting for rescue. Months of hospital and skin-grafts followed as a patient of the pioneering plastic surgeon Archibald McIndoe. Thus, the teleology of *The Last Enemy* does not end with the death of the pilot, but rather his re-entry into the world as a scarred and damaged warning, stripped of the insouciance of his class and background. In the closing episode of his narrative, Hillary, caught in an air-raid in London, helps to dig out a wounded woman and her dead child. The woman looks up at him and speaks: 'I see they got you too' (244). This moment of empathetic connection brings on hysteria in Hillary:

> It started small, small but insistent deep inside me, sharp as a needle, then welling up uncontrollable, spurting, flowing over, choking me. I was drowning, helpless in a rage that caught and twisted and hurled me on, mouthing in a blind unthinking frenzy. (245)

Here the wounded pilot, whose laconic and detached mental state had seemingly survived his bodily abjection and his new carapace, is ultimately broken by connective sympathy.

Another remaking of the airman occurs in the later works of John Sommerfield. After a spell fighting in the Spanish Civil War, Sommerfield returned to Britain, became entangled with the Mass Observation Movement and was then conscripted as a member of RAF ground crew before being posted to the Far East. His wartime writings were collected in *The Survivors* (1947), and their uneven lengths and tone give a structural corollary to their anti-heroic contingency. A memorable scene comes in a piece Sommerfeld wrote for 'The Way We Live Now' in *Penguin New Writing*. Here, as in his 'Worm's Eye View' (1941), he depicts the crushing monotony of life in an aerodrome, but then turns, with reverence, to the main hangers:

> Here planes are dismantled and overhauled. Little fighters, with fish-shaped bodies, have their sides laid open, disclosing elegant and complex silvery bones. Multicoloured electric cables branch and ramify like a nervous system amongst the bewildering confusion of tightly packed metal entrails. [. . .] Tenderly, intently, surgeons

operating with spanners, the mechanics replace each reassembled organ into the plane's body cavities, put back the dural skin, and make ready for the moment of reawakening. The cylinders inhale petrol breaths, the propellers turn, oil circulates through copper arteries, wires are charged with nervous energy, and a powerful creature roars with hungry voice, moves and flies. (The pilot socketed into his tiny cockpit, hands and feet fitted to controls, eyes linked with dials and gauges, seems only the final piece that completes the puzzle). (Sommerfield 1947: 117)

After this luscious detailing of materiality being cosseted into a near-corporeal state, the pilot emerges only at the close of the paragraph as a literal afterthought in parentheses; he is bracketed off into a capsule and suborned to the machine. This is a trope with its own long history, but it gets reused repeatedly in the Second World War as aircraft became more sophisticated and the role of the pilot more determined by the technology, as, for example, in one of Roald Dahl's bleakest short stories, 'Death of an Old Old Man' (1946).

Such gifting of animism on to machines also shapes some of the most memorable writings by the artist Paul Nash. Famous for his work in the First World War and his interwar negotiations with abstraction and surrealism, he returned to work again as a war artist in 1939–45. But alongside his painting he was writing about his subject-matter. In 'The Personality of Planes', first published in *Vogue* in 1942, he described why this war was different from the last: 'I first became interested in the war pictorially when I realised that machines were the real protagonists' (Nash 1949: 250). The essay then lists the aspects, in the different types of aircraft, which triggered his tendency to ascribe characteristics – and to read characteristics for personalities - such as '[t]he Wellington is very human in one way. It is jolly, on the plump side.' Then the machines become more animalistic than human: 'A Whitley, as Blake said of a tear, is an intellectual thing, and as obscurely so, perhaps [. . .] it is a queer birdlike creature reminding me of a dove! [. . .] but if it is a dove it is a dove of death' (256). These creatures are filled with a blind and terrifying death-urge, but they also eclipse the human; this is typified in another essay where Nash saw in a hanger – a 'lair' – some 'huge mammalian carcases of the bombers with their great heads and erect tail-fins. Their steady gaze was as threatening as their jutting maws, but seemingly oblivious' (Nash 2000: 154). In 'Aerial Flowers' (1945) – the most haunting piece, written just before his death – the very possibility of flight itself becomes a way of thinking about, and imagining, death (161).

Yet alongside the elision of the human by these newly animated aircraft came a counterpointing tendency. Nash painted extraordinary pictures of air battles, crashed bombers in cornfields and details of pitted fuselages, but his most haunting visual work of the Second World War was of the gigantic dump at Cowley in Oxfordshire, filled with broken carcasses of German planes: *Totes Meer (Dead Sea)* (1940–1). Nash described his inspiration in the film, *Out of Chaos* (1944), which was made about the painting:

The thing (the salvage dump) looked to me, suddenly, like a great inundating sea. You might feel – under certain circumstances – a moonlight night, for instance, this is a vast tide moving across the fields, the breakers rearing up and crashing on the plain. And then, no, nothing moves, it is not water or even ice, it is something static and dead. It is metal piled up, wreckage. It is hundreds and hundreds of flying creatures which invaded these shores (how many Nazi planes have been shot down or otherwise wrecked in this country since they first invaded?). Well, here they are, or some of them. By moonlight, the waning moon, one could swear they began to move and twist and turn as they did in the air. A sort of rigor mortis? No, they are quite dead and still. (Hall 1996: 31)

Here the bodies of crashed aircraft have *themselves* become a landscape, or rather a seascape owing much to Casper David Friedrich's Romanticism and especially his massive *The Sea of Ice* (1824). The aircraft have now become a vista akin to the one they once observed, and the form in which it has been rendered is another reuse of German (albeit aesthetic) skill and technology.

Nash offers one version of the refiguring of both the airman and the aerial view, a process which, this chapter has shown, occurred across some very different texts. Auden's double insight in the *Orators* – that the view from the plane offers a connective way of seeing patterns, both those spread out below and those implicit within culture; *and* that such vistas affect the body doing the perceiving, especially in ways that language has to struggle to describe – is a truly potent one. But it also belongs to a very historically specific period of the long 1930s – of pre-supersonic flight and of non-pressurised cabins – and one which was decisively ended by the deployment of atomic weapons. Therefore my final text, Constance Babington Smith's memoir *Evidence in Camera: The Story of Photographic Intelligence in World War II* (1958), offers a strange farewell to such an era. It was published sufficiently long after the war for the techniques she described to be declassified, many of the people to have died, and the worldview rendered into history by the Cold War. Babington Smith, who went on to become an acclaimed biographer and literary critic, narrated how she became part of a vast, delicate and profoundly frustrating process of discerning meaning: 'I tried in vain to say something about those wooly-looking photographs. It had been like peering through an overlay of tracing paper - you could see blurred shapes but you couldn't possibly hint what they were' (Babbington Smith: 206). This memoir of the evolving nature of photoreconnaissance and interpretation pivots on a sense of unease and estrangement, but not one to be found in the pilots swooping over German territory, nor in the actual camera views from above. But rather – alert, secretive, prone to hunches – it is the solitary young woman in an underground bunker, reading the landscapes with a wary suspicion and a desire for signs, who might prove the inheritor of what Auden diagnosed years earlier. But she is now doing so in artificial light, replete with the nascent technologies of data-mining and aided by primitive computing, gathering multiple copies and comparing them by stereoscopes, presaging a simulacrum of the actual world which might eventually come to pass in the planetary panopticon that is Google Maps.

Notes

1. For a cultural history see Dorian and Pousin (2013).
2. A range of theoretically different but useful ways of thinking about how and why aeriality mattered to interwar British culture include Beer (1996: 149–78), Saint-Amour (2015) and Holman (2014).

3. See Mellor and Salton-Cox (2015: 1–9).
4. For a discussion of the loaded term 'airmindedness' see Holman (2014: 1–11).
5. For imagined terrors of the future see Clarke (1992).
6. See, for example, Gertrude Stein's *Everybody's Autobiography* (1937) and Anni Albers's artworks such as *Tapestry* (1948).
7. See Francis (2011).

Works Cited

Anthony, Scott (2011), 'The Future's in the Air: Imperial Airways and the British Documentary Film Movement', *Journal of British Cinema and Television*, 8, pp. 301–21.

Auden, W. H. (1977), *The English Auden, Poems, Essays and Dramatic Writings 1927–1939*, ed. Edward Mendelson. London: Faber.

Babington Smith, Constance (1958), *Evidence in Camera: The Story of Photographic Intelligence in World War II*. London: Chatto.

Beer, Gillian (1996), 'The Island and the Aeroplane: The Case of Virginia Woolf', in *Virginia Woolf: The Common Ground: Essays by Gillian Beer*. Edinburgh: Edinburgh University Press, pp. 149–78.

Bowen, Elizabeth (1987), *To the North*. Harmondsworth: Penguin.

Caudwell, Christopher (2015), *Death of an Airman*. London: British Library.

Clarke, I. F. (1992), *Voices Prophesying War: Future Wars, 1763–3749*. Oxford: Oxford University Press.

Cunningham, Valentine (1988), *British Writers of the Thirties*. Oxford: Oxford University Press.

Dorian, Mark and Frederic Pousin, eds (2013), *Seeing from Above: The Aerial View in Visual Culture*. London: Bloomsbury.

Ellmann, Maud (2003), *Elizabeth Bowen: The Shadow Across the Page*. Edinburgh: Edinburgh University Press.

Francis, Martin (2011), *The Flyer: British Culture and the Royal Air Force, 1939–1945*. Oxford: Oxford University Press.

Greene, Graham (1935), *The Bear Fell Free*. London: Grayson and Grayson.

Greene, Graham (1970), *England Made Me*. Harmondsworth: Penguin.

Greene, Graham (2007), *Mornings in the Dark: The Graham Greene Film Reader*, ed. David Parkinson. Manchester: Carcanet.

Gwynn-Browne, Arthur (2002), *FSP: An NCO's Description of His and Others' First Six Months of War, January 1st–June 1st, 1940*. Bridgend: Seren.

Hall, Charles (1996), *Paul Nash: Aerial Creatures*. London: Lund Humphries.

Hauser, Kitty (2007), *Shadow Sites: Photography, Archaeology & the British Landscape 1927–1955*. Oxford: Oxford University Press.

Hillary, Richard (1956), *The Last Enemy*. London: Pan.

Holman, Brett (2014), *The Next War in the Air: Britain's Fear of the Bomber, 1908–1941*. Farnham: Ashgate.

Lewis, Cecil (2014), *Sagittarius Rising*. New York: Penguin.

Lowry, Malcolm (2014), *In Ballast to the White Sea*, ed. Patrick McCarthy. Ottawa: University of Ottawa Press.

Mellor, Leo and Glyn Salton-Cox (2015), 'Introduction', *Critical Quarterly*, 57: 3, Special Issue on the long 1930s, pp. 1–9.

Nash, Paul (1949), *Outline: An Autobiography and Other Writings*. London: Faber.

Nash, Paul (2000), *Writings on Art*, ed. Andrew Causey. Oxford: Oxford University Press.

Saint-Amour, Paul (2015), *Tense Future: Modernism, Total War, Encyclopedic Form*. Oxford: Oxford University Press.

Smith, Stan (1994), 'Remembering Bryden's Bill: Modernism from Eliot to Auden', *Critical Survey*, 6: 3, pp. 312–24.
Sommerfield, John (1947), *The Survivors*. London: J. Lehmann.
Sommerfield, John (2010), *May Day*. London: London Books.
Thompson, E. P. (1995), 'Christopher Caudwell', *Critical Inquiry*, 21: 2 (Winter), pp. 305–53.
Trotter, David (2013), *Literature in the First Media Age: Britain Between the Wars*. Cambridge, MA, and London: Harvard University Press.
Waugh, Evelyn (2000), *Vile Bodies*. London: Penguin.
Woolf, Virginia (2008), *Selected Essays*, ed. David Bradshaw. Oxford: Oxford University Press.

7

Robots: Gendered Machines and Anxious Technophilia

Katherine Shingler

THE CONCEPT OF the robot or humanoid machine has always been closely bound up with notions of sex, gender and reproduction. In Karel Čapek's play *R.U.R.*, whose 1923 English production first introduced the term 'robot' to the English language, the humanoid machines are presented as a 'sexless throng' (Čapek 1961: 78). Outwardly gendered along binary lines in order to cater to consumer demand (for 'female' domestic servants, notably), they are nevertheless devoid of biological sex and lack sexual desire; indeed, their inability to procreate, to reproduce themselves, is what differentiates them from and makes them dependent on humans. Čapek's play brings out a number of threats posed by this imagined technology: we see on stage the disastrous consequences that ensue when technology built to serve us escapes our control, when the apparently servile robots begin to think for themselves and overcome their human masters. And yet it is the robots' disruption of categories of sex and gender that is most central to the play's apocalyptic scenario, as the very existence of the 'sexless throng' mysteriously engenders an epidemic of infertility amongst humans, a phenomenon presented in the play as a kind of 'punishment' for humans' hubristic meddling in nature (41).

Although *R.U.R* was not created under the aegis of any modernist movement or sensibility, I begin with it here principally because it raises a number of intersecting concerns that can be traced through a broader late nineteenth- and early twentieth-century technological imaginary. In its suggestion that the destructive power of machine technology (which finds its ultimate expression in the imagined figure of the robot) lies in its ability to destabilise or undo categories of sex and gender, Čapek's play evokes the spectre of a 'civilization without sexes' – a notion which, as Mary Louise Roberts (1994: 4) has shown, haunted the French cultural imagination during the First World War and its aftermath. Fears about a degenerate technologised society, in which the status quo of sexual relations would be upended, may have been particularly prevalent in France in this period. This was due to a number of factors, including, first, a crisis of masculinity related to the technologies of war, which not only significantly dented the male population but subjected soldiers to psychological disorders disarmingly close in appearance to the 'female' disease of hysteria (Showalter 1987: 167–74). A second key factor was the protracted French demographic crisis, which resulted in a renewed emphasis on pronatalism and the nuclear family as the cornerstone of society, and a heightened awareness of the threats posed by the 'New Woman', in her various guises as flapper or *garçonne*, to patriarchal order (Silverman 1989: 63–7; Roberts 1994: 120–47).

Intersecting fears about degeneracy, gender and technology were also present in other national contexts,[1] however, as the international popularity of Čapek's play suggests. If this chapter focuses particularly on texts and works of art produced in metropolitan France, it does so with one eye on transnational currents, and in full acknowledgement of the fact that the works under consideration circulated within modernism's transnational networks – and are, in the case of Duchamp's *Large Glass* and Picabia's mechanomorphs, just as heavily imbricated in New York Dada as in the Parisian avant-garde. As such, the disruptions to sex and gender threatened by the imagined figure of the robot, and the ambivalent responses of modernist writers and artists to that figure, are far from a uniquely 'French' phenomenon.

Čapek may be responsible for popularising the term 'robot', but he was certainly not the first to imagine the robot itself. The idea of the automaton or mechanical doll has been around since ancient times, and real automatons proliferated from the mid-eighteenth century onwards, with industrial manufacture peaking around the 1880s (see Wosk 2015: 34–41). Although both male and female automatons were produced, it is notable that fictional representations tend overwhelmingly to identify such figures as female. Andreas Huyssen explains this in the following terms:

> [A]s soon as the machine came to be perceived as a demonic, inexplicable threat and as harbinger of chaos and destruction – a view which typically characterizes many 19th-century reactions to the railroad to give but one major example – writers began to imagine the *Maschinenmensch* as woman. There are grounds to suspect that we are facing here a complex process of projection and displacement. The fears and perceptual anxieties emanating from ever more powerful machines are recast and reconstructed in terms of the male fear of female sexuality, reflecting, in the Freudian account, the male's castration anxiety. (Huyssen 1986: 70)

If the robot itself can be seen to crystallise fears about the changes that technology might inflict upon human life, to engender a vision of the posthuman (well in advance, indeed, of the digital technologies to which the emergence of posthuman theory has sought to respond), and even to envision the possible displacement of the human by the machine, then casting the robot as female allowed authors to give voice to a yet more complex set of anxieties. In particular, it allowed them to assimilate technology to female sexuality and the female body in order to figure it as simultaneously alluring – an object of desire and fascination – and threatening, or potentially 'castrating'. This set of representational strategies culminates in what Rosi Braidotti, taking her cue from Huyssen, terms the 'machine vamp', as exemplified by Fritz Lang's robot Maria in his 1927 film *Metropolis* (Braidotti 2013: 106). But the identification of woman and machine also allowed for male fantasies of domination to be exercised, as with the android (or 'andréide', in its feminised form) of Villiers de l'Isle-Adam's 1886 novel *L'Ève future*. In Villiers's science-fiction scenario, the robot-woman Hadaly (whose name means 'ideal' in Persian) is designed by a fictionalised version of the inventor Thomas Edison to correspond totally to the desires of his friend Lord Ewald, in a reworking of the Pygmalion myth for the electric age. In creating this machine-woman, Edison attains a god-like creative power – but, as in *R.U.R.*, is ultimately punished for his audacity when Hadaly dies at sea, nature (or divine creation) reclaiming its supremacy over the artificial and the man-made.

Hadaly is unambiguously *feminine*, at least in her surface features; and yet her status as *female* is very much open to question, since she is sterile, unable to reproduce (creative power being afforded only to men in the framework of Villiers's narrative). In terms of sex, then, she is framed as not-quite-female, and provides a close counterpart to another late nineteenth-century instance of the robot that functions as an emblem of gender trouble. The automaton that appears at the end of Rachilde's 1884 novel *Monsieur Vénus* presents as male; yet this gruesome effigy (part-flesh, part-machine, with its transparent rubber skin, and its hair, teeth and fingernails torn from the dead body of the female protagonist's lover, Jacques) is framed as the culmination of a long series of 'perverse' gender inversions. Over the course of the novel, Jacques is progressively emasculated, so that he is eventually reduced to a passive sex doll, moulded to the desires of the cross-dressing Raoule, who has become the dominant, 'male' figure. Rachilde's novel thus presents a kind of playful, wilfully decadent inversion of the myth of Pygmalion and Galatea that would be taken up shortly afterwards by Villiers.

Both of these *fin-de-siècle* texts by Villiers and Rachilde put into play intersecting anxieties about gender and technology. Villiers's text seeks to counter these anxieties through recourse to Pygmalionesque fantasy, and justifies its own misogyny by appealing to an association between women and the artificial that Villiers clearly holds to be self-evident (Villiers de l'Isle-Adam 1993: 209). Rachilde's novel, however, is more subversive, playfully unsettling gender categories, yet situating the male-but-female automaton as a more disturbing figure that points to the emasculation to be suffered by men if the emancipated woman incarnated by Raoule gets her way. In this respect, the automaton of *Monsieur Vénus* looks forward to the close association, as demonstrated by Debora L. Silverman (1989: 67–72), between technology and the New Woman that marked debates about gender around the turn of the century; but it also looks beyond this to the post-war fear of a 'civilization without sexes', and, as I shall argue here, to a range of modernist representations of technology that appear to echo this fear. Taking my cue from Alex Goody's suggestion that 'the mechanomorphic portraits of New York Dada and their negotiations of gender sit in a tradition that stretches from the late-nineteenth century to the technosphere we presently inhabit' (Goody 2007: 79), I seek to highlight the continuity between the *fin-de-siècle* technological imagination and the modernist response to technology as formulated in the period extending from the *avant-guerre* to roughly 1930. One advantage of placing this continuity in the foreground of our discussion is that it allows us to bring out the critical significance of sex and gender in modernist visions of the robot. It also allows us to underline the deep ambivalence embedded in these visions, and hence to avoid simplistic equations between modernism and the cult of the machine, or straightforward oppositions between a forward-looking modernism and a more inward-looking, reactionary *fin de siècle*.

One might assume modernism to be less fearful, to take a less reactionary attitude towards technology, than the years of Symbolism and Decadence, characterised by a turn away from the psychologically damaging industrial world and towards a cushioned domestic interior. Modernism is commonly held to be characterised by an 'openness to possible futures' (Armstrong 2018: 237) and, as Marjorie Perloff has shown, by a literal openness to the sounds, images and textures of the technologised modern city, all of which are incorporated into the work of poets such as Guillaume Apollinaire and Blaise Cendrars (Perloff 2003: 2–79). From the emphasis in the *Blast Manifesto* on industry and 'mechanical inventiveness' (Lewis 1914: 39), to Italian Futurism's praise of the motorcar as an emblem of modern beauty (Marinetti 1909a: 1), to *The Little Review*'s professed vision of the machine as 'the religious expression of today' (Heap 1925: 22), literary modernism appears to welcome the dawning of the machine age with open arms. We similarly see artists replicating the forms and dynamics of the machine in various works of visual art, from Sonia Delaunay's 'prismes électriques' to Fernand Léger's engagements with the machine across the domains of painting, film and art theory (Léger 2009: 81–109), and in the many intersections between modernist performance and the mechanical imagination documented by Émilie Morin in this volume.

As was the case for Villiers de l'Isle-Adam in the 1880s, part of the appeal of the gendered machine for the male-dominated modernist generation was that it provided a space to exercise fantasies of patriarchal control and domination. This is particularly visible in a short statement by the Franco-American writer Paul Haviland, published on the front page of his friend Alfred Stieglitz's magazine, *291*, in 1915:

> Man made the machine in his own image. She has limbs which act; lungs which breathe; a heart which beats; a nervous system through which runs electricity. The phonograph is the image of his voice; the camera the image of his eye. The machine is his 'daughter born without a mother'. That is why he loves her. [. . .] After making the machine in his own image he has made his human ideal machinomorphic. But the machine is yet at a dependent stage. Man gave her every qualification except thought. She submits to his will but he must direct her activities. Without him she remains a wonderful being, but without aim or anatomy. Through their mating they complete one another. She brings forth according to his conceptions. (Haviland 1915)

Haviland unambiguously genders machine technology as female, and with the description of the machine as being made 'in his own image' (and the human ideal in turn becoming 'machinomorphic'), it is difficult not to imagine it as taking on a humanoid, specifically female, form. The text thus gestures towards the female robot as an ideal technological creation. The virtual robot-woman of this text is a direct creation of man, made according to his precise specifications, much as Villiers's Hadaly is made to correspond to Lord Ewald's desires. The 'girl born without a mother' (a concept that, as we shall see, is key to Francis Picabia's visual representations of the machine-woman) is the direct result of her (male) creator's will, but also provides a conveniently passive tool or vessel to enable his further creative acts. Through their 'mating' (which, while perhaps intended metaphorically, hints at the erotic potential of the robot-woman, as a perennially available love object), she will 'bring forth according to his conception', enabling his creativity. As such, and as David Hopkins has argued in relation to Duchamp and Picabia (2008: 81), Haviland's conception of technology as female seems to create space for fantasies not just of male domination over women but also of male creation *qua* procreation, the male artist-scientist-creator usurping the female role in giving birth and claiming this ultimate act of creation entirely for himself.

Filippo Tommaso Marinetti's 1909 play *Poupées électriques* (*Electric Dolls*) occupies a similar thematic terrain, but projects these fantasies of female robots on to women themselves, figuring them as compliant, machine-like bodies animated by 'electric' sexual impulses. The robots seen on stage here resemble stuffy bourgeois figures (reminiscent of eighteenth-century automatons in frock coats and wigs) and are not themselves the object of erotic interest, except insofar as they add spice to the sex life of the play's central couple, who pursue their trysts under the noses of the imperious 'dolls'. More pertinent, however, is Marinetti's insistence on the notion of women themselves as machines, such that the inventor of the robots is able to declare his wife a 'dynamo' (Marinetti 1909b: 131) and to compare her directly to his automatons, stating that 'vos mécaniques sont identiques . . . Et c'est toujours l'électricité qui fait vibrer vos nerfs comme des fils bons conducteurs de volupté' ('your mechanisms are identical . . . And it's always electricity that vibrates along your nerves, wires conducting your sexual impulses') (132). While the play's conventional romantic storyline sits awkwardly in relation to the emerging Futurist movement, it prefigures the Futurists' interest in electric technologies, and its conception of woman-as-machine speaks to the movement's conservative sexual politics.

Marinetti and Haviland's visions of the machine-woman are a long way from the disturbing 'machine vamp' figure of Lang's *Metropolis*, both of them possessing a sexuality that runs like clockwork and is easily mastered by the male creator/lover, rather than threatening to run out of control. Elsewhere, however, the female robot provides instead a cipher through which a more ambivalent position on machine technology, and the technologised New Woman, may be articulated. To paraphrase Michel Benamou (1980: 71), this position can helpfully be characterised as *anxious technophilia*, understood as a somewhat paradoxical mode of response which combines excitement, fascination or adulation with a keen awareness of the threats posed by the machine. My attention to the modernist ambivalence towards the machine also bears similarities to Roger Rothman's account of 'modernist melancholy and the presence of an anti-modernist nostalgia at the heart of the avant-garde' (2009: 5–6). I propose to show how this ambivalence, this anxious technophilia, operates across a number of works, both visual and verbal, by Marcel Duchamp, Francis Picabia, Marius de Zayas and Guillaume Apollinaire.

Marcel Duchamp began to create works of art responding to the machine from 1912, commencing with his *Mariée (Bride)* (Figure 7.1) and *Passage de la vierge à la mariée (Passage from Virgin to Bride)*. His *Nu descendant un escalier, no. 2* (1912, Figure 11.7) also arguably represents a robotic form – albeit a distinctly ungendered one. However, by far Duchamp's best-known intervention in machine aesthetics (indeed, perhaps *the* best-known avant-garde take on the machine and its gendered implications) is his *Mariée mise à nu par ses célibataires, même (Bride Stripped Bare by her Bachelors, Even)*, often referred to simply as *The Large Glass*, created between 1915 and 1923, a period corresponding roughly with his close friend Picabia's engagement with the machine. Inspiration for this mechanical turn in both Duchamp and Picabia's work derived from a number of sources which have been painstakingly excavated by scholars (Hopkins 2008: 76; Camfield 1966: 311; Borràs 1985: 153–4). Our concern here, however, is not to uncover such points of origin, but rather to examine how Duchamp and Picabia articulated ambivalent responses to machine technology through the figure of the robot-woman.

Duchamp's 1912 *Bride* is formed of a group of overlapping and interlinked tubes, vessels and levers. Some of the vessels are suggestively uterine in form, the tubes perhaps fallopian; the more delicate strings and levers suggest muscular tendons or connective

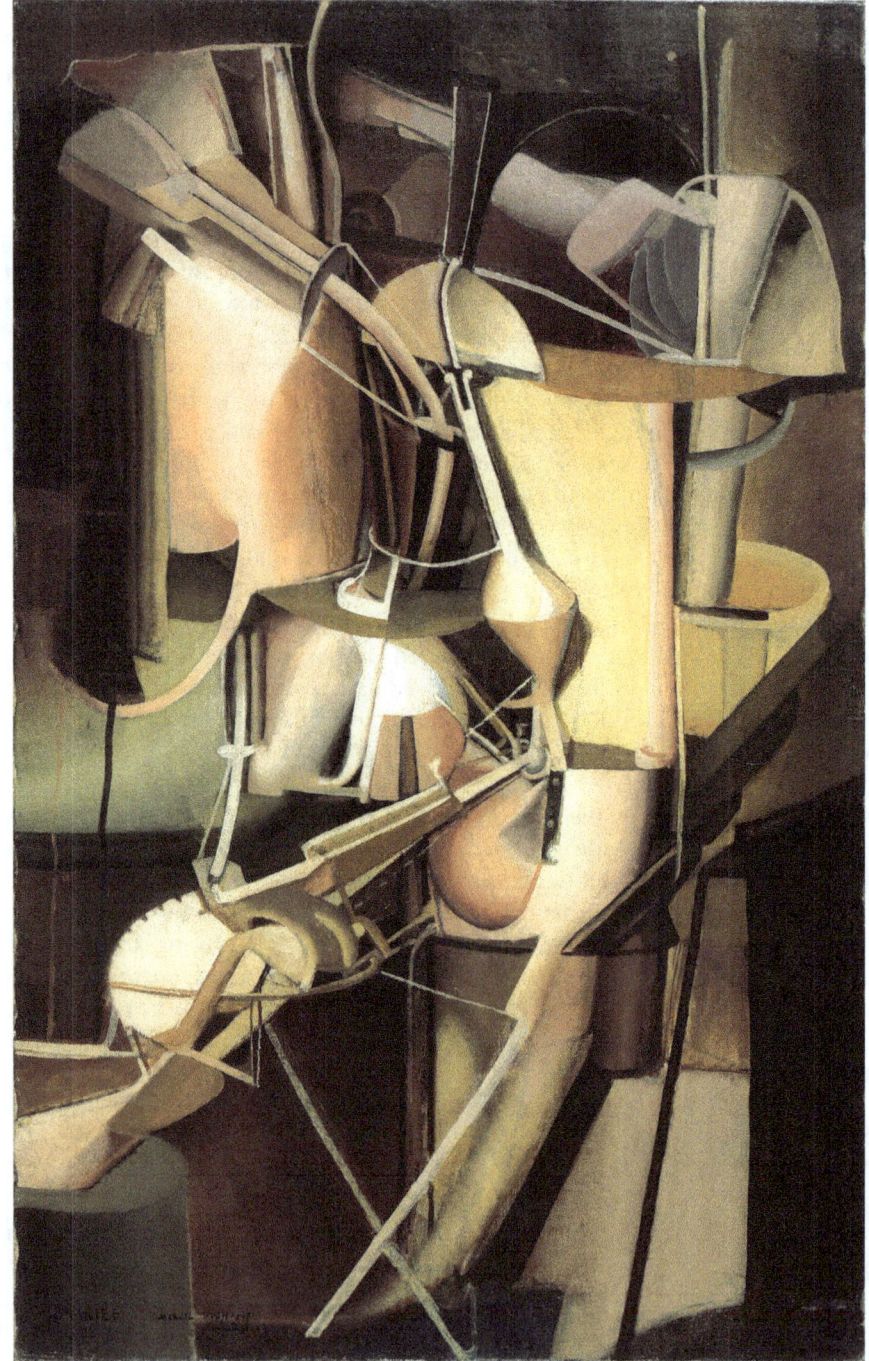

Figure 7.1 Marcel Duchamp, *Mariée* (*Bride*), 1912. Philadelphia Museum of Art, The Louise and Walter Arensberg Collection, 1950. © Photo SCALA, Florence. © Succession Marcel Duchamp / ADAGP, Paris and DACS, London 2021. / © Jacques Villon / ADAGP, Paris and DACS, London.

tissue. The palette is restricted to a relatively narrow range of oxidised browns and fleshy pinks. This is, then, a machine-body, a cyborg form, and yet it is also amorphous, without defining contours, without 'skin'. What we are looking at, it seems, is the interior of the Bride's body: it is the Bride flayed, her inner workings exposed to the spectator's gaze, much like Hadaly's anatomy which is stripped bare for the benefit of the male spectator Lord Ewald, in the lengthy dissection scenes of *L'Ève future* (Villiers de l'Isle-Adam 1993: 213–69).

If the machine-woman's status as 'bride' inevitably suggests her potential as love object and/or sex object (just as the title of the contemporary, very similar painting, *Passage from Virgin to Bride*, evokes her deflowering), this is taken yet further in Duchamp's *The Large Glass* (Figure 7.2).[2] *The Large Glass* is essentially a window split into two panes, the upper of which is occupied by the 'Bride' or female form, while the lower is occupied by the male forms of multiple 'Bachelors'. As suggested by the title, the Bride is 'stripped bare' by the Bachelors, her body exposed to their (and our) gazes. This body is, if anything, even more amorphous than the 1912 Brides, although the forms at the left of the top panel directly recall the connecting vessels and levers of those earlier paintings. The main part of the bride, however, which extends across the top of the work, is a sort of cloud-like, pinkish, fleshy form, with three blank panels at its centre: a looming absence or lack at the centre of the female body; in Duchamp's notes for the work, these are described as 'pistons' or 'nets' (1973: 36). The very solidity of this 'flesh' is open to question, its cloud-like shape suggesting gaseous emissions, perhaps fumes from the 'love gasoline' that the Bride, according to Duchamp's notes, is supposed to hold in her reservoir (Duchamp 1973: 42–3). If she is conceived by Duchamp as a sort of love machine, however, her purpose is surely frustrated, as there is no contact between her and the 'Bachelors' below. These 'Bachelor' forms, 'malic moulds' that seem hard but nevertheless hollow, are connected by an intricate wired mechanism to a form that resembles a water wheel (without water to turn it), and in turn to a schematic chocolate grinder.[3] The Bachelor machine, then, might turn and grind – although, as with most of Picabia's mechanomorphs of the same period, it is not clear *how*, or what powers it, exactly – but its movement is independent of the isolated Bride. If this work presents an 'erotics of the machine' (Grenville 2001: 19), it is first and foremost masturbatory, a bleak (if somewhat humorous) emptying-out of sexual relations in favour of purely mechanical actions; a vision of a machine-people which appears to maintain some sort of notion of biological sex and yet blocks meaningful bodily contact across the glass's central, gendered divide. While this is a hermetic work, and it certainly cannot be reduced to a single stable meaning, what is reasonably clear is that it reflects broader cultural anxieties about the impact of the machine on human culture, and in particular the notion that machine technology stands as a threat to biological sex and to sexual reproduction. The fact that the work contains traces of these anxieties should not, however, be taken to imply that Duchamp's discourse is itself fundamentally conservative or that it constitutes an implicit plea for the re-establishment of reassuring binary categories of sex and gender; indeed, the artist's gender-bending performances elsewhere in his work (via his female alter ego, Rrose Sélavy) rather suggest a more amused, playful stance in relation to these issues.

Francis Picabia's own erotics of the machine, and his generation of a discourse on the figure of the 'New Woman', are perhaps most easily visible in two works, *Portrait d'une jeune fille américaine dans l'état de nudité* (*Portrait of a Young American Girl in*

Figure 7.2 Marcel Duchamp, *La Mariée mise à nu par ses célibataires, même (The Large Glass)*, 1915–23. Philadelphia Museum of Art, bequest of Katherine S. Dreier, 1952. © Photo SCALA, Florence. © Association Marcel Duchamp / ADAGP, Paris and DACS, London 2021.

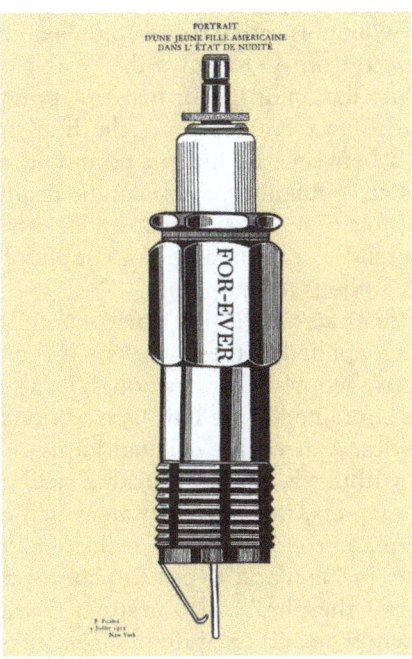

Figure 7.3 Francis Picabia, *Jeune fille américaine dans l'état de nudité*, 291, 5–6 (July–August 1915), p. 4. © ADAGP, Paris and DACS, London 2021.

a State of Nudity; 1915, Figure 7.3) and *Américaine* (*American Woman*; 1917).[4] The first of these is a simple, clean-lined drawing of a spark plug, reminiscent of technical drawings and diagrams. Here, the nude female body of the title is supplanted by and assimilated to a machine (or not even that: the girl is rather rendered here as a machine part, dependent on her contact with other parts, with a larger 'body' of connections, to function). Soft, yielding female flesh is replaced, then, with hard metallic contours. The branding of this machine-body with the word 'FOR-EVER' seems both to appropriate the slogans of modern advertising and to suggest a romantic promise that veers into a sexual joke: the girl in question, whose desires are implicitly likened to electrical charges, can be counted on to 'go' forever. (Indeed, the French for spark plug, 'bougie d'allumage', itself contains a host of sexual innuendos, with 'allumer' meaning 'to turn on', while the related term 'allumeuse' suggests a flirt or prick tease.) It is significant, too, that the machine-girl presented here is American, and not just because Picabia was particularly inspired by the machine cultures he encountered in New York on his visits in 1913 and 1915–17, as he indeed stated in an oft-quoted article (Anon. 1915: 2). Rather, the American girl is attractive because she was held to be more liberal in outlook than her French counterpart: less bound by the strictures of marriage, more open to extra-marital affairs, and hence more available to the artist-lover. This is reflected in the 1917 *Américaine*, a representation of a light-bulb whose electrical capacity to 'turn on' is again understood, and is echoed in the reflected words 'flirt' and 'divorce'.

This type of assimilation of woman to machine might seem to be a somewhat crass celebration of the New Woman's liberated sexuality, along the lines of Marinetti's vision of woman as electrically charged 'doll'. Elsewhere, however, Picabia's engagement with the figure of the machine-woman is rather more complex, and more anxious. Across a large body of work produced from 1915 onwards, Picabia envisages a range of different figures of the robot: 'mechanomorphs' or machine-portraits, often naming friends and acquaintances as the subject but replacing the human body with the machine; ambiguous confrontations between the human body and machine parts, very often presented as female or as an ambiguous combination of interacting male and female characteristics. It is impossible to make sweeping statements about the meaning of this varied body of work; I intend to examine only a couple of examples that I consider representative of Picabia's anxious technophilia.

One of the running themes across Picabia's mechanomorphic output – indeed, the title that Picabia most often applied to these works – is the 'Fille née sans mère' ('Girl born without a mother'). As George Baker has noted, Picabia derived this notion from the index of Latin phrases contained in the Larousse dictionary – as he did for many of his polyvalent, punning titles. And yet the original Latin phrase is 'Prolem sine matre creatam', or '*child* born without a mother': Picabia deliberately feminises it (Baker 2007: 281). The phrase suggests, first, the way in which an imagined robot-people would be 'born' not of human procreation and of the female body, but of pure (male) technological creativity, as in Haviland's very similar formulation, discussed above. The pointed feminisation of the phrase also gestures towards the possibility of the 'fille' herself as not-fully-feminine and not-fully-female: since woman did not bear her, the implication is that she too lacks the means of sexual reproduction. Like Hadaly, then, the 'fille née sans mère' is sterile. This sterility – indeed the impossibility of meaningful intercourse with the robot-woman – is reflected in the very first of Picabia's mechanomorphs, published in *291* in June 1915 (Figure 7.4).

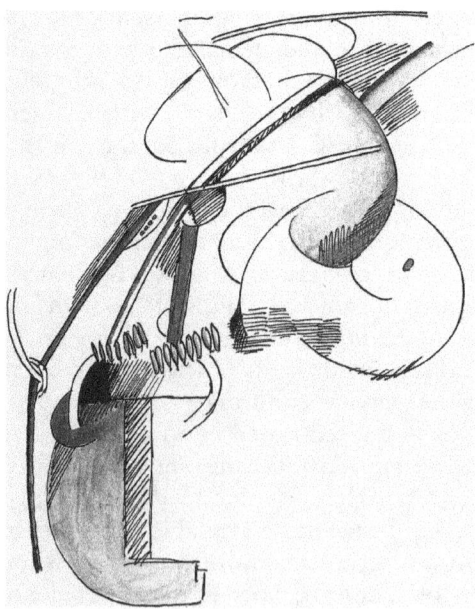

Figure 7.4 Francis Picabia, *Fille née sans mère*, *291*, 4 (June 1915), p. 2. © ADAGP, Paris and DACS, London 2021.

The rounded forms of this drawing, towards the upper right of the page, suggest female flesh: breasts, buttocks, perhaps an eye; the delicate shading might even indicate coyly blushing cheeks. Towards the left of the image, however, we see harder forms, metallic connecting levers which perhaps recall the ambiguously interconnecting parts of Duchamp's 1912 Brides. Beneath these are coiled springs, suggesting the back-and-forth movement of parts. A connecting part (a string or wire) on the far left remains incomplete, leading us to ask who or what causes the machine's movement: what, if anything, 'turns it on'? In the lower portion of the image, we see an apparent downpipe, a conduit for waste. If this is indeed a female body, then it would appear to be one reduced to its basic sexual and digestive functions; and even then, it is not clear how this body works. It is not clear, especially, whether it is a body waiting to be fucked or a machine that fucks itself. How and where does the (male) spectator gain access? Despite the invitingly rounded forms seen in the upper right of the image, this is not an enticingly sexualised robot-woman, much less a scurrilous joke, as in the two 'American girls' discussed above. It is not an 'open' body, or a body ready for penetration like Duchamp's Brides. It is, instead, an altogether more disturbing vision: a 'machine-vamp' whose sexuality disturbs because it is so confused, because it is situated beyond binaries of sex and gender.

This avoidance of binaries is also present in Picabia's 'Voilà ELLE' (Figure 7.5), in spite of the title which seems to indicate an unambiguously female body. The most prominent form here is the dark, phallic 'gun' that seems poised to shoot at a target at the upper right of the image. Both of these elements are connected to a

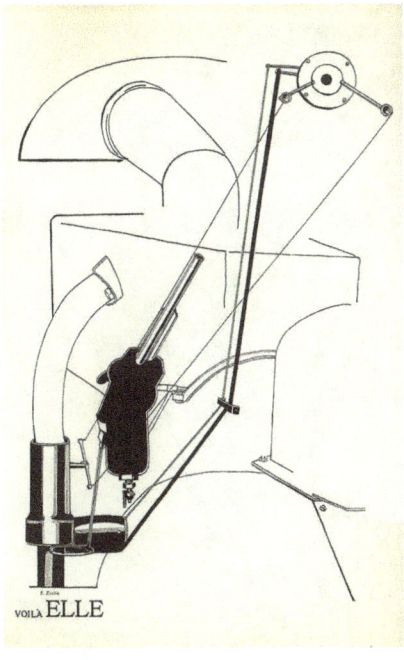

Figure 7.5 Francis Picabia, *Voilà ELLE*, *291*, 9 (November 1915), p. 3. © ADAGP, Paris and DACS, London 2021.

trigger mechanism which seems simultaneously to hold the target open and to start the action again. Behind this contraption, there is a central chamber with pipes connected to it, carrying air perhaps. The lower pipe connects in turn to what appears to be a microscope, its viewfinder trained on the word 'ELLE' directly below: woman, then, is to be seen, to be examined, and is conceived as the passive 'target' of male attention. At the same time, the image as a whole suggests a 'hardened, masculinized' woman, along the lines suggested by Caroline Jones (1998: 153): she is 'public, phallic'. As figures of the 'New Woman' go, this particular example seems to foreground her self-containment, the fact that she seems to 'go' by herself. The spectator is once again left forlorn, confused and deprived of points of penetration.

That 'Voilà ELLE' does indeed represent an implicit portrait of the 'New Woman' is suggested by Marius de Zayas's visual poem 'Elle', which was placed on a facing page in *291* (Figure 7.6). The lines positioned at the top left of the page, 'Femme! Tu voudrais bien te lire dans ce portrait' ('Woman! You'll willingly see yourself in this portrait'), address the poem directly to the modern female reader (the sort of forward-looking woman, presumably, who would have read a magazine like *291*). De Zayas also refers, notably, to the fact that the woman in question 'n'a pas la peur du plaisir' ('has no fear of pleasure'), and to the 'absence absolue de cilice' ('absolute absence of cilice' – that is, a penitential hair shirt), suggesting that she refuses to repent for her pleasures. Elsewhere in the poem he depicts her as driven by sexual pleasure, a willing slave to 'jouissance'. Unlike in Picabia's 'Américaine' images, which seem to celebrate a liberated female sexuality, de Zayas peppers his portrait with critical judgements,

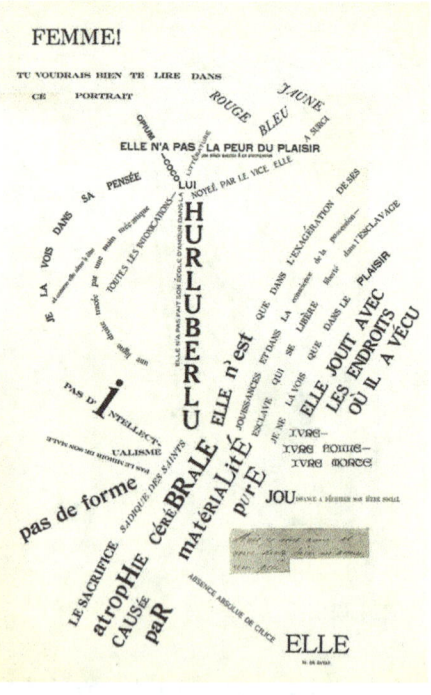

Figure 7.6. Marius de Zayas, 'Elle', *291*, 9 (November 1915), p. 2.

noting that the woman in question is brainless, a pure, unthinking mechanism: 'pas d'intellect/ualisme' ('no intellect/ualism'), he declares, following this with the notion of 'atrophie cérébrale causée par matérialité pure' ('cerebral atrophy caused by pure materiality'). She is, moreover, more machine than human, the curved forms suggestive of the female body ironically being constituted by the words 'une ligne droite tracée par une main mécanique' ('a straight line traced by a mechanical hand'). The robot-woman of de Zayas's poem is, then, an artificial, mechanical 'fille née sans mère'.

If this robot-woman is no more than an unthinking sex machine, this is no fantasy: it is, instead, a searing critique of the 'New Woman', rendered terrifying not just because her desires are seen to run out of control but through her association with the machine, itself situated beyond the province of patriarchal authority. Despite Baker's objections to feminist readings of Picabia's mechanomorphs (objections presented without either citing or engaging with the scholars who have presented these readings), it seems impossible to deny the fundamental misogyny that underlies both de Zayas's poem and Picabia's visual response to it (Baker 2007: 258, 437). That both de Zayas's poem and Picabia's images proceed from an anxiety about the threats posed by the figure of the 'New Woman' is also suggested by the handwritten text included in the poem: a plaintive 'Mais je vous aime et vous devez bien m'aimer, un peu' ('But I love you and you must love me, a little'), a plea to the wayward, uncontrollable technologised woman to love the male poet-artist back, to return his affections, to allow patriarchal order to be restored. This anxious response to the machine-woman thus contains the reassuring possibility that the threat may be contained, the machine-vamp placed back under male control.

Guillaume Apollinaire, of course, occupied a central position in the same Parisian avant-garde networks as Duchamp and Picabia. He wrote about both artists in his 1913 critical text *Méditations esthétiques: les peintres cubistes*, and they in turn responded to his work, Duchamp via his 1917 collage *Apolinère Enameled*, and Picabia via a 1918 mechanomorphic portrait.[5] What I argue here is that, despite a well-known conservative turn in Apollinaire's writing (associated with a broader cultural 'rappel à l'ordre', or 'return to order', bound up in the war and a will to take refuge in classical and specifically French aesthetic traditions), he shares with Duchamp and Picabia an ambivalent position with regard to machine technology, which he expresses through the figure of the robot-woman in his poem '1909'.

First published in Apollinaire's collection *Alcools* in 1913, '1909' (Apollinaire 1965b: 138–9), in its final version, contains lines from another poem, 'Vendémiaire', dating from 1909, and so is believed to have been composed in that year (Décaudin 1996: 210). Technological accomplishments such as Blériot's first cross-Channel flight captured the public imagination in 1909, and it is difficult to ignore a possible connection with Marinetti's Futurist Manifesto of the same year. This connection is especially evident in the Manifesto's displacement of the Victory of Samothrace, as a much-fêted classical representation of feminine beauty, with the sharp machine forms of the modern automobile, which finds a direct echo in Apollinaire's vision of a delicate feminine beauty absorbed into the alluring yet disturbing figure of the robot-woman.

The first stanza of '1909' consists of a portrait of a woman showcasing the fashions of 1909, which were dominated by purple and mauve fabrics, and tunic-style dresses with loose panels (Bohn 2017: 91). The poet goes on to focus on the woman's face, which, we are told, has the colours of France, implying that the woman embodies a singularly French femininity, and perhaps bringing to mind Marianne as archetype. The image of a 'tricolore' face is initially jarring, the woman's highly fashionable and conventional beauty (not to mention her status as a well to-do 'lady') being undercut here by a hint at her unnaturalness, her monstrousness. Apollinaire undoes this initial impression of shock by explaining that the woman's eyes are blue, her teeth white and her lips red; but the jarring effect perhaps stays with the reader and looks forward to the disturbing elision between the delicate 'lady' and the unnatural machine-women who appear later in the poem.

Apollinaire then describes, in the third stanza, a display of female flesh: his gaze settles on the woman's plunging neckline, her bare arms, and her hairstyle which is reminiscent of that of Juliette Récamier. The latter was the most prominent society beauty of the Napoleonic era, and Apollinaire's reference to her necessarily brings to mind the well-known portraits by Jacques-Louis David (1800) and François Gérard (1805), which themselves privilege the coy exposure of flesh: the arms, the décolleté, the neckline exposed to the gaze by the signature piled-up hair. This seems, then, to be a model of femininity that looks back to the ideals of a hundred years previously – although the piled-up Récamier hairstyle might also refer to the Gibson Girl up-do that was fashionable in the years running up to the First World War (and came, of course, from America, which, as we have seen in Picabia's slightly later mechanomorphs, was associated with a particular understanding of the New Woman as sexually liberated). This is a woman, then, who is simultaneously of the moment and yet looks back to the past; her flesh is very much on display and yet inaccessible to the poet who lusts after her, but laments, 'She was so beautiful/You wouldn't have dared love her.' All of this reflects, I contend, the desire and confusion generated by the emerging figure of the New Woman.

Towards the end of the poem, Apollinaire's gaze seems to turn away from this woman, to focus instead on the very new, exciting and yet anxiety-provoking technological forms of modernity:

> J'aimais les femmes atroces dans les quartiers énormes
> Où naissaient chaque jour quelques êtres nouveaux
> Le fer était leur sang la flamme leur cerveau
> J'aimais j'aimais le peuple habile des machines
> Le luxe et la beauté ne sont que son écume
> Cette femme était si belle
> Qu'elle me faisait peur
>   (Apollinaire 1965b: 138–9)

> I loved atrocious women from crowded districts
> Where each day a few new beings were born
> Iron was their blood flame their brains
> I loved I loved the clever tribe of machines
> Luxury and beauty are merely their spume
> That woman was so beautiful
> That she frightened me[6]

Here, Apollinaire tells of a terrifying breed of women, of 'new beings' made of iron and flame, belonging to the 'clever tribe of machines'. Willard Bohn has read this final stanza as referring straightforwardly to working-class women, translating 'peuple habile des machines' as 'people *skilled with* machines' (Bohn 2017: 96). In doing so, his reading overlooks the poem's futuristic vision, and the fact that this is a description of a new kind of 'being', of a metallic robot-people. Moreover, Bohn argues for a straight contrast between the fashionable woman, whom he sees Apollinaire as ridiculing, and the 'femmes atroces', whom Bohn claims Apollinaire prefers 'because they are more down to earth' (2017: 96). It is, of course, possible that the characterisation of luxury and beauty as frothy 'spume' on the surface of a more earthy machine culture does imply a ridicule of the woman in the first part of the poem. However, the way in which the final stanza returns suddenly to the singular figure of the woman from earlier in the poem, and to the fear she provokes, suggests an elision between the two figures of femininity that are deployed here. As Clive Scott has argued, the woman of the first part of the poem

> absorbs the present of the industrial city, is in fact created by it; the lines of the 'femmes atroces' and the 'peuple habile des machines' are as it were enveloped by the beauty of the woman [. . .] and her transformation from 'dame' to 'femme' is dependent upon her coming into contact with her industrial counterparts. (Scott 2014: 143)

The fashionable, delicate beauty of the first part of the poem does not so much stand in opposition to the robot-women of the last stanza, as morph into one of them. She is no longer warm, yielding flesh but something else, a melding of human and machine that delights the poet, and yet 'frightens' him too.

The poem thus reflects what may be cast as a broader ambivalence towards machine technology in Apollinaire's work. Apollinaire insists that poetry should 'machiner le monde' – manipulate or reconfigure the world through machine technology – in the same way that science has done (Apollinaire 1991: 954). And yet this technophilia can be seen to sit alongside more disturbing images of chewed-up, fragmented human bodies as figures of a subjectivity whose integrity is threatened by the machine, as in the headless mannequins and detachable hands of the poem 'L'Émigrant de Landor Road', for instance (Apollinaire 1965b: 105–6). As in Duchamp, Picabia and de Zayas, Apollinaire chooses to figure this ambivalence in '1909' through the robot-woman, and the dual desire and terror that she provokes.

It is worth emphasising that the anxious technophilia evoked through the robot-women examined in this chapter is not intended to be understood as the sole modernist response to machine technology, but rather as a useful pattern or conceptual framework against which other works might be judged. It is also worth emphasising that this anxious technophilia remains distinct from the fundamentally reactionary view of conservative commentators such as Georges Duhamel, who objects to an encroaching cult of the machine that he associates with American imperialism, and who envisions a future in which the working classes become part of a 'sexless', robotic 'human machine' (1931: 196–7). Insofar as the various imagined robot-women examined here also query stable notions of sex and gender, gesture towards new iterations of femininity, and simultaneously awaken and deny male desire, they register a similar set of anxieties about the rise of machine technology and its association with the emergence of the 'New Woman'. And yet there is still a certain excitement, a certain technophilic urge, in these modernist works: an openness to technology, as suggested earlier, rather than a reactionary turning away. We remain some way off, nevertheless, from the posthuman as it is envisioned, in celebratory terms, by Donna Haraway (1991): a liberatory movement beyond binaries of male and female, of human and machine, of warm 'meat' and cold machine parts. Despite modernist artists and writers' interest in such posthuman futures, it appears that they cannot help but look to these, through their robot-women, with some degree of trepidation and fear.

Notes

1. See, for instance, Maclaren's (2012: 2) suggestion that 'reproduction was a key site for many of those debating the merits of the modern mechanised world' in the interwar period in Britain.
2. Marcel Duchamp, *Passage de la vierge à la mariée* (1912), Museum of Modern Art, New York, available at: <https://www.moma.org/interactives/exhibitions/2012/inventingabstraction/?work=81> (last accessed 12 February 2020).
3. The chocolate grinder was itself the subject of two works of 1913–14, both in the collections of the Philadelphia Museum of Art: see <https://www.philamuseum.org/collections/permanent/51518.html> and <https://www.philamuseum.org/collections/permanent/51530.html> (last accessed 12 February 2020).
4. Francis Picabia, *Américaine*, *391*, no. 6, July 1917, cover. See <https://monoskop.org/391#/media/File:391_6_1917.jpg> (last accessed 13 February 2020).
5. Marcel Duchamp, *Apolinère Enameled* (1917), Philadelphia Museum of Art, available at: <https://www.philamuseum.org/collections/permanent/51563.html>; Francis Picabia, *Portrait d'Apollinaire (irritable poète)* (1918–19), collection Natalie et Léon Seroussi, available at: <https://www.artsy.net/artwork/francis-picabia-guillaume-apollinaire> (last accessed 12 February 2020).
6. The translation is adapted from Anne Hyde Greet's version, in Apollinaire (1965a: 183–5).

Works Cited

Anonymous (1915), 'French Artists Spur on an American Art', *New York Tribune*, 24 October, part IV: pp. 2–3.
Apollinaire, Guillaume (1965a), *Alcools*, trans. Anne Hyde Greet. Berkeley and Los Angeles: University of California Press.
Apollinaire, Guillaume (1965b), *Œuvres poétiques*, ed. Marcel Adéma and Michel Décaudin. Paris: Gallimard, Bibliothèque de la Pléiade.
Apollinaire, Guillaume (1991), *Œuvres en prose complètes*, vol. II, ed. Pierre Caizergues and Michel Décaudin. Paris: Gallimard, Bibliothèque de la Pléiade.
Armstrong, Tim (2018), 'Modernism, Technology, and the Life Sciences', in *The Cambridge Companion to Literature and Science*, ed. Steven Meyer. Cambridge: Cambridge University Press, pp. 223–41.
Baker, George (2007), *The Artwork Caught by the Tail: Francis Picabia and Dada in Paris*. Cambridge, MA: MIT Press.
Benamou, Michel (1980), 'Notes on the Technological Imagination', in *The Technological Imagination: Theories and Fictions*, ed. Teresa de Lauretis, Andreas Huyssen and Kathleen Woodward. Madison, WI: Coda Press, pp. 65–75.
Bohn, Willard (2017), *Reading Apollinaire's 'Alcools'*. Newark: University of Delaware Press.
Borràs, Maria Lluïsa (1985), *Picabia*. London: Thames and Hudson.
Braidotti, Rosi (2013), *The Posthuman*. Cambridge: Polity Press.

Camfield, William A. (1966), 'The Machinist Style of Francis Picabia', *Art Bulletin*, 48: 3–4, pp. 309–22.
Čapek, Karel (1961), *R.U.R. (Rossum's Universal Robots)*, in *R.U.R and The Insect Play*, by The Brothers Čapek. London: Oxford University Press.
Décaudin, Michel (1996), *Le Dossier d'"Alcools'*, 3rd edn. Geneva: Droz/Paris: Minard.
Duchamp, Marcel (1973), *Salt Seller: The Writings of Marcel Duchamp (Marchand du Sel)*, ed. Michael Sanouillet and Elmer Peterson. New York: Oxford University Press.
Duhamel, Georges (1931), *America the Menace: Scenes from the Life of the Future*, trans. Charles Miner Thompson. Boston and New York: Houghton Mifflin.
Goody, Alex (2007), 'Cyborgs, Women and New York Dada', *The Space Between: Literature and Culture 1915–1945*, 3: 1, pp. 79–100.
Grenville, Bruce (2001), 'The Uncanny: Experiments in Cyborg Culture', in *The Uncanny: Experiments in Cyborg Culture*, ed. Bruce Grenville. Vancouver: Vancouver Art Gallery/ Arsenal Pulp Press, pp. 13–48.
Haraway, Donna (1991), 'A Cyborg Manifesto: Science, Technology, and Socialist-Feminism in the Late Twentieth Century', in *Simians, Cyborgs and Women: The Reinvention of Nature*. New York: Routledge, pp. 149–81.
Haviland, Paul (1915), 'We are Living in the Age of the Machine', *291*, 7–8 (September–October), n.p.
Heap, Jane (1925), 'Machine-Age Exposition', *The Little Review*, Spring, pp. 22–4.
Hopkins, David (2008), 'Male Poetics', in *Duchamp, Man Ray, Picabia*, exhibition catalogue, ed. Jennifer Mundy. London: Tate, pp. 76–87.
Huyssen, Andreas (1986), 'The Vamp and the Machine: Fritz Lang's *Metropolis*', in *After the Great Divide: Modernism, Mass Culture, Postmodernism*. Bloomington and Indianapolis: Indiana University Press, pp. 65–81.
Jones, Caroline A. (1998), 'The Sex of the Machine: Mechanomorphic Art, New Women, and Francis Picabia's Neurasthenic Cure', in *Picturing Science, Producing Art*, ed. Caroline A. Jones and Peter Galison. New York and London: Routledge, pp. 145–80.
Léger, Fernand (2009), *Fonctions de la peinture*. Paris: Gallimard.
Lewis, Wyndham (1914), 'Manifesto I' and 'Manifesto II', *Blast*, 1, pp. 11–43.
Maclaren, Angus (2012), *Reproduction by Design: Sex, Robots, Trees, and Test-Tube Babies in Interwar Britain*. Chicago and London: University of Chicago Press.
Marinetti, F. T. (1909a), 'Le Futurisme', *Le Figaro*, 20 February, p. 1.
Marinetti, F. T. (1909b), *Poupées électriques*. Paris: E. Sansot.
Perloff, Marjorie (2003), *The Futurist Moment: Avant-Garde, Avant-Guerre, and the Language of Rupture*, 2nd edn. Chicago and London: University of Chicago Press.
Rachilde (1977), *Monsieur Vénus*. Paris: Flammarion.
Roberts, Mary Louise (1994), *Civilization without Sexes: Reconstructing Gender in Postwar France, 1917–1927*. Chicago and London: University of Chicago Press.
Rothman, Roger (2009), 'Modernist Melancholy: Guillaume Apollinaire and Francis Picabia after 1912', *French Cultural Studies*, 20: 1, pp. 5–26.
Scott, Clive (2014), *Translating Apollinaire*. Exeter: University of Exeter Press.
Showalter, Elaine (1987), *The Female Malady: Women, Madness and English Culture, 1830–1980*. London: Virago.
Silverman, Debora L. (1989), *Art Nouveau in Fin-de-Siècle France: Politics, Psychology, and Style*. Berkeley: University of California Press.
Villiers de l'Isle-Adam, Auguste de (1993), *L'Ève future*, ed. Alan Raitt. Paris: Gallimard.
Wosk, Julie (2015), *My Fair Ladies: Female Robots, Androids, and Other Artificial Eves*. New Brunswick, NJ: Rutgers University Press.

Part II
Media

8

MATERIALS: GLASS, IRON AND GHOSTLY FABRIC

David Trotter

'Useful matter' is the definition the materials scientist Christopher Hall proposes of the topic of this chapter. According to Hall, materials should, in the first instance, be taken to include obvious 'engineering stuff' such as steel, concrete, rubber, plastics, wood, glass and aluminium. But the term also extends to oil, gas, foodstuffs, agrochemicals, pharmaceuticals, explosives and textiles, as well as 'oddball things like ivory and invar, graphite, grease, porcelain, and paint'. All these substances have an evident use (Hall 2014: xiii). My concern here is with the representation of useful matter in modernist writing. What might the representation of useful matter tell us about the distinctiveness of literary modernism? What might literary modernism tell us about the distinctiveness of the uses to which particular materials were put in cultures undergoing widespread economic, social and technological transformation?

Useful matter has customarily been examined with the aid of the concept of 'material culture', which has over the last thirty years or so shaped a wide range of enquiries in the arts, humanities and social sciences. In archaeology and socio-cultural anthropology, where the concept first took hold, the focus has remained on the object or thing: that is to say, more often than not, on the artefact. People make things, things make people (Miller 2010: 42–78). Much the same could be said of highly informative studies of modernist material culture from Douglas Mao's *Solid Objects* (1998) to Juli Highfill's *Modernism and its Merchandise* (2014) and beyond. There, too, the artefact is key. But what about the materials out of which the things are made that make people? Hall rightly reminds us that, with some notable exceptions such as ceramics, manufacture has, for the most part, been a two-step process: making the material, making the artefact. A ship is made of steel, a garment of fabric: someone makes the steel or the fabric; someone else acquires it and makes a ship, or a garment. The two steps create a division of labour and skills, between ironmaster and shipwright, weaver and garment-maker (Hall 2014: 83). It is not self-evident how research into representations of that first step in the process of manufacture might further the enduring ambition of material cultural studies to 'connect people and things' (Deetz 1967: 138).

To be sure, some modernist writers took an interest in the ways in which either decay or the circumstances in which it is used might expose an artefact's materiality. Bill Brown's careful distinction between the concepts of 'object' and 'thing' enables him to locate Virginia Woolf's short story 'Solid Objects' (1920) within a 'continuum of modernist attention to materials' (Brown 2015: 60). By Brown's account, the protagonist's encounter with material fragments – pieces of glass, china and iron – 'bears witness' not only to the genealogies of avant-garde aesthetic theory, but to crises resulting from the wartime scarcity of basic materials and the post-war flood of cheap imports of iron and glass in particular (56). Freed from their incorporation into the 'familiar object world', these fragments assume 'lives of their own' (59), a 'thingness' at once 'intimate' and 'unassimilated' (65). Or we might want to ask why D. H. Lawrence should bother to mention that Connie Chatterley, having dined with her husband, and roundly condemned him in her own mind as a dead fish of a gentleman, has put on 'rubber tennis-shoes' before slipping out of the house to spend the night in the gamekeeper's cottage (2006: 195). One possible answer is that British rubber growers, alarmed by an apparently irreversible fall in the price of the raw material, had spent much of the 1920s promoting new uses for it, such as the soles of sports shoes. Crepe rubber, in particular, proved ideal for the purpose, since the proportion of raw material to added minerals (sulphur) in any commodity made from it was very high indeed. A rubber-soled tennis shoe thus combined nature with culture, the raw with the cooked, ancient energies with ultramodern refinement. In a later chapter, after Connie and Mellors have met at the hut in the forest in which they first made love, she dances naked in the rain: 'She slipped on her rubber shoes and ran out with a wild little laugh' (221). Those ancient–modern rubber shoes have immunised her against too much wildness as well as too little (Trotter 2013: 89–107).

In 'Solid Objects', however, as Brown admits, it is not 'material as such' but the 'whole process' of the retrieval and reanimation of fragments of iron, glass and china that sustains the protagonist's interest, and the reader's (2015: 70). Material as such could be said to inform the view we are encouraged to take of Connie Chatterley. But many readers will have noted Connie's tennis shoes without pausing to reflect on the fact that they are made out of rubber. It seems fair to say that criticism has not yet found a way to define the formal and thematic implications for our understanding of a text of the representation within it, either fleetingly or at length, of material(s) as such. This chapter constitutes a step in that direction. Its primary aim is to explore the as yet unidentified formal and thematic resonance of two materials in particular, iron and glass, in a range of texts from the era of high modernism. While there are exemplary cultural histories of modern materials such as concrete (Forty 2012), they tend to have little to say about literature, which, unlike architecture or the visual arts, cannot really be said to involve the shaping or manipulation of a substance. A writer's 'materials' are their subject-matter, not pen and paper. The methods I will propose for the study of the representation of materials as such in modernism owe less to the study of material culture than they do to two more recent initiatives: the study of the relation of literature to science (Beer 1996, Whitworth 2001, Morrisson 2017, Saunders 2019), and the study of sound in literature (Murphet et al. 2017). I conclude on a ghostly note because I suspect that materiality of a less tangible kind will continue to force itself on our attention.

We are used to the idea that the rapid development of X-ray technology during the early years of the twentieth century provided not only a topic (and a spectacle) of widespread public interest, but an opportunity for modernist writers (Danius 2002: 55–90, Garrington 2013: 92–7). The body's skeletal structure had finally been laid bare, the barrier between its inner and outer spaces breached. What may now merit further consideration is the fact that the same thing was about to happen to substances even more solid-seeming than human flesh. For the application of X-ray technology transformed the science of materials. In experiments conducted in 1912, Max von Laue and his colleagues at the University of Munich found that a beam of X-rays passing through a crystal of copper sulphate would diffract so as to create a pattern of discrete spots on a photographic plate. William and Lawrence Bragg, at the University of Cambridge, devised a method for the analysis of these patterns. A wide variety of materials could be shown to consist of a regular 'spatial lattice' of atoms, ions and molecules. X-ray diffraction made a detailed knowledge of the crystal structure of metals, ceramics and minerals readily available. It soon became apparent that polymer materials such as wool, silk and cellulose also formed crystals (Hall 2014: 25–6). Cultural historians have yet to describe these dramatic advances in detail. But even the most perfunctory of thumbnail sketches might indicate the scope thus created for a distinctively modernist understanding of materiality as spatial lattice.

Nobody was about to underestimate the significance of X-ray diffraction. In March 1920, the University of Cambridge announced the funding of a chair in the science of radiology, or 'radiometallography', which afforded 'great possibilities for examining the internal structure of metals and other materials'. According to the chair's distinguished sponsors, these possibilities had already begun to transform a range of projects from aircraft design to the manufacture of glass, steel and explosives ('X-ray Research' 1920: 13). In September 1923, the *Times* reported enthusiastically on a gathering of eminent physicists and chemists for the purpose of 'a joint discussion on cohesion and molecular forces'. Contributors included Oliver Lodge, Ernest Rutherford and William Bragg. The metallurgist Walter Rosenhain spoke of the distortion produced in the lattice of single atoms in a substance by the introduction into it, as in metallic alloys, of atoms from another element:

> In such alloys, when the interspaces of the atoms of the two metals were closely similar, the result was a solid solution; but when the interspaces differed, the result was a chemical compound. When stress was applied, the crystals slipped along certain definite planes of weaker attachment, and the process of hardening metals was in reality a process of reducing the facility for slip. ('Molecular Forces' 1923: 6)

The cohesion of a material like iron, hitherto evident enough to lay perception, and when necessary subjected to more strenuous mechanical testing by the engineer, had been shown to depend on the interaction of molecular forces within it: on the meshing of lattices, on slippage along planes of weak attachment. The problem, as *The Times* explained in December 1925, with reference to Bragg's recent Romanes Lecture at Oxford, was that the term 'solid', unlike 'gaseous' and 'liquid', describes 'qualities which are in a sense accidental': 'X-ray photography shows the true solid, or crystalline state, as marked off from all other states of matter by a definite orientation, an arrangement of the molecules with respect to each other' ('Progress' 1925: 7). Solidity was henceforth to be understood as a function of a material's internal structure, or spatial lattice. Not all seeming solids revealed such lattices, however. I begin my account of literary modernism's interest in materials with glass because the new science had sought in vain for any evidence of internal structure in it.

Glass

Glass, a combination of sand and other minerals fused at a high temperature, fulfils a variety of functions, from intricately wrought decorative object to ubiquitous feature of the built environment. Glass manufacture was an ancient technology and its products have exerted a powerful fascination in many cultures since (at least) the early modern period (Garrison 2015). Isobel Armstrong has shown that, during the nineteenth century, dramatic advances in the quality and quantity of the material produced led to the creation of an 'environment of mass transparency' and a corresponding 'glass consciousness' (2008: 1). Glass, Armstrong proposes, 'became a third or middle term: it interposed an almost invisible layer of matter between the seer and the seen – the sheen of a window, the silver glaze of the mirror, the convexity or concavity of the lens' (3). In the first decades of the twentieth century, further advances established the material's versatility, and its potential as a form of theatre (Misa 2004: 158–89). The plate-glass walls with which some of the most influential architects of the period chose to sheathe their most innovative buildings were thought to embody the International Style's vision of the radiant city of the future. These buildings propose transparency, above all (Gropius 1937: 19–29). 'To live in a glass house', Walter Benjamin declared, 'is a revolutionary virtue par excellence' (1929: 541).

Studies of modernist representations of glass have tended to concentrate either on the substance's transparency (Siraganian 2012: 79–109, Duffy 2015) or on its brittleness (Trotter 2013: 126–32): qualities which become manifest during the process of manufacture into an object, and can therefore be examined as aspects of material culture. These are representations of the things people make which make them. That was not, however, how the materials scientists saw it. While the property of transparency 'is at once suggested by the word "glass"', Walter Rosenhain wrote in a book first published in 1908, there are a number of 'true glasses' which are not transparent at all, while some are not even translucent. Brittleness is a more reliable criterion but not entirely so. 'Perhaps the only really universal property of glasses', Rosenhain concluded, 'is that of possessing an amorphous structure.' Vitreous bodies as a whole should be understood primarily as '"structureless" solids' (1919: 1). Such bodies are characterised by an 'entire absence' of crystalline structure. Their molecules possess the 'same arrangement, or rather lack of arrangement', as is found in liquids. Glasses are 'congealed liquids'. The process of congealing involves 'no change of structure, no re-arrangement of the molecules', but rather a 'gradual stiffening of a liquid until the viscosity becomes so great that the body behaves like a solid' (2). The advances in the chemical testing and analysis of materials that Rosenhain was able to draw on in the second (1919) edition of his book could be said to have created a properly modernist consciousness of glass as a structureless solid, for writers, too, did not concern themselves only with transparency and brittleness. They found something to say about what Alan Griffith, who led research into the chemical composition of glass at the Royal Aircraft Establishment in Farnborough, was to term 'The Phenomena of Rupture and Flow in Solids' (Griffith 1921).

Griffith's research was, of course, conducted at a level of technicality well beyond the layperson's grasp. But the muted eloquence of his title does at least propose a theme compatible, on the face of it, with experiment in literature and the visual arts. What was modernism if not a poetics of rupture and flow? The case could most plausibly be made, I suggest, with regard to the decisive part played by women writers in developing modernism's 'key formal innovations' (DuPlessis 2016: 533). This is a familiar topic. My aim here is simply to ask what difference an account of the representation of a particular material as such might make to our understanding of two experimental texts published in the years during which one version of modernism was taking shape in London: Dorothy Richardson's *Honeycomb* (1917), the third of the thirteen volumes of *Pilgrimage*; and May Sinclair's *Mary Olivier: A Life* (1919). The bourgeois interiors described in great detail in these texts are replete with objects made of glass: windows, mirrors, lamps, tableware, ornaments, beads and so on. But their resistance to the conventions of domestic realism, and to the patriarchy it could be said to sustain, involves a grasp of something other than the object: of usable matter, of glassiness, or glass-ness.

Pilgrimage, set for the most part in turn-of-the-century Britain, and largely in the mind of the protagonist, Miriam Henderson, is now acknowledged as the exemplary female modernist *Bildungsroman*. It is a work best known for the 'first-person pulsing of multiple, impressionistic vectors' (DuPlessis 2016: 549), which generates a narrative rhythm of rupture and flow. 'Stream of consciousness' was the term May Sinclair coined for that pulsing when she reviewed the first three volumes of *Pilgrimage* in the *Egoist* in April 1918. Richardson, Sinclair wrote, had seized reality 'alive'. 'The intense rapidity of the seizure defies you to distinguish between what is objective and what is subjective either in the reality presented or the art that presents' (1918: 446). In Chapter 6 of *Honeycomb*, fragments set out on the page like prose poems render Miriam's reverie in Regent Street.

> She pulled up sharply in front of a window. The pavement round it was clear, allowing her to stand rooted where she had been walking, in the middle of the pavement, in the midst of the tide flowing from the clear window, a soft fresh tide of sunlit colours ... clear green glass shelves laden with shapes of fluted glass, glinting transparencies of mauve and amber and green, rose-pearl and milky blue, welded to a flowing tide, freshening and flowing through her blood, a sea rising and falling with her breathing. (Richardson 1917: 127)

Reality (Miriam's reality) has been seized by the shift of emphasis from 'in the middle of the pavement' to 'in the midst of the tide flowing from the clear window'. In the middle of the pavement, Miriam is a subject among objects. In the midst of the tide flowing from the window, she is at once subject and object. The term Richardson chooses to define that fusion – '*welded* to a flowing tide' – draws attention to material as such. Welding temporarily reduces pieces of iron or steel to a 'plastic, coherent, and amorphous, non-crystalline (but not fluid) state' in order to join them together (Greenwood 1884: 7). Richardson wants both the 'reality presented' and the 'art that presents it', in Sinclair's phrase, to *remain* amorphous (or non-crystalline) even after it has solidified – as glass does, but not iron and steel.

For Sinclair, Richardson's method amounted to a philosophy, or guide to living. She had a sophisticated grasp of contemporary philosophies of perception, as her robust *Defence of Idealism* makes amply clear (1917: 53–66, 156–88, 209–25). But what she appears to have found in *Pilgrimage* is an original understanding of the mutual determination of perception and affect. Everything Miriam ever wanted has been withheld or taken from her. She has been reduced to the 'barest minimum on which it is possible to support the life of the senses and the emotions'. And yet she is happy. What really matters, when it comes to personal well-being, is 'a state of mind, the interest or the ecstasy with which we close with life' (1918: 446). Sinclair's next novel, *Mary Olivier: A Life*, aimed to convert Miriam's inexhaustible enthusiasm for 'life' into a feminist politics, or 'affective militancy' (Truran 2017: 79). The key to that conversion is a figurative dialectic (Sinclair was an admirer of Hegel), established by attention to materials as such.

The novel's five parts, or 'Books', follow Mary Olivier from infancy through childhood and adolescence, to maturity and middle age. Mary is a generation older than Miriam Henderson, and a lot less urban: her most powerful connections are with rural Essex and North Yorkshire. The vicissitudes of a dysfunctional Victorian family – alcoholic father, remote mother, siblings who fall regularly by the wayside – reduce her, too, to a bare minimum. Her first experience of a secure basis for the life of the senses and the emotions is prompted by an excursion into the Essex countryside: 'A queer white light everywhere, like water thin and clear.' Returning from the excursion, she sees Five Elms, the family home, as if for the first time. Its salient feature is the 'black glassy stare' of the windows (Sinclair 1980: 48). Henceforth, glassiness, or glass-ness, will be what welds her to the 'queer' light flowing from the world into her blood. It defines her moments of 'sudden, secret happiness' (93). Those moments provide the foundation for affective militancy. The greatest threat to them derives not from the social and moral conformity they have violated, but from an alternative emancipation through the fulfilment of desire. Although they undoubtedly belong to her 'real life' (211), the men she desires acquire a different – indeed, opposite – metaphorical association to that possessed by the moments of queer, glassy happiness. Maurice Jourdain, for example, boasts smoky black eyes, tired eyelids and a 'crystal mind, shining and flashing' (211). The object of desire has continually to be provoked into revealing its crystalline structure: 'If only she could set his mind moving; turn the crystal about; make it flash and shine' (212). The crystal's flashing and shining, however, serve to remind Mary that her moments of queer happiness do not flash and shine at all, but rather weld her into the world's glassy flow. Her own most profound desire is to remain amorphous. So the dialectic unfolds. Subsequent encounters with crystalline men – Professor Lee Ramsden of the University of London, and the eminent classicist Richard Nicholson, with whom she falls deeply in love – at once clarify and renew her passionate belief in the supreme value of rupture and flow: 'The globed light showed like a ball of fire, hung out in the garden, on the black, glassy darkness, behind the pane' (321). When all her potential lovers have proved unsatisfactory and her mother, who claimed her from them, has died, the queer happiness finally comes into its own. We owe any sense we have gained of what that happiness might consist of to Sinclair's interest in materials as such.

Iron

There is, of course, more than one way in which particular materials might have achieved historical and critical significance for our understanding of modernism. Coincidences of preoccupation between fields as distinct as literature and materials science do not occur all that often, while detailed familiarity on the part of one group of innovators with the decisive work of another is hard to prove at the best of times. The second material I have chosen to concentrate on was not notable, during the first decades of the twentieth century, for the enthusiasm it inspired among metallurgists. Steel, an alloy of iron and carbon, had long since superseded its own main component as one of the most widely used of all man-made materials. The idea of iron, however, seems not to have been deprived by that supersession of its menacing aura. Lecturing on the material in Tunbridge Wells in February 1858, John Ruskin felt obliged to expound its function not only in nature and art, but in 'policy'. Iron, forever capable of 'bearing a pull, and receiving an edge', was notable above all for its 'tenacity': 'These powers, which enable it to pierce, to bind, and to smite, render it fit for the three great instruments by which its political action may be simply typified; namely, the Plough, the Fetter, and the Sword' (1858: 395). Iron had become the embodiment or realisation of the will to pierce, bind and smite. So it remained, in association with law, necessity, the Duke of Wellington, the 'heel of despotism', and any number of acts of real or imaginary violence up to and including the 'curtain' which fell across Europe in the aftermath of the Second World War. By 1900, global capitalism had also staked its claim to a share of the menace. The financier Holroyd, in Joseph Conrad's *Nostromo* (1904), presides over 'immense silver and iron interests' from his headquarters in San Francisco: 'an enormous pile of iron, glass, and blocks of stone at the corner of two streets, cobwebbed aloft by the radiation of telegraph wires' (1983: 90, 97).

During the early years of the twentieth century, that High Victorian sonority fed into, and was brought down to earth by, a new, scientifically enhanced preoccupation with urban noise. William Bragg devoted one of six Royal Institution lectures he gave in December 1919 to 'Sounds of the Town' (1921: 67–98). What distinguished the city street as a sonic environment was the capacity of one sound arising within it to cancel or muffle another. 'One of the most interesting of town sounds', Bragg noted, 'is the reverberation sometimes found in public buildings, an effect which makes it difficult to hear a speaker' (81). 'Interference' had long been the term used by sound and light engineers to describe the way which in two waves reinforce or neutralise each other when their paths meet (Barton 1908: 42). Its use expressed an increasing preoccupation with what would subsequently come to be known as 'signal-to-noise' ratio. Bragg concluded his Royal Institution series with a lecture on 'Sound in War', which describes the use of listening devices to track submarines and aeroplanes, or incoming gunfire (Bragg 1921: 161–96). In this case, the problem was how to distinguish the identifying sound emitted by a target from noise in and beyond the channel created by the device. We can see here the beginnings of an informational approach to sound-waves.

Iron, of course, was not the only material which sounded in the modern city. But it seems to have acquired a particular – menacing – association with interference, or noise. 'Terrible the noise of *iron* all the while, breaks my head', D. H. Lawrence reported from San Francisco in 1922, 'and the black, glossy streets with steel rails in ribbons like the path of death itself' (1987: 290). The terrible noise was industrial capitalism's most damaging emanation, an iron cacophony. By the end of the decade, in 'What Is a Man to Do?', Lawrence was decrying the fate of the millions dancing the 'dry industrial jig' of 'corpses entangled in iron': a dance from which there was no escape, 'for the iron goes through their genitals, brains, and souls' (2013: 1. 545). Iron *sounds*, in modernist literature. It sounds at the point at which sound itself becomes indistinguishable from, or lost in, noise. The sound it makes is the sound of noise.

There is a striking example of the literary use of iron as an index to interference or noise in a scene in another novel by Conrad, *Chance* (1914). The scene involves a conversation in the East India Dock Road in London between Conrad's go-to narrator, Charlie Marlow, and young Flora De Barral, the daughter of a disgraced financier. This being Conrad, the circumstances are too complicated to explain in full. Suffice it to say that the conversation turns on (or skirts around) a letter Flora has sent to the sister of the man she has just eloped with. The letter amounts to an 'unreserved confession' (2002: 159). An intimacy develops between her and Marlow, as their glances meet 'in contact more familiar than a hand-clasp, more communicative, more expressive' (155). Needless to say, internal constraints abound on this exchange of confidences about love and death between a teenager and a middle-aged sea-captain. Conrad, however, wants also to insist on interference from outside the channel of communication established by the meeting of glances. As they converse on the pavement outside a hotel, Marlow, at least, has trouble in blocking out 'the odious uproar of that wide roadway thronged with heavy carts' (157). The uproar climaxes as Marlow confirms that he has not read Flora's letter: 'Just then the racket was distracting, a pair-horse trolly lightly loaded with loose rods of iron passing slowly very near us' (159). The sound made by those loose rods is an index to the ultimate determination of her predicament not so much by the 'chance' the novel's title advertises as by the mechanisms of the industrial and finance capitalism it has otherwise done no more than sketch in outline.

Iron sounds, too, as noise from the street, from public life, in Katherine Mansfield's short story 'Revelations' (1920). The protagonist, Monica Tyrell, suffers terribly from her nerves in the hours from eight o'clock in the morning until about half-past eleven. On the day in question, her suffering is exacerbated by the fierce wind which rattles the house, and by a cry of 'Coal! Coal! Coal! Old iron! Old iron! Old iron!' sounding from the street below her bedroom window (2001: 192). She seeks sanctuary at the hairdresser's salon. But there will be no respite from noise: 'The wind rattled the window frame; a piece of iron banged' (195). As in *Chance*, the iron banging compounds the difficulties that self-absorption has already created for communication and mutual understanding. It turns out that the hairdresser's young daughter had died in the early hours of the morning.

The sound of iron in the streets could be said to have acquired the status of an official acknowledgement of mortality. In another of Mansfield's stories, 'The Wrong House' (1919), the similarly fearful Mrs Bean shuts the door of her house on the noise made by the hooves of the horses pulling a hearse: '*Clockety-clock-clock. Cluk! Cluk! Clockety-clock-cluk!* sounded from outside, and then a faint *Cluk! Cluk!* and then silence. They were gone' (2001: 666). In the 'Calypso' episode of James Joyce's *Ulysses* (1922), Leopold Bloom, emerging from the jakes, reminds himself to check the time of Paddy Dignam's funeral: 'A creak and a dark whirr in the air high up. The bells of George's church. They tolled the hour: loud dark iron.' The darkness in the sound of the bells alters Bloom's mood significantly: 'Poor Dignam!' (1993: 67). Like Conrad and Mansfield, Joyce needed a way to indicate how public systems impinge all the time, even on those private lives they do not thereby alter fundamentally. There is always interference. In the 'Sirens' episode of *Ulysses*, Bloom arrives at the Ormond Hotel shortly after Blazes Boylan has set out for 7 Eccles Street, where he will soon have sex with Molly. The barmaid-sirens, bronze Miss Douce and gold Miss Kennedy, seem well equipped to offer distraction to an assembly of bar-flies. But the episode opens on another sound altogether – on noise, in fact: 'Bronze by gold heard the hoofirons, steelyringing' (245). The steely-ringing hoof-irons belong to the horses in the viceroy's cavalcade, which passes by outside the hotel. The noise they make is the least of Bloom's problems, we might imagine. Joyce nonetheless insists upon it, weaving its harshness into an otherwise melodious soundscape.

> Miss Kennedy served two gentlemen with tankards of cool stout. She passed a remark. It was indeed, first gentleman said, beautiful weather. They drank cool stout. Did she know where the lord lieutenant was going? And heard steelhoofs ringhoof ring. No, she couldn't say. But it would be in the paper. O, she needn't trouble. No trouble. She waved about her outspread *Independent*, searching, the lord lieutenant, her pinnacles of hair slowmoving, lord lieuten. Too much trouble first gentleman said. O, not in the least. Way he looked that. Lord lieutenant. Gold by bronze heard iron steel. (259)

These unnamed gentlemen are interlopers at the Ormond. They have no narrative significance. By thus cordoning off interference by official public occasion from the imminent fates of the novel's main and subsidiary protagonists, Joyce insists all the more powerfully on its ubiquity. It is there, even (or especially) when we do not notice it.

Something similar occurs in Henry Green's *Living* (1929), which is set in and around a Birmingham iron foundry, and so comes as close as modernist fiction ever did to a description of the manufacture of materials. In the foundry, the signals transmitted by the human voice struggle to penetrate the ubiquitous and perpetual din of machines. The black sand strewn on the floor adds a note of darkness. On one occasion, a worker – summoned into the narrative for this purpose only, like Joyce's two gentlemen – sings to celebrate the birth of a son. The song is said to come out from 'behind' the din. 'Everything in iron foundries is black with the burnt sand and here was his silver voice yelling like bells. The black grimed men bent over their black boxes.' The song gladdens all of the listeners except one, who 'had bitterness inside him like girders and when Arthur began singing his music was like acid to that man and it was like that girder was being melted and bitterness and anger decrystallized, rising up in him till he was full and would have broken out' (Green 2017: 76). The man appears to have iron's harshness inside him, which the song's silvery message somehow decrystallises. Once again, a material's reputation has served to dramatise the fineness of the adjustment of signal-to-noise ratio necessary under more or less all circumstances, and the unpredictability of its effects.

Ghosts

I have chosen to concentrate on traditional solid materials like iron and glass because I want to demonstrate that the scientific and technological advances of the early decades of the twentieth century created a context for literary experiment. But one result of those advances was the rapid development of new synthetic and semi-synthetic substances, most notably plastic: cellulose nitrate (celluloid), from the 1860s; viscose rayon, from the 1890s; cellulose acetate and cellophane, from the late 1920s; PVC and polystyrene, from the early 1930s; Perspex, from 1935; nylon and polythene, from 1938 (Trotter 2013: 32–4, 132–65). These undoubtedly deserve further attention.

I suspect, however, that future research may take the direction of the less tangible and less sonorous among materials. Steven Connor, for example, has described a 'hazy' or 'nebular' modernism whose abiding preoccupation was 'how to write, paint, photograph, compose, from within the condition of the atmosphere' (2006: 16). We might well think that haze does not constitute usable matter, although gas, a not dissimilar particulate substance, most certainly does (Connor 2003). The point is, however, that 'atmosphere' had begun to acquire – as much in technological as in aesthetic discourse – a certain materiality, as a space or dimension in which stuff happened. When Walter Benjamin used the term '*Medium*', he did not mean to refer to the development of film, radio or television. For these, he reserved the term '*Apparat*' or '*Apparatur*'. '*Medium*' refers instead, Antonio Somaini notes, to 'the spatially extended environment, the *milieu*, the atmosphere, the *Umwelt* in which perception occurs' (2016: 6). In its first appearance in essays written during the 1910s, the term indicates a realm or domain (colour, the pictorial mark, language, criticism, memory) in or through which relations can be established. Thereafter, it solidified into the concept of *milieu* which underpins, often in opposition to the concept of apparatus, Benjamin's foundational enquiries into the nature of modernity. One effect of the experiments he conducted with hashish between 1927 and 1934 was to suggest that the drug significantly enhances the user's capacity to perceive 'aura', which he thought of as a notable density in the 'medium' or atmosphere surrounding a person, place or object. His topic now was the ways in which a series of rapidly evolving technical *Apparate* had begun to reconfigure the *milieu* or *Umwelt* constituting what he was to describe in 'The Work of Art in the Age of its Technological Reproducibility' as the 'medium of perception' (Benjamin 1936). Such an emphasis is not all that far removed from the account Virginia Woolf had given in 'Modern Fiction' (1925) of the novelist's proper subject-matter or 'stuff': 'Life is not a series of gig lamps symmetrically arranged; life is a luminous halo, a semi-transparent envelope surrounding us from the beginning of consciousness to the end' (1984: 150). That semi-transparent envelope has the feel of usable matter.

Such considerations may have been behind the otherwise rather surprising interest shown by some modernist writers (women, in particular) in that quintessentially late Victorian or Edwardian genre, the ghost story. The period of the composition of the 'uncanny stories' May Sinclair began to write in 1910, and eventually published under that title in 1923, was also that of her closest association with the literary avant-garde: Ford Madox Ford, Ezra Pound, H. D., T. S. Eliot. In 1933, Mary Butts published a substantial commentary on the uses of the supernatural in fiction in four consecutive issues of *The Bookman* (Butts 1998). Then there were the two anthologies edited by Lady Cynthia Asquith: *The Ghost Book: Sixteen New Stories of the Uncanny* (1930) and *The Second Ghost Book* (1952). The latter contains a characteristically thoughtful introduction by Elizabeth Bowen, as well as her story 'Hand in Glove'. Traditional ghosts had been confined to antique manors, graveyards, yew walks, cliff edges and the like, Bowen wrote, but modern ghosts roam at will: 'They know how to curdle electric light, chill off heating, or de-condition air. Long ago, they captured railway trains and installed themselves in liners' luxury cabins; now telephones, motors, planes, and radio wave-lengths offer them self-expression' (1962: 102). The modern ghost converts atmosphere into usable matter.

Wavelengths may have worked for some. Others, like those operative in Butts's 'With and Without Buttons' (1932), still required the more tangible medium of fabric. The story takes place in a 'very old' cottage, now divided into two dwellings, in a 'remote village in Kent' (1962: 22). The narrator and her sister live in one half of the cottage; Trenchard, a retired colonial civil servant, lives in the other. The sisters decide to punish Trenchard for his obstinate, contemptuous rationalism by staging an apparition. They will leave odd kid gloves lying around in unexpected places. It soon dawns on them, however, that gloves have begun to turn up in unexpected places without anyone actually having put them there. The sisters join forces with Trenchard in a search for the source of the infestation. Their attic yields a cardboard box full of gloves which stink abominably: '"I know what it is," said Trenchard: "smelt it in Africa in a damp place. Bad skins"' (31). If iron is revealed as a material by the harshness of the sound it emits when struck, then the animal skin out of which a glove has been made persists most forcefully as a sickening odour: as a reputation filtered, in this case, through colonialism. The leather smells of Africa. But the ghosts at work in the cottage have devices other than odour at their disposal. On two occasions, shapeless pieces of fabric, revolting to touch, somehow infiltrate themselves into the cottage by way of the attic skylight. One of these ends up wrapped around Trenchard's head. The nausea he feels is what the story leaves us with. Someone, something, has created an atmosphere out of usable matter.

This final example should have served to reinforce my main contention: that the several potentially fruitful directions in which the study of materials as such might lead us do not include material culture, for while the material culture paradigm has produced some exemplary studies of modernist clothing (Marshik 2017; Plock 2017; Wallenberg and Kollnitz 2019), it is unlikely to tell us much about the stink of leather and the feel of shapeless pieces of cotton or calico. Here, people are not making things, nor things people. Materials as such have a different story to tell.

Works Cited

Armstrong, Isobel (2008), *Victorian Glassworlds: Glass Culture and the Imagination, 1830–1880*. Oxford: Oxford University Press.
Barton, Edwin H. (1908), *A Text-Book on Sound*. London: Macmillan.
Beer, Gillian (1996), *Open Fields: Science in Cultural Encounter*. Oxford: Oxford University Press.
Benjamin, Walter (1996–2003a [1929]), 'The Destructive Character', in *Selected Writings*, trans. Rodney Livingstone and others, ed. Michael W. Jennings, Howard Eiland and Gary Smith, 4 vols. Cambridge, MA: Harvard University Press, vol. 2, pp. 541–2.
Benjamin, Walter (1996–2003b [1936]), 'The Work of Art in the Age of its Technological Reproducibility', in *Selected Writings*, trans. Rodney Livingstone and others, ed. Michael W. Jennings, Howard Eiland and Gary Smith, 4 vols. Cambridge, MA: Harvard University Press, vol. 4, pp. 251–83.
Bowen, Elizabeth Bowen (1962), 'The Second Ghost Book', in *After-Thought: Pieces about Writing*. London: Longmans Green, pp. 101–4.
Bragg, William (1921), *The World of Sound*. London: G. Bell and Sons.
Brown, Bill (2015), *Other Things*. Chicago: University of Chicago Press.
Butts, Mary (1962), 'With and Without Buttons', in *From Altar to Chimney-Piece: Selected Stories*. Kingston, NY: McPherson and Company, pp. 22–38.
Butts, Mary (1998), 'Ghosties and Ghoulies', in *Ashe of Rings and Other Writings*. Kingston, NY: McPherson and Company, pp. 333–64.
Connor, Steven (2003), 'An Air that Kills: A Familiar History of Poison Gas', <http://stevenconnor.com/gas.html> (last accessed 20 January 2022).
Connor, Steven (2006), 'Haze: On Nebular Modernism', <http://stevenconnor.com/haze.html> (last accessed 20 January 2022).

Conrad, Joseph (1983), *Nostromo: A Tale of the Seaboard*. Harmondsworth: Penguin Books.
Conrad, Joseph (2002), *Chance: A Tale in Two Parts*, ed. Martin Ray. Oxford: Oxford University Press.
Danius, Sara (2002), *The Sense of Modernism: Technology, Perception, and Aesthetics*. Ithaca, NY: Cornell University Press.
Deetz, James (1967), *Invitation to Archaeology*, Garden City, NY: Natural History Press.
Duffy, Enda (2015), 'Irish Glass', *Critical Quarterly*, 57: 3, pp. 80–92.
DuPlessis, Rachel Blau (2016), 'Newer Freewomen and Modernism', in *The Cambridge History of Modernism*, ed. Vincent Sherry. Cambridge: Cambridge University Press, pp. 533–54.
Forty, Adrian (2012), *Concrete and Culture: A Material History*. London: Reaktion Books.
Garrington, Abbie (2013), *Haptic Modernism: Touch and the Tactile in Modernist Writing*. Edinburgh: Edinburgh University Press.
Garrison, John (2015), *Glass*. London: Bloomsbury Academic.
Green, Henry (2017), *Living*. New York: New York Review Books.
Greenwood, William Henry (1884), *Steel and Iron*, 2nd edn. London: Cassell.
Griffith, Alan Arnold (1921), 'The Phenomena of Rupture and Flow in Solids', *Philosophical Transactions of the Royal Society*, 221, pp. 163–98.
Gropius, Walter (1937), *The New Architecture and the Bauhaus*, trans. P. Morton Strand. London: Faber and Faber.
Hall, Christopher (2014), *Materials: A Very Short Introduction*. Oxford: Oxford University Press.
Highfill, Juli (2014), *Modernism and its Merchandise: The Spanish Avant-Garde and Material Culture, 1920–1930*. University Park: Pennsylvania State University Press.
Joyce, James (1993), *Ulysses*, ed. Jeri Johnson. Oxford: Oxford University Press.
Lawrence, D. H. (1987), *Letters*, vol. 4, ed. Warren Roberts, James T. Boulton and Elizabeth Mansfield. Cambridge: Cambridge University Press.
Lawrence, D. H. (2006), *Lady Chatterley's Lover*, ed. Michael Squires. Harmondsworth: Penguin Books.
Lawrence, D. H. (2013), *Poems*, ed Christopher Pollnitz, 2 vols. Cambridge: Cambridge University Press.
Mansfield, Katherine (2001), *Collected Stories*. Harmondsworth: Penguin Books.
Mao, Douglas (1998), *Solid Objects: Modernism and the Test of Production*. Princeton, NJ: Princeton University Press.
Marshik, Celia (2017), *At the Mercy of Their Clothes: Modernism, the Middlebrow, and British Garment Culture*. New York: Columbia University Press.
Miller, Daniel (2010), *Stuff*. Cambridge: Polity Press.
Misa, Thomas J. (2004), *Leonardo to the Internet: Technology and Culture from the Renaissance to the Present*. Baltimore: Johns Hopkins University Press.
'Molecular Forces' (1923), *Times*, 14 September, p. 6.
Morrisson, Mark S. (2017), *Modernism, Science, and Technology*. London: Bloomsbury Academic.
Murphet, Julian, Helen Groth and Penelope Hone, eds (2017), *Sounding Modernism: Rhythmic and Sonic Mediation in Modern Literature and Film*. Edinburgh: Edinburgh University Press.
Plock, Vike Martina (2017), *Modernism, Fashion, and Interwar Women Writers*. Edinburgh: Edinburgh University Press.
'Progress of Science, The' (1925), *The Times*, 28 December, p. 7.
Richardson, Dorothy (1917), *Honeycomb*. London: Duckworth.
Rosenhain, Walter (1919), *Glass Manufacture*, 2nd edn. London: Constable.
Ruskin, John (1903–12 [1858]), 'The Work of Iron, in Nature, Art, and Policy', in *Works*, ed. E. T. Cook and Alexander Wedderburn, 39 vols. London: Longmans, Green), vol. 16, pp. 375–411.

Saunders, Max (2019), *Imagined Futures: Writing, Science, and Modernity in the To-day and To-morrow Series, 1923–31*. Oxford: Oxford University Press.
Sinclair, May (1917), *A Defence of Idealism: Some Questions and Conclusions*. London: Macmillan.
Sinclair, May (1980 [1919]), *Mary Olivier: A Life*. London: Virago.
Sinclair, May (1990 [1918]), 'The Novels of Dorothy Richardson', in *The Gender of Modernism*, ed. Bonnie Kime Scott. Bloomington: Indiana University Press, pp. 442–8.
Sinclair, May (2006), *Uncanny Stories*. Ware: Wordsworth Editions.
Siraganian, Lisa (2012), *Modernism's Other Work: The Art Object's Political Life*. Oxford: Oxford University Press.
Somaini, Antonio (2016), 'Walter Benjamin's Media Theory: The *Medium* and the *Apparat*', *Grey Room*, 62, pp. 6–41.
Trotter, David (2013), *Literature in the First Media Age: Britain between the Wars*. Cambridge, MA: Harvard University Press.
Truran, Wendy (2017), 'Feminism, Freedom and the Hierarchy of Happiness in the Psychological Novels of May Sinclair', in *May Sinclair: Re-Thinking Bodies and Minds*, ed. Rebecca Bowler and Claire Drewery. Edinburgh: Edinburgh University Press, pp. 79–97.
Wallenberg, Louise and Andrea Kollnitz, eds (2019), *Fashion and Modernism*. London: Bloomsbury Visual Arts.
Whitworth, Michael (2001), *Einstein's Wake*. Oxford: Oxford University Press.
Woolf, Virginia (1984), 'Modern Fiction', in *The Common Reader: First Series*. London: Harcourt, pp. 146–54.
'X-ray Research' (1920), *Times*, 6 March, p. 13.

9

Advertising: Magazine Ads and the Creation of Femininity in Early Twentieth-century America

Einav Rabinovitch-Fox

During the last third of the nineteenth century, the United States experienced the rise of a new mass market that reshaped social, political and economic relationships. Changes in transportation and development of new technologies, as well as shifting trends in immigration and labour, brought with them a restructuring of business practices and a surge in mass production that ushered in a modern era of consumption. New patterns of merchandising, display and distribution enabled more and more people to gain access to new products, creating a distinct culture that historian William Leach defines as 'Consumer Capitalism'. This culture was based on celebration of the 'new', the valorisation of individual pleasure and the heralding of monetary value as the predominant measure of worth, and placed consumption and the circulation of goods at the centre of its aesthetic and moral sensibilities (Leach 1994: xiii–xiv). The advertising industry, together with other consumer institutions such as department stores and the press, was instrumental to the development and entrenchment of this modern consumer culture through the shaping of social and cultural attitudes. By promoting a modernist aesthetics and using new print technologies, advertising offered Americans, who had traditionally welcomed modernisation and technological progress, advice on how to negotiate their search for identity in a changing world, pushing products as answers to the public's concerns and fears (Marchand 1985: 9–13).

Advertising – both as communication technology and as a profession – created a new visual language that capitalised on the increasingly visual orientation of a society that emphasised appearance and personality. The use of images for commercial purposes grew in conjunction with the popularisation of mass media and technological improvements in printing. By the 1890s, many big monthly magazines – *Ladies' Home Journal, Good Housekeeping, McCall's, Delineator, Woman's Home Companion* and *Pictorial Review* among them – dropped their price to ten cents, becoming more dependent on advertising revenues than on subscribers for profits. This move not only expanded these magazines' circulation and outreach dramatically, but also turned them into a profitable arena for advertisers, who tapped into potential new consumers. The gradual introduction of colour printing and the increasing numbers of illustrations added to the visual appeal of magazines as an advertising space. As advertisements became an integral part of magazine content, their commercial message also entered contemporaries' daily lives and homes (Scanlon 1995: 9; Laird 1998: 220–7; Peiss 1998a).

Yet advertising not only promoted the consumption of goods, but also served as a means for promoting social values and ideologies. Just like trends in architecture and art, which gave a tangible expression to modernist ideas, advertising was a medium that operated as an agent of modernisation. As historians of advertising have shown, advertisements function both as a mirror of social attitudes and as an efficient medium for shaping popular notions, especially regarding gender, race and class (Davis 2000; Lears 1994; Marchand 1985). Particularly during the early twentieth century, a time of tremendous social change, advertising became a potent medium through which contemporaries made sense of these changes. Both as a technological form of communication and as a form of art, advertising encapsulated modernist ideas and aesthetics. The vision that advertising offered was commercial in its nature and was targeted towards the white middle class. However, while advertisements' messages were almost never too radical or too subversive for the potential consumer to relate to, advertising did function as an agent of change and as a modernising force, promoting new images, new identities and new values.

Since women comprised the bulk of magazine readership and consumers, advertisers largely catered to their tastes and wills by selling an image of femininity that appealed to large segments of the population. As a 1917 promotion piece for the ad agency J. Walter Thompson Company argued, 85 per cent of all retail purchases were made by women, and thus it was important to address them directly and efficiently (Women in Advertising 1917: 7–8). Indeed, as advertisers' assumption that the consumer was a 'she' became an undisputed truth in the industry, advertising became a tool to define her image and its meanings. In their attempts to win women's hearts, minds and wallets, advertisers constructed their own standards of what the 'modern woman' should look like and how she should behave, also shaping public discourses and understandings in the process. However, the power of advertising to mould public opinion was never absolute. Although new technologies enabled advertisements to become more persuasive and powerful, the construction of female modernity in the interwar period was a constant process of negotiation. Often advertisements presented conflicting messages, simultaneously celebrating women's freedom and demarcating its boundaries.

This chapter examines how advertising provided new spatial and visual means to shape modern feminine identities and their meanings in the early twentieth century. During the 1920s and 1930s, American advertising content and style adopted a distinctly modern look that transformed both the industry and Americans' attitudes towards consumption. By focusing on advertisements for consumer products that became associated with modern living – cosmetics, cigarettes, cars and electrical appliances – I argue that the advertising industry constructed modernity as a distinctly female experience, using the appeals of consumer culture to define what it meant to be a modern woman. These consumer products not only facilitate a more convenient, prosperous and mobile way of life, but were themselves new technologies that constructed modern female bodies and selves. Advertising played a crucial role in the mainstreaming of these techniques, highlighting the process of (re)shaping women's bodies and movement as crucial to the production of modernity (Nicholas 2015: 38).

While the vision that advertisements and ad people (many of them women) created was often limited in terms of race and class, it promoted female modernity as a liberating and a democratic experience, offering women tangible ways to imagine their new roles in society. Furthermore, women were not passive objects on which modernity was imposed through consumerist ideology, but played an active role in shaping the identity of the 'modern woman'. In understanding these women's negotiation of both the possibilities and limits that consumer culture enabled them, this chapter recentres advertising as an important realm where modernity, gender notions and questions of power were being redefined in the interwar period in America. I shift the focus from the masculine gaze and technologies of production as the defining experiences of modernity to highlight the important role that women's consumption had in shaping modernity. Far from being a superficial or ephemeral medium, advertising enables us to put women back into the narrative of modernism, not only as objects but as active agents.

* * *

Advertising as a promotional technology had developed in the early nineteenth century with the mercantile revolution that brought consumer goods to the American public. Yet, if in the 1920s advertising was not a new technique, it became more sophisticated, creative and innovative than in previous decades, and thus also more influential. Moving away from carnivalesque, chaotic and sometimes even dubious forms of marketing by peddlers and hustlers, ad agencies that formed in the late nineteenth century adopted more systematic, corporate and scientific methods of promotion (Lears 1994; Peiss 1998a). Advertisers began in the 1920s to implement new psychological theories about motivation and identity that shifted the marketing viewpoint from the product to the consumer. Increasingly, the main emphasis was on targeting women's emotional yearnings, which were formulated as if they were tangible objects attainable through the acquisition of goods. Rather than providing information about a product, advertisements began to sell a state of mind, a lifestyle – a worldview and constitutive reflection of the consumer for whom the product was intended (Marchand 1985: 9–13). Advertising copy included participatory anecdotes and illustrations, and used more direct, colloquial language that propelled consumers to imagine themselves in certain environments and scenes not necessarily connected directly to use. For example, an advertisement for Camel cigarettes invited the reader to imagine herself at the horse track, applying her good taste and 'fine breeding' not only to her 'good clothes, good manners, good society', but also to her selection of cigarette brand (Camel Ad 1929a: 152a).

Technological and commercial developments in print and photography were instrumental to these changes. In particular, the evolution of photolithography, photoengraving, halftones and electrotype techniques facilitated the production of images and improved the overall appearance of ads in magazines. Increasingly, small, non-visual copy, confined in half-columns and the corners of pages, was replaced by full-page displays with bolder headlines and large images. These technological improvements turned magazines into a more visually oriented medium. But more importantly, they made print content much more consumer-oriented (Garvey 1996: 9–11; Laird 1998: 218–20). In periodicals such as *Ladies' Home Journal*, *The Delineator*, *Vogue* and *Saturday Evening Post*, distinctions between editorial and promotional content were often blurred. Many advertisements were disguised as advice columns, stories and op-eds, and editorials in general promoted a consumerist agenda which, even if not promoting a specific brand, solidified the connections between consumption, beauty, modernity and progress (Scanlon 1995: 202; Peiss 1998a).

Moreover, the gradual introduction of colour printing made images not only more realistic and authentic, but – most importantly to advertisers – eye-catching (Leach 1994: 45, 50). According to historian Roland Marchand, in the early 1920s, ads in colour had grown to occupy between twelve and thirty-eight per cent of magazines' pages, creating a powerful statement against the greyish blandness of other pages. The use of colour in ads contributed to the process of turning utilitarian products into fashion goods, thus enhancing the message that ads were selling a lifestyle more than a product (Marchand 1985: 121–2). A colour advertisement for Cannon towels, for example, marketed its product as a fashionable accessory, arguing that, like the fashionable woman, a 'Bathroom needs new clothes' (Figure 9.1). Describing the towels as if they were a collection of clothes, the ad described the '[f]all fashions' as 'more handsome and helpful than ever'. Offering the choice of six bright colours, ranging from yellow to red and purple, the ad informed the reader that they 'were chosen by a noted stylist, after a careful study of the new bathroom tones'. Depicting two fashionably dressed women in a bathroom surrounded with colourful towels, the copy situated towels not as an everyday product but as part of a fashionable wardrobe (Cannon Ad 1931: C3).

Notions of gender, as well as class, played an important role in influencing the visual language of ads. Framing women as experts in style and fashion, advertisements used colourful images that spoke directly to the potential consumer's sense of taste. However, although advertisers put great effort into trying to understand women's motives, desires and worldviews, these efforts were often based more on predetermined assumptions regarding women's roles and character. In general, Victorian gender notions that viewed the female consumer as passive, capricious, irrational and ignorant maintained their hold on advertisers even into the 1920s and 1930s (McGovern 2006: 36–7). Advertising expert Carl Naether, for example, advised copywriters to use soft and more suggestive terminology, poetic images, French phrases and delicate touches, arguing that such techniques would be more effective on women than on men. Moreover, despite acknowledging the importance of presenting a 'woman's point of view' in ads, Naether believed that 'copy for sales letters, booklets and advertisements intended for feminine reading should, in general, be first prepared by men' (Naether 1928: 19). This approach led to a limited view of women's experiences as advertisers treated all female consumers as a universal group, united by their supposed natural inclination to beauty, motherhood and 'inarticulate longing' for material goods (Peiss 1998a). Ads for women tended to focus more on the benefits of consumption, deliberately and carefully appealing to the consumer's subjective desires and fears (Marchand 1985: 11–16, 66–9). While, overall, advertisers saw women as rational consumers, they promoted social mobility and popularity as the most desirable effects of a product. Slogans such as 'You Can Look Younger' on the one hand, and 'She looks old enough to be his mother' or 'Once she was welcomed ... now she isn't invited' on the other, entailed both promises and warnings for social consequences in relation to product use (Madame Jeannette Ad 1926: 101; Listerine Ad 1931: 115; Lysol Ad 1928: 77). This new form of emotional marketing was seen as more suitable for targeting women and it increasingly became part of the mainstream style of advertising in the interwar period in America.

If the malleable and gullible 'Mrs. Consumer' image maintained its popularity, changes in women's lives as well as in the advertising business helped to revise some

Figure 9.1 Cannon Towels advertisement, *Vogue*, 1 October 1931. Image published with permission of ProQuest LLC. Further reproduction is prohibited without permission.

of the attitudes towards women. New informational technologies, such as market research and customer surveys implemented by the industry in the 1920s, offered a more nuanced depiction of the female consumer. A 1924 article in the leading trade journal *Printers' Ink* divided female consumers into four groups: the housewife, toward whom 'the largest percentage of advertising is aimed'; the 'society woman', who was identified as a young girl being 'the chief consumer of fashionable clothing, cosmetics, toilet articles, and all sorts of high-priced luxuries'; and lastly, the 'club woman' and the 'business woman', two new types of consumers, whose needs differed from those of 'the woman in the home' (Maule 1924: 105). While there were many overlaps between these groups, this classification expanded the variety of feminine cultural types, allowing a more complex understanding of the modern woman.

In addition, the growing numbers of women working in the business also helped to change attitudes towards consumers. These highly educated, middle-class, white women, often involved in reform or suffrage work prior to their careers in advertising, brought with them a more complex 'woman's point of view', which created a less monolithic understanding of the 'typical' female consumer (Davis 2000: 80–1; McGovern 2006: 40–1; Sivulka 2012: 151–2). Frances Maule – a veteran suffragist who made a career as an executive copywriter at J. Walter Thompson Advertising Company – argued that '[w]hen we sit down ... to try to visualize the woman purchaser, we should do well to recall to our minds the fact – so well expressed in the old suffrage slogan – that "Women Are People."' Maule rejected the 'good old conventional "angel-idiot" conception of women', which was 'hard to find in real life' or unlikely 'to be true of any wide class of modern women', and instead suggested that women be seen as a more complex group of types and interests (Maule 1924: 105). Based on her own experience as a market researcher at a department store sales counter, Maule argued that advertisers should treat women first and foremost as rational consumers. She stressed that despite differences between them, as consumers, all women were practical, used a good deal of shrewdness, were capable of good judgement and thus deserved the utmost respect from advertisers (Maule 1922: 9–11).

Although women like Maule comprised a small minority (women made up only about three per cent of professionals in advertising in 1930) and these women were generally relegated to gender- segregated departments and occupations in ad agencies, their status as 'experts in femininity' enabled them to gain some influence in the industry (Peiss 1998a). 'Having all these domestic and personal interests in addition to what is strictly her "job" is what makes [a woman] a better advertising person,' argued one of Maule's colleagues, Aminta Casseres. Unlike men, Casseres claimed, adwomen could get intimately acquainted with products targeted at women to create better and more effective copy that appealed to female consumers (Casseres 1926: 87). Embodying a unique position both as representatives of the 'modern woman' and as an influential authority in shaping her image, these female professionals created the ideal consumer in their image. They portrayed her as a competent, independent and fashion-savvy woman who sought to take advantage of the new possibilities that became available. While this was a fairly narrow image that heralded the young, white, middle-class career woman, it posed an important alternative to the Victorian 'Mrs. Consumer', expanding the visual vocabulary with which women could identify. Indeed, while many ads celebrated the society woman who lived a life of leisure, no small number of ads, like the one for Ford (Figure 9.2), specifically targeted the modern businesswoman, depicting women in

Figure 9.2 Ford advertisement, *Vogue*, 1 April 1924. Image published with permission of ProQuest LLC. Further reproduction is prohibited without permission.

work settings and offices and appealing to their specific needs as working women (Ford Ad 1924a: 128; Good Shepherd Ad 1935: 110).

Yet, these adwomen not only used their position to create a more complex view of the female consumer or to legitimise women's work for wages. Many – especially those who entered the profession after working for women's suffrage – harnessed advertising to promote more feminist agendas that celebrated women's independence and freedom. In a campaign for Pond's Cream that used celebrities' testimonials to promote the product, the female copywriters intentionally secured the wealthy suffragist and feminist Alva Belmont to give the first endorsement. Although it was unclear what commercial value Belmont brought to the campaign, particularly as she refused to put her face on the ad, the copywriters insisted on launching it with an interview that associated the cause of women's rights with the importance of skin care (Scanlon 1995: 192–6; Pond's Ad 1924: 65). Thus, although their feminist message was always entangled in a consumerist agenda, adwomen played an important role in diversifying attitudes towards female consumers. Through their ad copy, they helped in the mainstreaming of feminism in popular culture, providing legitimacy for women's demands for freedom and equality.

Indeed, American advertisers, regardless of their gender, were not ignorant of the changes in women's status and consciousness as a result of their mobilisation during the First World War and the success of women's suffrage. As more women entered education, the labour force and politics, they used their role as consumers to advance social agendas and bolster their claims for citizenship. Women organised boycotts and 'buycotts', protesting against rising food prices, labour conditions and public health hazards (Glickman 2009; Cohen 2003; Frank 1994; Orleck 1995; Storrs 2000). Yet they also used their power as consumers to claim individual freedoms and to challenge gender norms regarding propriety and sexual expression (Rabinovitch-Fox 2016; Nicholas 2015). Advertisers capitalised on this new reality by reshaping the image of the female consumer and adjusting commercial messages to appeal to this sentiment. Rather than portraying the career woman or the young, sexually liberated girl as a threat, advertisers marketed these 'types' as new feminine role models in the interwar period.

In particular, advertisers capitalised on women's new sense of political citizenship to promote sales. Framing consumption as a political exercise, advertisements equated marketplace choices with political freedom, thereby emphasising women's 'natural' role as consumers as the manifestation of their political rights (McGovern 2006: 67–8, 70). According to advertising consultant Christine Frederick, consumers 'vote in broad democratic fashion at great popular elections, the polls being open every day at a million or more retail stores' (Frederick 1929: 322–3). Frederick suggested that advertisers should take note of this power and use it to boost sales. A General Electric advertisement implemented Frederick's advice, harnessing women's new sense of freedom as a sales tactic. Titled 'The Suffrage and the Switch', the ad conflated the achievement of women's suffrage with the progress that electricity brought to domestic life (Figure 9.3). Portraying a fashionable woman turning an electrical switch next to a smaller picture of a woman's hand casting a ballot, the copy announced that '[w]oman suffrage made the American woman the political equal of her man. The little switch which commands the great servant Electricity is making her workshop the equal of her man's' (General Electric Ad 1923: 69). Similarly, an ad for Campbell's

Figure 9.3 'The Suffrage and the Switch', General Electric advertisement, *The Independent*, 18 August 1923.

Soups encouraged the American Housewife to 'cast her daily vote for Campbell's at the grocery store' (Campbell's Soup Co. Ad 1923: 91) Another ad for Nujol Laboratories adopted the suffrage slogan 'Equal Rights for Women' in promoting their product, assuring the reader that 'Every woman has the right to be as healthy, vigorous and efficient as her husband, son, brother, or friend' (Nujol Ad 1919: 58). By providing a prescription for modern femininity, one in which women perform their household duties while also realising their political citizenship, advertisements like these framed consumption not as a frivolous act, but as a parallel arena for choice and control, one where women could exert their rationality as citizens and express their modern selves (Cott 1987: 172; McGovern 2006: 81–5). Yet in framing consumption as citizenship, these empowering messages also reduced political participation to a consumer choice, equating political power with buying products.

Advertisers also promoted a democratic message, suggesting that through consumption all women could become part of modern culture. 'You are not barred from beauty,' an advertisement for a face cream announced (Daggett & Ramsdell Ad 1926: 131). Marketing beauty as a right every woman was entitled to possess, an ad for Palmolive soap claimed that 'This Beauty Every Girl Can Have' (Palmolive Ad 1922: 75). This type of marketing constructed modernity as an attainable goal and as a right. However, it also constructed modernity as an individual choice, disregarding more structural economic and racial social barriers that might have prevented women from fully participating in consumer culture. 'Perhaps the only trouble with your complexion is just – lack of will-power,' a 1924 ad for Woodbury soap suggested. Putting the onerous task of achieving beauty on women's personal decisions, it told the reader that the reason 'why so many women fail to keep a lovely skin after they have passed their twenties' was because they were too lazy or too incompetent to maintain a 'simple daily care' regimen for their skins (Woodbury Soap Ad 1924: 95). Moreover, while advertisements celebrated individuality, they also encouraged conformity, using peer pressure and claims for the national popularity of their products in order to entice sales. An ad for Camel cigarettes argued that while gowns and jewellery – 'these things [that] are so much a part of the subtle web of personality' – reflect 'the clever woman's' distinct taste, their choice in cigarettes 'is strikingly uniform' (Camel Ad 1929b: C4). Instead of encouraging one's individual taste, the Camel ad promoted adherence to a conformist ideal to which all women should aspire.

Advertisers also played an instrumental role in the popularisation of a new youth culture that arose after the war, which put an emphasis on sexual expression and individual self-fulfilment (D'Emilio and Freedman 2012: 233–4, 241). Capitalising on the image of the 'flapper', the beauty ideal of the post-war decade, advertisements positioned her youth as the epitome of freedom and modernity. A 1929 Franklin Automobile Company ad, for example, argued that their car was 'as smart and as modern as youth itself', and a Cadillac advertisement claimed that 'one quality that women deeply admire in the Cadillac is its unrivalled capacity of *remaining young*', thus making youth synonymous with modern technology (Franklin Ad 1929: C2; Cadillac Ad 1924: 105). The flapper image, itself reminiscent of modern skyscrapers and vertical simplicity, became associated with technological progress and its benefits. An ad for Edison Mazda Lamps titled 'Let Me SEE Your Wares', also exploited the connection between the flapper's image and modernity by depicting a fashionable flapper on a background of New York City. Announcing that she was 'the purchasing agent of America', the ad targeted store owners who wanted to be associated with what the flapper represented. 'I must see things well displayed in good light,' the flapper in the copy advised. 'Good lighting in your display windows draws me into your store. Good light inside shows me that your store is neat, clean, sanitary, modern – a safe place to buy' (Mazda Ad 1929: 149). By celebrating the modern flapper as a positive selling point, ads like this helped to popularise her image and legitimise her behaviour. Yet, they also constructed the flapper not as a passive consumer, but as an independent agent of modernity who had the power to bring technological advancement. As they depicted women driving cars, using appliances or just enjoying the perks of modern living, advertisements framed women's freedom not as a threat to gender norms but as a necessary component of the modern woman and of modern living (Jordan Ad 1926: 140). It was through their use of technology and its celebration in advertising that women became crucial to the dissemination of modernism. Rather than through production, the flapper's affinity with technology was through her consumption of modern products. Ads framed consumption in itself both as a testament for technological savviness and as the route to achieve it.

Women's freedom thus became associated with modernity and the advancement of science, positioning technology as the enabler of women's sexual, economic and political freedoms. Advertisers framed modernity as a female trait, turning consumption into the vehicle through which the liberated modern woman could claim her independence. An advertisement for Ford Motor Company, for example, encouraged women to 'venture into new and untried places', asserting their freedom to challenge conventions and break social limitations (Ford Ad 1924b: 47). Similarly, an advertisement for Perfection Oil Cook Stoves and Ovens heralded its product as providing women with a 'New Freedom' from long kitchen hours and the domestic realm. Depicting a young, fashionably dressed woman stepping into a car driven by another woman, the advertisement alluded to the possibility that modern consumption enabled women (Cleveland Metal Products Co. 1925: 141). By connecting consumption and women's liberation, advertising constructed the modern consumer not as a submissive housewife, but as an independent and modern woman. Through the use of technology, women could free themselves not only from the drudgery of household chores, but also from traditional gender conventions and roles. Technology thus became the conduit through which women could both experience freedom and claim it.

The theme of freedom was most pronounced in a campaign for Kotex disposable sanitary pads. First launched on the national market in 1921 by Kimberly-Clark, the Kotex disposable sanitary pads were themselves a new technological invention that signified modernity in their production and function, but also through their marketing tactics. Often depicting a single woman or a group of women in active, leisurely settings, ads appealed to women's desire to participate in modernity without barriers of tradition or propriety. By alluding to the technological and military origins of the product – developed from bandages used in hospitals during the First World War – the ads touted the scientific knowledge invested in creating the pads and emphasised their sanitary and hygienic qualities. Yet, Kimberly-Clark moved beyond marketing the pads as mere technological solution. The Kotex campaign turned the consumption of mass-made sanitary pads into a lifestyle choice for modern women, allowing them to exhibit their bodies even while menstruating. It also turned technological savviness into a crucial component of modern femininity, furthering the connection between women's bodies and progress (Mandziuk 2010: 43, 46–8).

While using women's sexual appeal as a selling strategy had been a common theme in advertisement since the 1910s, the Kotex campaign specifically connected sexuality to ideas of women's mobility, independence and active lifestyle. Although ads never discussed menstruation explicitly, the campaign offered a new understanding of women's sexuality, seeing it not as a burden but as a thing to be celebrated. Ads promoted the idea that a woman could and should be active outside of the home, even during their menstrual period. 'Active outdoor days demand this comfortable, lasting sanitary protection,' one copy announced (Kotex Ad 1930a: 25). Depicting two young women dressed in masculine riding attire and close-fitting hats in front of a car, the ad offered a visual template for the modern woman who was not afraid to challenge social taboos regarding both her sexuality and her appearance.

Moreover, despite presenting menstruation as a 'bodily problem' and not as a natural phenomenon, ads offered women a route to claim their freedom by adopting not only a modern technology but also a modern lifestyle. 'Active Women of Today are Free,' announced another ad, legitimising the freedoms that women were beginning to claim for themselves. Depicting a group of three young, fashionable women, one holding a tennis racket and the others golf clubs, the ad asserted that women are now free from the 'handicap of yesterday's hygienic worries' and can wear sheer frocks, engage in sports and live their lives to their full potential (Kotex Ad 1927: 15). Yet, the freedom that Kotex offered was not without limitations. One ad suggested that although women were free to engage in various activities, they still had to maintain rigid standards of beauty and behaviour. Modern living demands both freedom and perfect poise, no matter what day of the month, or if engaging in sports, business or 'some other interest', it argued (Kotex Ad 1930b: 16a).

Thus, although advertising provided a space for women to imagine new freedoms and alternatives to the Victorian model of femininity, the commercialised nature of advertisements also set the boundaries of these freedoms. Indeed, advertisements often sent conflicting messages to their readers. On the one hand, advertisers characterised female consumers as potentates ruling over the market, naturalising their sovereignty and public power as political subjects. Yet, on the other hand, they were also careful not to portray women as too independent, emphasising that their status as 'citizen consumers' was limited to the realm of domesticity and women's traditional gender roles (McGovern 2006: 75, 79–80; Davis 2000: 81–3). An advertisement for Libby's canned beef boasted this kind of message, arguing that a woman can 'be a good mother and home-maker without sacrificing the time she needs for her own self-development'. If the copy promoted a feminist message that women could and should pursue their own interests beyond the domestic sphere, it did not challenge more traditional gender conventions that it was a woman's responsibility to make dinner for her family. While canned beef helped save time on household chores, the ad did not call for a more equal division of labour within the house, or advocated for women to forgo their familial duties. Rather than providing a challenge or reconfiguring gender roles, the ad reinforced them by bounding them in a consumerist discourse. Modern technologies like canned beef and hygienic pads could offer women freedom from the home but not from the confines of femininity (Libby's Ad 1920: 57).

Advertisements also did not offer all women the possibility to enjoy the promises of the modern consumer culture. The segregated nature of the advertising business meant that the ideal American consumer was often imagined very narrowly, as a middle-class, white and, as the 1920s progressed, young woman. Indeed, although advertisements offered variety in terms of age and marital status, they also delineated clear boundaries in terms of class and race. Especially in popular magazines, non-white women were never depicted as modern or young, and most certainly not as potential consumers (Scanlon 1995: 171, 211, 219–23). African Americans, for example, were commonly represented as servants or chauffeurs, or as stereotypical 'mammy' characters, most notably 'Aunt Jemima' (Aunt Jemima Mills Company Ad 1925: 114).[1] Perpetuating racist notions and visions of slavery, advertisements counterpoised the Black female body with ideals of technological modernity and feminine beauty that were always presented as white (Scanlon 1995: 220; Manring 1998: 88–9, 131–3).

Depictions of other women of colour were no less stereotypical. In a campaign for Palmolive soap, the promises of modern beauty, presented by an image of a young, modern, bobbed-hair flapper, were touted as the triumph of modern science over ancient traditions. The ad juxtaposes the image of the flapper in the top right corner with a depiction of two Middle Eastern women dressed in ethnic clothes in the bottom left corner (Figure 9.4). The two women, one with white skin and the other Black, represent the 'Oriental' allure of the product, based on a 'blend of rare oriental oils, famous for 3,000 years as cosmetics'. Yet they were not depicted as models of beauty but as a primitive version of the modern woman. Moreover, the position of the women also conveyed the superiority of modern science. Not only was the Black Middle Eastern woman kneeling in front of her white partner, but it was the modern flapper who looked down at both of them, creating a clear hierarchy of both race and progress (Palmolive Ad 1922: 75). Other ads from the campaign positioned the modern woman with images of ancient Greece or Egypt, capitalising on the exotic allure of these cultures. The depiction of

Figure 9.4 'This Beauty Every Girl Can Have', Palmolive advertisement, *The Ladies' Home Journal*, January 1922. Image published with permission of ProQuest LLC. Further reproduction is prohibited without permission.

'Oriental others' in advertising, especially from Asia, was used to demarcate class and racial hierarchies, validating the white American middle-class woman's modern superiority and power as consumer (Takagi 2003: 301–19).

If women of colour were barred from modernity, advertising offered more options for ethnic white minorities in America to engage with modern consumer culture. Ads for cosmetics and beauty products provided Southern and Eastern European women, and even Latinas, with 'a route to whiteness' via hair removal and skin-bleaching products that promised to change their appearance. According to these ads, through this intervention of cosmetic technologies that were meant to alter their bodies, ethnic white women could access modernity and its promise of progress. Some ads capitalised on the 'exotic' designation of ethnic white minorities, appealing specifically to immigrant women and encouraging them to embrace their looks. For example, an advertisement for Armand Beauty Products promoted the diversity of 'beauty types', alluding to the oriental origins of types like Cleopatra and the Queen of Sheba. Defined as 'dark and mysterious', these types suggested that non-Anglo-Saxon women could also be beautiful if they would use the right product. However, despite the inclusive message, the variations between the looks were minuscule: all 'types' represented white, young women who differ only in hair style and colour. Such framing pointed to the limitations that advertising could offer to women who could not fit with the white, middle-class image of the flapper (Peiss 1998b: 145–9). In the end, advertising afforded the promise of modernity only to those who had access to certain class and race privileges, constructing femininity in narrow terms.

Indeed, the vision advertisements presented was full of contradictions. As Marchand has argued, the casting of women as modern subjects in ads relied on a complex balance that defined modernity both as the realm of business rationality (efficiency, control, technological sophistication) and as the realm of fashion (expressiveness, changeability, luxury). Yet despite women's progress in the business sense of the term 'modern', it was their modernity in the fashion sense of the term that was more dominant (Marchand 1985: 168). Readers had to navigate between empowering messages that credited them with the agency to shape their lives, and a limiting perspective on how their lives should look and what the important things were to which they should aspire. Yet in these navigations, advertising also opened up a space, albeit subtle and non-radical, to negotiate more complex understandings of the modern woman and her changing roles in society. As advertisements depicted women in scenes of leisure and work, driving cars and playing sports, they acted as agents of change, turning these activities into part of the everyday life of American women. They not only positioned women as the beneficiaries of technological progress, but turned technology into the main route through which female modernity was manifested and made possible. And as advertisements convinced women to enact their independence, their freedom or their right to be beautiful, they also framed consumption as a tangible route to achieve these goals. While only a minority of women could live up to the ideal that was presented in ads, the modern woman's image became a cultural standard that has shaped contemporaries' views of femininity in this period.

* * *

Advertising in the early twentieth century served as a cultural barometer for changing attitudes and values in society. Ads provided a prescriptive template for engaging with modern life, in which young, white, middle-class, slender and beautiful women achieved freedom through the consumption of goods. Advertising offered women new ways to invent themselves, an access to independence and a legitimisation of their sexuality. Yet, these promises were often limited by class and racial barriers that prevented a full participation in the market and enjoyment of the opportunities it provided. Nevertheless, the use of gendered discourse and imagery that was based on emotional appeal and use of colour shifted the focus to the role of women as consumers and provided contemporaries with a visual vocabulary to shape the meanings of modern feminine identities. While advertising did not invent the modern woman, it played a crucial role in demarcating the boundaries of her image and her freedom. Connecting modernity and technological savviness to understandings of gender, advertising became the medium through which the modern woman and her meanings came to be defined in public discourse.

Note

1. The racist image of Aunt Jemima has come under scrutiny as a result of the Black Lives Matter movement and the protests following the death of George Floyd. After years in which Aunt Jemima stood for Black oppression and the romanticising of slavery, the company announced, as of 17 June 2020, it will no longer use the image on its products.

Works Cited

'Aunt Jemima Mills Company Ad' (1925), *The Ladies' Home Journal*, March, p. 114.
'Cadillac Ad' (1924), *Vogue*, 15 September, p. 105.
'Camel Ad' (1929a), *Vogue*, 12 October, p. 152a.
'Camel Ad' (1929b), *Vogue*, 8 June, p. C4.
'Campbell's Soup Co. Ad' (1923), *Harper's Bazaar*, November, p. 91.
'Cannon Ad' (1931), *Vogue*, 1 October, p. C3.
Casseres, Aminta (1926), 'Agencies Prefer Men!', *Printers' Ink*, August, pp. 35, 82, 85–7.
'Cleveland Metal Products Co. Ad' (1925), *The Ladies' Home Journal*, May, p. 141.
Cohen, Lizabeth (2003), *Consumers' Republic: The Politics of Consumption in Postwar America*. New York: Knopf.
Cott, Nancy F. (1987), *The Grounding of Modern Feminism*. New Haven, CT: Yale University Press.
'Daggett & Ramsdell Ad' (1926), *The Ladies' Home Journal*, January, p. 131.
Davis, Simone Weil (2000), *Living Up to the Ads: Gender Fictions of the 1920s*. Durham, NC: Duke University Press.
D'Emilio, John and Estelle B. Freedman (2012), *Intimate Matters*, 3rd edn. Chicago: University of Chicago Press.
'Ford Ad' (1924a), *Vogue*, 1 April, p. 128.
'Ford Ad' (1924b), *The Delineator*, October, p. 47.
Frank, Dana (1994), *Purchasing Power: Consumer Organizing, Gender and the Seattle Labor Movement 1919–1929*. Cambridge: Cambridge University Press.
'Franklin Ad' (1929), *Vogue*, 22 June, p. C2.
Frederick, Christine (1929), *Selling Mrs. Consumer*. New York: Business Bourse.
Garvey, Ellen Gruber (1996), *The Adman in the Parlor: Magazines and the Gendering of Consumer Culture 1880–1910*. New York: Oxford University Press.
'General Electric Ad' (1923), *The Independent*, 18 August, p. 69.

Glickman, Lawrence B. (2009), *Buying Power: A History of Consumer Activism in America*. Chicago: University of Chicago Press.
'Good Shepherd Ad' (1935), *Vogue*, 1 September, p. 110.
'Jordan Ad' (1926), *Vogue*, 1 June, p. 140.
'Kotex Ad' (1927), *Vogue*, 1 September, p. 15.
'Kotex Ad' (1930a), *Vogue*, 13 October, p. 25.
'Kotex Ad' (1930b), *Vogue*, 29 September, p. 16a.
Laird, Pamela Walker (1998), *Advertising Progress: American Business and the Rise of Consumer Marketing*. Baltimore: Johns Hopkins University Press.
Leach, William (1994), *Land of Desire: Merchants, Power, and the Rise of a New American Culture*. New York: Vintage Books.
Lears, Jackson (1994), *Fables of Abundance: A Cultural History of Advertising in America*. New York: Basic Books.
'Libby's Ad' (1920), *The Ladies' Home Journal*, February, p. 57.
'Listerine Ad' (1931), *Harper's Bazaar*, July, p. 115.
'Lysol Ad' (1928), *The Ladies' Home Journal*, May, p. 77.
McGovern, Charles (2006), *Sold American: Consumption and Citizenship 1890–1945*. Chapel Hill: University of North Carolina Press.
'Madame Jeannette Ad' (1926), *The Ladies' Home Journal*, September, p. 101.
Mandziuk, Roseann M. (2010), '"Ending Women's Greatest Hygienic Mistake": Modernity and the Mortification of Menstruation in Kotex Advertising, 1921–1926', *Women's Studies Quarterly*, 38: 3/4, pp. 42–62.
Manring, Maurice M. (1998), *Slave in a Box: The Strange Career of Aunt Jemima*. Charlottesville: University Press of Virginia.
Marchand, Roland (1985), *Advertising the American Dream: Making Way for Modernity 1920–1940*. Berkeley: University of California Press.
Maule, Frances (1922), 'How to Get a Good "Consumer Image"', *JWT News Bulletin*, 84 (March), pp. 9–11, JWT archives, Box MN5: JWT News Bulletin 1922–1930, Hartman Center for Sales, Advertising and Marketing History, David M. Rubenstein Rare Book & Manuscript Library, Duke University, Durham, NC.
Maule, Frances (1924), 'The "Woman Appeal"', *Printers' Ink*, 31 January, pp. 105–10.
'Mazda Ad' (1929), *Saturday Evening Post*, 11 May, p. 149.
Naether, Carl (1928), *Advertising to Women*. New York: Prentice-Hall.
Nicholas, Jane (2015), *The Modern Girl: Feminine Modernities, the Body, and Commodities in the 1920s*. Toronto: Toronto University Press.
'Nujol Ad' (1919), *The Delineator*, March, p. 58.
Orleck, Annelise (1995), *Common Sense and Little Fire: Women and Working-Class Politics in the United States 1900–1965*. Chapel Hill: University of North Carolina Press.
'Palmolive Ad' (1922), *The Ladies' Home Journal*, January, p. 75.
Peiss, Kathy (1998a), 'American Women and the Making of Modern Consumer Culture', *Journal for Multimedia History*, 1: 1, <https://www.albany.edu/jmmh/vol1no1/peiss-text.html> (last accessed 20 January 2022).
Peiss, Kathy (1998b), *Hope in a Jar: The Making of America's Beauty Culture*. New York: Henry Holt.
'Pond's Extract Co. Ad' (1924), *The Ladies' Home Journal*, February, p. 65.
Rabinovitch-Fox, Einav (2016), 'Baby, You Can Drive My Car: Advertising Women's Freedom in 1920s America', *American Journalism: Journal of Media History*, 33: 4, pp. 372–400.
Scanlon, Jennifer (1995), *Inarticulate Longings: The Ladies' Home Journal, Gender, and the Promises of Consumer Culture*. New York: Routledge.
Sivulka, Juliann (2012), *Soap, Sex, and Cigarettes: A Cultural History of American Advertising*. Boston: Wadsworth.

Storrs, Landon R. Y. (2000), *Civilizing Capitalism: The National Consumers' League, Women's Activism, and Labor Standards in the New Deal Era*. Chapel Hill: University of North Carolina Press.

Takagi, Midori (2003), 'Consuming the "Orient": Images of Asians in White Women's Beauty Magazines, 1900–1930', in *Sexual Borderland: Constructing an American Sexual Past*, ed. K. Kennedy and S. Ullman. Columbus: Ohio State University Press, pp. 303–19.

'Women in Advertising' (1917), *Printers' Ink*, 23 August, pp. 7–8.

'Woodbury Soap Ad' (1924), *Vogue*, 1 May, p .95.

10

Photography: Gertrude Käsebier and the Maternal Line of Sight

Alix Beeston

To misquote Freud's apocrypha: sometimes a lollipop is just a lollipop. Even though the photograph is named for them – rather, because the photograph is named for them – the lollipops in the girls' hands are a distraction, a mischievous diversion (Figure 10.1).[1] If, as seems likely, the sweets were a means of occupying the girls' attention, keeping them still before the large-format camera, then the title of the image extends the beguilements of the portrait scenario. My eyes are drawn to the lollipops, as to the huge bow in little Mina's hair, as to the white kitten cuddled under her cousin Elizabeth's arm. But they are also turned away from these cute details, from these girls, who are drenched in a brightness that obscures almost as much as it illuminates. Pooling at the bottom of the stairs, washing about the room, this same light carries the series of looks that structure the image. Mina looks sidelong at Elizabeth, as Mina's mother, Hermine, looks over at her from the doorway by the stairs, and as her grandmother, Gertrude – who operates the camera – looks on at them both. In this chapter, I argue that this scene of looking, with its circuit of women's and children's gazes, offers a new vantage on the practices and effects of modernist photography in the United States, as they developed in proximity to the material, vernacular and feminised visual cultures of modernity.

At the turn of the twentieth century, Gertrude Käsebier was one of the most successful portrait photographers in the US, celebrated especially for her luminous, dreamy depictions of white mothers and their children. 'Lollipops' was taken in 1910, and it sits alongside Käsebier's earlier and better-known pictures of motherhood, such as 'Blessed Art Thou among Women' and 'The Manger (Ideal Motherhood)' (Figures 10.2 and 10.3). Like these images, as Laura Wexler argues, 'Lollipops' 'glorifies white women's role within the domestic sphere' and reflects Käsebier's investment in discourses of child education that emerged in the late nineteenth century (2000: 182). Hermine Turner, Käsebier's daughter, is presented as the modern, middle-class mother following the methods advocated by Friedrich Froebel's kindergarten movement. As Ann Taylor Allen has explained, Froebel's doctrine of 'spiritual motherhood' called for child-rearing practices that balanced attention and inattention, 'careful tending and unforced growth' (1982: 319, 322). In Käsebier's image, Hermine's gaze slips through the banisters to sustain the girls with, in Wexler's words, 'just the right mixture of maternal shelter and freedom' (2000: 188).

Meanwhile the photograph, in representing this delicate system of relations, also reproduces that system. As Käsebier's gaze arranges this tableau of daughter and

Figure 10.1 Gertrude Käsebier, 'Lollipops', ca. 1910. Digital positive from the original gelatin silver negative. Library of Congress, Gift of Mina Turner, 2006684252.

granddaughters, it models more perfectly the ideal mother's view. After the invention of photography in the 1830s and throughout the modernist period, the actions of the camera challenged conceptions of the art object in its oscillations between the human and the mechanical, between artistry and automation, and here the camera's doubled modality is phrased as a specifically maternal problem, for Käsebier, more decisively than her daughter, is active and passive, hands on and hands off, there and not there. Once her surveilling presence was taken for granted in the daily lives of her family members: 'We were neither bored nor excited by the picture taking', recalled Mina after her grandmother's death; 'it was just one of those things that happened, like sneezing or brushing your teeth' (cited in Michaels 1992: 134). Now Käsebier's presence inheres in her photographs as an open secret – as if she remains under her focusing cloth still today, hidden in plain sight.

In more than one sense, then, the philosophy of mothering that Käsebier passes down to Hermine is extended by and folded back into her photographic work. Part of the first cohort of American women photographers to achieve significant commercial and artistic success, Käsebier promulgated a sentimental mythology of white motherhood that underwrote the US imperialist construct in the late nineteenth and early twentieth centuries. Although the famous studio portraits Käsebier took of Lakota people in the late 1890s and early 1900s were lauded for their empathy, those images interact with her icons of white motherhood to normalise raced and classed logics of dominance.[2] In the case of 'Lollipops', it is not difficult to see a representation of the mother's supporting function within the white supremacist and imperialist modern nation, as the network of vertical and horizontal lines creates a visual symmetry between the upright figure of Hermine and the columns that line the stairs. And yet: why is 'Lollipops' so eerie? Why do the children invite and refuse my gaze? How should I parse Hermine's solemn expression, which feeds the larger feeling of the image, a sombre mood that shades into the sinister? Käsebier's image is distinguished by this combination of poignancy and ominousness, telescoped to Hermine's face, as she watches the children without, presumably, being seen by them. But of course she is seen – by Käsebier, and also by us. To look with impunity at those who do not see you is the risky spectatorial pleasure of all portrait photography. As gazes multiply in 'Lollipops', the image puts pressure on its visual operations, to some degree destabilising them. If the mother–photographer charms us with lollipops, does she also surveil us? Or are we otherwise implicated in this circuit of seeing, this maternal line of sight?

'Lollipops' is inexactly aligned with Progressive-era discourses of white motherhood, and it works in excess of those discourses. Beginning with the questions raised but not resolved in Käsebier's image, this chapter attends to it – along with a number of other family photographs Käsebier made in and around her New York City studio in 1909 and 1910 – as an index of a crucial moment of transition in the cultures and traditions of modernist photography in the US. The period in which Käsebier posed Hermine and her grandchildren for these images was also the period in which she was making a break from the photographer Alfred Stieglitz and his influential Photo-Secession: a break, that is, from the artists and organisations that we most readily associate with American modernist photography. Käsebier is an unusual figure within the field of modernist cultural production, even though she was one of the most prominent photographers working in New York in the years when the city's association with modernism and modernity became entrenched. She was thirty-seven years old when

Figure 10.2 Gertrude Käsebier, 'Blessed Art Thou among Women', 1899. Photogravure. Brooklyn Museum, Gift of Mr and Mrs Miguel LaSalle and Peter Sinclair, 83.263.

Figure 10.3 Gertrude Käsebier, 'The Manger (Ideal Motherhood)', 1899. Platinum print. J. Paul Getty Museum, 84.XM.160.1.

she enrolled at art school, in 1887, and approaching fifty when she opened her first studio in the Women's Exchange on East 30th Street, off Fifth Avenue. The height of her career coincided with her becoming a grandmother and she was soon known as 'Granny' not only within her family but also in photography circles. She sat uneasily between the archetypes of the True Woman and the New Woman, remaining beholden to the nineteenth-century cult of motherhood and yet committed to photography, in her words, as a medium 'especially adapted' to women and primed to yield for them 'gratifying and profitable success' as artists and professionals. These remarks are from a lecture Käsebier gave at the Photographic Society of Philadelphia in 1898, in which she also attested to how she 'had to wade through seas of criticism' on account of her heretical views – before joking, with characteristic wit, about 'the advantage of a vocation which necessitates one's being a taking woman' (1898: 270, 272).

Käsebier is not quite True, not exactly New. Even so, I turn to her as a way of not turning to Stieglitz, or Paul Strand, or Ansel Adams, or Edward Weston – the host of men who are most often cited as the 'fathers' of modernist photography in the US. My focus on Käsebier's family photography – and, more specifically, on work that dates from the later and less studied part of her career – also serves to reroute the critical tradition that relates to photography in modernism. To conceive of modernist photography as 'mothered' by Käsebier rather than 'fathered' by Stieglitz – to emphasise how, around 1910, Käsebier quits Stieglitz, rather than the other way around – is to recalibrate our understanding of photography as technology and art in the late nineteenth and early twentieth centuries. It is to see modernist photography as shaped in tandem with, not in opposition to, the materiality and dailiness of modern experience. Käsebier's 'mothered' photography stages 'touching', affective encounters between subject and object, viewer and viewed, formulated through a line of sight which is also a line of descent. Her work anticipates Roland Barthes's account, in *Camera Lucida* (1980), of photographic light as a 'carnal medium' that 'links the body of the photographed thing to [the spectator's] gaze' via a 'sort of umbilical cord' (2000: 80–1). Barthes's account has been reimagined in recent work by feminist scholars that theorises a relational and transferential model of the photographic medium.[3] Similarly, Käsebier's work foregrounds the embodied labour of photography as, to return to Mina's phrase, 'just one of those things that happened, like sneezing or brushing your teeth'.

As 'Lollipops' indicates, the photograph is an enigmatic object, even a volatile one. According to Barthes, 'Society seeks to tame the Photograph, to temper the madness which keeps threatening to explode in the face of whoever looks at it' (2000: 117). Karen Beckman interprets this madness in relation to the medium's silence, its stubborn refusal to speak: the 'illegible messages' that condense the vital complexities and conceptual lability internal to any photographic image (2013: 317). I have argued elsewhere that the most vital affordances of photography in modernism are those associated with its rupturing of the visual field, its diffusing of the truths it was meant to guarantee.[4] Because of its indexicality, its apparent fidelity to the real, the camera seemed poised to fulfil the fantasies of Cartesian perspectivalism, the dominant (if not uncontested) scopic regime of modernity. Yet these fantasies – of human individuation, of epistemic objectivity, of the mastery of the eye that knows what it sees and sees what it knows – were in fact frustrated by photography. The photograph disclosed too much and too little. It contradicted the actions of the human eye in focus, perspective and framing, revealing Walter Benjamin's 'unconscious' substratum of visual experience

(2007: 237). At once, the photograph multiplied optical mistakes and puzzles, introducing a 'new magic of the visible', in Jean-Louis Comolli's terms, which burdened 'the human eye . . . with a series of limits and doubts' (1980: 123).

Photographic practice in modernism (and beyond) was conditioned by these paradoxical effects, which were made legible in the photograph's privileging of equivocality and incongruity and, importantly, in the unfixed relations it establishes between observed objects and observing subjects. The photograph's allusive meanings and motile viewing relations also augment the conceptual possibilities of interpreting modernist photography today. I therefore model the medium's defamiliarising and decentring impulse by engaging Käsebier's work between high-modernist and low-popular spheres, between art gallery and family photographic album, and between professional and domestic space. Including this work within the frame of modernist photography – more than that, approaching it as an important context for the development of modernist photography, at a remove from Stieglitz and the others – disrupts and disorders our conventionalised, masculinised understandings of its aesthetics and conditions. From within the purview of Käsebier's home–studio, modernist photography appears in a new light: as a relational and affective form, deeply embedded in the lived realities of modern (family) life.

Pictorialist/Straight

Gertrude Käsebier's first studio at the Women's Exchange, opened in 1897, was only a block away from the New York Camera Club, where Alfred Stieglitz was busy hosting events and exhibitions that sought to situate the medium of photography within the traditions of fine art.[5] The two photographers became friends, and in February 1899 Stieglitz organised the first solo exhibition of Käsebier's work. Stieglitz promoted Käsebier in his magazines, *Camera Notes* and *Camera Work*, and he counted her as one of the core members of the Photo-Secession at its formation in 1902. Her work appeared in every major Photo-Secession exhibition until 1907; it amounted to a full tenth of the images on display at the first group exhibition at the Little Galleries of the Photo-Secession, which opened in November 1905 at 291 Fifth Avenue (Michaels 1992: 111).

However, by 1907, Käsebier and Stieglitz's relationship had begun to sour. This was in part a reflection of shifting ideas about what modern art photography looked like. The Photo-Secession was conceived after the model of artistic secessions in Europe, notably the English Linked Ring, with which Käsebier and Stieglitz were both affiliated. It was meant to secede from traditional modes of picture-making, to break with the past in order to establish the apparatuses of photographic capture, development and printing as 'pliant tools and not mechanical tyrants', as Stieglitz put it in an 1899 essay (529). In the last two decades of the nineteenth century, as the messy and cumbersome collodion wet-plate technique was replaced by gelatin dry-plate negatives, and as albumen printing paper was replaced by neutral silver prints and a range of alternative printing processes, modern photography emerged as a newly expansive and multifaceted medium, offering 'an unprecedented ease in securing negatives [and] a new malleability in the making of prints from those negatives' (Peterson 2013: 11).

When Stieglitz spoke of photography's 'pliant tools' in 1899, he had in mind the techniques of pictorialist photography, a subjective genre that emulated painting and etching through methods of manipulation: soft focus, filters and lens coatings, darkroom editing, and the use of platinum printing or the hand-applied gum bichromate process. For Mary Fanton Roberts, writing as Giles Edgerton in *The Craftsman* in April 1907, Käsebier's 'The Manger (Ideal Motherhood)' was 'a study in shades of white' – a description that, like the image itself, encodes the racial politics of whiteness (92). Simply but elegantly composed, its mother veiled by the photograph's lack of definition as by her billowing gown and gauzy headdress, 'The Manger' exemplifies the pictorialist mode and Käsebier's success with it. In fact, in 1899 Käsebier sold a print of this image for US $100, an unprecedented price for a photograph. But a few months after the publication of Roberts's positive review of Käsebier's work, Stieglitz registered his growing antipathy toward pictorialism's painterly, subdued visions by including in *Camera Work* a parody of Roberts's essay. Written by the critic Charles Caffin, who several years earlier had praised Käsebier's work in this same magazine, the October 1907 article was a genuinely nasty attack piece against 'Mr. Theodosius Bunny', a thinly veiled stand-in for Käsebier. The article routes its critique of Käsebier's 'emotional art' through sexist remarks about her weight and her sex life ('it is no light matter I take it, to be the sleeping partner of an emotional artist'; 32).

According to her biographer Barbara Michaels, Käsebier was deeply offended by this article and saw it as part of a larger effort by Stieglitz to exclude her from his circle (1992: 124–5). Between 1907 and 1912, when Käsebier made her final, definitive break from the Photo-Secession, she experienced a series of slights from Stieglitz. Yet his rejection of her – and her rejection of him – played out more generalised conflicts within the aesthetic and political project of American modernist photography. 'Käsebier is a queer creature; she's touchy like all women', Stieglitz wrote in 1901 in a letter to the photographer Joseph T. Keiley (cited in Michaels 1992: 120). In the intervening years, Käsebier's touchiness, her 'womanly' sensitivity, collapsed into the touchiness of her artistic practice – its touching sentimentalism, as well as the material touchings and retouchings through which she achieved her style of self-conscious refinement and aestheticisation. Increasingly, as Kathleen Pyne has argued, Stieglitz cast 'Käsebier as the emblematic figure of a stagnant, even corrupt, feminized pictorialist aesthetic', displacing on to her all the bourgeois repressions he had come to associate with genteel, progressivist American culture (2008: 3). Käsebier morphed from a pioneer of modern photography to its antithesis, 'an impediment to the emergence of a more virile and vital modernism' (16, 15). Pictorialist methods of manipulation were reformulated as contaminating gestures, seen to require a kind of aesthetic (and erotic) desublimation: a clearing away, a clarifying, of pictorialism's blur and haze by the sharpness and facticity of 'straight' or 'pure' photography.[6]

Our histories of modernist photography have often followed Stieglitz's lead, proceeding under the sign of straight photography. This masculinised rhetoric promoted a narrow, straightened view of photography's uses and effects in the early decades of the twentieth century.[7] Not merely downplaying the significance of pictorialism in modernism's development, it obfuscated the extent to which modernism was conceptualised and constituted in a series of breaks with the past. In these repeated acts of secession, the definitions of the modern and the anti-modern were under active and uneven negotiation. In asserting the medium's difference to other artistic forms, the precision and rich detail of straight photography served as the visual syntax of its formalist aesthetics. Purity is, as ever, a form of negation, a sloughing off of excess;

it hangs on, and on to, its exclusions and refusals. And the refusals of straightness at the level of style are commensurate with other refusals. Stieglitz's working methods, as Mary Woods notes, 'projected ideas about masculine prowess and strength. . . . Working in fog, rain, ice, and snow, he courted frostbite and pneumonia' as he stood for hours on New York streets, waiting, in Stieglitz's words, for 'the moment when everything is in balance' (Woods 2009: 18; Stieglitz 1981 [1897]: 216). Responsive to the shifting light and movement of the urban environment, the modern photographer nevertheless claims a macho imperviousness to that environment.

Drenched and shivering, Stieglitz cultivated that very modernist, very masculinist myth of the autonomous artist, aloof and apart from the quotidian realities of the world – as the rain, dripping from his coat, makes tangible the limits of that myth. The clean, clear surfaces of straight photography are haunted by the materiality of the world its practitioners were committed to representing with such immediacy and directness. Hence Stieglitz's disdain for the vulgarities of commerce, his belief that an artist's work was desecrated by the pursuit of money. It was through a discourse of anti-commercialism that Stieglitz alienated those members of the Photo-Secession who needed or wanted to make a living from photography. This included Käsebier, who saw no contradiction between art and commerce and who measured her achievement as an artist in part through her commercial success. Käsebier's husband, who ran a prosperous shellac business, offered only grudging support for her career, but her work quickly became profitable, largely because she was willing to trespass the borders between artistic and professional worlds, displaying her commissioned portraits in galleries and selling her uncommissioned work to popular magazines (Hutchinson 2002: 60). When her husband died after a long illness in late 1909, Käsebier was left a wealthy woman, yet as she told Lord Northcliffe, a prominent British newspaper publisher who sat for her about this time, 'I love to work. I would pay for the privilege.' As Käsebier knew, Stieglitz could afford to ignore the costs of living and working because he had access to his wife's fortune, the profits of his late father-in-law's brewing business. She, on the other hand, 'didn't have a brewer's daughter for [her] cash register'. 'I thought Stieglitz was grand', she recalled later in life. 'When I saw he was only hot air, I quit. I remember saying to myself . . . I earn my own money. I pay my own bills. I carry my own license' (Michaels 1992: 128).

Secede/Succeed

Käsebier secedes from the Photo-Secession by succeeding, in financial terms, declaring her independence from the anti-lucre programme of modern art through a series of deliberate public gestures. As Michaels explains, Käsebier raised Stieglitz's ire in 1909 by choosing to enter the Professional rather than the Artistic Section of the Dresden International Photography Exhibition. And then, for the first time in years, she entered a photograph into a corporate advertising competition run by Kodak – and won third place and US $250 in prize money (1992: 128–9). The image Käsebier submitted to the competition shares something of the same recursive structure as 'Lollipops' (Figure 10.4). Käsebier photographs her daughter, Hermine, as Hermine directs her daughter, Mina, in photographing her son, Mason. As Mason looks out and away from these acts of picture-making, the image connects the female gaze and the apparatus of the camera as mechanisms of artistry and control.

Figure 10.4 Gertrude Käsebier, Hermine and Mina Turner photographing Mason Turner on the roof of Käsebier's studio at 315 Fifth Avenue (variant of prize-winning photograph in Kodak advertising contest), ca. 1909. Platinum print. George Eastman Museum, Gift of Hermine Turner. Courtesy of the George Eastman Museum.

In the context of the growing rift between Käsebier and Stieglitz, Käsebier's entrance of the photograph in the competition was an impressively 'knowing' gesture that contrasted with 'the innocent and playful picture-taking activity' depicted in the image (Peterson 2013: 24–5). Just as Käsebier moved between the technical skill and elaborate staging of 'Lollipops' and the effects of spontaneity and ease in the composition of the rooftop photograph, the latter image works through the productive interaction of the modernist art tradition and amateur family photography. Stieglitz, as we have seen, positions himself on the cold, wet city street in order to differentiate his methods from simpler, more domesticated ones – particularly those associated with Kodak's point-and-shoot cameras, which were introduced in 1888. When Käsebier was establishing her portraiture business in the 1890s, she too sought to align herself with artists rather than hobbyists, not least by setting up her studio 'at the heart of the New York art scene' (Hutchinson 2002: 47). Such efforts are unsurprising, and not only for financial reasons. Despite the centring of the figures of mother and child within pictorialism, the movement was established in opposition to the feminised photographic practices alongside which it emerged: namely, the family portraiture and travel photography made possible by the Kodak camera. The Kodak girl, who graced advertising copy from 1893, was a young woman of freedom and gumption, the camera slung around her neck a passport for exploration outside the home. But one could just as readily be 'At Home with the Kodak', as an early twentieth-century catalogue declared (Figure 10.5).

Figure 10.5 Kodak catalogue cover, ca. 1900s. Courtesy of the Martha Cooper Collection.

Käsebier's prize-winning photograph of her daughter and grandchildren is thus a version of a scenario already familiar from Kodak's advertisements. In playing to the company's marketing strategies, Käsebier's image openly acknowledges the traditions of popular, mass-cultural photography that she participates in and works to reformulate. As Carol Armstrong observes, Käsebier's photographs across her career 'articulate the intimate dialectical structure of the relationship between amateurism and art photography that marked her period much more overtly than the work of any of her male cohorts could or did' (2000: 104). Käsebier is not so much selling out to commercial culture as she is paying her debts to it. To be sure, modernism coincided with the 'golden age of home portraiture', which Christian Peterson dates from the 1890s to the 1940s (2011: 374). The expanded practices of home portraiture were ushered in by the many middle-class, mostly white women who took to photography in the 1880s and 1890s as a means of recording the lives of their children. Käsebier was one of these women, and family photography remained her privileged genre throughout her career. By the 1900s, images of her family were displayed at the Little Galleries of the Photo-Secession and included in her own family albums alongside postcards and Kodak snapshots.[8]

A material and relational object, the family album was a key vernacular use of photographic technologies from the second half of the nineteenth century on, particularly for women. Whereas the album has usually been understood as a 'decent, reassuring, and edifying' genre, producing the family's 'imagination of its own integration' (Bourdieu 1990: 31, 26), Daniel Novak has argued persuasively that the actions of collage essential to the album worked to disintegrate and denaturalise the body – and the family – by producing it as fragmented, distorted and infinitely malleable (2008: 14–15). Indeed, by the account of Käsebier's granddaughter, Mina, practices of collage and other idiosyncratic reworkings of photographic materials were at home in Käsebier's studio (Figure 10.6). In an undated, handwritten account of her childhood, Mina describes how she 'loved to go to Granny's studio' at 315 Fifth Avenue, where Käsebier worked between 1907 and 1914, and especially to 'a little dark attic' that was to her 'a treasure house':

> It was full of boxes of discarded prints and mounting materials etc. – Granny gave me crayons and old bits of pastels and I amused myself by the hour coloring the photographs and drawing pictures of my own on the back of them. . . . [T]here were always strips of paper by the chopping board – trimmed edges – I loved to gather them up and make things with them.

Mina then turns to describe how Käsebier herself 'experimented with every medium & technique she could learn about', implicitly connecting her own playful, 'touching' work with photographs to her grandmother's photographic labour. She continues to attest to the imbrication of the creative work of grandmother and granddaughter by relating a time when Käsebier's studio assistant, Alice Boughton, helped her to draw a human figure: '[S]he sat down and drew me a skeleton – then she put muscles on it, then flesh & hair & features. Next she dressed it and there was a complete human being. I was much impressed and delighted' (Turner n.d.).

Figure 10.6 Gertrude Käsebier's photographic workroom, ca. 1915. Special Collections, University of Delaware Libraries, Gift of William I. Homer.

Käsebier's mixed practices of exhibition and display reveal the entanglement of feminised, popular forms and apparatuses with those of masculinised, elite art in modernism, while also underscoring the market forces that shaped these intersecting arenas of culture.[9] But as her camera mediates between and is remediated in high and low culture, gallery and album, and public and private spheres, it is framed emphatically as a technology of family life, the varied and embodied practices of which are passed down from grandmother to granddaughter: women who make human figures materialise in one form or another.

Home/Work

In photographing Hermine in the guise of the Kodak girl, Käsebier's duplication of a popular type is recapitulated in the image through Hermine's own act of duplication: her teaching Mina to operate the camera. In Käsebier's studio on Fifth Avenue, as Mina scribbles on photographs, 'making things with them', she understands herself to be her grandmother's heir; and in the rooftop image, on the top of the building that houses that studio, Mina is given to us as Hermine in miniature – just as her name is a compacted version of her mother's. Käsebier makes Hermine a photographer, Hermine makes Mina a photographer, and the family is presented in a kind of *mise-en-abîme*, an infinitely recurring sequence of copies and copies' copies, smaller and smaller all the way down. The image is patterned after and destined for Kodak's mass-produced advertisements in illustrated magazines or on billboards, and it obliquely figures the technological reproduction of the photographic medium through the reproduction of the family, and of the family business. Like mother, like daughter: Käsebier's portraits of her family reference the iterative – procreative – functions of her medium, which synch with the imperatives of capitalistic production and trade. And as they take these reproductive functions as their theme, both Käsebier's portraits and Kodak's advertisements give new significance to the position of the cameras held by the women at their bellies.

Together with 'Lollipops', the rooftop portraits mark an evolution not only in the style and aims of modernist photography but also in the life and work of Käsebier's family. The family she photographed around 1910 is made up of women and children; it is a family conspicuously without men. I am tempted to read this absence of men as an extension of Käsebier's rejection of Stieglitz and his ilk. Yet it is Käsebier's recently deceased husband, Eduard Käsebier, who is the more palpable ghost in these photographs. There is little record, as Michaels notes, of the effect on Käsebier of Eduard's death in December 1909 – and this absence too is suggestive (1992: 130). Certainly, Käsebier was unsentimental about marriage when, in 1915, she gave the title 'Yoked and Muzzled: Marriage' to a photograph of two oxen, likening one form of constraint with another.

The death of her husband, combined with her break from the Stieglitz circle, seemed to afford Käsebier a new independence, expressed in her merging of work and home. The boundaries between the two had always been permeable for Käsebier, as is suggested by the setting of her photographs of Hermine and the children in 1910: the rooftop is and is not her studio, and it equivocates, in any case, between the interior and the exterior. Indeed, part of what distinguished as modern the portraiture studios Käsebier occupied in this period was how they deliberately simulated the home. Repudiating the ostentatiousness of Victorian decoration, as well as the theatrical props associated with earlier photographic portraiture, Käsebier made over her studios in the manner of a domestic parlour in an unfussy Arts and Crafts style. Art covered the walls; vases of flowers and decorative pitchers sat atop carved-wood furniture; and her camera was hidden behind a tasteful screen until her (mostly women) subjects began to feel as comfortable as she was, swathed in her signature silk kimono (Michaels 1992: 56–8).

In 1914, Käsebier moved from Fifth Avenue and took a large apartment on West 71st Street as a combined home and studio; she continued her thriving portraiture business there until 1920, when she moved to another apartment in Greenwich Village. In 1924, Hermine's marriage ended in divorce and she moved in with her ageing mother, to care for her and to continue the portraiture business. Soon after that, Mina joined them, and the three women lived together and supported themselves as a multigenerational family firm until the outbreak of the Second World War (Michaels 1992: 139, 156–8). 'Lollipops' and the rooftop images thus reflect and forecast a photographic practice that exists on a continuum with domestic life and that is identified as women's labour, the collaborative (home)work of mothers and daughters.

The portraiture business operated by Käsebier with her daughter and granddaughter during her late career – as it is conjured in the portraits of this family taken in 1909 and 1910 – situates the intersubjectivity of the photographic scenario, which is lately elaborated by feminist scholars. Extending Barthes's metaphor of the 'umbilical cord' of photographic light, which enjoins observer and observed in an experience of haptic immediacy, Elizabeth Abel theorises the 'dense intermediate viewing space' of photography, in which subject and object intermingle and exchange (Abel 2014: 99). For Margaret Olin, in a similar vein, the photograph is a tactile, relational object, poised to 'participate in and create relationships and communities' (2012: 15). Käsebier and her contemporaries tended to mystify the transferential and social effects of her portraiture, stressing the sympathy of the method by which she was able to coax her subjects into modes of self-disclosure. In 1910, for instance, the critic H. Snowden Ward described how Käsebier set her subjects at ease in the studio, taking a number of exposures and speaking with them until 'at last (as Mrs. Käsebier said afterward) the sitter began to lose self-consciousness, and his temperament began to reveal itself'. The photographs she produced were praised as 'human documents' – unaffected, vital and personal (591). Käsebier cultivated this vision of herself and her work, playing into cultural conceptions of the mother as a responsive and intercessory figure, while also shrouding her images in the aura of the symbolist 'mystical moment': surfacing the ineffable, giving form to psychological and spiritual truths. This mythology found its fullest expression in Käsebier's account of 'Real Motherhood' (Figure 10.7), a photograph she took in 1900, shortly after she became Granny through the birth of her first grandson. As she recalled in 1907,

> While posing my daughter there suddenly seemed to develop between us a greater intimacy than I had ever known before. Every barrier was down. We were not two women, mother and daughter, old and young, but two mothers with one feeling . . . and the tremendous import of motherhood which we both realized seemed to find its expression in this photograph. (Roberts 1907: 91–2)

It is easy to dismiss these remarks for their overt sentimentalism. Yet Käsebier's relational photographic method – more precisely her 'motherly' one, tethering mother

Figure 10.7 Gertrude Käsebier, 'Real Motherhood', 1900. Platinum on tissue. Museums Collections, Special Collections and Museums, University of Delaware, Gift of Philip and Laura T. Shevlin, 1994.07.003.

to mother in the space of the studio-as-home and the home-as-studio – subtends the decentring of the modern observer, in Jonathan Crary's terms. If Käsebier's method collapses the relation between object and subject, then it also admits the subjective, bodily formation of sight. In her hands, the photographic camera serves what Crary calls the 'uprooting of vision from the stable and fixed relations incarnated in the camera obscura' (1990: 14). Käsebier may have wanted to document the essential form and character of her subjects, but her camera was not the objective, detached eye of the *camera obscura* (as is made clear by the theatrical and atmospheric style of her pictorialist work).[10] It was instead an optical toy that resembled the modern stereoscope, in Crary's formulation: a fixture of and for her body, fastened to and guided by her corporeal subjectivity. Käsebier's emphasis on the production of her portraits through an active, affective engagement with her subjects, a social dynamic 'proper' to women and to mothers in particular, denies the discontinuity of observing self and observed other – and disrupts the continuity between seeing and knowing.

In this respect, we might well understand Käsebier's family photographs not simply as relevant to modernism's visual cultures, but as representing some of her most characteristically modernist work. Käsebier's late family portraiture unsettles the evidentiary claims of the medium, frustrating ideals of visual mastery and control, as it foregrounds the unstable, intersubjective structure of the photographic scenario. These aspects of photography were central to its uses in modernism, whether pictorialist or straight, commercial or artistic, in the shelter of the home or out on the street – or, as with Käsebier, some combination of the same.

Order/Disorder

'Lollipops', too, sits in the break between seeing and knowing. I find this image as distracting as the sweets surely were for the girls it pictures. I return to it again and again, pulled in (and pushed away) by its indeterminacy of meaning, its refusal to explain; above all, its pervasive sense of loss. Much more than the rooftop portraits, this vigil of mothers and mothers' mothers suggests the terrible promise baked into any genealogical line, the way that maternity is caught up with mortality, the assurance of death in every birth. Is family portraiture not a kind of visual cemetery, chronicling the yield of the everyday to the more essential evanescence of every generation? In at least potentially outliving the family itself, the pages of the family album are suffused with the 'catastrophe' and 'defeat of Time', Barthes's *noème*, the *that-has-been* of the photographic subject: '*that* is dead and *that* is going to die' (2000: 96).

In *Camera Lucida*, Barthes enmeshes a loose, paradoxical philosophy of photography with an elegy for his dead mother, or vice versa; and in this, too, Käsebier foreshadows Barthes, as her family photographs stage an anxious meditation of the affinities between death and motherhood, on the one hand, and between death and photography, on the other. Connecting (or reconnecting) subject to object, living and dead, from navel to navel, both Barthes and Käsebier conceive of the photograph as a surrogate maternal body. Since the mother is the 'originary matrix for all other reproductive acts', as Elissa Marder argues, 'the maternal body tends to become associated and confused with other forms of cultural labor' defined by reproduction (2012: 3). Hence photography, like the maternal function, 'opens up a strange space in which birth and death, *bios* and *technē*, the human and the nonhuman are brought into intimate and disturbing proximity with one another'. Yet as Marder demonstrates, the mother, as the sign for the event of birth – that most unaccountable, unknowable event in psychoanalytic thought – disrupts systems of representation and inspires 'alternative, nonmimetic, nonlinear conceptions of time and space', in Barthes's writing as in other cultural reckonings with the maternal body (2).

As much as subjects and objects are enfolded in Käsebier's work, touching one another by her touchy method, her photographs also thematise a fragmentation of the family. Like the denaturalising effects of collage in the family album, Käsebier's photographs disorder that which they seem most insistently to order. It is notable that the gazes that activate 'Lollipops' are gazes that never meet one another. One look does not cede to or join with the next; the circuit of seeing is repeatedly broken. Similarly, in many of Käsebier's portraits of mothers and children, as Armstrong explains, the unity of mother and child is disrupted by the child's outward glance, which 'seize[s] upon the viewer's attention, here and now outside of its space and time' (2000: 132). This outward glance – what Barthes would call the *punctum* of the image – 'disorganizes the family into an atomized series of separate, secretive cells', intimating, finally, 'the intrusion and germination of death within the heart and hearth of the family' (135).

Käsebier's discontinuous line of sight, and her disorganised family unit, allegorise the alternative genealogy of modernist photography her work also promotes. Barthes's theory of photography, notes Armstrong,

> runs counter to the dominant attitudes of art photography, which would have it be an aesthetic medium fit to vie authoritatively with others in the same discursive domain: yielding a canon of 'great' professional artists; predicated on visual intention and mastery of its optical apparatus, the camera; producing fine and original prints, formally unified, tonally pristine, and archivally preserved. (2000: 109)

No one shaped these attitudes so much as Stieglitz. But the alternative genealogy of photography we might trace from Käsebier, not the father of modernism but its heretical Granny, does not simply replace one single, coherent lineage with another lineage, equal but opposite to it. To the contrary, it frustrates a desire for originary, solitary geniuses and their orderly line of successors – for genius turned genus, the one become a type – including as it foregrounds the practical, material and social conditions of photography in modernism.[11]

As Judith Fryer Davidov has argued, our male-centric and hierarchical histories of photography must be revised toward 'the more amorphous configuration of a net', incorporating professional women photographers such as Käsebier alongside amateurs 'who worked from home [and] learned from each other at camera clubs' (1998: 30). In 'Lollipops', even as the spectre of death attenuates the generational logic of this family of women and children, we can also trace Davidov's network in the subjects' replicating lines of sight, which track in multiple directions about the space, shooting off in their own directions. Primed less for the articulation than the disarticulation of linear, teleological formulations, the reproductive gaze of the mother–photographer maintains the generative madness of the photograph's silence, hastens the defining crisis of the scopic regime of modernity, and defamiliarises our view of modernist photography – as the light at the bottom of the stairs lures and repels our gaze, sending us away blinking and dazzled.

Notes

1. I am grateful to the volume's editors for their incisive input into this chapter, as well as to Emily Burns, Louise Hornby, David Shackleton and Lorraine Sim, who each provided helpful feedback on early drafts. My thanks, too, to those participants and interlocutors at seminars where I presented this work in development, hosted by the Humanities Institute and the Department of English, Drama and Film at University College Dublin, and the Modern and Contemporary Workshop at the School of English, Communication and Philosophy at Cardiff University. This chapter's treatment of 'Lollipops' extends my brief analysis of this image in *Object Women* (Beeston 2018b).
2. On the imperialist logics of Käsebier's portraiture, see Wexler (2000: 177–208).
3. See Beeston (2018a) and the readings of Barthes in Smith (2013: 23–38) and Olin (2012: 51–70). The links between Käsebier's practice and Barthes's theory of photography are elaborated by Armstrong (2000), whose larger claims about the importance of the 'lady amateur' in photography history and the self-reflexivity of Käsebier's work are compatible with my argument.
4. On photography's erosion of Cartesian perspectivalism, see Beeston (2018a: 1–11).
5. For a general account of Stieglitz's development as a photographer, including his involvement with the New York Camera Club and the Photo-Secession, see Rose (2019).
6. Käsebier's rejection on these terms feeds into a tradition, described by Michel Orin, of associating women's photography with slipshod technique and a lack of quality or sharpness (1991: 123–4).
7. As Kirsten Swinth notes, the shift from pictorialism to straight photography registered a reconceptualisation of high culture in modernism, as the art world moved 'from a realm of (feminized) genteel refinement to a space of heroic (masculine) self-expression', largely in reaction to women's advances in art during the late nineteenth and early twentieth centuries (2001: 5–6). Meanwhile, according to Christian Peterson, pictorial photography flourished after the demise of Stieglitz's Photo-Secession in 1910, becoming less 'aesthetically homogenous and politically elitist' (1997: 13).
8. On these mixed practices of display, see Peterson (2013: 23–4).
9. A classic account of how the categorical distinction between high–elite and low–popular art in modernism reflects a 'paranoid' resistance to a mass culture that is pejoratively gendered is given in Huyssen (1986). On the complex relationship of modernity and femininity, see Felski (1995).
10. For an explanation of how pictorialist aesthetics staged a 'flight from the "real"' that resisted photography's production of the body as 'legible scientific sign', see Smith (2013: 39–72).
11. It is true that the photographer Imogen Cunningham once stated that her career was inspired by Käsebier's motherhood images, which she saw when she was in high school (Davidov 1998: 232). Cunningham was one of a number of women photographers, apart from Käsebier's daughter and granddaughter, whom Granny mentored and supported. But when Cunningham visited Käsebier in 1910, she observed that although Käsebier was 'nice, warm and encouraging' to her, she 'tended to boss Hermine in the studio' (cited in Michaels 1992: 158). Käsebier's studio was collaborative and multigenerational, but it was not exactly egalitarian.

Works Cited

Abel, Elizabeth (2014), 'Skin, Flesh, and the Affective Wrinkles of Civil Rights Photography', *Feeling Photography*, ed. Elspeth H. Brown and Thy Phu. Durham, NC, and London: Duke University Press, pp. 93–123.

Allen, Ann Taylor (1982), 'Spiritual Motherhood: German Feminists and the Kindergarten Movement, 1848–1911', *History of Education Quarterly*, 22: 3, pp. 319–39.
Armstrong, Carol (2000), 'From Clementina to Käsebier: The Photographic Attainment of the "Lady Amateur"', *October*, 91, pp. 101–39.
Barthes, Roland (2000 [1980]), *Camera Lucida: Reflections on Photography*, trans. Richard Howard. London: Vintage.
Beckman, Karen (2013), 'Nothing to Say: The War on Terror and the Mad Photography of Roland Barthes', in *On Writing with Photography*, ed. Karen Beckman and Liliane Weissberg. Minneapolis and London: University of Minnesota Press, pp. 297–317.
Beeston, Alix (2018a), *In and Out of Sight: Modernist Writing and the Photographic Unseen*. New York: Oxford University Press.
Beeston, Alix (2018b), *Object Women: A History of Women in Photography*, <www.instagram.com/objectwomen> (last accessed 21 January 2022).
Benjamin, Walter (2007 [1935]), 'The Work of Art in the Age of Mechanical Reproduction', in *Illuminations: Essays and Reflections*, trans. Harry Zohn, ed. Hannah Arendt. New York: Schocken Books, pp. 217–52.
Bourdieu, Pierre (1990), *Photography: A Middle-Brow Art*, trans. Shaun Whiteside. Stanford, CA: Stanford University Press.
Caffin, Charles H. (1907), 'Emotional Art (After Reading the "Craftsman," April, 1907)', *Camera Work*, 20, pp. 32–4.
Comolli, Jean-Louis (1980), 'Machines of the Visible', in *The Cinematic Apparatus*, ed. Teresa de Lauretis and Stephen Heath. New York: St Martin's Press, pp. 121–42.
Crary, Jonathan (1990), *Techniques of the Observer: On Vision and Modernity in the Nineteenth Century*. Cambridge, MA: MIT Press.
Davidov, Judith Fryer (1998), *Women's Camera Work: Self/Body/Other in American Visual Culture*. Durham, NC, and London: Duke University Press.
Felski, Rita (1995), *The Gender of Modernity*. Cambridge, MA: Harvard University Press.
Hutchinson, Elizabeth (2002), '"When the Sioux Chief's Party Calls": Käsebier's Indian Portraits and the Gendering of the Artist's Studio', *American Art*, 16: 2, pp. 40–65.
Huyssen, Andreas (1986), 'Mass Culture as Woman: Modernism's Other', in *After the Great Divide: Modernism, Mass Culture, Postmodernism*. Bloomington and Indianapolis: Indiana University Press, pp. 44–64.
Käsebier, Gertrude (1898), 'Studies in Photography', *Photographic Times*, 30: 6, pp. 269–72.
Marder, Elissa (2012), *The Mother in the Age of Mechanical Reproduction: Psychoanalysis, Photography, Deconstruction*. New York: Fordham University Press.
Michaels, Barbara (1992), *Gertrude Käsebier: The Photographer and Her Photographs*. New York: Harry N. Abrams.
Novak, Daniel A. (2008), *Realism, Photography, and Nineteenth-Century Fiction*. Cambridge: Cambridge University Press.
Olin, Margaret (2012), *Touching Photographs*. Chicago and London: University of Chicago Press.
Orin, Michel (1991), 'On the Impurity of Group f/64 Photography', *History of Photography*, 15: 2, pp. 119–27.
Peterson, Christian A. (1997), *After the Photo-Secession: American Pictorial Photography, 1910–1955*. New York and London: Minneapolis Institute of Arts and W. W. Norton and Co.
Peterson, Christian A. (2011), 'Home Portraiture', *History of Photography*, 35: 4, pp. 374–87.
Peterson, Stephen (2013), 'The Complexity of Light and Shade: Gertrude Käsebier and the Field of Modern Photography', in *Gertrude Käsebier: The Complexity of Light and Shade*, ed. Stephen Peterson and Janis A. Tomlinson. Newark: University of Delaware Press, pp. 7–30.
Pyne, Kathleen (2008), *Modernism and the Feminine Voice: O'Keeffe and the Women of the Stieglitz Circle*. Berkeley: University of California Press.

Roberts, Mary Fanton [Giles Edgerton] (1907), 'Photography as an Emotional Art: A Study of the Work of Gertrude Käsebier', *Craftsman*, 12, pp. 80–93.
Rose, Phyllis (2019), *Alfred Stieglitz: Taking Pictures, Making Painters*. New Haven, CT, and London: Yale University Press.
Smith, Shawn Michelle (2013), *At the Edge of Sight: Photography and the Unseen*. Durham, NC, and London: Duke University Press.
Stieglitz, Alfred (1899), 'Pictorial Photography', *Scribner's*, 26: 5, pp. 528–37.
Stieglitz, Alfred (1981 [1897]), 'The Hand-Held Camera – Its Present Importance', in *Photography in Print: Writings from 1816 to the Present*, ed. Vicki Goldberg. New York: Simon and Schuster, pp. 214–17.
Swinth, Kirsten (2001), *Painting Professionals: Women Artists and the Development of Modern American Art, 1870–1930*. Chapel Hill and London: University of North Carolina Press.
Turner, Mina (n.d.), 'Mina Turner at Gertrude Käsebier's studios', Gertrude Käsebier Papers, MSS 149, F18, Special Collections, University of Delaware, <http://udspace.udel.edu/handle/19716/11745> (last accessed 21 January 2022).
Ward, H. Snowden (1910), 'Gertrude Käsebier and Her Work', *Amateur Photographer and Photographic News*, 52, p. 591.
Wexler, Laura (2000), *Tender Violence: Domestic Visions in an Age of U.S. Imperialism*. Chapel Hill and London: University of North Carolina Press.
Woods, Mary N. (2009), *Beyond the Architect's Eye: Photographs and the American Built Environment*. Philadelphia: University of Pennsylvania Press.

11

X-RAYS: TECHNOLOGICAL REVELATION AND ITS CULTURAL RECEPTIONS

Tom Slevin

THE DISCOVERY OF the 'X-ray' had profoundly significant effects upon modern culture: it pushed the boundaries of science and medicine, operated as spectacle for public entertainment, nourished beliefs in the paranormal and provided a subject through which printed media could raise emerging modern social and ethical issues. The fascination with X-rays, as Lisa Cartwright writes, was a 'mania [that] swept the West at the turn of the century' (1995: 109). Wilhelm Röntgen submitted the first research paper on X-rays on 28 December 1895 and within days the discovery appeared in newspapers, gracing the front page of the Viennese *Die Presse* on 5 January 1896. Knowledge of one invisible force was disseminated through another as the news was telegraphed across the world through pulsating electrical signals that circulated information with wired instantaneity. At least forty-nine books and 1,044 scientific essays on X-rays appeared in 1896 alone (see Natale 2011: 347). Whilst X-radiation generated an incredible cultural and scientific fascination, it was also enveloped into other media, from writing and literature to film and painting. Indeed, the very moment of the discovery attests to its position within intermedial modernism: Röntgen submitted his paper on X-rays on the same day as the Lumière brothers' first public cinematic screening at the Salon Indien du Grand Café. As with the Röntgen rays, so news of the Lumières' work spread across the world; both made a deep impact upon society, creating visible spectacles through technology's harnessing of invisible matter. Marconi, again in 1895, achieved his first wireless telegram, creating physical effects from immaterial process through signal transmission and reception. While these new media, including X-rays, transformed and revealed hitherto concealed energies, they also invoked the realm of the dead. Marconi sought to develop an instrument for listening to the dead; photography also contained the fantastic possibility of capturing the spirits of the dead and auras of the living. Upon observing her X-rayed hand, Anne Berthe Röntgen reportedly exclaimed 'I have seen my death!' (Tuniz 2012: 3) (Figure 11.1). Modern technologies were folding, collapsing and transforming existing regimes of space, time, distance, speed, interiority and exteriority in different ways. The X-ray embodied technology's promise of harnessing forces towards the expansion and increase of humanity's powers, whilst it simultaneously contained a concurrent hauntological spectre at the heart of modernity's 'progress'.

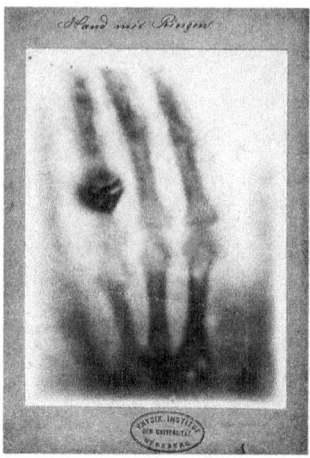

Figure 11.1 Wilhelm Röntgen, X-ray photograph of Anne Berthe Röntgen, 22 December 1895.

'These Naughty, Naughty Roentgen Rays'

The impact of X-rays upon the imagination and visualisation of the human body was immediate. Otto Glasser (1993: 29), Linda Dalrymple Henderson (1988: 324) and Bettyann Kevles (1997: 116) all describe the profound, widespread and immediate impact of the discovery upon both scientific and public thought. Henderson considers that it 'produced a sense that the world had changed irrevocably' (1988: 336). Within a month, X-rays were used in surgical processes, and within six months, were harnessed by surgeons to identify bullets inside soldiers' bodies. X-rays featured in popular public entertainment: stories and cartoons frequently appeared in the press, and X-ray machines quickly appeared as spectacular fairground attractions. X-ray equipment and images featured in shop windows, and commercial X-ray photography offered imaging services to the public (see Reiser 1990: 60). People from different backgrounds began purchasing the equipment to experiment with X-rays (Busch 2017: 329); some amateurs even built their own machines from X-ray kits. Indeed, the production of induction coils could not initially meet the overwhelming public demand (Glasser 1993: 38).

Within the X-ray 'mania', however, an anxiety emerged about the technology and its uses. This was reflected in popular media representations, which dwelt on the erasure between public and private boundaries. A concern with this erasure is clear in the comic poem *X-actly So!* by 'Wilhelma', published in *Electrical Review* in April 1896:

X-actly So!

The Roentgen Ray, the Roentgen Rays,
What is this craze?
The town's ablaze
With the new phase
Of X-ray's ways.

I'm full of daze,
Shock and amaze;
For nowadays
I hear they'll gaze
Thro' cloak and gown – and even stays,
These naughty, naughty Roentgen Rays.
(qtd in Glasser 1993: 44)

Such anxiety lies within a broader cultural concern involving private and public perceptions. Albert Robida's illustrations in 'Variations sur les rayons X', featured in *La Nature* of May 1896 (Figure 11.2), caricatures such fears, with scenario eleven depicting people wearing suits of armour in public. This reflected the actual sale of clothing designed to protect its wearers against invasive X-ray vision. Other scenarios, for example, involved prohibiting the use of X-rays in theatre glasses. Although scientists and doctors were the first purchasers of X-ray equipment, exhibition entrepreneurs joined the queue as they saw the entertainment potential of the latest visual spectacle. Exhibition audiences were increasingly familiar with a range of inventions that demonstrated the technological expansion of perception for visual entertainment, from the panoramic to developments in window dressing and the theatre to modernity's new vision machines such as the stereoscope, camera, stereograph, kaleidoscope, diorama, zoetrope, phenakistoscope and film projector. Thomas Edison, for example, promoted popular demonstrations of X-rays just as he promoted cinema; he encouraged commercial interest from businesspeople, inventors and entrepreneurs, believing it would become the foremost spectacular modern medium (Cartwright 1995: 109). Indeed,

Figure 11.2 'Variations sur les rayons X', *La Nature*, May 1896.

tickets were sold for X-ray exhibitions, and it existed as visual entertainment alongside early cinematic projections. Tom Gunning has documented 1890s showbusiness trade journal advertisements of travelling exhibitors wanting to exchange film projectors for X-ray equipment – evidence, he argues, that 'impresarios thought x-rays showed even greater potential than "animated pictures"' (2008: 52). The visual spectacle of a screen illuminated by an intangible, quasi-invisible force was a fantastic modern technology that bordered on 'the realm of fantasy or magic' (Gunning 2008: 53). Some projectionists exhibited X-ray photographs whilst others amazed audiences with live physical demonstrations. Both X-ray and cinematic media projected a new, alternative regime of space and experience through technologically enhanced vision. Unlike the optical intensification of the microscope or telescope, the X-ray and cinema were open, public visual experiences, aligned more with theatre and the fairground.

Whilst the history of the technical intermediality between film and X-rays lies outside the scope of this chapter, it is worth briefly considering the convergence of content between the media. Three short films from the late 1890s capture how X-rays raised issues concerning gender and social behaviour, the separation of one's lived, experiential embodied being and the technological representation of the body as a disturbing 'Other'. George Albert Smith's 1897 British short film *The X-Rays* featured real-life partners Laura Bayley and Tom Green in a romantic sketch. A camera marked 'X-Rays' appears, and through a jump cut, the two figures become skeletons. The camera exits and the scene is returned to 'normal' vision, but Bayley is furious with Green and leaves. Her reaction is perhaps a response to Green's motivations stripped bare as she perceives his 'inner' motives. However, this is unclear, as the innovative use of jump cuts indicate that the audience is in a privileged epistemic position over the characters involved. The film's alternative title, *The X-Ray Fiend*, hints at further implications: either that the cameraman is the 'fiend' for his penetration and revelation of the two bodies, or perhaps that Green is complicit, seeking to 'know the inside' of the female body as a sexual and visual pun. The film reflects contemporaneous anxieties about the 'revolting indecency' (Kevles 1997: 166) involved in the external display of one's internal body. In Georges Méliès's lost 1897/8 film *Les Rayons Röntgen*, a scientist separates a patient's skeleton from its flesh using an X-ray machine. The boneless body folds into a structureless heap and the skeleton dances; the process is reversed, and the skeleton is reinserted back into the body to 'restore' the person. Whilst far from the realm of possibility, the film nevertheless captured technological modernity's potential for creating alienating, uncanny images of the human body distinct from the reality of lived experience. This emphasis on the associations between X-rays and uncanny visualisations is similarly apparent in Wallace McCutcheon's film *The X-Ray Mirror* (1899), which features a woman trying a hat in front of a mirror. As she judges her appearance, her reflection transforms into that of a ballet dancer, and she faints at the surprise. Whilst there is little to suggest the actual intervention of X-rays, there is nevertheless an interest in the body's transformation and a split between actual and visualised body. The narrative of each film is premised upon the potential duality of the technology: insightful yet invading, alienating or traumatising.

'The New Light'

The relatively low cost and accessibility of the X-ray as an imaging technology were significant in its appeal to entrepreneurs, amateurs and medical communities alike (see

Reiser 1990: 62). The first X-ray department was created at the Glasgow Royal Infirmary in 1896, led by John Macintyre, who had lectured on 'The New Light – X-rays' (see Thomas 2017: 333). It was here that 'roentgenology' (radiology) first became a medical specialism (see Busch 2017: 329). In 1897 Glasgow opened its modern 'New Electrical Pavilion'. Prior to modern inventions that imaged bodily interiority – such as the X-ray, ophthalmoscope and laryngoscope – medical diagnosis largely consisted of haptic, tactile and acoustic processes. Internal corporeality was not visible without the physical act of being turned inside out. However, nineteenth-century visual technologies overturned prior forms of tactile and acoustic diagnosis. Reiser argues that 'X-rays directly challenged the use of touch in diagnosis' (1990: 63), embodying a shift from physical exploration to visual medical diagnosis through the exterior imaging of bodily interiority. Unlike acoustic diagnosis, the image produced by X-ray photography provided evidence and testimony independent of the patient, something that Reiser identifies as part of a wider modern shift within Western medical practice towards isolating and separating the condition and its symptoms from the subject. The technological process incurs the fragmentation of patient experience and clinical diagnosis in 'an increasing alienation between doctor and patient' (Reiser 1990: x), further distancing one's own lived embodiment from the body-as-image.

Technical instrumentation fragments the body into specific sites of disorder – rather than generating wider, holistic knowledge – in the process of diagnosis. X-rays emerged within a wider context of an expanded visual field; the 1870s witnessed inventions that rendered the body transparent through positioning intense electric illumination within the body to render the skin a quasi-X-ray surface. The design of these 'scopes' reflected the specific bodily forms required for illumination. Although some medical practitioners raised objections to the new techniques, this did not 'undermine the widely held belief within medicine that the most significant advances in diagnosis would come from new ways of visualizing pathology' (Reiser 1990: 56). Indeed, photographic evidence reinforced and enhanced this belief. An 1859 article, 'Photography in Medical Science', published in the foremost medical journal *The Lancet*, described photography as the 'art of truth'. Medical attitudes perceived this technique as providing objective, observable evidence that would transform diagnosis. As photographic technology developed – and formerly elaborate preparation and exposure times became more practical – it became an increasingly common technique through the 1890s. Figure 11.3 shows how the 'fluoroscope', a quasi-cinematic projection of radiation upon a fluorescent screen, even eliminated the prolonged photographic process involved in using X-ray plates by providing real-time imaging.

The potential medical benefits of the invisible rays were apparent to anyone who witnessed the display of bodily interiority. It is understandable, in the new age of technologically expanded vision, that these invisible forces might have helped to combat fears around things such as the newly discovered pathogens evidenced by microphotographic developments. However, through its revelation of bodily interiority, the X-ray also created the *unheimlich* image of a living skeleton. The iconography of this specific form is, of course, the gothic figure of death. Figure 11.4, featured in *Life* magazine just weeks after the discovery of X-rays, evidences an immediate connection between the body and mortality; day becomes night and the cheery farmer becomes a doppelgänger in the form of a grim reaper, replete with scythe for harvesting life. As Cartwright proposes, 'the X-ray is both gothic and modernist' (1995: 107); hence Anne

Figure 11.3 'An X-ray shadow picture', *Popular Electricity in Plain English* magazine, May 1909.

Figure 11.4 Illustration from *Life* magazine, February 1896.

Berthe Röntgen's exclamation that the X-ray image foretold her death. Hopes for the therapeutic use of X-rays were increasingly tempered by emerging scientific evidence and media reports of the deleterious relationship between X-radiation and the human body. Matthew Lavine notes that the 'hazards that x-radiation presented provided an early and perennial stream of newspaper stories . . . For all the general exuberance in the press towards the potential of x-rays, newspapers also made clear that the same rays could burn, maim, or kill' (Lavine 2012: 596–7). Indeed, Thomas Edison embodies such ambivalence; his entrepreneurial exuberance was replaced by growing reluctance after his own illnesses. Following the horrific, prolonged, bodily degeneration of his assistant Clarence Dally, Edison would infamously declare in 1903, 'Don't talk to me about X-rays . . . I am afraid of them' (quoted in Lavine 2012: 596).

Hearts of Darkness and Mists of Flesh

The X-ray's ability to provide penetrative vision, render bodies transparent and transform interior structure into an exterior surface was an important and pervasive metaphor around the turn of the twentieth century, not least in the work of Joseph Conrad. Conceptual metaphors involving skin, bone, transparency and identity are embedded in Conrad's X-ray character diagnoses through recurring tropes of light, technology and the body. Indeed, Conrad had a prior interest in, and direct experience of, X-rays. The writer Neil Munro recounted, in his later pseudonymous 'Random Reminiscences' newspaper column, a dinner in September 1898 that included himself, Conrad and John MacIntyre, the medical X-ray pioneer who had established the Glasgow Royal Infirmary's X-ray department. Munro described the event wherein 'all the wizardry of Röntgen rays were [sic] turned on' (1990: 94) as he was subjected to X-rays whilst Conrad and MacIntyre observed his ribs, backbone and 'the more opaque portions of my viscera'. Munro also recalled having 'our hands X-rayed' – presumably 'our' included Conrad's own hand – before receiving photographic images hours later. Conrad's own letter to Edward Garnett in September 1898 corroborates these events, describing a conversation that ranged from the important role of X-rays in medicine to a discussion of the secrets of the universe and 'the nonexistence of [. . .] matter' (1928: 143). Conrad remarked upon Munro's X-ray: 'we contemplated his backbone and his ribs. The rest of that promising youth was too diaphanous to be visible' (1928: 143).

This fascination with the literal and metaphorical powers of X-rays is apparent in *Heart of Darkness*, which Conrad began writing in December 1898, just two months after his evening with Munro and MacIntyre. There is a clear connection between Conrad's experience of Munro's X-ray, of his 'backbone', 'ribs' and 'diaphanous body', and the perceptions of the narrator Marlow. For example, the physical, bodily description of enslaved, chained Africans notes their 'every rib, the joints of their limbs [. . .] like knots in a rope' (1995: 15). As Marlow continues his journey into the darkness, the environment's geology becomes biomorphic, in line with what Martine Hennard Dutheil de la Rochère identifies as a widespread 'land-as-body analogy' (2004: 188). Marlow conflates the structure of a sandbank in shallow water with the human skeletal structure beneath the skin's veil: 'exactly as a man's backbone is seen running down the middle of his back under the skin' (1995: 43). Prior to Marlow's encounter with Kurtz, the narrative's antagonist, he perceives at a distance Kurtz's gothic, skeletal figure, an 'atrocious phantom', an 'apparition' with 'eyes . . . shining darkly in its bony head'

(1995: 59). Marlow describes Kurtz's body with striking similarity to an X-ray's penetration and uncovering of the skin and flesh to reveal a skeleton:

> His covering had fallen off, and his body emerged from it pitiful and appalling as from a winding-sheet. I could see the cage of his ribs all astir, the bones of his arm waving. It was as though an animated image of death carved out of old ivory had been shaking its hand with menaces at a motionless crowd of men made of dark and glittering bronze. (Conrad 1995: 59)

Again, protruding ribs and presence of bone come to the fore, resembling the gothic, deathly image of the X-ray. As with MacIntyre's image of Munro, although the skeleton is present, the rest of what makes someone human is absent. Whilst Conrad described Munro's image as 'too diaphanous to be visible', Marlow describes Kurtz as 'hollow at the core' (1995: 58); like the X-ray, Kurtz's inhumanity reveals a 'heart of darkness'.

Conrad's metaphors do not just articulate different ways of thinking and observing in response to a new visual technology; in Conrad's treatment, X-ray technology itself is a metonym for rendering transparent the brutality of colonialism and the effects upon its victims. Conrad describes Kurtz's transformation of native African bodies into living corpses resembling X-rays; just as the process of X-rays penetrates and pervades bodies – destroying them both physically through radiation and conceptually as a fragmented image – so European imperialism diminishes the native body into bones bound by chains. The X-ray, as a metaphor of truth and enlightenment, is also turned in on itself, as through this operation Marlow's 'X-ray vision' also reveals the imperialist motives of 'hollow' officials and 'shadow' men, and he 'see[s] through' the civilising mission and the 'vacuity of colonial discourse' (Hennard Dutheil 2004: 192). Whilst the 'heart' is often represented as a 'core', it is also an organic pulse, an alive, beating condition that is used to describe the jungle. However, Kurtz himself can be understood as the story's heart of darkness, underlying his status as a white European male shining a 'civilising' colonial light. Indeed, Conrad's narrative is counter to the enlightenment shone upon Africa by European male voyages such as Henry Morton Stanley's exploration of Africa. Stanley's search for David Livingston continued to popularise this metaphor in his accounts *Through the Dark Continent* (1878) and *In Darkest Africa* (1890). Conrad's recurring metaphors of body and light, vision and knowledge, surface and depth, solidity and vacuity all suggest how X-ray technology provided an apposite metonym; the X-ray was a technology of clarity and truth, but is used here to perceive the problematic ideological histories and destructive practices inherent within colonial power.

Conrad was not the only writer to consider X-rays within their work. Figures such as Jack London, Virginia Woolf, D. H. Lawrence, Thomas Mann and H. G. Wells, among others, were all influenced by this new technology. Woolf's writing was influenced by cinema, photography and a broader notion of visual culture, including X-rays. Margaret Humm proposes that the incorporation of the new capacities for revelation and representation created by a visual culture obsessed with new visual technologies such as photography, stereoscope, X-rays and cinema was fundamental to Woolf's modernism: 'Woolf concerns herself both with visible and "invisible" vision, with what contemporary physics was recognising in Einstein's theories of space time, as kinesis, that is the flow of differing perspectives' (2010: 214, 215). In a diary entry on 9 January 1897, written at the age of fourteen, Woolf describes accidentally attending a lecture and live demonstration of 'Rontgen [sic] Rays' (Woolf 1990: 9, see also Whitworth 2001a and 2001b). Woolf later incorporated direct reference to X-rays in her 1922 review of Percy Lubbock's literary criticism, *The Craft of Fiction*:

> Mr Lubbock applies his Röntgen rays. The voluminous lady submits to examination. The flesh, the finery, even the smile and witchery, together with the umbrellas and brown paper parcels which she has collected on her long and toilsome journey, dissolve and disappear; the skeleton alone remains. It is surprising. It is even momentarily shocking. Our old familiar friend has vanished. But, after all, there is something satisfactory in bone – one can grasp it. (Woolf 1986: 341)

Woolf describes Lubbock's approach almost as male violence upon a submissive female body. For Michael Whitworth, Woolf's reference to the X-ray here is a 'metaphor for reductiveness' (2001b: 153). Unlike Conrad's portrayal of the body as a hollow shell for an absent soul, Woolf appears to find comfort, something 'satisfactory', in the permanence of material solidity following the reductive process (see also Crossland 2014). Criticism and 're-reading' enact a process of stripping to reveal something essential as the (male) X-ray becomes a metaphor for revealing a (female) novel's structure. Later, in *To the Lighthouse* (1927), Woolf draws upon X-rays to penetrate inner motives behind the thin façade of behavioural etiquette at a social gathering. Woolf writes of Lily Briscoe's perception – 'as in an X-ray photograph' – of Charles Tansley's discomfort as his tense, restless ribs and bones become a symptom of his desire to impress 'lying dark in the mist of his flesh'. Lily then reflects upon behavioural social codes that compel her to provide an opportunity for which a man 'may expose and relieve the thigh bones, the ribs, of his vanity, of his urgent desire to assert himself' (Woolf 2004: 107). In distinction to Conrad's metaphor of the X-ray as a measure of a person's solidity, contrasting solid backbones of men of character to those merely hollow physical husks, Woolf perceives a permanence in one's skeletal deportment, even if it is made uncomfortable by social behaviour. Both writers problematise the very binary concepts of exterior and interior created through the X-ray by entangling one's inner and outer being; each dimension, inside and outside, is symptomatic of the other and fundamentally entwined. The X-ray not only reveals human interiority, but also serves as a metaphor to dissect social and political behaviours, with these examples laying bare the violent impositions of colonialism and patriarchy alike.

(De)Materialised Bodies

The relationships between interior and exterior, surface and depth, movement and perspective were of profound interest not only to modernist novelists but also to the European artistic avant-gardes. They incorporated their fascination with X-rays into a wider set of influences concerning the visual articulation of non-perceptible matter and forces influenced by the modern world such as new speeds of travel, electricity, prosthetically expanded vision, non-Euclidean and n-dimensional geometries and notions of the 'fourth dimension'. These forces reflected 'modern' experience and reality, with artists engaged in rethinking and reconfiguring the terms of visual representation.

Indeed, the long-established representational structure of three-dimensional perspective could no longer sustain and articulate such a new, dynamic, modern world. The French Puteaux group of artists and thinkers – including the painters Fernand Léger, Robert and Sonia Delaunay, Francis Picabia and František Kupka, and writers such as Guillaume Apollinaire – explored a range of modern concepts across philosophy, literature, technology, science, art and mathematics. Many ideas were nourished by an increase of books, journals, magazines and newspaper articles, and translations publishing the latest, radical, modern thinking (see Henderson 1983). The revelation of X-radiation was received within a larger context of profound cultural change (see Kern 2003) that inspired new visual articulations of transformed concepts of space, time, form, objecthood, energy and matter. The avant-garde's artistic experiments referred to processes of penetration, duration, movement and recomposition of objects, spaces and people to encode their 'reality' according to a different order. Cubism, a term advanced by Apollinaire and consisting broadly of the Puteaux artists and Montmartre painters such as Picasso and Georges Braque, presented a radical new vision by instituting a process of rupturing pictorial form and re-presenting objects. The abandonment of linear perspective and the integration of multiple perspectives through different interconnected, semi-opaque planes embodied the concept of dynamic 'becoming', inspired by the philosophy of Henri Bergson, in the articulation of an object whereby its structure was an expression of its relationship to temporality and an emanation of its interiority. Kevles insists that 'The first to portray the transparency and simultaneity of seeing through the body were the cubists' (1997: 124).

The Italian Futurists were also inspired by the increasing dissemination of new ideas (see Kern 2003; Lista 2001). Umberto Boccioni's 1910 'Technical Manifesto of Futurist Painting' addressed the need for representation to embody modern forces and an energistic interconnectivity between states of matter: 'Our bodies penetrate the sofas upon which we sit, and the sofas penetrate our bodies. The motor bus rushes into the houses which it passes, and in their turn the houses throw themselves upon the motor bus and are blended with it' (Boccioni 1968a: 290). The Futurists disavowed the permanence and 'opacity' of objects and figures in the new age of technological modernity: 'Why should we forget in our creations the doubled power of our sight, capable of giving results analogous to those of x-rays?' (1968a: 290). The new culture of vision and speed – from the X-ray to the motorcar – required new forms of visual encoding. Indeed, the Futurists perceived a radical deanthropocentrism occurring in the realisation of the profound limitations of human perceptual faculties and a destabilisation of their presupposed priority over perceptual reality: 'Our renovated consciousness does not permit us to look upon man as the centre of universal life' (1968a: 290).

Futurist painters experimented with a set of ideas, supported by the concept of X-rays, in articulating how 'movement and light destroy the materiality of bodies' (1968a: 293) and how a two-dimensional surface could synthesise concepts of force, dynamism and Bergsonian *durée*. Umberto Boccioni's writing referenced X-rays, and he used sculpture – traditionally a static medium – to express dynamic movement in his *Unique Forms of Continuity in Space* (1913) through a synthesis of Bergsonian concepts of 'relative' and 'absolute' time. Boccioni's prior sculpture, *Development of a Bottle in Space* (1912) (Figure 11.5), exposes the bottle's interior structure, in 'an explicit affirmation of positive negative space' (Kern 2003: 159). The sculpture moves

Figure 11.5 Umberto Boccioni, *Development of a Bottle in Space*, 1912. Metropolitan Museum of Art, Bequest of Lydia Winston Malbin, 1989.

beyond the surface in order to penetrate its interiority; the internal curvature and rotation of the bottle become fundamental to its exterior representation. The result is a synthesis of material and temporal conditions defining the bottle's status as an object. Resembling Woolf's and Conrad's synthetic vision of interior core and exterior surface, the bottle is simultaneously solid and hollow, static and rotating.

Boccioni's 'Technical Manifesto of Futurist Sculpture' of 1912 described an aspiration for sculpture to develop as Futurist painting had – through the synthetic interpenetration of planes that interconnect matter and states of being. He wrote, 'Futurist painting has overcome this conception of rhythmic continuity of the lines in a human figure and of the figure's isolation from its background and from its INVISIBLE INVOLVING SPACE' (Boccioni 1968b: 302). The potential role that X-ray images had in the development of Boccioni's notion that 'the sculpture will contain within itself the architectural elements' (Boccioni 1968b: 302) is significant. His conclusion – 'We proclaim that sculpture is based on the abstract reconstruction of the planes and volumes that determine the forms, not their figurative value' (Boccioni 1968b: 303) – summarises how the very process should become the form, for sculpture inherently to incorporate a dimension of Bergsonian temporality and the object's own 'becoming'. As Rosalind Krauss writes on *Development of a Bottle in Space*, 'it not only treats the viewer as a consciousness capable of encompassing the object's exterior in a single instant but it also guarantees the unity and clarity of this knowledge by giving him access to the object's very core' (1981: 45). Krauss understands Boccioni's reference to X-ray vision in the 'Technical Manifesto of Futurist Painting' as a 'turn to science to peel away the mute surfaces of things that make them unintelligible' (1981: 46). We can further understand Boccioni's approach by examining the resemblances to X-rays in the arcing structures of his drawing *Table + Bottle + House* (1912) (Figure 11.6).

Futurism's explorations in synthesising form and temporality into visual representation initially extended to photography and had briefly concerned Futurism's foremost artists – Boccioni, Carlo Carrà, Luigi Russolo, Giacomo Balla and Gino Severini. However, the medium was ultimately rejected as antithetical to Futurist aspirations

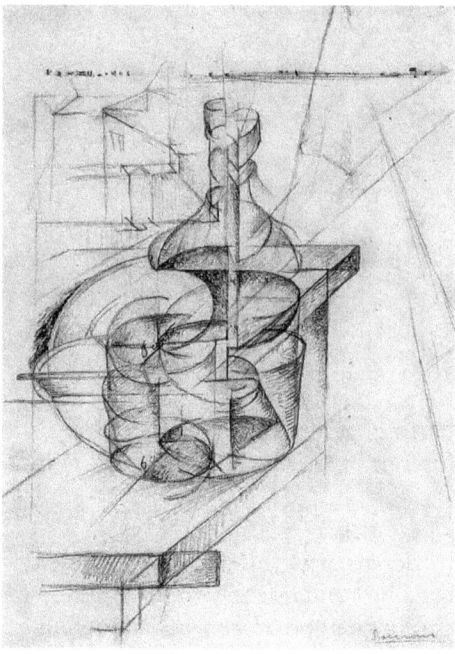

Figure 11.6 Umberto Boccioni, *Table + Bottle + House*, 1912. Pencil on paper. Civico Gabinetto dei Desegni, Castello Sforzesco, Milan.

(see Lista 2001). As the X-ray was an instrument of revelation, so photography initially promised similar possibilities. Giovanni Lista writes:

> By translating the infrasensorial and metaperceptive dimensions for the first time, by transfixing the transience or invisibility of the interaction between matter and energy, thereby revealing the unconscious dimension of the gaze, photography seemed to penetrate the very mystery of life. (2001: 10)

Futurism's most active photographic practitioner, Anton Giulio Bragaglia, developed a theory of 'Photodynamism' to accompany Filippo Tomaso Marinetti's 'free-verse dynamism', Boccioni's 'pictorial dynamism' and Francesco Ballila Pratella's 'musical dynamism' (Lista 2001: 21). Bragaglia was influenced by different sources, including Bergsonian philosophy, Étienne-Jules Marey's chronophotography, X-ray technology and parascientific photography (see Lista 2001).

Bragaglia would have been aware of contemporaneous experiments in the Italian photographic journals *Il Dilettante di Fotografia* and *Il Progresso Fotografico*. They featured images of 'Roentgen rays' alongside the parascientific – the 'photography of thought', spirit and ectoplasmic photography – and the more legitimate scientific work of Ernst Mach's dynamography, Marey's chronophotography, and microphotography (Lista 2001: 9). It is important to consider that the distinction between 'legitimate' and spurious forms of photographic innovations, and the revelations made possible by their images, was neither clear nor established, given photography's own nascent development and the wider cultural fascination for hitherto concealed dimensions of perception. Indeed, there are numerous examples of scientists and engineers engaged in both paranormal and parascientific research. One particularly apposite example here is the attempts by British scientist William Crookes – whose 'Crookes tube' was a prerequisite for discovering X-rays – to validate paranormal activity scientifically and objectively; he concluded that 'Psychic Force', emanating from the 'soul or mind' (1874: 23), had an objective existence. Exploring the limits of a technology was, understandably, considerably attractive within the scientific community; Gunning notes that spiritualist ideas actually encountered greater resistance and objection from religious organisations than from scientists and rationalists engaged in its research (2008: 62).

The X-ray existed within this ambivalent cultural and artistic context, at an intersection between reality and metareality, science and parascience. Indeed, other sorts of 'rays' were 'discovered' that similarly entwined rationality and the mysterious. French Commandant Louis Darget developed 'thought photography', capturing invisible rays projected from the human soul. He claimed this proved the existence of 'V-rays' ('V' for 'vital'). This was contemporaneous with French physicist Prosper-René Blondlot's disproven 1903 claims around radioactive 'N-rays' ('N' for Nancy University). Dr Hippolyte Baraduc, neurologist at the renowned Parisian hospital La Salpêtrière, had made photographic 'studies' of the soul, and had been influenced by Baron Carl von Reichenbach's concept of 'Od-rays' (after 'Odic force', referencing the Norse God Odin). 'Discoveries' of such invisible forces demonstrated an entanglement between scientific, parascientific, amateur, spiritualist and public spheres. This clear desire to go beyond the visible, to investigate the immaterial, was reflected in Futurist concerns with synthetic concepts of exterior and interior, absolute and relative. For Bragaglia, his concept of 'Photodynamism' was inspired by, and incorporated, such diverse influences.

The influence of X-rays upon the 'Orphism' of František Kupka and Marcel Duchamp has been studied in detail by Linda Henderson (1998) and Virginia Spate (1979). The appellation 'Orphism' was coined by the poet Guillaume Apollinaire, who attempted to cluster several painters into a distinct facet of Cubism. Like the Italian Futurists, Kupka and Duchamp were deeply inspired by new imperceptible dynamic forces and energies. Both artists attended the Puteaux group meetings on contemporary science, literature and philosophy, where, as Spate writes, there was an 'artistic transformation [following] the scientific and technological discoveries which were creating a new awareness of the physical world' (1979: 23). The X-ray directly inspired a number of those artists. For example, Francis Picabia's *Mechanical Expression Seen Through Our Own Mechanical Expression* (1913) – anticipating his later 'mechanomorphs' that hybridised the human body and industrial machine – refigured the film star and dancer Stacia Napierkowska as a machine, consisting in part of an X-ray-emitting Crookes tube. Picabia's figure is a construction of machine sexuality, exhibitionism and energy. However, Picabia's imagery is strikingly different from that of Kupka, a practising spiritualist and Theosophist. Kupka was a Czech painter living in Puteaux and sought to create non-representational (abstract) art to articulate 'soul impressions' (Spate 1979: 12) through treatment of form, line and colour. His description of the artist's mind used the metaphor of 'ultrasensitive film, capable of seeing even the unknown worlds of which the rhythms would seem incomprehensible to us' (Kevles 1997: 127). Kupka's interest in X-rays was supported by his studies of biology, physiology and neurology at the Sorbonne whilst he 'encountered numerous references to x rays [sic] and radioactivity in occult literature in this period' (Henderson 1988: 328), such as in the Theosophical works of Annie Besant and Charles Leadbeater. Paintings such as *The Dream* (1909) and *Planes by Colours, Large Nude* (1909–10) articulate Kupka's ideas, whilst his notebook reveals a Kantian concern with 'perception of matter under its exterior form [and] . . . perception of the form in itself' (Henderson 1988: 329).

Marcel Duchamp's famous *Nude Descending a Staircase, No. 2* (1912) (Figure 11.7) developed the concern between interior thought and exterior action in his 1910 *Portrait of Chess Players*, whilst unfolding from an intersection of further converging modern influences. Duchamp himself cited the impact of Cubism, Marey's stroboscopic chronophotography and the poetry of Jules Laforgue and Stéphane Mallarmé (see Duchamp and Cabanne 1979: 30–4). Duchamp recounted how he made illustrations for Laforgue's poetry and derived the idea for *Nude Descending* from *Encore à cet astre* (Sweeney 1946: 19; see also Steefel 1976). Laforgue's significance may have unfolded from his technique of combining disparate content through a unifying rhyming form, together with ascribing living features to inanimate objects (certainly observable in Picabia). Duchamp was also influenced by cinema, had seen Futurist depictions of movement, knew of Eadweard Muybridge's pioneering photographic studies and had been attached to the Puteaux Cubist group (Sweeney 1946: 19–20). Linda Henderson also argues that *Nude Descending* was significantly influenced by the X-ray and chronophotographic work of Albert Londe, upon which Professor of Anatomy Paul Richer developed anatomical diagrams. Richer published his schematic, simplified figures in *Physiologie artistique de l'homme en mouvement* (1895); in the image 'Deux doubles pas successifs de la descente d'un escalier', Richer's drawn figure descends two steps in nine layered, successive positions. For Henderson, 'Richer's diagram is almost the prototype for Duchamp's composition' (1988: 332). Duchamp's painting incorporates a similar sense of planar rotation but moves beyond the schematic to imbricate interior and exterior, rhythm and movement, to extract temporal and spatial essence. According to Henderson, Duchamp created a 'painterly equivalent to the transparent and fluid reality suggested by x rays' (1988: 336). Within the cultural anxiety over X-ray invasiveness, Duchamp desexualised his nude into something resembling mechanical form, whilst Picabia explored a machine 'erotics' with its parts, orifices, connections and biomorphic elements. Whilst Duchamp and Picabia became increasingly closer in their shared concern for imagining human-machine assemblages, Duchamp's *Nude* articulated something more akin to Futurism's interest in X-rays: penetrating exterior surfaces to reveal the interior structures upon which figures and forms unfold. The visual technologies of the X-ray, cinema and chronophotography inspired new modes of artistic figuration that had been nourished by new, modern ideas concerning duration, dynamism, interconnectivity and dimensionality.

The X-ray was a profoundly intermedial technology; the intangibility of radiation required a medium through which to manifest its presence. Indeed, the very condition of the X-ray's discovery was contingent upon an accidental photographic process. As such, the X-ray was rapidly harnessed by medical and scientific communities, commercial enterprises and entertainment entrepreneurs – all purchasing equipment for different contexts and audiences. X-rays also prompted significant modernist innovations. For example, the influence of Conrad's direct participation in an X-ray experiment can be traced in *Heart of Darkness*, where Marlow's gothic X-ray perceptions transform the landscape and penetrate the surfaces of its phantom figures. In contrast, Duchamp was inspired through a wider, more indirect set of X-rays' intermedial entanglements – from the painterly

Figure 11.7 Marcel Duchamp, *Nude Descending a Staircase, No. 2*, 1912. Philadelphia Museum of Art. The Louise and Walter Arensberg Collection. © Association Marcel Duchamp / ADAGP, Paris and DACS, London 2021.

innovations of his contemporaries, to photographic revelations, poetic experimentation and medical research. The forms that X-rays took were clearly both technical and metaphorical. As the discovery of X-rays was concurrent with the Lumières' first cinematic projection and Marconi's wireless communication, so it also occurred in the same year as the publication of works such as H. G. Wells's *The Time Machine* and Freud and Breuer's *Studies on Hysteria*. Both foundational works, of science fiction and psychoanalysis respectively, they also articulated something fantastic and disturbing beyond the visible. The duality inherent within the exterior and interior, surface and repressed, is inherent in the X-ray: visual media gave it spectacular presence whilst that very visibility generated a hauntological spectre within modernism. Within these contexts and through such works, Röntgen's discovery provided modernity's own metaphoric figure from which to 'know thyself'; the skeletons that had once occupied anatomical theatres waving their banners proclaiming 'Nosce te ipsum'('Know thyself') could be replaced by ubiquitous, photographic images of human interiority, first realised through Anne Berthe Röntgen's hand.

Works Cited

Boccioni, Umberto (1968a), 'Futurist Painting: Technical Manifesto (1910)', in *Theories of Modern Art*, ed. H. Chipp. Berkeley, Los Angeles and London: University of California Press, pp. 289–93.
Boccioni, Umberto (1968b), 'Technical Manifesto of Futurist Sculpture (1912)', in *Theories of Modern Art*, ed. H. Chipp. Berkeley, Los Angeles and London: University of California Press', pp. 298–304.
Busch, Uwe (2017), 'Wilhelm Conrad Röntgen: The Discovery of X-Rays and the Creation of a New Medical Profession', in *Handbook of X-Ray Imaging: Physics and Technology*, ed. P. Russo. Boca Raton. London. New York: CRC Press, pp. 327–30.
Cartwright, Lisa (1995), *Screening the Body: Tracing Medicine's Visual Culture*. Minneapolis: University of Minnesota Press.
Conrad, Joseph (1928), 'Letter to Edward Garnett, 29 September 1898', in *Letters from Joseph Conrad 1895–1924*, ed. E. Garnett. Indianapolis: Bobbs-Merrill.
Conrad, Joseph (1995), *Heart of Darkness and Other Stories*. Ware: Wordsworth Editions.
Crookes, William (1874), 'Enquiry into the Phenomena Called Spiritual', *Quarterly Journal of Science*, January, pp. 3–23.
Crossland, Rachel (2014), 'Exposing the Bones of Desire: Virginia Woolf's X-ray Visions', *Virginia Woolf Miscellany*, 85, Spring, pp. 18–20.
Duchamp, Marcel and Pierre Cabanne (1979), *Dialogues with Marcel Duchamp*, trans. R. Padgett. London: Da Capo Press.
Glasser, Otto (1993), *Wilhelm Conrad Röntgen and the Early History of the Roentgen Rays*. San Franciso: Norman Publishing.
Gunning, Tom (2008), 'Invisible Worlds, Visible Media', in *Brought to Light: Photography and the Invisible, 1840–1900*, ed. C. Keller. New Haven, CT: Yale University Press, pp. 52–65.
Henderson, L. D. (1983), *The Fourth Dimension and Non-Euclidean Geometry in Modern Art*. Princeton, NJ: Princeton University Press.
Henderson, L. D. (1988), 'X Rays and the Quest for Invisible Reality in the Art of Kupka, Duchamp, and the Cubists', *Art Journal*, 47: 4, pp. 323–40.
Hennard Dutheil de la Rochère, Martine (2004), 'Body Politics: Conrad's Anatomy of Empire in "Heart of Darkness"', *Conradiana*, 36: 3, pp. 185–205.

Humm, Maggie (2010), 'Virginia Woolf and Visual Culture', in *The Cambridge Companion to Virginia Woolf (Second Edition)*, ed. S. Sullers, pp. 214–30.

Kern, Stephen (2003), *The Culture of Time and Space 1880–1918*. Cambridge, MA, and London: Harvard University Press.

Kevles, Bettyann (1997), *Naked to the Bone: Medical Imaging in the Twentieth Century*. New Brunswick, NJ: Rutgers University Press.

Krauss, Rosalind (1981), *Passages in Modern Sculpture*. Cambridge, MA, and London: MIT Press.

Lavine, Matthew (2012), 'The Early Clinical X-Ray in the United States: Patient Experiences and Public Perceptions', *Journal of the History of Medicine and Allied Sciences*, 67: 4, pp. 587–625.

Lista, Giovanni (2001), *Futurism and Photography*. London: Merrell.

Munro, Neil (1990), 'Conrad's X-Ray', in *Joseph Conrad: Interviews and Recollections*, ed. M. Ray. Iowa: University of Iowa Press.

Natale, Simone (2011), 'The Invisible Made Visible: X-rays as Attraction and Visual Medium at the End of the Nineteenth Century', *Media History*, 17: 4, pp. 345–58.

'Photography in Medical Science' (1859), *The Lancet*, 22 January, p. 89.

Reiser, Stanley Joel (1990), *Medicine and the Reign of Technology*. Cambridge: Cambridge University Press.

Spate, Virginia (1979), *Orphism: The Evolution of Non-Figurative Painting in Paris 1910–1914*. Oxford: Clarendon Press.

Steefel, Lawrence D. (1976), 'Marcel Duchamp's "Encore à Cet Astre": A New Look', *Art Journal*, 36: 1, Autumn, pp. 23–30.

Sweeney, James Johnson (1946), *The Bulletin of the Museum of Modern Art*, VIII: 4–5.

Thomas, Adrian (2017), 'History of Radiology', in *Handbook of X-Ray Imaging: Physics and Technology*, ed. P. Russo. London and New York: CRC Press, pp. 331–54.

Tuniz, Claudio (2012), *Radioactivity: A Very Short Introduction*. Oxford: Oxford University Press.

Whitworth, Michael (2001a), *Einstein's Wake: Relativity, Metaphor, and Modernist Literature*. Oxford: Oxford University Press.

Whitworth, Michael (2001b), 'Porous Objects: Self, Community, and the Nature of Matter', in *Virginia Woolf Out of Bounds: Selected Papers from the Tenth Annual Conference on Virginia Woolf*, ed. J. Berman and J. Goldman. New York: Pace University Press, pp. 151–6.

Woolf, Virginia (1986), 'On Re-reading Novels', in *The Essays of Virginia Woolf, Vol. 3: 1919–1924*, ed. A. McNeillie. London: Hogarth Press, pp. 336–46.

Woolf, Virginia (1990), *A Passionate Apprentice: The Early Journals 1897–1909*, ed. M. A. Leaska. London: Hogarth Press, 1990.

Woolf, Virginia (2004), *To the Lighthouse*. London: Collector's Library.

12

Cinema: Notes on Germaine Dulac's 'Integral Cinema', Form and Spirit

Felicity Gee

WRITING ABOUT CINEMATOGRAPHY in the 1920s and 1930s involved an extraordinary, celestial vocabulary, which both derived and departed from scientific and philosophical ideas of the previous century.[1] Prior to the invention of cinema, scientists, photographers, astronomers, meteorologists and psychoanalysts of the mid-nineteenth century debated the potential wonders (and dangers) of seeing at a lesser or greater speed than one-tenth of a second, the unit of 'microtime' then believed to represent the standard time a human being took to react to external stimuli.[2] Consequently, '[n]ew arrangements between keys, bodies, wires, clocks, texts, images, and screens were set in place to understand this moment and solve the problems it posed' (Canales 2009: 217). The Transit of Venus (which took place in 1874 and 1882), lightning storms, electrical sparks, and solar and lunar events were some of the camera's early muses. These natural and man-made phenomena occurred at a pace or velocity, a distance or scale, that required the focal range and mobility of early cinematographic technologies.

Until the arrival of the Lumière cinematographic camera in 1895, advances in cinematography were often battles fought in laboratories and observatories, but these advances also presented philosophical conundrums. Frances Guerin argues that 'Technologies such as electrical light and cinema – with their impetus toward instantaneity, fragmentation and ephemerality – arguably frustrate the totalities and hinder the reconciliation between the world of things and that of the spiritual in technological modernity' (Guerin 2005: 20). As technologies pushed humans to attempt ever more accurate recordings of the exterior world, the unreliability of the observer, and the discrepancy between individual reactions to events and memories of them, became clearer, as did categorical factors such racial and ethnic discrimination based on an assumed biological determinism. The quest for the technological expansion of human ocular and neurological faculties necessarily invoked a rethinking 'of basic conceptions of the self [. . .] the difference between subjectivity and objectivity. [. . .The camera] was used to investigate what was distinctly personal and individual about particular observations and about the testimony of these observations' (Canales 2009: 215). For example, artist–filmmakers of the early twentieth century were entranced by cinematography's potential to capture sensory impressions, rather than its ability to augment verisimilitude and improve representational accuracy: 'If instruments decompose motion and explore the infinitesimal in nature,' wrote experimental filmmaker Germaine Dulac in 1928, 'it is to show us visually the dramas or beauties that our eye, a powerless lens, cannot perceive' (Dulac 2018: *Le Rouge et le Noir* (July 1928)).

This chapter is concerned with the various ways in which a new affective and philosophical vocabulary emerged through experiments in cinematic language across the world. Most of the examples I draw upon are from the work of avant-garde filmmakers and artists in Europe in the 1920s and 1930s, but the impact of cinema in the early twentieth century is world-wide, and illustrative of intellectual and economic flows across sometimes vastly unequal and difficult geopolitical boundaries. While the Third Cinema movement did not emerge in Latin America until the 1960s, for example, it took inspiration from the European avant-gardes of the century's early decades (including Soviet montage, Italian neo-realism, French surrealism and documentary). Thanks to individuals lugging canisters home from their travels, 35mm film reels often circulated abroad; these films included Man Ray's *L'Étoile de mer* (The Sea Star, 1928) and Dulac's much-discussed Surrealist work *La Coquille et le clergyman* (The Seashell and the Clergyman, 1927; scenario by Antonin Artaud), which reached Japan from France in this manner and were screened at small public gatherings (Nada 1992). Critical reviews also proved transformative in disseminating new trends and opinions beyond Europe. For example, Cuban novelist and musicologist Alejo Carpentier, exiled in Paris from 1928 to 1939, wrote reviews for viewers in Latin America who did not yet have access to the range of films that he saw at the Vieux Colombier cinema in Montparnasse (see Gee 2021). Typical of the balance of cultural specificity and international exchange, and discussed later in this chapter, are the work of Japanese filmmaker Kinugasa Teinosuke and the writing of Greek filmmaker Ado (Adonis) Kyrou, which, while created in dialogue with the European avant-garde, clearly articulate histories and traditions through a regional, socio-political lens.

In another sign of the internationalist potential of interwar cinema, the 1920s and 1930s saw an increase in polysemic film criticism that attacked racism in Hollywood and elsewhere. Anna Everett offers an overview of this critical trend:

> The preponderance of the literature bifurcates along familiar lines in African American political thought, that duality of accommodation and radicalism. Along the accommodationist axis are criticism and commentary concerned with effecting a progressive reform of Hollywood in matters of race and representation; along the radical line are those critiques defined by a politics of opposition to dominant film-making practices and their attendant bourgeois ideologies. (Everett 2001: 179–80)

In 1929, the film periodical *Close-Up* (1927–33) – a little magazine founded in Switzerland and later housed in the UK, edited by poet and novelist Winifred Bryher and Kenneth Macpherson – published a special issue on race to promote better and more sophisticated cinematic representation of Black subjects that might arrive with the coming of sound. Harry A. Potamkin's 'The Aframerican Cinema' makes some racist missteps but was nevertheless an earnest attempt to address discrimination in the industry:

> The cinema, through its workers, has been content to remain ignorant. It might have saved itself a great deal of trouble and many failures and much time had he [sic] studied the experience of the other arts. Well, what can the negro cinema learn from The White Man's Negro and The Black Man's Negro in art, in literature, in theatre?' (1929: 5.2, 1998: 66)

Even the most intellectually bourgeois or avant-garde film magazines took on political subjects and educational matters alongside articles on film as a serious art form. For some cinéphiles, such as Dulac, cinema seemed a miraculous uniting force:

> The films of each country bear their stamp of origin [. . .] but beyond local customs, spiritual and social internationalism shines through. Cinema is the marvelous Volapük[3] and, by being a universal language, creates affection and understanding between peoples. (Dulac 2018: 'The Meaning of Cinema' (December 1931))

This chapter considers the revelatory potential of film as it was perceived by artists and writers of the time through their often effusive philosophical and experimental prose. What is so striking in these examples of early twentieth-century cinema and cinematic writing is how modernist cinema inspired a wealth of approaches to filmmaking, including essayistic and philosophical approaches to montage, thereby indexing the flux and instability of the period. And what is also clear is that the line between practice and theory is, like the line between fantasy and reality, a permeable boundary. As such, we find ideas bridging Romanticism (awe at the natural world; metaphysics; and emotionality) and modernity (the cinematic apparatus as augmenter of reality; a perceived waning of human agency; and questions of the non-anthropocentric). A medium capable of expressing everything from inner thought to exterior everydayness in a synaesthetic rush of new combinations and juxtapositions, the moving image was by turns derided – as merely mimetic, 'an industry governed by sordid market forces incapable of distinguishing a work of the mind from a sack of flour' (Péret 2000 [1951]: 59) – and extolled: 'Cinema will be able to construct the synthesis-temple of our intense inner life, in the heavens that its new strength will illumine and "illustrate" by means of the incomparable findings of Science' (Canudo 1993 [1923]: 293–4). Navigating the vast constellations of schools, movements and industrial centres of interwar cinema, this chapter draws on the work of French filmmaker, producer and critic Germaine Dulac to thread these key concepts and ideas together. Dulac, one of few female filmmakers of the modernist avant-garde, made a significant contribution to film-philosophy. Resolutely detailed in her notes, she eschewed improvisation and focused on the detail of experience, specifically of women's boredom, habitual movements, domesticity and labour, centring, as Dulac scholar Tami Williams identifies, female desire and fear. Her counter-hegemonic observations necessitated a certain opacity of style in the male-dominated and oft-conservative milieux of filmmaking and journalism: 'Dulac's use of a less direct, cumulative system of symbolist association supported a more subversive and liberating discourse' (Williams 2014: 89). Her lectures and film criticism further underline a philosophical approach to human interiority and phenomenological experience.

Movement and the Senses: Dulac and Stein

Dulac was excited about film's potential to bring media as well as the senses into communication:

> In listening to the second Arabesque of Debussy, [. . .] I had the completely personal vision of the earth turning, rejuvenated by the sun, a vision of flowers, of sap, of

fountains of water rising and falling back, of joy, of rebirth, of physical well-being. I chose the visual rhythms to compose a 'film ballet' made from the very material of the Seventh Art, in other words, of motion, of light, of form, of connections. Would I claim that 'This is the entirety of cinema?' No. Better than that: it is a possibility of cinema. (2018: 'Within Its Visual Frame Cinema Has No Limits' (9 May 1931))

She writes here of her film *Étude cinégraphique sur une Arabesque* (aka *Arabesques*) (1929), a dance in light combining linear patterns of foliage and figural composition, woven in rhythmic, interlacing lines of the decorative Baroque style from which it takes its title. The spiritual art of Islamic cultures is set in motion with inspiration from Claude Debussy's impressionistic Baroque and the graceful poise of ballet dancers. An arabesque typically slows time in the unfolding of its ornamental, free-form melody. Dulac's *Arabesques* celebrates the cycles of routine and the slow beauty of natural forms in her cinematic poetry. Its rhythm has a softer, more harmonious ebb than in the pulsing and spinning of the better-known film *Le Ballet mécanique* (1924, directed by Fernand Léger and Dudley Murphy). These rhythmic differences remind us that, in this vibrant period, consensus was rare and transient, as views and movements emerged, clashed and separated. Terms such as 'pure', 'impressionist', 'absolute', '*photogénie*', 'Dadaist' and 'Surrealist' find philosophical as well as aesthetic purchase in a dialectics of formal innovation. Accompanying film criticism was frequently experimental and naïvely enthusiastic. Filmmakers also worked as critics, discussing and underlining the aesthetic, philosophical and utopian aims of their medium, often with an undeniable effusiveness. Dulac's *Arabesques* (Figures 12.1 and 12.2) and her written reflections on it, emblematise the dialectics of the cinematic avant-garde through a

Figure 12.1 *Arabesques*, Germaine Dulac, 1929.

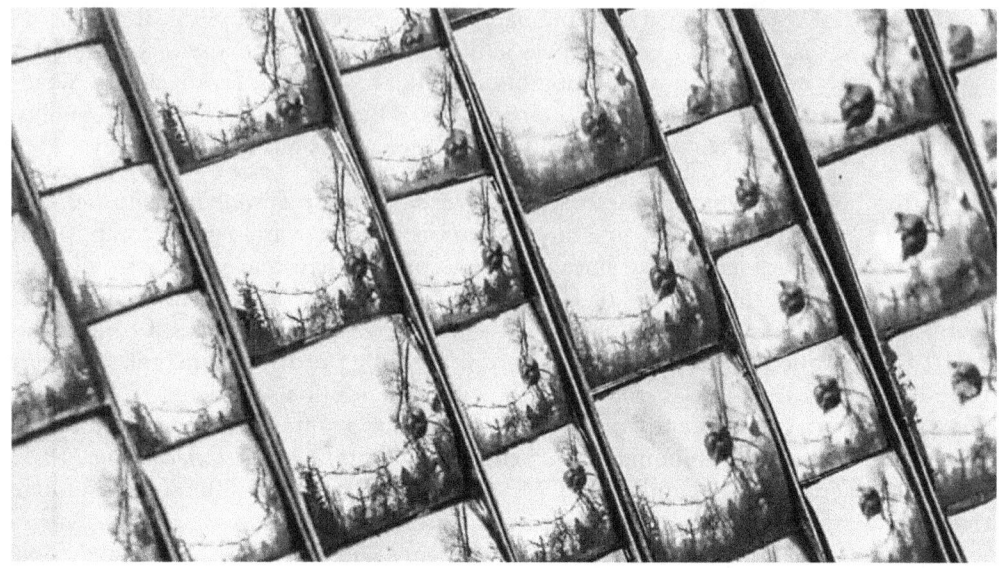

Figure 12.2 *Arabesques*, Germaine Dulac, 1929.

self-reflexive awareness. She combines thoughts on technological experimentation and the politics of the gaze with commentary on the challenges of representing the rhythms of emotion. The choice to foreground women's bodies, rhythmic association and the role of the senses lends her films an essayistic–feminist style, repeating and returning to affective resonances and motifs.

In Dulac's film-ballet, the viewer is encouraged to fall into the images, and while this visual world may appear discordant or incongruous, the cuts are not. The dissolves and edits are slower than Debussy's rather frenetic 'Arabesque No. 2', but thanks to time-lapse photography, life – the miraculous life of plants, for example – speeds up mechanically. In a lecture given on 17 June 1924, she explains how

> Distortions, like superimposition, are a way to make imaginary phantasmagoria real. The superimposition comes as a reaction, the lap dissolve as a link, distortion and soft focus as commentary. When recoiling from an emotion, do we see things as they are? Don't we tend to enlarge or shrink things? (Dulac 2018: 'The Expressive Processes of Cinematography' [1924])

Distortion and soft focus, she continues, 'can bring a whole philosophy to cinema' – as in the girl dying of hunger in her film *Gossette* (1923), or her contemporary Jacques Feyder's *Crainquebille* (1922), where the titular character's 'ingenuous soul' and inner turmoil are revealed through soft focus (Dulac 2018: 'Cinematography' [1924]). Not only is distortion linked to the inconsistency and unreliability of human perception, but in Dulac's hands it also describes a metamorphosis of things, ideas, that cinematography brings into being. The 'beautiful dream' of the avant-garde, in Dulac's eyes, was to counterbalance the commercial side of cinema, 'break down barriers, open new paths, and break new ground' (Dulac 2018: 'The Avant-Garde Cinema' [1932]).

Debussy's and Dulac's respective œuvres have been labelled 'French Impressionist'. In *Arabesques* this corresponds to a predominant lightness or haziness in the image, a fluidity of shot transitions, and an emphasis on sensation rather than narrative action. Jets and ripples of water are overexposed to lend an ethereal or otherworldly aspect; flowers appear in frames like specimens on contact sheets, seeming to stand in for humans; a seated woman is shot from behind, the succeeding shots apparently emanating from her mind; the weft of a coarse material meets the sharp lines of objects reflected in water. Dulac used effects such as the vignette of an iris, or the blur of overexposure in natural, rather than studio, lighting to contribute to the soft, impressionistic life of objects in motion:

> Impressionism made the audience consider nature and objects as elements contributing to the action. A shadow, a light, a flower, had first a meaning as a reflection of an inner soul or a situation, then little by little became a necessary addition with their own intrinsic value. We tried hard to make things move and, with the intervention of the science of optics, tried to transform their lines according to the logic of a state of mind. (Dulac 2018: 'Aesthetics, Obstacles, Integral Cinema' [1927])

Dulac's 'logic' does not follow a cause-and-effect linearity. This is the logic of things in perpetual metamorphosis, finding parallels in Debussy's seizure of movement via the decorative Baroque of 'Arabesque no. 2', which in its meandering modes and keys seems rather to connote a flutter of butterflies, a circular or spiral poetry in natural movement. Dulac's version of impressionism is in harmony with Maurice Merleau-Ponty's description of Paul Cézanne's 'instantaneous perception, without fixed contours, bound together by light and air' (1964: 11), which similarly attempts to grasp the fleeting. But instead of the painter's 'sunlit colours', which are used to represent sensations derived from the position of objects, Dulac employs a tonal spectrum from the powderiest cloud-white to the inkiest jet-black silhouette.

Writing on film in the early twentieth century often overflows with dynamic superlatives. It reaches into the depths of the personal and phenomenological. Poet and novelist H. D.'s wordy reviews for *Close-Up* accumulate layer upon layer of descriptive fascination:

> We moved like moths in darkness, we were hypnotized by cross currents and interacting shades of light and darkness and maybe cigarette smoke. Our censors, intellectually off guard, permitted our minds to rest. We sank into this pulse and warmth and were recreated. (1998: 116)

There is a sense of freedom in such regenerative abandon, a state appreciated by many artists to similar and divergent ends. Despite admitting to hardly ever watching films, Gertrude Stein was similarly obsessed with form, creating a textual shorthand for her sensory portraits of exterior reality through cinematography's technical expression of new ontological experience: 'The business of Art as I tried to explain in Composition as Explanation is to live in the actual present that is the complete actual present, and to completely express that complete actual present' (Stein 1988: 104–5). If immediacy springs from repetition, and 'each time the emphasis is different just as the cinema has each time a slightly different thing to make it all be moving'

(1988: 201), then, Stein believed, the mechanism of film art could act as a metaphor for intense experience.

When asked to contribute to *Close-Up* by Macpherson in 1927, Stein sent 'Mrs Emerson', a short piece that is formally entertaining and elusive. It begins:

> The regular way of instituting clerical resemblances and
> neglecting hazards and bespeaking combinations and heroically
> and heroically celebrating instances [. . .] (1998: 23)

and continues:

> The way to show shapes is to realise rightly that
> Mentionings are abominable.
> I can't help it I can't help hearing carrots.
> I do help it, I do help it fastening chocolate.
> A secret time in spinning. (1998: 27)

This experimental prose tells a partial story resembling an experimental film. It processes sensation, perception and thought in a synaesthetic rush. The irony of the line 'I cannot see I cannot see I cannot see. I cannot see. I cannot see beside always' (24),[4] in a response to cinema, forces the reader to 'see' elsewhere.

Susan McCabe's exquisite reading of Stein's incorporation of 'cultural tropes of bodily dislocation' in 'Mrs Emerson' reveals the significance of *Close-Up*'s editorial decision to juxtapose her portrait directly with a text by Man Ray on his experimental *ciné-poème*, *Emak Bakia* (1928): 'Stein's recuperations of viscerality did not assert bodily wholeness; rather, Stein's alternate modernism depended upon the incarnated, "existing," and dismembered body materialized by the avant-garde film' (2001: 403). Ray's film typically fragments the female body into legs, lips, torsos; and, similarly to Stein's appeal to the senses to register the present moment of existence, Ray ruminates on sight. The film is bookended with gags on looking: in the opening sequence Ray looks into a moving-image camera, with an eye superimposed onto one of the lenses, and in the closing sequence Kiki de Montparnasse 'looks' into the camera with her eyes closed, and eyes drawn over her closed eyelids. Stein, Ray and Dulac each comment on the affective experience of experiencing bodies in space, and on the screen, in differing but interrelated ways.

The art of writing on film embraced the spatial, social and time-based experience of cinema-going: the cine-clubs, cinephilia and popular and modernist magazines (for fans and critics, respectively). Stein's intellectual and phenomenological response to cinema seems aligned with Dulac's 'vision' in their shared attention to the sensory effects of the medium; other film critics, meanwhile, emphasised film's industrial and technological methods to challenge common perceptions of the cinema as lowbrow entertainment. The cinematic apparatus is a shining example of technology as muse: a means of seeing and sensing anew, bringing a kaleidoscopic world closer. To the already well-established connections between magic, occultism, science and montage[5] were added new ideas based in synaesthetic experiences (H. D., Stein, Eisenstein) and phenomenological–philosophical writing (Bergson, Bachelard, Merleau-Ponty). Film criticism moved beyond its ocularcentric focus to explore avant-garde cinema's potential to capture and interrogate the trauma and hope of the interwar years. An overwhelming desire to comprehend human reaction (and error) through measurement in science-based research contributed to the many philosophical debates on modernist time. Merleau-Ponty mused that cinematic time was exclusively tied to perception (as opposed to ordered thought):

> [A] movie has meaning in the same way that a thing does: neither of them speaks to an isolated understanding; rather, both appeal to our power tacitly to decipher the world or men and to coexist with them. It is true that in our ordinary lives we lose sight of this aesthetic value of the tiniest perceived thing. It is also true that the perceived form is never perfect in real life, that it always has blurs, smudges, and superfluous matter, as it were. (1964: 58)

Dulac's philosophy of film art draws fruitfully on the imperfection of the image. Writing for *Le Rouge et le noir* in July 1928, she vented her frustration at modern cinema's tendency to drift back towards narrative at the expense of all else. For her, as for many others, film art (no matter whether silent, sound or colour) was participatory, and therefore extended beyond the screen:

> The visual shock is ephemeral, it is an impression one gets that suggests a thousand thoughts. A shock analogous to the one which creates a musical harmony. [. . .] The story is the surface. The Seventh Art is the art of the screen, making the depth that stretches out below this surface perceptible, it is musical intangible. (Dulac 2018: 'Visual and Anti-Visual Films' [1928])

Her paradoxical description pinpoints the fleeting but palpable energy that is unlocked in the simultaneous unspooling and projection of celluloid frames. Here film montage is not simply a matter of rhythmic editing or musical notation; it interpellates the viewer anew with each fragment and sensation. In his 1960 *Theory of Film*, Siegfried Kracauer was similarly interested in the affective qualities of 'more or less free-hovering images of material reality' that '[n]otwithstanding their latent or ultimately even manifest bearing on the narrative' escape from the events on screen: 'their cinematic quality lies precisely in their allusiveness' (1997: 71). From this perspective, cinema is not a mausoleum, nor the 'flawless storage' that vanquishes death (Doane 1996: 338), but the point of genesis where the encounter between human and apparatus sparks life. Although Dulac was concerned that advances in technology and production should further her ability to make films internationally and connect with other professionals that she admired, such as D. W. Griffith or Jacques de Baroncelli (Williams 2014: 87–8), her artistic aims, as the images in her films, are blurry. This is both literal (in the sense that images can be out of focus, over- or underexposed, or deliberately distorted) and, by extension, philosophical: a 'deep, categorical blurring involving a transgression of boundaries', as Rosalind Krauss describes the heightened disregard for order or tradition found in Surrealist works (1999: 13). Surrealist emphasis on black humour, chance, irrational juxtaposition and a non-hierarchised blurring of low- and highbrow art and culture is similarly favoured by Dulac, who is concerned neither with perfection, nor with mastering a technology to achieve greater mimetic clarity.

In a similar vein, Greek filmmaker Ado Kyrou called for cinema to reveal unexplored and extraordinary facets beneath, and beyond, the surface of everyday life.

'Eroticism, imagination, exaltation, infernal tension', he writes, 'are the elements of a cinema that will have at last rejected the void to forever advance with giant strides toward "something else"' ('Romanticism and Cinema' [1951], qtd in Hammond 2000: 4). I find Kyrou's 'something else' evocative and mysterious, an important intervention in the dialogues between cinema, psychoanalysis and surrealism. Cinematography seemed to materialise individual and collective lack into 'something else' – it offered a form of proxy fulfilment (much explored in later psychoanalytic film theory, from Metz and Mulvey to Marcus[6]), but also a dialectical means (montage) to test philosophical concerns with no preconceived outcomes. 'Our lives are not limited to external manifestations,' Dulac repeats, 'but above all, and even more, consist of internal impressions which transform us into different mirrors of an identical action' (2018: 'Within Its Visual Frame' [1931]). Dulac refers here, of course, to the collected throng of possible responses elicited from a given audience. But on an individual level, the words also seem to encapsulate the encounter between a cinema screen and a viewer's sensing body, which creates a *mise-en-abîme* of selves and identities. Standing in front of a Cubist painting, a body multiplies in the repeated figural representation of 'movement'; for the viewer in front of moving forms on the screen, shapes perform in four-dimensional space, the fourth dimension being 'the image-dimension, which is also mind, thought, dream, memory' (Mariën 2015: 62). Thoughts and impressions collide at a pace dictated by the image/sound, the rhythm of edits, superimpositions and dissolves, and the manipulation and fragmentation of bodies and objects.

In 'Non-Scientific Treatise on the Fourth Dimension' [1944], Belgian Surrealist Marcel Mariën articulates a process of *sensing* reality that chimes with Dulac's cinematic aims. For her, depth is intangible; for Mariën, modern life is surface, the viewer never quite apprehending 'volume', which is 'the realm of hypotheses and legends' (2015: 62). The proliferation of images (a pear becomes a new object when peeled, the bark of a tree a new surface when detached from the tree) requires the viewer's imagination as the foundation upon which to evaluate 'the content and intimate nature of things' (2015: 63). In contradistinction to the Metzian view of film, where a lack of tactility is what constitutes the difference between a real object and its representation (Metz 1974: 9), Mariën and Dulac locate tactility and a psychological depth (perhaps paradoxically) in proliferating 'surface' images imbued with mental matter. All unfolds in the present, whether past or future; the viewer apprehends presence but senses absence, a lack or gap that contributes depth. This is not, then, only a cinema of attractions revelling in 'pure instance' (Gunning 2004: 49), but, as Stein also suggests, an opportunity for sensation to create new avenues for intellectual as well as emotional pursuit. Unlike in an essay, the viewer cannot pause the flow of ideas (the possibilities of home video were yet out of reach) but succumbs to them, perhaps reordering later in their own interior post-production. Mariën's 'treatise' is an exemplar of early twentieth-century obsessions with the intersection of art, technology and a form of affective neuro-non-science or playful psychoanalysis.

Time and space in the first half of the twentieth century were like nothing before: cinema brought far-flung regions into view, it combined new research in ethnology and ethnography, reanimated the dead and tracked the cosmos. It circulated globally, thanks to both commercial and private exhibition, and, most importantly, staged the 'intimate nature of things'. Mariën's description of the dimensions (height, width, depth, image) of objects found dynamism ultimately in the succession and surpassing of their surfaces (*images*), thereby locating meaning in gaps and ellipses, and aligning with Dulac's theories of composition. Significantly, one of the most powerful sections of Henri Bergson's *Creative Evolution*, where he writes substantially about cinematographic approaches to experiential time, focuses on absence, or nothing-ness. I have already suggested that the allure of early twentieth-century essays on the cinema rests in their fascination with the unknown, the unnoticed, the gaps. Bergson considers the ancient Eleatic school's philosophical questioning of 'eternal' time against duration, where the immutable becomes impossible in the reality of perpetual flux and change. Although cinematographic art is considered as an analogy, he unspools a philosophical line that articulates the schisms between reality/representation and shot/flicker (or image/cut):

> It is [. . .] something negative, or zero at most, that must be added to Ideas to obtain change. In that consists the Platonic 'non-being,' the Aristotelian 'matter' – a metaphysical zero which, joined to the Idea, like the arithmetical zero to unity, multiplies it in space and time. By it the motionless and simple Idea is refracted into a movement spread out indefinitely. In right, there ought to be nothing but immutable Ideas, immutably fitted to each other. In fact, matter comes to add to them its void, and thereby lets loose the universal becoming. It is an elusive nothing, that creeps between the Ideas and creates endless agitation, eternal disquiet, like a suspicion insinuated between two loving hearts. [. . .] As to sensible reality, it is a perpetual oscillation from one side to the other of this point of equilibrium. (Bergson 2008: 317)

Bergson does not consider the role of the filmmaker at all. However, what this idea has in common with Dulac's concept of cinematic art is its phenomenological focus, which oscillates between facticity (the object in front of you – real or represented) and the invisible or not-yet-understood or materialised. Gaston Bachelard viewed time and space very differently and is equally provocative in analyses of modernist image-making. Where Bergson philosophises 'becoming' in image succession, Bachelard hypothesises a non-rational perspective opening into time and space that anticipates the cinematic intensities described by Gilles Deleuze in *Cinema 2: The Time-Image* (1985): 'we must be fully attentive to the image at the very moment it appears, both as itself and as a vibration of the psyche' (Bachelard, qtd in Kearney 2014: xix). The thrill and beauty of the rupturing instant, 'the very ecstasy of the newness of the image' (Bachelard 2014: 1), has the potential to interrupt flow, something prioritised in Dulac's cinematography and editing choices for *La Coquille*, which, despite its oneiric associative montage flow, introduces shock and incongruity, vertically.

Describing the feminist montage of Dulac's 1923 film *La Souriante Madame Beudet* (The Smiling Madame Beudet), Tami Williams observes how Dulac employed 'a specifically cinematic system of signification based on the isolation and the opposition or synthesis of expressive gestures, which she used as "social critique", and which were later developed in Eisenstein's "intellectual montage"' (Williams uses the example of the juxtaposition of Madeleine's hands gracefully playing Debussy at the piano, with Monsieur Beudet's hands counting money) (2014: 129). *La Coquille*, filmed towards the end of the decade, develops a far greater subtlety and confusion in its montage, imploring the viewer to be 'fully attentive to the image' and its instantaneous affect.

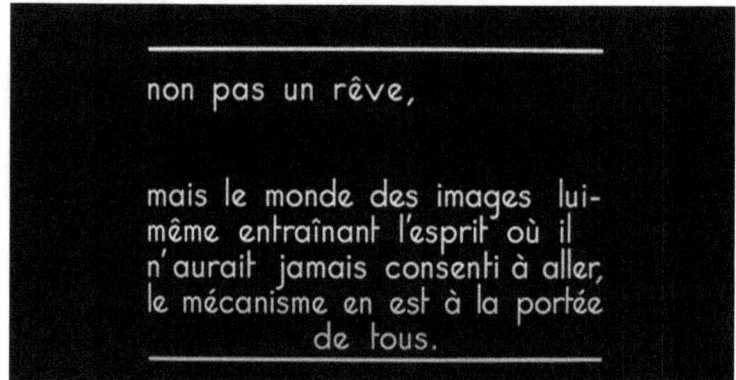

Figure 12.3 Intertitle, *La Coquille et le clergyman*, Germaine Dulac, 1927.

The psychological mechanism that drives the images is desire, a desire that appears out of nowhere, unannounced and all-consuming. As in all Surrealist films, neither the outcome nor the psychological reasoning behind it is important; what is significant is the affect generated at the moment of creation and in the work's interaction with an audience.[7] The intertitle at the beginning of *La Coquille* (Figure 12.3) states plainly Dulac's cinematographic intent:

[not a dream,
but the world of images itself, enticing the spirit where it
would never have consented to go,
the mechanism is within reach
of everyone.]

Dulac's images condense desire not in the grabbing hands and lascivious leer of the clergyman, but in the alchemical transfer of objects: liquid into glass, solid whole into shards, human body into mythical sea creature, dance into labour, landscapes into cityscapes, monarchical hierarchies into chess, water vapour into steel. One thing becomes another, at times bearing resemblance or matching movement, at others completely defined by difference, and all the while set within the fourth dimension of images. Dulac asserted that to know or understand was less important than to feel and to challenge. Her oneiric and object-centred films harness technology in-camera, and in post-production, reproducing human mental life. Mirroring the gaze and interior thought processes of male desire, she deliberately shifts focus to that of the female human and her temporality.

Kinugasa's *A Page of Madness*: Reality, Surreality and the Migration of Ideas

Witness and participant in countless world and civil wars, cinema reordered 'things' and gave to them new dimensions: 'like those between different worlds and thoughts:

struggle between madness and reason, the known and the unknown, you and me' (Mariën 2015: 64). This section illustrates how an example of early Japanese experimental film, which takes the tension between so-called madness and order as its guiding principle, creates a vision and aesthetic that resonates with Dulac's. Cinema's ability to 'reorder' reality, recording both its known and its unknown aspects, straddled boundaries of discipline and medium, appealing to artists and writers such as those in the Paris Surrealist group. The ideas set out in André Breton's *Manifeste du surréalisme* (1924) reverberated across the globe. It is a pioneering modernist text which provoked and sustained transnational collaboration, political and exilic tracts, and revolutionary art, including cinema. In the 'Manifesto of Surrealism' Breton instructs his reader (or viewer) to adopt a state of readiness to enable *automatic* thought unfettered by logic to appear (1972). In the mid-1920s, thanks to a small number of writers and artists, Breton's ideas started to circulate in Japan. The Japanese word for surrealism – *chō-genjitsushugi* – was coined by poet Muramatsu Masatoshi in his essay 'Reality and Surreality', published in the May 1925 issue of the *Bungei Nihon* (Literary Japan) (Stojkovic 2020: 2). The Japanese translation is separated into two parts; *genjitsushugi* refers to the principle of realism/reality, while, as Miryam Sas explains, '*chō-* signifies transcendence as well as transgression – something that moves beyond the everyday, breaks the mold of the category it modifies' (1999: 8). Significantly, this formal modification of reality through the transcendence of logic, order and the ordinary results, nevertheless, in an expansion that does not depart from reality. The Japanese government perceived surrealism to be dangerous, transgressive and Marxist:

> [Surrealism] aims to liberate the human mind by overcoming various inconsistencies in human psychology. It claims that the psychological phenomena cannot exist without a relation to the realms of material, that the psychological inconsistencies are reflections of inconsistencies of capitalist society and tyranny.[8]

This proclamation illustrates the power of formal dislocation to make tangible political interventions (as Dulac's commentary on the clergyman's odious desire demonstrates). To return to Kyrou's concept of 'something else', we might consider how experimental film reproduces the everyday tension that is both anchored in, and transcendent of, lived experience. It should also be noted that while the European avant-gardes provided inspiration for new formal experimentation, the ideas were not often followed wholesale, but fed into a burgeoning film culture that tackled homegrown social issues.

In Japan in 1926, a year after the publication of Muramatsu's essay, an extraordinary silent experimental film about madness was made by Kinugasa Teinosuke. Based on a treatment written by Nobel Prize-winning novelist Yasunari Kawabata, *A Page of Madness* (*Kuruta ippeiji*) tells the story of a young woman incarcerated in an 'asylum' (most likely driven to illness after her child drowns), and her husband, a retired sailor who takes up the position of janitor at the asylum to watch over her. The film's poetic form evinces a pleasure in incongruity, irrationality and fantasy that has much in common with Surrealist principles. Stylistically, *A Page of Madness* shares a vocabulary with several European films of the 1920s – Murnau's *Der letze Mann* (The Last Laugh, 1924), for example, or that trigger for 'collective hypnosis' (Kittler 1999: 146), Robert Wiene's *Das Cabinet des Dr. Caligari*

(The Cabinet of Doctor Caligari, 1920) – and its illusory sequences, dominated by graphic lines and oblique angles, resemble the only surviving Futurist film, Anton Giulio Bragaglia's *Thaïs* (1917). However, *A Page of Madness* might be the most audacious visual portrayal of the fourth dimension of its time. Its depiction of what Mariën called the 'struggle between madness and reason' is chaotic: the edits are frenetic, figures and objects are constantly in motion, and moments of genuine reflective sadness emanate from the film's relational (dis)order. Kinugasa's film hinges on the performances of the incarcerated woman, and a dancer whose presence symbolises the male inpatients' fantasies, as well as embodying liberation. The viewer is unable to discern the seam between anguish and erotic spectacle, and that is the point. Spatio-temporal logic disappears in the overwhelming perspectival shifts. Standard shot-reverse shot logic, which would denote relational movement or an individual character's interiority, is blurred, allowing emotion to bleed across and between the web of voyeuristic and alienated gazes. *A Page of Madness* invites the viewer to enter a Surrealist landscape which nonetheless never departs from reality, delivering a nightmarish vision of the human cost of state institutions. Whip pans, canted angles, spinning and blurred images, and eradication of contextual markers experiment with space at the service of the human mind in crisis. The viewer slips in and out of seemingly solid iron cell bars, both voyeur and participant in the opaque interior lives of the film's uprooted protagonists.

The film begins *in media res* during a heavy storm. The overexposed images of rain and overflowing water flicker in rapid succession: horizontally, vertically. Suddenly the viewer is plunged into a new plane of reality as a costumed dancer embraces the air, framed against a Futurist set. Then, a series of cell number plates appear and dissolve before we meet the first inpatients, the camera uniting their individual worlds cut by cut, rendering the environment kaleidoscopic. Like Breton's state of readiness, so famously enacted in Luis Buñuel's and Salvador Dalí's series of match cuts which culminate in the slicing of an eye in *Un Chien andalou* (1928), Kinugasa's *tabula rasa* creates an active viewer, awakened to a strange technological uncanny. The effect recalls the associative montage of early European Surrealist films, such as *La Coquille*, where, as Artaud explains, 'The kind of virtual power images have goes rummaging in the depths of the mind for hitherto unused possibilities' (2000: 104). For James Peterson, the poetic rebellion of *A Page of Madness* requires that

> viewers are not only challenged to separate the 'real' world of the primary story level from the level of character subjectivity, they must also distinguish between two types of subjective images: images of past events (memories) and images of imaginary events (fantasies, hallucinations, and dreams). (1989: 41)

In its exploration of criminality, desire and desperation, *A Page of Madness* is an example of Japanese modernist avant-garde cinematography that is clearly underpinned by specific geopolitical concerns: imperialism, its status in the East Asian region, and discrimination against working-class, minority, migrant and mentally ill citizens. Kinugasa understands the power of cinematography to mobilise a rebellious anti-establishment sentiment. The film's associative montage combines Japanese traditional arts – calligraphy, *shunga* (woodblock prints depicting sensual, erotic scenes), dance – with cropped and fragmented images of a reality torn from the mind.

Desire and Fear – Between Avant-Garde and the Mainstream

The process of identifying with one's 'like' on screen (Mulvey 1975: 17–18), of desiring or fetishising an object, or of simply being prompted into a succession of thoughts triggered by a film and its transient objects, might seem to repeat or parallel the mechanics of a psychoanalytic session or a dream. The cinematic unconscious is *all image*, as Stephen Heath reminds us, 'its provision of a residue of signifying traces [. . .] something only *analytically* calculable' from individual viewer experience (Heath 1999: 27). In contrast, the human unconscious is embedded within layers of linguistic, pre-cognitive and emotional strata that are not presented externally in the same way; nor, as Bergson argued, are they subject to time. Film's 'blending of movement and stillness' mirrors the 'transformation of the animate into the inanimate', a 'point of uncertainty' that plays on the difficulty of living with the reality of death (Mulvey 2006: 30). Lack, latency and lacunae generated by desire each may be set into play in the act of watching a film; a film narrative might fully cohere to Freud's Oedipal scenario or reveal a protagonist's neurosis or obsession (a thread that delighted Surrealists such as Breton, who was both attracted and repulsed by psychoanalytic theories – Freud and Jean-Marie Charcot, respectively); the orchestration of the gaze may align with objects of desire. Ultimately, Mary Ann Doane argues, scientists (she discusses chronophotographer Étienne-Jules Marey) and Freud 'resisted the cinema because it adhered to the senses and was not amenable to the abstraction required either to illustrate the basic concepts of psychoanalysis or to produce scientific knowledge' (Doane 1996: 343). Doane's reference to psychoanalytic abstraction (or a mental reduction represented in the image) differs from the cinematic term abstraction as it used by Dulac, who deploys it in reference to the very representation of the senses that Freud seemingly dismisses.

In *Thèmes et variations* (1928; Figures 12.4 and 12.5), Dulac mobilises her theoretical ideas, juxtaposing the graceful repetitions of a female dancer with matched

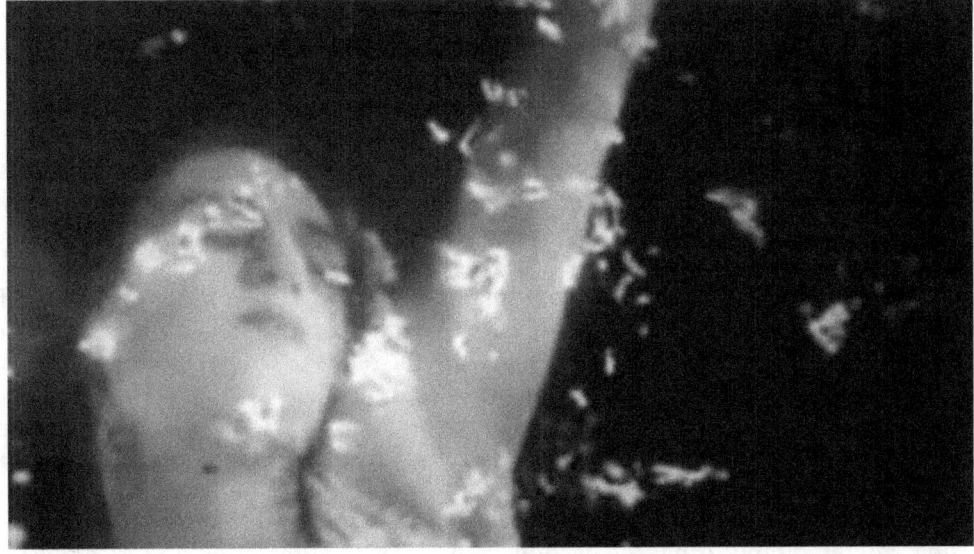

Figure 12.4 *Thèmes et variations*, Germaine Dulac, 1928

Figure 12.5 *Thèmes et variations*, Germaine Dulac, 1928.

movement in the mechanical turns of pistons, wheels and bells. The viewer follows these themes and variations, musically imagined, and materialised in the ethereal dancer and the faster, glinting rotations of the machinery. Something is lost; it escapes, perhaps unnoticed, or too quickly replaced by the successive images? The human eye cannot see all. What occurs between the woman and the machines, or between the body and the impressionistically fashioned landscape and plant-life at the end of the short film? The possibilities teem. The hard and the delicate (masculine/feminine) might suggest Kyrou's eroticism; on the other hand, the lack of synthesis in this strange and vivid pas-de-deux is suggestively critical. The viewer must enter the ellipses, a blink or moment of distraction giving way to a flicker effect: 'Lines, surfaces, volumes directly changing, without anything artificial, in the logic of their forms, stripped of all overly human meaning to better rise towards abstraction and give more room to feelings and dreams: INTEGRAL CINEMA' (Dulac 'From Sentiment to Line' [February 1927], qtd in Williams 2014: 158). Dulac's words are, like H. D.'s, Stein's and Kyrou's, filled with freedom. Synthesis transpires in the completion of the image by the viewer, where the inner life (she refers to souls, emotions, dreams) rises to meet the forms and figures dancing on screen. These sentiments were echoed in the film practice of certain filmmakers of the period who crossed over into commercial studio filmmaking; F. W. Murnau's work for Ufa Studios laboratory (*Universum Film-Aktien Gesellschaft*, 1917–45) and 20th Century Fox stands out. His ultimate desire was to create a fully 'architectural' film that captured 'the interplay of lines rising, falling, disappearing; the encounter of surfaces, stimulation and its opposite, calm; construction and collapse; the formation and destruction of a hitherto almost unsuspected life' (Eisner 1973: 84). The contrast between the implied order and stability of architectural form and its impermanent cinematic equivalent relies upon minor and minute aspects to convey the bipartite reality of conscious and unconscious life. The conscious portion leans towards the philosophical (unsuspected life) rather than the analytical, with the cyclical movement of formation and destruction deliberately courting a lack of resolution or fixity. As Kracauer, commenting in 1947 on Murnau's *Schloss Vogelöd* (The Haunted Castle, 1921) well understood, this was achieved in '[the] unique faculty of obliterating boundaries between the real and the unreal. Reality in his films was surrounded by a halo of dreams and presentiments' (Kracauer 2004: 78).

Angela Dalle Vacche's reading of Count Orlok (aka Nosferatu, played by Max Schreck, in Murnau's silent film *Nosferatu, eine Symphonie des Grauens* (Nosferatu: A Symphony of Horror, 1922) articulates how the character has two sides, one eliciting desire, the other inspiring fear. This lonely figure 'can be seen as an embodiment of Romantic painting, of the supernatural in daily life, of an unfulfilled yearning toward the divine' (1996: 162). In a thrilling sequence as the Count recoils at the threatening sunrise at an open window, his body is rendered partially transparent in a dissolve, becoming half flesh, half phantom, a negative reversal of divinity. In Murnau's films humans are not ontologically favoured above nature or objects 'but are revealed together'; fantasy and reality cannot be separated when 'the world is already drawn by fantasy' (Cavell 1971: 102). In *Nosferatu* the emotional and 'spiritual' emerge in a technical incorporeality that relies on translucence, magnification, superimposition and oblique editing to blur the distinction between phantom and human, or natural and artificial. In his commentary on the film (2013), Murnau's friend and partner, the painter Walter Spies, notes how the director harnesses technical detail (focal length, telescopic lenses and stop motion) to portray the 'other side' of reality. Seeming to anticipate Làzsló Moholy-Nagy's late 1920s teaching of X-ray photography, microphotography and astrophotography at the Bauhaus, *Nosferatu*'s Professor Bulwer studies the habits of carnivorous plants under a microscope. The resulting tinted microphotographs yield fantastic images ('almost incorporeal', Bulwer comments), which are intercut with shots of the imprisoned 'madman', Knock. This associative montage foregrounds scientific and technological 'facts' to establish an altered reality, not as self-reflexive trickery to showcase the apparatus or display cleverness, but to 'photograph thought',[9] thereby capturing subtleties of prismatic interiority.

This chapter has explored only a few of the marvellous examples of film and film criticism that constitute a history of modernist cinema. I have deliberately focused on avant-garde films that sought to capture something of the ephemeral sensations of modern life. In his manifesto 'Le Peintre de la vie moderne' (The Painter of Modern Life), Charles Baudelaire describes how 'Modernity is the transient, the fleeting, the contingent; it is one half of art, the other being the eternal and the immovable' (1972: 397). With the impossibility of 'newness' comes a different understanding of tradition, and for much of European modernism and its avant-gardes this meant a re-engagement with Romanticism, and with the place of human beings in the exterior world. Baudelaire favours the 'transient' flows above the sublime and 'eternal' view of nature, where humans are not overcome by the world, but share a mutual space and time with it (as Dulac's and Murnau's films hypothesise). The Romantic perspective engaged with:

a philosophy of nature that presupposed dynamism, dialectic, animated nature [. . .] In such a cosmos, magical exchanges occur between humans and minerals, spirits and matter, poles and forces. In such a vision all is alive, historical, subject to change and movement. (Leslie 2005: 13)

Much of this is evidenced in the films and essays that I have cited, where cinematography holds a paradoxically Romantic and occult charm, despite its clearly cutting-edge technology and ability to reimagine modern human existence. In these works, emotional depth reveals latent affect in technological surface: Dulac's soft and rhythmic abstraction, Kinugasa's experimental form, H. D. and Stein's affective engagement with cinematography, all offer resubjectivised views of their respective realities. Surrealism is a central component of this renewed view of the world. Murnau's philosophical experiments in studio-funded film projects exemplify the need to see oneself not only in nature, but in technology and artifice. It is Dulac, however, who offers the most urgent revision to our understanding of modernist cinema: her resolutely non-anthropocentric film-philosophy emphasises the world of objects through a deliberately female gaze. She insists that the future of cinema be technically marvellous: 'An art of feelings' (2018: [1923] 'Mon ciné').

Notes

1. Thanks to Phil Wickham at the Bill Douglas Cinema Museum for providing me with an original copy of Gertrude Stein's 'Mrs Emerson' from *Close-Up* magazine. Accessing artefacts from the period, like watching the films in their original format, brings the reader closer to their wonder.
2. See Canales, *A Tenth of a Second*, which connects creative and technological modernist mediums to the nineteenth-century European preoccupation with an oft-universally accepted unit of measuring affect and cognition in humans. This unit was problematically deployed to determine the slowness or speed of a given human's sense of perception, leading to key debates in physical, psychical and metaphysical existence, as well as being central to Walter Benjamin's theories of film (2009: 223–4).
3. Volapük was a universal language created in 1879/80 by Johann Martin Schleyer. It was eclipsed by Esperanto (invented by Ludwig Zamenhoof in 1887) by the turn of the century.
4. Stein's original article contains deliberate rhythmic spacing, which is not reproducible here given the specificity of print layout.
5. In Russia, Sergei Eisenstein popularised a theory of montage which he saw as being at the service of the audience: 'Revolutionary form is the product of correctly ascertained technical methods for the concretisation of a new attitude and approach to objects and phenomena – of a new class ideology' (1998: 55).
6. See, for example, Metz (1982), Mulvey (1975, 1996 and 2006) and Marcus (2014).
7. Both Williams (2014) and de Julio (2013) cite Alain Virmaux's essay, 'La Coquille et le clergyman: essai d'élucidation d'une querelle mythique' (2009), which discusses the correspondence between Dulac and screenwriter Antonin Artaud in detail.
8. The anti-establishment Surrealist spirit of the 1920s culminated in an annual government report entitled 'The Condition of Social Movements During the 16th Year of Shōwa' (1931), which posited surrealism as Communism's cultural face, discussed in Tezuka (2005: 122–3).
9. Taken from an interview with Murnau in *Theatre Magazine*, January 1928. In Petrie (2002): 94.

Works Cited

Artaud, Antonin (2000 [ca. 1928]), 'Sorcery and Cinema', in *The Shadow and Its Shadow: Surrealist Writings on the Cinema*, trans. and ed. Paul Hammond. San Francisco: City Lights Books, pp. 103–5.
Bachelard, Gaston (2014 [1958]), *The Poetics of Space* [La Poétique de l'espace], trans. Maria Jolas. New York: Penguin Books.
Baudelaire, Charles (1972 [1863]), *Baudelaire: Selected Writings on Art and Artists*, ed. P. E. Charvet. Cambridge: Cambridge University Press.
Bergson, Henri (2008 [1911]), *Creative Evolution*, trans. Arthur Mitchell. New York: Henry Holt and Company, <https://www.gutenberg.org/files/26163/26163-h/26163-h.htm> (last accessed 24 January 2022).
Breton, André (1972 [1924]), 'Manifesto of Surrealism', in *Manifestos of Surrealism*, trans. Richard Seaver and Helen R. Lane. Ann Arbor: University of Michigan Press, pp. 3–47.
Canales, Jimena (2009), *A Tenth of a Second: A History*. Chicago and London: Chicago University Press.
Canudo, Ricciotto (1993 [1923]), 'Reflections on the Seventh Art', in *French Film Theory and Criticism: A History /Anthology 1907–1929, Volume 1*, ed. Richard Abel. Princeton, NJ: Princeton University Press, pp. 291–303.
Cavell, Stanley (1971), *The World Viewed: Reflections on the Ontology of Film*. Cambridge, MA: Harvard University Press.
Dalle Vacche, Angela (1996), *Cinema and Painting: How Art is Used in Film*. London: The Athlone Press.
De Julio, Maryann (2013), 'Another Look at Germaine Dulac's The Seashell and the Clergyman', *Senses of Cinema*, 69 (December), <https://www.sensesofcinema.com/2013/feature-articles/another-look-at-germaine-dulacs-the-seashell-and-the-clergyman/#1> (last accessed 24 January 2022).
Doane, Mary Anne (1996), 'Temporality, Storage, Legibility: Freud, Marey, and the Cinema', *Critical Inquiry*, 22 (Winter), pp. 313–43.
Dulac, Germaine (2018), *Germaine Dulac: Writings on Cinema (1919–1937)*, trans. Scott Hammen, ed. Prosper Hillairet. Paris: Paris Expérimental and Eyewash Books, Kindle Edition.
Eisenstein, Sergei (1998 [1925]), 'The Problem of the Materialist Approach to Form', in *The Eisenstein Reader*, trans. Richard Taylor and William Powell, ed. Richard Taylor. London: BFI Publishing, pp. 53-9.
Eisner, Lotte (1973), *Murnau*. London: Secker and Warburg.
Everett, Anna (2001), *Returning the Gaze: A Genealogy of Black Film Criticism 1909–1949*. Durham, NC, and London: Duke University Press.
Gee, Felicity (2021), *Magic Realism, World Cinema, and the Avant Garde*. London and New York: Routledge.
Guerin, Frances (2005), *A Culture of Light: Cinema and Technology in 1920s Germany*. Minneapolis and London: University of Minnesota Press.
Gunning, Tom (2004), '"Now You See It, Now You Don't": The Temporality of the Cinema of Attractions', in *The Silent Cinema Reader*, ed. Lee Grieveson and Peter Krämer. London and New York: Routledge, pp. 41–50.
Hammond, Paul (2000), 'Available Light', in *The Shadow and Its Shadow: Surrealist Writings on the Cinema*, ed. Paul Hammond. San Francisco: City Lights Books, pp. 1–45.
H. D. (1998 [November 1927]), 'The Mask and the Movietone', in *Close-Up 1927–1933: Cinema and Modernism*, ed. James Donald, Anna Friedberg and Laura Marcus. Princeton, NJ: Princeton University Press, pp. 114–20.

Heath, Stephen (1999), 'Cinema and Psychoanalysis: Parallel Histories', in *Endless Night Cinema and Psychoanalysis: Parallel Histories*, ed. Janet Bergstrom. Berkeley: University of California Press, pp. 25–57.
Kearney, Richard (2014), 'Introduction', in Gaston Bachelard, *The Poetics of Space* [La Poétique de l'espace], trans. Maria Jolas. New York: Penguin Books, pp. xvii–xxvii.
Kittler, Friedrich A. (1999 [1986]), *Gramophone, Film, Typewriter*. Stanford, CA: Stanford University Press.
Kracauer, Siegfried (1997 [1960]), *Theory of Film: The Redemption of Physical Reality*. New York: Oxford University Press.
Kracauer, Siegfried (2004 [1947]), *From Caligari to Hitler: A Psychological History of the German Film*. Princeton, NJ, and Oxford: Princeton University Press.
Krauss, Rosalind E. (1999), *Bachelors*. Cambridge, MA: MIT Press.
Kyrou, Ado (2000 [1963]), 'The Marvellous is Popular', in *The Shadow and Its Shadow: Surrealist Writings on the Cinema*, trans. and ed. Paul Hammond. San Francisco: City Lights Books, pp. 68–71.
Leslie, Esther (2005), *Synthetic Worlds: Nature, Art and the Chemical Industry*. London: Reaktion Books.
McCabe, Susan (2001), '"Delight in Dislocation": The Cinematic Modernism of Stein, Chaplin, and Man Ray', *Modernism/modernity*, 8: 3 (September), pp. 429–52.
Marcus, Laura (2014), *Dreams of Modernity: Psychoanalysis, Literature, Cinema*. Cambridge: Cambridge University Press.
Mariën, Marcel (2015 [1944]), 'Non-Scientific Treatise on the Fourth Dimension', in *The Surrealism Reader: An Anthology of Ideas*, ed. Dawn Ades and Michael Richardson, with Krzysztof Fijalkowski. London: Tate Publishing, pp. 59–64.
Merleau-Ponty, Maurice (1964 [1948]), *Sense and Non-Sense*, trans. Hubert L. and Patricia Allen Dreyfus. Evanston, IL: Northwestern University Press.
Metz, Christian (1974 [1971]), *Film Language: A Semiotics of the Cinema*, trans. Michael Taylor. Chicago: Chicago University Press.
Metz, Christian (1982), *The Imaginary Signifier: Psychoanalysis and the Cinema*, trans. Celia Britton, Annywyl Williams, Ben Brewster, and Alfred Guzzetti. London: Macmillan Press.
Mulvey, Laura (1975). 'Visual Pleasure and Narrative Cinema', *Screen* 16.3 (Autumn), pp .6–18.
Mulvey, Laura (1996), *Fetishism and Curiosity: Cinema and the Mind's Eye*. London and Bloomington: BFI Publishing and Indiana University Press.
Mulvey, Laura (2006), *Death 24x a Second: Stillness and the Moving Image*. London: Reaktion Books.
Nada, Hiroshi (1992), 'An Aspect of the Reception of Avant-Garde Films in Japan', *Iconics*, 2, pp. 47–74.
Péret, Benjamin ([1951] 2000), 'Against Commercial Cinema', translated in *The Shadow and Its Shadow: Surrealist Writings on the Cinema*, ed. Paul Hammond. San Francisco: City Lights, pp. 59-60.
Potamkin, Harry A. (1998 [August 1929]), 'The Aframerican Cinema', in *Close-Up 1927–1933: Cinema and Modernism*, ed. James Donald, Anna Friedberg and Laura Marcus. Princeton, NJ: Princeton University Press, pp. 65–72.
Peterson, James (1989), 'A War of Utter Rebellion: Kinugasa's "Page of Madness" and the Japanese Avant-Garde of the 1920s', *Cinema Journal*, 29: 1 (Autumn), pp. 36–53.
Petrie, Graham (2002), *Hollywood Destinies: European Directors in America, 1922–1931*. Detroit: Wayne State University Press.
Sas, Miryam (1999), *Fault Lines: Cultural Memory and Japanese Surrealism*. Stanford, CA: Stanford University Press.
Stein, Gertrude (1998 [1927]), 'Mrs Emerson', *Close-Up*, 1: 1–6, pp. 23–9.
Stein, Gertrude (1988 [1935]), *Lectures in America*. London: Virago Press.

Stojkovic, Jelena (2020), *Surrealism and Photography in 1930s Japan: The Impossible Avant-Garde*. London: Routledge.
Tezuka, Miwako (2005), *Jikken Kōbō [Experimental Workshop]: Avant-Garde Experiments in Japanese Art of the 1950s*, PhD thesis, Columbia University.
Virmaux, Alain (2009), *Artaud-Dulac: La Coquille et le clergyman: essai d'élucidation d'une querelle mythique*. Paris: Editions Paris Expérimental.
Williams, Tami (2014), *Germaine Dulac: A Cinema of Sensations*. Urbana: University of Illinois Press.

Filmography

A Page of Madness (2015 [1926]), directed by Teinosuke Kinugasa, Blu-ray. Japan: Flicker Alley.
Le Ballet mécanique (2018 [1924]), directed by Fernand Léger and Dudley Murphy. San Francisco: Kanopy Streaming, Filmmakers Showcase.
La Coquille et le clergyman (2008 [1927]), directed by Germaine Dulac, DVD. France: Light Cone / Paris Expérimental.
Étude cinégraphique sur une Arabesque aka *Arabesques* (2002–8 [1929]), directed by Germaine Dulac, on *Cinexpérimentaux 8: Cooperative Lightcone* by Frédérique Dévaux and Michel Amarge, DVD. France: Light Cone / Paris Expérimental.
Nosferatu: A Symphony of Horror [1922] (2013), directed by F. W. Murnau, Blu-ray. Germany: Eureka Entertainment.
La Souriante Mme. Beudet (2019 [1922]), directed by Germaine Dulac, on *Early Women Filmmakers Collection*, Blu-ray. UK: BFI.
Thèmes et variations (2008 [1928]), directed by Germaine Dulac. France: Light Cone / Paris Expérimental.

13

Radio: Blindness, Disability and Technology

Emily C. Bloom

The first generation of radio scholars labelled radio 'the blind medium' and returned obsessively to cataloguing the benefits and drawbacks of blindness. Not only was blindness a ubiquitous metaphor for defining the non-visual qualities of the radio medium, but early radio dramatists often used blind characters to orient listeners to the auditory space of the radio play. Looking back at this literature, a pattern emerges in which scholars evoke the experience of the blind, only to discount the blind listener as the imagined audience of radio broadcasting. This chapter will consider the central role of disability in defining early radio for producers, writers and critics, and also its significance for blind listeners. Radio broadcasters could evoke blindness, but they were only rarely – and opportunistically – willing to define the medium by its accessibility to blind listeners.

The proliferation of audio technologies in the late nineteenth and early twentieth centuries brought about a renewed interest in sound, an interest that sparked anxieties about the hierarchy of the senses. This hierarchy positions sight as 'higher' than hearing and has been, according to Martin Jay, a pervasive thread in Western thought, reaching back to Plato and leading to an understanding of sight as the 'master sense of the modern era' (1993: 543). Jonathan Sterne describes the dominance of what he calls an 'audio-visual litany' in American and European philosophy and cultural criticism, which characterises hearing as 'manifesting a kind of pure interiority', while either praising or blaming vision as a sense that allows distance and, with it, reason (2003: 15). The literature around one twentieth-century sound technology – radio – reveals that an underlying concern in these debates about hearing versus seeing is a preoccupation with disability, and particularly blindness. In *Enforcing Normalcy*, Lennard J. Davis describes how the rise of print focused attention on deafness among a public acclimatising to silent reading. If, as Davis writes, 'Europe became deaf during the eighteenth century' (1995: 51), then blindness came to define the sonic landscape of the early twentieth century as radio producers, writers and listeners learned to communicate with what was, for many, an unnervingly auditory medium.

Over the last ten years, modernist studies has seen a new wave of work in radio studies, often under the label of 'radio modernism', first coined by Todd Avery (2006).[1] Much of this scholarship borrows theoretical frameworks from sound studies to examine the epistemologies of auditory technologies and their relationship to literary works. Following recent trends in new modernist studies, this work sheds light on the role of popular forms and genres in the production of modernist literature. This scholarship, in many ways an expansion of periodical studies, embraces the role of the broadcast medium as a site for the dissemination of modernist texts in the form of talks, poetry and prose readings and radio drama. Formalist approaches in this vein show how the aesthetics of radio motivates, influences or is sympathetic with modernist aesthetics, while also paying close attention to the political stakes of the medium, which allowed for the dissemination of competing ideologies on an unprecedented scale. While much work has focused on domestic broadcasting by Anglo-American institutions, there has been a gradual expansion of the field to encompass global modernism.[2]

At the same time, modernist studies has seen a proliferation of work in disability studies that recognises the central importance of neurodiversity and bodily vulnerability among modernist themes, as well as the ways in which modernism was shaped in the shadow of eugenics.[3] Maren Tova Linett argues that in breaking apart traditional narrative, modernists 'inquired into the metaphoric meanings disabilities had come to bear, often challenging normative understandings of embodiment' (2016: 2). Radio studies and disability studies may seem quite distinct, with one highlighting a supposedly disembodied medium and the other focusing on the imbricated bodymind. This perceived difference belies the fact that many communication technologies, including radio, were promoted as accessibility aids for a range of disabilities or as technologies intended to eradicate disability.[4]

Within disability studies, calls for 'disability media studies' and 'crip technoscience' are exploring new connections between media, science, technology and disability. The collection *Disability Media Studies*, edited by Elizabeth Ellcessor, Mack Hagood and Bill Kirkpatrick, argues for linking the fields of disability studies and media studies in order 'to better address media's materiality and a wide range of practices of reception' (Ellcessor et al. 2017: 18). Rather than treating technological media like radio in terms of disembodiment, these critics highlight the materiality of media and its impact on embodied subjects. In providing an overview of this emerging field, the editors chart a shift from early work that focuses on representations of people with disabilities in media (especially film and television), to more recent work that studies 'the lived experiences of people with disabilities – who often use media quite differently' (18). Aimi Hamraie and Kelly Fritsch, the co-editors of 'Crip Technoscience', a special issue of *Catalyst: Feminism, Theory, Technoscience* (2019) begin with a similar premise: that disability studies approaches to science, technology and media must focus on the experience of disabled users. Drawing upon recent work in critical disability studies with its focus on justice and intersectionality, Hamraie and Fritsch emphasise the role of disabled people as users and developers of their own technological systems and, while repudiating the notion that technology could or should provide a 'cure' for disability, they argue that 'technoscience can be a transformative tool for disability justice' (3). Bringing these insights into modernist radio studies involves paying closer attention to the materiality of a supposedly 'disembodied' medium and challenging normative constructions of the listening public.

Debating Blindness

The use of disability metaphors is pervasive in radio studies, a phenomenon that Mara Mills identifies across a range of scholarship in media, science and technology, which, she argues, exploits disability 'as a metaphor and exemplar' (2015: 177). Moreover, as

David Mitchell and Sharon Snyder have observed, 'Disability underwrites the cultural study of technology writ large' (2000: 8). New inventions in the modernist period drew alarmist concerns about disablement or, on the other hand, futurist claims about curing or eradicating disability; but in both cases, disability served as a spectre against which all innovation must contend. The first generation of radio broadcasters and critics in the 1920s and 1930s relied extensively on disability metaphors to explain the difficulty of radio-listening for a public unused to acousmatic sound. Blindness became a common metaphor for explaining the audience's relationship to a space inhabited by speakers, characters and scenes that they could not see. Significantly, the blind listener evoked by radio critics was rarely understood to be actually blind.[5]

In one of the earliest theoretical books on radio, Rudolf Arnheim writes, 'wireless rules out a certain range of sense in a most startling way. It seems much more sensorily [sic] defective and incomplete than the other arts – because it excludes the most important sense, that of sight' (1936: 135). Arnheim draws upon the hierarchy of the senses to describe radio's reliance on audition as a sign of its defectiveness. Yet he goes on to champion these very features of radio broadcasting in a chapter titled 'In Praise of Blindness', in which he claims that the formal possibilities and constraints of radio – what later critics might call its protocols or affordances – give radio drama a sense of unity through its exclusive focus on the auditory.

Following a similar line of reasoning, the BBC producer Donald McWhinnie asks his readers in *The Art of Radio* (1959) to consider the ways in which radio's blindness enables the development of auditory expertise. McWhinnie was a significant presence in radio modernism, producing Samuel Beckett's works for the BBC's Third Programme and promoting experimental drama on air. In his treatise on radio drama, he begins by describing audition as a more difficult sensory experience than vision, one that individuals must learn to master at a later developmental stage; children, he argues, prefer visuals until they learn to appreciate language. He then evokes blind men and women as exemplars of advanced audition. He describes the experience of his archetypal blind man as follows:

> There are no hypnotic flickers of light to shield him from the knives of reality; he must apprehend reality, interpret it and react to it in a split second, and by a hypersensitive ability to create the whole out of a part [. . .] His vision of the world he cannot see might well be alarming to the sighted because it is necessarily so penetrating, so little influenced by embellishment or distraction. (23)

McWhinnie's imagined blind man is not only the ideal radio listener, but the modernist audience *par excellence* – someone with a preternatural ability to shape sonic cacophony into a vision of the world shed of its illusions. McWhinnie relies on what disability theorists describe as supercrip stereotypes to attribute hypersensory abilities to the blind.[6] Like Arnheim, McWhinnie praises blindness, but he also follows Arnheim in evoking blindness only to dispense with it. He goes on to write:

> although the experience of the radio listener is similar to that of the blind man, there is this important difference: the sound-complex the listener hears has been carefully calculated in advance and designed to achieve a certain emotional and physical effect: it is not just a random collection of noises but a prefabricated pattern. (24)

According to this logic, the blindness experienced by a blind person is a 'random collection of noises', whereas the blindness experienced by the sighted radio listener has aesthetic value. McWhinnie does not stop to consider the aesthetic experiences of blind radio listeners or producers in his distinction between the blind person and the radio listener.

In contrast to the use of these disability metaphors in early radio studies, scholars of blindness have shown the complexity and value of aesthetic experiences by the blind, which make use of the senses of sound, touch and sight (though not always sight as understood by the non-blind). Foremost among this scholarship is Georgina Kleege's *Sight Unseen*, which is, incidentally, also the title of a critical study of radio drama by Elissa S. Guralnick.[7] Writing as a blind scholar, Kleege describes various aesthetic experiences: looking at a painting by Matisse at a museum, watching films, reading books in various formats (braille, codex and audio) and also listening to radio. Her description of a radio broadcast focuses on an interview between Liane Hansen and the photographer Howard Schatz on the subject of his book *Homeless: Portraits of Americans in Hard Times*. Kleege describes Schatz and Hansen as 'engaged in the difficult task of describing a visual phenomenon to an audience that cannot see it, an audience temporarily blind' (1999: 130–1). Kleege does not challenge the trope of radio's blindness, but modifies it with an emphasis on its temporal limitations. The radio programme about photography radically puts the blind and sighted listener on an equal footing, if only for a moment. Kleege's disappointment in the programme is that the participants 'fall back on certain figures of sighted speech which point to the eyes as not only the focal point of every face but as the site of all significant experience' (131). Even if all radio listeners are temporarily blind in their reliance on audio description in order to 'see' the photographs, there is no doubt raised in the conversation between Schatz and Hansen that the listener is missing out on something by not having access to the images. The sighted listener can rectify this by buying a copy of the book once the programme ends. The blind listener cannot.

One common theme among scholars of blindness is the ways in which the non-blind take for granted the self-evidence of vision. As Kleege writes, 'The sighted can be touchingly naïve about vision. They apparently believe that the brain stays out of it' (96). By paying attention to blindness, Kleege argues, we can better understand the slippery relationship between the bodymind and the world. Building upon this theme, Rod Michalko writes in an essay, 'What's Cool about Blindness?', that 'We know of the existence of sight because of its opposite, the existence of blindness. It might even be said that sight owes its existence to blindness' (2010). Returning to early debates on radio's blindness through contemporary disability studies, blindness emerges as a more complex and more enabling discourse for media studies than either its early proponents or detractors allowed. Moving beyond disability metaphors, a critical approach to blindness in modernist radio should allow for interpretations of aesthetic experiences that do not take for granted the self-evidence of sight. As the blind detective Lee Masters says in the South African radio series 'The Sounds of Darkness', 'when a man can see, he gets lazy' (O'Shaughnessy 1967).[8] Blind characters in radio drama, like Masters, often served as native informants to sighted listeners who needed to be re-educated in the use of their senses. In the following sections, I will shift focus from radio criticism to modernist radio drama in order to examine how the metaphor of radio's blindness was translated into the trope of the blind character.

Blind Characters

Including blind characters in the diegetic world of the radio play became a common device to link the viewer's experience of temporary blindness with the action taking place in the drama. It allowed the dramatist to include additional explication when another character appeared to apprise the blind character of events that were happening that they, and by extension the audience, could not see. In his radio adaptation of Sergei Eisenstein's film *Alexander Nevsky*, for instance, Louis MacNeice invents a new character, Blind Iuri, as what Ian Whittington calls 'a diegetical surrogate for the listener' (2018: 100). The audience is placed in a position of unique intimacy with blind characters who become their guides. In a compilation of American radio programmes, the Old Time Radio Catalog lists 108 programmes that are on the topic of blindness or that feature blind characters ('Blind Tales in Old Time Radio'). Popular programmes capitalised on blind characters to create suspense, evoke pity or sympathy, tell tales of triumph over adversity, or exploit blindness for humour. In the suspense or horror genre, the listener could find themselves in the position of the blind character who is the potential victim, perpetrator or detective of a crime and must listen for auditory clues about what would happen next.

The over-representation of blind characters in radio drama helps explain the popularity of H. G. Wells's 'The Country of the Blind' on the airwaves. This story flipped the usual radio script by introducing not one blind character, but rather an entire village of blind characters. Here, the listener surrogate is not the blind character, but instead the lone sighted person who must learn to navigate in a world created by and for the blind. It was the first Wells story broadcast on the BBC in an adaptation that the author himself approved, which was written by E. G. King-Bull and produced by Lance Sieveking (9 January 1933). Later broadcasts in the US included the series *Escape* (CBS, 1947), Ronald Colman's *Favorite Story* (1949, as 'Strange Valley'), Laurence Olivier's *Theater Royal* (NBC, 1954) and *Suspense* (CBS, 1957).

'The Country of the Blind' tells the story of a mountaineer, Francisco Nunez, who stumbles upon a valley in the Andes inhabited by a community of blind men and women who have been cut off from the rest of society for fifteen generations. The first generation was blinded by a mysterious illness and later generations inherited this trait until every man, woman and child was blind. Nunez discovers that in the valley of the blind, his sight does not make him king, as the proverb claims, but rather becomes an impairment. Disability studies scholars have singled out the story for its illustration of the social model of disability, which argues that social, institutional and environmental factors produce disability (Kleege 1999: 78–80; Linett 2016: 63–6). In 'The Country of the Blind' the native people do not experience their blindness as an impairment because they have built their world to accommodate their other senses. Their bodies are not in conflict with their surroundings, but rather they exist seamlessly within their environment. In contrast, Nunez's sighted body and mind clash with the world around him. His sense of hearing is less refined than that of the villagers, he cannot navigate in the dark, he speaks more loudly and coarsely than they do, and he cannot curb his use of metaphors that rely on the importance of sight, which become meaningless in this new environment. The villagers find him to be unintelligent, unattractive and dangerous. When he falls in love with Medina-Saroté, the daughter of his master, the village elders offer to 'cure' him by removing his eyes as a condition to allow him to marry one of their own. Wells struggled with the story's ending, writing several different versions: in one early manuscript, Nunez flees, only to return to face the surgeons, whereas in the published version of 1904, he escapes to the mountains, where he faces near-certain death (Parrinder 1990). In an ironic twist in the *Escape* script written by John Dunkel (1947), Nunez manages to make it over the Andes mountains, but the perilous journey through the wind, glaring sun and bitter cold has rendered him blind at last.

Each radio adaptation introduced important differences into the story, but in all of them the radio listener is positioned close to Nunez – much closer, in fact, than in Wells's original story. The radio versions consistently replaced Well's third-person omniscient narrator with Nunez as narrator, often through the use of a frame narrative in which Nunez returns to tell a former member of his expedition the tale of his disappearance. In the *Escape* version, the actor playing Nunez is physically closer to the microphone than the actors playing blind villagers in an example of what Neil Verma calls 'intimate audioposition'. Verma argues that in radio scripts that use 'intimate audioposition', the first-person narrator '"carries" the listener not just because the story tells us so, but also because on a visceral level he or she is "closer" to us than anyone else, as indicated by volume in narration' (2012: 62). Just as Nunez must strain to understand the inhabitants of the country of the blind, the listener has to lean closer to the radio set to make out their words.[9] In the final scene of the frame narrative, Nunez finishes recounting his adventures to the mining engineer Ibara, who only then realises that the man telling the tale is blind. The twist here is that once Nunez reveals that he is now blind, the audience discovers that they have been listening to a blind man all along. After bringing the listener close to the protagonist, singling him out as the relatable sighted man against a muffled backdrop of blind villagers, the script turns this identification on its head by revealing Nunez, in the present moment, to be blind himself.

Whereas the *Escape* episode of 'The Country of the Blind' draws upon radio's intimacy to push the listener surreptitiously towards a closer identification with a blind character, Dylan Thomas's *Under Milk Wood* introduces listeners to a blind perspective that they are asked, ultimately, to transcend. One way of understanding these different approaches is through Verma's distinction between two forms of audioposition – the intimate version that we see in this episode of *Escape*, which positions the listener closer to the consciousness of a particular character, and 'kaleidosonic audioposition', which presents a cast of many different voices on a relatively equal footing (Verma 2012: 58–73). We see an example of the latter in *Under Milk Wood*, which introduces the listener to a symphony of different voices, one of which is a blind retired sea captain, Captain Cat.

Under Milk Wood, one of the few canonical plays written for the radio medium, is set in an imaginary Welsh seaside town called Llareggub. There is no main protagonist, but among the villagers, Captain Cat emerges as a central figure. The play was written in close collaboration with the BBC Features Department, which often eschewed traditional dramatic conventions of setting and plot while pioneering radiogenic formal experimentation.[10] The Feature programme was characterised by a collage-like approach that introduced many voices and moved quickly through time and space. The producer of *Under Milk Wood*, Douglas Cleverdon, described the feature as follows:

> A radio feature is, roughly, any constructed programme (that is, other than news bulletins, racing commentaries, and so forth) that derives from the technical apparatus of radio (microphone, control-panel, recording gear, loud-speaker). It can

combine any sound elements – words, music, sound effects – in any form or mixture of forms – documentary, actuality, dramatized, poetic, musico-dramatic. It has no rules determining what can or cannot be done. And though it may be in dramatic form, it has no need of a dramatic plot. (1969: 17)

Cleverdon goes on to say that, in moving away from dramatic conventions and encouraging formal experimentation, the feature programme was ideally suited to poets.

In early drafts of the script, Thomas toyed with the idea of making Captain Cat the narrator and central character (Cleverdon 1969: 5). The final version of the play does away with the character–narrator in favour of two voices – simply First Voice and Second Voice – who speak directly to the listener, introducing the villagers and weaving in and out of the narration. The rest of the play is comprised of the voices of sixty-two characters; and yet Captain Cat remains central to the story and his blindness plays an important role in framing the experience of the listener.

The play begins with a 'First Voice' speaking 'very softly' to the audience. The voice sets the opening pre-dawn scene as follows: 'The houses are blind as moles (though moles see fine to-night in the snouting, velvet dingles) or blind as Captain Cat there in the muffled middle by the pump and the town clock' (Thomas 1954: 1). Thomas presents two versions of blindness: the blindness of the mole that thrives in the dark, and the blindness of Captain Cat, a former sailor. Towards the end of the play, the First Voice will describe Captain Cat thus: 'Like a cat, he sees in the dark' (92). Unlike the other residents of Llareggub, moles, cats and Captain Cats can see in the dark and are therefore excellent conduits for listeners asked to see in the dark.

Captain Cat (always described by the First Voice as Blind Captain Cat) is the first character introduced to the listener and remains an important focal point for the stream of voices to follow. He is the one who pulls the rope of the townhall bell, waking the sleepers from their dreams and literally opening their eyes (26). He also 'hears all the morning of the town', interpreting sounds with great specificity: he deciphers a child's cry as Billy Swansea hitting Maggie Richards and a knock on the door as the work of Willy Nilly, the postman. In so doing, he introduces the listener to a number of characters through their sonic shibboleths – crying, knocking, feet on cobblestones, slamming doors and organ music – and teaches them how to interpret these sounds.

In the opening monologue, the First Voice speaks to the radio listener directly, telling them that they have been gifted with unique modes of sensory perception:

Only you can hear the houses sleeping in the streets in the slow deep salt and silent black, bandaged night. Only you can see, in the blinded bedrooms, the combs and petticoats over the chairs, the jugs and basins, the glasses of teeth, Thou Shalt Not on the wall, and the yellow dicky-bird-watching pictures of the dead. (3)

The listener here is gifted with supernatural abilities of sight and hearing, able to see past the 'blinded bedrooms' and into the very dreams of the townspeople. Captain Cat's extra-sensory insight is therefore placed a step below the listener's supernatural abilities to see and hear through the magic of radio. The listener's senses ultimately transcend those of Captain Cat, whose abilities are circumscribed to the world of Llareggub and whose blindness, unlike the listener's, is not temporary.

Captain Cat teaches the listener to navigate an auditory environment, but the listener is then expected to move beyond blind audition towards an omniscience that is only possible through the radio performance. Blind characters like Captain Cat serve as guides for the temporarily blinded listener, who will be able to shrug off the posture of blindness once the play is over. The listener, presumably sighted, will better appreciate and sharpen their senses of hearing and sight by imagining a state of blindness. Whereas blind characters proliferated in radio broadcasting, Matthew Rubery notes that in the production of audiobooks for the blind, works with representations of blindness were often *de facto* censored in order not to offend blind listeners (2016: 178). Comparing these disparate approaches to two audio formats – one for a general population and one for the blind – we see blindness as a trope deployed to speak to a sighted radio audience, whereas blind listeners to audiobooks were, rightly or wrongly, often spared from these representations.

Radio for the Blind

Even if radio producers and writers did not consider blind listeners as their audience, blind listeners were quick to consider radio. From the emerging scholarship on blind radio listeners, notably work by Rebecca Scales and Bill Kirkpatrick, a few themes emerge. First, when broadcasters did consider blind listeners, it was often in the context of charity work that, in turn, helped to legitimise the public role of radio. Radio for the blind and other disabled groups emerged as a notable social benefit of the medium, one that broadcasters could periodically foreground for strategic purposes. Second, blind listeners, like other radio listeners, were voracious correspondents who articulated their own programming preferences, not all of which point in the same direction. And finally, blind listeners not only were the passive recipients of broadcasts, but also played important, and often unheralded, roles in the development of the medium.

Some of the earliest and most well-documented blind listeners were veterans of the First World War, many of whom had been blinded by poison gas. Rebecca Scales and Bill Kirkpatrick have described the role of radio in endeavours to rehabilitate the war blind in France and the US, respectively. The war blind were a strategically important group for early radio boosters who sought legitimacy for the medium. Scales describes how broadcasters in France promoted the wireless as a means of rehabilitating war veterans into national life and in so doing 'vigorously promoted this concept of radio as a media that should serve the nation's citizens' (2016: 65). Schemes to put radios in hospitals and to provide free radios to veterans appealed to patriotism while touting the benefits of radio in connecting the war blind to the wider community and, especially, to national life. Organisations like Radio for the Blind (France), Wireless at the Hospital (France) and the British Wireless for the Blind Fund drew upon the patriotic appeal of serving the war blind and widened their scope from there to include the benefits to the broader blind community.

A notice for the BBC's annual Christmas Day appeal for the British Wireless for the Blind Fund in *Radio Times* tells readers, 'There is no need to stress here what wireless means to the blind listener. It is his newspaper, his theatre, his cinema' ('Appeal' 1931). The Fund began in 1928 as an endeavour to provide a free radio to every blind person in the UK and the Christmas Day appeals were delivered by Prime Ministers Winston Churchill and Lloyd George, among others.[11] During the Christmas appeal of 1934 and

Figure 13.1 'Blind listener, Mr Oransby (right), listening to his Crystal Radio Set with headphones, December 1929'. Reproduced with permission from the BBC Photo Library.

again in 1939, listeners were addressed by an 'Unknown Blind Man' who, *Radio Times* reported in 1939, 'made so many friends when he spoke about himself and his fellows five Christmases ago' ('Wireless for the Blind'). It is with a curious mixture of anonymity and intimacy that *Radio Times* refers to the speaker as an 'Unknown Blind Man' and yet emphasises his success in making friends with his listeners through the act of broadcasting. Intimacy is another site where radio and blindness share a discourse. Radio, by bringing the voice of the speaker into the private home, created affective bonds between broadcasters and their listeners in the form of 'fireside chats' and other intimate modes of address. On the other hand, Linett argues that modernist writers viewed 'blindness as conducive to intimacy' because 'the absence of vision makes way for greater attention to hearing and touch, two senses understood to foster human attachment' (2016: 84). The blind man addressing an audience of sighted listeners could appeal to this understanding of sound-mediated intimacy, even while the BBC refuses to call him by his name.

For all the advantages that radio offered to blind broadcasters and listeners, enumerated by the 'Unknown Blind Man', it could also present other obstacles; Kirkpatrick points out that the radio set itself, with its 'fiddly tuning knobs and often hard-to-read dials—could itself be a disabling technology for much of its history, even as it enabled new forms of cultural participation' (2018: 474). Radio's elevation of the auditory, moreover, was disabling for deaf people in the era before transcription services were widely available.[12] Broadcasting institutions were also forceful gatekeepers of access, blocking individuals with a range of disabilities, especially those, like stuttering, that had an impact on the 'good' radio voice, and preventing access on the grounds of race, gender and nationality.[13] Expanding on the metaphor of blindness, radio broadcasters claimed to be 'colour-blind', a claim that belied the actual discriminatory practices of broadcasting corporations.[14]

In letters to broadcasters and within publications for the blind, blind listeners articulated their programming preferences and described both the tremendous benefits they found in listening to radio drama, news reporting and music, and the areas that they wished to change. Scales describes debate in France among blind radio enthusiasts about whether programming should speak directly to the needs of the blind, or whether the benefit of radio was in providing the same services to the blind as to sighted listeners. Programmes specifically for the blind, such as the BBC's *In Touch*, which was pioneered by Janet Quigley in the 1950s, addressed (and continues to address) a blind audience with programmes on employment opportunities and other issues of interest to the blind community.[15] Other programmes ostensibly targeted at the blind, like France's Radio for the Blind and Wireless at the Hospital's variety shows, ended up being enormously popular with a general audience.[16]

Blind men and women saw radio not only as providing an opportunity to listen in new ways, but also as opening up potential employment possibilities. In an article titled 'Radio-Criticism a New Profession for the Blind', published in *Outlook for the Blind*, a publication of the American Foundation for the Blind, Marjory Stewart is introduced to readers as a 'blind radio-critic for the Westinghouse Electric and Manufacturing Company' (1923: 31). The article goes on to describe 'radio criticism as a profession that is fraught with tremendous possibilities for blind persons of particular endowment'.[17] While some blind men and women found traditional occupations like piano tuning and musical accompaniment under threat with the introduction of sound technologies, others saw new opportunities in radio manufacturing, repairs and broadcasting.[18] If a radio broadcaster spoke to an unseen audience, then a blind announcer might find themselves at an advantage.

Looking beyond the major broadcasting institutions – commercial and public alike – there are glimpses of an even broader range of broadcasters and publics. Here one can discover amateur radio stations run from schools for the blind and letters written to broadcasters by blind men and women outlining programming preferences (Kirkpatrick 2018: 474, 477–8). We also find articles about broadcasting in publications like *Outlook for the Blind* and first-hand accounts of radio programmes by blind listeners embedded in first-person narratives like Kleege's.

The history of radio broadcasting reveals an alternating process of access and disablement, as well as a broad spectrum of needs, desires, inclusions and exclusions among broadcasters and their listening publics. Technologically driven literary forms like radio drama were shaped by disability metaphors and tropes in ways that could be exploitative and stereotyping, but that also fundamentally reconfigured the imagined audience as disabled, if only temporarily. This understanding of the 'blind listener' can serve as a gateway to considering listeners with disabilities on whom broadcasting had a profound impact and who often sought experiences with the medium beyond those intended by its inventors or mainstream practitioners. An approach to modernism and radio that attends to the use of these metaphors and tropes, as well as to sensory and neurodiversity among its users, allows for a deeper understanding of modernist genres like radio drama and their various publics.

Notes

1. A short list of monographs on Anglophone radio modernism includes Damien Keane (2014), Melissa Dinsman (2015), Emily Bloom (2016), Ian Whittington (2018) and Angela Frattarola (2018); edited collections such as *Broadcasting Modernism* (ed. Debra Rae Cohen et al., 2009) and *Samuel Beckett and BBC Radio: A Reassessment* (ed. David Addyman et al., 2017); as well as special issues in the journals *Modernist Cultures* (ed. Debra Rae Cohen and Michael Coyle, 2015) and *Media History* (ed. Aasiya Lodhi and Amanda Wrigley, 2018).
2. See Daniel Ryan Morse (2020), Julie Cyzewski (2018) and Jessica Berman (2019).
3. See Maren Tova Linett (2016), Michael Davidson (2019) and Rebecca Sanchez (2015) for recent examples.
4. Early radios were seen, in part, as prosthetic devices for the hard of hearing. Rebecca Scales describes how early radios were deconstructed by hard-of-hearing men and women, and rebuilt as hearing aids (2016: 99-100). For more on disability as a driving force in the development of communication technologies, see Jonathan Sterne (2003) and Mara Mills (2011).
5. For an overview of debates regarding radio's blindness, see the entry on 'Blindness' in Hugh Chignell (2009).
6. Sami Schalk describes three typologies of the 'supercrip' narrative – the 'regular supercrip' narrative in which someone with disabilities is praised for doing 'normal' things; the 'glorified supercrip' narrative wherein someone with disabilities performs tasks that most able-bodied people cannot; and 'the superpowered supercrip' narrative often seen in comic books where the disabled person discovers extraordinary powers. What I describe as McWhinnie's use of the supercrip stereotype connects to Schalk's definition of the 'glorified supercrip', in that he ascribes exceptional auditory powers to the blind, which he suggests that the sighted are not capable of attaining.
7. I point out this coincidence only to further emphasise the cross-currents and common discourse between radio and blindness.
8. Special thanks to Neil Verma for bringing 'Sounds of Darkness' to my attention. The series ran from 1967 to 1974 on Springbok Radio.
9. The blind villagers in the *Escape* script also speak with vaguely Hispanic accents even though Nunez, who is from Bogotá, speaks with a US accent. This distinction creates another layer of intimacy between the narrator and the imagined American listening public, and another means of othering the blind villagers.
10. Features began as a research unit in 1924; after the Second World War it was made into an autonomous department led by Laurence Gilliam until his death in 1964 (Lodhi and Wrigley 2018: 162). Feature producers included Louis MacNeice, D. G. Bridson, Edward Sackville-West, Tyrone Guthrie, Lance Sieveking, Mary Hope Allen and W. R. Rodgers. I will not attempt a comprehensive list of modernist writers who wrote Feature programmes here, but the special edition of *Media History* on 'Radio Modernisms: Features, Cultures and the BBC' (2018), edited by Aasiya Lodhi and Amanda Wrigley, provides a helpful overview.
11. The British Wireless for the Blind Fund was organised by the National Institute for the Blind and was presided over by the Prince of Wales. The Fund continues to operate today, providing free audio equipment to blind men and women in the UK. See Matthew Rubery (2016) for more on the organisation's work with audiobooks.
12. More recently, the popularity of podcasts has renewed discussion of unequal access for deaf audiences in auditory formats. For more on this discussion and resources for podcasting transcription, see the Healing Justice Collective's Accessibility Guide, available at: <https://www.healingjustice.org/access> (last accessed 24 January 2022).

13. While there were many women in broadcasting, they were often sequestered in women's and children's programming and, with some notable exceptions, were rarely found in leadership positions. For more on women at the BBC see Kate Murphy (2016).
14. For more on radio and 'colour-blindness' see Jennifer Lynn Stoever (2016) and Max Shulman (2016).
15. See Kate Murphy (2016) for more on Quigley's career at the BBC. In 1969, C. Stanley Potter and Robert Watson launched the Minnesota Radio Talking Book Network, which was the first radio reading service in the US. Broadcasting on a subchannel, the service focused on news-reading services for the blind.
16. Rebecca Scales describes how these variety programmes, which aired on France's commercial stations Radio-Vitus and Radio LL, and the state-run station Paris PTT, were ranked as listener favourites among the general population in a public survey (2016: 79).
17. Stewart appears to have been an in-house critic for Westinghouse. *The New Outlook for the Blind* describes the duties of the radio critic as providing 'a consistent check on progammes by eliminating worthless or negligible numbers, and so establishing a system of standardization, and as a medium through which announcers may be schooled in matters of style, pronunciation and so forth' ('Radio-Criticism': 31).
18. One sensational headline from *The Evening Journal* (1930) read 'Blind Lose Jobs: Radio Blamed'. In 1923, the French Association Valentin Haüy formed a radio club to offer occupational training programmes for the blind in radio construction and maintenance (Scales 2016: 73–4).

Works Cited

Addyman, David, Matthew Feldman and Erik Tonning, eds (2017), *Samuel Beckett and BBC Radio: A Reassessment*. New York: Palgrave Macmillan.
'Appeal on Behalf of the British Wireless for the Blind Fund' (1931), *Radio Times*, 429 (25 December), p. 67.
Arnheim, Rudolf (1936), *Radio*. London: Faber and Faber.
Avery, Todd (2006), *Radio Modernism: Literature, Ethics, and the BBC, 1922–1938*. Burlington, VT: Ashgate.
Berman, Jessica (2019), 'Re-Routing Community: Colonial Broadcasting and the Aesthetics of Relation', in *Modernist Communities Across Cultures and Media*, ed. Caroline Pollentier and Sarah Wilson. Gainesville: University Press of Florida.
'Blind Lose Jobs: Radio Blamed' (1930), *The Evening Journal*, 8 March, p. 8.
'Blind Tales in Old Time Radio' (n.d.), Old Time Radio Catalog, <https://www.otrcat.com/p/blind-tales-in-old-time-radio> (last accessed 4 June 2020).
Bloom, Emily C. (2016), *The Wireless Past: Anglo-Irish Writers and the BBC, 1931–1968*. Oxford: Oxford University Press.
Chignell, Hugh (2009), *Key Concepts in Radio Studies*. Los Angeles: Sage Publications.
Cleverdon, Douglas (1969), *The Growth of Milk Wood*. New York: New Directions.
Cohen, Debra Rae and Michael Coyle, eds (2015), 'Broadcast Traces/Tracing Broadcasting: Modernism and Radio', *Modernist Cultures*, 10: 1.
Cohen, Debra Rae, Michael Coyle and Jane Lewty, eds (2009), *Broadcasting Modernism*. Gainesville: University Press of Florida.
Cyzewski, Julie (2018), 'Broadcasting Nature Poetry: Una Marson and the BBC's Overseas Service', *PMLA*, 133: 3, pp. 575–93.
Davidson, Michael (2019), *Invalid Modernism: Disability and the Missing Body of the Aesthetic*. New York: Oxford University Press.
Davis, Lennard J. (1995), *Enforcing Normalcy: Disability, Deafness, and the Body*. New York: Verso.

Dinsman, Melissa (2015), *Modernism at the Microphone: Radio, Propaganda, and Literary Aesthetics During World War II*. New York: Bloomsbury.

Dunkel, John (1947), 'The Country of the Blind', *Escape*, directed by William N. Robson. CBS, Radio Broadcast.

Ellcessor, Elizabeth, Mack Hagood and Bill Kirkpatrick (2017), 'Introduction: Toward a Disability Media Studies', in *Disability Media Studies*. New York: New York University Press, pp. 1–26.

Frattarola, Angela (2018), *Modernist Soundscapes: Auditory Technology and the Novel*. Gainesville: University Press of Florida.

Guralnick, Elissa S. (1996), *Sight Unseen: Beckett, Pinter, Stoppard, and Other Contemporary Dramatists on Radio*. Athens: Ohio University Press.

Hamraie, Aimi and Kelly Fritsch (2019), 'Crip Technoscience Manifesto', *Catalyst: Feminism, Theory, Technoscience*, 5: 1, pp. 1–34.

Jay, Martin (1993), *Downcast Eyes: The Denigration of Vision in Twentieth-Century French Thought*. Berkeley: University of California Press.

Keane, Damien (2014), *Ireland and the Problem of Information: Irish Writing, Radio, Late Modernist Communication*. University Park, PA: Pennsylvania State University Press.

Kirkpatrick, Bill (2018), 'Disability, Cultural Accessibility, and the Radio Archive', *New Review of Film and Television Studies*, 16: 4, pp. 473–80.

Kleege, Georgina (1999), *Sight Unseen*. New Haven, CT: Yale University Press.

Linett, Maren Tova (2016), *Bodies of Modernism: Physical Disability in Transatlantic Modernist Literature*. Ann Arbor: University of Michigan Press.

Lodhi, Aasiya and Amanda Wrigley, eds (2018), 'Radio Modernisms: Features, Cultures and the BBC', *Media History*, 24: 2, pp. 159–65.

McWhinnie, Donald (1959), *The Art of Radio*. London: Faber and Faber.

Michalko, Rod (2010), 'What's Cool about Blindness?', *Disability Studies Quarterly* 30: 3/4, <http://www.dsq-sds.org/article/view/1296/1332> (last accessed 2 February 2020).

Mills, Mara (2011), 'Hearing Aids and the History of Electronics Miniaturization', *IEEE Annals of the History of Computing*, 33: 2, pp. 24–44.

Mills, Mara (2015), 'Technology', in *Keywords for Disability Studies*, ed. Rachel Adams, Benjamin Reiss and David Serlin. New York: New York University Press, pp. 176–9.

Mitchell, David T. and Sharon L. Snyder (2000), *Narrative Prosthesis: Disability and the Dependencies of Discourse*. Ann Arbor: University of Michigan Press.

Morse, Daniel Ryan (2020), *Radio Empire: The BBC's Eastern Service and the Emergence of the Global Anglophone Novel*. New York: Columbia University Press.

Murphy, Kate (2016), *Behind the Wireless: A History of Women at the BBC*. New York: Palgrave.

O'Shaughnessy, Brian (1967), 'Traitor Beware' (7 July), directed by Gerrie van Wyk, *The Sounds of Darkness*, SABC- Springbok Radio, <http://otrarchive.blogspot.com/2013/04/sounds-of-darkness-sa.html> (last accessed 2 February 2020).

Parrinder, Patrick (1990), 'Wells's Cancelled Endings for "The Country of the Blind"', *Science Fiction Studies*, 17: 1, pp. 71–6.

'Radio-Criticism a New Profession for the Blind' (1923), *Outlook for the Blind*, 17: 1, p. 31.

Rubery, Matthew (2016), *The Untold Story of the Talking Book*. Cambridge, MA: Harvard University Press.

Sanchez, Rebecca (2015), *Deafening Modernism: Embodied Language and Visual Poetics in American Literature*. New York: New York University Press.

Scales, Rebecca P. (2016), *Radio and the Politics of Sound in Interwar France, 1921–1939*. New York: Cambridge University Press.

Schalk, Sami (2016), 'Reevaluating the Supercrip', *Journal of Literary and Cultural Disability Studies*, 10: 1, pp. 71–86.

Shulman, Max (2016), 'Tuning the Black Voice: Colour-Deafness and the American Negro Theatre's Radio Dramas', *Modern Drama*, 59: 4, pp. 456–77.
Sterne, Jonathan (2003), *The Audible Past: Cultural Origins of Sound Reproduction*. Durham, NC: Duke University Press.
Stoever, Jennifer Lynn (2016), *The Sonic Color Line: Race and the Cultural Politics of Listening*. New York: New York University Press.
Thomas, Dylan (1954), *Under Milk Wood: A Play for Voices*. New York: New Directions.
Verma, Neil (2012), *Theater of the Mind: Imagination, Aesthetics, and American Radio Drama*. Chicago: University of Chicago Press.
Whittington, Ian (2018), *Writing the Radio War: Literature, Politics and the BBC, 1939–1945*. Edinburgh: Edinburgh University Press.
'Wireless for the Blind' (1939), *Radio Times*, 847 (25 December), p. 30.

14

MUSIC: MODERNIST REMEDIATION AND TECHNOLOGIES OF LISTENING

Josh Epstein

LUDWIG VAN BEETHOVEN, if not exactly a modernist, offers ample fodder for modern artists looking to defend – or expand – their turf. While producing *City Lights* (1928), Charlie Chaplin responded to the newly popular 'talkies' by proclaiming that 'Moving pictures need sound as much as Beethoven symphonies need lyrics' (qtd in Crafton 1999: 296). It might be tempting to retort that Beethoven's last symphony did have lyrics – and still turned out okay – but taking Chaplin's maxim seriously is more useful (if less instantly gratifying) than the easy dismissal. Chaplin, who composed the score to *City Lights*, understood the supple relationship between image and music even in the 'silent' picture (which, as film historians repeatedly note, was never truly silent). Music in 1920s film was increasingly tasked with sustaining the narrative development, on-screen action and extra-diegetic affect of films such as *City Lights*, itself part pantomime and part melodrama (literally, 'music-drama'). Chaplin's later score for *Modern Times* (1936), a sort of semi-talkie, enhanced these tensions: the main love theme, influenced by Puccini's *Tosca* and written to narrate the Tramp's refuge from technology in the arms of sentimental domesticity, attached to the popular imagination two decades later as the popular song 'Smile'. From operatic melodrama to silent film melodrama to *melos* without drama, this music was churned through a dialectical factory-wheel to which lyrics added considerable exchange value.

Emerging alongside Chaplin's melodramatic pantomimes were 'city-symphonies' by Dziga Vertov (*Man with a Movie Camera*, 1929), Walter Ruttmann (*Berlin: Die Sinfonie der Großstadt*, 1927), Fritz Lang (*Metropolis*, 1927) and Alberto Cavalcanti (*Rien que les heures*, 1926), as well as avant-garde experiments such as Fernand Léger's *Ballet mécanique*, which features Chaplin ('Charlot') in puppet form. Even without the noisy accompaniment of George Antheil's score, composed and performed independently for pianolas, sirens, electric bells and percussion, the film's gestures to Chaplin invoke the rhythmic physicality of a 'mechanical ballet' and disrupt any pretence to pure formal abstraction. Films had sound, whether they 'needed' it or not: the presence of music and speech was not silenced by film but reanimated by it and helped to act on the sensorium in unexpected ways.

This chapter examines how modernist radio and film remediate musical expression, not only leveraging music's appeals to sentiment but representing music as a media technology in its own right. I focus primarily on two films produced by the British General Post Office (GPO) Film Unit: Stuart Legg's *BBC: The Voice of Britain* (1936), featuring a set-piece in which Beethoven's Fifth Symphony is performed for a broadcast audience, and Humphrey Jennings's *Listen to Britain* (1942; edited by Stewart McAllister). By depicting the performance and broadcasting of music in a different medium, these films remediate the technological propensities embedded in musical sound, using the technologies of cinema to extend those propensities further. Modernist composers conceived of their own music as something technological, wired into the material networks of communication, machinery and infrastructure that we reflexively associate with 'modernity'. Before turning to Legg and Jennings, then, some attention is due to the intermedial aesthetics of modernist music, which the GPO films extend: though the music in Jennings's and Legg's films is not modernist (Beethoven, Mozart, dance music, Welsh folk song), it is rendered modernist in effect through exactly such hybridised juxtapositions of genre and medium.

Modernist Music as Media

Modernist texts seek ways to transport the voice across media and spatio-temporal limits. In perhaps the most canonical modernist example, T. S. Eliot's typist, listening to 'a record on the gramophone' in the aftermath of an indifferent assault, exemplifies modernists' preoccupations with recorded music, as it remediates a subject's recuperation from trauma, and dissociation from her own voice, by inscribing distant voices on to the perceptual texture of the present. Decades later, at the tail end of 'modernism' as conventionally defined, the protagonist of Francis Poulenc's *La Voix humaine* (1958), named Elle, talks to her former lover on the telephone, and hears the sounds of a jazz record emanating from the other end. The audience does not quite listen along with her; as in Cocteau's original 1928 stage play and Gian Carlo Menotti's opera *The Telephone* (1947), and in the tradition of radio dramas such as Lucille Fletcher's *Sorry, Wrong Number* (1943), we hear only Elle's reactions to the conversation and to the failures of the technology. We participate partially in Elle's aural discovery, however. An outburst of classicised jazz locating Elle's 'ex' in a new lover's home marks a moment of semi-diegetic music: an orchestral imitation of what she hears, and an interruption of the opera's formal self-containment, as if to echo the telephone's fragmentary effects. Dropped calls, hang-ups and wrong numbers limn a failed human connection and an alienated relationship with technology (marked even by the name/pronoun 'Elle'). This 'monodrama' soon turns melodrama, as Elle pleads insanity and dies, strangled by the telephone cord.

La Voix re-enacts recurring modernist concerns about technologies that may expand the cultural status of music or threaten its aura. Elle's singing voice both signals her instability and awakens modernist anxieties about the 'material practices and technologies through which voices become audible' (Weidman 2013: 236). In short, *La Voix* alerts us to the technological character of music itself. Poulenc imbues his onstage and offstage music, and Elle's description of the music she hears, with all the qualities of a technology that mediates information and interacts with other technologies. Entwined with Elle's elliptical narrative, the telephone's mediations are remediated by Poulenc's music, tasked with both the narrative work of filling in half of a conversation and the thematic work of redoubling Elle's alienation. Inasmuch as the orchestra and Elle's voice must suggest an acoustic presence on the other end of the line, these sounds mediate the act of listening; Elle's singing and the orchestral accompaniment must do the work of recomposing Elle's disjointed auditory engagement.

Poulenc and Cocteau had long participated in a modernist musical milieu that synthesised art with technology. The scandalous 1917 Ballets Russes production of Erik Satie's *Parade* reinvents ubiquitous media images in order to uproot aesthetic hierarchies and 'reconfigur[e] the fashionable life' (Davis 2006: 129). Satie's mechanical noises, musical loops and parodies of ragtime complement Cocteau's scenario, drawn from a barrage of popular American media: 'The *Titanic* – "Nearer My God to Thee" . . . The *New York Herald* . . . gramophones . . . posters . . . Charlie Chaplin' (qtd in Perloff 1991: 113). The media savvy of *Les Six* – a group of composers, including Poulenc, known for their fashionable 'lifestyle modernism' and distaste for the 'sauce' of nineteenth-century music – yielded compositions such as Arthur Honegger's *Pacific 231* (1923), an orchestral homage to the locomotive, and *Les Mariés sur la Tour Eiffel* (1921), a ballet collaboratively composed by five of *Les Six* in which 'human gramophones' comment on a series of *tableaux vivants*. The soundscape is no mere 'background' for dramatic action: the music and the gesturing body simulate the presence of other visual, textual and recording media.

A text, such as *La Voix* or *Parade*, that is openly intermedial – situated between different media and their clashing 'signifying systems' (Clements 2019: 46)[1] – understands music as a technology in both form (as media begin to resemble each other) and function (as we experience these technologies' alienating effects). 'All mediation', Jay Bolter and Richard Grusin write, 'is remediation': each medium enters into 'relationships of respect and rivalry with other media', just as a medium's 'representational power' presumes familiarity with a media ecology (2000 [1999]: 65). Modernist art partakes in a similar 'heightening [of] medial awareness' (Murphet 2009: 4). Sara Danius (2002) argues that as the modernist novel reconstructs a crisis of perception, it approximates a Wagnerian *Gesamtkunstwerk*, contending with compartmentalised sense experiences by abstracting and then subsuming them into a genre-bending synthesis. Danius's theatrical analogy suggests that modernist aesthetic forms – literary, musical, visual and cinematic – are constantly staging a confrontation with modernity's sensory assaults, through explicit reference or through immanent formal development.

Julian Murphet notes that the figureheads of the European avant-garde (Marinetti, Ball, Apollinaire, Tzara), and later artists whom they influenced, were 'aware of themselves as media artifacts' (2009: 4), an apt description of musical as well as literary practices. The so-called Bruitistes accompanied asemantic 'sound poetry' with mechanical noises, turning the poet-performer's body into an anti-technological technology, a resonant mediator for sounds that recuperate (often through primitivist kitsch) an essential irrationality. In Futurist texts such as F. T. Marinetti's *Zang Tumb Tumb* (1914) and Luigi Russolo's manifesto, *The Art of Noise* (1913), and composition *Awakening of a City* (1914), the sensationalised noises of mechanised warfare are glorified as the basis of a sonic art that 'conquer[s] the infinite variety of noise-sounds' (Russolo 1986 [1913]: 25). Futurist music aimed to explode music's autonomy by heightening its contradictions, using the noisy soundscape to break down Art-with-a-capital-A, which built its 'respectability' on acoustic technologies and cultural norms that excluded noise (or tried to) from both stage and audience (Bailey 1998).

The noises of Futurism and Bruitisme were absorbed by French and Anglo-American musical modernists, including and beyond Cocteau, Poulenc and *Les Six*. Edgard Varèse's *Amériques* (1926), a homage to New York City in which duck-calls and air-raid sirens share space with the conventional orchestra, was an instant sensation. Antheil's riot-inducing concert versions of *Ballet mécanique* earned him the fandom of the Anglo-American modernist literati, including Pound, Yeats, Joyce and one Hedy Lamarr (with whom Antheil collaborated on a 'frequency-hopping' torpedo patent). Though defended by the composer in the language of neoclassical formalism, Antheil's *Ballet mécanique* prompted a noisy debate over the relationships between music and capitalism, joined by Ezra Pound's tracts comparing the piece to a musical factory (Epstein 2014). William Carlos Williams felt that, with Antheil's help, they had 'gone up over' the noise of the New York subway (qtd in Thompson 2002: 143); Antheil's music seemed to recalibrate the 'audile technique' of urban listening.[2]

At the centre of this soundscape was jazz, soon to become, in Geoffrey Jacques's words, 'a standard against which the modernity of other art forms was measured' (2001: 74). Especially early in the century, 'jazz' encompassed a multifaceted range of idioms that, in their mass-distributed forms, served as a 'transmitter' of verbal conventions – vernacular dialects and minstrelsy 'cross-talk' – coextensive with the linguistic hybridity of modernism (Jacques 2009: 14, 78; North 1994). Perhaps because the term itself is so elastic, jazz found itself appreciated and appropriated by the European avant-garde in overdetermined ways. Glorified and vilified as a symptom of war trauma and mechanised city life, both celebrated as raw emotional expression and fetishised as a kindred spirit to the 'anti-art' sensibilities of Futurism, Dada and Cocteauvian 'lifestyle modernism', jazz was 'affixed to . . . activities of the avant-garde like a decal on a traveler's bag' (Rasula 2003: 14).

Modernist music, and jazz specifically, was thus positioned as a technological intervention into a 'battle over the significance and value of modernity' (Chinitz 2000: 10). Modernist studies has (mercifully) abandoned the rhetoric of a 'cultural divide' that exempts 'high art' from the technological dependencies of popular art – or has worked to historicise the vested interests that invented such a divide. Discourses of 'absolute' music (music that claims no extramusical 'meaning') are no less subject to technological mediation, both extensional (sound recording) and intensional (the technical means of musical language). The experiments of the Second Viennese School, conceived not as an avant-garde attack on art so much as an extension of Austro-German Romanticism, struck Theodor Adorno as a 'musical technology' that revealed the mutual dependence between technical discipline and a 'blind state of nature' (2002 [1934]: 207). As Arved Ashby (2010) argues, the *ethos* of sound recording supports an 'absolute' ideal of music by rendering a sound autonomous from its context. This severing heightens questions of authenticity, performance style, subjective sense-memory and textuality with which music contends. As Rick Altman writes, with respect to film sound, 'Recordings do not reproduce sound, they represent sound' (1992: 40): a recording is an interpretation and inscription of the sound's performed materiality. For Igor Stravinsky, who ostensibly resisted individual interpretations of his music, a recording was functionally 'coincident with the work without . . . displacing or replacing it' (Ashby 2010: 201–2). Stravinsky's formalism, in any case, was a rhetorical posture as much as a compositional practice. His fascination with Russian folk traditions invokes contemporaries such as Béla Bartók, Leoš Janáček and Percy Grainger, for whom the phonograph was not only a tool to preserve 'authorial intention' but a means of investigating indigenous vernaculars.

In these and other ways, the modernist musical text represents a technology of form built on technologies of performance, recording, distribution and ethnography. Modernist music – however 'absolute' in conception – is remediation all the way down.

The GPO: Documenting Musical Intermediality

The intermedial qualities of opera, film, ballet and narrative radio give an additional thrust to music's technological character, employing new musical noises and actively representing music as a social actor; exploiting the affective qualities of music (as in non-diegetic background music); and making visible its technological circulation. If cinema was often imagined, after Kandinsky, as the *telos* of the synaesthetic total artwork (Murphet 2009: 147–8), modernist films often defamiliarise their own synthesis, unfolding a dialectic between the artwork and its material substructure. The technological self-awareness of these films, like that of *Parade* or *Les Mariés*, produces what Matthew Wilson Smith (2007) calls the 'crystalline' total artwork: one that foregrounds its own 'hypermediacy' by spotlighting its multiple constituent media (of which some, like cinema, seemed 'total' to begin with).

Similarly, Legg's *BBC: The Voice of Britain* and Jennings's *Listen to Britain* capitalise on the effects of music while characterising the technological structures that disseminate it. As Janice Ho argues in her contribution to this volume, GPO Film Unit documentaries formally represent a social contract defined by the technologies and media that bind a citizenry. This ideal of mediated citizenship motivates the use of musical noise and rhythm in several GPO productions. In Harry Watt's *Night Mail* (1936), a paean to the postal train, a W. H. Auden poem is accompanied by Benjamin Britten's noisy score using industrial objects as percussion. Just as it muddies distinctions between diegetic and non-diegetic sound, *Night Mail* 'redraws geographical and intersubjective boundaries' through intermedial rhythmic play (Milian 2019). Jennings, too, juxtaposed 'art music' with provincial music and industrial noises; films such as *Spare Time* (1939) critique the pressures of wartime production by creating separate 'sonic spaces' that use 'musical temporality [as] refuge from the noisy reality of modern life' (Claydon 2011:183; Mansell 2011: 166).

The GPO's artistic and ideological rifts, though beyond my present scope, offer additional context for Legg's and Jennings's uses of music. Sensibilities clashed, for example, over the relative merits of 'city-symphony' films such as Ruttmann's *Berlin* and Vertov's *Man with a Movie Camera*. Directors who championed a realist aesthetic, such as Paul Rotha, found these films too ideologically vague to effect social reform; *Night Mail* seemed to Rotha to have 'no social purpose whatsoever' (qtd in Richards 2011: 3). John Grierson, who admired Eisenstein but found Vertov's films aimless, left the Unit in 1937, dismayed with its new direction. With the hiring of Surrealists including Jennings and Cavalcanti, the GPO gravitated away from documentary realism toward experiments with montage and sound-image counterpoint, influenced by Vertov's deployment of music as both method and diegetic subject. *Man with a Movie Camera*, for example, opens with the tuning of an orchestra; the conductor and players await the projectionist, their motions captured and conducted into being by the film strip, which is then pruned throughout the film's narrative (Roberts 2000: 49–50).

GPO films, too, use music as a symbol of national community and institutional command, a self-aware technological actor marshalled for cultural repair. Though neither Legg's nor Jennings's film employs modernist music, both remediate 'classical' music as a modernist form within a modern media ecology. Beethoven serves as Legg's primary example of musical sublimity, reracinated by the sounds of politics. *Listen to Britain* cross-fertilises the industrial, military and urban sounds of Blitz-era London with music-hall numbers, Welsh folk songs ('The Ash Grove'), North American folk songs (Canadian soldiers singing 'Home on the Range') and Mozart. Through layered remediations, Legg and Jennings defamiliarise how the production of music feeds into 'second-nature' daily rituals – which, in times of national distress, may have ceased to feel natural and found themselves in need of reconstruction.

Aiming to cultivate public listening habits and shape a coherent 'imagined community' of tuned-in listeners, BBC music programming served as a support system for cultural production. The BBC programme *Music While You Work*, which *Listen to Britain* quotes directly, designed its programming to increase industrial productivity in concert with the rhythms of the working body.[3] Synchronising the BBC with images of labour, Legg and Jennings weave music into a process through which British subjects constitute, in lived time, a cohesive public that both whistles and listens while they work. Simultaneously, these films strive to preserve music's integrity as a (contingently) self-sufficient medium through which citizens can realise themselves. *Voice* and *Listen* reconstruct music as a 'technology of the self': a mediated 'cultural resource' that actors 'mobilize for their ongoing self-construction' (DeNora 1999: 32).

Conducting the Voices of Britain

'Classical' music fit the BBC's pedagogical aims for the new medium. Promoting the BBC as a 'sustained endeavour to ... build up knowledge, experience and character', founding Director General John Reith argued that programming 'high-brow' music would popularise it to the improvement of national tastes (qtd in Doctor 1999: 27–8). This approach would, Reith hoped, prove democratic, enabling the 'shepherd on the downs, or the lonely crofter in the farthest Hebrides' to 'sit side by side with the patron of the stalls and hear some of the best performances in the world' (*BBC Handbook* [1928], qtd in Scannell 1981: 244). The programming of modernist composers (including those discussed above) met with mixed responses, but rather than change the programming, the BBC supplemented it with the *Radio Times*, *The Listener*, school pamphlets and listener handbooks (Scannell 1981: 245; Briggs 1995 [1965]: 181–2). According to Debra Rae Cohen, the BBC constructed its 'voice' intermedially through collaborations of sound and print, propping its public image on *The Listener*, which endeavoured to train listeners as discriminating 'aural citizen[s]' (2012: 579). And if *The Listener* was used to 'assuage anxieties about broadcasting' with 'oracular' pronouncements about the 'magic of radio', it did so only by 'eliminat[ing] that "noise" that validates the radio signal' and 'underscore[s] its immediacy' (Cohen 2012: 585).

In the late 1920s, the conductor Edward Clark pulled off successful radio performances of Stravinsky's *L'Histoire du soldat* (1918) and Schoenberg's *Pierrot lunaire* (1912) and *Gurre-Lieder* (1913), showing that British listeners were prepared to engage with the 'new music' (even the proudly late Romantic music of *Gurre-Lieder* offers its share of challenges for listeners). After the hiring of Adrian Boult as Music Director in 1930, the BBC Symphony Orchestra emerged as a world-class ensemble; the BBC established a concert hall in Broadcasting House for both live and broadcast audiences (Briggs 1995 [1965]: 164–5). While underscoring the BBC's confidence in its musicians, *Voice* presents the production of culture, 'high' and 'low', as an interactive process, tempering the BBC's self-seriousness with a playful respect for the music itself.[4] And as Legg accompanies Boult's performance with images of the *Radio Times* flying off the presses, music's intermediality both broadens its civic influence and leaves it more prone to desacralisation.

A film that depicts, à la Joyce or Woolf, a 'day in the life' of BBC operations, *Voice* emphasises the 'unifying and integrative nature' of radio (Richards 2011: 7), counterpointing Beethoven with comedy acts, dance music, children's programming and a production of *Macbeth* (featuring a baby-faced Jennings as a Weïrd Sister). A series of opening dissolve cuts introduces Reith's pontifical inscription on Broadcasting House, which in workmanlike Latin dedicates '[t]his temple of the arts and muses . . . to Almighty God' with a prayer that 'the people inclining their ear to whatsoever things are beautiful and honest and of good report may tread the path of virtue and wisdom'. The film then pivots to the sounds of a morning service, dubbed over images of rural citizens listening on the wireless. Returning to the BBC offices, the mail is sorted, the contradictory injunctions of complaint letters heard in choric voiceovers ('More variety! Less variety!') as an army of typists responds. A 'gramophone specialist' tries, and then destroys, a crooning new record; professional 'practisers of noise' prepare noise-making devices for *Macbeth*; a voiceover extols the station's extensive gramophone library; a producer casually eats an apple during the 'Dancing Daughters'. The studio work is treated with more irony than reverence – a tone that throws into relief, if only temporarily, the gravitas of Beethoven's Fifth.

If the choice of this symphonic warhorse, rather than Schoenberg or Poulenc, avoids debates over the niche appeal of 'modern' music, it accentuates a recurring modernist interest in Beethoven's music. In an excellent recent monograph, Nathan Waddell reads 'Beethovenian' modernism as both a Romantic challenge to 'restrictive aesthetic norms' and a 'valuing of the artist as a socially and politically transformative figure' (2020: 6). Literary modernists 'buried' Beethoven in their work, showing how 'music seemingly available for all to enjoy is bound up with the economic hierarchies it is so often said to transcend' (Waddell 2020: 49). In E. M. Forster's *Howards End*, a narrator remarks that 'all sorts and conditions are satisfied' by Beethoven's Fifth, proceeding to show competing interpretations of its 'sublime noise' being 'broadcast' over a metaphorical 'field of battle' (Forster 1998 [1910]: 25). Similarly, Legg's *BBC* extends outward, showing the music's production and then mapping out a cultural 'field' over which it is 'broadcast'. This field, and its 'hierarchies', matriculate into the rest of the film; Boult's performance is 'bound up with' the radio's daily operations, as the BBC's social mission is bound with the music's immanent tensions. This set-piece reads as a defence of reflective listening – the interruption of which does not devalue music, but humanises it, reintegrating it with other fare and with the 'sorts and conditions' listening back.

Legg frames the Beethoven performance with images of medial self-consciousness, at the scenes of both production and reception. A voiceover names the four movements of Beethoven's Fifth as the presses churn out the *Radio Times*. Accompanied by an oscillating chime, an announcer lists imperial outposts where the broadcast will be heard. We then hear the voice of Reith – a somewhat sinister radio talk promoting the Empire Service, which promises to induce 'greater sympathy' to imperial subjects across the globe. Legg cross-hatches a synthesis between technological infrastructure and musical performance: first, a series of angular cuts between orchestra musicians and radio engineers (Figure 14.1) – complete with the whirring howls of the technology generating the signal – then Boult and his antenna-like baton empowered by a series of low-angle shots (Figures 14.2–3). Interrupted briefly by a hand at a dial panel (Figure 14.4), Boult's con-

Figure 14.1 BBC Engineer, in *BBC: The Voice of Britain*, dir. Stuart Legg (BFI).

Figure 14.2 Sir Adrian Boult conducting the BBC Symphony Orchestra in a performance of Beethoven's Fifth Symphony, in *BBC: The Voice of Britain*.

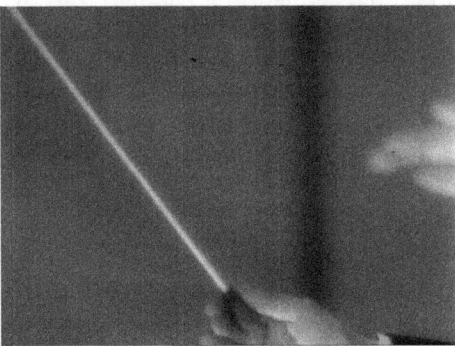

Figure 14.3 Sir Adrian Boult's baton giving a downbeat in *BBC: The Voice of Britain*.

ducting downbeat – and Beethoven's opening motif – create a circuit among the technology of broadcast, the body of an engineer, and the body and baton of Boult himself. The music runs for some five minutes, dubbed first over fragmentary shots of the orchestra, then over images of domestic 'attentive listeners', explicitly linking the players to their fellow citizens in whose ears and name the music resonates.

Figure 14.4 Hand of a BBC engineer during Beethoven performance, in *BBC: The Voice of Britain*.

The symphony's generative power is thus remediated by the signals that disseminate it for (global) consumption. Having established the BBC's imperial cultural heft, Beethoven's music opens into the spheres of politics; as in Forster, the music generates unifying connectivity which is dispersed into conflicting modes of reception. Formally, the disorienting cuts and angles that establish Boult's dominance also create an effect of distraction rather than 'attentive' absorption. Beethoven's music is interrupted, moreover, by an SOS signal to a trawler at sea, interrupting sublimity with the contingencies of work. Legg presents a litany of 'leaders of opinion' in closeup, including H. G. Wells on the conditions of socialist Russia, and a wry speech by George Bernard Shaw proclaiming that the 'microphone is the most wonderful tell-tale in the world', a medium that renders a politician's (in)sincerity immediately detectable. Once Beethoven and Boult fade, 'high culture' gives way to Henry Hall's Dance Band, over shots of a policeman on his beat and a couple unceremoniously necking on the street. In a final sequence, a pacing father tells his son to stop whistling along with the performers on air. Boult's reign does not run here; music now produces not reverent absorption, but immodesty and restlessness, the voice (and lips) of a whistling bandleader reflexively mimicked by those of distracted listeners. Interrupted by naval exigencies and boat races, Boult's conducting hand, and Reith's extended imperial handshake, are subsumed – with a few ironic remainders – into quotidian rituals.

Beethoven and Boult may not generate the 'attentive listening' behaviours meant to edify public taste, but they do conduct productive listening habits. By treating music as both an object of representation and an acoustic substructure, *The Voice of Britain* capitalises on music's emotional force while connecting it to a material process. The film presents music as a mediation of the labour of production, used to make both trifles and 'warhorses', and the cultural labour of reception, performed by those domestic subjects whom radio music proposes to 'educate'. In practice, the film enacts the dialectic articulated by Walter Benjamin (1969 [1936]): if the aura of Boult's performance aestheticises politics, that aura is abruptly punctured by material noises and collisions, allowing a listening public to absorb (rather than be absorbed by) the sacralised artwork.

Listening (Out) to Britain: Music and Civic Soundscape

Beginning his career as a Surrealist painter, poet and literary critic (trained by I. A. Richards) before cofounding the ethnographic group Mass Observation, Jennings long understood media forms as interdependent. His unfinished anthology, *Pandaemonium*, organises a literary history of the Industrial Revolution as 'images . . . in an unrolling film', exploring the history of the senses and the structures of feeling[5] revealed in writing. Sound and music provide a pulse for this rhythmic literary montage, which juxtaposes Samuel Pepys on the nature of sound and Daines Barrington on birdsong, Robert Hooke's experiments with vibration and John Tyndall's comparisons of air disturbances in vowels and consonants. *Pandaemonium* hears music as a physical disturbance of matter and as raw material for the imagination, a dialectic that 'unrolls' alongside the engines of capital. Jennings's film aesthetic draws from these same Surrealist and materialist instincts, and in particular, the use of formal and generic ambiguity to destabilise 'referential or functional aspects' of concrete 'found objects' (Miller 2002: 232). In Jennings's and Len Lye's *Birth of a Robot*, an animated film made for Shell-Mex, puppets in the vestments of Roman gods use high-grade motor oil to 'lubricate' a dead motorist back to life in the Egyptian deserts. Lye uses the music of Gustav Holst's *The Planets*, likewise a synthesis of nostalgic mythology and outward exploration, to enact oneiric free-play rooted in the object-world: an aesthetic that meets the material needs and medial self-awareness of both advertising and surrealism.

If Jennings's version of surrealism feeds into late modernists' 'anthropological turn' – a reversal of modernism's fractured imperialist gaze on to a self-examination of England's own rituals (Esty 2004) – *Listen to Britain* takes a similarly dialectical tack, using concrete sonic particulars to unfold patterns of musical production and consumption. For Thomas Davis, *Listen to Britain* absorbs the ruptures of wartime within a broader sense of everyday ordinariness, suggesting that 'even a day at war is not all that extraordinary' (Davis 2015: 45), and constructs this sense of the ordinary through the formal approximation of consensus, which compensates for the impoverishment of visible meaning. That consensus is reconstructed in the modality of the audible – in intersubjective acts of 'listening out' (Lacey 2013) that constitute the public sphere.

Listen to Britain expands this intersubjectivity of listening across the spheres of work, play and education – creating a total artwork while preserving the porous openness of sound in the world. Jennings connects a playground clapping routine, lovingly surveilled by a woman nearby (Figure 14.5), to military preparations – the work these children may some day join – through distorted sounds of engine noise and Bren gun carriers. As we move into a montage of travel – starting with a plane's-eye-view of the English landscape, cutting to a lorry moving forward through a tunnel as a train horizontally crosses the screen – we hear the music of 'Calling All Workers', Eric Coates's rousing theme to *Music While You Work*, over the 'keynote sound' of helicopters.[6] An assembly line of women factory workers sing along as 'Yes, My Darling Daughter' is piped through a speaker (Figure 14.6), which sets the beat for the assembly line and the singing workers (in that order) (Figure 14.7). Work, study, play and war, moving along the X, Y and Z visual axes, create a shared habitus of listening, conducted by the BBC.

This factory sequence pivots on an 'acousmatic' voice: a sound without a visible presence. Acousmatic sound, as Brian Kane writes, functions as a 'node in the tensile

Figure 14.5 Schoolyard round game, in *Listen to Britain*, dir. Humphrey Jennings and ed. Stewart McAllister (BFI).

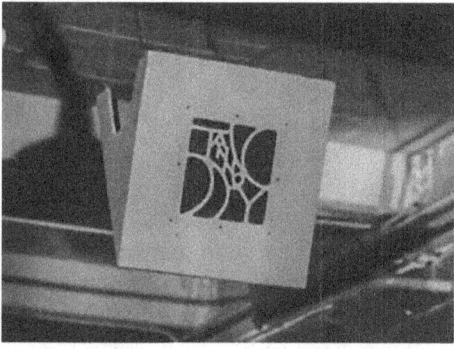

Figure 14.6 Factory loudspeaker, in *Listen to Britain*.

Figure 14.7 Women singing to *Music While You Work*, in *Listen to Britain*.

mesh of a form of life', a 'point where disparate auditory and cultural practices intersect' (2014: 226). Here, a loudspeaker amplifies the materiality of this 'mesh', disciplining us to listen to the 'absolute' sound-object, while recalling the phantasmagoric technology that occludes its material source (Kane 2014: 119–20). Jennings's depiction of sound piped through speakers connects the music to affective and economic mobilisations of war, an act of mediated listening both compulsory and voluntary, conducted by an invisible voice in defence against an unseen enemy.

Music While You Work (hereafter *MWYW*) was initiated in 1940 in response to a concern that as women's labour grew increasingly repetitive, production and morale would diminish. As Keith Jones (2010) and Christina Baade (2012) have detailed, the implementation of *MWYW* on the BBC and in the factories (and, eventually, for home listeners) was provoked by a surge of studies in the 1930s and 1940s speculating on how music might ease boredom and obviate the need for frequent breaks. *MWYW*, Baade writes, was based on 'research in industrial efficiency that focused on workers' bodies, psychology and welfare; and the conviction that, in a state of total war, the contributions of every citizen mattered' (2012: 61). BBC administrators used listener research surveys and interviews with factory workers and managers to parse the effects of musical elements – tempo, rhythm, melody – on workplace productivity. Managers hoped that *MWYW* might 'restore the rhythm of the work within the chaos of mechanical din', though new acoustic and practical difficulties emerged (Bijsterveld 2008: 87). Wynford Reynolds, the first producer, claimed in a 1942 directive that *MWYW* would have the effect of a cup of tea, a 'tonic' for worker morale (qtd in Kirkpatrick 1942) – as long as the music was neither too spiritual nor too sentimental, neither too *rubato* nor too syncopated. The complex rhythms of 'hot' music, Reynolds warned, would create 'a confusion of sound' that interfered with the rhythms of workers' bodies and machines, building on a 'deeply rooted symbolism of sound which associated noise with chaos and rhythm with order' (Bijsterveld 2006: 327).

MWYW was conscripted in the service of health, tasked with increasing (without overstimulating) the body's output. Such efforts to standardise workers' bodies, and nurture the body politic, buttress Jennings's images of cheerful labourers tunefully whistling along to a speaker that regulates their movements from afar. This factory scene thus represents an administered technology of production, conducted by the *acousmêtre*. If, as Baade argues (quoting Michel Foucault's *Discipline and Punish*), *MWYW* 'subjected music to a "mechanics of power" in order to render it useful to the war effort' and made itself akin to 'the systems of factory discipline that transformed workers into docile bodies' (2012: 66), Jennings locates this internalised docility in the mediated structure of listening itself, placing music not outside but at the nexus of technology and labour. The injunction to 'listen to Britain' enjoins us also to listen to listening, to hear music as part of an ongoing process of cultural labour both patriotic and disciplinary.

Listen to Britain's most formally innovative moment occurs when Jennings transitions from the music hall, featuring the comic duo of Flanagan and Allen singing 'Underneath the Arches', to a performance in London's National Gallery of Mozart's Piano Concerto no. 17 in G major, K.453, by pianist Myra Hess and the Royal Air Force Orchestra. Moving from an interactive ritual to a solemn one, Jennings connects two forms of listening through a musical pivot chord: the penultimate dominant chord of the music-hall song is Mozart's tonic chord. Jennings claimed this to be a happy accident of editing, nurturing his Surrealist faith that unconscious structures reveal themselves in material coincidences. What Grierson called the 'umbilical cord' between spectator and state, his ideal for documentary film, is here replaced with what we might playfully term an umbilical *chord* – a modulating musical resonance that binds, without equating, listening habitus of different classes.

If 'high' and popular art are 'torn halves of an integral freedom to which, however, they do not add up' (Adorno 1977 [1936]: 123), to connect high and popular forms through the umbilical chord of listening is to fashion a synthesis that unfolds its own social tensions. From rear-angle shots of Flanagan and Allen playfully conducting their audience, Jennings cuts to medium-shots of the active spectators, then to shots of the National Gallery's exterior, then to its interior. As a counterpoint to Flanagan and Allen's participatory whistlers, Hess's audience listens blissfully, sanctified by the presence of the Queen Mother (smiling with arms folded) alongside a wounded soldier and an economically diverse audience. Hess's lunchtime Gallery concerts, which cost a shilling, were noted for their cross-class appeal and cosmopolitan programming[7] – a reputation confirmed by a shot of the programme, which features Mozart, Smetana and Howard Ferguson (*Four Diversions on Ulster Airs* [1942], newly composed for the BBC in Northern Ireland). The Steinway piano, revealed in a deep-focused shot from the audience, features as a mediator of this internationalism: a material instrument and a synecdoche for the 'House of Steinway' (founded in 1850s New York by a German immigrant), and no less a cosmopolitan technology than radar or radio. The image of Hess (a Steinway loyalist) at the piano produces music as a network of auditory mediations.

The film closes by merging material technologies with idealised music: over a shot of metal being forged, a chorus of 'Rule, Britannia!' fades in asynchronously with shots of the earth and air. 'Rule, Britannia!', like the title of the film, speaks in the imperative mood, instructing the Empire to rule itself through acoustic introspection. Presenting the 'voice of Britain' as an acousmatic collective, this chorus can be heard as non-diegetic (externally imposed) or diegetic (produced by land and sky, sublated from the noises of labour and aerial warfare). In either reading, the anthem frames the music of Britain as a remediated artefact, by acknowledging (through violation) the artificiality of the film's formal premise, or by unpacking the material sounds and social practices that produce this ethereal chorus. The final frame presents a snippet of 'Rule, Britannia!', in the key of B-flat, overlaid by a cannon crossed over a violin. The musical notation ends not with the song's final words, however, but with the leading tone: the A-natural, corresponding with the word 'waves', that a listener expects resolved to the tonic (Figure 14.8). Closing mid-thought, this musical image attenuates the film's final words – 'Britons never, ever shall be slaves' – a message that, like the title of Jennings's *London Can Take It!* (1940), raises more anxiety than closure about Britain's absorption of trauma.

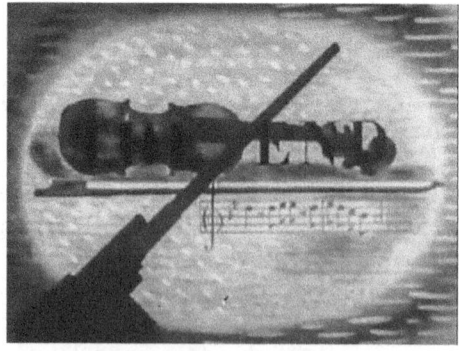

Figure 14.8 Final frame of *Listen to Britain*.

Jennings, a classmate of William Empson, may have felt this a necessary ambiguity, a gesture to the 'radical openness', 'plurality' and 'intersubjectivity' of a listening 'public sphere' premised on acts of 'faith in the act of listening that there will be some resonance with the address' (Lacey 2013: 7–8). What exactly does it mean to 'listen to Britain', anyway? Who is listening to whom? Jennings captures the ambiguity of the acousmatic address: the possibility that no one is listening, that no one perceives the human behind the voice, and that we must continue listening still. The injunction to 'rule' lies in suspended tension with the injunction to 'listen': Jennings implicates the 'human voice' with human listeners, their auditory acts of 'faith' reciprocally inscribing a material network of musical technologies. In these films, all music is 'music while you work', conducted in the context of factory labour, the theatre of war and the field of cultural production.

Notes

1. Clements employs this definition of intermediality in a discussion of Gertrude Stein's and Virgil Thomson's opera *Four Saints in Three Acts*, building on Rajewsky's excavation of 'intermediality' as an 'umbrella term' for other discourses (2005: 44). See also Lewis (2020) on the visual elements of intermedial form; Lewis employs the concept of intermediality, in congress with methods of 'new formalism', to show how intermedial forms awaken newly mobile and 'protean' spatial and temporal reading practices.
2. For an exceptionally lucid explication of Pound's *Antheil* treatise, see Moss: 2019. The phrase 'audile technique' is Sterne's (2003).
3. Braun compares *Music While You Work* to noise-abatement campaigns and industrial music management in Germany, under the Nazi regime as well as in the German Democratic Republic (2012: 62–4). See also Bijsterveld's foundational work on *MWYW* in relation to industrial noise (2006).
4. Inevitably, Legg's film sidesteps debates over the material interests of working musicians and institutional tensions between national and regional programmes. See Scannell (1981: 251).
5. Upon Jennings's untimely death, Raymond Williams's name was offered as a potential editor of *Pandaemonium*. (Williams, finishing his *Culture and Society: 1780–1950*, was unavailable.)
6. 'Keynote sound' is R. Murray Schafer's term for sounds that establish a soundscape's basic tonality and 'become listening habits in spite of themselves' (1994: 9).
7. Forster praised Hess in a BBC radio talk, contrasting her liberal internationalism with the Nazis' xenophobia (Deutsch 2016: 220); he would rehearse this claim in a screenplay for Jennings's *A Diary for Timothy* (1945), which extols Beethoven's humanism.

Works Cited

Adorno, Theodor (1977 [1936]), Letter to Walter Benjamin, 18 March 1936, in *Aesthetics and Politics*, ed. Ronald Taylor. London: Verso, pp. 120–6.

Adorno, Theodor (2002 [1934]), 'The Dialectical Composer', trans. Susan Gillespie, in *Essays on Music*, ed. Richard Leppert. Berkeley: University of California Press, pp. 203–9.

Altman, Rick (1992), 'Introduction: Four and a Half Film Fallacies', in *Sound Theory/Sound Practice*, ed. Rick Altman. London: Routledge, pp. 35–45.

Ashby, Arved (2010), *Absolute Music, Mechanical Reproduction*. Berkeley: University of California Press.

Baade, Christina L. (2012), *Victory Through Harmony: The BBC and Popular Music in World War II*. Oxford: Oxford University Press.
Bailey, Peter (1998), *Popular Culture and Performance in the Victorian City*. Cambridge: Cambridge University Press, 1998.
BBC: The Voice of Britain (2013 [1936]), directed by Stuart Legg, on *Land of Promise: The British Documentary Movement, 1930–1950*, DVD. London: British Film Institute.
Benjamin, Walter (1969 [1936]), 'The Work of Art in the Age of Mechanical Reproduction', trans. Harry Zohn, rpt. in *Illuminations*, ed. Hannah Arendt. New York: Schocken, pp. 217–51.
Bijsterveld, Karen (2006), 'Listening to Machines: Industrial Noise, Hearing Loss, and the Cultural Meaning of Sound', *Interdisciplinary Science Reviews*, 31: 4, pp. 323–37.
Bijsterveld, Karen (2008), *Mechanical Sound: Technology, Culture, and Public Problems of Noise in the Twentieth Century*. Cambridge, MA: MIT Press.
Bolter, Jay David and Richard Grusin (2000 [1999]), *Remediation: Understanding New Media*. Cambridge, MA: MIT Press.
Braun, Hans Joachin (2012), 'Turning a Deaf Ear? Industrial Noise and Noise Control in Germany since the 1920s', in *The Oxford Handbook of Sound Studies*, ed. Trevor Pinch and Karin Bijsterveld. Oxford: Oxford University Press, pp. 58–78.
Briggs, Asa (1995 [1965]), *The Golden Age of Wireless*, vol. 2 of *The History of Broadcasting in the United Kingdom*. Oxford: Oxford University Press.
Chinitz, David (2000), 'A Jazz-Banjorine, Not a Lute: Eliot and Popular Music before *The Waste Land*', in *T. S. Eliot's Orchestra: Critical Essays on Poetry and Music*, ed. John Xiros Cooper. New York: Garland, pp. 3–24.
Claydon, E. Anna (2011), 'National Identity, the GPO Film Unit, and their Music', in *The Projection of Britain: A History of the GPO Film Unit*, ed. Scott Anthony and James G. Mansell. London: Palgrave Macmillan, pp. 179–87.
Clements, Elicia (2019), 'How to Remediate; or, Gertrude Stein and Virgil Thomson's *Four Saints and Three Acts*', *Modern Drama*, 62: 1, pp. 45–72.
Cohen, Debra Rae (2012), 'Intermediality and the Problem of the *Listener*', *Modernism/modernity*, 19: 3, pp. 569–92.
Crafton, Donald (1999), *The Talkies: American Cinema's Transition to Sound, 1926–1931*. Berkeley: University of California Press.
Danius, Sara (2002), *The Senses of Modernism: Technology, Perception, and Aesthetics*. Ithaca, NY: Cornell University Press.
Davis, Mary E. (2006), *Classic Chic: Music, Fashion, and Modernism*. Berkeley: University of California Press.
Davis, Thomas (2015), *The Extinct Scene: Late Modernism and Everyday Life*. New York: Columbia University Press.
DeNora, Tia (1999), 'Music as a Technology of the Self', *Poetics*, 27, pp. 31–56.
Deutsch, David (2016), *British Literature and Classical Music: Cultural Contexts, 1870–1945*. London: Bloomsbury.
Doctor, Jennifer (1999), *The BBC and Ultra-Modern Music, 1922–1936: Shaping a Nation's Tastes*. Cambridge: Cambridge University Press.
Epstein, Josh (2014), *Sublime Noise: Musical Culture and the Modernist Writer*. Baltimore: Johns Hopkins University Press.
Esty, Jed (2004), *A Shrinking Island: Modernism and National Culture in England*. Princeton: Princeton University Press.
Forster, E. M. (1998 [1910]), *Howards End*, ed. Paul Armstrong. London: Norton.
Jacques, Geoffrey (2001), 'Listening to Jazz', in *American Popular Music: New Approaches to the Twentieth Century*, ed. Rachel Rubin and Jeffrey Melnick. Amherst: University of Massachusetts Press, pp. 65–92.

Jacques, Geoffrey (2009), *A Change in the Weather: Modernist Imagination, African American Imaginary*. Amherst: University of Massachusetts Press.

Jones, Keith (2010), 'Music in Factories: A Twentieth-Century Technique for Control of the Productive Self', *Social and Cultural Geography*, 6: 5, pp. 723–44.

Kane, Brian (2014), *Sound Unseen: Acousmatic Sound in Theory and Practice*. Oxford: Oxford University Press.

Kirkpatrick, Forrest H. (1942), 'Music and the Factory Worker', *The Psychological Record*, 5, pp. 197–204.

Lacey, Kate (2013), *Listening Publics: The Politics and Experience of Listening in the Media Age*. Cambridge: Polity Press.

Lewis, Cara L. (2020), *Dynamic Form: How Intermediality Made Modernism*. Ithaca, NY: Cornell University Press.

Listen to Britain (2013 [1942]), directed by Humphrey Jennings, on *Land of Promise: The British Documentary Movement, 1930–1950*, DVD. London: British Film Institute.

Man with a Movie Camera (1929), directed by Dziga Vertov, Alexander Street. Available at: <https://video.alexanderstreet.com/watch/dziga-vertov-s-man-with-a-movie-camera>.

Mansell, James G. (2011), 'Rhythm, Modernity, and the Politics of Sound', in *The Projection of Britain: A History of the GPO Film Unit*, ed. Scott Anthony and James G. Mansell. London: Palgrave Macmillan, pp. 161–7.

Milian, Patrick (2019), '"A Quickening of the Heart": *Night Mail*, *Paul Bunyan*, and the Multimodal Rhythms of Late Modernism', *Modernism/modernity Print-Plus*, 4: 3, <https://doi.org/10.26597/mod.0137> (last accessed 25 January 2022).

Miller, Tyrus (2002), 'Documentary/Modernism: Convergence and Complementarity in the 1930s', *Modernism/modernity*, 9: 2, pp. 226–41.

Moss, Gemma (2019), 'Pound as Music Theorist: *Antheil and the Treatise on Harmony*', in *The Edinburgh Companion to Ezra Pound and the Arts*, ed. Roxana Preda. Edinburgh: Edinburgh University Press, pp. 347–58.

Murphet, Julian (2009), *Multimedia Modernism: Literature and the Anglo-American Avant-Garde*. Cambridge: Cambridge University Press.

North, Michael (1994), *The Dialect of Modernism: Race, Language, and Twentieth-Century Literature*. Oxford: Oxford University Press.

Perloff, Nancy (1991), *Art and the Everyday: Popular Entertainment and the Circle of Erik Satie*. Oxford: Oxford University Press.

Rajewsky, Irina O. (2005), 'Intermediality, Intertextuality, and Remediation: A Literary Perspective on Intermediality', *Intermediality: History and Theory of the Arts, Literature and Technologies*, 6, pp. 43–64.

Rasula, Jed (2003), 'Jazz as Decal for the European Avant-Garde', in *Blackening Europe: The African-American Presence*, ed. Heike Raphael-Hernandez. London: Routledge, pp. 13–34.

Richards, Jeffrey (2011), 'John Grierson and the Lost World of the GPO Film Unit', in *The Projection of Britain: A History of the GPO Film Unit*, ed. Scott Anthony and James G. Mansell. London: Palgrave Macmillan, pp. 1–9.

Roberts, Graham (2000), *The Man with a Movie Camera: The Film Companion*. London: Tauris & Co.

Russolo, Luigi (1996 [1913]), 'The Art of Noises', trans. Barclay Brown, in *The Art of Noises*. New York: Pendragon Press, pp. 23–30.

Scannell, Paddy (1981), 'Music for the Multitude? The Dilemmas of the BBC's Music Policy, 1923–1946', *Media, Culture, and Society*, 3, pp. 243–60.

Schafer, R. Murray (1994), *The Soundscape: Our Sonic Environment and the Tuning of Our World*. Rochester, VT: Destiny Books.

Smith, Matthew Wilson (2007), *The Total Work of Art from Bayreuth to Cyberspace*. London: Routledge.

Sterne, Jonathan (2003), *The Audible Past: Cultural Origins of Sound Reproduction*. Durham, NC: Duke University Press.
Thompson, Emily (2002), *The Soundscape of Modernity: Architectural Acoustics and the Culture of Listening in America, 1930–1933*. Cambridge, MA: MIT Press.
Waddell, Nathan (2020), *Moonlighting: Beethoven and Literary Modernism*. Oxford: Oxford University Press.
Weidman, Amanda (2013), 'Voice', in *Keywords in Sound*, ed. Matt Sakakeeny and David Novak. Durham, NC: Duke University Press, pp. 232–45.

15

Performance: Machine Dances and the Avant-garde's Technological Imaginary

Emilie Morin

'Not against technology, but with it!' (Blume 2008: 51): László Moholy-Nagy's motto for the Bauhaus theatre workshop during the 1920s resonates with the proliferation of ideas about mechanised performance that swept across avant-garde movements in Europe in the aftermath of the First World War. The emergence of a machine art shaped by industrial modes of production and technologies of image, sound and light is illustrated in the architectural plans for total, mechanical or spherical theatres drawn by Walter Gropius and his Bauhaus pupils; in theories of movement, such as Rudolf Laban's eukinetics and Vsevolod Meyerhold's biomechanics; in Constructivist acting machines and in contraptions such as Luigi Russolo's experimental noise intoners and Moholy-Nagy's Light-Space Modulator; and in Dadaist affirmations such as Kurt Schwitters's 'Rrrrummmm!!!!' and Tristan Tzara's 'Boum boum boum' (Schwitters 1993: 60; Gordon 1987: 38). To artists associated with the Dadaist, Futurist, Constructivist, *De Stijl* and Bauhaus movements, the machine – always a nebulous notion – offered a convenient shorthand for modernity as a whole, enabling imaginative metaphor and imitation, as well as new explorations of form and content that conveyed varying sensibilities to war and its legacies, to urbanisation and industrialisation, to theories of progress and to art's changed purpose (see Salter 2010; Vaingurt 2013; Ovadija 2013; Broeckmann 2016). 'The machine has become more than a mere adjunct to life. It is really part of human life – perhaps the very soul,' Francis Picabia observed in 1915 ('French Artists' 1915: 2). Not everyone shared Picabia's enthusiasm. Some wondered where the reign of the machine would take humanity. For Hugo Ball, notably, the 'crass error' of war was all too easy to understand: 'We have confused men with machines. We should be decimating machines instead of people' (qtd in Fijalkowski 1987: 235).

In the wake of the First World War, and throughout the 1920s and early 1930s, performance provided a focus and a channel for modernism's varied and discordant technological enthusiasms, and avant-garde artists who had little or no experience of the stage came to perceive the theatre, in particular, as the ideal outlet for creative energies that had nowhere else to go, as El Lissitzky observed of his painter colleagues (Drain 1995: 40). This chapter shows how performance gave form and voice to a technological imaginary that was, in principle, motivated by an aspiration to offer a synthesis between the arts but was, in practice, messy, haphazard and idiosyncratically out of step with the realities of technology. Indeed, the technological fantasies that I discuss here are neither precise nor consistent, but draw upon a whole range of vocabularies and techniques indebted to mechanisation and assign a new artistic purpose to industrial designs, motor sounds and geometric forms recalling factory machines and domestic appliances. There are some constants, which derive from artists' persistent attraction to the puppet show, the circus, the ballet and the cabaret during this period. There is also great variety: some performances sought to assimilate visual and auditory references drawn from recognisable and already available technologies, while others created a new apparatus of their own; some involved banal idealisations of the machine and trite reflections on dehumanisation, while others offered probing investigations of pure movement, the rules of abstraction and the human form, and attempted to dismantle relations between cause and effect traditionally enshrined in playwriting and theatrical performance.

The avant-garde's machine art, as this chapter demonstrates, was built on grand visions of technologised performances, buildings and bodies as much as it was built on cardboard simulacra of cogs, pistons and wheels, the skills of trained and untrained dancers, trained and amateur actors, and costumes improvised from whichever materials were at hand. It was also a collaborative art, the work of painters, composers, stage designers, choreographers, writers and filmmakers, open to chance, error and discovery. Sergei Diaghilev's Ballets Russes and Rolf de Maré's Ballets Suédois, its Swedish–Parisian counterpart, keenly encouraged these collaborations, leading Oskar Schlemmer – who kept a keen eye on their innovations – to quip that the main ambition of the Ballets Russes was to enable every famous painter living in Paris to have a go at designing a theatre set (Schlemmer 1978: 54). The artists involved had a sustained interest in mechanisation as a form of aesthetic creation; Fernand Léger, notably, theorised the beauty of the machine in essays published in 1923 and 1924 in *Bulletin de l'effort moderne*. In an essay dedicated to de Maré, he describes a modern world ruled by speed and movement, in which 'the eye must know "how to choose" in the split second during which it plays out its existence, while driving the machine, on the street, or behind the scientist's microscope' (Léger 1924: 4; my translation).

Léger's vision of technology as a force capable of changing not simply how the world is experienced but how the eye and the mind function resonates with the ad hoc collisions of human performers, machine-like assemblages and new media shaping the stage work of the Ballets Russes, the Ballets Suédois and beyond. The libretti composed for the Ballets Russes included Georgi Yakulov's Constructivist ode to industrial labour, *Le Pas d'acier* (1927), a collaboration with Léonide Massine and Kasimir Malevich in which the dancers and scenery imitated machine parts, and Jean Cocteau's *Parade* (1917), with music by Erik Satie, choreography by Massine and décor and costumes by Picasso, with a contribution from the Futurist Fortunato Depero (Pizzi 2019: 98). Satie's score for *Parade* was initially driven by Cocteau's wish (which was partially frustrated) to have 'dynamos – Morse code machine – sirens – express train – airplane' feature as 'trompe l'oreille' or auditory illusions in a manner emulating Georges Braque's integration of mundane objects into his collages (Cocteau 1948: 58). The Ballets Suédois honed a whole repertoire of skits, including Cocteau's libretto *Les Mariés de la Tour Eiffel* (1921), with music by Darius Milhaud, Arthur Honegger and the rest of the Six; the set resembled the Eiffel Tower photographed from above and the dialogue involved two actors dressed as speaking phonographs, commenting upon the miscellany of machines before them, including a bicycle, a camera and an imaginary train. Other pieces performed by the Ballets Suédois included Paul Claudel's 'plastic poem', *L'Homme et son désir* (1921), with music by Milhaud; the 'symphonie choréographique' or 'dance-poem' *Skating Rink* (1922) by Ricciotto Canudo, Léger and Honegger; Blaise Cendrars's ballet *La Création du monde* (1923), a collaboration with Léger and Milhaud; Pirandello's libretto *La Jarre* (1924), with costumes by Giorgio de Chirico; and *Relâche* (1924), Picabia's 'instantaneist ballet', with music by Satie. Both Honegger and Milhaud composed scores foregrounding machines: Honegger's *Pacific 231* (1923) was a musical recreation of a moving locomotive, while Milhaud's *Machines agricoles* (1919) set to music descriptions of farming machinery collected from farming exhibitions catalogues (Milhaud 1998: 105). *Relâche*, meanwhile, partially emerged from ideas put forward by Satie and André Derain to perform 'a parody of the Cinema' in which the characters 'would have the appearance of emerging from the screen' (McCarren 2003: 118); the collaboration inspired from this idea and led by Picabia featured a film by René Clair, *Entr'acte* (1924), animated by flashing electric signs and powerful stage lights (Gordon 1987: 163). These pieces illustrate the many forms that the new machine art took on the stages of Europe, from pieces that drew on mime, puppetry and idealised automata to performances that revolved around costume and stage designs aligned with innovations in painting and sculpture, through to collaborative skits featuring film projections and dance performances, and abstract pieces involving mobile figures and the play of colour and light.

Throughout the 1920s, the label 'mechanical' proved seductive, and was deployed to qualify experiments with dance choreographies and animated figures long before Fernand Léger, Dudley Murphy and Georges Antheil made their 'film without scenario', *Ballet mécanique* (1924). Machine pieces included Vilmos Huszár's *Mechanical Dancing Figure* (completed in 1920); Ivo Pannaggi and Vinicio Paladini's *Futurist Mechanical Dance* (1922), which was performed to the noise of two motorcycles (Poggi 2009: 326); *Machine Dances* (1922 and 1923) by Bronislava Nijinska, sister of Nijinski; and Nikolai Foregger's *Dance of the Machines* (1923). Mechanical fantasies also dominated the experimental performances devised at the Bauhaus, where a considerable proportion of the staff developed a strong interest in theatre and mechanical performances, particularly between 1923 and 1926, despite inadequate facilities (Michaud 1978: 68, 151–2, 162, 168). Kurt Schmidt and Georg Teltscher's *Mechanical Ballet* was the centrepiece in a Bauhaus event baptised *The Mechanical Cabaret* (1923); Schmidt planned ballets called *Man+Machine* and *Man–Machine* (1924); Moholy-Nagy published a *Sketch for a Score for a Mechanised Eccentric* (1925), which envisioned a kinetic performance of moving panels, machines and light in which no body appeared (see Michaud 1978: 162); Joost Schmidt and Heinz Loew designed different models for a 'Mechanical Stage' (1926 and 1927); and Andor Weininger crafted plans for a 'Spherical Theatre' (1926), conceived as 'the home of the mechanical play' and offering 'a new mechanical synthesis' of space, body, line, point, light, sound and noise (Gropius 1961: 89). The relationship between machine and inventor provided fodder for other performances – notably, *The Man at the Control Panel* (1924), a pantomime about a man possessed by electricity, with a set and costumes designed by Schmidt to suggest coils, tension and speed (Schawinsky 1971: 32). Schlemmer's *The Figural Cabinet* (1922), a fantasy about machine and inventor inspired by E. T. A. Hoffmann, featured a stage shaped like a shooting gallery and multicoloured figures marching by, their bodies and interchangeable heads stuck on rolling panels moving in opposite directions (Michaud 1978: 82–3). The surviving script shows that only

Hoffmann's Spalanzani, the inventor, was impersonated, 'spooking around, directing, gesticulating, telephoning, shooting himself in the head, and dying a thousand deaths from worry about the function of the functional' (Gropius 1961: 40).

These performances called for new conceptions of staging: the stage – often approached as a space that followed its own rules and logic, dictated not by convention but by the vision of the artist – became a receptacle for visionary scripts that did not necessarily need to remain within the order of the feasible, but could reach for the unachievable and illustrate pure aesthetic aspirations. That some of these pieces hankered for formal abstraction does not mean that their content was also abstract or attempted to question social norms, however; as in the many robot-inspired texts discussed by Katherine Shingler in this volume, the worship of technology did not go hand in hand with a neutral or, indeed, progressive social vision. In *The Figural Cabinet*, for example, the heads moving like shooting targets include that of a woman called Gret, who has 'a blabbermouth and a swivelhead / and a nose like a trumpet', and a figure called 'the Turk' (Gropius 1961: 40). Other scripts were mostly a glorification of masculinity, with women featuring as men's prey. The script of *Relâche*, notably, calls for a woman wearing a 'very elegant evening dress', who 'disrobes down to pink silk tights, skin tight' while 'thirty men in black suits, white ties, white gloves and opera hats' circle around her (the second half of the performance suggests an attempt to reverse the gaze, albeit in an unimaginative and formulaic way: the woman, still in pink tights, watches the men disrobe) (Gordon 1987: 162); the weakness of the plot contrasts with the spectacular set imagined by Picabia. In a similar mode, Ivo Pannaggi and Vinicio Paladini's *Futurist Mechanical Dance* presented the dilemma of a man – a 'proletarian Man-Machine' – torn between his attraction for a machine and for a nightclub dancer (Berghaus 1998: 425–6; Pizzi 2019: 144–7), while Xanti Schawinsky's Bauhaus pantomime, *Feminine Repetition*, involved two men, one wearing beach attire and the other dressed as a tap dancer, courting the same woman (Michaud 1978: 166).

For some artists, finding suitable content with which to experiment remained a perennial problem: in 1930, in the wake of performances of Mozart's *Marriage of Figaro*, for which he had devised scenery in the industrial style of the Bauhaus, Moholy-Nagy observed: 'Grand opera and Total Theater don't blend. One can't dress obsolete content with modern design. One could, but the guardians of tradition won't let us' (Moholy-Nagy 1950: 50). The focus on machine-like performance made new types of notation a necessity; Schlemmer, in particular, became acutely aware of the difficulties inherent in scripting kinetic performances. Reflecting on the score for his *Dance of Gestures* (1926), he remarked upon 'the difficulty of the problem of preparing a script for dance and other stage action': a diagram can indicate tempo and sound, but cannot give 'precise indications of gesture (movements of torso, legs, arms, and hands), of mimetics (motions of the head, facial expression), of voice pitch, and so on' (Gropius 1961: 86). 'The more completely such a script tries to fix the total action,' he concluded, 'the more the multitude of essential details complicates the matter and obscures the very purpose of such a score, namely, legibility' (Gropius 1961: 86). Performance was not necessarily the ultimate goal; in some radical experiments on abstraction and notation – such as Moholy-Nagy's *Sketch for a Score for a Mechanised Eccentric* and Wassily Kandinsky's *Yellow Sound* and other 'colour-tone' dramas – the idea that the script should facilitate a performance is secondary, and the script is entirely driven by its attempt to imagine a choreography of sound, light and movement. Such pieces were not staged during their authors' lifetimes, like other scripts hankering after technologies yet to be born, the most noteworthy of which include Schwitters's choral theatre piece, *Above and Below* (1925–9), in which voices attempt to mimic the sounds of industrial production, only to reveal their inability to do so ('Howl howl/ Screech screech / Blast blast / Turn turn'; Schwitters 1993: 195), and the plays that Mina Loy wrote during her Futurist phase. The opening of Loy's *Two Plays* (1915) features a man pressing an 'electric button', triggering off 'shattering insistant noise' and pandemonium: 'intermittently arc-light extinguishes – varicolored shafts of lightning crash through fifty-nine windows at irregular heights – the floor worked by propellers – rises and falls irrhythmically – the disymetric receding and incursive planes and angles of walls and ceiling interchange kaleidescopically to successive intricacies' [sic] (Loy 1996: 8).

In these attempts to imagine and craft a radically new kind of performance some familiar ideas reverberate: that theatre, as a medium overly laden with conventions of acting and writing, had become its own worst enemy, and that the social foibles and delusions upon which it relied had become obvious with the advent of cinema. Responding to claims that cinema was in the process of superseding theatre, Antonio Gramsci argued, in 1916, that cinema and theatre offered the same kind of entertainment, but cinema did so 'under better conditions, without the choreographic contrivances of a false intellectualism, without promising too much while delivering little' (Gramsci 1985: 55). For Gramsci, cinema had an honesty and a transparency that theatre did not have: 'It is silent; in other words it reduces the role of the artists to movement alone, to being machines without souls, to what they really are in the theatre as well' (Gramsci 1985: 55).

The 'cult of the puppet' (to borrow Olga Taxidou's phrase; Taxidou 2007: 16), influenced by Edward Gordon Craig's views on the unreliability of the human form and Heinrich von Kleist's reflections on the marionette's unique grace, also looms large in many of the experimental performances and scripts glorifying the machine aesthetic (see Koss 2003). The idea of transforming the actor into a partially mechanised being is an avant-garde commonplace: giant puppets, papier mâché heads, cardboard contraptions and costumes transforming actors and dancers into the semblance of marionettes recur in performances from the period. At the Bauhaus, which saw an efflorescence of puppet-making and marionette theatre between 1920 and 1923, the reflection on performance was led by Schlemmer, who was fascinated by Kleist's and Craig's writings on the marionette. Schlemmer – for whom the marionette remained a theoretical interest, rather than part of his practice – cited them frequently in essays on theatre and dance, and enjoyed recalling how the Russian Symbolist Valery Briusov had once wished for a theatre that could 'replace actors with mechanised dolls, into each of which a phonograph shall be built' (Schlemmer 1978: 66; Gropius 1961: 28). To others too, semi-automated beings could provide the solution to performance challenges: Lissitzky, for example, felt that the difficulties posed by the Russian Cubo-Futurist opera *Victory Over the Sun* (which called for '[a] traveller through the centuries arriv[ing] in the wheels of an airplane' and '[a] machine gun of the future country appear[ing] on stage and stop[ping] at a telephone pole'; Kruchenykh 1971: 110, 112) could be resolved with puppets. He modelled a performance based on the play, an 'electromechanical peepshow', in which '[a]ll the parts of the stage and all the bodies are set in motion by means of electromechanical forces and devices' (Lissitzky-Küppers 1968: 352). As part of the set and costumes designed by Kasimir Malevich in 1915, the actors wore Cubist costumes made of cardboard and large papier mâché heads, and performed the piece on a narrow strip of stage, with puppet-like gestures (Goldberg 1979: 24). Likewise, Jean Cocteau's *Le Bœuf sur le toit* relies upon the idea that the cast are 'props that move'; the script indicates that they should all wear 'cardboard heads, three times the normal size' and move 'in slow-motion, heavily like divers, and in opposition to the music' (Cocteau 1972: 34).

Ultimately, the origins of the new machine art are uncertain. Some of its underlying concerns can be traced back to the three-dimensional architectural objects that Vladimir Tatlin started making in 1914, using basic industrial materials such as metal, wood and iron; these works proved important for Dada, as well as Futurism (Broeckmann 2016: 9–11; Salter 2010: 13). In any case, the birth of a theatre free from all the old trappings of plot, scenery and acting had long been wished for; we can trace such aspirations back to Alfred Jarry, who, in 1896, provocatively listed scenery and actors at the top of 'an index of certain things that are notoriously horrid [. . .] and that encumber the stage uselessly' (Drain 1995: 11). These dreams of simplicity find concrete form in some Bauhaus realisations – in the improvisation *Meta or the Pantomime of Places* (1924), which presented 'a simple plot [. . .] freed from all accessories and paraphernalia' and signalled the progression of the action 'by means of placards' (Gropius 1961: 44); or in Loew's model for a 'Mechanical Stage', which sought to dispense with human input and presented rotary discs and movable objects that could be controlled mechanically, 'undisguised and as an end in itself' (Gropius 1961: 84). These plans for mechanised performances were also exercises in synthesis, not simply between technologies and visions of the machine, but also between artistic forms, media and the senses. Moholy-Nagy labelled his *Sketch for a Score for a Mechanised Eccentric* as a 'synthesis of form, movement, sound, light (color) and smell' (Gropius 1925: n.p.). Huszár's *Mechanical Dancing Figure* was the centrepiece in a mechanical stage performance that he called 'Plastic Drama', which he wanted to be performed 'with electro-mechanical or coloristic-cinematographic' means; if this proved impossible, he indicated that marionettes could be considered in order to realise the piece in its most 'primitive' form (Huszár 1921: 126; Troy 1984: 649). Indeed, during the Dada tour of the Netherlands in 1923, the piece was realised using a marionette projected as a shadow on a screen (White 2003: 39).

The Italian Futurists, who hailed the 'reign of the Machine' and its corollary, 'multiplied Man', with unconditional enthusiasm from early on (Rainey et al. 2009: 89–92), created performances that integrated real machines and paid tribute to motor noises, the motorised body and the piston engine (see Berghaus 1998; Pizzi 2019) while attempting to transcend the machine's earth-bound parameters and transforming it into a cipher for any worthwhile artistic pursuit. The idea that artistic creation should proceed in symbiosis with the machine is central to several manifestos, including F. T. Marinetti's 'The Founding and Manifesto of Futurism' (1909) and Enrico Prampolini's call for 'mechanical introspection' (Prampolini 1922); it also shapes Futurist conceptions of a technologised theatre – notably, Prampolini's model for a 'Magnetic Theatre', which involved kinetic elements and a chromatic light show (Berghaus 1998: 445–6), and Depero's *Anihccam del 3000* (Anihccam being an anagram of *macchina*), a ballet in which two dancing locomotives express their love for a stationmaster (Pizzi 2019: 101). The 'Manifesto of Futurist Mechanical Art' (1922) by Pannaggi and Paladini – who also celebrated the machine in their paintings – argued for a complete symbiosis of feeling with the machine, claiming an irresistible attraction to '[p]ulleys and flywheels, bolts and smokestacks, all the polished steel and odor of grease': 'We feel mechanically, and we sense that we ourselves are also made of steel, we too are machines, we too have been mechanised by our surroundings' (Rainey et al. 2009: 272). Marinetti often resorted to analogies with the piston engine and the moving wheel when defining the movements to be used by Futurist performers and dancers; his manifesto defining 'Dynamic and Synoptic Declamation' (1916) advised the Futurist declaimer to 'Gesticulate geometrically, so giving his arms the sharp rigidity of semaphore signals and lighthouse rays in order to indicate the direction of forces, or of pistons and wheels, to express the dynamism of words-in-freedom' (Rainey et al. 2009: 272). His 'Manifesto of Futurist Dance' (1917), accompanied by scripts for dances glorifying war – 'The Shrapnel Dance', 'The Machine-Gun Dance' and the 'Dance of the Aviatrix' – argued for a Futurist dance practice able to 'imitate the movements of machines assiduously paying court to steering wheels, tires, pistons, and so preparing for the fusion of man with the machine' (Rainey et al. 2009: 235). His vision had already been realised: in 1914, Giacomo Balla gave a private performance for Diaghilev of *Printing Press* (*Macchina tipografica*), a dance based on the workings of a newspaper typesetting machine which involved six performers simulating a piston and another six simulating a wheel driven by the piston; all were arranged in a geometrical pattern, and each uttered specific onomatopoeias keyed to their movements (Goldberg 1979: 16; Poggi 2009: 120).

The fascination that Balla and Marinetti expressed for the interplay between piston-operated engines and wheels resonates in later mechanical dances that also foreground tempo. Massine's choreography for *Le Pas d'acier*, notably, ended with a scene in which 'the wheels and pistons on the rostrums moved in time to the hammering movements of the young factory workers' (Massine 1968: 172), transforming the dancers into 'a kinetic, mechanised, interdependent mass to express the movement of cogs, levers, transmissions, wheels and pistons' (Norton 2004: 113). Likewise, the dancers in Nijinska's *Machine Dances* simulated different machine parts and were trained to perform a machine-like 'dynamic rhythm' that could accommodate 'unexpected nervous breaking' (Salter 2010: 233). One part of Foregger's *Dance of the Machines* imitated an engine transmission; another, a mechanical saw (Goldberg 1979: 28); Foregger wanted his audience to grasp 'the rhythm that is so essential in all labour processes' (Braun 2012: 90). He praised 'the precision and accuracy of machines' when describing the rhythm of the piece and perceived 'the dancer's body as a machine and the volitional muscles as the machinist' (Foregger 1975: 77, 75). A contemporary, René Fülöp-Miller, described *Dance of the Machines* as 'a cinematics of the living organism, an analysis in dance of the human mechanism', concluding: 'Dancing is intended to be nothing but a vivid demonstration of the adequate organization of the human machine' (Fülöp-Miller 1927: 182). Other dance creations focused on rhythm without requiring a sophisticated physical performance: Schmidt and Teltscher's *Mechanical Ballet* – which involved five actors dancing against a black backdrop, rhythmically, to a uniform and monotone music, and wearing black leotards, black tights and geometric cardboard costumes (Michaud 1978: 85) – sought to express 'the technical spirit' of the period through a 'uniform, constant rhythm [. . .] with no changes of tempo', as Schmidt later explained (Droste 1990: 102). A world separates the makeshift and minimalist arrangements of Bauhaus performances from the well-oiled choreographies of Russian Constructivism, which strive for a total vision and total method; yet within these performances we can discern a shared fascination for the suggestive power of the machine as artistic idea, dissociated from the mundane realities of technology and its production imperatives, and reduced to a repetitive tempo and movements that have no aim beyond the performance itself.

Avant-garde visions of mechanised performance did not develop in isolation but as part of a transnational dialogue, conducted across languages and cultural borders, and through the little magazines and other publications in which performances were sometimes described (see White 2003: 39). The note in *De Stijl* in which Huszár described the 'Plastic Drama' hosting his Mechanical Dancing Figure, for example, proved particularly important for Schmidt, and helped him shape his own *Mechanical Ballet* at the Bauhaus (Michaud 1978: 96). Festivals and exhibitions – notably, Friedrich Kiesler's International Exhibition of New Theatre Techniques (1924) – also played a key role in disseminating ideas. Kiesler's exhibition, a veritable who's who of the interwar avant-garde, brought to Vienna avant-garde artists from the Bauhaus, Futurism, Dada, *De Stijl* and Constructivism, exposing them to a wide range of theories and work on theatre and dance in which technology and mechanics featured strongly. Léger's *Ballet mécanique* was first shown on this occasion; Schawinsky also recalled performing his piece *The Circus* (1924), a pantomime featuring the Bauhaus theatre group dressed as puppet-like animals and circus performers, and remembered hearing Léger and witnessing his ballet *La Création du monde* (Schawinsky 1971: 33). Alongside these events, Kiesler – then renowned for the striking set he had designed for Karel Čapek's robot play *R.U.R.* in 1922 – curated a large exhibition of theatre paraphernalia from across Europe, including models of theatre sets, designs and costumes. The exhibition catalogue, framed by commentaries on theatre and dance, shows that designs, models and sketches by ninety-five contemporary artists from across Europe were exhibited, including materials from mechanical performances conceived by Schlemmer, Moholy-Nagy, Schmidt, Depero, Pannaggi and Paladini, as well as pieces created for the Ballets Suédois by Léger and for Cocteau (Kiesler 1975). The Austrian–Hungarian journal *MA* reproduced some of these exhibits that same year, in a richly illustrated issue featuring essays by Marinetti, Schwitters, Lissitzky, Grosz, Picasso, Prampolini, Moholy-Nagy and others, commenting on the theatre of the future and the potential of the mechanical (Kassák 1924). Here, the avant-garde's machine art is framed as a coherent artistic endeavour across the Continent: photographs from Meyerhold's stage machinery accompany an essay by Marinetti; Schwitters's description of Merz theatre features alongside remnants of El Lissitzky's 'electromechanical show'; Léger's designs for Cendrars's *La Création du monde* are shown alongside a theatre composition by Hans Suschny; and an image from Picasso's costumes for *Parade* appears alongside a figure from Schmidt and Teltscher's *Mechanical Ballet* and an essay by Hans Heinz Stuckenschmidt on the mechanisation of music.

For the artists associated with the Bauhaus, who worked in a world shaped by patents and collaborations with industry, there was nothing to fear about technology or about modes of industrial production; rather, technology could enable the conception of art forms better suited to life and to the needs of humankind. 'Even a complete mechanization of art might not, it seems to me, imply a menace to its essential creativeness,' Moholy-Nagy observed in a 1936 essay describing mechanised representation and reproduction as the nexus of new interrelations within the visual arts of the present, past and future: 'Painting, photography, film and light display no longer have any exclusive sphere of activity jealously isolated from one another. They are all weapons in the struggle for a new and more purposive human reality' (Kostelanetz 1970: 43). An extensive corpus of theoretical texts on performance and technology reveals the dedication with which Moholy-Nagy and others looked towards technology to move away from figuration. In their view, the task of the artist was to give a clear direction to the proliferation of possibilities opened up by the new technological reality, and to create new artistic forms that bridged the multiple worlds of photography, film, architecture, design, typography, theatre and dance. Schlemmer, who had first trained as a painter like Moholy-Nagy, saw mechanisation and abstraction as the twin poles of modernity; he argued that within technology and invention lay the promise of a new future for art in general and for theatre in particular, and sought to integrate the human figure into 'the geometry of calisthenics, eurhythmics, and gymnastics', to produce movements 'determined *mechanically and rationally*' (Gropius 1961: 17, 23). Kandinsky pointed to 'the collapse of the wall dividing art from technology' and imagined the rules of abstraction through a variety of media including photography, stage design and dance, extracting point-line compositions from diverse photographs including electric pylons and Gret Palucca dancing (Kandinsky 1994: 714, 520–3, 624–5). These reflections on a new mechanised art often served to affirm an undefeated humanism: Moholy-Nagy asserted that he placed his faith not in art but in humankind (Kostelanetz 1970: 18), while Schlemmer emphasised that he did 'not want to produce what industrial manufacture already does better, what engineers do better', but wanted to focus on 'the metaphysical element: art itself' (Harrison and Wood 2003: 307).

In this context, the sound and letter poems of the Expressionist, Futurist and Dadaist poets held particular significance: for Moholy-Nagy, these works finally put 'an end to the rule of logical-intellectual evaluation' in a way that could be applied to the theatre and enabled the artist to dispense with the traditional representational logics assuming that theatre and performance should present a relation between cause and effect (Passuth 1987: 299). In his landmark essay 'Theatre, Circus, Variety', he claimed affinities with Schwitters's Merz, Dada and Italian Futurism, which had succeeded in showing that 'phonetic word relationships were more significant than other creative literary means' (Gropius 1961: 52). Dadaist and Futurist synthetic performance strategies were of particular interest to him, as well as the effect produced by 'the *repetition* of a thought in the same words, in the same or a varying inflection, by several performers at the same time' (Passuth 1987: 300). He imagined a new kind of dramatic performance emulating sound poetry, but in another form, and observed that 'similar effects can be obtained from the simultaneous, synoptical, and synacoustical reproduction of thought (with motion pictures, photographs, loud-speakers), or from the reproduction of thoughts suggested by the construction of variously meshing gears' (Gropius 1961: 62). When it came to the stage itself, his imagination was boundless, and he pondered various types of machinery that went much further than Meyerhold's constructivist stage. Nothing was off limits: 'film, automobile, elevator, airplane, and other machinery, as well as optical instruments, reflecting equipment, and so on'; 'suspended bridges and drawbridges running horizontally, diagonally, and vertically within the space of the theater; platform stages built far into the auditorium'; 'rotating sections' and 'movable space constructions and DISLIKE AREAS, in order to bring certain action moments on the stage into prominence, as in film "close-ups"' (Gropius 1961: 67, 68). These ideas remained mostly unrealised, but energised experiments with performance at the Bauhaus as well as his own work and his film scripts.

These mechanical visions and experiments with play-acting, dance, scenery and costumes contributed to shaping the performing arts as we know them today, and yet we know little about what some of these performances looked and felt like to their early audiences. The 1932 recording of Schwitters reading the *Ursonate* for the Süddeutscher Rundfunk is the only record of live performance to have survived from the interwar period, and it gives a sense of the great challenges posed by the avant-garde fascination with mechanisation: the alphabet becomes a synthesis of noises mimicking the train, the factory and the mechanics of mass production in a more abstract sense. A few landmark performances have been recreated: Günter Berghaus reconstructed some Futurist mechanical performances in 1995 and 1996 (Berghaus 2011: 82), and in 1987 and 1988 the music theatre company Theater der Klänge created a performance around Moholy-Nagy's *Sketch for a Score for a Mechanised Eccentric* and reworked *The Mechanical Ballet*, granting a more contemporary form to it. Footage of the latter production (see Mertens 2008) shows how closely the geometrical figures conceived by Schmidt resemble piston engine parts, once animated, and how far removed they seem from the purely abstract forms appearing on historic photographs. Overall, nonetheless, this strand of experimental work has left few traces, consisting mainly of black-and-white photographs, sketches, costumes and first-hand recollections expressing bewilderment and admiration. It can be difficult to square these records – the photographs in particular, which can alternate between marvellously eerie visions and something resembling a fancy-dress party gone awry (see Figure 15.1) – with the revolutionary character of the live event as described in contemporaneous sources. Recollections from audience members and friends are not necessarily reliable: avant-garde performance has proved particularly prone to selective recollection and conflicting memories, as Thomas Postlewait has shown in relation to the iconic premiere of Jarry's *Ubu Roi* (Postlewait 2009). Yet, on occasion, marginal evidence shows how deeply affecting these spectacles could be. Hans Richter described Schwitters's performance of his *Ursonate* in Potsdam in 1924 or 1925 as a moment of great joy and wonder: at first, Schwitters's audience, 'who had no experience whatever of anything modern', was 'completely baffled'; then the spectators 'lost control' and 'shrieked with laughter, gasped for breath, slapped their thighs, choked themselves', and eventually 'came to Schwitters, again with tears in their eyes, almost stuttering with admiration and gratitude. Something had been opened up within them, something they had never expected to feel: a great joy' (Schwitters 1993: xxi). Similarly, T. Lux Feininger wrote of his 'breathless excitement, admiration, and wonder' upon witnessing a performance of Schlemmer's *Dance of Gestures* and *Dance of Forms* (Feininger 1960: 272). 'The stage elements were assembled, re-grouped, amplified, and gradually grew into something like a "play,"' he recalled many years later (Feininger 1960: 273).

In spite of the grand ambitions that framed it, avant-garde machine aesthetics remained shaped by a visible lack of means: the machine art that the Dadaists greeted in 1920 ('Long live the machine art of Vladimir Tatlin') was also an art of poor materials and leftovers (Broeckmann 2016: 9–11). At the Bauhaus, costume-making mostly

Figure 15.1 Copy print: Members of the Bauhaus Stage Workshop on the Roof of the Studio Building, 1927 (printed ca. 1948), Harvard Art Museums/Busch-Reisinger Museum, Gift of Herbert Bayer, © President and Fellows of Harvard College, © T. Lux Feininger, © Estate of T. Lux Feininger, BR48.121.

involved cardboard cut-outs and 'papier-mâché work over plaster sculptural forms', as Schawinsky recalled (Schawinsky 1971: 32); as for the theatre workshop, it began with little more than a bare platform (Schlemmer 1978: 46). The costumes that have been photographed – particularly the kapok-filled costumes made for Schlemmer's dances – have a handmade feel and look as though each stitch would be visible when seen up close. Today, these iconic performances would come across as 'more or less serious experiments in kinetic art', as Torsten Blume observes (Blume 2008: 25). No one had trained formally in acting or dance, but there was interest aplenty. As Feininger diplomatically put it, 'the Bauhaus stage did not train pupils in ballet or choreography, but it attracted persons who had ideas and interest in this field and gave them an opportunity to lend their talent to the work' (Feininger 1960: 273). Those who were involved in the stage workshop did so as part of their extra-curricular activities, and the syllabus did not offer formal training in theatre and costume design, nor indeed in acting, dance and music (Blume 2008: 23). This lack of training and paucity of means provided the ideal circumstances for experiment. Here is how Stuckenschmidt described the moment when the *Mechanical Ballet* came into being:

[Schmidt's studio] was full of man-high constructions of cardboard, wire, canvas and wood, all in elementary forms: circles, triangles, squares, rectangles, trapezia, and naturally all in the primary colours yellow, red and blue. Schmidt put on a red square, fastening it with leather straps in such a way that he disappeared behind it. Two of his colleagues did the same with a circle and a triangle. These strange geometric figures, their wearers completely invisible behind them, then danced an eerie round. There was an old piano against the wall. It refused to stay in tune and sounded appalling. I improvised a few chords and aggressive rhythms. The cardboard figures immediately began to react. An abstract dance of square, circle and triangle was performed ad lib. After about a quarter of an hour, Kurt Schmidt got out of his square, rather out of breath but thoroughly satisfied. I had instinctively guessed and performed something he had wanted but only vaguely imagined: a primitive accompaniment roughly corresponding to the primary geometric forms . . . From now on we rehearsed every day, from morning till night . . . After two or three weeks the programme of 'The Mechanical Ballet,' or rather 'The Mechanical Cabaret,' of which it was a part, had been created. (Droste 1990: 102–3)

These visions of the makeshift work taking place behind the scenes seem difficult to reconcile with the reverence and enthusiasm with which the Bauhaus and other avant-garde movements greeted the idea of automatised and technologised performance, and with their aspirations for efficient and streamlined machines. To the modernist avant-garde, technology was more of a dream than a reality; yet in the many gaps between their visions of mechanical forms and the poor materials of theatre and dance, artists found the freedom to imagine new forms of performance.

Works Cited

Berghaus, Günter (1998), *Italian Futurist Theatre, 1909–1944*. Oxford: Clarendon Press.
Berghaus, Günter (2011), 'From Avant-Garde to Mainstream: Futurist Theatre in the 1920s', in *Historische avant garde en het theater in het Interbellum*, ed. Peter Benoy and Jaak van Schoor. Brussels: ASP, pp. 75–93.
Blume, Torsten (2008), 'The Historic Bauhaus Stage – A Theatre of Space', in *Bauhaus. Bühne. Dessau/Bauhaus. Theatre. Dessau*, ed. Torsten Blume and Burghard Duhm. Berlin: Jovis, pp. 22–64.
Braun, Edward (2012), 'Futurism in the Russian Theatre, 1913–1923', in *International Futurism in Arts and Literature*, ed. Günter Berghaus. Berlin: De Gruyter, pp. 75–99.
Broeckmann, Andreas (2016), *Machine Art in the Twentieth Century*. Cambridge, MA: MIT Press.
Cocteau, Jean (1948), *Le Rappel à l'ordre*. Paris: Stock.
Cocteau, Jean (1972), *Le Bœuf sur le toit or The Nothing-Doing Bar*, trans. N. E. Nes, in *The Puppet Issue, TDR: The Drama Review*, ed. Michael Kirby, 16: 3, pp. 33–5.
Drain, Richard, ed. (1995), *Twentieth Century Theatre: A Sourcebook*. Abingdon: Routledge.
Droste, Magdalena (1990), *Bauhaus, 1919–1933*, trans. Karen Williams. Berlin: Taschen.
Feininger, T. L. (1960), 'The Bauhaus: Evolution of an Idea', *Criticism: A Quarterly for Literature and the Arts*, 2: 3, pp. 260–77.
Fijalkowski, Krzysztof (1987), 'Dada and the Machine', *Journal of European Studies*, 17: 4, pp. 233–51.
Foregger, Nikolai (1975), 'Experiments in the Art of the Dance', trans. David Miller, *TDR: The Drama Review*, 19: 1, pp. 74–7.
'French Artists Spur On an American Art' (1915), *New York Tribune*, 24 October, p. 2.
Fülöp-Miller, René (1927), *The Mind and Face of Bolshevism: An Examination of Cultural Life in Soviet Russia*, trans. F. S. Flint and D. F. Tait. London: G. P. Putnam's Sons.

Goldberg, Roselee (1979), *Performance: Live Art, 1909 to the Present*. New York: Harry N. Abrams.
Gordon, Mel, ed. (1987), *Dada Performance*. New York: PAJ Publications.
Gramsci, Antonio (1985), *Selections from Cultural Writings*, ed. D. Forgacs and G. Nowell-Smith, trans. W. Boelhower. Cambridge, MA: Harvard University Press.
Gropius, Walter, ed. (1925), *Die Bühne im Bauhaus: Bauhausbuch Nr. 4*. Munich: Albert Langen.
Gropius, Walter, ed. (1961), *The Theatre of the Bauhaus*, trans. A. S. Wensinger. Middletown, CT: Wesleyan University.
Harrison, Charles and Paul Wood, eds (2003), *Art in Theory, 1900–2000: An Anthology of Changing Ideas*, 2nd edn, Malden, MA: Blackwell.
Huszár, Vilmos (1921), 'Kurze technische Erklärung von der "Gestaldende Schauspiel", Komposition 1920–21', *De Stijl*, 4: 8, pp. 126–8.
Kandinsky, Wassily (1994), *Complete Writings on Art*, ed. K. C. Lindsay and P. Vergo. New York: Da Capo Press.
Kassák, Lajos, ed. (1924), *Musik und Theater Nummer/Musique et théâtre/Külön Szám*, MA, 2: 8–9, n.p.
Kiesler, Freidrich, ed. (1975 [1924]), *Internationale Ausstellung neuer Theatertechnik*. Vienna: Löcker & Wögenstein.
Koss, Juliet (2003), 'Bauhaus Theater of Human Dolls', *The Art Bulletin*, 85: 4, pp. 724–45.
Kostelanetz, Richard, ed. (1970), *Moholy-Nagy: An Anthology*. New York: Da Capo Press.
Kruchenykh, Alexei (1971), '*Victory over the Sun* Prologue', trans. E. Bartos and V. Nes Kirby, *TDR: The Drama Review*, 15: 4, pp. 107–25.
Léger, Fernand (1924), 'Le Spectacle', *Bulletin de l'effort moderne*, 7, pp. 4–7.
Lissitzky-Küppers, Sophie, ed. (1968), *El Lissitzky: Life, Letters, Texts*. London: Thames and Hudson.
Loy, Mina (1996), *Two Plays*, *Performing Arts Journal*, 18: 1, pp. 8–17.
McCarren, Felicia (2003), *Dancing Machines: Choreographies of the Age of Mechanical Reproduction*. Stanford, CA: Stanford University Press.
Massine, Leonide (1968), *My Life in Ballet*, ed. P. Hartnoll and R. Rubens. London: Macmillan.
Mertens, H. (2008), *Ausschnitte aus ausgewählten Aufführungen auf der Bauhausbühne/ Excerpts from Selected Performances of the Bauhaus Stage*, DVD, in *Bauhaus. Bühne. Dessau/Bauhaus. Theatre. Dessau*, ed. T. Blume and B. Duhm. Berlin: Jovis.
Michaud, Eric (1978), *Théâtre au Bauhaus (1919–1929)*. Lausanne: La Cité-L'Age d'Homme.
Milhaud, Darius (1998), *Ma vie heureuse*. Bourg-la-Reine: Zurfluh.
Moholy-Nagy, Sibyl (1950), *Moholy-Nagy: Experiment in Totality*. New York: Harper and Brothers.
Norton, Leslie (2004), *Léonide Massine and the 20th-Century Ballet*. Jefferson, NC: McFarland & Company.
Ovadija, Mladen (2013), *Dramaturgy of Sound in the Avant-Garde and Postdramatic Theatre*. Montreal: McGill-Queen's University Press.
Passuth, Krisztina (1987), *Moholy-Nagy*. London: Thames and Hudson.
Pizzi, K. (2019), *Italian Futurism and the Machine*. Manchester: Manchester University Press.
Poggi, Christine (2009), *Inventing Futurism: The Art and Politics of Artificial Optimism*. Princeton, NJ: Princeton University Press.
Postlewait, Thomas, ed. (2009), 'Cultural Histories: The Case of Alfred Jarry's *Ubu Roi*', in *The Cambridge Introduction to Theatre Historiography*. Cambridge: Cambridge University Press, pp. 60–86.
Prampolini, Enrico (1922), 'The Aesthetic of the Machine and Mechanical Introspection in Art', *Broom*, 3: 3, pp. 235–7.
Rainey, Lawrence, Christine Poggi and Laura Wittman, eds (2009), *Futurism: An Anthology*. New Haven, CT: Yale University Press.

Salter, Chris (2010), *Entangled: Technology and the Transformation of Performance*. Cambridge, MA: MIT Press.
Schawinsky, Xanti (1971), 'From the Bauhaus to Black Mountain', *TDR: The Drama Review*, 15: 3, pp. 30–44.
Schlemmer, Oskar (1978), *Théâtre et abstraction (L'Espace du Bauhaus)*, ed. and trans. E. Michaud. Lausanne: L'Age d'Homme.
Schwitters, Kurt (1993), *Pppppp: Poems Performance Pieces Proses Plays Poetics*, ed. J. Rothenberg and P. Joris. Philadelphia: Temple University Press.
Taxidou, Olga (2007), *Modernism and Performance: Jarry to Brecht*. Basingstoke: Palgrave Macmillan.
Troy, N. J. (1984), 'Figures of the Dance in De Stijl', *The Art Bulletin*, 66: 4, pp. 645–56.
Vaingurt, Julia (2013), *Wonderlands of the Avant-Garde: Technology and the Arts in Russia of the 1920s*. Evanston, IL: Northwestern University Press.
White, Michael (2003), *De Stijl and Dutch Modernism*. Manchester: Manchester University Press.

16

AMPLIFICATION: AT HOME WITH *MARLENE DIETRICH OVERSEAS*

Damien Keane

DROP THE NEEDLE on the record and the voice of the chanteuse fills the living room: *Sei lieb zu mir / komm nicht / wie ein dieb zu mir / sag nicht immer Sie zu mir / wenn andere dabei sind.* Mixed in front of the swelling strings, the tinkling piano, a fitfully ardent accordion, her voice is close to listeners, the studio microphone having rendered its sighs and hesitations and quavering holds with full presence, but without reverberation. For listeners sitting at home, these production techniques are meant to evoke the nostalgic and melancholy intimacies associated with the small café or cabaret. It is a quiet record that amplification has made possible. The arrival of high-fidelity, long-playing microgroove vinyl records on the commercial market in 1948 ushered in what Roland Gelatt called the 'renaissance at a new speed', or what has since come to be known as the LP era (Gelatt 1955: 290–304). Although long-playing discs made from a variety of materials and spinning at various speeds had been employed in the broadcasting industry for close to two decades, the war had accelerated research into plastics, which had resulted in both a durable base for magnetic tape and the vinylite products used in the production of long-playing records. It was Columbia who first brought out the 33-rpm vinyl record and called the new format the 'LP', in so doing promising the listening public a revolution in how music could be played back and stored at home. For listeners, the plastic base produced noticeably less surface noise and a greater dynamic range, while the slower rate of rotation and narrower grooves allowed for more music and better continuity (Schicke 1974: 114–30). Record labels initially marketed 'high fidelity' recordings as the realisation of a sonic documentary ideal, as the capability to bring the concert hall or night club faithfully into any domestic space. Yet the new format's finer sonic definition also offered a challenge to this aspiration toward mimetic auditory realism, precisely through the enhanced ability to arrange and manipulate sounds within the field of the recording. Rather than 'duplicat[e] the sound of an original performance', engineers and producers might instead construct 'a soundscape specifically for the home listener' (Barry 2010: 120). While exceeding purely technological considerations, and by no means new, this tension between documentation and fabrication during the first decade of the LP era was a notable characteristic of the acoustic envelope of modernism.

It was in this context of limits, pressures and changes over time that Columbia Masterworks released *Marlene Dietrich Overseas* as a 10-inch long-playing record in 1951.[1] As the front cover announces – to the exclusion of the record's actual title, which appears only on the back cover – the album consists of 'American songs in German for the O.S.S.', or Office of Strategic Services, the wartime intelligence bureau that was the direct precursor to the Central Intelligence Agency (CIA). Late in the war, under the auspices of its Morale Operations division, Dietrich had recorded a handful of American pop songs with specially adapted German lyrics, which were then clandestinely broadcast to military and civilian audiences in Axis and Axis-occupied countries as part of the effort to erode morale. The work was top secret at the time, and this chapter will return to it in its final section. For now, the note to accent is that the album does not present the wartime recordings, but provides in their place high-fidelity recordings of the same material. The question therefore arises why rerecordings of these songs were thought to have been appropriate for an audience of American hi-fi listeners: what did songs meant to undermine morale in one theatre of total war mean to do in the post-war home theatre? The sleeve notes describe how

> these songs went to war, did their work and vanished into the OSS files at Washington. Miss Dietrich, however, had copies of the recordings, and played them for Columbia's Mitch Miller. He felt they were the best she had ever made, and asked her to remake them for Columbia Records. The result is this collection, a remarkable combination of completely personal popular singing and a working demonstration of part of the propaganda battle of World War II.

In this gloss, the music on the LP has been redirected to home listeners, in recognition of the capacities of the new format to make 'the best she ever made' better, even as the propaganda function behind the music remains politically operative. With a wartime photograph of Dietrich in army boots and fatigues adorning the front cover, the notes on the back promise that the

> collection brings to the ear all the haunting, nostalgic allure one expects from Miss Dietrich, but, because of the unique nature of the material and the purpose for which these records were made, you will also hear undertones of deep sadness and feeling which represent Marlene Dietrich at her best.

Meeting the expectations of nostalgia, yet also substantiating the once-secret motivation of the wartime recordings: here seems to be the pitch for the post-war rerecordings. Like so much good pop music, the album seeks to confirm expectations, in order to do something new or surprising with them – only in this case, the significance of the undertones of feeling and emotion the microphone renders has less to do with affective experience or subjective truth than with the rise of the national security state. When the needle drops, the new format serves as a medium not only of storage, but of amplification.

Intelligence Records: Bureaucratic Stacks

One index to the work being done in that relationship of storage and amplification can be found in another set of records that 'went to war, did their work and vanished' into the stacks: this is the file the Federal Bureau of Investigation (FBI) kept on Dietrich during these years. The extant documents in the file were declassified for the most part in 1996, and digitised copies of these items are currently accessible through the FBI's electronic Freedom of Information Act library, known as The Vault.[2] In the form now available, the file runs to 230 pages, all but the final 30 of which were made during the war years. These pages are marked by frequent redactions, primarily of names and other details that could be used to identify sources and methods, although in several instances larger portions of documents are blacked out. In addition, notations throughout the file indicate that documents were destroyed at various times between the creation of the original pages and the later process of duplication, first to microfilm and then as digital images. During the long and not always linear passage from classified to declassified status, redaction and document destruction were both routine means of handling protected or sensitive (or illegally obtained) material at intelligence agencies. In this, there is nothing odd or exceptional about the Dietrich file, as it moved from operational storage at the Bureau to institutional holding at the National Archives and Records Administration. While the stakes are not as high for the file on Dietrich as they are for those on other individuals and organisations subject to government surveillance, the range of agency prerogatives and procedures on display in her file still bears blunt witness to the unhampered intensity of the Bureau's investigations. Even so, the significance of the file derives more from what it demonstrates about the administrative function that records serve than from the descriptive content of its documents. Beyond the evidential and informational values on which the appraisal and disposition of its documents rest, and for which they have been preserved, the Dietrich file is significant because of what it shows about the practice of records management within the Bureau.[3] As items were added to the dossier over the years, they both took on and reinforced its prosecutorial demeanour. A study in control, the file exemplifies the organisational ability to define the relations among the documents collected within it and, still more decisively, to assimilate these relations to the Bureau's system of operational knowledge.[4] In short, the storage system was also a mechanism of amplification.

The file on Dietrich provides an odd counterpoint to the political work of *Marlene Dietrich Overseas*. In his study of German émigrés in the wartime United States, Alexander Stephan provides a useful list of (some of) the federal agencies that undertook monitoring activities during these years. The jurisdictional outline alone testifies to how pervasive these activities were, while also suggesting the extent to which the government ignored or betrayed the history, experience and privacy of those falling under scrutiny. Based on extensive work with security files, Stephan notes:

> What the refugee writers scattered from New York to Los Angeles did not know and for the most part did not even guess was that almost all of them, admirers and critics of the United States alike, were under surveillance by secret agencies of their host nation, especially the FBI and the forerunner of the CIA, the Office of Strategic Services, along with the Immigration and Naturalization Service, the State Department, the army's Military Intelligence Division, the Office of Naval Intelligence, [and] the Un-American Activities Committee of the House of Representatives. (Stephan 2000: 2)

Owing to its seniority and its zeal, the FBI was at the apex of this surveillance apparatus, a commanding and increasingly autonomous position that its records helped to guarantee:

> an ingenious system of card indexes and files, telephone tapping, mail interception, and a whole network of spies and informers supplied [J. Edgar] Hoover with

information that allowed him to steer the decisions of other agencies, intervene in political developments, and influence legal proceedings. (Stephan 2000: 3)

Compulsively maintained, these records were instrumental to the functioning of an array of other government agencies, which had to rely on cooperation, or compliance, with the Bureau. Because it was able to regulate access to its extensive files so thoroughly, the FBI also had considerable authority over their meaning and implications. As David Jenemann has observed, 'such oversight and interpretation [were] not part of a grand conspiracy but, rather, [of] the day-to-day life of refugees and citizens alike in 1940s America' (Jenemann 2007: xiv).

In these efforts, record-keeping provided needed gain to items that, on their own, were thin or altogether lacked it. The earliest pieces in Dietrich's file date from May 1942, almost three years after she had become an American citizen and nearly a decade after she had first come to the country. Whatever her legal status and regardless of her celebrity, the fact of her German birth made her a person of suspicion, and it is precisely this suspicion that the steady accumulation of documents in the file sustains and amplifies. Three items from across its span attest to this point. In a report from June 1942, agents in the Los Angeles field office follow up on rumours that Dietrich has hosted meetings of the German American Bund, the domestic, pro-Nazi group, in her home, and relay what their sources have told them:

> [Redacted] was interviewed by Agent [redacted]. She resides at [redacted] telephone [redacted] and upon interview she stated that she had no information; that she had heard from [redacted] whose name she could not recall, who was at one time working in a house near DIETRICH'S, that there were frequent meetings held in her home which [redacted] thought were Bund meetings. [Redacted] was going to obtain the name and address of [redacted] and advise this office. To date same has not been done, but should she have any information of interest to the Bureau, it will be reported. (Federal Bureau of Investigation 2003a: 38)

The subsequent redaction only makes graphically literal how little there is, beyond suspicion, in this chain of negations, hedges and deferrals. Yet this suspicion echoed two and a half years later while Dietrich was on tour in Europe performing for troops with the United Service Organizations (USO), when the Bureau received this lead from an informant: 'Dear Mr. Hoover,' begins the typed letter. 'It strikes me as rather strange that Miss Dietrich intends to do as the inclosed [sic] news item implies. She is German born.' The enclosure is a small newspaper clipping of a wire service bulletin, which quotes Dietrich saying that she will forego making movies for the remainder of the war in order to devote herself to entertaining GIs. In thanks for the tip, the Bureau's Communications Section sent the informant a form letter from J. Edgar Hoover: 'Your courtesy and interest in bringing this information to my attention are indeed appreciated, and you may be assured your letter will receive appropriate consideration' (Federal Bureau of Investigation 2003c: 25–7). While this reply seems only to say nothing in response to nothing, the letter's formal acknowledgement of receipt in fact marks the completion of a scene of communication. Indeed, its semantic barrenness is a demonstration of the phatic function of the letter: its ritualised bureaucratese serves no other purpose than to comment on the channel or format of exchange, as a means of recognising the social conditions and expectations that link the parties engaged in the exchange.[5] In doing so, the letter certifies the informant's suspicion as something shared and 'appreciated', and this relationship in turn registers in the Bureau's retention of a copy of the letter for its file.

The reverberations of this boilerplate acknowledgement could still be discerned twenty-two years later. Giving ear to chatter and official sanction to cranks can perhaps be chalked up to wartime exigencies, yet a final, post-war item captures the amplifying effect of the entire file. Dating from March 1967, the third item is the summary of a background check the Bureau ran on Dietrich at the request of staff at the White House, where she had been invited to attend an unnamed affair:

> Captioned individual, well-known Hollywood personality, was the subject of a limited security-type inquiry conducted by the FBI in the early 1940's based on allegations of a pro-Nazi nature. The investigation failed to substantiate those allegations and our files contain no additional pertinent information concerning her. (Federal Bureau of Investigation 2003d: 6)

In phrasing the summary's findings in this manner, the Bureau does not state that these allegations about Dietrich were false or baseless, but rather merely that they could not be verified. That the language of the summary may follow a generic standard or be an example of administrative jargon in no way obviates the point. It instead demonstrates the additive and amplificatory protocol governing the creation and maintenance of this paperwork. Documenting the tips of informants had achieved the taxonomic conversion of suspicion into allegation, but the post-war summary shows how allegations were available to be operationalised through the record-keeping at the Bureau. The item stands less as the residue of past defamation or insinuation or even misguided alarm than as the product of a filing system organised to retrieve active and actionable records. Decades after its creation, then, this repository of unsubstantiated 'allegations of a pro-Nazi nature' remained the measure against which Dietrich's life was compared and checked.[6] Designed to serve the Bureau's agenda of keeping tabs, the system of records also came to authorise the perpetuation of its surveillance mandate. Here is the rationale for the Bureau's practice of records control.

The file now accessible online is the product of the conditions of secrecy and denial that shaped its creation and handling at the Bureau. The agency's chequered compliance with the Freedom of Information Act stems directly from this administrative culture of unaccountability and unimpeded autonomy (Theoharis 1981; Theoharis 1984; Steinwell 1986). Although much of what it logs is drawn from casual observation, second-hand news and celebrity gossip, the file itself is information that never wanted to be free. Throughout its pages, aspects of Dietrich's everyday life are singlemindedly enumerated: agents note that she drives a 1940 Buick convertible coupé and a Ford station wagon (estate car); that she orders flowers from a favourite florist; that she rents a safe deposit box; that she frequents the lunch counter at Schwab's Drugstore at the corner of Sunset Boulevard and Laurel Canyon, where an eavesdropping employee recounts she is often heard speaking German. Her cables are stopped and read; her postman is enlisted as an informant, with agents explicitly instructed not to divulge this relationship to the Post Office. Other details now severely redacted are listed as being for 'near future use' or of 'possible future interest to [the] record'.

Industry people appear to have been quite accommodating of agents' enquiries, some equivocating on the question of Dietrich's political allegiances and others pointedly clearing her: 'Informant described DIETRICH as being too stupid to be a spy, that she is effeminately cruel and further described her as being "bitchy"' (Federal Bureau of Investigation 2003b: 13). Still others tendered open secrets and innuendo for the profile the Bureau was assembling, and the documents often directly quote this brand of testimony:

> With reference to her personal history, Source [redacted] continued that 'despite her marriage to [Rudolf] SIEBER, with whom she has not lived for many years, at least as long as she has been in the United States, DIETRICH has been promiscuous in a bland, glamorous sort of way. She, of course, was [Josef] VON STERNBERG'S mistress. DIETRICH has never been able to "hold a man." She gets them and loses them in periods of amour ranging from "quickies" to "six months." During her Paramount days, she verged from the norm for an affair with KAY FRANCIS (known Lesbian), and since that time has been involved in similar experiences, although less known. [Redacted]'s wife, [(]also a known Lesbian), reportedly once was given a large sapphire ring by DIETRICH in a night club on the Strip. Her usual technique, insofar as men are concerned (and her temporary success) was evinced by the way she went after JOHN WAYNE on Universal's "Seven Sinners." She saw him, liked him, and made advances. WAYNE is the father of three children and was at that time seemingly happily married. He repulsed DIETRICH, but she kept coming. She finally got him. This affair lasted about six months.['] (Federal Bureau of Investigation 2003a: 42)

Scarcely paraphrased, these particulars would later appear in a memorandum on the investigation into Dietrich that the Los Angeles field office prepared for J. Edgar Hoover, who is known to have maintained a considerable trove of information on sexual allegations: in the memo reproduced in the file, a reader has studiously underlined each line of the paragraph (Federal Bureau of Investigation 2003b: 3). Yet these details seem straight out of the scandal sheets and, indeed, now read like the forerunner to *Hollywood Babylon*, Kenneth Anger's notorious dilation on the whispers and half-truths of the movie industry's early decades.[7] Tasteless echoes aside, the surveillance dossier should not be mistaken for the sensationalism of the gutter press, with its limited repertoire of generic moves and reliable set of prompted reactions. The FBI file is, instead, a reference work, its emphasis less on its contents than on the amplificatory and self-confirming definitional power it exercises over them. For all the intensity of its focus, there is nothing quite personal about the dossier. The odd intimacy of its pages stems only from the proliferation of cross-references, forever held close by the Bureau and always of 'possible future interest'.

In retrospect, this material stands at an unpleasantly auspicious spot, where media persona shades into bureaucratic profile and everything is transfigured as an aggregate of data points. This tendency is most evident when agents enter Dietrich's voice into her own file. With national mobilisation in full swing, Dietrich went to work on behalf of the war effort, travelling throughout the country to encourage Americans to buy war bonds and touring military camps with USO revues to entertain troops preparing to go overseas (Federal Bureau of Investigation 2003a: 53–60). As the course of the war in Europe then began to shift, she learned that she too would be sent to the fighting. While readying to depart in early 1944, Dietrich contacted the FBI about a letter she had received from a German prisoner of war claiming to be her cousin, who wished to begin a correspondence with her: in the file, a memorandum titled 'Re: Marlene Dietrich; Offer of Services' announces her approach to the Bureau. What follows is a remarkable section of the dossier. The memo notates what has caught her attention:

> Dietrich said the thing that disturbed her was [the prisoner's] statement that he had so much to communicate to her. Also she observed that he addressed her as 'Dear Marlene,' using the German word which is not used unless one knows another rather well. A casual fan would have addressed her with a more formal word.

Her apprehensions raised by this inappropriate intimacy, she asks the Bureau whether it would like her to respond and, if so, how. Before answering, however, the Bureau sends the letter to its criminal laboratory for cryptographic analysis, which does not 'disclose anything indicative of a concealed code or cipher message or any evidence of double meaning'. With this report to hand, it decides to pursue her offer, and a translated copy of the dictated response to the prisoner, signed 'Marlene', appears later in the file. What, if any, channel of communication this reply opened the file does not describe. Instead, this section of the dossier ends with a note of instruction Hoover sent to agents in Paris and London in November 1944, while Dietrich was performing for the troops. After recapitulating the various allegations of disloyalty made against her, the dispatch concludes with an ode to control:

> Investigation has not been able to substantiate any such information. To the contrary, Miss Dietrich, as you know, has been developed into a special service contact of the Bureau prior to her present trip. Despite this proffer of assistance, the above information [on past investigations] is being brought to your attention so that you may exercise the requisite degree of judgment and caution in any future contacts you may have with Miss Dietrich. (Federal Bureau of Investigation 2003c: 6–23)

Checked against the records, her own voice here serves to validate the procedures of record-keeping simply by becoming the latest entry in the file. In turn, Hoover's memo provides phatic confirmation of this bureaucratic fact when it is shared with his subordinates. Having announced its wariness of unsolicited and undue familiarity, Dietrich's voice here briskly assumes its place in the Bureau's dossier as only one more item among its amplifying cross-references.

Intelligence Records: Bureaucratic Wax

Whereas Hoover knew exactly what the circumstances were behind Dietrich being 'developed into a special service contact of the Bureau', it is not clear to what extent he would have been aware or informed of her work with the OSS. Several disputed jurisdictional boundaries and the reality of inter-agency rivalries make it difficult to sort out this relationship, and nothing about it appears in the Bureau's file on Dietrich. At the same time, the agencies were like two grand chordal inversions arranged around a common tonal centre, with the activities of domestic law enforcement and foreign subversive operations working as complements within the totalised system of national security. The Morale Operations division at the OSS had been established in January 1943 and was modelled on Britain's Political Warfare Executive, which oversaw the deployment and coordination of all forms of psychological warfare. In its sphere, the American division was given responsibility for 'the conduct of subversion other than physical', a mandate that soon gained a sharper operational focus:

> it is the function of the Morale Operations Branch to attack the morale and the political unity of the enemy through any primarily psychological means operating within or purporting to operate within the enemy or occupied territories. The principal means to be employed are field agents, native residents of the enemy and occupied countries, rumors, printed matter, and radio. (Roosevelt 1976 [1947]: 212, 215)

While duplicity and guile were critical parts of the work of the division, its machinations were nevertheless most effective when belief could be manipulated in service to strategic ends, when the affirmed or plausible could become the source of dismay, as an internal evaluation of the OSS makes plain:

> Propaganda of ideas, in which truth should be the weapon and conversion the objective, must make room for 'black' propaganda which, through judicious mixture of rumor and deception with truth as a bait, fosters disunity and confusion to support military operations. (Roosevelt 1976 [1947]: 2)[8]

It was in this context of weaponised truth and calculated misrepresentation that Dietrich was recruited to work with Morale Operations. In mid-1944, not long after she had approached the FBI with the dubiously informal letter from the prisoner of war, the OSS division had received a request from the Political Warfare Executive to provide recordings of American pop songs with German lyrics for one of its clandestine radio stations known as *Soldatensender West*, which purported to be a German-run station broadcasting news and entertainment to the Wehrmacht. In order to entice listeners to the station's talk programming, it was felt that popular music of the highest – indeed, the best – quality was necessary to capture the attention of the audience and hold it, to keep enemy soldiers tuned in for the spun features and tailored reports that comprised this form of psychological warfare. At the OSS, responsibility for this endeavour was given to members of J. Walter Thompson Company, an advertising agency based in New York, whose experience with writing catchy creative copy and integrating jingles into on-air programming would enable techniques of promotion and publicity to be used for purposes of subversion. Rather than hector or abuse listeners, these recruits mostly avoided overt ideological themes or conflicts and instead 'approached psychological warfare as though they were selling toothpaste' (Soley 1989: 99). For them, luring the greatest number of listeners to the secret station and its news bulletins was the goal, and all of their white-collar proficiencies and professional contacts within the entertainment industry were marshalled in the effort to reach it. Around the radio dial, the use of music as a kind of moral correlative in propaganda broadcasting was widespread, with musical selections meant to provide emotional cues and affective associations for the ongoing demands of total mobilisation (Bronfen 2012: 74–106; Fauser 2013: 76–134). For this clandestine assignment, the ad agency crew would create product that had no moral as such, but relied instead on its quality and the intensity of its appeal to listeners. The music could thus serve as an effective bridge to the news because it aimed only to be good entertainment. Their innovation was to recognise that audiences were increasingly aware of how music was being employed in propaganda broadcasting and to play to this awareness: listeners could remain knowing or suspicious consumers, yet still be entranced and get hooked by the songs. Like today's clickbait, their work in this venture could trace its genealogy back to the methods of yellow journalism and the scandal pages, in which headlines attracted eyes and then rarely delivered quite what had been promised. This subterfuge was exactly what Morale Operations wanted. With the directive to begin their undertaking, the ad agency personnel set up a front corporation in New York in order to begin hiring musicians and booking studio time. Music would not be the message, but an adjunct to the messaging.

This conjoining of advertising and entertainment under the aegis of psychological warfare became known within Morale Operations as the Muzac Project. In condensed form, the moniker announced the need for 'musical action', while also gesturing to the fact that work behind the project was done primarily in the studios of the Muzak Corporation in New York.[9] There, arrangers, musicians and singers were told they were making recordings for the Voice of America and most often found themselves slightly recasting stock settings of popular songs and standards in order to 'suit the German personality' (Soley 1989: 125). Responsibility for translating lyrics fell largely to Lothar Metzl, an Austrian-born cabaret playwright who would later work as a research analyst for the CIA. With their crisp expression and semantic care, his translations earned the approval of his superiors, who in particular reserved praise for the manner in which his lyrics conveyed feelings of longing, loneliness and sadness to their intended audience. Whether with subtle humour or elegant melancholy, Metzl's work used the specific qualities of the German language to carry the motivated sentiment of the songs (Mauch 2003: 151–62). Fine as his translations were, however, the songs became potent only once they were performed for the studio microphone, and it was in this position that Dietrich proved to be one of the Muzac Project's greatest assets. For all the secrecy surrounding its work, she was informed of the true nature of the project, with her recording sessions taking place while she recovered in New York from a bout of pneumonia that had developed during one of her extended tours of the European frontlines. Despite this respiratory condition (which, in any case, would have been less evident to listeners of medium- and short-wave transmissions), her vocal performances have been hailed for their affective candour and expressive impact: 'for an actress known for her emotional remove, the strength of her German-language performances was her sincerity' (Baade 2012: 95). This quality was an effect of the studio microphone, which enabled her voice not only to be the vehicle of Metzl's wistful lyrics, but to be rendered within the musical setting precisely as a German voice, with its own articulatory gestures, prosodic features and phonetic rhythms (Frith 1996: 183–202). As objects of the studio microphone, that is, Dietrich's vocal performances were available to be amplified in the recording process and thereby to communicate elements of tenderness and familiarity across the separation and absence of wartime. Like all 312 made for Morale Operations between July 1944 and April 1945, Dietrich's recordings were pressed to 16-inch, 33-rpm vinylite discs and sent to London for broadcast (Soley 1989: 127). In the words of the War Department's report assessing the work of the OSS, the Muzac Project was 'one of MO's most proficient and worthwhile achievements' (Roosevelt 1976 [1947]: 219).

To ask again the opening question of this chapter: why might an album of rerecordings of these clandestine songs of war have been deemed appropriate for a post-war audience at home? For one thing, the business model of the entertainment industry asserted the commercial appeal of such material. The sleeve notes recount how, when Dietrich had played her personal copies of the wartime recordings for Mitch Miller, the legendary Artists and Repertoire (A&R) man at Columbia, he had suggested that she rerecord the songs. Years later, to one of her biographers, he stressed the importance to this decision of the technological advantages of the LP era:

> 'I talked to her about breathing . . . and the conscious things she could do with it. We recorded on monaural high-fidelity tape, on which only the most minimal kind of cutting and splicing was possible, and when she concentrated on the artistic, rather than the "historical" value of what she was doing, her ear took over. It was all spontaneous craft, no tracking, no splicing, *all* performing.' (qtd in Bach 1992: 363–4, emphasis in original)

In this telling, the enhanced sonic definition of the recording medium promises a kind of immediacy to Dietrich's performance, a faithfulness that would render her 'breathing' and 'the conscious things she could do with it' as though not rendering them at all. The kind of closeness that Miller extols and that listeners hear as intimacy nevertheless relies on extreme vocal isolation. It is a premier effect of amplification. Recorded close to the microphone and in an acoustically dead studio room or vocal booth, Dietrich's voice has no reverberation, and this lack of sonic reflection causes it to sound as though it comes from a very nearby point. In the field of the recording, this sonic space is distinct from that of the instrumental accompaniment, with her voice presented higher than and in front of the musicians. Recorded and mixed in this way, the high-fidelity versions of the songs place Dietrich's voice in a singular position, at once close by and quite alone. This placement is particularly evident in the album's rendition of 'Mean to Me', for which Dietrich gave this paraphrase of its German lyrics on the back sleeve: 'Be good to me; don't come to me like a thief at night. My love for you is so far greater than you think. Be good to me; all I have done was to love you and be good to you.' This note gives the gist of the translation, but leaves out its lyrical hook. Where the English original resolves on a double entendre ('You're mean to me / why must you be mean to me? / You shouldn't for can't you see / what you mean to me'), Metzl's German version centres on the use of the formal second-person pronoun: 'Sei lieb zu mir / komm nicht / wie ein dieb zu mir / sag nicht immer Sie zu mir / wenn andere dabei sind' ('be good to me, don't come like a thief to me, don't always say [formal] You to me, when others are around').[10] In the recording, the voice asks why her lover addresses her only as one does a stranger, an intimate question about unreliable or betrayed or altogether dubious intimacy. It is an untranslatable hook that sounds twice, first as a sung and then as a spoken entreaty; and although the repetition amplifies the plea, it also suggests that it has remained unreceived, that the condition of intimacy remains at best uncertain. To what audience of listeners was this song of feigned closeness addressed? While American home listeners very likely did not follow the lyrical turn, they could still hear the 'haunting, nostalgic allure' of the close-miked voice placed in their domestic midst. In the living room, this sound effect is not one of intimacy, but only of amplification.

Taking a cue from the design of the front sleeve of the album, however, it is possible to discern another reason for its release beyond the cash nexus. Alongside the wartime photograph of Dietrich, and the words 'Columbia Records' and the LP logo that appear between her combat boots, the visual field of the cover is completed by the large letters 'OSS', printed in imitation military stencil, and it is this triangulation of graphic features that points to the final amplification at issue. The OSS had been disbanded at the end of the war, and much of the work it had done in the conflict remained classified and unknown to the American public. Before the conclusion of hostilities, its leadership had already begun to seek ways quietly to publicise its role in the war effort and, in this way, to certify and promote its function as an agency of government. Like using truth as bait, these overtures played up its support for and assistance to the service branches, but kept silent about the practical import of the organisation for life after the end of declared war. In the War Department's report on the agency, the rationale behind this stratagem is spelled out:

> The public did not realize, and it is quite possible that some of the initiated did not comprehend fully, the significance and potential value to America of developing the doctrine of unorthodox warfare; in providing a foundation for the American practice of espionage and counter-espionage which could be projected into the future; in providing a basis of experience for the various aspects of morale and physical subversion which could be used in the future should a war crisis arise; and in promulgating the principle of a central intelligence agency. (Roosevelt 1976 [1947]: 120)

As in the clandestine wartime operations, these promotional activities leveraged connections to the worlds of advertising and entertainment, in order to sell the national security state and its intelligence apparatus as the necessary guarantors of civilian life (Mauch 2003: 217–20). Even after the formation of the CIA in 1947 had instituted the 'principle' and practices of the OSS as a permanent part of the American state, the aura of wartime service remained an alluringly useful means to validate the claims and assumptions underlying the successor agency's function. When Dietrich and Miller first thought to revisit the wartime material for commercial release, she had to request formal permission to do so from none other than William Donovan, the former director of the OSS, so that they might proceed with the rerecording plan (Mauch 2003: 285 n83). His consent to the project indicates how, in official circles, the value of the material lay not with wartime recordings, but with wartime mystique and the sanction it would provide to the ongoing affirmation of the 'principle of a central intelligence agency'. In its way, then, the resulting album is 'a working demonstration of part of the propaganda battle of World War II' that, for domestic listeners, continues on new terrain. For while *Marlene Dietrich Overseas* stores a wide range of complicated historical dynamics, the album was a platform for propagating and amplifying the founding ideology of the national security state. That it remains such a platform the CIA has confirmed with one of the tweets it sent out in 2017 to mark the seventy-fifth anniversary of the establishment of the OSS: 'During #WWII, Marlene Dietrich recorded a number of anti-Nazi albums in German for the #OSS' (Central Intelligence Agency 2017). Framed by hashtags, the historical errors of the message only reaffirm the phatic value of 'haunting, nostalgic allure' to the political work being done on behalf of its sender. Accompanying this text is an image of the front cover of the album of songs Dietrich had rerecorded sixty-six years earlier, as once more the LP is pressed into the service of those who wage war by other means.

Notes

1. This being an unsettled moment in the record business, the album was also released as a 45-rpm double 7-inch, before it eventually appeared, with several bonus tracks, as a 33-rpm 12-inch record.
2. For the homepage, see <https://vault.fbi.gov> (last accessed 25 January 2022). The Bureau notes the digital copies have been made available online 'so you can read them in the comfort of your home or office'.
3. The language of 'evidential' and 'informational' values within the process of document appraisal comes from Schellenberg (1956) and (2003 [1956]).
4. James Beniger defines control as 'purposive influence toward a predetermined goal' and strongly links it to information processing and communication (Beniger 1986: 7–9).
5. The phatic function in communication has a distinctly modernist history. In 1923, Bronislaw Malinowski gave the name 'phatic communion' to the 'type of speech in which ties of union are created by a mere exchange of words', to the kind of speech that created and maintained social bonds among speakers, but outside of the need to impart information (Malinowski 1966 [1923]: 315). In 1958, Roman Jakobson revised this notion in order to account for the function that addresses the qualities of the channel, or what he calls the 'contact', between addresser and addressee (Jakobson 1987 [1958]: 66–9).
6. Beniger notes that the word 'control' derives from 'the medieval Latin verb *contrarotulare*, to compare something "against the rolls," the cylinders of paper that served as official records in ancient times' (Beniger 1986: 8).
7. For comparison's sake: 'By all accounts a joyous bisexual with an appetite for many loves, Marlene kept the magpies chirping right through the Thirties. Her passel of girlfriends was dubbed "Marlene's Sewing Circle." They were not lesbians . . ., but good-time Charlenes who, like Marlene, swung both ways.' The passage continues with a paean to Dietrich's trousers (her 'man-drag') and an account of her relationship with Sternberg ('her Svengali') (Anger [1959] 1975: 246–55).
8. A shorter version of this statement, but attributed to William 'Wild Bill' Donovan, director of the OSS, appeared in the catalogue to a commemorative exhibition on the wartime agency (Central Intelligence Agency 2015: 26). In this source, 'black propaganda' is defined as 'information that looked and sounded like it originated with the enemy' (13).
9. Different sources offer variant spellings of the name of this project. I follow Roosevelt's official report in giving it as 'Muzac', although even there it is rendered entirely in capital letters.
10. I am grateful to my friend and colleague Jasmina Tumbas, who provided me with an English translation of Metzl's German lyrics.

Works Cited

Anger, Kenneth (1975 [1959]), *Hollywood Babylon*. New York: Dell.

Baade, Christina (2012), 'Between the Lines: "Lili Marlene," Sexuality, and the Desert War', in *Music, Politics, and Violence*, ed. Susan Fast and Kip Pegley. Middletown, CT: Wesleyan University Press.

Bach, Stephen (1992), *Marlene Dietrich: Life and Legend*. New York: William Morrow and Company.
Barry, Eric D. (2010), 'High-Fidelity Sound as Spectacle and Sublime, 1950–1961', in *Sound in the Age of Mechanical Reproduction*, ed. David Sussman and Susan Strasser. Philadelphia: University of Pennsylvania Press.
Beniger, James (1986), *The Control Revolution: Technological and Economic Origins of the Information Society*. Cambridge, MA: Harvard University Press.
Bronfen, Elisabeth (2012), *Specters of War: Hollywood's Engagement with Military Conflict*. New Brunswick, NJ: Rutgers University Press.
Central Intelligence Agency (2015), *OSS Exhibition Catalogue*. Washington, DC: Center for the Study of Intelligence.
Central Intelligence Agency [@CIA] (2017), 'During #WWII, Marlene Dietrich recorded a number of anti-Nazi albums in German for the #OSS', Twitter, 27 June, <https://twitter.com/cia/status/879741645062893569> (last accessed 25 January 2022).
Dietrich, Marlene (1951), *Marlene Dietrich Overseas*. Columbia Records ML 2615, LP.
Fauser, Annegret (2013), *Sounds of War: Music in the United States during World War II*. New York: Oxford University Press.
Federal Bureau of Investigation (2003a), 'Subject: Marlene Dietrich (Part 1)', Washington, DC, <https://vault.fbi.gov/Marlene%20Dietrich%20/Marlene%20Dietrich%20Part%201%20of%205/view> (last accessed 25 January 2022).
Federal Bureau of Investigation (2003b), 'Subject: Marlene Dietrich (Part 2)', Washington, DC, <https://vault.fbi.gov/Marlene%20Dietrich%20/Marlene%20Dietrich%20Part%202%20of%205/view> (last accessed 25 January 2022).
Federal Bureau of Investigation (2003c), 'Subject: Marlene Dietrich (Part 3)', Washington, DC, <https://vault.fbi.gov/Marlene%20Dietrich%20/Marlene%20Dietrich%20Part%203%20of%205/view> (last accessed 25 January 2022).
Federal Bureau of Investigation (2003d), 'Subject: Marlene Dietrich (Part 4)', Washington, DC, <https://vault.fbi.gov/Marlene%20Dietrich%20/Marlene%20Dietrich%20Part%204%20of%205/view> (last accessed 25 January 2022).
Frith, Simon (1996), *Performing Rites: On the Value of Popular Music*. Cambridge, MA: Harvard University Press.
Gelatt, Roland (1955), *The Fabulous Phonograph*. Philadelphia: Lippincott.
Jakobson, Roman (1987 [1958]), 'Linguistics and Poetics', in *Language in Literature*, ed. Krystyna Pomorska and Stephen Rudy. Cambridge, MA: Harvard University Press.
Jenemann, David (2007), *Adorno in America*. Minneapolis: University of Minnesota Press.
Malinowski, Bronislaw (1966 [1923]), 'The Problem of Meaning in Primitive Languages', in *The Meaning of Meaning*, ed. C. K. Ogden and I. A. Richards. New York: Harcourt Brace Jovanovich.
Mauch, Christof (2003), *The Shadow War Against Hitler*, trans. Jeremiah M. Riemer. New York: Columbia University Press.
Roosevelt, Kermit, ed. (1976 [1947]), *War Report of the OSS (Office of Strategic Services)*, Vol. 1. New York: Walker and Company.
Schellenberg, T. R. (1956), *The Appraisal of Modern Public Records*. Washington, DC: US Government Printing Office.
Schellenberg, T. R. (2003 [1956]), *Modern Archives: Principles and Techniques*. Chicago: Society of American Archivists.
Schicke, C. A. (1974), *Revolution in Sound: A Biography of the Recording Industry*. Boston: Little, Brown and Company.
Soley, Lawrence (1989), *Radio Warfare: OSS and CIA Subversive Propaganda*. New York: Praeger.
Steinwell, Susan (1986), 'Appraisal and the FBI Files Case: For Whom Do Archivists Retain Records?', *American Archivist*, 49: 1 (Winter), pp. 52–63.

Stephan, Alexander (2000), *Communazis: FBI Surveillance of German Émigré Writers*, trans. Jan van Huerck. New Haven, CT: Yale University Press.

Theoharis, Athan (1981), 'The FBI and the FOIA: Problems in Access and Destruction', *The Midwestern Archivist*, 5: 2, pp. 61–74.

Theoharis, Athan (1984), 'Researching the Intelligence Agencies: The Problem of Covert Activities', *The Public Historian*, 6: 2 (Spring), pp. 67–76.

Theoharis, Athan (2004), 'Secrecy and Power: Unanticipated Problems in Researching FBI Files', *Political Science Quarterly*, 119: 2 (Summer), pp. 271–90.

Part III
Bodies

17

Sex: Hypnosis, Hormones, Birth Control and the Modernist Body

Jana Funke

Towards the end of *A Room of One's Own* (1929), Virginia Woolf introduces the imaginary figure of Mary Carmichael, the young female author of a book called *Life's Adventure*. Carmichael represents a new generation of modern writers that has the potential to 'light a torch in that vast chamber where nobody has yet been' (Woolf 2001: 72). Woolf's narrator hopes that Carmichael will write in novel ways about aspects of life that have not yet received adequate treatment in literature, including love, desire and intimate friendship between women, the experiences of the 'harlot' and 'courtesan', and other previously obscure or taboo topics (Woolf 2001: 76). The name of Woolf's modern author is a reference to Marie Carmichael Stopes, a trained palaeobotanist, who, by the end of the 1920s, had established herself as the leader of the British birth control movement and as a key voice in eugenic circles. She had also made a name for herself as the author of marital and sexual advice literature, including the bestseller *Married Love* (1918). Woolf's nod to Stopes's controversial work suggests that the production of modern literature, especially by women, was inevitably connected not only with questions around sexuality, the body and reproduction, but also with scientific and technological innovation, including birth control.

Following Woolf's lead, this chapter explores the link between modernist literature, scientific and eugenic constructions of bodily sex and sexuality, and new technologies of intimacy and the body. Literary modernism and sexual science emerged in tandem in the late nineteenth and early twentieth century (Bauer 2009; Kahan 2019; Leng 2018; Peppis 2014; Schaffner 2011). The modernist period is also associated with an acceleration of technologies that opened up new ways of understanding and controlling sex and sexuality. This chapter focuses on three interrelated technological interventions that played a prominent role in sexual scientific and literary modernist writings: hypnosis and attempts to influence sexual orientation, hormonal interventions to control physical markers of sex and age, and birth control. While sexual scientists and literary writers were often drawn to the idea that human bodies and desires could be manipulated and controlled, the chapter also demonstrates that scientific and literary authors were equally fascinated by the potential inadequacies and productive uncertainties associated with modern technologies.

The late nineteenth and early twentieth centuries witnessed important changes in the construction of 'sex', a term that held various unstable meanings at the time, cutting across biological sex, gender identity and gender presentation, and sexual desire. Different markers of bodily sex abounded in this period. British physiologist Ernest

Starling formally coined the term 'hormones' in 1905 to refer to blood-borne chemical messengers (Starling 1905: 6). His discovery renewed interest in glandular secretions, which were seen to control mental and physical sex characteristics (Sengoopta 2006). The same year, American geneticists Nettie M. Stevens and Edmund B. Wilson proposed that two kinds of microscopic entities, the X- and Y-chromosomes, determined sex in most biological organisms (Brush 1978). With regard to sexual desire, late nineteenth-century Western European sexual scientists began to construct sexuality as an object of scientific study. They invented new identity categories, including 'the homosexual', 'the sadist', 'the masochist' and 'the transvestite', to classify people on the basis of their sexual interests (Bland and Doan 1998). In the first decades of the twentieth century, knowledge about sexological categories was circulated via mass print media and film, thus reaching wider audiences who began to identify with these new labels. For heterosexual and bisexual people, and women in particular, increased knowledge about new methods of birth control opened up freedoms to control and limit reproduction and to renegotiate the meanings of intimacy between men and women (Cook 2004). Birth control was also misused as a eugenic technology to try to limit the reproduction of people deemed 'unfit' (Childs 2001; English 2004; Turda 2010).

Such new scientific and technological discoveries promised to make the sexed body and its desires transparent and controllable. As Foucault and many others have argued, nineteenth- and early twentieth-century sexual science sought to discipline the body, its pleasures and reproductive functions (Foucault 1990). This was achieved both through the power of science to assert the truth status of its knowledge claims and through the marketisation of a range of techno-scientific products, including hypnotic techniques, hormonal transplants and stimulants, and birth control devices – to name but a few. Modernist scholars have shown that literary modernist writers and sexual scientists shared a fascination with attempts to discipline the body. Tim Armstrong, for instance, has influentially examined a 'surgical' or 'prosthetic' branch of modernist culture that partakes in this project through literary innovation (Armstrong 1998). In this reading, modernism is most clearly aligned with techno-scientific interventions when seeking to control the body and offer prosthetic augmentation for its perceived lack.

This chapter provides much evidence to support this important argument, but also considers other resonances between modernist literature and sexual science. Sexual scientific studies and technological interventions rarely delivered straightforward truths or solutions. The perceived or actual novelty of these discourses also acted as a constant reminder that sexual possibilities were radically open to renegotiation in the modern world. As we shall see, literary modernists responded to the uncertainties and failures of techno-scientific modernity not only by seeking disciplinary power, but also by amplifying and embracing the unknowable and uncontrollable aspects of the sexed body and desire. This gave rise to constructions of fractured modernist subjects deeply entangled with techno-scientific frameworks that not only served to control and contain, but also to open up new questions about the meanings and purposes of sex and sexuality.

Hypnotic Control and Sexual Attraction

Late nineteenth- and early twentieth-century sexual scientists were fascinated with questions of aetiology. In particular, they debated whether and to what extent sexuality could be shaped by external influences and modified through biological, psychological or behavioural interventions. Partly in response to public fears that young people could be corrupted and seduced into same-sex relationships, reform-oriented sexual scientists like Havelock Ellis in Britain and Magnus Hirschfeld in Germany began to present sexual orientation as congenital or inborn (Funke 2013; Funke and Fisher 2019). Presenting homosexuality as a natural and unchanging trait that affected only a small, biologically predisposed minority offered a powerful means to oppose arguments about so-called corruption and seduction, and to counter the moral condemnation and criminalisation of same-sex desire. However, the congenital model was not the only construction of sexuality to be found in early twentieth-century sexual science. Even sexual scientists invested in congenital explanations acknowledged that there were external factors that could powerfully shape an individual's desire, including the weather, diet or 'obscene' literature and art (Kahan 2019: 1). There were also widespread fears that modernity, urbanisation and new technologies like 'tubes and cinema shows' could disrupt individuals' allegedly natural heterosexual desires (Stopes 1918: 12–13). According to Stopes, this could lead to a lack of heterosexual intimacy and diminish women's 'spontaneous sex-impulse' altogether (Stopes 1918: 33). Ellis went further in suggesting that 'there are many influences in our civilisation today which encourage' expressions of homosexual desire (Ellis and Symonds 2008: 177). Accordingly, constructions of sexuality were closely intertwined with understandings of and anxieties around technology and influence.

The idea that sexuality could be shaped by external influences also inspired sexual scientists like Auguste Forel, Albert Moll or Albert von Schrenck-Notzing to explore technologies that could be used to alter same-sex attraction and reduce other 'undesirable' sexual behaviours, including masturbation (Forel 1906: 229; Moll 1921; Schrenck-Notzing 1895). Although the efficacy of such interventions was widely debated, sexual scientists were particularly interested in the use of hypnotic technologies (Wolffram 2009: 94–5). The term hypnotism was coined by the surgeon James Braid in 1840, originally in an attempt to reclaim earlier states of trance associated with Franz Anton Mesmer, an eighteenth-century physician who had claimed to use magnetic forces to put his patients in a trance. Towards the end of the nineteenth century, hypnosis became a topic of vibrant debate among researchers situated within and across the fields of sexual science and psychical research, the scientific study of occult phenomena. The concerns of psychical research – including hypnosis, telepathy and mediumistic communication with the dead – offered rich frameworks to theorise intimacy, attraction and desire and spoke to a wider modernist fascination with technologies of 'cultural transmission and communication' (Thurschwell 2001: 16).

Central to this discourse of *magia sexualis*, as Benjamin Kahan has called the sexual scientific fascination with the magical and occult (2019: 66–84), was a tension between a desire for the control of inner states and the recognition that the individual mind was porous and vulnerable to external influences. While hypnosis was presented as a technology that could help individuals manage sexual impulses, hypnotic suggestion could never quite free itself from associations with quackery and abuses of power, going back to its disavowed mesmeric roots in the early nineteenth century. Freud, like many other clinicians, moved away from hypnosis as a therapeutic method, but nevertheless saw it as a useful way of understanding the experience of love in which the ego is at risk of becoming consumed (Freud 2001: 111–16). Similarly, literary modernist authors drew on the language of hypnosis within their works to explore interpersonal bonds and flows of communication between individuals. In Mina Loy's novel *Insel*, published posthumously in 1991, for instance, the highly ambiguous relationship between the art dealer and writer Mrs Jones and the elusive Surrealist painter Insel is conducted through the mysterious magnetic rays that Insel emits and which Jones is capable of receiving like a radio or a 'televisionary machinery' (Loy 1991: 167; Gaedtke 2008). Through this non-verbal communication, which is presented as analogous to new communication technologies, Jones can access and derive pleasure from Insel's surreal visions. She also feels, however, that her sense of self is at risk of being corrupted and invaded by these foreign hypnotic rays. Loy's feminist novel uses the language of hypnosis to expose both the pleasures and the risks that individuals can experience in intimate relationships with others.

Paradoxically, given attempts to use hypnosis to 'cure' homosexuality, hypnotic influence was also evoked to caution against the alleged dangers of same-sex desires. In the UK, Oscar Wilde was presented as having magnetic and hypnotic powers that would seduce younger men (Thurschwell 2001: 37–8). This association of hypnosis with queer corruption persisted in the 1920s, when Radclyffe Hall was accused of seducing the married Una Troubridge 'through psychical research' (Medd 2012: 77). In 1928, Hall was famously charged with writing *The Well of Loneliness*, a book that was banned as obscene because of its allegedly poisonous and corruptive influence on England's youth. In this context, literature itself was constructed as a technology that could lead to what Valerie Rohy has theorised as homosexual reproduction, the passing on of queer desire (2015: 22–55).

Queer modernist authors challenged and reworked the seduction argument through an engagement with hypnotic frameworks. Towards the end of E. M. Forster's *Bildungsroman*, *Maurice*, largely written in 1913–14 and published posthumously in 1971, the protagonist seeks the help of an American hypnotist, Dr Lasker Jones, to try to rid himself of his desire for other men. The attempt fails and backfires: Maurice's encounter with the doctor only serves to affirm his self-identification as 'a young invert', a person experiencing '[c]ongenital homosexuality' (Forster 2005: 190, 160). Here, Forster seems to embrace the inborn model promoted by sexual scientists like Ellis in Britain. The hypnotic session is not without effect, however, and Forster does rely on a hypnotic understanding of desire in the novel. While the hypnotist cannot alter the patient's desires, the hypnotic session confirms that Maurice is 'open to suggestion' and ends with one of his recurrent homoerotic dreams in which he hears the beckoning voice of a mysterious male friend, which has infiltrated his imagination, seemingly against his will (Foster 2005: 162). Hypnosis does not allow Maurice to redirect his sexuality at will; rather, it enables him to connect more deeply with his body and its desires, and to realise that his lover, Alec's, hypnotic influence is not 'against his will' or, indeed, his nature (Forster 2005: 189). In this sense, hypnotic suggestion reveals a desire that is already natural for Maurice, but that nevertheless needs to be accessed through hypnotic technologies and forms of exchange. With Alec, who is explicitly written as a bisexual character for whom 'it's "natural" to care both for women and men' (Forster 2005: 197), Forster goes further in suggesting that even men who are not 'congenital inverts' can be drawn to other men through the hypnotic pull of attraction. In *Maurice*, as in other queer modernist works, 'mesmeric exchange enables the flow of desire', to such an extent that even so-called 'natural' desires become accessible only through technological mediation (Armstrong 2018: 124).

Forster also engages critically with anxieties about the potentially damaging impact of modern technologies. As mentioned above, some of his contemporaries believed that modern technologies could have a harmful impact on allegedly natural heterosexual desires. Forster turns this heteronormative argument on its head when Maurice's first partner, Clive, is converted to heterosexuality, partially due to his touristic travels in Greece and his engagement with the hypnotic technologies of mass culture, including 'the advertisements, the daily papers' and the 'cinema palace' (Forster 2005: 104). This conversion is described in strikingly pathological terms as a form of 'illness' that results in Clive's ultimately unfulfilling heterosexual marriage (Forster 2005: 103). Here, Forster suggests again that desire is always mediated through and vulnerable to technological influences, which can either alienate individuals from themselves or connect them more deeply with their own feelings and needs.

Hormonal Interventions, Rejuvenation and Sexual Mobility

Hypnosis was not the only technology that was used to influence and even change sexual desire. The early twentieth century also witnessed the rise of hormonal interventions, which were believed to affect a wide range of physical and mental phenomena. Although the study of glandular secretions was not new in itself, the 1910s and 1920s witnessed the rise of endocrinology as a medical discipline. Sexual scientists like Ellis, Freud and Hirschfeld quickly began to engage with endocrinological models according to which hormones regulated 'not only primary, but also secondary sexual characteristics as well as sexual orientation and even certain forms of behaviour, speech or thoughts that could be read as gendered' (Sengoopta 2006: 3). They hoped that endocrinology could provide new ways of understanding and treating what was, at the time, understood as the nexus of sex, gender and sexuality, cutting 'across the psyche–soma boundary' (Hausman 2006: 38). Before the arrival of synthetic hormones, sex glands were implanted or manipulated through surgical and electric technologies. The goal was to regulate hormonal secretions in order to restore youth and sexual proficiency, change sexual orientation or carry out gender-affirming interventions (Armstrong 1998: 131–83; Gill-Peterson 40–56; Sengoopta 2006; Stark 2020: 24–67).

The dream that hormonal interventions might make it possible to control human bodies and minds in previously unimaginable ways found expression in the rejuvenation hype of the 1920s, a decade that Chandak Sengoopta has described as 'the heroic age of the endocrine glands' (2006: 69). Russian-born surgeon Serge Voronoff suggested that animal sex glands should be transplanted into humans to reinvigorate their glandular secretions. Austrian physiologist Eugen Steinach pioneered a less invasive alternative: for male patients, the so-called 'Steinach treatment' consisted of the ligation of the vas deferens, a treatment that would nowadays be described as a vasectomy. Influential modernist figures like Jean Cocteau, Freud and W. B. Yeats underwent the procedure in the hope of restoring lost youth, virility, potency and energy. This fascination with male rejuvenation was closely tied to concerns about gender and sexuality. Armstrong argues that anti-ageing treatments for men were 'a response to contemporary fears, in America and Europe, of masculine decline' (1998: 149). Especially during and after the First World War, the promise that technological interventions could help to restore male strength and virility alongside sexual desire resonated with eugenic concerns about the health and fitness of the nation. Steinach and his followers maintained that rejuvenation was harder to achieve for women, but could be attempted by using electric technologies, especially X-rays and natural or artificial ultraviolet light, to stimulate the function of the ovaries (Stark 2020: 38–9). While reinforcing normative eugenic ideals of youthful beauty, health and productivity, rejuvenation procedures were also subversive in eliminating women's reproductive functions, thus presenting an image of desirable femininity that was not necessarily tied to procreative duties (Sengoopta 1998: 94).

The prospect of female rejuvenation inspired diverse responses from literary authors in the interwar period and, at times, opened up feminist and queer possibilities. Gertrude Atherton, who had herself received the Steinach treatment from sexual scientist Harry Benjamin to cure her writer's block, celebrated the intervention in her popular novel *Black Oxen* (1923) (Sengoopta 1998: 90–4). The book features a successfully rejuvenated middle-aged heroine who regains her vitality, beauty and sexual allure. Marie Corelli's *The Young Diana: An Experiment with the Future* (1918) offers a more critical feminist assessment of the cult of youth. Corelli's protagonist is a spinster who is 'considered useless' and 'superfluous' by society (Corelli 1918: 75). Unsatisfied with life, she decides to fake her own death and leave her parents to undergo a dangerous medical experiment and recover her youth. In the process, Diana gains youthful beauty and energy, but also loses access to human emotions and vulnerabilities. She becomes 'enwrapt in a strange world of unknown experience' and transcends the patriarchal society that has previously rejected her (Corelli 1918: 380; Hallim 2002: 90). The rejuvenation plot also inspired queer writers like Radclyffe Hall. The protagonist of Hall's short story 'Miss Ogilvy Finds Herself', written in 1926 and published in 1934, is a spinster who has served in the First World War and experiences deep frustration upon return to England. During a spontaneous trip to an island off the coast of Devon, Ogilvy travels in time and magically transforms into a youthful Stone Age man, who finds sexual fulfilment with a female partner. In an earlier draft of the text, which remained unpublished during Hall's lifetime, Ogilvy transforms into a youthful Stone Age woman with a male lover. In this version, the narrative trajectory is even more closely aligned with other rejuvenation stories of the period (Hall 2016: 171–82). In either case, for Hall, as for other modernist writers, rejuvenation was closely intertwined with other forms of transitioning related to the sexed body, gender and sexuality.

Concerns with youth are also central to Lili Elbe's semi-fictional co-authored memoir *Man into Woman*, which engages explicitly with contemporary medical constructions of the hormonal body (Meyer 2015: 79–221). Modernist scholars have tended to read the text as an early trans memoir that reflects wider modernist concerns with gender performativity (Caughie 2013) or attempts to control and remake the plastic body through technological and literary interventions (Armstrong 1998: 159–83). Yet, as Emma Heaney has shown, what this allegorical reading of trans femininity obscures is the fact that '[m]odernists responded to the new modern mobility of femininity and feminization, not the breakdown of gender' (2017: 17). As Heaney explains, trans femininity does not signal a queer undoing of gender, but rather demonstrates that the category of woman has never been defined by a narrow cisnormative standard in the first place (2017: 20). At the same time, *Man into Woman* reveals that the surgical interventions Elbe sought in the late 1920s and early 1930s, which included the transplantations of ovaries and a uterus, were available only within a healthcare system that was built to uphold precisely this standard. This medicalising framework, as Kadji Amin has demonstrated in his important reading of Elbe's memoir as a rejuvenation narrative, reinforced a eugenic ideal of 'youthful, vigorous, feminine European womanhood' (2018: 598) that Elbe, as a white European woman, could access. Although Elbe has generally been read as a trans woman, she understood herself to be intersexed and believed that her underdeveloped ovaries needed to be reactivated through the transplantation of younger gonadal tissue. For Elbe and her doctors, her surgeries 'are as much about *rejuvenation* as they are a means of changing the markers of Lili's bodily sex: by obtaining the ovaries of a woman in her twenties, Lili becomes young again' (Amin 2018: 592). As such, Elbe's memoirs can usefully be read as part of wider modernist explorations of feminine mobility that were often informed by eugenic ideologies.

While popular reports of rejuvenation treatments and gender-affirming surgeries in the interwar period suggested that the hormonal body could be controlled at will, such treatments also inspired widespread scepticism about the powers of modern science and technology. Literary authors often presented glandular experiments and the (usually male) doctors who carried out these procedures in highly satirical and critical ways, as novels like Corelli's *The Young Diana*, discussed above, as well as Bertram Gayton's *The Gland Stealers* (1922) and Aldous Huxley's *Brave New World* (1932) and *After Many a Summer* (1939), demonstrate (Armstrong 2018: 232–3). Literary caricatures of megalomaniac endocrinologists aside, many scientists openly acknowledged that the hormonal body and its secretions remained a mystery that could not yet be manipulated at will. The notion that organisms were controlled by a delicate mixture of internal secretions also drew attention to the fact that bodily sex, gender and sexual desire were open to change and could not easily be labelled or categorised on the basis of rigid taxonomic systems. In an article published in the inaugural issue of the journal *Endocrinology* in 1917, for instance, geneticist Richard Goldschmidt described his experiments with intersex moths that were bred to combine male and female markers (Linge 2021; Richmond 2007). Some of these moths initially presented as female and then as male, whereas others started out as male and then developed as female. According to Goldschmidt, this observation reveals how little was known about sexual development:

> The knowledge of the mechanism which distributes in the right way those things which are responsible for the ultimate differentiation of male and female sex might be compared with information about the system of tracks and switches within a railroad station, which direct the trains into different directions. But this knowledge does not furnish any information about the material, the destiny, the loads, or the moving power of the trains. (1917: 436)

Goldschmidt compares sex development and, by extension, the living organism to railway networks, which featured prominently in the Victorian and modernist imagination. This use of technological metaphors of transport and communication was characteristic of early twentieth-century constructions of the hormonal body. In his influential 1905 Croonian Lectures, Starling described hormones as 'chemical messengers [. . .] speeding from cell to cell along the blood stream' (1905: 6). In so doing, he evoked a 'body-as-communication-network metaphor' that resonated with later scientists (Jensen 2015: 335; Koerber 2018: 85–6). In Goldschmidt's article, likening the organism to a moving train puts emphasis on mobility and change rather than presenting sex as fixed and static. The metaphor also foregrounds the complexity of sex development, which is presented as a largely unpredictable process involving multiple intersecting parts. Far from presenting bodily sex as fully controllable or even knowable, endocrinological studies drew attention to the mystery and open-ended nature of developmental processes, which were not necessarily linear or teleological.

This dimension of endocrinological science resonated strongly with modernist writers. Woolf's *Orlando* (1928) is overtly written in opposition to a modern scientific project that seeks to understand and categorise the human body and its desires. Yet, the novel's recognition that '[d]ifferent though the sexes are, they intermix' (Woolf 2008: 181), its wider celebration of sexual fluidity and its playful engagement with delayed ageing can also be read in dialogue with contemporary scientific constructions, especially of the hormonal body (Kahan 2013: 355–6). Modernist authors and scientists even made use of similar imagery to convey this sense of sexual mobility. Like Goldschmidt, Woolf draws on metaphors related to modern technologies of travel and transportation in her work: *Orlando* concludes with a joyful ride in a motorcar and the thrilling apparition of an aeroplane, which signal queer and trans possibilities in the text. Travel via car, train and boat also offers Hall an important means to represent sexual mobility in 'Miss Ogilvy Finds Herself', as Laura Doan has shown (2007). As such, the hormonal body held various conflicting meanings, representing the promise of complete technological control, as well as the fascination with the mystery and variability of sexual development.

Birth Control and Heterosexual Possibilities

In addition to hypnotic and hormonal treatments, the early twentieth century witnessed increased debate about contraceptive technologies, especially for women. This was despite the fact that birth control was considered an 'obscene' topic that could be censored under laws like the 1857 Obscene Publications Act in the UK or the 1873 Comstock Act in the US. Birth control advocates like Stopes and her American counterpart, Margaret Sanger, promoted female birth-control technologies like the cervical cap, coitus interruptus or spermicides. They argued that only reliable birth control could free women from the physical and economical 'strain' of successive births and ensure the health and happiness of the married couple (Stopes 1918: 89). This concern with individual reproductive rights and needs was underpinned by the eugenic belief that birth control would also serve to protect the health of the nation, 'race' and 'Empire' by preventing the birth of 'unfit weaklings and diseased individuals' (Stopes 1919: 7). These quotes, which are characteristic of Stopes's rhetoric, demonstrate that the feminist ambitions of birth control movements led by white women tended to exclude people who did not fit eugenic standards as defined by ableist, classist, colonial, heteronormative and racist ideologies.

As Aimee Armande Wilson has shown, birth control activism and literary modernism need to be understood as mutually co-constitutive and influencing movements. Birth-control rhetoric presented a fundamentally divided human subject that was at the mercy of biological processes and external forces, which technology and science promised to control (Wilson 2016: 12). Some modernist authors embraced the possibilities of birth control to liberate the individual from these pressures. Woolf, for instance, as already mentioned above, indicates in *A Room of One's Own* that contraception would play an important role in allowing women to think and write. Woolf also foregrounds the stifling effects of uncontrollable reproduction on creativity in *Orlando*, suggesting that 'the strand of the modernist movement focused on the life of the mind is due in part to the increasing availability of birth control' (Wilson 2016: 72). Contraceptive technologies allow Orlando to control biological reproduction and turn attention to the production of literary works that are expressive of the modern spirit. They also make it possible for Orlando and husband Shelmerdine to cocreate a modern marriage that is no longer restrained by Victorian marital expectations.

In contrast to *Orlando*, Nella Larsen's *Quicksand* (1928) demonstrates that birth control was not an uncomplicated technology of liberation for all women. The bleak ending of the novel exposes the stifling impact of uncontrollable reproduction on women: Larsen's protagonist, Helga Crane, slowly dies because of the seemingly endless cycles of repeated childbirth. This is despite the fact that, earlier in the book, Crane explicitly resists the eugenicist sentiments expressed by her former fiancé, James Vayle, who insists that it is her duty, as a Black woman 'of the better class', to secure the future of 'the race' through reproduction with an equally 'fit' partner (Larsen 1969: 231–2). As Daylanne K. English has demonstrated, Vayle represents the eugenic Black bourgeois uplift politics that were articulated by leading thinkers like W. E. B. DuBois and E. Franklin Frazier, and that existed alongside mainstream eugenic movements targeting white women (English 2004: 55–9). Larsen was highly critical of eugenic thought and used her fiction to expose and challenge eugenic ideologies (English 2004: 133–6; Macharia 2011; Schalk 2015). In *Quicksand*, Crane resists the eugenic pressures placed on Black women, initially, by refusing to reproduce at all and, later, by reproducing in ways that would be considered 'irresponsible' within a eugenic framework: she knows very little about her husband and endangers her own health and that of her increasingly 'sickly' children by reproducing 'too much' (Larsen: 1969: 283). It is precisely through her refusal to reproduce 'well' or 'responsibly' – for instance, by accessing contraceptive technologies – that Crane resists eugenic ideologies, even if this comes at the cost of her own unravelling as a subject.

White male modernist authors like D. H. Lawrence felt ambivalent about birth control for other reasons. In *Lady Chatterley's Lover* (1928), as part of his wider 'attack on technologization' (Goody 2011: 33), Lawrence presents birth control as one of many modern technologies that society needs to reject to return to a more natural state of living in connection with the body and other people. Early on in the novel, Connie, her upper-class husband and their educated friends debate a 'future, when babies would be bred in bottles and women would be "immunised"' (Lawrence 2006: 74). An enthusiastic female friend explains that these new technological interventions can bring about an emancipated future in which 'a woman can live her own life' without being 'dragged down by her *functions*' (Lawrence 2006: 74). Within the logic of the novel, artificial reproduction and birth control are part of a dystopian vision that Lawrence's readers are meant to reject. Indeed, Connie discovers strong maternal desires through her extra-marital relationship with Mellors. Although the couple discusses birth control briefly (Lawrence 2006: 168–9), neither of them uses contraception, and Connie is pregnant with Mellors's child at the end of the book. Mellors's much more ambivalent attitude towards reproduction complicates the novel's overt technophobic dismissal of birth control, however. This is indicative of Lawrence's wider anxieties about procreative sex and pregnancy. He feared that the focus on biological reproduction and children could prevent heterosexual individuals from truly connecting with each other and stop them from experiencing the transformative power of sex (Bond 2016). As Lawrence explains in his *Study of Thomas Hardy*, 'the sexual act [. . .] is not for the depositing of seed. It is for leaping off into the unknown' (Lawrence 1985: 53). Similarly, Mellors stresses in *Lady Chatterley's Lover* that sex is 'a creative act that is far more than procreative' (Lawrence 2006: 279).

This exploration of non-procreative sexual intimacy between men and women was part of a broader rearticulation of heterosexual erotics in the modernist period that was partially enabled by the availability of more reliable forms of birth control, as well as increased public debate around their use. Even though Lawrence criticised Stopes for being 'wise and scientific' about sex (Lawrence 2004: 247), the way in which he wrote about heterosexual intimacy on its own terms instead of as a means to have children shares important similarities with Stopes's *Married Love*. Like Stopes, Lawrence uses rhythmic language and repetition to try to depict the bodily and mental sensations his characters experience during sex rather than focusing on the reproductive futures such acts might engender. In terms of content and style, Lawrence's work was thus part of broader technologically enabled attempts to reimagine love, intimacy and sex between men and women. For Lawrence, the goal was not to discipline the body and its desires, but to enable what he called the 'leap into the unknown', the fusion of two embodied selves that, he believed, could remake the individual and the modern world.

As this chapter has shown, techno-scientific interventions inspired diverse responses from literary modernist authors. Some celebrated the emancipatory and empowering dimensions of technological innovations that promised to make the body and its desires and functions subject to rational human control. Others were cautious and critical of the ways in which technologies could be marshalled in harmful ways, for instance, when used for eugenic purposes. What the literary authors and sexual scientists discussed in this chapter have in common – despite their many differences – is an understanding of bodily sex and sexuality as deeply entangled with techno-scientific frameworks. In addition, many of them shared an appreciation of the fact that modern science and technology often failed to control and contain, but rather made it possible to imagine the open-ended and as yet unknowable possibilities of bodies and desires.

Works Cited

Amin, Kadij (2018), 'Glands, Eugenics, and Rejuvenation in Man into Woman', *TSQ: Transgender Studies Quarterly*, 5: 4, pp. 589–605.

Armstrong, Tim (1998), *Modernism, Technology and the Body: A Cultural Study*. Cambridge: Cambridge University Press.

Armstrong, Tim (2018), 'Modernism, Technology, and the Life Sciences', in *The Cambridge Companion to Literature and Science*, ed. S. Meyer. Cambridge: Cambridge University Press, pp. 223–41.

Bauer, Heike (2009), *English Literary Sexology: Translations of Inversion, 1860–1930*. Basingstoke: Palgrave Macmillan.
Bland, Lucy and Laura Doan, eds (1998), *Sexology in Culture: Labelling Bodies and Desires*. Chicago: University of Chicago Press.
Bond, Candis (2016), 'Embodied Love: D. H. Lawrence, Modernity and Pregnancy', *The D. H. Lawrence Review*, 41: 1, pp. 21–44.
Brush, S. G. (1978), 'Nettie M. Stevens and the Discovery of Sex Determination by Chromosomes', *Isis*, 69: 2, pp. 162–72.
Caughie, P. L. (2013), 'The Temporality of Modernist Life Writing in the Era of Transsexualism: Virginia Woolf's *Orlando* and Einar Wegener's *Man into Woman*', *Modern Fiction Studies*, 59: 3, pp. 501–25.
Childs, D. J. (2001), *Modernism and Eugenics: Woolf, Eliot, Yeats, and the Culture of Degeneration*. Cambridge: Cambridge University Press.
Cook, Hera (2004), *The Long Sexual Revolution: English Women, Sex, and Contraception 1800–1975*. Oxford: Oxford University Press.
Corelli, Marie (1918), *The Young Diana: An Experiment with the Future*. New York: George H. Doran Company.
Doan, Laura (2007), '"Miss Ogilvy Finds Herself": The Queer Navigational Systems of Radclyffe Hall', *English Language Notes*, 45: 2, pp. 9–22.
Ellis, Havelock and John Addington Symonds (2008), *Sexual Inversion: A Critical Edition*, ed. I. Crozier. Basingstoke: Palgrave Macmillan.
English, D. K. (2004), *Unnatural Selections: Eugenics in American Modernism and the Harlem Renaissance*. Chapel Hill: University of North Carolina Press.
Forel, August (1906), *Hypnotism, or Suggestion and Psychotherapy*. London: Rebman.
Forster, E. M. (2005), *Maurice*. London: Penguin.
Foucault, Michel (1990), *The History of Sexuality: The Will to Knowledge*. London: Vintage.
Freud, Sigmund (2001), 'Group Psychology and the Analysis of the Ego', in *Complete Psychological Works of Sigmund Freud. Volume 18*, ed. J. Strachey. London: Vintage, pp. 67–144.
Funke, Jana (2013), '"We Cannot Be Greek Now": Age Difference, Corruption of Youth and the Making of *Sexual Inversion*', *English Studies*, 94: 2, pp. 139–53.
Funke, Jana and K. Fisher (2019), 'The Age of Attraction: Age, Gender and the History of Modern Male Homosexuality', *Gender & History*, 31: 2, pp. 266–83.
Gaedtke, Andrew (2008), 'From Transmissions of Madness to Machines of Writing: Mina Loy's *Insel* as Clinical Fantasy', *Journal of Modern Literature*, 32: 1, pp. 143–62.
Gill-Peterson, Jules (2018), *Histories of the Transgender Child*. Minneapolis: University of Minnesota Press.
Goldschmidt, Richard (1917), 'Intersexuality and the Endocrine Aspect of Sex', *Endocrinology: The Bulletin of the Association for the Study of the Internal Secretions*, 1, pp. 433–56.
Goody, Alex (2011), *Technology, Literature and Culture*. Cambridge: Polity Press.
Hall, Radclyffe (2016), *The World and Other Unpublished Works by Radclyffe Hall*, ed. J. Funke. Manchester: Manchester University Press.
Hallim, Robyn (2002), *Marie Corelli: Science, Society and the Best Seller*, PhD Thesis, University of Sydney.
Hausman, B. L. (2006), *Changing Sex: Transsexualism, Technology, and the Idea of Gender*. Durham, NC: Duke University Press.
Heaney, Emma (2017), *The New Woman: Literary Modernism, Queer Theory, and the Trans Feminine Allegory*. Evanston, IL: Northwestern University Press.
Jensen, R. E. (2015), 'Improving Upon Nature: The Rhetorical Ecology of Chemical Language, Reproductive Endocrinology, and the Medicalization of Infertility', *Quarterly Journal of Speech*, 101: 2, pp. 329–53.

Kahan, Benjamin (2013), 'Queer Modernism', in *A Handbook of Modernist Studies*, ed. J.-M. Rabaté. Chichester: Wiley, pp. 347–62.
Kahan, Benjamin (2019), *The Book of Minor Perverts: Sexology, Etiology, and the Emergences of Sexuality*. Chicago: University of Chicago Press.
Koerber, Amy (2018), *From Hysteria to Hormones: A Rhetorical History*. Philadelphia: Pennsylvania State University Press.
Larsen, Nella (1969), *Quicksand*. New York: Negro Universities Press.
Lawrence, D. H. (1985), *Study of Thomas Hardy*, ed. B. Steele. Cambridge: Cambridge University Press.
Lawrence, D. H. (2004), 'Pornography and Obscenity', in *Late Essays and Articles*, ed. J. T. Boulton. Cambridge: Cambridge University Press, pp. 233–53.
Lawrence, D. H. (2006), *Lady Chatterley's Lover*. London: Penguin.
Leng, Kirsten (2018), *Sexual Politics and Feminist Science: Women Sexologists in Germany, 1900–1933*. Ithaca, NY: Cornell University Press.
Linge, Ina (2021), 'The Potency of the Butterfly: The Reception of Richard B. Goldschmidt's Animal Experiments in German Sexology around 1920', *History of the Human Sciences*, 34: 1, pp. 1–31.
Loy, Mina (1991), *Insel*. Santa Rosa, CA: Black Sparrow Press.
Macharia, Keguro (2011), 'Queering Helga Crane: Black Nativism in Nella Larsen's *Quicksand*', *Modern Fiction Studies*, 57: 2, pp. 254–75.
Medd, Jodie (2012), *Lesbian Scandal and the Culture of Modernism*. Cambridge: Cambridge University Press.
Meyer, Sabine (2015), *'Wie Lili zu einem richtigen Mädchen wurde': Lili Elbe - zur Konstruktion von Geschlecht und Identität zwischen Medialisierung, Regulierung und Subjektivierung*. Bielefeld: Transcript.
Moll, Albert (1921), *Behandlung der Homosexualität: Biochemisch oder Psychisch?* Bonn: Marcus and Webers.
Peppis, Paul (2014), *Sciences of Modernism: Ethnography, Sexology, and Psychology*. Cambridge: Cambridge University Press.
Richmond, M. L. (2007), 'The Cell as the Basis for Heredity, Development, and Evolution: Richard Goldschmidt's Program of Physiological Genetics', in *From Embryology to Evo-Devo: A History of Developmental Evolution*, ed. M. D. Laubichler and J. Maienschein. Cambridge, MA: MIT Press, pp. 169–211.
Rohy, Valerie (2015), *Lost Causes : Narrative, Etiology, and Queer Theory*. Oxford: Oxford University Press.
Schaffner, A. K. (2011), *Modernism and Perversion: Sexual Deviance in Sexology and Literature, 1850–1930*, Basingstoke: Palgrave Macmillan.
Schalk, Sami (2015), 'Transing: Resistance to Eugenic Ideology in Nella Larsen's *Passing*', *Journal of Modern Literature*, 38: 3, pp. 148–61.
Schrenck-Notzing, Albert von (1895), *Therapeutic Suggestion in Psychopathia Sexualis: Pathological Manifestations of the Sexual Sense, with Especial Reference to Contrary Sexual Instinct*. Philadelphia: F. A. Davis Company.
Sengoopta, Chandak (2006), *The Most Secret Quintessence of Life: Sex, Glands, and Hormones 1850–1950*. Chicago: University of Chicago Press.
Stark, J. F. (2020), *The Cult of Youth: Anti-Ageing in Modern Britain*. Cambridge: Cambridge University Press.
Starling, E. H. (1905), *The Croonian Lectures on the Chemical Correlation of the Functions of the Body: Delivered Before the Royal College of Physicians of London*. London: publisher not identified.
Stopes, Marie (1918), *Married Love: A New Contribution to the Solution of Sex Difficulties*. London: A. C. Fifield.

Stopes, Marie (1919), *Wise Parenthood: A Sequel to 'Married Love'*. London: A. C. Fifield.
Thurschwell, Pamela (2001), *Literature, Technology and Magical Thinking, 1880–1920*. Cambridge: Cambridge University Press.
Turda, Marius (2010), *Modernism and Eugenics*. Basingstoke: Palgrave.
Wilson, A. A. (2016), *Conceived in Modernism: The Aesthetics and Politics of Birth Control*. London: Bloomsbury.
Wolffram, Heather (2009), *The Stepchildren of Science: Psychical Research and Parapsychology in Germany, c. 1870–1939*. Amsterdam: Brill Rodopi.
Woolf, Virginia (2001), *A Room of One's Own and Three Guineas*. London: Vintage.
Woolf, Virginia (2008), *Orlando*. Oxford: Oxford University Press.

18

RACE: FORDISM, FACTORIES AND THE MECHANICAL REPRODUCTION OF RACIAL IDENTITY

Joshua Lam

Toward the end of the nineteenth century, understandings of the human body underwent a radical revision. With the advent of new medical technologies that could perceive corporeal interiors, such as the ophthalmoscope (1847) and the X-ray (1895), bodies became subject to new regimes of perception. Scientists began to view the body in terms of thermodynamics, and Frederick Winslow Taylor's scientific management sought to economise physical labour, while inventions such as the typewriter (1873), phonograph (1877) and cinema (1891) began to incorporate bodies into new media environments. As the techniques of mass production formalised by Henry Ford spread across the globe, the manufacture of new technologies of mobility like the car and the aeroplane produced a more interconnected world. Each of these phenomena participated in the recasting of racial relations and ideologies: the X-ray, for example, was used for 'epilation' (cosmetic hair removal) to clear 'dark shadow[s]' from ambiguous skin colour, participating in the technological 'refashioning of white racial identity' (Herzig 2005: 162–3). New media pluralised methods of bodily and cultural transmission, from the commercialisation of recorded African American music ('race records') in the interwar period to ethnographic sound recordings and cinematic depictions of the body. Taylorism depended upon implicit beliefs about racial and national aptitudes; Fordism utilised neo-colonial theories of 'race development'.

Despite these confluences, scholars now recognise that, as Bruce Sinclair notes, 'The history of race in America has been written as if technologies scarcely existed, and the history of technology as if it were utterly innocent of racial significance' (2004: 1). Although scholars like Rayvon Fouché (2005) and Alondra Nelson (2002), and fields including Afrofuturism, have gone to great lengths to address such gaps, modernist studies has produced little comparable work.[1] Pioneering studies of modernism and technology by Tim Armstrong (1998) and Sara Danius (2002), for example, make few references to race or racial identity, despite their investment in the 'socially constructed' meanings and perceptions of the body (Armstrong 1998: 4). This is one symptom of what Michael Bibby calls the 'racial formation of modernist studies', which 'overwhelmingly focuses on white authors', even as the 'new modernist studies' have sought to produce a more inclusive field (2013: 486). The fact that technophilic modernist movements like F. T. Marinetti's Futurism persistently construed Africa and Africans as representing 'nature, the primitive, *and* the pretechnological' also helps to explain the persistence of the 'reified binary between blackness and technology' (Chude-Sokei 2016: 31;

Nelson 2002: 6). As Marianna Torgovnick (1990), Michael North (1994) and Hal Foster (2004) have shown, the 'primitive' became one of modernism's primary fetishes, along with the machine to which it was ostensibly opposed. Yet as Nelson notes, African American thought has produced 'over a century's worth' of critical 'tools' that challenge such oppositions, beginning with W. E. B. Du Bois (2002: 3).

If scholars have not yet turned sustained attention to intersections of race and technology in modernist literature, it is not for a lack of material. In the US context alone, a brief glance at Black modernist writers reveals numerous engagements and opportunities for study. In addition to protesting against the social and legal injustices of Jim Crow that regulated so many aspects of their bodies and lives (including access to social space, employment, medical treatment and geographic mobility), Black modernist writers also viewed their bodies, and their texts, in technological terms. Consider, for example, Jean Toomer's celebration of a 'machine aesthetic' that sought to remake the image of the perfectible body (Whalan 2002: 464). Consider futuristic inventions like the 'megascope' in Du Bois's 'The Princess Steel', which features a posthuman African princess with hair of steel; consider George Schuyler's satirical *Black No More*, which revolves around a 'formidable apparatus of sparkling nickel' that transforms skin from Black to white (1999 [1931]: 16). Zora Neale Hurston's œuvre, too, is dependent upon the machines she used to collect her folklore, including her automobile, 'Sassie Susie', and the acetate discs upon which she recorded folk songs, sermons and children's games (Brooks 2010). The language of mechanisation also pervades Claude McKay's novels, which despair at 'the super-mechanical Anglo-Saxon-controlled world' (1929: 325); Richard Wright's accounts of the Great Migration and urbanisation; and Ralph Ellison's masterpiece, *Invisible Man* (1952). Though none of these works has been ignored by scholars – many are canonical works of African American, if not modernist, literature – the lack of sustained scholarly attention to the intersection of race and technology in modernist studies is indicative of the work left to be done.

In the US context, the year 1903 serves as a fitting moment to consider the co-constitution of race and technology. As Elizabeth D. Esch observes, Henry Ford incorporated the Ford Motor Company during the same year that Du Bois declared the problem of the twentieth century to be 'the problem of the color line' (Du Bois 1999: 17). In subsequent decades, Ford's Model-T would become the best-selling automobile in the world, just as his company's pioneering techniques of mechanised mass production spread across the globe. These practices were so influential that Ford's name has come to characterise the modernist era itself. Marxist thinkers, in particular, have regarded Fordism as the mode of production governing the modernist era (Jameson 1991; Harvey 1989, 1990). As Michael Denning puts it, 'modernism itself might be understood as the culture of Fordism' (1997: 28).

Ford's products and manufacturing techniques were distributed, like virtually all technologies – and like modernism – unevenly. As Esch notes, the uneven development of Fordism allowed the company to employ 'the color line' in varied and flexible ways, even as it consistently used 'white supremacist ideas and racial segregationist practices' across the globe, from Detroit and the Southern US to Brazil, South Africa and Nazi Germany (Esch 2018: 1). In addition to pioneering a mode of industrial production, Ford's company was also committed (since 1914) to 'making men' (1). The formidable combination of Ford's mass production and the company's cultural endeavours, such as the five-dollar day and the Ford English School, prompted Antonio Gramsci to identify Fordism with 'Americanism', claiming that 'Hegemony here is born in the factory' (1988: 278). Through the regulation of its employees' homes and social lives, including their marital status, languages, clothing, leisure and more, Ford sought to produce not just cars, but also consumers who would purchase them. Although Ford's boast of 'making men' is typically understood in terms of his desire to expand his base of consumers, his company was also engaged in what Roediger and Esch (2012, 2017) have called 'race management', a set of practices that used racial beliefs to structure labour relations. Developing this insight, this chapter will turn to the site of the factory in modernist literature, surveying the ways in which writers such as Aldous Huxley, Richard Wright and Ralph Ellison have deployed the fictional factory to scrutinise the technological mediation of class and race relations. As the complex literary depictions of the factory by each of these writers shows, Fordism did more than merely use race to manage labour. Indeed, the company and its followers used new systems of industrial organisation, scientific management and racial ideologies actively to produce the racial categories we have come to recognise as modern.

The Factory and the World

The prospect of humanity's subordination to a technologised world disturbed many modernist writers, particularly during the economic and cultural crises of the 1930s. Aldous Huxley's *Brave New World* (1932), for example, imagines a dystopian society structured according to Fordist principles. Set in the year A.F. 632 (After Ford), the novel depicts a planet ruled by a World State that has chosen 1908, the year the Model-T was first produced, as the first 'Year of Our Ford'. Anticipating later scientific innovations such as in vitro fertilisation and cloning, the novel's society is founded upon the 'principle of mass production at last applied to biology' (1932: 7). New members of society are mass manufactured on an assembly line via extracted ovaries in an enormous 'hatchery', where the 'Bokanovsky Process' makes one egg produce nearly 100 identical individuals. Explicitly linking industrial production with reproduction, this process is geared towards principles of efficient labour: 'The whole of a small factory [is] staffed with the products of a single bokanovskified egg' (7). Above all, the novel warns against the submission of humankind to mechanisation. As Huxley declaimed elsewhere:

> Fordism demands that we should sacrifice the animal man . . . not indeed to God, but to the Machine. There is no place in the factory, or in that larger factory which is the modern industrialized world, for . . . artists, mystics, or even, finally, individuals. (1931: 180)

By extrapolating Fordist principles to its dystopian society, the novel envisions a world where a 'philosophy of industrialism' conspires with eugenics and Pavlovian conditioning to produce indistinct masses rather than individuals (180). The disturbing promise of Fordism, for Huxley, is that all distinctions between the factory and the world will collapse.

Underneath this familiar dystopian image lurks a less familiar aspect of Fordism: the production of rigid caste divisions formalised via segregated housing, transportation and colour-coded uniforms. Houses and helicopters are reserved for the upper castes, barracks and a monorail for the lower; Alphas wear grey, Epsilons wear black. The caste divisions are implicitly racial and explicitly eugenic: Alpha and Beta characters are white or unmarked, and most lower-caste figures fit the mould of racial stereotypes, from a pair of 'small, black and hideous' Delta attendants to an 'Epsilon-Plus Negro porter' (Huxley 1932: 64, 101). Racial stereotypes of fertility and sexuality are also present: 'You should see the way a negro ovary responds to pituitary!,' the Director of Hatcheries declares: 'It's quite astonishing, when you're used to working with European material' (9). Unlike his satirical approach to Fordism, Huxley does not mock such stereotypes; critics have noted that the author 'openly favoured caste-based social models' and supported eugenic theories at this time (Waddell 2016: 33; Greenberg 2016: 113).

Beyond the implicit racism and colourism of *Brave New World*, Huxley's nightmarish portrayal of Fordist rationalisation is aptly (if unconsciously) linked to contemporaneous notions of 'race' in two fundamental ways. First, through eugenics, Huxley's Fordist society renders 'eternal and biological' not just the 'system of class relationships', as Theodor Adorno observes, but also the implicit racial hierarchies that intersect with that system (1967: 100). Applying mass production to biological reproduction, the World State mechanically reproduces the character of race relations governing Huxley's present: white supremacy and a racially coded caste system. With the addition of Pavlovian conditioning, through which individuals are taught to enjoy their social position and fear all others, this rationalised but unequal society is able to reproduce itself by literalising what Walter Lippmann famously called 'the manufacture of consent' (1941 [1922]: 248).

Second, the correlation between specific races and castes is governed by Fordist principles of labour and efficiency. Specific racial and ethnic groups are selected for specific tasks in Huxley's society. Beyond the assignation of jobs like 'porter' and 'attendant' for dark-skinned individuals, the systematised nature of race-based roles, assigned at birth, is most visible in a scene where an outsider, John the Savage, visits one of the World State's factories in London.

> 'Each process,' explained the Human Element Manager, 'is carried out, so far as possible, by a single Bokanovsky Group.'
> And, in effect, eighty-three almost noseless black brachycephalic Deltas were cold-pressing. The fifty-six four-spindle chucking and turning machines were being manipulated by fifty-six aquiline and ginger Gammas. One hundred and seven heat-conditioned Epsilon Senegalese were working in the foundry. (159)

Numerous other 'Bokanovsky' groups, characterised by caste and physiognomy, follow this list, each connected with a specific function in the factory. With labourers bred for specific types of (dis)ability and conditioned for specific work environments, eugenics works in tandem with race management to realise Ford's doctrine of continuous improvement on a mass scale.

Though Huxley's dystopian vision projects far into the future, *Brave New World* captures several aspects of the Fordist ethos with striking accuracy. In his writings and public comments, Henry Ford frequently touted his utopian pretensions. His *My Life and Work*, for example, imagines what 'will happen when this world is put on a production basis' (1922: 79). Throughout the book, Ford seeks to extend his manufacturing and managerial principles to 'the largest application – . . . they have nothing peculiarly to do with motor cars or tractors but form something in the nature of a universal code' (3).

At the same time, scholars have shown that the universalist principles promoted by Henry Ford were at odds with his company's varied application of what Esch calls 'racial knowledge' (Meyer 1981; Esch 2018). Though the Ford Motor Company has been viewed as progressive for hiring large numbers of Black workers at its River Rouge complex in the 1920s, two decades before most car manufacturers, this specific policy (exceptional among other Ford factories) masks the company's deeper inequities. As Esch demonstrates, this hiring policy existed alongside the notorious anti-Semitism of Henry Ford's *Dearborn Independent* and public support for eugenics; company hiring practices that routed Black workers into the most dangerous jobs; colonial practices that exploited racial hierarchies in Brazil and South Africa; assimilationist practices of 'race development' that sought to whiten European immigrants; and a belief in 'white managerialism' that drew upon so-called 'racial knowledge' pioneered in Southern US plantation slavery (2018: 2, 9). It is for many of these reasons that the radical journalist George Seldes declared in 1943, 'The Ford Empire is the Hitler Nazi Empire on a small scale' (1943: 138). If the Ford factory became a 'repressive state in miniature', acting as an inspiration and even a model for 'management-as-social-control among fascists' like Hitler and Mussolini (Esch 2018: 52), *Brave New World* anticipates these developments by amplifying the company's racial capitalism to the level of the World State. Indeed, many of the company's racial practices are echoed in Huxley's World State, which is also a colonial empire; it appears to have achieved world domination, with the exception of a few 'Savage Reservations', which remain unconquered only because they are not 'worth the expense of civilizing' (Huxley 1932: 162). Taking Fordism as his model for world-wide technocracy, Huxley's *Brave New World* thus stands as a reminder that US industrialism has long been explicitly linked with practices of racial exploitation and colonisation.

The Mechanical Production of Racial Optics

While Huxley's novel offers the best-known fictional representation of Fordist principles extended to a global scale, Black modernist writers also turned to the site of the factory to index how deeply racial ideologies were inscribed upon class relations. As the mechanised assembly line came under greater scrutiny in the 1930s for its dehumanising qualities, epitomised by the slapstick antics of Charlie Chaplin's *Modern Times* (1936), novelists Richard Wright and Ralph Ellison sought to reveal the uneven impacts of these degradations. In key scenes from Wright's memoir *Black Boy* (1945), his novel *Lawd Today!* (1963) and Ellison's *Invisible Man*, the factory emerges as a space where prohibition of industrial education for Black workers coexists alongside the exploitation of their physical labour; where surveillance intended to promote industrial efficiency operates according to a racial optics; and where whiteness is accorded a managerial function that defines itself in terms of technological proficiency and racial knowledge. In short, for Wright and Ellison, the factory becomes a site where race relations are manufactured every bit as much as the objects and commodities it produces.

Wright recounts one such site in his memoir. As a teenager in Jackson, Mississippi, Richard gains employment with the American Optical Company, 'a tiny factory filled with many strange machines smeared with red dust' (1945: 187).² The factory initially operates as a site of promise that will help him earn enough money to leave the South and 'learn a trade' (186). Viewing industrial education as a means to upward economic and geographic mobility, the factory initially symbolises the prospects of the North. Soon, however, Richard learns a lesson of a different sort. Despite the intent of the manager, a 'Yankee', to 'train a Negro boy in the optical trade . . . to help him, guide him', the two white men instructed to 'break [Richard] in' and teach him about 'the mechanics of grinding and polishing lenses' refuse to do so (187). After a month of sweeping floors and watching the intractable white men work in silence, he is told by one of them, 'This is *white* man's work around here' (188). Facing weeks of intimidation, open hostility and death threats, Richard soon realises he 'would never learn to operate those machines as long as those two white men in there stood by them' (192). Despite the sympathy of his employer, Richard leaves the job, fearing for his life.

Wright's account of oppression in the optical factory offers a compact lesson in technologically mediated race relations. As the white men jealously guard their trade and their machines, they enact a widespread process that Ronald Takaki (2000) and Michael Adas (1989) have described: the identification of white, Anglo-Saxon, US masculinity with technological ingenuity, and the use of technology to subordinate women and minority populations, who were often construed as incapable of achieving technological competence. Despite the popularity in the South of accommodationist positions like Booker T. Washington's, which advocated for industrial education and trade training instead of higher education for Southern Black workers, even basic access to technical training was often refused to Black Americans, who were restricted instead to manual or deskilled (not 'unskilled') labour. As Wright noted in *12 Million Black Voices*, his impressionistic work of photo-journalism narrativising the Great Migration, 'The Bosses of the Buildings decree that we must be maids, porters, janitors, cooks, and general servants' (1941: 102–3).

Beyond these labour inequities, *Black Boy* also demonstrates how uneven technological development across racial lines helps to enforce geographical segregation. Wright frames his experience at the optical factory by prefacing it with two violent racist encounters that juxtapose the discreet mobility of the bicycle with the (white) power of the car. In the first, Richard returns from a delivery in the suburbs with a punctured bicycle tyre. A group of young white men offer him a lift on the running board of their car, but they soon assault him and throw him from the vehicle for neglecting to say 'sir' to one of the passengers. A second encounter shows Richard making a bicycle delivery in a white neighbourhood, only to be 'jammed . . . into the curbing' by a police car; he is violently searched at gunpoint, then warned not to enter white neighbourhoods at night (181). In each case, cars are used to keep Richard 'in his place' socially and geographically, just as white managerialism at the factory does so in terms of economics and employment.

The threat of physical violence that precedes and pervades Richard's experience at the optical factory is one component of white supremacist terrorism that seeks to regulate his and other Black Americans' access to technical education and employment (among other social privileges). Another component, hinted at in the name of the company, is rendered on a more figurative level. As Mikko Tuhkanen suggests, Wright's discussion of 'the optical trade' also marks a Foucauldian shift from spectacles of punishment towards forms of racial violence that depended upon 'a more economically disseminated disciplinary regime' (2009: 110). Chief among the latter is a form of self-surveillance that Wright construes in visual terms. As Richard struggles to 'see' why he continues to be fired from low-paying jobs, he devotes increasing effort to scrutinising his own behaviour. 'White people make it their business to watch niggers,' his friend Griggs explains to him. 'And they pass the word around. . . . You're marked already' (1945: 183). The irony of Richard's inability to 'see' the racial optics governing Jim Crow while employed in an optical factory will not be lost on readers.

Black Boy portrays an internalised form of surveillance that replicates the type of managerial oversight practised in Ford's factories. In the 1920s, particularly in the River Rouge complex, where large numbers of African Americans were employed, the Ford Motor Company 'pioneered new levels of surveillance, segregation, repression, and fraternalism, all under the umbrella of the exaltation of managerial leadership' (Esch 2018: 52). Extending managerial oversight beyond the factory and into the home through the company's infamous Sociological Department, Black workers at Ford were 'particularly surveilled' (91). In his memoir, Wright's emphasis on 'disembodied surveillance' mirrors what Tuhkanen calls 'the panoptic regime's superior efficacy over the spectacle of punishment in ensuring subjection' (2009: 108–9).

Wright's account of the optical factory demonstrates precisely how the remote threat of violence undergirds a discipline that coerces Black subjects to watch themselves. Even when his paternalistic 'Yankee' employer, Mr Crane, asks Richard to explain how the white machinists have mistreated him, Crane continually reminds him: 'Keep control of yourself. No matter what happens, keep control . . .' (192). In the wake of his termination, Richard tries to instil this lesson in himself. However, the pervasive threat of violence thwarts his attempts to naturalise a docile, servile manner. Though Richard goes to work 'resolving to watch [his] every move', this self-surveillance paralyses him; he forgets tasks, drops items and freezes when white customers address him (195). In such instances, Richard's expectation of violence obstructs his efficiency as a worker. If the point of panoptic discipline is 'to induce in the [subject] a state of conscious and permanent visibility that assures the automatic functioning of power' (Foucault 1977: 201), Richard's failure to internalise social codes mandated by his employer *and*, simultaneously, to work efficiently dramatises a tension between the imperatives of racial subjection and productive labour.

In casting himself as the melancholy individual who remains heroically maladapted to harmful social expectations, Wright emphasises the struggle of the individual against mass society in a manner that parallels Huxley's *Brave New World* and many other modernist texts. Though its status as memoir demands a localised attention that contrasts with Huxley's fantastical extension of Fordism to a global scale, *Black Boy* also emphasises the systematic and disciplinary nature of racial inequality. Reflecting upon his time at the American Optical Company, Wright declares that the white workers who tormented him 'did not seem to be individual men, but part of a huge, implacable, elemental design toward which hate was futile' (194). Much as Richard's body continually rejects his attempts to incorporate racist social codes, Wright's memoir consistently throws off the notion that racism exists solely in the conscious hatred of prejudiced individuals. Instead, *Black Boy* dramatises the systematic and manufactured nature of such inequities as they are encoded in relations of management and production.

Race Management and the Technological Reproduction of Whiteness

Wright's autobiographical observations about racial optics and social automatism, grounded in the site of the factory, are uncannily echoed in a key scene from Ralph Ellison's *Invisible Man*. During his brief employment at the Liberty Paint Company, Ellison's narrator begins to learn how to produce the company's most successful paint, 'Optic White'. Described by one employee as 'the purest white that can be found', the paint and the company use the barely coded language of white supremacy (1980: 201–2). A 'huge electric sign' (196) outside the plant makes this abundantly clear:

> KEEP AMERICA PURE
> WITH
> LIBERTY PAINTS

As Harryette Mullen notes, this episode of Ellison's novel offers an 'astute parable of the production of whiteness' by using 'technological metaphors of production' (2012: 134, 138). Working under a white supervisor named Kimbro, the narrator is asked to use a device like 'a battery hydrometer' to put ten drops of 'dead black' liquid into each bucket of 'Optic White' (Ellison 1980: 200). Though the drops spread upon the surface and 'become blacker still, spreading suddenly out to the edges', Kimbro emphasises the mindless nature of the task: 'You just do what you're told and don't try to think about it' (200). Eventually, the black liquid disappears, rendering a white paint 'that'll cover just about anything' (202). In this evocative image, the production of whiteness itself depends upon the concealment of Black labour, Black materials and Black death ('dead black[s]'); it is a product that elides its miscegenated origins, even as it seeks to cover 'just about anything' with a supreme shade of white.

The invisibility of Black contributions to the formation of an implicitly white US culture, and to industrialisation, is taken one step further when Ellison's narrator is sent to the plant's basement to work under Lucius Brockway, an elderly Black worker in charge of many mysterious machines. Though he lacks technical education, Brockway functions as an unofficial engineer. Wary of racial competition, he recounts with glee his ousting of an 'Italian fellow', 'one of them so-called engineers', whose official training could not compete with Brockway's extensive experience:

> A fool! He wanted to boss *me* and I know more about this basement than anybody, boilers and everything. . . . I knows the location of each and every pipe and switch and cable and wire and everything else. . . . I got it in my head so good I can trace it out on paper down to the last nut and bolt; and ain't never been to nobody's engineering school neither. (215–16)

Brockway also participates in the company's marketing; he produces the company's slogan, 'If It's Optic White, It's the Right White,' for which he receives a $300 bonus. He brags to the narrator: 'We make the best white paint in the world . . . Our white is so white you can paint a chunka coal and you'd have to crack it open with a sledge hammer to prove it wasn't white clear through!' (217). Brockway thus hyphenates the roles of an Uncle Tom and a trickster. He dissembles before his white employers (as Richard in *Black Boy* could not) and exploits the paternalism of the company's owner, 'the Old Man', for his own benefit; yet he is also complicit with the company's racist rhetoric and is eager to remain in his exploited position.

The exploitation of Black labour and its implication in the industrial production of whiteness are made especially clear in one of Brockway's formulations: 'They got all this machinery, but that ain't everything; *we the machines inside the machine*' (217). As he elaborates, it is his own concealed labour that produces 'Optic White' and keeps the machines running.

> They thinks 'cause everything down here is done by machinery, that's all there is to it. They crazy! Ain't a continental thing that happens down here that ain't as iffen I done put my black hands into it! Them machines just do the cooking, these here hands right here do the sweeting. Yes, sir! Lucius Brockway hit it square on the head! I dips my finger in and sweets it! (218)

Brockway's claim to technical skill, despite his relative invisibility, fits into a larger trend in twentieth-century US modernity: the attempt to prove and perform masculinity through technological mastery. Mullen identifies this as 'the black man's potential assimilation/mastery through technological rather than reproductive power', an attempt that is limited by Brockway's feminised status as a 'cook', which prevents him from acquiring social and economic power (2012: 139). More broadly, such factory scenes highlight how historical shifts in gender roles have been inscribed in mechanical labour. Paule Marshall's *Brown Girl, Brownstones* (2009 [1959]), for example, compares the traditionally feminine work of cooking with one character's mastery at an 'old-fashioned lathe' resembling 'an oversize cookstove' in a munitions factory during the Second World War (84). As the young protagonist, Selina, witnesses her Barbadian mother, Silla, at work, she views her mother's movements, 'attuned to the mechanical rhythms of the machine-mass', as evidence of Silla's 'formidable force' (84). Observing 'the same transient calm' Silla emits when cooking, Selina feels her mother 'was like the machines, some larger form of life with an awesome beauty all her own' (85). In a plot that pits the mother's desire to remain in Brooklyn against the father's dream of returning to Barbados, the mother's mechanisation underscores how industrial capitalism forcefully assimilates racial and national difference, while also hinting at the economic empowerment that accompanied the mass employment of women during the Second World War. As with Ellison's Brockway, feminised domestic labour is mapped onto the traditionally masculine space of the factory in order to signal shifting hierarchies of race, class and gender, even as each scene acknowledges the technical skills necessary for domestic and industrial labour alike.

Brockway's unofficial status and obscure placement in the factory basement also make him a kind of antecedent for Ellison's unnamed narrator, who will eventually become another 'invisible man', living in a 'hole in [a] basement' that he has 'wired' with 1,369 lights, using stolen electrical current from 'Monopolated Light & Power' (3, 7). Both characters push against the myth of Black resistance to technology, even as they demonstrate how subversive the notion of Black technical mastery is to a society that affiliates technological expertise, and the figure of the engineer, with white masculinity. Ellison's depiction of these technologically adept Black men is evidence of what Jennifer L. Lieberman calls his 'technological humanism', a position that resists the notion that 'new inventions will [necessarily] liberate or harm people' (2017: 172). Instead of maintaining simplistic associations between social and technological progress, Ellison reminds readers that technologies are fundamentally ambiguous, and that they are, in Lieberman's words, 'shaped by the institutions and powers that control them' (172).

While Wright's memoir portrays the disciplinary implications of racial optics in a small factory setting, Ellison's *Invisible Man* further engages large-scale institutions typified by the Ford Motor Company: the Liberty Paint Company 'looks like a small city' (197). As with Seldes's analogy between the Ford and Nazi empires, Ellison turns to the site of the factory to emblematise a widespread form of techno-scientific control. This is most apparent in an episode following the protagonist's encounter with Brockway. After a mechanical explosion in the basement of the paint factory, the protagonist is admitted to a 'factory hospital', where doctors administer X-rays and electric shocks while discussing him in psychological, sociological, medical and racial terms (243). As Scott Selisker notes, Ellison 'combines institutions as a strategy for underlining their similarities and pervasive control over U.S. culture' (2016: 76). The novel is 'proto-Foucauldian' in its emphasis on the 'isomorphism between institutions' like factories, schools, hospitals and prisons (73). Playing upon the figurative aspects of technological language, Ellison thus uses technological tropes, especially the figure of the human automaton, to indict widespread forms of social control.

At the same time, these episodes of the novel also point towards ideologies enacted in specific Fordist practices. Though there is figurative power in Ellison's play with isomorphic institutions, the Ford Motor Company had already formalised such combinations of industrial technique, scientific management and sociological knowledge in the early twentieth century. The Ford Sociological Department is an instructive example. Though the company made headlines in 1914 for its drastic increase in wages with the 'five-dollar day', the Sociological Department determined which employees were permitted to participate in the profit-sharing plan. To qualify, employees needed to demonstrate efficiency not only on the assembly line, but also in their private lives. To that end, the company sent 'investigators' into employees' homes to collect personal data, including leisure habits, marital status, savings, ostensibly 'moral' issues (alcohol consumption, gambling, monogamy) and perceived cultural habits (language, sanitary conditions, dress). The company's goal was thus to 'remake social and cultural values for men to fit the regimen of the mechanized plant' (Meyer 1981: 123). By entwining the home, the hospital and the factory, the Ford Motor Company combined different forms of disciplinary knowledge in its project of 'making men'. It is precisely these kinds of interconnections that Ellison satirises in his portrayal of the factory as an emblematic site of social control – one in which the narrator is broken down, retrained and remade into a new man.

Far from being universal in its design and application, Ford's quest for maximum efficiency was a response to a racialised labour problem. In the Highland Park factory in Detroit, where a vast majority of workers were immigrants from Eastern and Southern Europe, the company experienced massive labour turnover due to the increasing demands of mechanised assembly lines. The five-dollar day was intended to stem this tide by inducing employees to remain with competitive wages, while the Sociological Department sought to Americanise immigrant employees in order to reduce the chances of their returning to their native countries. As Esch notes, this labour problem 'was also a "race" problem, in the sense that managers, reformers and scholars used the word race to describe European nationalities in the Progressive Era' (2018: 35). Indeed, the Sociological Department required little surveillance for US-born and white-collar workers, and devoted most of its coercive scrutiny to immigrant workers (and later, at the Rouge, to Black workers).

The Fordist policies described above fall under the rubric of what Roediger and Esch (2012, 2017) call 'race management', a set of practices that sought to mobilise racial knowledge (better described as 'managerial race lore') to maximise profit, including racial competition, racial development and white managerialism (2017: 148). Though these practices emerged in the US through settler colonialism and racial slavery in the antebellum era, they combined with Taylorism at the turn of the century and found their fullest expression in Ford's factories after the First World War. While 'paternal fantasies of generalized racial uplift' form one component of race management, the hallmark of the white managerial impulse lies in the way 'Americans developed a sense of themselves as white by casting their race as uniquely fit to manage land and labor and by judging how other races might come and go in the service of that project' (2017: 142, 123). Such management was also overtly technological in many ways. From control over tools and patents to ownership of land, firms and factories, white Americans in the early twentieth century sought to contour the colour line by welding technological management to racial hierarchies.

The disparate threads of race management are brilliantly drawn together in Richard Wright's early modernist novel *Lawd Today!*, written between 1934 and 1938 but published posthumously in 1963. With a significant nod to James Joyce's *Ulysses*, the action of the novel follows the protagonist, a Black postal worker named Jake Jackson, as he moves through Depression-era Chicago over the course of a single day.[3] The novel's second section, 'Squirrel Cage', devotes considerable space to technical descriptions of the Chicago Post Office, which is portrayed as a highly rationalised industrial factory. Preceded by an epigraph from Waldo Frank's *Our America*, which describes 'long, rigid rows of desiccated men and women', Wright uses the space to portray the rote, deadening dimensions of modern industrialism (qtd in Wright 1963: 113). In addition to naturalistic passages that describe the detailed workings of mail-sorting machines and their devastation of the human sensorium, the novel depicts the racial dimensions of labour and management. Key among Wright's observations is his emphasis on managerial surveillance:

> For eight long hours a clerk's hands must be moving ceaselessly, to and fro, stacking the mail. At intervals a foreman makes rounds of inspection to see that all is going well. Under him works a legion of catfooted spies and stoolpigeons who snoop eternally. Along the walls are slits through which detectives peep and peer. (129)

By the 1930s, portrayals of on-the-job factory surveillance could be found in works as disparate as Chaplin's *Modern Times* (1936) and the social realist historical fiction of Upton Sinclair's *The Flivver King: A Story of Ford-America* (1936). Yet Wright goes further, picking up on practices pioneered by Ford, by demonstrating how white employers would surveil the home lives of non-white employees, combining moral policing with managerial power. A key plot point in *Lawd Today!* revolves around Jake's fear that his wife, Lil, will report an episode of Jake's domestic violence to his employers. When he appeals to the Board of Review for a loan, the white supervisors question him about his spending habits, his commitment to his job and his relationship with his wife; they bring up prior citations for 'drinking on the job' and 'debt dodging' (124). Other passages portray Jake's encounters with racist foremen and inspectors, racial competition brewing between Jake and other races and ethnicities ('West Indian Negroes', 'Filipinos') and a racial glass ceiling: 'When a black man gets a job in the Post Office he's done reached the top,' one character notes with irony (148, 118). Like Ellison's fiction and Wright's memoir, *Lawd Today!* demonstrates how race management combines with scientific management and technological restriction to enforce racial and class-based inequities that pervade not only the factory floor and the post room, but the whole of life, rendering it all one massive 'squirrel cage'. As Wright declared elsewhere, combining images of the animal and the automaton:

> It seems as though we are now living inside of a machine; days and events move with a hard reasoning of their own. We live amid swarms of people, yet there is a vast distance between people, a distance that words cannot bridge. (1941: 100)

More than a decade before Ellison's Brockway would call the Black workers of America '*the machines inside the machine*', Wright turned to the site of the factory, and the imagery of mechanisation, to portray how intimately industrialisation worked according to a racial and racist logic.

If Ellison's treatment of the Liberty Paint Company in *Invisible Man* functions as a parable about the production of racial difference in the US, it is crucial to note that modernist works by Ellison, Wright and others also address the construction of race beyond the level of the symbolic. In their scrutiny of labour, management, industrial education and the inequities of mechanisation, Black modernist writers in the US have attended closely to what Rebecca Herzig calls 'the *tools* of race-making' (2004: 157). Decades before historians of technology came to consider 'the technological constitution of racial identity and difference', these writers were exploiting the 'metaphoric flexibility' of race and technology in order to expose the intractable myths of US civilisation (Herzig 2004: 156; Chude-Sokei 2016: 15). Thus Ellison's narrator uses his own technological ingenuity as a metaphor for the power of words to subvert the racial ideologies and uneven technological developments that characterise US modernity: 'Though invisible, I am in the great American tradition of tinkers. That makes me kin to Ford, Edison and Franklin. Call me, since I have a theory and a concept, a "thinker-tinker"' (1980: 7). Placing himself at the centre of this 'great American tradition', Ellison's nameless protagonist – like Ellison, Wright and other paragons of Black modernism – tinkers with the myth of whiteness itself, exposing it as a tool of racial capitalism reproduced in the Fordist factory and predicated on narratives of technological mastery and Western domination.

Notes

1. One significant exception to this critical inattention lies in the field of modernist sound studies, where scholars often draw upon African American texts, especially Du Bois's *The Souls of Black Folk* (1999 [1903]) and Ralph Ellison's *Invisible Man* (1980 [1952]), which bookend the modernist era. Recent scholarship by Mark Goble (2010), Louis Chude-Sokei (2016) and Julie Beth Napolin (2020) has turned to literary modernism to consider how written narratives engage simultaneously with racial ideologies and recording technologies

such as the phonograph. As Napolin argues, literature itself often functions as 'a sound recording technology, documenting vocal rhythms, tones, and idiolects' in ways that are implicated in a *'technological racial unconscious*' (2020: 190, 192).
2. In what follows, I use 'Wright' to refer to the author, and 'Richard' to refer to the autobiographical subject of *Black Boy*.
3. Wright was employed at the Chicago Post Office numerous times between 1929 and 1937 (Ward and Butler 2008: 76). According to biographer Michel Fabre, the central post office was marked by 'the worst working conditions of all United States post offices', with 'discipline worthy of a penitentiary' (1993: 78).

Works Cited

Adas, Michael (1989), *Machines as the Measure of Men: Science, Technology, and Ideologies of Western Dominance*. Ithaca, NY: Cornell University Press.

Adorno, Theodor W. (1967), 'Aldous Huxley and Utopia', in *Prisms*, trans. Samuel and Shierry Weber. Cambridge, MA: MIT Press, pp. 95–118.

Armstrong, Tim (1998), *Modernism, Technology, and the Body: A Cultural Study*. Cambridge: Cambridge University Press.

Bibby, Michael (2013), 'The Disinterested and Fine: New Negro Renaissance Poetry and the Racial Formation of Modernist Studies', *Modernism/modernity*, 20: 3, pp. 485–501.

Brooks, Daphne A. (2010), '"Sister, Can You Line It Out?": Zora Neale Hurston and the Sound of Angular Black Womanhood', *Amerikastudien / American Studies*, 55: 4, pp. 617–27.

Chude-Sokei, Louis (2016), *The Sound of Culture: Diaspora and Black Technopoetics*. Middletown, CT: Wesleyan University Press.

Danius, Sara (2002), *The Senses of Modernism: Technology, Perception, and Aesthetics*. Ithaca, NY: Cornell University Press.

Denning, Michael (1997), *The Cultural Front: The Laboring of American Culture in the Twentieth Century*. London: Verso.

Du Bois, W. E. B. (1999 [1903]), *The Souls of Black Folk*, ed. Henry Louis Gates, Jr, and Terri Hume Oliver. New York: Norton.

Ellison, Ralph (1980 [1952]), *Invisible Man*. New York: Vintage Books.

Esch, Elizabeth D. (2018), *The Color Line and the Assembly Line: Managing Race in the Ford Empire*. Oakland: University of California Press.

Fabre, Michel (1993), *The Unfinished Quest of Richard Wright*, trans. Isabel Barzun, 2nd edn. Urbana: University of Illinois Press.

Ford, Henry, with Samuel Crowther (1922), *My Life and Work*. Garden City, NY: Doubleday, Page & Company.

Foster, Hal (2004), *Prosthetic Gods*. Cambridge, MA: MIT Press.

Foucault, Michel (1977), *Discipline and Punish: The Birth of the Prison*, trans. Alan Sheridan. New York: Vintage.

Fouché, Rayvon (2003), *Black Inventors in the Age of Segregation: Granville T. Woods, Lewis H. Latimer, and Shelby J. Davidson*. Baltimore: Johns Hopkins University Press.

Goble, Mark (2010), *Beautiful Circuits: Modernism and the Mediated Life*. New York: Columbia University Press.

Gramsci, Antonio (1988), *The Antonio Gramsci Reader: Selected Writings 1916–1935*, ed. David Forgacs. New York: New York University Press.

Greenberg, Jonathan (2016), 'What Huxley Got Wrong', in *Brave New World: Contexts and Legacies*, ed. Jonathan Greenberg and Nathan Waddell. London: Palgrave Macmillan, pp. 109–26.

Harvey, David (1989), *The Urban Experience*. Baltimore: Johns Hopkins University Press.

Harvey, David (1990), *The Condition of Postmodernity: An Enquiry into the Origins of Social Change*. Cambridge: Blackwell.

Herzig, Rebecca (2004), 'The Matter of Race in Histories of American Technology', in *Technology and the African-American Experience: Needs and Opportunities for Study*, ed. Bruce Sinclair. Cambridge, MA: MIT Press, pp. 155–70.
Huxley, Aldous (1931), *Music at Night & Other Essays*. London: Chatto & Windus.
Huxley, Aldous (1932), *Brave New World*. New York: Harper Perennial.
Jameson, Fredric (1991), *Postmodernism: Or, the Cultural Logic of Late Capitalism*. Durham, NC: Duke University Press.
Lieberman, Jennifer L. (2017), *Power Lines: Electricity in American Life and Letters, 1882–1952*. Cambridge, MA: MIT Press.
Lippmann, Walter (1941 [1922]), *Public Opinion*. New York: Macmillan.
McKay, Claude (1929), *Banjo: A Story Without a Plot*. San Diego: Harcourt Brace & Company.
Marshall, Paule (2009 [1959]), *Brown Girl, Brownstones*. Mineola, NY: Dover.
Meyer III, Stephen (1981), *The Five Dollar Day: Labor Management and Social Control in the Ford Motor Company, 1908–1921*. Albany: State University of New York Press.
Mullen, Harryette (2012), *The Cracks Between What We Are and What We Are Supposed to Be: Essays and Interviews*. Tuscaloosa: University of Alabama Press, pp. 130–54.
Napolin, Julie Beth (2020), 'Unrecordable Sound: Media History, Technology and the Racial Unconscious', in *Sound and Literature*, ed. Anna Snaith. Cambridge: Cambridge University Press, pp. 190–208.
Nelson, Alondra (2002), 'Introduction: Future Texts', *Social Text*, 20: 2, pp. 1–15.
North, Michael (1994), *The Dialect of Modernism: Race, Language & Twentieth-Century Literature*. New York: Oxford University Press.
Roediger, David R., and Elizabeth D. Esch (2012), *The Production of Difference: Race and the Management of Labor in U.S. History*. Oxford: Oxford University Press.
Roediger, David R. and Elizabeth D. Esch (2017), '"One Symptom of Originality": Race and the Management of Labor in U.S. History', in *Class, Race, and Marxism*, by David Roediger. London: Verso.
Schuyler, George S. (1999 [1931]), *Black No More*. New York: The Modern Library.
Seldes, George, assisted by Helen Seldes (1943), *Facts and Fascism*. New York: In Fact.
Selisker, Scott (2016), *Human Programming: Brainwashing, Automatons, and American Unfreedom*. Minneapolis: University of Minnesota Press.
Sinclair, Bruce (2004), 'Integrating the Histories of Race and Technology', in *Technology and the African-American Experience: Needs and Opportunities for Study*, ed. Bruce Sinclair. Cambridge, MA: MIT Press, pp. 1–17.
Takaki, Ronald (2000), *Iron Cages: Race and Culture in 19th-Century America*, rev. edn. New York: Oxford University Press.
Torgovnick, Marianna (1990), *Gone Primitive: Savage Intellects, Modern Lives*. Chicago: University of Chicago Press.
Tuhkanen, Mikko (2009), *The American Optic: Psychoanalysis, Critical Race Theory, and Richard Wright*. Albany: State University of New York Press.
Waddell, Nathan (2016), 'Signs of the T: Aldous Huxley, High Art, and American Technocracy', in *Brave New World: Contexts and Legacies*, ed. Jonathan Greenberg and Nathan Waddell. London: Palgrave Macmillan, pp. 31–49.
Ward, Jerry W. and Robert J. Butler, eds (2008), *The Richard Wright Encyclopedia*. Westport, CT: Greenwood Press.
Whalan, Mark (2002), 'Jean Toomer, Technology, and Race', *Journal of American Studies*, 36: 3, pp. 459–72.
Wright, Richard (1941), *12 Million Black Voices*. New York: Basic Books.
Wright, Richard (1945), *Black Boy (American Hunger): A Record of Childhood and Youth*. New York: Harper Perennial.
Wright, Richard (1963), *Lawd Today!* Boston: Northeastern University Press.

19

Technics: Education and Pharmakon in Lawrence, Simondon and Stiegler

Jeff Wallace

In *Fantasia of the Unconscious* (1922), D. H. Lawrence wrote with emphasis: 'The great mass of humanity should never learn to read and write – never' (Lawrence 2004: 118). Lawrence's post-First World War writings on education can seem to epitomise the democracy-shy paranoia of a certain strain of high modernism. His proposition (or provocation) concerning literacy follows from what he called at *Fantasia*'s outset 'an age of mistaken democracy' (62). In a prior essay, 'Education of the People' (1920), Lawrence had claimed that the modern aspiration to universal literacy was wrongheadedly based on the notion that all humans are equally capable of, and would equally benefit from, intellectual or 'mental' development. The untruth of this notion is apprehended, Lawrence insisted, by all actual teachers (he had been a schoolteacher himself for some six years, three as a pupil-teacher in Nottinghamshire, and three, qualified and salaried, in Croydon, South London): 'every teacher' knows that they are always confronted by a majority of 'uninstructibles', the extent of the latter varying, within the unstable rhetoric of Lawrence's essay, between 'at least fifty-per cent' of scholars and 'a very large majority' (Lawrence 1988: 96).

For the liberal education system of the early twentieth-century British state to insist on administering culture and literacy to such scholars was, Lawrence maintained, to 'allow nothing except in terms of itself' (1988: 96). Given (it is a considerable assumption) the inaptitude of the young people themselves, Lawrence's concern was that such a policy was directly harmful to them – 'psychologically barbaric' – and also a form of idealist bullying (Lawrence reserved some of his most scathing moral disapprobation for the violence of bullying) (2004: 115). Conversely, he argued, the same children are clever enough to realise – with what might be called the alternative intelligence of the uninstructible – that only the 'smatterings' or 'imbecile pretence' of culture were on offer to them, through which the state could assuage its conscience whilst maintaining the necessary division of labour between minds and bodies (1988: 112).[1] Beyond this schooling, they knew, lay their own inevitable capture by the industrial system – the laundry and the bottle factory. Either way, Lawrence insisted, the political correlative of this system could not be an educated democracy. 'A little learning *is* a dangerous thing,' he warns; the uninstructible majority will come to see the educated classes as 'tricksters' – 'And once *that* happens, what becomes of your State?' (1988: 96).

To avert this threat of (presumably) chaos and insurrection within actually existing democracy, educational and political systems alike should turn, Lawrence argued, towards the 'true democracy' of leadership (1988: 109). In order to make crucial decisions about their pupils' aptitudes and subsequent placement within a new system of education (of which more below), leading educators would have to be 'priests of life, deep in the wisdom of life' (107). Inevitably, this system would give rise to a hierarchy of new and distinct classes where class is defined, no longer by money, but by 'life-quality' or 'quality of being' (107–8). As if grappling with an enveloping conceptual organicism that will not provide him with a precise analogy, Lawrence writes: 'As the leaves of a tree accumulate towards blossom, so will the great bulk of mankind at all time accumulate towards its leaders' (109).

This chapter will not be an exercise in exonerating Lawrence for his views on education; throughout, I sustain as an absolute the conviction that the denial of universal literacy is toxic. At the same time, through the lenses of technics and of the pharmakon, my discussion works to differentiate Lawrence from those surrounding contexts of anti-democratic literary modernism. Within such contexts a construct such as '*the great mass of humanity*' would normally connect Lawrence's educational thinking to the discourse and pseudo-science of eugenics. As Tim Armstrong has suggested, a general cultural-modernist desire 'to *intervene* in the body' brought it into inevitable if complex relation with the political interventionist aspirations of eugenics (1998: 6–8). The collective body that was the 'great mass' existed for eugenics both as a threat – if, in the wake of the universal elementary education established by the reforms of the later nineteenth century in Britain, it became defined as an expanded public eager to read and write – and as an opportunity: that is, for the shaping of racialised identity and destiny. In previous work, I have suggested an element of paradox in Lawrence's relation to eugenic dehumanisation, encapsulated in the tension between his overt reaction to Wilfred Trotter's *Instincts of the Herd in Peace and War* (1915) as 'a great lie' and 'loud-mouthed impertinence', and the ease with which his own views might be assimilated into eugenic policies of collective manipulation (Wallace 2005: 44–8, 152–5). Where bold pronouncements on the denial of literacy to people defined as a great mass is concerned, what price loud-mouthed impertinence?[2]

Undoubtedly, Lawrence's critique of liberal-democratic education and of the extension of literacy finds resonances across the field of a eugenically oriented literary modernism. In the opening Vorticist salvo of *BLAST 1* (1914), Wyndham Lewis declared education's propensity to 'destroy the creative instinct'; art therefore flourished where education was absent, but in a sense of the 'popular' that emphasised individuals rather than 'the People' (2009: 7). In later writings such as *The Art of Being Ruled* (1926), Lewis continued to allude to the democratic illusion of educational systems. W. B. Yeats's *On the Boiler* (1939) is seen by Donald J. Childs as a culmination of degenerationist fears held by the poet since the turn of the century: 'Forcing reading and writing on those who wanted neither was the worst part of the violence which for two centuries has been creating that hell wherein we suffer,' Yeats wrote (qtd in Childs 2001: 149). T. S. Eliot's poetry is held by John Carey (1992) to embody a distaste for those urban masses who were spiritually dead yet insistent on reading. Yet the actually more nuanced and sustained position of Eliot's *The Idea of a Christian Society* (1939) bears some comparison with Lawrence's defence of the working-class child. By 'substituting instruction for education' and 'fostering a notion of *getting on* to which the alternative is a hopeless apathy', Liberalism facilitated 'its own negation' and demonstrated the 'chaos of ideals and confusion of thought in our large scale mass education' (Eliot 1939: 16, 40). Eliot's firm if reluctant conclusion – 'however undemocratic it may sound' – is that a coherent culture could be maintained only by a 'positive distinction . . . between the educated and the uneducated' (40). Before tracing a eugenical subtext in *Mrs Dalloway*, Donald J. Childs highlights the visceral nature of Virginia Woolf's diary response to a group of institutionalised patients she had 'had to' walk past in public – 'They should certainly be killed' (qtd in Childs 2001: 23). Woolf's terminology – 'a long line of imbeciles' – recalls the reliance of Aldous Huxley's prose writings on such categories. Huxley's essays from the late 1920s through the 1930s are steeped in degenerationism, posing an intriguing question about their relationship with the satire on eugenics that *Brave New World* (1932) seemed to be. Huxley's abiding concern with 'varieties' of inherited intelligence led to periodic reflections on how this might be squared with the democratic expansion of education and literacy. In the essay 'Education', contemplating the self-evidently 'enormous' defects of the current 'ordinary system of mass education', Huxley's endorsement was of a system aspiring to meet the needs of individual students (1927: 113). Whilst more overtly individualist than Lawrence's thinking, Huxley's scepticism about the 'hopes of the ardent educationists of the democratic epoch' when these are based on the fallacy that 'all minds are alike and can profit by the same system of training' resonates strongly with Lawrence's slightly earlier condemnation of educational bullying (Huxley 1927: 98–9).

Lawrence certainly had more lived experience than any of these peers as an educator within the state systems under critique. This experience informed an educative drive in his work that has begun to attract more scholarly attention.[3] The two essays by Lawrence under discussion here are distinctive, within literary modernism's attention to education, in their scale, creative experimentalism and directness of intent. Through a comparison with the concept of technics as this is elaborated in the philosophies of Gilbert Simondon (1924–89) and Bernard Stiegler (1952–2020), my aim will be to open out the complexity of what it meant for Lawrence to educate bodies as much as to educate people or 'the People'. Where Aldous Huxley could briskly assert that the 'problem of bodily training has been solved', more or less, because the body is visible, whereas the continuing problem of mental education was that 'we are unable to see the mind' (1927: 89, 91), Lawrence's far less reductive deployment of mind–body dualism warrants new attention. This therefore will be to reapproach the scandal of '*The great mass of humanity should never learn to read and write*', but without seeking to redeem it: I reiterate here that Lawrence's proposition is toxic. Rather, the chapter is a way of testing out the possibility of taking such toxicity at its word, by applying to Lawrence's views the ambivalent concept of the pharmakon that is associated with toxicity itself. How might a poison relate to its inherent potential as antidote or cure? Conversely, in what sense did the strong curative or benevolent motivation of Lawrence's educational thinking – 'But particularly', he writes in *Fantasia of the Unconscious*, 'let us take care of the children' – become so poisonous (2004: 119)?

The principle of the pharmakon is itself at the heart of technics as this is elaborated implicitly in Simondon but more overtly in Stiegler. In each, to think of technics is effectively to take up Martin Heidegger's injunction to consider more carefully the meaning of technology in human lives; it is also, both in Simondon's 'social pedagogics' (Bardin and Menegalle 2015: 15) and in Stiegler's tireless critiques of early twenty-first century industrial populism, to think about the principle of care, particularly the care of children. Care is at the heart of the pharmakon's ambivalence, as Stiegler, following D. W. Winnicott, notes in defining the pharmakon as a transitional object first encountered in the form of the mother's care for the child. It is not something that ex-ists so much as con-sists, and which begins to transmit to the child the feeling that life is worth living:

> The *pharmakon* is at once what *enables* care to be taken and that *of which* care must be taken – in the sense that it is necessary to *pay attention*: its power is *curative to the immeasurable extent (dans la mesure et la démesure)* that it is also destructive. (Stiegler 2013: 4)

In each of the two closely related essays upon which this chapter draws, Lawrence meditates upon the potential of education to be both curative and destructive. The first version of 'Education of the People' was drafted late in 1918, while the second and only published version was begun in mid-1920. Neither appeared in Lawrence's lifetime, being successively rejected by the *Times Educational Supplement* and Stanley Unwin. *Fantasia of the Unconscious* was begun in June 1921 and published in New York on 23 October 1922. In what follows I take the latitude to move freely between 'Education' and *Fantasia*, on the grounds of the significant emphases they share, and despite certain differences of orientation. 'Education' sets out as an ideological critique of the British elementary and secondary education system, containing within it a detailed blueprint and rationale for an alternative system. Yet insofar as this alternative system is grounded in the call for 'a new mode of human relationship', based in its turn on 'a different notion of the nature of children' (Lawrence 1988: 115, 117), the essay presents one of Lawrence's first elaborations of an idiosyncratic schema for the understanding of human consciousness – the so-called solar plexus theory, a physiology of four dynamic centres in the body.

Fantasia, setting out as an essay on 'child consciousness', reprises this schema by developing the passing pronouncement made in the intervening essay, *Psychoanalysis and the Unconscious*, that 'Education now is widely at sea,' and that we must understand the nature of consciousness at the four dynamic centres 'before we can even begin to consider a genuine system of education' (2004: 31–2). But it also directly returns to the scene of 'Education'; the latter's suggestion, for example, that 'We should be wise if by decree we shut up all elementary schools at once, and kept them shut' (1988: 100) becomes in *Fantasia* the (ventriloquised) decree itself: 'Parents, the State can no longer be responsible for the mind and character of your children. From the first day of the coming year, all schools will be closed for an indefinite period' (2004: 114). Both essays reflect upon the parental responsibilities ensuing from this fantasy scenario, notably *Fantasia*'s chapter on the nature of parental love, tying parenting to a set of highly heteronormative nostrums on sexual relationships and family roles – concerns with which 'Education' had also concluded.

Another injection of toxin, then, into the body politic: the closure of schools, to help deliver illiteracy. Driving each gesture is a technics, concerning a human relation to materiality, where the latter signifies both the physical world to which we belong and the tools and technologies we generate within it. Its core in Lawrence is situated thus: 'In the early years, a child's education should be entirely non-mental'; 'There should be no effort made to teach children to think' (1988: 142; 2004: 112). 'Early years' means pre-school only; *Fantasia* proceeds to construct a blueprint for a subsequent school system which actually adheres to a universal if differentiated literacy. Elementary education between the years of seven and twelve would consist of mornings given over to reading, writing and arithmetic, and afternoons given over to martial sports, games, exercise and workshops in which each child would be trained in a highly gender-specific 'domestic craft'. This system, Lawrence proposes, would provide 'a common human basis, a common radical understanding' (1988: 98). At the age of twelve, those less amenable to intellectual study would continue with two hours of 'mental' education per day, while those attending secondary schools with a curriculum extending to languages and science would continue with an hour a day in craft workshops and physical training. When apprenticeship and semi-apprenticeship paths are taken at the age of fourteen, provision for reading and mental education continues for all; conversely, those who proceed to colleges at sixteen for the further study of science, liberal arts or pure and technical arts would continue and emerge with a training in at least one technical skill or craft.

Despite, then, this system's seemingly inflexible categorisations, locking young people into the strata of a new class society through the decisions of priestly educators, the division between 'mental' and 'non-mental' in Lawrence's educational thinking was not a division of people as such. Not even the scholar deemed to have 'no capacity for true learning or understanding' would receive a non-mental education (1988: 96). Rather, the non-mental as such becomes in Lawrence's writing a rebalancing principle of physical relatedness infinitely extending beyond the school years – a kind of lifelong unlearning, or permanent pursuit of the knowledge of 'how *not to know*' (2004: 111). 'A good part of the life of every human creature', he asserts, 'should pass in mindless, active occupation . . . Busy, intent, absorbed work, forgetfulness, this is one of the joys of life' (1988: 154). It is both typical and apposite that Lawrence should offer concrete and sensuous examples of this joy of life, and here is the first of two such examples around which I want to weave a comparison with the realm of technics.

> Supposing we are to learn to solder a kettle . . . . It is a question of *knowing*, by direct physical contact, your kettle-substance, your kettle-curves, your solder, your soldering-iron, your fire, your resin, and all the fusing, slipping interaction of all these. A question of direct knowing by contact, not a question of understanding . . . . Know by immediate sensual contact. Know by the tension and reaction of the muscles, know, know profoundly but forever untellably, at the spontaneous primary centres. (154)

Let us take a detour around and back to this scenario of direct knowing, of kettle-substance and kettle-curves, through Gilbert Simondon. Simondon's principal commentator, Muriel Combes (2013), maintains that the apparently stark difference of orientation between his two major works, *On the Mode of Existence of Technical Objects* (1958) and *L'Individu et sa genèse physico-biologique* (*The Individual and its Physico-Biological Genesis*) (1964), for some time obscured their common ground as studies of ontology. As Elizabeth Grosz puts it, Simondon's concern was with 'the various processes of self-formation that create what is', whether these entities are human or technological, organic or inorganic (2017: 170). Combes alludes to the debt to Simondon in Gilles Deleuze and Félix Guattari, and insofar as Deleuze and Guattari located in experimental modernist fiction (that of Lawrence and Woolf in particular) a sense of the impersonal forces that bring beings and their haecceities into play, we might see in Simondon's conception of transindividuation a key element in modernist theories of becoming. This is implicit in the way Simondon takes up the Heideggerian challenge to think the 'essence' of technology as a means of human bringing-forth or revealing, rather than as a mode of instrumentality simply defined by use. Heidegger had argued that, in the context of the centrality of technology to the project of modernity, the instrumentalist attitude was extended to the physical world as mere raw material for human disposition, and to humans within that world as 'standing-reserve' – a general orientation of the Anthropocene which is now widely acknowledged to have helped precipitate environmental crisis. Within this state of unfreedom, technology's essence could never be approached if simply on its own terms: 'the essence of technology is by no means anything technological' (Heidegger 2011: 217). We may at this point recall Lawrence's questioning of the refusal of educational idealism to be understood on any but its own terms – as if the essence of literacy were by no means anything defined by reading and writing. For Simondon, the precondition of an emancipated thinking of technology was closely comparable to Heidegger's emphasis upon the Greek root word *technē* as signifying the activity or skill both of the craftsman and of the artist, linked in turn to *epistēmē* where both are general terms for knowing but, in the latter case, as a state of immersion that at least invites comparison with the 'direct knowing' we might need to solder a kettle: 'to be entirely at home in something, to understand and be expert in it' (Heidegger 2011: 222).

How, then, does technics, or technicity, differ from technology? In Simondon, this is a question of the equivalence of culture and technology as forms of human making, modulating into a way of teaching technology that assumes this equivalence with culture whilst maintaining a meaningful distinction between them. As a pedagogical enterprise, Simondon's technics was a way of heading off a Two Cultures divide before it could even begin to take root. Like Lawrence, Simondon endorsed a rebalancing approach to technical instruction; culture and technology would ideally be a 'simultaneous encounter' from elementary education onwards, though culture 'should be focused more towards adulthood' while technical education 'should begin sooner' (Simondon 2015: 22). In a 1965 essay, Simondon is strident about the 'murderous and noxious' primacy of cultural education (2015: 23); literary culture, he had earlier claimed, is 'enslaved' to historical retrospect, with the literary work as '*social witness*' to the existence and authority of 'determinate social groups' (2017: 124). Culture's subsequent misunderstanding of technological objects was a 'facile humanism' (Simondon 2017: 15) based on fearful idolatry of the machine and framed by a master–slave morality: the technical object is either an assemblage of inert matter awaiting instrumental use, as in Heideggerian standing-reserve, or a threat to the integrity and mastery of the human, typified by the modern(ist) demonisation of the robot.

Restoring the necessary 'human dynamisms' to education therefore entailed for Simondon conferring upon technology the same kind of 'pure' or autonomous value as enjoyed by the cultural artefact or scientific theory: 'A child ought to know what self-regulation is, or what a positive reaction is, in the same way a child knows mathematical theorems' (Simondon 2017: 124, 19). This remained a 'minority' knowledge, 'implicit, non-reflective, and habitual', and based on the everyday encounter with technical objects in the heart of the child's environment; an adult could not go back to childhood to acquire new aspects of it. Yet, as Thomas LaMarre argues, this minority/majority distinction transcends that between juvenility and maturity, and must instead be understood in Deleuze and Guattari's sense of a relation within the politics of knowledge (LaMarre in Combes 2013: 106–7). Hence the relation of the minor to the major in technological education contains both equivalence – 'It would be entirely wrong to consider this technical training as necessarily inferior to a training using intellectual symbols' – and necessity: the 'encyclopedism' which, for Simondon, characterises the abstract and conceptual technics of the adult 'must integrate the education of the child' (Simondon 2017: 108, 122).

For this technics 'learned by the child', however, Simondon requires a discourse on irrationality, instinct and intuition, and of bodily affect, that carries broader and surprising historical ramifications. As in Lawrence's 'direct knowing' and 'untellable' sensual knowledge of the soldering process, the young child apprehends technology 'in the form of a dynamic intuition', a 'very profound acquisition' made through 'early habitual immersion' and forming the basis of a *manual dexterity* possessed almost by instinct' (Simondon 2017: 124, 106). Simondon arrives at a comparison of the craftsman with the magician, 'endowed with a power of intuition and complicity with the world that will give him a very remarkable aptitude' that is 'operational rather than intellectual'; the 'true technician loves the matter upon which he acts', is 'on its side', forming a 'couple' with it, and is loved by matter in return – indeed, obeyed 'with the faithful docility of an animal who has recognised his master' (Simondon 2017: 109). Appropriately, *On the Mode of Existence of Technical Objects* here makes its only reference to imaginative literature, citing E. T. A. Hoffmann's story 'The Mines of Falun' for its figure of the old miner who loves the mine as part of a 'co-natural relation with underground nature', and whose ghost warns the young sailor of the fate awaiting anyone who 'is not endowed with the power of participation' (2017: 107). Technical 'skill', for Simondon, is not then a 'violent despotism' but a relationship of 'complicity', a 'participation' driven by a 'force' of 'recurrent causality' (2017: 109).

Concurrent with this arresting metaphysic, Simondon's technics also insist upon an empirical grounding. The fact that 'there is something alive in a technical ensemble' follows from the inventive life invested in it by human purpose: 'What resides in the machines is human reality, human gesture fixed and crystallized into working structures' (Simondon 2017: 140, 18). In this, as LaMarre explains, Simondon retains the ontological distinction between humans and machines, resisting recruitment for any post-human kinship or blurring of boundaries (LaMarre in Combes 2013: 80). Yet, again, an egalitarianism emerges, positing an ontological equality or 'reciprocity of exchange' between humans and machines: the human is 'between machines rather than above them' (Simondon 2017: 150). At the heart of this equality is inevitably a rethinking of the machine itself. Simondon insists on exposing the widespread error of misconstruing all mechanism as automatism. To make a machine automatic is to limit strictly its functionality; to raise a machine's technicity requires, on the contrary, the creation of a margin of indeterminacy enabling sensitivity to information, and hence modification, from outside. The 'open machine' therefore emerges in Simondon as the realisation of a progressive technics in which all such machines together presuppose the human as both 'permanent organiser' and 'living interpreter' (2017: 17).[4] At one level, this translates into the physical pleasure or even 'euphoria' that accompanies the acquisition of a new, improved tool: for the craftsman in this instance, it is 'the entire corporeal schema that expands against his limitations, that dilates and frees itself; the impression of awkwardness diminishes ... for the tool is an extension of the organ' (Simondon 2017: 130).

At another level, that of the philosophy of transindividual becoming, the open machine's sensitivity to information and improvement expresses that principle of 'transduction', common to 'the human being, and the living being more generally', by which energy and information are not merely stored but assimilated and then form the materials for modification (Simondon 2017: 155–7).

It is important to stress that, for Lawrence, the 'immediate physical contact' of soldering a kettle perpetuates a 'mode of childish intelligence'; this surely resonates with the 'implicit, non-reflective, and habitual' technical knowledge that, for Simondon, is held by the child (Lawrence 2004: 124; Simondon 2017: 103). In somewhat cosmological mode, Lawrence could characterise this 'clue to early education' as 'the attuning of the kinetic energy of the motor centres to the vast sway of the earth's centre'; in more empirical mode, the child was 'a small vital organism which has direct dynamic *rapport* with the objects of the outer universe' (1988: 144; 2004: 121). Lawrence pushed against the boundaries of humanistic representation in thus describing the 'circuit' that henceforth comes to exist between any person and an 'external object with which he has an affective connection' (2004: 153). The said object may be 'human, or animal, or plant, or quite inanimate', but there is nevertheless a 'vital flow' as 'definite and concrete' as the electric current in tram cars, lamps or radio wires, and felt equally, Lawrence asserts, in the 'magnetism' and 'dynamic vibratory connection' he has with his dog or canary, the cells of the ash tree he loved as a child, or his old boots (153). As Tim Armstrong has noted, the fictions of Lawrence and other modernists register a fascination with that 'vibrating world' consequent upon the discovery of electro-magnetic energy and field theory in late nineteenth-century physics (2005: 115–34). The 'fusing, slipping interaction' of elements in the temporary soldering ensemble conveys a radical instability which is yet also participatory ('your kettle-substance, your kettle-curves') – what Simondon characterises as the 'entire corporeal schema' that 'dilates and frees itself', and in which 'intuition and complicity' are manifest in neither 'consciousness' nor 'discourse'. Simondon is as ready as Lawrence to frame such direct knowing in terms of the physical grace and pride of an overtly ableist definition of human worth: the diminishing of 'awkwardness' that, he states, accompanies the splicing of tool and organ(ism) resonates with Lawrence's assertion that, without such technical dexterity, we 'are nothing: clumsy, mechanical clowns, or pinched little automata' (1988: 144). We arrive at the second of my key illustrations from 'Education of the People' – its subject, the 'quick' and 'infinite' complexity of washing dishes:

> The actual doing things is in itself a joy. If I wash the dishes I learn a quick, light touch of china and earthenware, the feel of it, the weight and roll and poise of it, the peculiar hotness, the quickness or slowness of its surface. I am at the middle of an infinite complexity of motions and adjustments and quick, apprehensive contacts. Nimble faculties hover and play along my nerves, the primal consciousness is alert in me. Apart from all the moral or practical satisfaction derived from a thing well done, I have the *mindless* motor activity and reaction in primal consciousness, which is a pure satisfaction. If I am to be well and satisfied, as a human being, a large part of my life must pass in mindless motion, quick busy activity in which I am neither bought nor sold, but acting alone and free from the centre of my own active isolation. Not self-consciously, however. Not watching my own reactions. If I wash dishes, I wash them to get them clean, nothing else. (151)

While returning to ontological equality in the direct encounter with china- and earthenware-substance, the 'joy' of actual doing things is here expressed epistemologically and educatively – 'I learn', 'nimble faculties' and 'alert' primal consciousness, 'complexity', 'apprehensive contacts'. The principle of care reasserts itself; health and a varied 'satisfaction' are dependent upon a preponderance of 'mindless' motion. We have seen how 'childish intelligence' feeds into majority life: 'craftsmanship', for example, is a 'physical- spontaneous intelligence' (1988: 113). Washing the dishes introduces a yet more radical openness to alternative modes of intelligence because embedded in everyday, putatively unskilled activity, and pertaining to lives perhaps spent immersed in the so-called non-mental.

This pluralising of intelligence via technics has inevitable implications for the role of democracy in Lawrence's educational thinking. What, after all, of the rights of the 'uninstructible'? 'Is not radical *unlearnedness*', Lawrence asks, 'just as true a form of self-expression, and just as desirable a state, for many natures (even the bulk), as learnedness?' (1988: 95). Washing the dishes must not therefore be recuperated back into the ideal of the literate self-conscious subject; its intelligence as a form of mindlessness is adequate to itself, sheerly different and yet common to all. It becomes, with that peculiar Lawrentian faculty of powering on through the vulnerability to satire, an act of resistance to that realm of the 'bought and sold' which itself shapes the idea of modern democratic self-consciousness, at the same time distributing and constraining access to it. The first step towards a true ontological equality, Lawrence claimed, was therefore to recognise universal inequality or an 'equipoise in difference' (1988: 165), such that each person's uniqueness is deemed sufficient unto itself. As in Simondon's technics, this condition was also a life-equality with the world of things.

In such ideas of critique, resistance and alternative possibilities of healthy satisfaction, a path of comparison opens up to the elaboration of technics in the work of Bernard Stiegler. Since the first volume of his *Technics and Time* sequence in 1994, Stiegler has written a quickening succession of volumes, often overlapping in content, in response to a global process of technological capture generating a 'systemic stupidity' which he regards as 'spinning out of control' (Stiegler 2013: 22, 89). Ironically, Stiegler is less interested than Simondon in the essence and meaning of technological objects *per se*; his critique of the digital centres on its commercial and corporate ownership within late capitalism.[5] Yet Stiegler shares with Simondon an essentially affirmative theory of technics, explicitly related in his case to the principle of pharmacological care. Grammaticisation, or the history of the exteriorisation of human memory through a range of hypomnemata, all of which oscillate between poison and cure, is, Stiegler insists, a necessary human history; it stretches, we might say, from verbal literacy to the Internet of Things. The value of Jacques Derrida's rereading of the pharmakon in Plato was in unsettling the Platonic concept of anamnesic memory as the 'source of all knowledge' constituted by 'the pure autonomy of thinking for oneself' (Stiegler 2013: 18). Writing, as 'the discretrization of the flow of speech', is, for example, a notable stage in the process of grammatisation. Within this critical technics, it becomes less easy either to idolise or to demonise technology as the self's other. To simplify, writing and books are technologies, forms of hypomnesis or, in the modernist terms of Stéphane Mallarmé, our 'spiritual instruments' (quoted in Stiegler 2014: 6).

Lawrence's version of this might be found in his spirited endorsement of the human 'thought-adventure', from the 1924 essay 'Books':

> Man is a thought-adventurer. He has thought his way down the far ages. He used to think in little images of wood or stone: then in hieroglyphs on obelisks and clay rolls and papyrus. Now he thinks in books, between two covers. (1988: 197)

Changing cultural technologies are not simply repositories of thought: thought happens 'in' them, Lawrence holding books responsible for the tortured interiority of modernity whose counterpart became psychoanalysis. 'Education of the People', of course, identified the industrial class system as a material limitation on the possibility of this thought-adventuring. Reading and writing are both the instruments of the peoples' potential emancipation into the thought-adventure (quite obviously, Lawrence's own) and, in the existent system, the means of their being denied it. However, denial is effected not by exclusion or at least the tokenisation of literacy alone, but by its obverse, the presentation of universal literacy as a pure good. In what forms other than literacy might the thought-adventure occur? Lawrence, in a sense, insisted on thinking the technics of literacy pharmacologically, as poised between cure and poison, furiously critiquing a system that refused or was unable to see beyond its own educational dominant.

Where Lawrence located industrial capture in educational policy and the unequal distribution of an already idealised literacy, for Stiegler a much more overt and physically invasive mode of capture is at stake. He critiques the collusion between digital technology and global capitalism that issues in an industrialisation of the spirit. A 'constant industrial channelling' and 'generalised addiction' begins in infancy with exposure to 'psychotechnologies' now imbued with the same self-evidence of value that universal literacy once held (Stiegler 2013: 81, 27). 'Audiovisual transitional space' is, however, 'purely and simply toxic for the child's brain', rendering the psychic apparatus 'weakened' and 'fragile', and causing a 'massive destruction of attention' (Stiegler 2013: 69, 81–2). Stiegler cites the research of Katherine Hayles on the way in which the brains of the youngest children are becoming differently structured to those of previous generations, characterised by a diverse and oscillating 'hyperattention' rather than the 'deep' critical attention deriving from a training in reading and writing: this, Hayles contends, 'poses serious challenges to every level of education' (qtd in Stiegler 2010b: 73).

In adults the process of capture continues, Stiegler argues, through the decomposition of the libido or creative spirit into the merely acquisitional, short-term drives required by late capitalism. Transindividuation, Simondon's concept of the circuits by which individuals are thrown into being, is, for Stiegler, threatened and disabled. Instead, there is a generalised 'proletarianization', as the surrender of memory to computer and archival technologies creates 'economic actors who are without knowledge because they are without memory' – a proletarianisation, therefore, to which the middle classes are also subject (Stiegler 2010a: 35). With pharmacological thinking overridden by commercial motivation, the propensity of digital culture to act as a disempowerment and dispossession of the faculty of memory overbalances its potential to augment and assist that memory. Significantly, the knowledge lost is, Stiegler insists, a knowledge of practice rather than theory: whereas the industrial age produced 'labour power without *savoir-faire*', the post-industrial produces 'buying power without *savoir vivre*' (2010a: 43).

The diagnosis that Stiegler and Lawrence share is that modernity threatens the dispossession of practical and technical knowledge – the knowledge of what to do, how to live and, recalling the precarity of the pharmacological relationship between child and mother, of what makes life worth living. This is primarily a failure of care for the young, and is signalled in the polemics of each by an insistence on generational responsibility and maturity. For Stiegler, carelessness is built into our epochal psychotechnological organisation as its *'very principle'* (2010a: 126). Irresponsibility consists partly in the structural absence of regulation, whether of marketing practices targeting children, or of the technologies of social networking, 'for which no political economy and no system of care is prescribed by any public authority' (2010a: 44). Simondon had defined 'technical wisdom' as a responsibility for 'technical realities', advocating that 'every human being' should be responsible for taking part in technical ensembles, in the same way that travel is undertaken to acquire culture, in order to become 'connected with a network of universal technics' (2017: 159, 235). While Lawrence refused to conflate childish intuitive understanding with the 'deep wisdom of responsibility' required of parents, it is clear that, for him, the intelligence of the child extends into or even beyond a mature ethical responsibility: young 'creatures, not persons' can identify any adult falsehood or ideal-benevolent bullying, he writes, because 'children have an infinite understanding of the soul's passionate variabilities' (2004: 92; 1988: 54; 2004: 94).

For Stiegler, however, it is, in the main, the techno-capitalist transformation of adults into consumers that dispossesses parents of the maturity that would allow then to be responsible for their children. Lawrence's education essays often, too, read like manuals of parental guidance in the face of dispossession, sometimes enveloped in a rage directed at state and societal bullying and imbecility. In Stiegler's polemical voice, curiously alike yet different, we can perhaps hear something of Lawrence's direct provocation, as in this characterisation of a parental infantilisation based on

> the massive development of service-based societies that discharge them of the obligations of their own existences, that is, of their responsibilities as mature adults. In the end, this results in the elimination of their own desire as well as the desire of their own children, to the strict extent that the latter can no longer identify with them, both because these parents no longer know anything, and are no longer responsible for anything, having themselves become overgrown children, and also because the process of primary identification has been short-circuited by the psycho-power of psychotechnologies. (2013: 88)

In a certain unequivocal sense Stiegler's work nevertheless provides a corrective, or perhaps an antidote, to Lawrence's *'the great mass of humanity should never learn to read and write'*. In what he calls the current 'battle for intelligence', the late capitalist hegemony of psychotechnologies depends upon the dismantling of a prior model of critical literacy predicated upon reading and writing (Stiegler 2010b: 89). To repeat my earlier emphasis, this offers no redemption for Lawrence's scandalous proposition. Yet to think pharmacologically is to see any antidote as itself equivocal. As if in anticipation of sceptical or, indeed, hostile readers, progressive and democratic educationalists, Lawrence in 'Education' posed the teacherly question: have we 'become too conscious?' (1988: 130). The answer is 'Not at all'; merely, he asserts, 'we have become too *fixedly* conscious'. In this chapter I have posited the technics of Simondon and Stiegler as modes of alertness to the dangers of becoming too fixedly conscious in our technologies of intelligence. Lawrence's technics, with its soldering of kettles and washing of dishes, similarly strives to sustain a pharmacological understanding of these technologies, their precarious ability to oscillate between poison and cure, and the potential they might hold for participatory modes of knowledge, education and politics. My references to Lawrence's provocations therefore lead to a proposition that may seem as scandalous as anything else here: it is that Lawrence surely – clearly? – did not wish to terminate the pursuit of universal literacy or to close all schools. Perhaps we may consider the decrees and declarations of the essays as toxic textual effects, injected into educational debate, or alternatively as antidotes for current ills (administered safe, as it were, in the knowledge that no one would read or act upon them, as the Lawrence of *Fantasia* occasionally and rather archly reminds us: 'There is no danger of the working man ever reading my books, so I shan't hurt him that way'; 2004: 141).

It should not go amiss that Lawrence's writings on education contain their own overt pharmacology. 'We have almost poisoned the mass of humanity to death with *understanding*', he writes, while 'love and benevolence are our poison, poison to the giver, and still more poison to the receiver' (2004: 141, 114). Chillingly, in anticipating humanity's potential demise, Lawrence's education essays figure technological warfare as a seemingly ultimate embodiment of this idealism, and with it the diabolical invention of poison gas. 'We're making a careful study of poison-gases', the 'problem of the future' being the quest to find the strongest (Lawrence 2004: 163, 162). With the bitterness that had characterised his reaction to the outbreak of the Great War, Lawrence raged that any species that could warp its intelligence, that pharmacologically fragile, 'most double-edged blessing of all', to such an end only deserved its own fate: 'how you deserve your own poison-gases! How you deserve to perish in your own stink' (1988: 105; 2004: 162). Poison gas was the ultimate result of the failure to think human consciousness and its technologies as pharmacological – a failure to consider exactly how life is worth living. Bernard Stiegler, building on Simondon, proposes a sophisticated technics or 'pharmacological intelligence' leading to newly cultivated 'systems of care' that might become the concrete expression of an 'art of living' (2010a: 126). Through a dynamic balance of cure and poison, Lawrence's technics was dedicated to the elaboration and education of this 'art of living', in aspiring towards 'a common human basis, a common radical understanding' (1988: 98).

Notes

1. Ghosting the phrase 'the alternative intelligence of the uninstructible', and indeed this chapter as a whole, are Jacques Rancière's theories of the democracy of modern fiction and poetry. On this reading, modern writing proposes the destruction of the hierarchical model 'dividing humanity between an elite of active beings and a multitude of passive ones' (Rancière 2017: xxxiii). In the poetry of John Keats, for example, this issues in a new 'art of life' founded on the principles of education of each and all, and of an equivalence of intelligences (77). Natasha Periyan (2019) has noted that Lawrence would have known, from his teacher training, of the example of French schoolmaster Joseph Jacotot, who, in earlier work of Rancière's such as *The Ignorant Schoolmaster: Five Lessons in Intellectual Emancipation* (1991), is the educational figure for the model of equal intelligences.

2. Lawrence's counter-enlightenment rhetoric can be a gift to selective quotation. Thus *'The great mass of humanity . . .'* shows up in John Carey's notorious characterisation of modernism's collusion with eugenics, where Lawrence's 'hope', Carey contends, is that illiteracy would allow the masses to 'relapse into purely physical life' (1992: 15).
3. See, for example, Benjamin D. Hagen (2020), Natasha Periyan (2019) and the 2016 edition of Études Lawrenciennes on Education and Culture in Lawrence's work, available at <https://journals.openedition.org/lawrence/251> (last accessed 16 June 2020).
4. For an application of this 'open machine' to modes of resolution in two of Lawrence's short stories, see Wallace (2019).
5. For an apposite contrast between Simondon's 'humanism after the death of man', stressing human potentiality, and Stiegler's Lacanian sense of the lack for which technology provides 'massive overcompensation', see LaMarre (2013: 98).

Works Cited

Armstrong, Tim (1998), *Modernism, Technology, and the Body*. Cambridge: Cambridge University Press.
Armstrong, Tim (2005), *Modernism: A Cultural History*. Cambridge: Polity.
Bardin, Andrea and Giovanni Menegalle (2015), 'Introduction to Simondon', *Radical Philosophy*, 189, pp. 15–16.
Carey, John (1992), *The Intellectuals and the Masses: Pride and Prejudice among the Literary Intelligentsia*. London: Faber.
Childs, Donald J. (2001), *Modernism and Eugenics: Woolf, Eliot, Yeats and the Culture of Degeneration*. Cambridge: Cambridge University Press.
Combes, Muriel (2013), *Gilbert Simondon and the Philosophy of the Transindividual*, trans. Thomas LaMarre. Cambridge, MA, and London: MIT Press.
Eliot, T. S. (1939), *The Idea of a Christian Society*. London: Faber.
Grosz, Elizabeth (2017), *The Incorporeal: Ontology, Ethics, and the Limits of Materialism*. New York: Columbia University Press.
Hagen, Benjamin D. (2020), *The Sensuous Pedagogies of Virginia Woolf and D. H. Lawrence*. Clemson, SC: Clemson University Press.
Heidegger, Martin (2011 [1953]), 'The Question Concerning Technology', in *Basic Writings*, ed. David Farrell Krell. London: Routledge, pp. 217–38.
Huxley, Aldous (1927), *Proper Studies*. London: Chatto and Windus.
LaMarre, Thomas (2013), 'Afterword', in Muriel Combes, *Gilbert Simondon and the Philosophy of the Transindividual*, trans. Thomas LaMarre. Cambridge, MA, and London: MIT Press.
Lawrence, D. H. (1988), *Reflections on the Death of a Porcupine and Other Essays*, ed. Michael Herbert. Cambridge: Cambridge University Press.
Lawrence, D. H. (2004), *Psychoanalysis of the Unconscious and Fantasia of the Unconscious*, ed. Bruce Steele. Cambridge: Cambridge University Press.
Lewis, Wyndham, ed. (2009 [1914]), *BLAST 1*. London: Thames and Hudson.
Periyan, Natasha (2019), '*Women in Love* and Education: D. H. Lawrence's Epistemological Critique', *Modernist Cultures*, 14: 3, pp. 357–74.
Rancière, Jacques (2017), *The Lost Thread: The Democracy of Modern Fiction*, trans. Steven Corcoran. London: Bloomsbury.
Simondon, Gilbert (2015 [1965]), 'Culture and Technics', *Radical Philosophy*, 189, pp. 17–23.
Simondon, Gilbert (2017 [1958]), *On the Mode of Existence of Technical Objects*, trans. Cecile Malaspina and John Rogove. Minneapolis and London: Univocal/University of Minnesota Press.

Stiegler, Bernard (2010a), *For a New Critique of Political Economy*, trans. Daniel Ross. Cambridge: Polity.
Stiegler, Bernard (2010b), *Taking Care of Youth and the Generations*, trans. Stephen Barker. Stanford, CA: Stanford University Press.
Stiegler, Bernard (2013), *What Makes Life Worth Living: On Pharmacology*, trans. Daniel Ross. Cambridge: Polity Press.
Stiegler, Bernard (2014), *The Re-enchantment of the World: The Value of Spirit against Industrial Populism*, trans. Trevor Arthur. London: Bloomsbury.
Wallace, Jeff (2005), *D. H. Lawrence, Science and the Posthuman*. Basingstoke: Palgrave.
Wallace, Jeff (2019), '"The Art of Living": D. H. Lawrence's Technologies of the Self', in *D. H. Lawrence, Technology, and Modernity*, ed. Indrek Männiste. New York and London: Bloomsbury, pp. 115–26.

20

GERMS: THE SHOCKS, POLITICS AND AESTHETICS OF MICROBIAL MODERNISM

Maebh Long

IN 1927 AN article in *The Manchester Guardian* gave a wry account of the public acceptance of germs:

> By this time we take it for granted that everything we touch, taste, or handle in our relatively brief passage from cradle to grave is infested with germs. They float in the air we breathe, they swim in the water we drink; they squat malevolently on every coin in our pockets, they roost in their billions about our bedrooms, and hold a witches' sabbath over the breakfast table. Like infants in arms, they travel free of charge in railway carriages; they are superabundantly on the free list of every theatre and dance hall. They reside in kitchens and kinemas, they are equally at home in sausages and sarsaparilla; they bound forth at us from every book we open, and are acquired in almost incredible quantities from the handles of every door we close. ('The Generous Germ' 1927: 8)

When I first read this article in December 2019, I relished its sardonic description of life in an age of germ consciousness. It depicted a microbiological reality to which we, as much as *The Manchester Guardian*'s presumed readers, had adapted and to which we were mostly inured. By April 2020, however, when responses to the Covid-19 pandemic had caused countries across the world to declare states of emergency, shut all but essential services and insist on social distancing or complete isolation, and a new era of anxious hygiene had been ushered in, the irreverent acceptance of 1927 and 2019 seemed remote, and almost shockingly blasé. Covid-19, like the influenza that caused the 1918–19 pandemic, is a virus rather than a bacterium, but our new awareness of a virulent 'germ' of infection has caused us to view the world, and our contact with people within it, through heightened senses of omnipresent threat. We are having to learn about invisible transmission and the seeds of contagion all over again, and modify our behaviour to prevent devastating loss of life. Our new understanding of what we touch and how we protect ourselves places us – tragically – in a unique position to understand what it was like when the world first learned about germs, and how modernity adapted to them.

The gradual public awareness of germs over a century ago had turned the world into an overpopulated place, as spaces suddenly teemed with invisible threats. Shaking hands with strangers became a dangerous venture, and public coughing and spitting became a menace. Trains were seen as breeding grounds for germs, and bacteria in library books made reading perilous. The fly, which had generally been considered harmless, became a carrier of disease, and was denounced in 1911 by the *Ladies Home Journal* as 'The Most Dangerous Animal in the World' (McClary 1980: 37). Domestic tasks took on fresh urgency and precision, which simultaneously elevated women's chores to new levels of importance and scientific rigour while also making them more physically and emotionally burdensome (Tomes 1998: 10). Sending work out to be done was even more risky, however, and in 1912 *Good Housekeeping* warned that commercial laundries could well mix the 'soiled linen of persons suffering from tuberculosis, from typhoid fever, from pneumonia, from diphtheria, and a thousand and one diseases' (Balderston and Gunther 1912: 713).

In the late nineteenth and early twentieth centuries, as the public adjusted to a world in which, as Aldous Huxley punned in *Brave New World* (1932), 'civilisation is sterilization' (Huxley 1947: 137), germs and their omnipresent threat provided rich metaphors for writers of popular and literary works, as their invisible hordes conjured ideas of sly, insidious contagions to the body and the body politic. In 'A Room of One's Own' (1929) Virginia Woolf – who was born the year Robert Koch isolated the tubercle bacillus – refers to the social insistence on women's intellectual inferiority as an 'active and poisonous' germ (Woolf 1959: 82). In *Fantasia of the Unconscious* (1922) D. H. Lawrence describes ideas as 'the most dangerous germs mankind has ever been injected with. They are introduced into the brain by injection, in schools and by means of newspapers, and then we are done for' (Lawrence 2004: 115). By what right, Lawrence asks, do we 'inject into him [the child] our own disease-germs of ideas and infallible motives? By the right of the diseased, who want to infect everybody' (Lawrence 2004: 116). And in the same year Tristan Tzara embraced the germ's power of social disruption by describing Dada as 'a virgin microbe that insinuates itself with the insistence of air into all the spaces that reason hasn't been able to fill with words or conventions' (Tzara 1977: 112).

In this chapter we step back from our current viral disquiet to look at the presence of germs in the late nineteenth and early twentieth centuries, tracing the ways in which modernity responded to developments in germ theory and, later, bacteriology. The modern world was a contagious one, full of catching new ideas and social structures, and bacteria gave writers striking imagery of imperceptible but persistent infections, be they medical, social or intellectual. The growing interest in the microbial was, I argue, part of a modernist aesthetics we can understand as bacteriological – invested in the shock of the microscopic and the threat of the dimly perceived. The germs of a microbial modernism lurk in the corners with the dust, quietly but persistently infiltrating texts and lives.

Knowledge of the 'seeds' of disease predated the nineteenth century, but in Europe and America theories of disease transmission were dominated by the miasmic and the contagic: the former stipulated that illness was environmental, as it stemmed from the noxious gases produced by decaying matter found in certain countries or conditions, while the latter argued that disease was, so to speak, other people, as contagious diseases were transmitted by living hosts. When epidemics were not occurring, however, illness was thought to be internally rather than externally caused, as it was primarily constitutional – the result of inherited susceptibilities exacerbated by poor living habits. In the years before germ theory, contamination of foodstuffs and the dangers of casual contact with strangers were of concern to few, which meant that food was frequently left out all day, strangers often shared beds in hotels, water was drunk unfiltered, and chamber pots were emptied with little thought to water supplies (Tomes 1998: 3).

The mid-nineteenth century brought Louis Pasteur's discovery of the microorganisms involved in fermentation and putrefaction, Joseph Lister's insights into the antiseptic uses of carbolic acid and Robert Koch's identification of the causative agents of tuberculosis, cholera, diphtheria and anthrax, and gradually the germ theory of disease caught scientific and public attention. As Frederick T. Roberts explained to early twentieth-century audiences, germ theory stipulates that 'disease is the result of the direct action upon the body of one or more living pathogenic micro-organisms or bacteria'. The realisation that infectious diseases were caused by a 'contagium vivum' – that is, a living germ – led to the important knowledge that 'a specific organism is the cause of a particular disease, and of no other' (Roberts 1903: 234). The determination of the exact bacterial causes of a range of illnesses changed responses to disease by making medicine more targeted, as incubation periods, infectious periods, modes of contamination and resultant immunity could be determined. Koch's isolation of the tubercle bacillus in 1882, for example, brought bacteriological specificity to tuberculosis, which meant that ill-health was increasingly understood as governed by a particular bacterial aetiology, and less as a constitutional disorder. The modern doctor, then, was slowly becoming a bacteriologist and immunologist, 'one who would have his dwelling in a small apartment adjoining a huge laboratory, and who would carry with him test tubes and antitoxins when he set out to visit his patients by aeroplane' (Worboys 2000: 188).

There were, of course, dissenting voices such as G. W. Bulman's, who in 1893 insisted that cholera was a nervous disorder rather than an illness caused by germs (Bulman 1893: 506). G. B. Shaw was a vociferous opponent of germ theory: in his preface to *The Doctor's Dilemma* (1906) he criticised the medical establishment for making it seem a 'marvel that anyone could possibly survive three days in an atmosphere consisting mainly of countless pathogenic germs', and dismissed bacteriologists as monomaniacal 'witch finders' (Shaw 1922: xxxiii, xxxv). Anti-vivisection magazines regularly published diatribes against bacteriology, such as Shaw's letter in 1918 to the *Vaccination Inquirer*, in which he robustly denied that germs cause disease (Soloski 2014: 49). *The Abolitionist* added evocative imagery to its articles, and on 1 March 1919 showed a greedy bacteriologist counting his ill-gotten gains, all the while laughing at his witch doctor and necromancer predecessors for failing to make earlier superstition as profitable ('His Ancestors' 1919: cover). Peter Fifield's study of patent medicine advertisements in *Cassell's Family Magazine* finds that although cleaning products were drawing strongly on the language of bacteriology in 1895, nostrums continued to be advertised until at least 1905 with little regard to advancements in germ theory, and poor blood, imperfect digestion and fragile nerves were presented instead as the dominant aetiologies (Fifield 2019: 44–5). Older theories such as miasma were often slow to be abandoned, particularly as they offered a form of danger that the general public could sense, and turn-of-the-century novels such as Bram Stoker's *Dracula* (1897) and Joseph Conrad's *The Nigger of the 'Narcissus'* (1897) stage the tension between old and new theories (see, for example, Jørgensen 2015). In *Dracula*, when Lucy sickens from vampiric attacks, differing therapeutic responses clash and endanger her, as Mrs Westenra's commitment to miasma thwarts

Van Helsing's germ theory-indebted approaches (Willis 2007). Similarly, in *The 'Narcissus'*, the stages and transmission of Wait's tuberculosis are represented in terms of microbial infection, while the ship, and London itself, are blanketed by miasmic mists and vapours (Bock 2006).

Even for those convinced by germ theory, the isolation of bacilli did not always provide immediate solutions for treatment, and despite the image of the modern flying doctor, many therapeutic measures went unchanged. Large numbers of 'physicians gradually integrated the theory into their medicine bags as an additional "exciting cause" of the disease, without adjusting their practice' (Ott 1996: 53). However, beliefs in environmental impacts and constitutional weaknesses were gradually supplanted or modified, as scientists and the public began to think in terms of contamination through microorganisms on skin, in food and water, and via insects. Pathé's *Travellers' Nightmare* (1905) and *Sleeping Sickness* (1910), Edison's *Microscopic Pond Life* (1915, released 1917), and the wonderfully titled *The Germ in the Kiss* (1914), along with the pandemic-motivated *Dr Wise on Influenza* (1919) and films on the transmission of germs by flies and the spreading of tuberculosis bacteria, served to give the public insights into the bacteriological and offer graphic warnings about the necessity for hygiene. *Moving Picture World* describes *Sleeping Sickness* as showing the rapid progress of the disease, which served 'to inoculate the lay mind with a far better idea of what sleeping sickness is than the most simply worded treatise on the same subject could do' (*Moving Picture World* 1910: 989). In 1903 a series of short films by Francis Duncan, made for Charles Urban, were shown in London under the general title *The Unseen World: A Series of Microscopic Studies, Photographed by Means of the Urban-Duncan Micro-Bioscope*. Audiences watched shorts that showed the first cinematographic records of living typhoid bacteria, as well as the infamous *Cheese Mites* (1903).

Cheese Mites shows a man amusing himself by looking at his lunch through a magnifying glass, only to be horrified to realise that his Stilton is teeming with creatures previously invisible. The film caused a sensation, and was both hotly discussed and parodied (Berenbaum 2018: 68). In one comedic response, *The Unclean World* (1903), a man also becomes disgusted by the taste of his cheese, and dramatically spitting out his mouthful, reaches for the microscope sitting conveniently beside him. The next shot shows what seems to be a magnified view of minuscule bugs in his lunch, but when he touches them our sense of relative proportions are quickly destroyed, as the bugs and his hands are the same size. He then turns the bugs/bacteria upside down, to reveal that they were not 'living germs' but clockwork toys. Educational films, germ theory and scientific knowledge are thus brought sharply into question, and *The Unclean World* returns to a point made by Hilaire Belloc in his comic poem 'The Microbe' (1897):

> The Microbe is so very small
> You cannot make him out at all [. . .]
> But Scientists, who ought to know,
> Assure us that they must be so . . .
> Oh! Let us never, never doubt
> What nobody is sure about!
> (Belloc 1897: 47–8)

In consuming films with educational content, audiences presume that they are being given transparent, unmediated access to the real, but *The Unclean World* reminds viewers of the dissemblance of art, and through that, calls into question a science depending on the mediation of technology. If film cannot be trusted, how can the viewer rely on the microscope, or the scientific expert? Unlike the man in the silent short, members of the general public do not keep microscopes at the dinner table and cannot confirm the existence of bacteria themselves – they are as obliged to trust scientists as they are obliged to trust the filmmaker.

For the public, germ theory suggested that a constant state of vigilance was required, as places that looked and smelled clean could be perilous, and the public could no longer depend on the evidence of their eyes or noses. Previous understandings of the causes of illness – foul smells, damp conditions, the inheritance of bodily weaknesses – could be perceived by the public and followed an easily understood logic, but now life could be threatened everywhere by the undetectable. The public were being asked to accept the presence of that which is indistinct, unseen and seemingly other to common sense. As such, germs are connected to the indeterminate lines between appearance and actuality, which Woolf plays on in *Orlando* (1928). In a novel queering gender, love, language and the natural world, Woolf describes the love of literature as an infection caused by a

> germ [. . .] bred of the pollen of the asphodel and [. . .] blown out of Greece and Italy, which was of so deadly a nature that it would shake the hand as it was raised to strike, cloud the eye as it sought its prey, and make the tongue stammer as it declared its love. (Woolf 2011: 52)

This deadly germ of reading has, Woolf wryly reports, the fatal effect of making people confuse fiction and reality, and turn everything around them to mist. The next stage of the disease is the desire to write, and so malignant is the germ that men of a weaker constitution than Orlando would try, and fail, to compose great works, thereby falling into consumption and death. The germ of reading turns certainties into haze, which not only parodies anxious public perception of every germ but, appropriately for *Orlando*, mirrors the destabilisation of limits caused by the throng of germs on the body. Germs mean that the limits of the self extend uncertainly, and they also disrupt the self's singularity. Acknowledging the presence of germs means acknowledging that each individual is legion: inside and on the surface of each individual is a multitude. If Darwin unpicked the immutable, perfectly formed human, and Freud undid the self-knowing ego, bacteriologists rendered the body a metropolis full of dark corners and unknown threats, filled with entities that are us and not us. Germs not only represent contagion, but the dissolution of seemingly clear categories and identities.

Belief in the invisible is difficult, even when the majority of a population is religious, but social behaviour during this period was gradually modified in response to the general acceptance of unseen yet pervasive threats to health. In 1882 Clifford Allbutt announced, perhaps slightly prematurely, that 'Germ theory had become germ fact,' but despite some resistance the new century saw bacterial theories of disease become the lingua franca of public health medicine (Worboys 2000: 194, 275). Bacteriologists could map the circulation of germs, which helped growing public health services interrupt the spread of disease (Tomes 1998: 6). Through germ theory, surgical and hygienic standards in hospitals began to improve, and the public began to see reasons to change habits in dress, contact and general hygiene. Long skirts on women and long beards on men began to be considered unsanitary, to be abandoned for a more modern, antiseptic way of living. Modernist architecture, particularly after the First World War and the 1918–19 influenza pandemic, was deeply invested in promoting health and was influenced by germ theory, in particular by the tubercle bacillus. Defining features of modernist architectural style, such as flat roofs, balconies, summerhouses and the recliner chair that so impressed Hans Castorp in Thomas Mann's *The Magic Mountain* (1924), can be linked to the sanatorium movement, where rest, open air and sun were used in the treatment of pulmonary tuberculosis. Sunlight was thought to have antiseptic effects and inhibit germs, and so the modern aesthetic included long windows and sun traps (Wilk 2006: 255). Le Corbusier, for example, included sun parlours in his famous Villa Savoye in Poissy (1929), noting that they had 'proved so successful in the United States in combating tuberculosis' (Campbell 2005: 472). The asepsis of modernist design can be taken literally, as its well-lit rooms, smooth, washable surfaces and uncluttered interiors can be connected to the knowledge of germs. Nancy Tomes writes that the 'cult of the new and the gospel of germs were but two facets of the same enthusiastic pursuit of modernity' (Tomes 1998: 158), and this point is neatly exemplified in Rudyard Kipling's short story 'Wireless' (1902), in which the imperceptible tubercle bacillus is rendered as modern as imperceptible wireless telegraphy. While an enthusiast of the new technology tries to receive wireless messages from a different town, a consumptive chemist's assistant in the next room begins to receive fragments of John Keats's poem 'The Eve of St Agnes' from a different era, a transmission that comes via the 'bacillus, or Hertzian wave of tuberculosis' (Kipling 1904: 212). Germ theory and telegraphy have modernised not only health and communication, Kipling's story tells us, but time and space.

Growing public understanding of germ theory meant that even dust changed from the unsightly to the dangerous. In *Ulysses* (1922) Buck Mulligan describes Dublin's streets as 'paved with dust, horsedung and consumptives' spits' (Joyce 2008: 14), and in the 'Oxen of the Sun' episode he gives 'inhaling the bacteria which lurk in dust' as a prime cause of death in Dublin (Joyce 2008: 398). In his influential *Dust and its Dangers* (1890, but regularly reprinted until 1919) T. Mitchell Prudden had told the public that 'ordinary living-rooms, even though they be well ventilated, are actually dust and bacteria repositories' (Prudden 1910: 29–30). Bacteria from flies and the sputum from tuberculosis sufferers were thought to mix with the dust on the street and could contaminate domestic spaces when swept in on shoes or women's skirts. Readers of magazines and journals were often dramatically warned against the presence of germs on roads and in dusty homes, and as Martin Bock has noted, in 1906 *The Irish Homestead*, in which James Joyce published his early work, ran articles entitled 'The Ethics of Dusting' and 'Don't Spit'. When we understand the health concerns voiced in periodicals of the time, we realise that the dust haunting 'Eveline' in *Dubliners* is not merely an image of paralysis, but of infection (Bock 2007).

Similarly, in T. S. Eliot's *The Waste Land* (1922), the real horror in its famous warning – 'I will show you fear in a handful of dust' (Eliot 2002: 54) – is not the abomination of the barren, but the dread of the swarms of bacterial life in the seemingly lifeless: the terror of the unexpected threat in the seemingly moribund. The dangers of the syphilitic Mrs Porter and her daughter might be avoided by the moral, but the deathly crowd flowing over London Bridge, exhaling 'Sighs, short and infrequent', evoke ideas of endless, urban contaminations that were harder to circumvent – 'so many / I had not thought death had undone so many' (Eliot 2002: 55). As Elizabeth Outka notes, Eliot caught influenza during the terrible 1918–19 pandemic, and even though his case was a mild one, he felt it affected his brain (Outka 2014: 938). Indeed, the after-effects of the virus included depression, mental confusion and at times schizophrenia, the recognition of which adds a further biomedical layer to modernist styles (Outka 2019: 13). Modernism is associated with shock, anticipated harm and worry as the pace of modern life led to exhaustion and stress, and its trauma can be traced to microscopic, bacteriological levels.

Of course, once germs are known as a threat to be eliminated, they also become a transgressive joy to be embraced. Modernism is full of 'dirty' stories, not merely in the sexual sense, but in their engagements with places that are particularly sensitive to germs: bathrooms (Todd 2012; James 2017). Marcel Duchamp's *Fountain* (1917) displayed a urinal as high art, public toilets and chamberpots recur throughout *Ulysses*, Mulk Raj Anand's *Untouchable* (1935) explores Westernisation, social progress and individual agency through the tension between latrine cleaners and the technology of the flushing toilet, Jean Rhys's depressed women are frequently found in lavatories, Graham Greene's novels feature suicides in toilets and chases in sewers, and Samuel Beckett is frequently scatological. Toilets represent the delights of modern plumbing, the frisson of the private and the dalliance with the bacterial, whose threat is at times wantonly celebrated, and at times righteously contained by contemporary hygiene.

Modernity's rising rates of travel and immigration made the world seem a little smaller, and other communities' germs a little closer. Knowledge of the healthy carrier meant that the invisible germ had undetectable points of contagion, and *Harpers* announced in 1912 that the fear of ambient disease germs needed to be replaced by concern about other people (Wald 2008: 75). Bacteriology's war on germs can be figured, as Laura Otis has done, as an imperialist ideology, as its emphasis on attacks by external threats made people increasingly 'anxious about penetration and about any connection with other people – the same anxieties inspired by imperialism' (Otis 1999: 5). Late Victorian Gothic texts such as *Dracula* show disease, represented in this instance by the vampire, as an active, aggressive force deliberately hunting a prey, and needing violence and cunning to contain, cure and eradicate.

Bacteriology was also co-opted by growing eugenics movements, in all their varied forms, although for some advocates of eugenics germ theory had a dangerous disregard for the gene. For those suspicious of germ theory, presenting bacteriological causes for diseases such as tuberculosis ignored 'taints' of the blood caused by moral and bodily inferiority (Porter 1992: 197–9). As Charles Davenport wrote in 1911:

> Modern medicine is responsible for the loss of appreciation of the power of heredity. It has had its attention too exclusively focused on germs and conditions of life. It has neglected the personal element that help determines the course of every disease. It has begotten a wholly impersonal hygiene whose teachings are false in so far as they are laid down as universally applicable. It has forgotten the fundamental fact that all men are created *bound* by their protoplasmic makeup and *unequal* in their powers and responsibilities. (Davenport 1911: iv)

However, for many with eugenicist beliefs, germ theory added a further veneer of scientific objectivity and respectability to their evaluative ideologies. The scientific interest in the microbe meant that, frequently, the image of the bacillus stood for the disease, eventually becoming a substitute for the victims themselves (Ott 1996: 64), and in eugenicist contexts germs were replaced by people as the microbe of infection. Anti-Semitic propaganda in Germany drew on the potency of germ imagery to ensure that Jewish people were not depicted as *like* bacteria, but *as* bacteria, and in the UK and America, representations of class, and racial or religious others, as well as those with disabilities, were little better.

Those designated 'unfit' could be represented as threats to social hygiene, and in 1915, for example, the *American Journal of the Public Health* published a special issue on the 'Negro health problem', in which it represented Black Americans as a fundamentally inferior, germ-ridden population who were a constant threat to the well-being of white Americans (Krieger 2011: 113). Racist communities who were convinced by bacteriology lamented the fact that the 'disease germ knows no colour or race line, no class distinction and has little respect for distance, when it can fasten on a human carrier', and in 1909 the Atlanta *Constitution* reluctantly acknowledged that if white health was to be preserved, then sanitary reforms and medical assistance must be extended to Black communities (Patterson 2009: 541). The militaristic metaphors that became dominant in the early twentieth century aided this sense of social threat. 'Disease germs', a primer informed readers in 1914, 'are the greatest enemies of mankind', as between 'these germs and the body there is never-ceasing war. The germs attack the body. [...] To defend itself the body kills the germs. Day by day and year by year the struggle goes on, the germs attacking, the body fighting to keep out the germs (Ritchie 1914: 6, 11).

The weaponising of the germ figures in a number of popular texts from this period. In H. G. Wells's *The War of the Worlds* (1897) humanity is saved from Martian attack by an unexpected source – the germs to which humans had become immune. There are 'no bacteria in Mars', Wells informs readers, and so, 'directly these invaders arrived, directly they drank and fed, our microscopic allies began to work their overthrow' (Wells 1955: 210). But while the humans in *The War of the Worlds* are turned into bystanders in a microbial battle, in Wells's earlier short story, 'The Stolen Bacillus' (1894), bacteria are deliberately wielded in a struggle between human foes. In this story an anarchist steals what he thinks is a vial of cholera bacilli from a bacteriologist's home laboratory. After a comic but urgent chase in which the anarchist is pursued by the bacteriologist, who is hotly followed by his wife for leaving the house without his shoes and hat, it is revealed that the 'pestilence imprisoned' (Wells 1957: 196) in a test tube, and desperately swallowed by the anarchist, is merely a new species of bacterium that causes blue patches on monkeys. The crisis is not merely averted, but revealed to have never been. As humorous as the story's twist is, and while the anarchist's desire to become a germ in the body politic is reassuringly unfulfilled, the threat of genuine bioterrorism has nonetheless been raised, and the possibility suggested that science, even accidentally, can be complicit in attacks on the city, as bacteria are described as far more dangerous than bombs. If society created the anarchist, science provided the means through which the anarchist could retaliate: the anarchist attempts to take revenge on society's rejection – 'He would teach them yet what it is to isolate a man' (Wells 1957: 200) – by devastating the city with the cholera bacilli isolated by bacteriologists.

Bioterror moves from the large to the small scale in Arthur Conan Doyle's 'The Adventure of the Dying Detective' (1913), in which a bacteriologist is not simply a potential accessory, but a villain who uses his knowledge of germs to murder. Culverton Smith kills his nephew by infecting him with a little-known disease, and tries to murder Sherlock Holmes with the same microbe when the detective suspects foul play. In an important passage, Smith likens his bacteriological investigations to Holmes's detective work: 'He is an amateur of crime, as I am of disease. For him the villain, for me the microbe' (Conan Doyle 1974: 136–7). When science is wielded as a weapon, and the dangers of scientific progress emphasised, it is scientific methods and rigour – with a few theatrics – that restore order. The bad bacteriologist, Smith, is eventually bested by the good bacteriologist, Holmes, as Holmes not only is sufficiently conversant in germ theory to understand Smith's crime, but can also perform applied bacteriology, as he finds cures to social ills by scrutinising his cases with microscopic intensity, thereby solving large problems through small details. There will be those, the story comforts readers, who try to abuse scientific advances, but they will be bested by superior knowledge.

The strange microscopic world that germ theory brought to the fore had an alluring mystique. Paul de Kruif's popular book *Microbe Hunters* (1926) is replete with descriptions of drops swarming with 'curious dancing specks' and 'great tangled dancing masses of tiny rod-like things [. . .] all of them shimmying with a weird incessant vibration' (de Kruif 1996: 61, 62). A fascination with the microscopic existed before public knowledge of germ theory, as magic lantern slides showed enlargements of insects, but with the growing knowledge of a bacteriological world, audiences began to delight in the 'interplanetary travel' made possible through films made using microscopic lenses. Films showed fleas and flies on large screens – which gives a possible source for Gregor's monstrous transformation in Kafka's *The Metamorphosis* (1912) – as well as the spirals and rods of bacteria (Godbey 2004: 285). As Emily Godbey writes, 'audiences assimilated germ theory's messages and saw that this teeming universe was not located halfway around the planet, but was as close as their own skins' (Godbey 2004: 277). The bacteriological universe moved as evocatively as abstract and expressionist art, and Standish Lawder asserts that these films,

> no less than the pre-war paintings of Kandinsky, must have been experienced by sensitive minds as profound and uniquely modern revelations of an unknown world – images of organic forms in movement recalling telescopic views of swirling galaxies, full of the flux and flow of life itself, touching at the core of secret meanings of the universe, and, at the same time, paradoxically, palpably real, that is, objectively verified by moving photographic images of a biological, if not spiritual, inner life. (Lawder 1975: 13)

Both Walter Benjamin and Aldous Huxley connected modernist aesthetics and the images shown by the microscope. In a review of Karl Blossfeldt, Benjamin wrote that 'new painters like Klee and even more Kandinsky have long been at work establishing friendly relations between us and the realms into which the microscope would like to seduce us' (Benjamin 2005: 156). Similarly, Huxley argued that new microscopic technologies opened up 'processes that cannot be directly perceived, but only logically inferred – with the invisibles and intangibles, whose movements, patternings, and modifications are the physical causes of our immediate experience of the outer world and of our own ongoing life' (Huxley 2002: 87). Much of the technology through which we approach the bacteriological 'present[s] us with a two-dimensional universe of intricate patterning on a flat surface'. This 'microphotographic universe, in which there are no solids and no distances', is, Huxley argues, 'essentially similar to the universe of the Abstract Expressionist'. This connection, he insists, is no coincidence, as 'Seeking the essences of things, contemporary artists have turned, not unnaturally, to the images of reality furnished by modern technology in the service of science' (Huxley 2002: 89).

For many modernist writers the small and ambiguous became part of a new mode of insight and expression, as germ theory drove new engagements not merely with threat and contagion, but with meaning beyond the immediate or directly perceivable. In 'On Being Ill' (1926) Woolf calls for novels to be 'devoted to influenza; epic poems to typhoid; odes to pneumonia; lyrics to tooth-ache' (Woolf 2009a: 101). For too long, she argues, literature has rooted itself in the mind, and a 'new language' is needed to enable an aesthetic of the physical and the debilitated, a language 'more primitive, more sensual, more obscene' (Woolf 2009a: 102). Illness, for Woolf, causes her to look differently, as the 'dark cupboard of illness' takes the mind into different places within the body (Woolf 1978: 125). To be ill is to rise above the everyday and see the limits and extensions of the self differently, thereby turning the ill subject, as Kimberly Engdahl Coates suggests, into an artist whose body is an aesthetic instrument (Coates 2002: 247). When ill, we inhabit our bodies differently, as our aches and pains cause us to look within. How could the growing dominance of the microscopic and the bacteriological not influence a gaze into the body and into the minute, invisible depths of the self?

Similarly, in 'Modern Fiction' (1919; revised 1925) Woolf asks us to think of the myriad impressions received by an ordinary mind on an ordinary day, as from 'all sides they come, an incessant shower of innumerable atoms' (Woolf 2009b: 9). If we think in terms of the minor, the varying and the unknown, we will no longer take 'for granted that life exists more fully in what is commonly thought big than what is commonly thought small' (Woolf 2009b: 9). In allowing the accent to fall a little differently, we look beyond the obvious to consider the barely noticed, the poorly perceived and the seemingly inconsequential. Woolf makes few direct mentions of germs and bacteria, but her interest in the minor is part of a bacteriological age, in which thinking turns to the imperceptible. 'Kew Gardens' (1919), which was written in the same year, offers an almost microscopic reading of the gardens, as Woolf's focus zooms from deep within the flower beds to the people on the paths and out again to the streets outside and skies above. As medical knowledge was increasingly aided by devices that examined at deeper and smaller scales, we see an approach to the body that was, as Craig Gordon notes, 'no longer content to read the signs of disease on the body's surface and aims instead at penetrating its interiority, discerning the functioning of its mechanism, and quantifying the information thus obtained' (Gordon 2007: 46). This approach to the body extends, I argue, to the text.

Woolf's complaint that Edwardian tools stressed the surface rather than the depth – the houses in which people lived, rather than the people themselves – is an echo of the new diagnostic techniques, in which examination shifted from the body's surface to the body's cells. The body in bacteriology is fragmented: so intimate, interior and minute that individuality is difficult to recognise. This proximity enables the complexity as well as the flatness of modernism: the body can be plumbed to ever-increasing levels of detail and depth, while also etherised upon a table, trapped on a labelled slide, measurable through specific aetiologies. Bacteriology contributes to the details and extravagances of *Ulysses*, which Joyce described as an 'epic of the body' (Budge 1960: 21) that can be explored through increasing levels of microscopic refinement, which, like fractals or Zeno's Achilles and the tortoise, go on infinitely:

> the myriad minute entomological organic existences [. . .] of microbes, germs, bacteria, bacilli, spermatozoa: [. . .] of the universe of human serum constellated with red and white bodies, themselves universes of void space constellated with other bodies, each, in continuity, its universe of divisible component bodies of which each was again divisible in divisions of redivisible component bodies, dividends and divisors ever diminishing without actual division till, if the progress were carried far enough, nought nowhere was never reached. (Joyce 2008: 651–2)

Ulysses is a petri dish in which a large array of textual microbes are brought together to create a new cultural product – art imitating nature at a microbiological level.

Bacteriology, with its microscopes and slides, also leads to the clean lines of modernist design, and the Cubist tendency to reconfigure the body as an 'endlessly divisible series of flat surfaces and mobile networks', in which, as Clement Greenberg writes, we are presented with 'a completely two-dimensional transcription of three-dimensional phenomena. [. . .] The world was stripped of its surface, of its skin, and the skin was spread flat on the flatness of the picture plane' (Greenberg 1961: 172; Cartwright 1995: 91). This extends to poetic forms such as imagism, in which, as Pound dictates in 'A Few Don'ts by an Imagiste' (1913), poetic language should be stripped down, minimal and clean: a commitment that Judith Brown refers to as a 'technical hygiene' (Brown 2009: 625n26), and which we can recognise as part of a bacteriological era. For Victoria Rosner, 'modernism's commitment to an aesthetic of cleanliness and hygiene [was] articulated through a new emphasis on visual clarity in representation' (Rosner 2020: 115), and William Carlos Williams too had argued that 'the cleansing of the "word" [. . .] is the work poets have in hand' (Williams 1974: 6). Brown links modernism's interest in blankness and central abysses – she cites the Marabar Caves in E. M. Forster's *Passage to India* (1924), the missing main character in Woolf's *Jacob's Room* (1922), and the nothingness found in the works of Beckett and Kafka – not to an absolute absence, but to the signification of absence, which she figures in relation to the new technology of cellophane (Brown 2009: 615–17). But modernism's fraught engagement with invisible presences and absences in loud attendance can, like cellophane's ability to keep germs off food, also be situated within the bacteriological, where the ubiquity of the invisible recognises that barren gaps are also swarming with meaning, albeit ones that frequently threaten to disturb.

From clothing to housing, bodily hygiene to racial hygiene, a fascination with contagion to a dedication to the microscopic, germs linger in modernism, sometimes as an overt infestation, but more often as a pervasive, yet barely perceptible, presence. An inextricable aspect of the shock of modernity was the growing awareness of the prevalence of invisible threat in the air, on surfaces and on other people, and modernity was irrevocably transformed by social and aesthetic adjustments to the constant, shifting hazard of the germ. As we grapple with the isolation and contagion caused by the viral emergency that began in 2019, microbial modernism comes into sharp relief, but also reminds us that while we share the modernist period's fears of chronic exposure to infinitesimal seeds of disease, and suffer similar traumas of anticipated attack, this too will pass.

Works Cited

Balderston, L. R. and E. H. Gunther (1912), 'Sanitary Precautions in Laundry Work', *Good Housekeeping*, 54, pp. 712–15.
Belloc, Hilaire [verse] and Basil Temple Blackwood [illustrations] (1897), 'The Microbe', in *More Beasts for Worse Children*. London: Duckworth, pp. 47–8.
Benjamin, Walter (2005), 'News about Flowers', in *Selected Writings Volume 2, part 1, 1927–1934*, trans. Rodney Livingstone et al., ed. Michael W. Jennings, Howard Eiland and Gary Smith. Cambridge, MA: Belknap Press of Harvard University Press, pp. 155–7.
Berenbaum, May (2018), 'Cinema-tick Experience', *American Entomologist*, 64: 2, pp. 67–70.
Bock, Martin (2006), 'Joseph Conrad and Germ Theory: Why Captain Allistoun Smiles Thoughtfully', *The Conradian*, 31: 2, pp. 1–14.
Bock, Martin (2007), 'James Joyce and Germ Theory: The Skeleton at the Feast', *James Joyce Quarterly*, 45: 1, pp. 23–46.
Brown, Judith (2009), 'Cellophane Glamour', *Modernism/modernity*, 15: 4, pp. 605–26.
Budge, Frank (1960), *James Joyce and the Making of* Ulysses. Bloomington: Indiana University Press.
Bulman, G. W. (1893), 'Are Bacilli Causes of Disease?', *Westminster Review*, 139, pp. 500–7.
Campbell, Margaret (2005), 'What Tuberculosis Did for Modernism: The Influence of a Curative Environment on Modernist Design and Architecture', *Medical History*, 49, pp. 463–88.
Cartwright, Lisa (1995), *Screening the Body: Tracing Medicine's Visual Culture*. Minneapolis: University of Minnesota Press.
Coates, Kimberly Engdahl (2002), 'Exposing the "Nerves of Language": Virginia Woolf, Charles Mauron, and the Affinity between Aesthetics and Illness', *Literature and Medicine*, 21: 2, pp. 242–63.
Conan Doyle, Arthur (1974), 'The Adventure of the Dying Detective', in *His Last Bow: Some Reminiscences of Sherlock Holmes*. London: John Murray and Jonathan Cape, pp. 127–44.
Davenport, Charles Benedict (1911), *Heredity in Relation to Eugenics*. New York: Henry Holt and Company.
de Kruif, Paul (1996), *Microbe Hunters*. San Diego: Harvest.
Eliot, T. S. (2002), *The Waste Land*, in *Collected Poems, 1909–1962*. London: Faber and Faber.
Fifield, Peter (2019), 'On the Invisible Threat: Bacteriologists in Fiction and Periodical Advertisements, 1894–1913', *Journal of Victorian Culture*, 24: 1, pp. 33–52.
Godbey, Emily (2004), 'The Cinema of (Un)Attractions: Microscopic Objects on Screen', in *Allegories of Communication: Intermedial Concerns from Cinema to the Digital*, ed. John Fullerton and Jan Olsson. Bloomington: Indiana University Press, pp. 277–98.
Gordon, Craig A. (2007), *Literary Modernism, Bioscience, and Community in Early 20th Century Britain*. New York: Palgrave Macmillan.
Greenberg, Clement (1961), *Art and Culture: Critical Essays*. Boston: Beacon Press.
'His Ancestors' (1919), *The Abolitionist*, 1 March.
Huxley, Aldous (1947), *Brave New World*. London: Chatto & Windus.
Huxley, Aldous (2002), 'Science, Technology, and Beauty', in *Complete Essays Volume VI, 1956–1963*, ed. Robert S. Baker and James Sexton. Chicago: Ivan R. Dee, pp. 83–9.

James, Laura Natalie (2017), '"The Power of Filth": Dirt, Waste, and Gender in Modern Fiction, 1890–1945', unpublished PhD thesis, Stony Brook University, NY.
Jørgensen, Jens Lohfert (2015), 'Bacillophobia: Man and Microbes in *Dracula*, *The War of the Worlds*, and *The Nigger of the "Narcissus"*', *Critical Survey*, 27: 2, pp. 36–49.
Joyce, James (2008), *Ulysses*. Oxford: Oxford University Press.
Kipling, Rudyard (1904), *Traffics and Discoveries*. Leipzig: Bernhard Tauchnitz.
Krieger, Nancy (2011), *Epidemiology and the People's Health: Theory and Context*. Oxford: Oxford University Press.
Lawder, Standish D. (1975), *The Cubist Cinema*. New York: New York University Press.
Lawrence, D. H. (2004), *Psychoanalysis and the Unconscious and Fantasia of the Unconscious*, ed. Bruce Steele. Cambridge: Cambridge University Press.
McClary, Andrew (1980), 'Germs are Everywhere: The Germ Threat as Seen in Magazine Articles 1890–1920', *Journal of American Culture*, 3: 1, pp. 33–46.
Moving Picture World (1910), 11 June, p. 989.
Otis, Laura (1999), *Membranes: Metaphors of Invasion in Nineteenth-Century Literature, Science, and Politics*. Baltimore: John Hopkins University Press.
Ott, Katherine (1996), *Fevered Lives: Tuberculosis in American Culture since 1870*. Cambridge, MA: Harvard University Press.
Outka, Elizabeth (2014), '"Wood for the Coffins Ran Out": Modernism and the Shadowed Afterlife of the Influenza Pandemic', *Modernism/modernity*, 21: 4, pp. 937–60.
Outka, Elizabeth (2019), *Viral Modernism: The Influenza Pandemic and Interwar Literature*. New York: Columbia University Press.
Patterson, Andrea (2009), 'Germs and Jim Crow: The Impact of Microbiology on Public Health Policies in Progressive Era American South', *Journal of the History of Biology*, 42, pp. 529–59.
Porter, Roy (1992) 'The Case of Consumption', in *Understanding Catastrophe: Its Impact on Life on Earth*, ed. Janine Bourriau. Cambridge: Cambridge University Press, pp. 179–203.
Prudden, T. Mitchell (1910), *Dust and its Dangers*. New York: G. P. Putnam's Sons.
Ritchie, John W. (1914), *Primer of Sanitation and Physiology: Being Primer of Sanitation and Primer of Physiology in One Volume*. Yonkers-on-Hudson, NY: World Book.
Roberts, Frederick T. (1903), 'Address in Medicine: On Infective and Infectious Diseases', *British Medical Journal*, 1 August, pp. 233–40.
Rosner, Victoria (2020), *Machines for Living: Modernism and Domestic Life*. Oxford: Oxford University Press.
Shaw, George Bernard (1922), *The Doctor's Dilemma: A Tragedy*. London: Constable.
Soloski, Alexis (2014), 'The Playwright's Perplexity: Constitution, Contagion, and Consumption in The Doctor's Dilemma', *SHAW: The Annual of Bernard Shaw Studies*, 34, pp. 46–58.
'The Generous Germ' (1927), *The Manchester Guardian*, 8 June, p. 8.
Todd, Ian Scott (2012), 'Dirty Books: Modernism and the Toilet', *MFS Modern Fiction Studies*, 58: 2, pp. 191–213.
Tomes, Nancy (1998), *The Gospel of Germs: Men, Women and the Microbe in American Life*. Cambridge, MA: Harvard University Press.
Tzara, Tristan (1977), 'Lecture on Dada', in *Seven Dada Manifestos and Lampisteries*, trans. Barbara Wright. London: John Calder.
Wald, Priscilla (2008), *Contagious: Cultures, Carriers, and the Outbreak Narrative*. Durham, NC: Duke University Press.
Wells, H. G. (1955), *The War of the Worlds*. London: William Heinemann.
Wells, H. G. (1957), 'The Stolen Bacillus', in *The Short Stories of H. G. Wells*. London: Ernest Benn, pp. 195–202.
Wilk, Christopher (2006), 'The Healthy Body Culture', in *Modernism 1914–1939: Designing a New World*. London: V&A Publications, pp. 249–97.

Williams, William Carlos (1974), *The Embodiment of Knowledge*. New York: New Directions.
Willis, Martin (2007), '"The Invisible Giant", Dracula, and Disease', *Studies in the Novel*, 39: 3, pp. 301–25.
Woolf, Virginia (1959), *A Room of One's Own*. London: Hogarth Press.
Woolf, Virginia (1978), *The Diary of Virginia Woolf, Volume II: 1920–1924*, ed. Anne Olivier Bell. New York: Harcourt Brace.
Woolf, Virginia (2009a), 'On Being Ill', in *Selected Essays*. Oxford: Oxford University Press, pp. 101–10.
Woolf, Virginia (2009b), 'Modern Fiction', in *Selected Essays*. Oxford: Oxford University Press, pp. 6–12.
Woolf, Virginia (2011), *Orlando*. London: Penguin.
Worboys, Michael (2000), *Spreading Germs: Disease Theories and Medical Practice in Britain, 1865–1900*. Cambridge: Cambridge University Press.

21

NOISE: LABOUR, INDUSTRY AND EMBODIMENT IN INTERWAR FACTORY FICTION

Anna Snaith

IN EARLY TWENTIETH-CENTURY Britain, modernity became synonymous with the noise of technology. Increasing attention was paid to the sonic by-products of machines and their effects on the human body. Listening in to this chapter of sound history amplifies an often-silenced mode of response to technology and its impacts, as well as foregrounding multiple and competing discourses about noise and their indexing of cultural, social and political concerns. The designation of sound as noise is, of course, highly subjective: one person's music is another's torment. Noise can be both demonised and fetishised, signalling an intrusion into a soundscape understood as restorative or harmonious, or a means of protest and counter-cultural resistance. At once a sign of sociability, of existence (as vibration, everything is in noise), noise can also be unwanted, non-periodic sound, a form of torture or weaponry. Often associated with excess or background sound, noise slips between figure and ground as it carries or disrupts meaning.

While concerns about noise are ubiquitous, the modernist period saw an intensification of attention to noise and its mental and physical effects. Whether or not decibel levels rose, the first decades of the twentieth century were characterised by the proliferation of the sounds of technology. The rise of amplified and broadcast sound reshaped public and private soundscapes as well as modes of listening. Aptly called 'the age of noise' by Aldous Huxley, interwar Britain saw the publication of a plethora of books on noise. In one such publication, A. H. Davis describes how the 'irregular rattle of machinery, the shriek of brakes, the crescendo of violently accelerating motorcycles, the shattering explosions of road-breaking drills, burst rudely upon our consciousness and stir our resentment and fears' (Davis 1937: 5). Adjectival assault indicates the intrusive experience of shock and disturbance associated with mechanical sound. With the advent in the 1920s of a unit (the decibel) and machines (audiometers) with which to measure sound intensity objectively, noise became something to be charted, analysed and controlled. Background sound became undesirable noise through its continual foregrounding. As Davis notes, these acoustical developments led to 'an increasing consciousness of noise' (Davis 1937: 4); they made a sonic phenomenon visible through charts and audiograms. The interwar decades witnessed the growth of noise abatement work and experiments into the effects of noise in the newly active fields of industrial health and psychology. Attempts in the period to define noise – such as physicist G. W. C. Kaye's 'sound out of place' (qtd in Goldsmith 2012: 1) or psychologist F. C. Bartlett's 'any sound which is treated as a nuisance'

(Bartlett 1934: 2) – marked a broader move to analyse and control a sonic phenomenon perceived by some to encapsulate modernity's injurious qualities.

Retrospective ocularcentric definitions of modernity have done much to silence the sonic and auditory dimensions of early twentieth-century paradigms. Recent scholarship in sound studies and sound history is beginning to reconfigure such sensory hierarchies. In his study of the aural sectionalism of antebellum America, for example, Mark S. Smith argues that 'sounds and their meanings are shaped by the cultural, economic, and political contexts in which they are produced and heard' (Smith 2001: 7), such that the hum of industry was mobilised by Northern elites to designate 'the satisfying sounds of free and wage labor' (13), in contrast to the 'shrieks of slavery, the awful silence of oppression' (14). Kate Lacey, too, has written about a distinction that emerged in the late nineteenth century between '"productive" and "unproductive" or "unnecessary" noise [. . .] the dampening of noise in engines and machinery and domestic appliances coming to signify greater efficiency and rationalisation' (Lacey 2013: 77). In interwar Britain, I contend, a version of this narrative about 'needless' noise was harnessed to a preoccupation with waste that drew on Taylorisation, the European science of work and a language of maximising efficiency. Conversely, the rationalisation of industrial labour had a sonic dimension which is rarely acknowledged. The associations of noise with meaninglessness – not just sound without message but sound that interferes with communication – meant that it could rapidly be construed as a cynosure for the supposed inefficiencies in the methods of factory labour or, indeed, the workers themselves. Not only that, but the 'right' kind of sound and rhythm could be harnessed to enhance productivity and reduce fatigue.

This chapter will argue that interwar fiction plays a crucial role in the period's particularly vociferous debates, involving government and industry, about the effects of mechanical sound on the body. Noise abatement work, as carried out by the Anti-Noise League, employed a biopolitics which advocated acoustic self-regulation. The nerve-force of the nation, they argued, was at invisible risk from the surround sound emanating from the ever-increasing number of cars, car horns, aeroplanes, trains and drills. This was also a product of newly popular sound technologies which altered the sites and modes of listening to foreground the noise within the system or the machine. Technologies such as the telephone or radio required the operator or listener to learn to navigate or listen through noise: to hear and self-deafen simultaneously, or to practise auditory streaming. In contrast, non-discriminating sound-recording technologies, such as the phonograph, produced what Douglas Kahn has called '*all sound*' (Kahn 1999: 9). This foregrounding of mechanical noise, or sound perceived as being without message, hierarchy or system, created a semantic void within which competing noise narratives jostled.

With the increased attention to noise as a phenomenon in the modernist period came its increased potential to become figure rather than ground. Literature, I suggest, was central to the shaping, staging and resisting of definitions of noise. If noise is not a sound but an orientation towards sound, that process of orientation requires discursive pressure. Literary fiction was not only a key source for understanding the history of sound and auditory cultures, but a key site for the narration, and hence creation, of noise from sound and a demonstration of its effects. As James Mansell writes, 'turning a sound into a noise is the product of a good deal of cultural work' (Mansell 2020: 156). Modernist writers sought to make noise 'visible' through a wide range of experimental typographical and stylistic techniques displayed across genres and modes. For the Italian Futurists, technological noise generated new forms of aesthetic response, as well as providing a metaphor for the bombastic motivations of the avant-garde. Writer, composer and instrument maker Luigi Russolo's manifesto, *The Art of Noises* (1913), articulated an origin narrative for noise. Emerging with the Industrial Revolution, Russolo argues, noise is synonymous with the by-products of technology: natural sounds are not noise. An early advocate of the soundwalk, Russolo wrote that crossing 'a great modern city with our ears more alert then our eyes' will generate 'mental orchestrations of the crashing down of metal shop blinds [. . .] the varied racket of railroad stations, iron foundries, spinning wheels, printing plants, subways and electrical power stations' (Russolo 2009: 135). The acoustic emotion generated by the polyphony of technology meant that art music no longer provided adequate sensory stimulation to the modern ear. New aesthetic forms could be found in the widened soundworld generated by technology. But Russolo's project was as much about noise production as reception: he built and toured noise intoners (*intonarumori*), positing that by 'selecting, coordinating and controlling noises we shall enrich mankind with a new and unexpected pleasure of the senses' (Russolo 2009: 137). While the machines were named for particular sounds – crackling, gurgling, hissing – his work suggests not mimesis but the aesthetic control and ordering of noise within the concert hall or performance space.

One industrial noisescape became a multidisciplinary site of contestation in the interwar period: the factory. Given the extreme decibel levels in many factories, tuning in to the representation of machine sound in these environments can tell us much about how noise impacts were understood (or ignored). This chapter will read factory fiction of the 1930s and 1940s by writers such as Walter Greenwood, John Sommerfield, James Hanley and Inez Holden alongside state-sponsored experiments into the effects of industrial noise. The Industrial Fatigue (later Health) Research Board was founded in 1918, and by the 1930s its noise subcommittee was working closely with the Noise Abatement League (NAL) in carrying out a range of experiments into the effects of high-decibel noise on the labouring body. Published and archival materials detailing the findings of these experiments are part of a wider preoccupation with the implications of the sonic environment on worker morale and productivity. Mass Observation publications such as *People in Production* (1942), Celia Fremlin's *War Factory: A Report* (1943) or Amabel Williams-Ellis's *Women in War Factories* (1943) all discuss the correlation between noise and efficiency, and note the beneficial impacts of the 'right' kind of music on the factory floor, whether via radio, gramophone or Entertainments National Service Association concerts. The BBC's *Music While You Work* programme was introduced in June 1940 to air twice daily, explicitly to aid factory workers during wartime and as part of exactly these debates about sound, bodily rhythms and productivity.

Karl Marx included noise in his account of toxic, Victorian factory conditions: 'every sense organ is injured by the artificially high temperatures, by the dust-laden atmosphere, by the deafening noise, not to mention the danger to life and limb among machines' (Marx 1990: 552). But R. Murray Schafer, in *The Soundscape,* has noted literary fiction's unique position as ear witness to this form of aural bombardment: the 'only people to criticize the "prodigious noise" of machinery were the writers, figures like Dickens and Zola' (Schafer 1994: 75). Whereas, in novels such as Charles Dickens's *Hard Times* or Elizabeth Gaskell's *North and South*, the pandemonium of factory conditions becomes an aural symbol of pervasive hardship, in interwar proletarian factory novels we begin to find not only systematic attention to the worker's point of view but detailed representation of the sensory experience of labour in high-decibel noise. By and large written from first-hand or family experience of cotton mills, engineering or munitions factories, these texts also represent the impacts of aural overload on the body, thereby attending to the oft-overlooked place of noise in the history of industrial relations and workers' rights. Noise is registered as an industrial pollutant, one that enslaves, deafens and silences. This takes us to what Karin Bijsterveld has called 'repertoires for dramatizing sound' or the rhetoric, staging or 'auditory topoi' used to express the urgency of particular understandings of noise impacts (Bijsterveld 2008: 30). These novels, I posit, do not simply register the effects of extreme industrial noise but offer complex and competing narratives about the symbolism and semiotics of noise which, again, bring noise repeatedly into focus as figure rather than ground. While recent scholarship by Karin Bijsterveld, Emily Thompson and James Mansell has contributed to a layered and contextualised understanding of mechanical sound in this period, a fuller account of the role of literary fiction is long overdue.[1]

Not only that, but the act of representing extreme sound has implications for the phonographic capacity of the literary, and therefore for literary sound studies more broadly. How is the literary text sound-bearing: a multimedia event that registers and anticipates the effects of the newly available sound media such as radio and cinema? In the case of interwar factory fiction, I suggest, the challenges of writing high-decibel sound generated textual experiments that complicate familiar designations of social realism and the emphasis on authenticity that surrounds such texts. Walter Greenwood's *Love on the Dole* (1933) is set in the Hanky Park area of Salford and follows protagonist Harry Hardcastle as he moves from an exploitative factory apprenticeship at Marlowe's (based on Metropolitan Vickers at Trafford Park, Manchester) to unemployment. The novel culminates in a chapter entitled 'Historical Narrative', depicting the Battle of Bexley Square, a violent clash with police that ended a march organised by the National Unemployed Workers' Movement (NUWM) in Salford on 1 October 1931. Greenwood was from a working-class, activist family and responses to the novel from the 1930s to the present have revolved around measures of 'authenticity'. Contemporary reviews praised Greenwood for the ways in which his 'faithful representation' drew the country's attention to issues of poverty and unemployment (qtd in Gaughan 2008: 1). More recent scholarship has used the same lens to critique Greenwood: his localism is inaccurate, or he capitulates to a middle-class readership through his selective use of dialect and a singular class focus.[2] While these readings certainly bear investigation, attuning ourselves to an audile perspective reorients any discussion of labour conditions and class politics, as well as complicating notions of 'authenticity' through the act of writing sound.

Love on the Dole is saturated in sound, but like all the texts under consideration here, there is a central factory floor scene. The reader accompanies Harry Hardcastle as he is toured round the factory from foundry to forge and assaulted by the bedlam.

> Blocks of steel crashing up on the white hot forgings with a shattering BUMP. Earth shook, trembled beneath your feet. If you stood within yards of the largest hammers you actually were lifted off your feet. (Greenwood 1993: 49)

In the riveting shop, in particular, the din was 'insufferable' with 'every man stone deaf after a six months' spell of work here. Phew!' (50). Staged rather than described and using typographic variation and markers of affect, the text registers sound as touch and physical force. The effects of noise are multisensory, dispersed and corporeal, and linked immediately to injury (here noise-induced hearing loss). Greenwood offers a phenomenology of noise as nausea-inducing vibration through reference to 'giddiness' and its 'tickling of the stomach', which gestures towards the etymology of noise in *nausea* or seasickness (49). Michael Heller has used the term 'listener collapse' to describe the blurring of the distinction between exterior (sound) and interior (self) caused by high-decibel sound (Heller 2015: 45). Sound here is totalising, moving beyond the ear to an all-encompassing physicality and eliminating the 'possibility of detached listening' (Heller 2015: 45). While some communities of listeners seek out this kind of experience, in the context of labour, such physical, and at times painful, bodily impact can erode a sense of selfhood and bodily autonomy.

These interwar literary noisescapes were a crucial element of multidisciplinary attempts across the creative arts, psychology, acoustics, engineering and medicine to define, legislate against, measure and listen in to noise. This preoccupation was the sonic legacy of the First World War. Initial definitions of shell shock revolved around the force and sound of exploding shells and early experiments into the condition saw neurologists, such as Frederick Mott, attempting to find noise-induced lesions on nerves. Even though, early in the war, more psychologically orientated theories of war trauma entered the frame, the renewed interest in neurasthenia and nervous disorders caused or exacerbated by sound continued well into the interwar period. The prevalence of auditory injuries (acoustic shock, burst eardrums, deafness, tinnitus) resulting from the excessive decibel levels of the conflict zone led to scientific investigations into noise effects, particularly noise-induced hearing loss (NIHL) in the years during and after the First World War.[3] One of the legacies of war's noise impacts was a concern with *ordinary* urban din as physically and psychologically injurious to the individual and national body.

The Anti-Noise League (later Noise Abatement League [NAL]) was founded in 1933 by prominent doctor Thomas Horder and campaigned endlessly to have noise understood as a public health issue. The multidisciplinary organisation included medics, engineers, architects and writers (including H. G. Wells). They sought a range of noise-limiting legislation, but also advocated public education into the effects of noise on the nervous system and promoted sonic self-regulation and the 'proper' use of technology: 'acoustic civilisation', to use Horder's terminology.[4] Via the NAL's magazine, *Quiet* (1936–48), billboard campaigns, conferences and publications, the NAL employed a language of nerve-force to describe the impacts of this invisible yet 'unnecessary' pollutant. Horder described the threat and the solution like this:

> [A]s never before – does this nation need cool judgement, steady nerves and reserves of force. The untidiness of our civic lives and our health-arrangements are sapping these vital things and, among the chief causes we vaguely say 'greater nervous strain of modern life' is responsible. Much of this is due to noise outside and inside our homes. Avoidable noise, from the slammed door to the pneumatic drill.[5]

The focus of the NAL's advertising was the male professional unable to adapt to or cope with the onslaught of the machine. The ear became the locus for a body assaulted by the modern, thereby positing hearing and the ear (as opposed to the eye) as archaic or retrogressive.

The NAL's concern was primarily mechanical sound, but the association of noise with sonic waste drew connections to wider discourses of social and national efficiency in a new era of technological modernity. Horder spoke often of the protective capacities of the senses not keeping pace with technological innovation, but the absence of an earlid deepened the perception of vulnerability. The wide-ranging work of Horder and the NAL revolved around a desire to capture, anaesthetise or narrate ostensibly 'meaningless' sound as part of a wider reconsideration of the relationship between the human and the machine. High-decibel mechanical noise produced very real bodily effects (injurious, silencing, energising), but everyday noise became a cynosure for a network of concerns about the effects of modernity and techno–human relations. Furthermore, while noise abaters mobilised nostalgia for the quiet rural soundscape, their position was not one of technophobia. As with the rural preservation movements, with which the noise abaters were networked, a rational, technological modern was mobilised to counter its own effects.[6] As A. H. Davis wrote, through the 'proper' use of technology 'the way seems clearer for [noise] control both technically and by regulation' (Davis 1937: 4).

The factory, like the war zone, was a site in which decibel levels had the potential to cause injury. NIHL is now understood to be amongst the most prevalent occupational disorders, but it 'was not recognized as a compensable disorder by the workers' compensation system of any Western nation until after World War II' (Dembe 1996: 203). In the UK, it was not until 1989 that 'Noise at Work' legislation was introduced to protect workers' hearing. The history of objections to industrial noise, from prohibitions around coppersmiths in ancient Rome to early modern restrictions on placement of mills, largely consists of instances of noise emanating from rather than within the workplace (Bijsterveld 2008: 56). Accounts of workers' hearing loss are isolated and rare but include Bernardino Ramazzini's *De Morbis Artificum* (Diseases of Workers, 1713) with its inclusion of deafness in coppersmiths and the first scientific study into occupational hearing loss: John Fosbroke's 1831 investigation of blacksmiths' deafness (Dembe 1996: 163). Later in the century, in 1886, Thomas Barr tested the hearing of Glaswegian shipyard boilermakers with a ticking watch: not one worker had normal hearing (Dembe 1996: 168). For R. Murray Schafer, 'the inability to recognize noise during the early phases of the Industrial Revolution as a factor contributing to the multiplicitory toxicity of the new working environments is one of the strangest facts in the history of aural perception' (Schafer 1994: 76). There is an ironic, uncanny silence around industrial noise.

There are several reasons for this silence. The lack of evidence or medical records prior to large-scale auditory testing meant that the focus on industrial hazards registered in the Factory Acts was on air pollution, posture or mechanical injury. In addition, the 'putative regularity' of factory noise served to dampen the perception of its harm (Bijsterveld 2008: 74). And the longstanding emphasis on noise sensitivity in the middle- and upper-class brain worker meant that noise abatement work tended to direct its attention to urban, street noise rather than to industrial soundscapes. This changed in Britain when concerns about the health and efficiency of the labour force (particularly the military) during and after the First World War brought about growth in the study of industrial health and psychology. In 1918, the government's Industrial

Fatigue Research Bureau (which became the Industrial Health Research Board [IHRB] in 1926) emerged out of the wartime Health of Munitions Workers Committee, set up in 1915 in response to concerns about wartime productivity and labour management. The IHRB represented a 'state-led technocratic intervention' based on professional expertise and the use of 'rigorous and objective scientific techniques' (Mansell 2016: 100, 107). Its role was to conduct scientific studies into 'the human factor' and the 'health and efficiency problems created by modern industrial conditions' (McIvor 1987: 165).

Walter Fletcher, Secretary of the Medical Research Council, oversaw the setting up of the organisation and was keen to distance its work from F. W. Taylor's scientific management and its emphasis on profit maximisation through time-motion studies, 'task management' and reductions in wasted energy. Ostensibly, the IHRB's literature emphasised a commitment to research that would bring 'chief benefits to the workers themselves' and foregrounded fitting the worker to the task by investigating variation in energy levels and biorhythms (McIvor 1987: 163). But exploration of its experiments – particularly those related to industrial noise – indicates the extent to which the focus on 'healthy', energised and stimulated workers was understood as a productivity-maximising strategy.

A noise subcommittee commissioned a range of experiments into the effects of noise on different kinds of labour. In one of these, F. C. Bartlett, Professor of Experimental Psychology at Cambridge, and K. G. Pollock investigated the effects of various 'noise' environments (rattles, clicks, horns, jazz music) on the performance of a mix of motor and mental tasks in a group of Cambridge students (Pollock and Bartlett 1932). While the experiment showed a reduction in efficiency in the presence of noise, particularly when this was discontinuous or the tasks required concentration, in their conclusion the scientists sought to downplay the 'noise problem'. The effects of noise have been 'greatly exaggerated' in popular writing, they conclude, and are likely due to 'social causes': it is 'very easy for any person who is "off colour", or who fails to adapt himself to his social group, to make noise the butt of his grievance' (Pollock and Bartlett 1932: 33). The noise 'problem' is allied with the 'inefficient' worker by connecting it to pre-existing, individual malaise and mental health issues.[7]

Significantly for our context here, experiments were also carried out in 1932 and 1935 by H. C. Weston and S. Adams into the effects of high-decibel industrial noise on weavers in a Lancashire weaving shed, where sound intensity levels measured 96 dB (repeated exposure to levels over 85 dB has the potential to cause physiological damage) (Weston and Adams 1932). Ten weavers with 'normal' hearing wore Mallock Armstrong ear defenders, which reduced the sound intensity to 87 db, in alternate weeks for six months. The rationale for the experiment was not about workers' hearing (which went untested) but productivity measured through pick recorders (when the thread is passed across the loom). Given that weaving was a largely mechanised process, human efficiency related to reshuttling and tying broken ends and was found to increase by 12 per cent with ear defenders (Weston and Adams 1932: 58). A second experiment was conducted in 1935 with two groups of equally 'efficient' weavers measured over a twelve-month period. The group wearing ear defenders saw an increase in personal efficiency of 7.5 per cent (Weston and Adams 1935: 14). Weston and Adams concluded that 'excessive noise is to the human organism very much as excessive friction is to the machine: it wastes energy [. . .] Partial deafness appears to be the only effective protection which the individual can acquire' (Weston and Adams 1935: 14).

While acknowledging the difficulty in testing the effects of noise, given the range of other factors (climate, management, age, adaptability) in play, these experiments bypassed any consideration of auditory or physical injury or psychological impacts on the worker. Deafness became a recommended prophylactic for the decrease in productivity. Archival material indicates that, working with the NAL, Weston had planned a range of further noise experiments in factories during the mid-1930s (National Archives: FD1/4050). It is also clear that there was considerable industry interest in the noise experiments. These experiments not only rehearse the narrative of noise as waste or inefficiency used by the NAL but mark industrial noise as detrimental to labour capacity rather than the organ of hearing. While the IHRB set out to promote 'better knowledge of the effects of conditions of employment on the health and efficiency of the workers' (Culpin and Smith 1930: iii), the noise experiments in particular demonstrate the prioritising of efficiency over health. Not only that, but they indicate how the vocabulary of work science extended to the sonic.

Interwar factory novels provide a crucial counterpart to the IHRB's work. James Mansell has noted that 'working class voices rarely emerge on their own terms in the noise investigations', but in interwar factory novels we find representation of these voices and effects (Mansell 2016: 103). In *Love on the Dole*, Greenwood not only offers a recognition of the effects of high-decibel industrial noise on the worker but frames that recognition within an awareness of the biopolitics of a wider sonic regime. The factory din spills beyond its walls, and an auditory regime of bells, whistles and sirens operates within and without the workplace. In the novel's opening scene, the 'wakerer up' Joe Riley can be heard, at 5.30 a.m., rattling 'the wires against the bedroom windows' (Greenwood 1993: 14). The novel's soundtrack consists of the 'deep, loud, hoarse note of a siren' (24), the 'mill and factory hooters [. . .] shrieking and moaning' (239), the 'ping-ping-ping' of bells' (25) and the sounds of workers' clogs on cobblestones. Labour is harnessed through sonic regulation: the body trained to respond to these aural cues. Even when out of earshot, the sounds echo in the mind as a pervasive reminder of the body's internalised labour rhythms. Harry's sister Sal works in the weaving trade and hears the noise of the looms in her mind's ear: the 'clack-clack [. . .] hideous noise of the shuttle's traverse seared her brain with its intolerable dinning' (24). The invasive internalised noisescape is only amplified by the experience of unemployment represented in all these novels of interwar factory life. In Derbyshire miner Walter Brierley's *Means Test Man* (1935), the dehumanising effects of unemployment are exacerbated by the protagonist's continued and obsessive registering of the factory sounds: the 'varying-toned hooters and whistles' (Brierley 2011: 183). He experiences them as 'time-sound', given their marking of the temporal shape of the working day (183). These texts reveal the sonic and auditory aspects of more familiar accounts of the body's temporal harnessing to industrial labour conditions. Industrial sound prompts and conditions a physical response, thus making the ear, as well as the eye, a significant yet often ignored mode of control.

Such representations of the embodied effects of sound register a complex blend of the psychological, social and physiological impacts of factory noise. In James Hanley's story 'The Machines Stop', factory worker Mr Edmonds is bound to technology through noise:

> there was also something about them other than their power. It was their sound. Mr Edmonds liked to bury himself in that orgy of metallic sound. The concourse

of roar and rattle thrown up by them absorbed him. He became their slave, the prisoner of sound. (Hanley 1938: 249)

When the machines stop, Edmonds experiences headaches and physical collapse. The normal, physical connection between vibrating object and its auditor's eardrum is here writ large. The totalising vibrations yoke man to machine symbiotically and symbolically. The all-encompassing effects of the extreme conditions of his labour are registered through the body's dependence on noise. Edmonds's doctor declares: 'here is a man whose life has been one long surrender to noise' (253). In *Love on the Dole*, too, Harry's initial desire to escape his 'feminised' labour as a clerk is transferred on to his ascribing of magical properties to technology: the 'gods of the machine and forge' (Greenwood 1993: 21). The noise of the machines, and sensory overload more generally, are associated with the formation of the masculine body within capitalist modernity, initiated into its 'spellbinding' enchantment (Greenwood 1993: 21).

John Sommerfield's *May Day* (1936) is set in London over a three-day period some time in the 1930s. It depicts the exploitative working conditions in Langfier's Carbon Works during the lead-up to industrial action on 1 May. The novel documents the working body's regulation and enslavement through 'speeded-up' labour, piece work and inadequate safety procedures: the 'tired hands mangled in the machines [. . .] the invisible whiplash that drove the hurrying limbs' (Sommerfield 2010: 33). After a series of accidents, the factory strike is catalysed in part by the scalping of a woman worker whose hair is caught in the machinery. Noise is a prominent element in the toxicity of the working environment. In a key scene, Sommerfield registers the soundscape of a machine shop: as a door swings open and shut, a 'pandemonium of noise swelled out', the room 'shivering with the loud, undeviating music of machines [. . .] [A]fter a while the noise comes to seem a fearful, shattering silence' (48). The sound of machines is tactile, it 'jet[s] forth', 'cracking whips in the workers' ears' (126). This is a novel in which industrial modernity is continually registered through an 'avalanche of noise' (126). R. Murray Schafer has used the term 'sound imperialism' to describe the dominating power of extreme industrial noise: sound that numbs, overloads and disorientates (Schafer 1994: 76). The cacophony imposed long-term and temporary deafening just as it muted speech and singing. Workers in high-decibel environments, particularly women working in weaving sheds, were known for their capacity to lip-read (see Robertson et al. 2013: 161). Yorkshire writer William Holt worked, as a teenager, in a weaving shed with his aunt and describes the 'shattering din' of the machines, exacerbated by his inability to lip-read, unlike the women workers around him (Holt 1939: 35). Referencing a long history of workplace unison singing, Holt records: 'Sometimes all the weavers sang in unison. It was just possible to hear the high notes above the roar of the machinery' (35). He tracks the auditory impacts but also the persistent internalised sound: 'the noise of the looms completely deafened me at first, and I could hear them long after the engine had stopped and even in my bed at night' (35). Holt's autobiography is haunted by the looms; even the pandemonium of the Second World War is described through reference back to the weaving shed noisescape (66). In a text continually attuned to the auditory, the looms become a dominating and oppressive keynote sound. As Frances Dyson puts it: 'Noise deafens – the more you hear, the less you are able to hear, the less you can hear, the more noise you need in order to hear. Noise undoes its own hearing and in the process multiplies' (Dyson 2014: 7).

But industrial noise demands attention despite its deafening qualities. Survival depended on hyper-alert listening. Hillel Schwartz writes of factory workers' expertise in 'understanding anomalous sounds: the hoarse gasp of a rusty steam press, the wheeze of a worn belt on a high-speed lathe, the guttural gripe of an industrial stitching machine aching for oil [. . .] always "in hearing" of the noise of their machines' (Schwartz 2011: 349). While earplugs and ear defenders were worn in factories and conflict zones, these had limited success because survival depended on the ability to hear the irregularities of a faulty machine or the oncoming shells. In *May Day*, factory worker Jenny describes her 'long slavery of body and mind to the factory [. . .] the noise, the particular note of her machine sound amongst the others' (Sommerfield 2010: 119). The 'flap . . . flap . . . flap' of a loose belt in the machine shop is repeated ominously through the novel (204). The text's audile points – and those of its characters – oscillate between aural overload (sound impossible to register) and listening in to noise or writing its causes and effects.

In *May Day*, Sommerfield not only registers high-decibel noise but, to use Bijsterveld's terminology, 'dramatizes' sound through a sonic schema whereby 'meaningless' machine noise is transferred to meaningful vocal protest. The novel enacts a transfer of sonic power: noise is recuperated and transposed into the communal sound of 'revolutionary song' (240). In one particularly cinematic machine-shop scene, 240 women work to a 'savage, exact rhythm', a 'terrible mechanical ballet' where 'everything moves meaninglessly, repetitively'. The machines underscore the redundancy of the human: 'insatiable metallic jaws with a machine-gun rattle that drowns their motors' electric whining and slavering' (49). The withdrawal of labour – the word 'STRIKE in jagged red letters' – means a cessation of noise: 'the machines stopping with a stunning silence' (95). As the novel unfolds, print and sound technologies are co-opted and repurposed. Radios endlessly play 'without a caress / Life is meaningless', as though in both medium and message they are emptied of signification (166). Excess sound is recuperated as resistance: on the radio 'an alien voice, a hoarse shout of "Workers, all out on May Day!"' until the 'clangour sounded everywhere, until even the radio and the newspapers, the loudest instruments in the orchestra of suppression were forced to echo the undertone of a working class motif' (68). As Leo Mellor has argued, 1930s writers aimed to capture the street sounds of mass political protest and, in doing so, were trying to find 'analogies in prose for the absorptive power of early recording technologies', but they also were interested in not just representing noise but recreating it 'as an overtly political act' (Mellor 2016: 114). Literary fiction is not only central to our understanding of the phenomenological experience of audition but is one of the places where the cultural and political signification of sound is shaped and resisted.

In this way, *May Day* resists the musicalisation of machine noise. Industrial noise was often recalibrated as 'sonic communitarism', particularly in documentary films of the period such as Humphrey Jennings's *Listen to Britain* (1942) or the GPO Film Unit's *Night Mail* or *Coal Face* (Mansell 2016: 134). In these films, as Mansell has explored, we find a 'self-conscious attempt to reorient the dominant negative view of industrial and mechanical noise in Britain' (139). The sonic and physical rhythms of industry bring human and machine into supposed harmonic alignment as part of the depiction of national purpose. This preoccupation with industrial rhythms connects to the growth of state-sponsored programmes to counter the impacts of noise with workplace music designed to boost morale and productivity in wartime. The use of rhythmic and 'ordered' sound via factory gramophones and radios, as well as factory concerts run by the Entertainments National Service Association, tuned in to ideas about the benefits of particular kinds of sound in training the efficient and productive labouring body. The BBC's *Music While You Work* (from 1940) was the direct result of IHRB experiments into the effects of music on workers' productivity and fatigue.[8] In all these schemes, the type and style of music were carefully chosen and monitored, throwing into relief the distinction between 'ordered' sound and noise.

Inez Holden's novella *Night Shift* (1941) is another sonically minded factory text that represents a layered and itemised soundscape, as though the auditory streaming, categorising or 'orchestration' of sounds enacts control over an invasive noise environment. Holden's text also forms part of a gendered perspective on factory work found in novels such as Monica Dickens's *The Fancy* and non-fiction works like Amabel Williams-Ellis's *Women in War Factories* and Celia Fremlin's *War Factory* (all 1943). These texts, as Judy Suh has argued, act as a corrective to the male-dominated documentary realism of the interwar and wartime periods (Suh 2012). Set over six shifts at a factory, Braille's, making camera parts for war planes, *Night Shift*'s 'acute ear for sound' registers and itemises individual sounds with intense detail (Bluemel 2019: xvii). The text's earspective listens into noise, identifying its 'foundation' as the 'thump-hum-drum of the machinery', over which is overlaid the 'violent hissing of the steam jets' and the 'clattering sound of someone dropping or tripping over some castings' (Holden 2019: 3–4). The workers adapt to the auditory environment so that pain comes from the 'noise within the noise' when an unexpected sound runs 'along the workers' nerves like monkeys jumping on telephone wires' (4). *Night Shift*'s auditory field documents not only hypersensitive listening but a kind of wartime communal hyperacusis.

The factory noisescape is counterposed with an 'air-raid orchestra of airplane hum, anti-aircraft shell bursts, ambulance and fire bells' (4). On one level, the novella evokes the sound effects of radio or documentary film, but throughout, the sensing and streaming human ear is emphasised over mechanical all-sound recording. The ability to itemise and identify particular noises is central to survival and sensory navigation in wartime. When the factory is bombed in an air raid (a scene based on a raid of 16 April 1941), the event is bounded by sounds: 'I remembered again two clear sounds, the penny whistle at the beginning of the bombardment, the bird singing at the end of it' (85). Auditory memories and their accurate identification form part of spatial and temporal wartime orientation:

> I thought of the way in which we lived by sounds and in my mind I began to go through the sounds of the evening. The penny whistle, the siren wail, airplane hum, gunfire, penny whistle again, howling of dogs, a tear-sheet sound of bomb, crackling sound of fire, running feet, dragging of a stirrup pump along a floor, human voice [. . .] water jetting [. . .] the stones of a house falling [. . .] ambulance bells [. . .] breaking glass [. . .] machinegun fire [. . .] a noise like a barbed wire rug being rolled up, wardens' whistles [. . .] and so these same sounds again in two-sound, three-sound time, altogether or separately. (80)

This is partly about actuality recording and the documentary impulse, but the intensity and dominance of 'listening in', also found in Elizabeth Bowen's wartime fiction, illustrate the sensory reorientations of wartime.

As well as bringing attention to a neglected aspect of aural history, these phonographic texts amplify wider questions about writing sound, ever conscious of the gap between word and sense phenomena. The sonic disrupts the written precisely because it triggers and evokes a sense and medium other than the one used to experience it. Textual sound is inherently, as Justin St Clair puts it, 'dislocatory' or acousmatic (St Clair 2019: 355). The act of writing noise generates textual experiment and foregrounds the inadequacy of representation more generally. The high-decibel factory-floor scene in interwar texts prompts various modes of immediacy and extra-textual gestures, whether a shift to the second person in *Love on the Dole* (49) or the present tense in *May Day* (48). Attempts to describe high-decibel noise disrupt textual conventions and multiple representational modes are deployed given the decibel level under capture, whether analogy, onomatopoeia ('tat-tat-tat'), typographic experiment ('BUMP'), or the rhythmic push and pull of phonemes. Registers of affect, such as exclamation marks, abound too in these passages. Writing sound that troubles, confuses and overloads the senses inevitably 'troubles' the novel form. The very qualities that underscore these texts' commitment to proletarianism are also those that connect them to avant-garde noise art and characteristics conventionally associated with modernism. Attending to the representation of technological noise can reveal lines of influence that cut across literary critical categories that obscure such affiliations.

Like the complex, non-periodic frequencies of noise itself, these writers tune in to a range of different styles, modes, techniques of sound writing which could be said to complicate their texts' status as realist (as well as the discourse of authenticity within which they are often judged to be lacking). Noise punctures and interrupts the text in the moment of its evocation, that moment itself shifting between evoking and creating through the sound of the medium (whether heard in mind's ear or out loud). But perhaps what emerges most forcefully from these noise texts is the place of the listening, sensing body within these tussles over the signification of loud sound. As Julie Napolin argues, 'In its inclusion of a listening subject, literature is a particular kind of historical record: the linguistic presentation of sound – its tense and mood – does not record a positive event, but rather a site of contact' (Napolin 2020: 195). That site of aural overload has been silenced in histories of industrial health as in literary histories of interwar Britain. Bodies are drilled and controlled by the production line and repetitive labour, but the sonic by-product of technology also controls, invades and silences the body. Technology trains the senses and is, in turn, discursively formed by culture. Literature is one of the places where narratives about noise were constructed. Those narratives are intimately connected to understandings of technological modernity and human/machine relations.

Notes

1. See, for example, Thompson (2002), Bijsterveld (2008) and Mansell (2016). For more literary-orientated studies of modernism see Groth et al. (2018), Frattarola (2018) and Halliday (2013).
2. See, for example, Constantine (1928) or Stephen Ross (2004), 'Authenticity Betrayed: the "Idiotic Folk" of *Love on the Dole*', *Cultural Critique* 56: 189–209.
3. Dembe cites studies such as Jobson (1917), which concludes that 'exposure to gun-fire in the present war often produces rapidly a permanent deafness'.

4. Thomas Horder archive, Wellcome Institute, GP/31/B.2/24.
5. Thomas Horder archive, Wellcome Institute, GP/31/B.2/24, p. 9.
6. James Mansell writes extensively on these contexts in *The Age of Noise* (Chs 1 and 3).
7. See Mansell (2016: 25–60, 103-17) for more discussion of the debates concerning the psychological versus the physical impacts of noise between doctors and industrial psychologists.
8. See the 'Music While You Work' section of *People in Production: An Enquiry into British War Production* (Mass Observation 1942), which describes factory gramophone loan schemes and suggests that one-fifth of factories had radio installations. See also Wyatt and Langdon (1937), 'Fatigue and Boredom', IHRB Report No. 77 and Wynford Reynolds, *Music While You Work* (BBC 1942).

Works Cited

Bartlett, F. C. (1934), *The Problem of Noise*. Cambridge: Cambridge University Press.
Bijsterveld, Karin (2008), *Mechanical Sound: Technology, Culture and Public Problems of Noise in the Twentieth Century*. Cambridge, MA: MIT Press.
Bluemel, Kristin (2019), 'Introduction', in Inez Holden, *Blitz Writing: Night Shift & It Was Different at the Time*. Bath: Handheld, Press, pp. vii–xxxiv.
Brierley, Walter (2011), *Means Test Man*. Nottingham: Spokesman Books.
Constantine, Stephen (1928), '*Love on the Dole* and its Reception in the 1930s', *Literature and History*, 8: 2, pp. 232–47.
Culpin, Millais and May Smith (1930), 'The Nervous Temperament', *Industrial Health Research Board, Report No. 61*, pp. ii–46.
Davis, A. H. (1937), *Noise*. London: Watts & Co.
Dembe, Allard (1996), *Occupation and Disease: How Social Factors Affect the Conception of Work-Related Disorders*. New Haven, CT: Yale University Press.
Dyson, Frances (2014), *The Tone of Our Times: Sound, Sense, Economy and Ecology*. Boston: MIT Press.
Frattarola, Angela (2018), *Modernist Soundscapes: Auditory Technology and the Novel*. Gainesville: University Press of Florida.
Gaughan, Matthew (2008), 'Palatable Socialism or "The Real Thing"?: Walter Greenwood's *Love on the Dole*', *Literature and History*, 17: 2, pp. 47–61.
Goldsmith, Mike (2012), *Discord: The Story of Noise*. Oxford: Oxford University Press.
Greenwood, Walter (1993), *Love on the Dole*. London: Vintage.
Groth, Helen, Julian Murphet and Penelope Hone, eds (2018), *Sounding Modernism: Rhythm and Sonic Mediation in Modern Literature and Film*. Edinburgh: Edinburgh University Press.
Halliday, Sam (2013), *Sonic Modernity*. Edinburgh: Edinburgh University Press.
Hanley, James (1938), 'The Machines Stop', in *People are Curious*. London: John Lane.
Heller, Michael C. (2015), 'Between Silence and Pain: Loudness and the Affective Encounter', *Sound Studies*, 1: 1, pp. 40–58.
Holden, Inez (2019), *Blitz Writing: Night Shift & It Was Different at the Time*, ed. Kristin Bleumel. Bath: Handheld Press.
Holt, William (1939), *I Haven't Unpacked: An Autobiography*. London George G. Harrap & Co.)
Horder, Thomas, Speeches, Wellcome Institute, GP/31/B.2/24.
Jobson, T. B. (1917), 'Normal Gun Deafness', *Lancet*, 2, p. 566.
Kahn, Douglas (1999), *Noise, Water, Meat: A History of Sound in the Arts*. Cambridge, MA: MIT Press.
Lacey, Kate (2013), *Listening Publics: The Politics and Experience of Listening in the Media Age*. London: Polity.

McIvor, A. J. (1987), 'Manual Work, Technology and Industrial Health, 1918–1939', *Medical History*, 31, pp. 160–89.
Mansell, James (2016), *The Age of Noise in Britain: Hearing Modernity*. Urbana: University of Illinois Press.
Mansell, James (2020), 'Noise', in *Sound and Literature*, ed. Anna Snaith. Cambridge: Cambridge University Press.
Marx, Karl (1990), *Capital*, vol. 1. Harmondsworth: Penguin.
Mass Observation (1942), 'Music While You Work', *People in Production: An Enquiry into British War Production*. London: John Murray, pp. 175–7.
Mellor, Leo (2016), 'Listening-in to the Long 1930s', *Critical Quarterly*, 58: 4, pp. 113–32.
Napolin, Julie (2020), 'Unrecordable Sound: Media History, Technology and the Racial Unconscious', in *Sound and Literature*, ed. Anna Snaith. Cambridge: Cambridge University Press.
Pollock, K. G. and F. C. Bartlett (1932), 'Psychological Experiments on the Effects of Noise', *Industrial Health Research Board Reports*, 65, pp. 1–37.
Rabinbach, Anson (1992), *Human Motor: Energy, Fatigue and the Origins of Modernity*. Oakland: University of California Press.
Reynolds, Wynford (1942), *Music While You Work*. London: BBC.
Robertson, Emma, Marek Korczynski and Michael Pickering, eds (2013), *Rhythms of Labour: Music at Work in Britain*. Cambridge: Cambridge University Press.
Ross, Stephen (2004), 'Authenticity Betrayed: The "Idiotic Folk" of *Love on the Dole*', *Cultural Critique*, 56, pp. 189–209.
Russolo, Luigi (2009 [1913]), *The Art of Noises*, in *Futurism: An Anthology*, ed. Lawrence Rainey, Christine Poggi and Laura Wittman. New Haven, CT: Yale University Press, pp. 133–8.
Schafer, R. Murray (1994), *The Soundscape: Our Sonic Environment and the Tuning of Our World*. Rochester, VT: Destiny Books.
Schwartz, Hillel (2011), *Making Noise: From Babel to the Big Bang and Beyond*. New York: Zone Books.
Smith, Mark M. (2001), *Listening to Nineteenth-Century America*. Chapel Hill: University of North Carolina Press.
Sommerfield, John (2010), *May Day*. London: London Books.
St Clair, Justin (2019), 'Literature and Sound', in *The Routledge Companion to Sound Studies*, ed. Michael Bull. London: Routledge, pp. 353–61.
Suh, Judy (2012), 'Women, Work and Leisure in British Wartime Documentary Realism', *Literature/Film Quarterly*, 40: 1, pp. 54–76.
Thompson, Emily (2002), *The Soundscape of Modernity: Architectural Acoustics and the Culture of Listening in America 1900-1930*. Cambridge, MA: MIT Press.
Weston, H. C. and S. Adams (1932), 'The Effects of Noise on the Performance of Weavers', *Industrial Health Research Board Reports No. 65*, pp. 38–62.
Weston, H. C. and S. Adams (1935), 'The Performance of Weavers Under Varying Conditions of Noise', *Industrial Health Research Board Reports No. 70*, pp. 1–16.
Wyatt, S. and J. N. Langdon (1937), 'Fatigue and Boredom', *Industrial Health Research Board Reports No. 77*.

Part IV

Systems

22

NATION: GPO DOCUMENTARIES AND INFRASTRUCTURES OF THE NATION-STATE

Janice Ho

IN HIS 1941 wartime essay 'England, Your England', George Orwell attempted to define the components of national character. 'There *is* something distinctive and recognizable in English civilization,' he maintained, and '[i]t is somehow bound up with solid breakfasts and gloomy Sundays, smoky towns and winding roads, green fields and red pillar-boxes' (Orwell 1961 [1941]: 11, emphasis in original). Orwell's turn to the red pillar-boxes of the General Post Office (GPO) as an emblem of the nation, as integral to the fabric of everyday life as breakfast, was a sentiment widely echoed throughout early twentieth-century Britain. W. H. Auden's 1937 travelogue to Iceland, written in rhyme royal as a *Letter to Lord Byron*, notes that 'confession is a human want, / So Englishmen must make theirs now by post', reflecting on the affective intimacies circulated by the post office's 'modern methods of communication: / New roads, new rails, new contacts, as we know / From documentaries by the G.P.O' (1977a [1937]: 169). When Cambridge University Press commissioned a series of books on 'English Institutions', the first monograph was E. T. Crutchley's *G.P.O.* (1938), and a review in *The Observer* declared, 'No one can read this excellent book without a sense of pride at a great national achievement' ('G.P.O.' 1938: 21). Ivor Halstead's best-selling wartime account *Post Haste* (1944) evoked the continuous presence of the GPO through the lifespan of citizens from their cradles to their graves – anticipating the post-war Welfare State to come – with the 'young tak[ing] their earliest savings to the Post Office, [and] the old go[ing] to it for their pensions' (qtd in Robinson 1948: 415).

These expressed attachments to the post office as an institution at once ordinary and iconic, embedded into the daily rhythms of national life, are unsurprising, given the range of infrastructural and technological services under the purview of the GPO at this time. Although the nineteenth century is often seen as the moment of the institution's modernisation – with the establishment of the Penny Post in 1840, the Savings Bank in 1861 and exclusive rights to telegraph services in 1869 – the early twentieth century saw a radical expansion of the GPO's responsibilities. By the outbreak of the First World War, the GPO was the largest employer of labour in the country, with nearly a quarter of a million men and women in its workforce. It began functioning as the administrative interface between the public and state social services through the distribution of pensions and the sale of unemployment insurance stamps after the passage of the 1908 Old Age Pensions and 1911 National Insurance Acts, respectively. It took over the National Telephone Company in 1912 and, because the GPO also controlled licences for wireless sending and receiving apparatuses, it was the authority in charge of collecting radio and television fees for the BBC and ensuring the efficient operation of cable and wireless networks.[1] If, as David Trotter suggests, the modernist era might be characterised as the 'first media age' because there emerged, for the first time in history, 'a widespread awareness of the multiple coexistence of mass media' that reshaped 'the exercise of state power, [and] the construction of the citizen', the GPO was very much the institution at the centre of this critical mass with its monopoly over Britain's various communications networks (2013: 2).

Expanding on the lines of enquiry set up by historians of communications infrastructure, this chapter argues that the early twentieth century saw a reconfiguration of modes of national belonging insofar as affective ties to the nation and the relationship between citizen and state began to be construed and imagined materially, logistically – that is to say, infrastructurally. Nowhere is this more visible than in the interwar documentaries produced by the cultural arm of the GPO, the Film Unit, headed by John Grierson and subsequently Alberto Cavalcanti between 1933 and 1940, after which it was integrated into the Crown Film Unit. The Unit was tasked with explaining, educating and advertising the range of GPO state services to the public but, no mere propaganda machine, it soon became renowned for avant-garde experiments in documentary form. Indeed, Grierson is credited with coining the term 'documentary' in a film review, later defining it as the 'creative treatment of actuality' (qtd in Hardy 1966: 13). Such aesthetic experiments were also political experiments in how to imagine the nation and its citizens as part of an infrastructure state – a new Leviathan whose representational associations were very much in historical flux.

Connecting the Nation-State

In scholarship influenced by Benedict Anderson's seminal definition of the nation as an 'imagined political community', emphasis tends to fall on the imagination, on the profound fictiveness underlying national communities. No less important, however, is Anderson's analysis of the materiality on which this fictiveness is based: the capacity for national consciousness depends on the development of print capitalism, during which a 'system of production' converged with a 'technology of communications' best embodied by the eighteenth-century mass-produced forms of the realist novel and the newspaper (2006 [1983]: 6, 43). These cultural forms made possible the apprehension of 'homogeneous, empty time', the simultaneity of clock and calendar, thereby providing a 'precise analogue of the idea of the nation, which also is conceived as a solid community moving down (or up) history' (26). Imagine, Anderson posits, the citizen reading his morning newspaper:

> It is performed in silent privacy, in the lair of the skull. Yet each communicant is well aware that the ceremony he performs is being replicated simultaneously by thousands (or millions) of others of whose existence he is confident, yet of whose identity he has not the slightest notion. [. . .] What more vivid figure for the secular, historically clocked, imagined community can be envisioned? At the same time, the newspaper reader, observing exact replicas of his own paper being consumed by his subway, barbershop, or residential neighbors, is continually reassured that the imagined world is visibly rooted in everyday life. (35–6)

Anderson foregrounds the temporal coincidence that allows the citizen to scale up his imagined solidarities: we move from his private consumption of the newspaper to his concrete community of neighbours to the abstract national community, all participating in the same ritual at the same time. But although time is Anderson's main concern, the excerpt also gestures at the centrality of spatial and material connections: if the newspaper circulates from citizen to neighbour to subway (underground) and beyond, it does so thanks to a communications infrastructure – probably the post office – that facilitates this network of print distribution. It is not just a particular apprehension of time, then, that underwrites the imagined community of the nation, but a spatial connection produced not so much through territorial contiguity or the geographical circumscription of national borders, but rather, through infrastructural flows.

Anderson's discussion of the interrelations between print capitalism, the communications technology in which it is rooted and the rise of national consciousness thus anticipates more recent historical work by Jo Guldi and Patrick Joyce on the relationship between the governance of the nation-state and the establishment of infrastructural systems. Tracing the history of Britain's road-building, Guldi argues for the emergence of what she calls 'the infrastructure state' in the eighteenth century. Unlike the fiscal–military state, defined by the size of its army for the defence of the realm, the modern infrastructure state 'mediate[s] the relationship between individuals and infrastructure technology' by 'design[ing] the flow of bodies, information, and goods' (Guldi 2012: 4). Guldi charts the centralised efforts of Parliament to construct a national system of roadway arteries in the eighteenth century that displaced earlier, and rather uneven, road projects undertaken by local authorities. This process of state centralisation fell into disarray – indeed, reversed course – by the mid-nineteenth century, with the rise of libertarian lobbies agitating for local control against the rule of bureaucratic experts in Westminster, but the infrastructure state was to return in force during the modernist *fin de siècle*, with increasing calls for government intervention into multiple areas of urban planning, sanitation, telecommunications and transport. Patrick Joyce's chronology and terminology differ, but he too maps the growth of a different mode of governance: the 'technostate' grounded in everyday technologies like postal services, writing and filing systems, and educational institutions. For him, the older territorial state is superseded by the communications state of the nineteenth century, which, in turn, transforms into the more 'fully fledged technological state' by the early twentieth century, epochally marked by the Second Industrial Revolution and two world wars (Joyce 2013: 43).

In Guldi's and Joyce's social histories, the nation is newly envisioned as a system of flow, connection and circulation in which national belonging is constituted via shared infrastructure. This vision of the nation-state thus differs from longstanding conceptions of nationalism predicated on shared political praxis – say, the exercise of citizenship rights at the ballot box[2] – or shared racial identities, commonly described as civic and ethnic forms of nationalisms, respectively. Of course, this by no means implies that these more conventional modes of nationalism were supplanted or displaced, as their durability testifies otherwise. It is, however, to suggest that the articulation of the nation-state *as* infrastructural system is distinct from other ways in which the nation-state had previously been apprehended; and, furthermore, that infrastructure began to function as the material and symbolic ground on which many struggles over national belonging took place.

Although Guldi and Joyce date the origins of the infrastructure or techno-state much earlier, both historians acknowledge the centrality of the modernist era as the moment of its full realisation as a consequence of state centralisation and technological advancement. This claim is borne out by recent criticism in modernist studies: Michael Rubenstein, for instance, argues for the interrelations between the constitution of Ireland as an independent nation-state between 1922 and 1940 and the development of public utilities such as a national electrical grid and waterworks. As he suggests, the provision of such infrastructures allowed citizens to constitute 'a virtual relationship with the state'; when we turn on the tap or the lights, 'we commune with the material culture of the state, encountering its power and, when things are in working order, its benevolent provision' (Rubenstein 2010: 9–10). James Purdon too reads the late nineteenth and early twentieth centuries as marking a time of state transformation predicated on informatics – a set of 'new material, social, and technological practices of official communications' – that allowed for *'the government of information'*, with an entire infrastructure of memos, reports, records, passports and files underwriting the state's administration of its national population (Purdon 2016: 5–6, emphasis in original). In both these accounts, new technologies of infrastructure are instrumental to shaping both state governance and national identities.

The interwar films produced by the GPO, a state institution of unprecedented size and with unparalleled control over Britain's communications technologies, similarly index a national consciousness constituted by the mere fact of infrastructural connectivity. Flow, connection and circulation function as both themes and tropes in these documentaries. Consider the GPO's most critically acclaimed documentary, *Night Mail* (1936) – produced by Basil Wright and Harry Watt, with Alberto Cavalcanti, Benjamin Britten and W. H. Auden responsible for sound direction[3] – which follows the operations of the Travelling Post Office over the course of a single night, as the train departs from Euston Station in London at 8.30 p.m., travels north through the industrial Midlands and arrives in Scotland at sunrise. The film seeks, one critic notes, to 'demonstrate the integrative role of the GPO and the railways linking England and Scotland, North and South' and to stress 'social integration and interdependence, Britain being linked ever closer and more cohesively by modern technology' (Richards 2011: 4, 7). These infrastructural flows are evoked through carefully juxtaposed montages of smooth, parallel lines: railway tracks with the train travelling north (Figure 22.1), levers used to control the railway switches (Figure 22.2), hanging telegraph wires and poles (Figure 22.3). The voiceover reinforces the trope of connectivity, reciting over an aerial shot of the train moving through the countryside: 'Trains from Lincolnshire and Derbyshire connect to Tamworth, trains from Warwickshire and Leicestershire connect to Rugby.'

It is, of course, a critical truism that *Night Mail* is nationalistic in its projection of Britain as a progressive, technologically modern nation. But the newness and distinctiveness of this national imaginary are worth emphasising: the integration of the nation is achieved not through the unity of a singular national identity – an inherent Englishness or Britishness – but rather, by infrastructural linkages between disparate and heterogeneous parts equalised simply by virtue of their access to the railway and postal service. For instance, the Southern countryside gives way to industrial England after the train makes a short stop at Crewe, the main junction for the Midlands, where letters are collected and a handover occurs from the English to the Scottish crew. As the train begins its next leg, the voiceover narrates: 'North – with

Figure 22.1 Railway tracks, *Night Mail*. BFI National Archive; COI / Crown ©.

Figure 22.2 Railway switch levers, *Night Mail*. BFI National Archive; COI / Crown ©.

Figure 22.3 Telegraph wires, *Night Mail*. BFI National Archive; COI / Crown ©.

Figure 22.4 Pigeonholes, *Night Mail*. BFI National Archive; COI / Crown ©.

a hundred tons of new letters to sort. The postal special picks up and distributes the mail to industrial England. The mines of Wigan – the steelworks of Warrington – the machine shops of Preston.' The regionalism of the industries seems to foreground the particularity of place, leading Ian Aitken to argue that *Night Mail*'s 'thematic centre' is 'linked to representations of regional accents, forms of behaviour, place names and environments', with the film privileging 'the regional above the national' and above metropolitan London (1998: 19). Yet Marsha Bryant rightly notes that this sequence does not, in fact, display these regional specificities, aside from a tracking shot of smoking pitheads from the viewpoint of the moving train when 'the mines of Wigan' are mentioned (1997: 50).[4] Rather, the images focus tightly on the train's speed and movement, with the passing landscape increasingly blurred, followed by a dark screen illuminated only by the train lights, and ending with an external shot of the train picking up a leather pouch of mail from a bag exchange apparatus (which allowed mail to be collected and dispatched while the train was moving at full speed). Regional industries are cued not by the film's visuals, but by sounds evoking the different activities of steelworks and machines superimposed on the undercurrent rhythms of the travelling train. In this sequence, then, the heterogeneity of regional identities is indeed preserved in the soundtrack and in the voiceover's description of place, but regional affiliations are not elevated over those of the nation, as Aitken suggests. Instead, the sphere of the nation emerges as a deeper connective tissue of infrastructure that synchronises – in fact, equalises – these locations through the film's continued focus on the train in its visuals and audio, with the sounds of each region merely overlaid as the train passes through. Another image of infrastructural equality is visible in the sorting station in the Travelling Post Office (Figure 22.4), where each town is allocated a pigeonhole of the same size, with the postal workers updating the names of towns as the train travels on. Geographical particularities are equalised in a democracy of infrastructural access – since all places, no matter how big or small, central or remote, have postcodes – with the latter neither superseding nor erasing these local identities, but simply connecting them. Likewise, in W. H. Auden's verse which accompanies the documentary's final sequence, the train is

> the night mail crossing the Border
> Bringing the cheque and the postal order

> Letters for the rich
> Letters for the poor
> [. . . For those] Asleep in working Glasgow, asleep in well-set Edinburgh.
> (Auden 1977b [1936]: 290–2)

Equality of citizenship is defined not socio-economically, but logistically: there are the rich and the poor, cities with differing statures of wealth and power, and the postal system does nothing to alter such distinctions; yet a national consciousness is nonetheless made possible through a public infrastructure that circulates amongst all citizens.

Figures of the Infrastructure State

If the cohesion of the nation-state during the early twentieth century was increasingly articulated in terms of the logistical connections between different parts of the nation and an infrastructural commons shared by all, the GPO documentaries' varied and heterogeneous styles nevertheless reflect the imaginative challenges of representing this new Leviathan. In the famous frontispiece of Thomas Hobbes's 1651 *Leviathan*, which the Parisian engraver Abraham Brosse designed in collaboration with Hobbes, the political iconography visually embodies the social contract between the sovereign and the people, since the body of the sovereign is constituted by the individual bodies of the citizenry: the Leviathan, or the Commonwealth, is an 'artificial person' wherein 'the multitude [is] so united in one person' (Hobbes 1998 [1651]: 106, 114). The GPO documentaries faced a similar representational challenge in attempting to articulate a set of figures to concretise the modern infrastructure state, one whose existence is defined not by the representative body of the people, but by the invisible flows of technologies. As Trotter suggests in his account of the rise of connective media,

> representation was [. . .] the issue, or *an* issue, where the oddly unspectacular spectacle of connectivity was concerned. [. . .] The job of representational media was to render palpable again a connectivity that had become at once more necessary than ever before and more abstract. (2013: 21)

The diversity, even eccentricity, of the GPO documentaries is thus attributable not merely to the individual styles of the many directors associated with the Film Unit – for instance, in the well-known divide between John Grierson's commitment to social realism and Alberto Cavalcanti's preference for narrative-driven and human-interest stories – but also to the fact that the discursive matrix governing representations of the infrastructure state had not yet been consolidated, leading to a series of political thought experiments expressed in different aesthetic forms. Various figurations of the nation as infrastructural system emerge in these documentaries, which also invoke different tropes and generic forms: the infrastructure state is the embodiment of technocratic, scientific expertise in Stuart Legg's *The Coming of the Dial* (1933); of the democratic socialist cooperative in E. H. Anstey and Harry Watt's *6:30 Collection* (1934); of the organic lifeblood and nervous system of the nation, as natural as the cycle of the seasons, in Evelyn Spice's *Calendar of the Year* (1936).

The Coming of the Dial presents the telephone dial that links up to an automatic exchange – instead of calls manually connected through a human operator – as a technological machine originating from the modern frontiers of scientific enquiry, and casts the GPO as a laboratory staffed by scientific experts who control the circulation of British commercial life through telephony. The documentary begins with the voiceover announcing over a montage of rotating objects that culminates in the image of the whirling telephone dial:

> Research – the creative power behind the modern world. Building the future in the laboratory. The industrial chemist [. . .] The physicist [. . .] The plant breeder [. . .] These men are applying the laws of science to everyday problems. And research into the behaviour of electromagnets has revolutionized the telephone system and introduced the dial.

The film follows engineers conducting volume, durability, transmission and reception tests on the telephone apparatus, as well as designers of telephone exchanges measuring and calculating telephone traffic. The images deployed create an aura of expertise by foregrounding scientific equipment: oscillators, gauges, statistical tables, rulers, cables. The film consists primarily of extra-diegetic narration, the so-called 'voice of God', that underscores this external authority. In *The Coming of the Dial*, the infrastructure state is figured as a top-down, technocratic institution, governed by the rule of experts responsible for directing and overseeing the traffic of technology. This oversight – 'seeing like a state', to use James Scott's formulation (1998) – is quite literally figured as a product of the ocular power of expertise (Figure 22.5). The documentary offers a view into the inner workings of an institution that seems removed from the everyday life of the populace and anticipates the genre of 'infrastructural tourism' that seeks to showcase the spectacularity of modern technological systems (Mattern 2013).

By contrast, in a documentary like *6:30 Collection*, usually seen as a precursor to *Night Mail*, the hierarchical and distant nature of the infrastructure state is inverted, since this film depicts the GPO as something akin to a socialist cooperative insofar as the smoothness of infrastructural flows is facilitated by working-class labour and camaraderie amongst (male) postal workers. The film begins with an aerial shot of London's West End, but moves from the general to the particular by zooming in to track a single postman making his way to the sorting headquarters. Like *The Coming of the*

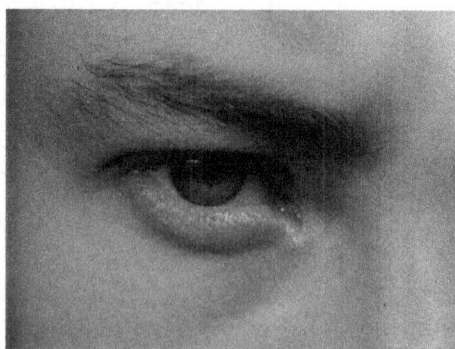

Figure 22.5 The ocular power of the expert, *The Coming of the Dial*.
BFI National Archive; COI / Crown ©.

Figure 22.6 Post office staff working together, *6:30 Collection*.
BFI National Archive; COI / Crown ©.

Dial, *6:30 Collection* aims to capture a set of post office operations: the sorting process when a collection of letters comes in. But the two films are quite different. Unlike *The Coming of the Dial*'s focus on the singular expert – the scientists and engineers appear individually, for the most part – *6:30 Collection* foregrounds the sorting process as a collaborative and collective enterprise with a large group of postal workers working seamlessly in tandem (Figure 22.6). And although this documentary too is narrated by a voiceover, albeit more sparsely, the film's soundtrack differs in that the voiceover overlays a rich and continuous auditory background of the workers' chatter – that occasionally rises to the surface with overheard phrases like 'Mind your back' or 'Make way, please' – their whistling, and the general hustle and bustle of their work. Steve Foxon observes that *6:30 Collection* 'is probably the first documentary made entirely with authentic sound [. . . with] the careful introduction of oddments of conversation on allotments, [with] the choral effort of the despatch men calling the destination of their bags across half the world, and [with] a beautiful scrap of whistling' (2008: 40–1). Insofar as it is, paradoxically, the background sounds of workers in conversation and of their quotidian labour that is *6:30 Collection*'s most interesting feature, the film reverses the authoritativeness of the voiceover to emphasise the demotic voices of the postal workers instead. The focus on how working-class labour facilitates the circulation of the infrastructure state is also visible in the documentary's depiction of the sorters' physical skill: a sequence portrays the workers sorting parcels by deftly tossing them into postal bags with unerring accuracy, much as basketball players shoot hoops. Far from a mode of alienation, working-class labour is a function of artisanal craft and bodily dexterity, literally embodying the effortless speed of the nation's technological connections. With its attention to the labouring body, *6:30 Collection*, like *Night Mail*, shares generic affinities with Soviet-style cinema celebrating the dignity of the worker.

In *The Coming of the Dial* and *6:30 Collection*, two radically opposed figures of the nation as infrastructure state emerge, the one vertical and technocratic; the other, horizontal and democratic. In the first, the infrastructural flows of the GPO are conducted from the top down by elite experts; in the second, they are orchestrated through the collaborative labour of GPO workers. These two contrasting depictions reflect the historically open-ended politics of infrastructural systems during the modernist era, as these could alternately signal more centralised and hierarchical forms of state control or promise an egalitarian and a collective access to a national public good. Furthermore, the growth of the infrastructure state and the consequent extension of governmental reach into private spheres of life also had to accommodate itself to a longstanding ideological self-image of a liberal nation, one predicated on a clear separation between state and civil society and a circumscribed role for the former. If '[c]onflict over the government's role in infrastructure is one of the primary features of the infrastructure state' (Guldi 2012: 18), this conflict is visible in controversies during the interwar years, which ranged from objections to new roads built too close to houses to concerns about the regulatory powers given to electricity suppliers to enter and inspect private residences to fears about the telephone as an intrusive medium, bringing the outside world inside the domestic home.[5] Because of the interlocking of public and private spaces effected by the rise of infrastructural systems which aroused liberal concerns regarding the limits of state power, GPO documentaries also frequently figured the infrastructure state in ways that sought to mitigate these anxieties.

In *Calendar of the Year*, for instance, the communications technologies of the GPO are depicted, not as artificial impositions or modern wonders, but rather, as natural accompaniments to the seasonal life of the nation. As the voiceover declares at the beginning, over shots of cliffs, seas and trees, 'Year in, year out, the life of this island country is held together by a vast network of communications.' The documentary follows the everyday activities of citizens and commercial enterprises across a cycle of seasons to depict the organic embeddedness of GPO infrastructure in the nation's quotidian existence. Beginning with winter, it shows the GPO as a rescuer of ships battered by storms, responsible for transmitting distress signals. From spring to summer and autumn, the telephone, telegraph and postal mail are presented as essential services to farmers sending their spring flower and potato crops to the market; to the London crowd in summer making bookings for the Russian ballet and mailing postcards from beach holidays; to the British public instantaneously finding out the outcomes of major sporting events and races like the Derby; to the national institutions of Lloyds, the Stock Exchange and the Bank of England that mediate the economic transactions of buying, selling and shipping harvest crops in autumn. Organic metaphors reinforce the naturalisation of these systems as a human body: for instance, in the comparison of the Stores Department – the GPO centre responsible for 'feeding materials [such as copper wires] to a hundred points' – to the 'nerve centre of a vast organisation'. The film ends in a cyclical fashion with a return to winter by foregrounding the GPO's role in delivering 10 million parcels during the three days before Christmas. *Calendar of the Year* figures the infrastructure state as an inconspicuous entity underwriting the ordinary lives of the nation's citizens; by doing so, it relocates state power into the realm of civil society, casting it as a natural force entirely compatible with liberalism's belief in the light touch of government.

Glitches in Infrastructural Flows

In GPO documentaries, the new Leviathan of the infrastructural nation could thus take on a variety of figurations, all with rather different political implications. Yet in spite of these differences, these documentaries share one thing in common: infrastructural flows always proceed smoothly, without disruptions, regardless of whether they are coordinated by technocratic experts from on high, conducted through a camaraderie of socialist solidarity, or channelled as a feature of the natural world. The synchrony of logistical connections acts as the corollary of national unity, integrating disparate parts of the country in an interdependent whole. To return to *Night Mail* as an example: in a central sequence, a novice postal worker learns how to swing out a leather pouch of mail, hung from a metallic arm, from the train moving at full speed in preparation for it to be caught by a mechanical bag exchange apparatus positioned near train stations. This device allowed for the delivery and pickup of mail without the train slowing down and the process was an operation with not inconsiderable risks: postal workers and train drivers were occasionally killed or had their arms ripped off, if they missed their timing (Anthony 2007: 32). *Night Mail*'s presentation of this sequence, however, emphasises the impeccable harmony of infrastructural networks: the human labour of the post office worker is continuous with the machinery of the bag exchange apparatus and with the speed and motion of the train, as the leather pouch of mail is flawlessly transferred via this chain of connections. Indeed, the sound of the train is incorporated as syncopated musical rhythm in the auditory track, reinforced by the veteran post office worker's instruction to the new hire to wait for '2 bridges and 45 beats' before he lowers the leather pouch; the film thus unifies the sphere of labour and leisure, train and music, and reflects the broader tendency of GPO documentaries to use 'industrial and ambient noise [. . .] *as* music', corresponding to the modernist genre of city symphony films such as Walter Ruttmann's *Berlin: Symphony of a Metropolis* (1927), wherein urban life is presented as rhythmic movement (Sargent 2011: 56, emphasis in original).[6] In his essay for this collection, Josh Epstein likewise points out that, in many modernist texts, the 'affective qualities of music [. . .] mak[e] visible its technological circulation' and that these texts frequently sought to enhance the relationship between music and industrial noise (230). *Night Mail* and other GPO documentaries predominantly cast the technologically networked nation as an infrastructural symphony.

But what happens when infrastructure breaks down? *Night Mail* never contemplates such a possibility and the film has 'often been mocked because its workers are too cheerful, its trains are too punctual [. . .and] [h]arsher critics assert that the film is less a documentary than a fantastical imagining of a model railway' (Anthony 2007:19). The documentaries' depiction of the infrastructure state as a harmonic unit means that they understand national infrastructure as primarily an organisational and technocratic challenge, rather than a political one. GPO filmmakers were themselves aware of this shortcoming, with the director of *Night Mail*, Harry Watt, complaining about *6:30 Collection* thus:

> Once you post a letter there is little that can happen to it, except the process of collecting, sorting and delivering. They have been known to be blown up by the IRA, or covered with a swarm of bees, or even eaten by a plague of snails, but such a scene would hardly fit into a film financed by the Post Office to emphasise its modernity. (qtd in Anthony 2007: 25)

Significantly, Watt points not only to natural glitches in postal circulation – bees and snails – but to political ones in the IRA's attempt to sabotage infrastructural flows. Because politics in an infrastructure state is invariably engendered by 'changes in infrastructure' and fought 'over issues of access to infrastructure', it is precisely in such moments of infrastructural glitches that political struggles are at their most visible

(Guldi 2012: 3). This is Lauren Berlant's argument when she observes that a glitch is 'an interruption within a transition, a troubled transmission. A glitch is also the revelation of infrastructural failure [...but] failure [also] opens up the potential for new organizations of life' (2016: 393). Glitches to logistical chains do not necessarily reflect mere technological breakdowns, but may signal alternative political imaginaries altogether. These glitches are ultimately foreclosed in the documentaries funded by the GPO Film Unit, given the institution's investments in the synchronic and symphonic circulation of infrastructure as the material embodiment of national integration and unity. But we can nevertheless turn to the historical record to gesture briefly at two central moments in the modernist era during which struggles over citizenship and national belonging took the form of a politics of infrastructure that deliberately sought to interrupt – to glitch – the nation-state's postal system.

The first is the Easter Rising of 1916, invariably memorialised as the founding act of the Irish Republic, when a group of Irish republican nationalists led by, among others, Patrick Pearse, James Connolly and Joseph Plunkett, seized prominent locations in Dublin – including Dublin City Hall, St Stephen's Green, Boland's Mill, Jacob's Biscuit Factory and the Four Courts – on 24 April and held them for nearly a week before British soldiers crushed the uprising and retook the buildings. The headquarters of this uprising was established at the Dublin General Post Office (Figure 22.7) and Patrick Pearse read out the Proclamation of the Republic at its steps. Historians have debated about the tactics of the rebels, especially their choice of particular landmarks, since 'buildings of obvious strategic or symbolic value – such as Trinity College and Dublin Castle – [were] not occupied', whereas 'positions

Figure 22.7 'Gutted GPO Dublin'. The Postal Museum ©.

of negligible military value, such as St. Stephen's Green, [were] seized' (McGarry 2012: 120). Yet no such ambiguity attends the siege on Dublin's GPO, with historians noting both the symbolism and the pragmatism of the location, as an attack on the infrastructural embodiment of the British imperial state, on one hand, and a way to seize control of the city's communications centre, on the other. Clair Wills observes that '[t]he rebels took over what would now be the television station' and quickly transformed its significance 'from an emblem of nineteenth-century British power and civil government to a barricade against shelling, to a national [Irish] symbol' (2009: 9, 20). W. B. Yeats subsequently mythologised the location in his poem 'The Statues', with the poetic speaker asking, 'When Pearse summoned Cuchulainn to his side / What stalked through the Post Office?' (1996 [1938]: 362). Yeats casts the GPO as an apocalyptic scene wherein past and present converge, as the ancient mythic Irish hero is brought forth by the rebels in their attempt to found an Irish Republic. Revolution takes the literal form of an infrastructural glitch since, in the uprising, the GPO is simultaneously a material network of communications being fought over as well as a symbolic monument to be reappropriated for Irish nationalism. Furthermore, as Christopher Morash details, the Easter Rising was 'a media event as much as it was a military operation', for besides seizing the GPO, the rebels also briefly occupied the Irish School of Wireless Telegraphy (situated directly opposite), where they sought to transmit the proclamation of the new Irish Republic, an act frequently held to be the first radio broadcast in history (2010: 127). Yet another group led by J. J. Walsh – future Postmaster General of the Irish Free State – tried to use telephones in the GPO's telephone exchange on Dame Street to spread news of the uprising, though they were unable to seize this building. The politics of citizenship – the assertion of Irish sovereignty – is thus played out on the grounds of the media infrastructure controlled by the GPO.

This was also the case during the heyday of the militant moment of the suffragette movement right before the First World War, when the GPO similarly became a site of contention. As is well known, women fighting for the vote smashed local Post Office windows, destroyed red pillar-boxes by setting them on fire, and poured ink to damage the mail inside. *The Suffragette*, the official newspaper of the Women's Social and Political Union, reported on 10 January 1913 that '[s]ince our last number was printed, there have been reports almost daily of attacks on pillar-boxes in London and the provinces' ('Pillar-Boxes' 1913: 184). The concerted attacks on the GPO generated anti-suffragette propaganda in return, with a cartoonist fantasising a design for a pillar-box able to repel the suffragettes' ink and arson vandalism by automatically booting them away (Figure 22.8). But the suffragettes did not just attempt to create glitches in the system through sabotage. Sylvia Pankhurst recalls in her account of the movement that, after the Postmaster General issued regulations that permitted individuals to be mailed by express, the suffragettes decided to orchestrate a publicity stunt, arranging for a Miss Soloman and a Miss McLellan to be posted to the Prime Minister, Herbert Asquith, on 23 January 1909. The women were escorted by a GPO messenger boy to 10 Downing Street but delivery was refused, with the official answering the door telling the women, 'You must be returned [. . .] The Post Office must deliver you somewhere else, you cannot be received here' (Pankhurst 1912: 363). Here, the suffragettes quite literally embody glitches in infrastructural flows, unable to be processed in the nation-state's logistical chain of connections. These historical incidents illustrate how

Figure 22.8 Dudley Buxton, 'Automatic Suffragette Exterminating Pillar-Box (Patent NOT Applied For) Postcard'. The Postal Museum ©.

the nation's postal system was both used and abused in the historical campaign for women's rights to vote.

If we understand the nation as an infrastructural system, what the Easter Rising and the militant suffragette movement reveal is that issues of citizenship, disenfranchisement and national belonging invariably manifest themselves through contests around infrastructure. The GPO documentaries of the interwar period articulate and experiment with this new way of apprehending the nation, but they ultimately fail to account for those excluded from this national imaginary. It is only by turning to the glitches in the nation's infrastructural systems – to the space of the colonies or to those domestically disenfranchised – that such exclusions become visible. This is a question that Jennifer Lieberman will take up in different ways in the very next chapter in this volume, when she asks what kinds of narratives of infrastructure were written by 'technologically disenfranchised people' and how the exclusions of race and gender shape counter-narratives to the teleology of infrastructural modernity (363). National politics in an infrastructure state raises questions about who has access to infrastructure and what types of infrastructure, where it circulates, who controls it, when it runs smoothly, who and what allow it to run smoothly, when it is disrupted and who might disrupt it. And the politics of infrastructure remains an integral part of our lives today, in our persistent struggles over access to clean water, healthcare and affordable housing, and in contests over the geographical placement of structures from oil pipelines to dams to broadband cables.

Notes

1. The above account has been synthesised from three key histories of the GPO: Robinson (1948), Daunton (1985) and Campbell-Smith (2011).
2. See, for instance, Hadley (2010) for an account of how the ballot box became a material embodiment of liberal conceptions of citizenship in the mid-nineteenth century.
3. The official credits of *Night Mail* were the subject of a fight within the GPO Film Unit: Basil Wright and Harry Watt were, in fact, its directors (and Watt felt he deserved sole credit), while John Grierson produced the film. Scott Anthony's *Night Mail* (2007) gives an account of this conflict.
4. Bryant reads this sequence as demonstrating an 'industrial unconscious' in which the reality of working-class labour is repressed (Bryant 1997: 48–53).
5. In a House of Commons debate on the Trunk Roads Bill on 19 November 1936, for instance, which centralised government control over the nation's main arterial roads, a Member of Parliament expressed concern about a scenario in which 'the construction of the new road involve[d] an injurious affectation or purchase of property or interference with private rights [of home ownership]' ('Trunk Roads Bill' 1936). Another House of Commons debate on 2 February 1934 about the Electricity Supply Bill sees a Member of Parliament insisting that tenants 'are entitled to the privacy of their own homes, unless they are given proper notice asking for inspection' ('Electricity [Supply] Bill' 1934).
6. See also John Grierson's 'First Principles of Documentary', where he discusses the tendency of most modernist documentaries to follow Ruttmann's aesthetic, rendering documentary a style 'principally concerned with movements and the building of separate images into movements' (1966 [1926]: 150).

Works Cited

Aitken, Ian (1998), 'Introduction', in *The Documentary Film Movement: An Anthology*, ed. Ian Aitken. Edinburgh: Edinburgh University Press, pp. 1–68.
Anderson, Benedict (2006 [1983]), *Imagined Communities: Reflections on the Origin and Spread of Nationalism*, revised edn. London: Verso.
Anstey, E. H. and R. H. Watt (2008 [1934]), *6:30 Collection*. London: British Film Institute.
Anthony, Scott (2007), *Night Mail*. London: BFI Film Classics.
Auden, W. H. (1977a [1937]), *Letter to Lord Byron*, in *The English Auden: Poems, Essays and Dramatic Writings 1927–1939*, ed. Edward Mendelson. New York: Random House, pp. 169–99.
Auden, W. H. (1977b [1936]), 'Night Mail', in *The English Auden: Poems, Essays, and Dramatic Writings 1927–1939*, ed. Edward Mendelson. New York: Random House, pp. 290–2.
Berlant, Lauren (2016), 'The Commons: Infrastructure for Troubling Times', *Event and Planning D: Society and Space*, 34: 3, pp. 393–419.
Bryant, Marsha (1997), *Auden and Documentary in the 1930s*. Charlottesville: University of Virginia Press.
Buxton, Dudley (n.d.), 'Automatic Suffragette Exterminating Pillar-Box (Patent NOT Applied For) Postcard', in 'The Suffrage Movement', *The Postal Museum*, <https://www.postalmuseum.org/blog/suffrage/> (last accessed 26 May 2020).
Campbell-Smith, Duncan (2011), *Masters of the Post: The Authorized History of the Royal Mail*. London: Allen Lane.
Daunton, Martin (1985), *Royal Mail: The Post Office Since 1840*. London: The Athlone Press.

'Electricity (Supply) Bill' (1934), *Hansard House of Commons*, 2 February, <https://hansard.parliament.uk/Commons/1934-02-02/debates/3a26f757-c481-4f2c-9b6f-061fb0e6ffc0/Electricity(Supply)Bill?highlight=privacy%20electricity#contribution-dd7bad81-3858-44be-8d73-0d3abe082e05> (last accessed 26 May 2020).

Foxon, Steve (2008), '*6:30 Collection*', in *Addressing the Nation: The GPO Film Unit Collection*. London: British Film Institute.

'G.P.O.' (1938), *The Observer*, 4 December. ProQuest Historical Newspapers.

Grierson, John (1966 [1926]), 'First Principles of Documentary', in *Grierson on Documentary*, ed. Forsyth Hardy, revised edn. Berkeley: University of California Press, pp. 145–56.

Guldi, Jo (2012), *Roads to Power: Britain Invents the Infrastructure State*. Cambridge, MA: Harvard University Press.

'Gutted GPO Dublin' (1916), in 'Dublin Has Risen', *The Postal Museum*, <https://www.postal-museum.org/blog/dublin-has-risen/> (last accessed 26 May 2020).

Hadley, Elaine (2010), *Living Liberalism: Practical Citizenship in Mid-Victorian Britain*. Chicago: University of Chicago Press.

Hardy, Forsyth (1966), 'Introduction', in *Grierson on Documentary*, ed. Forsyth Hardy, revised edn. Berkeley: University of California Press, pp. 13–49.

Hobbes, Thomas (1998 [1651]), *Leviathan*, ed. J. C. A. Gaskin. Oxford: Oxford University Press.

Joyce, Patrick (2013), *The State of Freedom: A Social History of the British State Since 1800*. Cambridge: Cambridge University Press.

Legg, Stuart (2008 [1933]), *The Coming of the Dial*. London: British Film Institute.

McGarry, Fearghal (2012), *The Rising: Easter 1916*. Oxford: Oxford University Press.

Mattern, Shannon (2013), 'Infrastructural Tourism', *Places Journal*, <https://placesjournal.org/article/infrastructural-tourism/> (last accessed 26 May 2020).

Morash, Christopher (2010), *A History of the Media in Ireland*. Cambridge: Cambridge University Press.

Orwell, George (1961 [1941]), *The Lion and the Unicorn: Socialism and the English Genius*. London: Secker and Warburg.

Pankhurst, Sylvia (1912), *The Suffragette: The History of the Women's Militant Suffragette Movement, 1905–1910*. Boston: The Women's Journal.

'Pillar-Boxes Again! Attacks in London and the Provinces' (1913), *The Suffragette*, 10 January. Accessed online from *Nineteenth Century Collections Online*. Available at: <link.gale.com/apps/doc/EMTFHH994906263/NCCO?u=coloboulder&sid=bookmark-NCCO&xid=9d1d689f> (last accessed 18 February 2022).

Purdon, James (2016), *Modernist Informatics: Literature, Information, and the State*. Oxford: Oxford University Press.

Richards, Jeffrey (2011), 'John Grierson and the Lost World of the GPO Film Unit', in *The Projection of Britain: A History of the GPO Film Unit*, ed. Scott Anthony and James Mansell. London: Palgrave, pp. 1–9.

Robinson, Howard (1948), *The British Post Office: A History*. Princeton, NJ: Princeton University Press.

Rubenstein, Michael (2010), *Public Works: Infrastructure, Irish Modernism, and the Postcolonial*. Notre Dame, IN: Notre Dame University Press.

Sargent, Amy (2011), 'Harry Watt: On Land, at Sea and in the Air', in *The Projection of Britain*, eds Scott Anthony and James Mansell. London: Palgrave, pp. 53–61.

Scott, James C. (1998), *Seeing Like a State: How Certain Schemes to Improve the Human Condition Have Failed*. New Haven, CT: Yale University Press.

Spice, Evelyn (2008 [1936]), *Calendar of the Year*. London: British Film Institute.

Trotter, David (2013), *The Literature of the First Media Age: Britain Between the Wars*. Cambridge, MA: Harvard University Press.

'Trunk Roads Bill' (1936), *House of Commons Hansard*, 19 November, <https://hansard.parliament.uk/Commons/1936-11-19/debates/9d004f6f-536a-4b2f-9fb5-3d69be76ff3b/TrunkRoadsBill?highlight=roads%20property%20values#contribution-f577e205-9534-43bc-9bc7-be2cd73af443> (last accessed 26 May 2020).

Watt, Harry and Basil Wright (2008 [1936]), *Night Mail*. London: British Film Institute.

Wills, Clair (2009), *Dublin 1916: The Siege of the GPO*. Cambridge, MA: Harvard University Press.

Yeats, W. B. (1996 [1938]), 'The Statues', in *Collected Poems of W. B. Yeats*, ed. Richard Finneran, revised edn. New York: Scribner.

23

INFRASTRUCTURE: WOMEN WRITERS CONFRONT LARGE TECHNOLOGICAL SYSTEMS

Jennifer L. Lieberman

ON 17 NOVEMBER 1847, Senator Daniel Webster gave a speech to commemorate the 'Opening of the Northern Railroad to Lebanon, N.H.'. Although the occasion for his speech was the extension of the railway, Webster does not limit himself to a discussion of train travel. He also invokes steam boats and telegraphy, as if these systems are interrelated. Using the first-person plural, he includes his listeners in a shared experience of awe: 'We see the ocean navigated and the solid land traversed by steam power, and intelligence communicated by electricity. Truly this is almost a miraculous era' (Webster 1858: 419). He yokes electricity and steam together because they changed the way that he and many of his contemporaries moved through space, conceptualised time and understood progress.

Senator Webster's example typifies the dominant narrative about technological development in the nineteenth and early twentieth centuries. New systems – however disparate – seemed to signify in aggregate that machinery and scientific knowledge could render the chaotic world more controllable to the individual user. Much has already been written about this understanding of nineteenth- and twentieth-century systems. For example, Stephen Kern (1983), Wolfgang Schivelbush (1997) and Armand Mattelart (1996) – to name only a few – have chronicled how the railway and other new systems altered the way Americans understood time. Schedules for arriving and departing trains homogenised the way towns marked time. And, although they function by dramatically different mechanisms, the steam engine and electric communication could make distant spaces seem more readily accessible. Communication and transportation systems also changed conceptualisations of space. As Robert MacDougall has shown, 'One of the nineteenth century's great clichés was that the rail and wire would "annihilate" space and time' (2014: 9). Analysing the violence inherent in that word choice, he adds,

> The pace of change in this era was exhilarating and at the same time wrenching and alarming to many Americans. Each advance in communication technology gave new powers to its users yet compounded the ability of distant people and events to affect those users' lives. (9)

Advertisers, system builders and people who perceived themselves as benefitting from technological development promulgated narratives about large-scale systems as progressive and modernising. Indeed, in the chapter that precedes mine, Janice Ho argues convincingly that infrastructures helped to reshape the idea of the nation as a space that coheres through infrastructural flows. While these accounts are not unilaterally positive, as we can see in MacDougall's and Ho's examples, they typically emphasised the awesome power of new inventions and systems while promising to enhance user control. As I have argued elsewhere, some advertisements even described electrical appliances as 'slaves' to exaggerate user control (Lieberman 2017: 176–83). But these narratives were subjective and incomplete; they were stories that people (especially from privileged positions) told about the systems that they used, built, maintained, modified and derived meaning from. As David E. Nye argues, 'A technological narrative is selective. It singles out particular objects while deemphasizing or even deleting others' (2003: 11). The same structures that seemed to annihilate space, enhance control or foster connections also created disjunctions that are downplayed or erased in prevailing narratives about progress. But technologically disenfranchised people wrote narratives, too, and their stories can help historians identify more expansive cultural meanings of the large-scale systems that Senator Webster describes.[1]

Consider, for example, Pauline E. Hopkins's essay on 'The New York Subway', written for *The Voice of the Negro* in 1904.[2] Hopkins crafts a brief narrative of progress that resonates with Webster's. She asserts that 'the American people owe a debt of gratitude to Robert Fulton' for his invention of the steam engine. She places the New York subway in this Fultonian tradition of 'stupendous exercises', along with the Erie Canal and Brooklyn Bridge (2). Even as Hopkins uses the idiom of linear progress, she tempers her approbation. She is careful to note, for example, that the new subway was not the first of its kind, even though it did solve interesting engineering problems in the crossing of the Harlem river. The subway, as she portrays it, was not a pinnacle of human achievement; it was a massive financial undertaking that employed labourers, benefitted investors, solved perplexing engineering problems and made travel more convenient for commuters.

Hopkins's extensive and well-illustrated account discusses how building the tunnel necessitated 'the displacement of hundreds of sewers, masses of intricate and interlaced electric wires, gas, water and steam-pipes and all this to be done without seriously interrupting the services of these essentials to the life of a great city' (4). She describes how

> All the water-pipes, gas-pipes and sewer-pipes were hung up by chains to the beams supporting the street until blasting was over and then forty-five miles of new pipes were laid in neat and orderly style thus bringing order out of former chaos. Miles of sewers were rebuilt mostly of concrete, that material being found to be cheaper than the old brick structures. (4)

This explanation stresses that new systems like the subway were not simply symbols of progress or bold new inventions: they were the result of assiduous planning and large sums of money, intensive labour and interlocking pieces of concrete and pipe.

While Hopkins's essay presents a detailed account of the subway and related systems, akin to those that Webster described, her stunning conclusion throws the preceding narrative into relief:

> We cannot close this article without again reverting to the greatness of the Empire City of the United States. Wonderful, indeed, is the country which produces so

magnificent a metropolis. But we hope that the warning words of Emerson will forever impress this country and its citizens:
'The civility of no race is perfect whilst another race is degraded.' (7)

With her final words, Hopkins insists that the subway might be a great work in a great city but that it constitutes only a superficial version of progress in a country where life is still structured according to violent white supremacy. Where Webster described railway travel as 'almost . . . miraculous', Hopkins insists that such new developments are limited in their usefulness. Her final line insinuates that the huge expenditure on this subway – $40 million in total (which adjusts to more than $1.1 billion today) – may have been misallocated, since it does not address the foremost problem facing Americans of her day.

Large technological systems like those that Webster and Hopkins described were significant developments that influenced how nineteenth-century and early twentieth-century Americans understood the world. But if we want to understand the cultural meanings of these systems, we must analyse alternative narratives that raise questions about prevailing discourses. Hopkins's article on 'The New York Subway' is one example; in the pages that follow I discuss Hopkins at greater length and compare her approach to Charlotte Perkins Gilman's. Since I discuss Gilman at length elsewhere,[3] I focus primarily on Hopkins's counter-narratives below. Still, Gilman offers a useful comparison, since her narratives do not quite rise to the level of counter-narratives. David E. Nye defines counter-narratives as decoding dominant narratives and recoding them as ironic (2003: 15). Hopkins recodes the dominant narrative by asking readers to consider how the idea of technological progress conflicts with ongoing racial degradation (as above) and by comparing speculative advanced technologies to slave cabins (as I argue below). Gilman criticises the sexism of existing systems, but she does not recode the dominant narrative in the same way. In fact, she adopts the idioms of utilitarianism and progress to her feminist ends. By comparing Gilman's *alternative* narratives to Hopkins's *counter*-narratives, this chapter elucidates a range of subversive literary responses to the early twentieth-century notion of technological progress.

Thoughts on Terminology

Gilman and Hopkins were both drawn to write about transportation, communication and power systems; we would now call those constructs 'technological' or 'infrastructural', but they did not describe those systems in such singular terms. In fact, they did not even use the word *system* to describe them, even though they both employ that term in different contexts. Recognising this conspicuous omission in the works of other nineteenth- and early twentieth-century writers (including Webster but neither Hopkins nor Gilman), Leo Marx argued that large-scale systems strained the vocabulary of Americans in the nineteenth and early twentieth centuries. Complex, sprawling projects like electrical power systems or railways could hardly be described as 'mechanic arts', although they were associated with and often employed machinery (Marx 1997: 568). Marx asserted that these developments created the 'semantic void' that would eventually be filled by the evolving meanings of the word *technology* – a 'hazardous' singular concept, which seems to invoke new and useful material objects but is surprisingly difficult to define (573).

Although I am well acquainted with the 'hazards' that Marx locates in the word *technology*,[4] I used the phrase 'large technological systems' in my title to refer to Thomas P. Hughes's work in this area. Hughes's 2012 essay on 'The Evolution of Large Technological Systems' delineates how the construction of systems entails more than the development of physical components. He argues: 'Persons who build electric light and power systems invent and develop not only generators and transmission lines but also such organizational forms as electrical manufacturing and utility holding companies' (46). Hughes defines the development of these systems as a specific kind of 'problem solving' that 'is concerned with the reordering of the material world to make it more productive of goods and services' (47). This definition resonates with Gilman and Hopkins's depictions of the systems of their day: both women wrote extensively about reordering the material world and the organisational systems that came with it. But, it must be noted, they cared less for 'goods and services' than for the way that different social and technical systems could nourish women and people of colour, respectively.

If the large systems that Gilman and Hopkins wrote about inspired the evolving definition of the word *technology*, those same systems also inflected the way we would come to understand *infrastructure*. First coined in 1927 and used in military contexts, the term *infrastructure* has come to be nearly as ubiquitous, important and elusive as *technology*. Both of these concepts conjure material structures but cannot be understood apart from organisational systems, knowledge, labour and practices. Paul N. Edwards's essay on 'Infrastructure and Modernity' is particularly useful in elucidating the nuances of the term *infrastructure*. That concept, he argues, 'has become a slippery term, often used to mean essentially any important, widely shared, human-constructed resource' (2003: 186–7). And, although it is often defined by its materiality, Edwards and Manuel Castells have both demonstrated that *infrastructure* is more helpfully defined by the 'flows' it facilitates (Castells 2010: xxxi–xxxii, 408–9; Edwards 2003: 187).

The terms *infrastructure* and *technology* overlap significantly: every infrastructure is a technology, but not every technology is an infrastructure. One distinction between these terms might be the way that infrastructures become woven into the patterns and habits of daily life. Generalising from Wiebe E. Bijker's 2007 study of dykes and dams, infrastructures gradually 'grow[] hard and obdurate', so that 'stable ways of thinking and fixed patterns of interaction [. . .] do emerge around them' (Bijker 2007: 122). For example, Americans today expect new and constantly improving consumer technologies. In contrast, they expect their infrastructures to continue working without paying much heed to the inner workings or maintenance of these systems. Paul N. Edwards compellingly describes how these systems keep various resources (such as water, energy or gas) flowing, so that people in the global North are less apt to notice these systems when they function than when they fail: 'Infrastructures are largely responsible for the sense of stability of life in the developed world, the feeling that things work, and will go on working, without the need for thought or action on the part of users beyond paying the monthly bills' (2003: 188). Michael Rubenstein takes this logic a step further, arguing that awareness of 'public utilities' can have an 'uncanny effect [which] results from the normally instantaneous forgetting by which they incorporate themselves into the modern habitus' (2010: 137). Infrastructures, then, might be understood as the large technological systems that users depend on but can also learn to ignore – when those systems function according to plan. Disruptions such as power failures, new construction or pandemics draw attention to dependencies that are otherwise invisible. These disruptions can be caused by forces that humans inflect but cannot control, such as the spread of disease or the destruction wrought by a storm, or – as Ho showed in the previous chapter – they can be intentional acts of sabotage and resistance.

Gilman and Hopkins did not use the word *infrastructure*, but they did write extensively about the flow of people, energy and information. Science and technology studies scholars differentiate between 'analyst terms' (terms we use as scholars) and 'actor terms' (the terms our subjects use). *Modern* is an actor term because Gilman and Hopkins both use it; they wanted women and people of African descent to be included in the definition of modernity, respectively. *Infrastructure* and *technology* are analyst terms. While I focus on the way Hopkins and Gilman described their world as they perceived it, I argue that these words can be useful tools to think with because (1) they help me describe themes that are present in their bodies of work and are frequently overlooked by previous scholars, and (2) they help illuminate how these historical examples can contribute to our understanding of enduring questions concerning infrastructure and technology, today.

Infrastructure is a particularly useful analyst term because it connotes large systems that transcend scales or frames of reference, and, thus, it encourages a multiscalar analysis. Edwards employs Thomas J. Misa's definitions of scales to describe the different levels on which we can think about them:

- micro: individuals, small groups; generally short-term
- meso: institutions, e.g. corporations and standard-setting bodies, generally enduring over decades or longer
- macro: large systems and structures such as political economies and some governments, enduring over many decades or centuries. (Edwards 2003: 197)

Edwards argues that attention to each of these scales enables different perspectives about the relationship between infrastructures and modernity. I propose that a similar attention to scale can also provide a useful tool for analysing some of the more complex, multiscalar aspects of Hopkins's and Gilman's writings.

Both Hopkins and Gilman shift haphazardly between scales, focusing on individual perspectives before suddenly including a distant, meso- or macro-scale perspective. Hopkins's novel *Of One Blood* describes systems and flows from the perspective of the protagonist, Reuel Briggs – but it also deals with the haunting history of the Civil War and with the fall and rise of Ethiopian civilisation. Gilman's treatises and utopian fictions fluctuate between the perspectives of individual women and a broader perspective that imagines all of society and its systems as one macro-organism. This tendency to change scales can baffle readers, but, as I argue elsewhere, the desire to write about systems that exceed the individual perspective 'inspire[d writers] to play with narrative in ways that anticipate the experimental rhetorical strategies [of] literary modernism' (Lieberman 2017: 12). In other words, although Gilman and Hopkins are not usually categorised as modernist writers, they employed the modernist rhetorical strategy of bricolage in their attempts to describe the systems and flows that we associate with infrastructure today. Analysing infrastructure in their work can help to make sense of a dance of scales that may otherwise appear incoherent.

While attention to infrastructure can help us interpret the shifting scales in Gilman and Hopkins's work, it can also help us understand their utopian impulses. Gilman and Hopkins both wrote during an era when systemic change seemed possible, if difficult. The systems we would come to think of as *infrastructures* were growing 'obdurate' but had not yet grown 'stable', to use Bijker's terms. 'The New York Subway' demonstrated that fact. When Hopkins describes how the subway could not be constructed without moving power lines and water, gas and sewer pipes, she hints at the difficulty of radical change in a stabilising physical environment. When city-dwellers depend on a tangle of systems that share conduits or power sources but are managed by disparate entities, a modification to one system can have cascading effects across others, rendering innovation complex and sometimes cost-prohibitive. Still, both writers believed that it was possible to change minds and the built environment. They imagined that social progress, in the forms of women's rights and anti-racism, would involve new architectural infrastructures as well as new ideas.

Charlotte Perkins Gilman

Gilman's depictions of 'modern' life foreground interconnection. In her treatise *Concerning Children* (1900), for example, she argues,

> The savage as an individual animal may be equal – in some ways superior – to the modern man; but, as a social constituent, he is like a grain of sand in a heap compared to some exquisitely fitted part of an intricate machine, – a living machine, an organism. (19–20)

In her estimation, 'modern' society is part-mechanical and part-organic macro-organism, comprised of people and the systems that interconnect them.

As that short excerpt demonstrates, Gilman's treatises can be difficult to follow. They weave together sociological, biological and philosophical discourses and metaphors in their attempts to describe interconnection on micro-, meso- and macro-scales. In the beginning of *Concerning Children*, Gilman claims: 'Our mechanical products in all their rich variety serve two purposes, – to show the measure of the brains that made them, and to help make better ones' (5). And in *Human Work* (1904), she credits 'steam and electric communication' for interconnecting human lives and therefore catalysing the evolution of the social organism (24). She claims that the systems we would now call technologies or infrastructures are what give a 'modern' society a coherent form. Her interpretation is clearly informed by her racism, as evidenced by her desire to differentiate the 'savage' from the 'modern man'. Gilman engages with the dominant and racist technological narratives of her day, but she repurposes them into arguments against sexism, creating an alternative, feminist narrative.

Gilman advocates for women's inclusion in America's increasingly interconnected public sphere, in part, by embracing stereotypes about women. For example, *Concerning Children* makes the conditional argument that if the domestic sphere is a woman's purview, then all of the systems connecting to the home should demand her supervision, as well. Gilman explains:

> Like an ostrich with his head in the sand, the mother shuts herself up in the home and imagines that she is safe and hidden, acting as if 'the home' was isolated in space. That home is not isolated we are made painfully conscious through its material

connections, gas-pipes, water-pipes, sewer-pipes and electric wires, – all serving us well or ill according to their general management. (Gilman 1900: 289–90)

Gilman builds her argument on a foundation of *infrastructure*: since a material substratum of water, power and gas connects homes to one another and to public spaces, she insists that the private sphere cannot be separated from the public sphere. Scale is also crucial to her argument. She repeatedly suggests that it is inefficient and illogical for women to focus on micro-scale, individual problems when there are meso- and macro-scale systems that demand their attention.

In the above passage, Gilman mentions how the systems connecting American homes 'serv[e] us well or ill'. This insinuation of vulnerability suffuses this treatise, as when she asserts that '[t]he accidents to little children from electric and cable cars are pitifully numerous. What mother has taken any steps to prevent these accidents?' (284). Gilman concludes women ought to be responsible for any system that can make homes and children vulnerable. It is worth noting that a similar rationalisation was eventually effective at changing policy in the UK, if not in the US. In the 1920s and 1930s, the Electrical Association for Women campaigned for policy reform, such as the grounding of electrical circuits in the home, and many of their demands were met.

Gilman used fiction as well as non-fiction to advocate for change. Her short story 'Bee Wise' (1913) provides one particularly succinct and illustrative example, though many of her utopias follow this pattern. 'Bee Wise' focuses primarily on a meso-scale perspective. Characters in this story do not even have names; rather, their titles are designated by their social roles, 'The Manager', 'The Engineer' and so on. This short story describes two fictional towns, 'Beewise' and 'Herways', designed to 'decrease the hours of labour, increase the value of the product, ensure health, peace, and prosperity, and multiply human happiness beyond measure' (234). Gilman imagines these radical changes could begin by using present-day systems but organising them anew:

> The first cash outlay of the Manager, after starting the cable line from beach to hill which made the whole growth possible, was to build a reservoir at either end, one of which furnished drinking water and irrigation in the long summer, the other a swimming pool and steady stream of power. The powerhouse in the cañon was supplemented by wind-mills on the heights and tide-mill on the beach, and among them they furnished light, heat, and power. (230)

By choosing an imagined, unpopulated plot of land near the California coast for her setting, Gilman makes widespread, structural change seem feasible. She imagines a fantastically blank canvas for innovation, rather than the tangle of pipes and wires that would need updating (not to mention the tangle of people who would need uprooting) in an existing city.

Gilman's vision for Beewise and Herways resonates with Hughes's definition of large technological systems as systems that solve problems in order to improve output: 'Later they set up a solar engine which furnished additional force, to minimize labour and add to their producing capacity' (230). As The Manager puts it, 'The whole thing must pay ... else it cannot stand' (231). She also invokes the materiality commonly associated with large technological systems when she describes, briefly, how those systems were built in her fictional towns by citizens who were essential personnel, including: 'the men who built and dug and ran the engines, the women who spun and wove and worked among the flowers, or vice versa if they chose' (233). The phrase 'vice versa' nonchalantly challenges gendered labour norms, although, as discussed above, Gilman typically insists her ideas would allow women to adhere to their stereotypical social roles more rationally and consistently than they can in actual twentieth-century American society.

Gilman's most radical proposition exemplifies what Polly Wyn Allen calls 'architectural feminism'. In addition to building the large-scale systems that provide power, water and other services to her fictional towns, Gilman describes ideal homes as conspicuously lacking kitchens: 'The dainty houses had no kitchen, only the small electric outfit where those who would might prepare coffee and the like. Food was prepared in clean wide laboratories' (Gilman 1913: 233). Her use of the word 'laboratories', rather than centralised kitchens, caterers or restaurants, frames her vision as a scientific advancement. The 'small electric outfit' replacing the kitchen represents the micro-scale detail in this meso-scale story: it implies the reorganisation of domestic labour need not infringe upon individual desires.

Gilman's reorganisation of domestic labour is also conspicuously white. She does not mention race in 'Bee Wise' but she does note that her model town eschews 'servants in the old sense' (233). Gilman calls up the racialised economy of domestic labour as a problem in the 'real' world that she supposedly solves in her realistic fiction. Intentional communities, Beewise and Herways accepted only 'carefully selected' tenants or visitors by application. Gilman frames this homogeneousness as a selling point. As her treatises show, she perceives the actual American home as vulnerable to any number of potentially risky connections. In contrast, her utopias imagine an alternative built environment where white women help to manage everything, but have less to manage within their own homes. Echoing dominant narratives, Gilman emphasises user control; she simply extends that fantasy to include white women better.

Pauline E. Hopkins

Hopkins did not propose implementable infrastructural or architectural changes in the way that Gilman did. As she demonstrated in her conclusion to 'The New York Subway', she considered technical innovations to be ancillary to the more pressing issue of civil rights. And, as Gilman's example demonstrated, even reform ideas that were labelled *radical* or *progressive* in the early twentieth century could still wilfully exclude people of African descent. In this context, it is unsurprising that Hopkins was dubious of the American conceptualisation of advancement and modernity. In her Pan-Africanist essay on 'The North American Indian' for her series on 'The Dark Races of the Twentieth Century' for *The Voice of the Negro*, she writes:

> If we let them [white people] tell it, the slightest advancement in art, science, and government removes all traces of Negro origin; therefore, East Indians, Indians, Japanese, Chinese, Arabs, Abyssinians, Zulus (including Kaffirs), and many others are not classed among the members of the great family of blacks. (Hopkins 1905a: 329)

In other words, she argues the very concept of *advancement* is defined by the anti-Black presumption that Blackness equals primitiveness. Hopkins's catalogue of work writes against this assumption.

Like Gilman, Hopkins uses non-fiction as well as fiction to argue for a more inclusive understanding of modernity. She published a stand-alone treatise, *A Primer of Facts Pertaining to the Early Greatness of the African Race and the Possibility of Restoration by its Descendants—with Epilogue* in 1905 that establishes the Ethiopian roots of modernity by using ethnology, history and biblical literalism.[5] Her last novel, *Of One Blood, or The Hidden Self*, which was serialised in *The Colored American Magazine* between 1903 and 1904, and recovered and republished in 1988, weaves similar information into a fictional form.[6] This speculative novel complements her realistic depictions of archaeological finds with quasi-utopian fiction. *Of One Blood* presents an alternate history of – and future for – modernity that is predicated on Black ingenuity and Black history.

Of One Blood is a byzantine novel that focuses on the interactions of three main characters: Reuel Briggs, a Harvard medical student; Aubrey Livingston, Reuel's false friend; and Dianthe Lusk, a Jubilee singer who has a mesmeric connection to Reuel. A brief summary of the first half of the novel can lend context to the infrastructural elements of the second half. The story begins in Boston, where Reuel reanimates Dianthe from apparent death. When he revives her, she has total amnesia. He recognises her as a Black singer but he keeps her identity a secret even as he courts her. Meanwhile, Reuel gains notoriety for resuscitating a patient other doctors had pronounced dead. Still, he cannot procure a job. Readers later learn that Aubrey, jealous of his friend's engagement to Dianthe, has broadcast the fact that Reuel is Black and passing to potential employers. The micro-scale interactions among these characters dramatise macro-scale problems about the history of American racism, and how that legacy is recapitulated by 'modern' institutions, including the hospitals that refuse to hire Reuel.

Reuel marries Dianthe but, before they can consummate their marriage, he accepts the only job available, as a medic on an expedition to Africa. His wealthy friend, Charlie Vance, joins him. Aubrey hires a stereotypically subservient Black man, Jim Titus, to join the mission trip as a saboteur. After his colleagues depart, Aubrey kills his own fiancé, Molly – Charlie's sister – and absconds with Dianthe to the plantation that was his childhood home, where he uses mesmerism to seduce her. Aubrey embodies an explicit, vicious form of white supremacy. He resembles his father, Aubrey Livingston, Sr, a slave owner who experimented with mesmerism on his slave, Mira; Livingston, Sr, published extensively about his plantation experiments before selling Mira because she angered him for predicting the Civil War while in a trance (Hopkins 1988: 486).[7]

In the second half of the novel, Reuel and Charlie arrive in Ethiopia. Their trip introduces the infrastructural dimension to the novel – a small but important facet of this complicated tale. Their experiences give Hopkins the opportunity to compare realistic and fictional systems in Ethiopia and America. These chapters ultimately overturn racialised assumptions about Africa's primitiveness. As one character puts it: 'from Ethiopia came all the arts and cunning inventions that make your modern glory' (Hopkins 1988: 560).

Reuel and Charlie's first impression of the continent of Africa compares it unfavourably to America. The third-person, limited narrator describes Tripoli (presumably the city in Libya and not in Lebanon) as 'a truly barbaric state, virgin of improvements' (512). The lack of 'improvements', especially as they pertain to communication, frustrates Charlie and Reuel. They had taken communication for granted in America, but in the African cities they visit it appears to be a luxury. Once they leave Tripoli and make their way overland to Ethiopia, waiting for the mail constitutes a significant fraction of this section of the novel. The lack of a postal service accords with the Americans' expectations that African nations would be primitive compared to America. But, when they learn that Aubrey had instructed Jim to hide the mail from them, Reuel and Charlie question their assumptions about the lack of advancement they witness. In today's terminology, the difficulty receiving post did not speak to Libya or Ethiopia's weaker infrastructures, but rather to the impediment of American racism; America is a less 'advanced' country than Ethiopia in that regard.

Reuel and Charlie remain unaware of Aubrey's treachery until the climax of the novel. While they long for the seemingly seamless communications of America from their micro-scale perspectives, the narrator hints that transportation and communication systems have been historically dangerous for Africans from a macro-scale perspective: 'Tripoli is the natural road by which Africa has been attacked by many explorers because of the facility of communication with the country of the Blacks' (512). When Reuel finds the hidden, ancient city of Telessar still very much in use, a high priest named Ai reinforces the idea that a *lack* of communication and transportation systems connecting to the outside world could be beneficial on the macro-scale: 'we wait behind the protection of our mountains and swamps, secure from the intrusion' (547). In the context of colonialism, the absence of transportation and communication infrastructure constitutes a clever defence system.

While Reuel learns to see the mountains and swamps as protection, Charlie continues to lament the apparent absence of development. Charlie reflects that he 'missed the march of progress attested by the sound of hammers on unfinished buildings that told of a busy future and cosy modern homeliness. Here there was no future. No railroads, no churches, no saloons, no schoolhouses . . .' (526). His impressions echo the stereotype that America is modernising while Ethiopia – and synecdochically the continent of Africa – is stagnating.[8] But Professor Stone, the researcher who organised their expedition, proposes an alternative interpretation of Ethiopia – and of progress. He claims that Ethiopia is the 'most ancient source of all that you value in modern life' (520). The Professor tells Charlie, 'Canals covered the land, serving the purposes of traffic, defence and irrigation. Lakes were dug and stored with water, dykes built along the banks of rivers to fertilize the land' (532). Charlie replies, 'Great Scott! . . . you don't mean to tell me that all of this was done by *niggers*?' (532). Charlie's disbelief represents a different kind of white supremacy from Aubrey's. Uninformed rather than underhanded, Charlie eventually learns to question his assumptions. After coming to see the beauty and advancement of Telessar, Charlie changes his opinions about race. He represents the possibility for white people to progress beyond their ignorant, tribalist views.

In keeping with Hopkins's tendency to invert expectations, Telessar discovers the explorers, rather than the other way around. The expedition's local guide is a citizen of the hidden city, who recognises Reuel has a birthmark that bespeaks his royal bloodline – a lotus flower mark he inherited from his mother, Mira, the Livingstons' former slave. When Reuel wanders near the edge of Telessar after receiving a false report of Dianthe's death, priests drug him and bring him into the palace. When he awakens, he finds himself in a wondrous land. Telessar is limned with lamps that are distinctly non-electrical; it has both wild natural areas and a 'perfect network of streams' (565); it has running water and interesting materials that are 'not glass, though quite transparent; it was not metal, though bright as polished steel' (575). America compares unfavourably to this alternative, African modernity: 'Used as he was to the improvements and luxuries of life in the modern Athens [a turn-of-the-century nickname for Boston], [Reuel] could but acknowledge them as poor beside the combination of Oriental and ancient luxury he now enjoyed' (548). The high priest who serves as Reuel's tour guide emphasises this contrast, saying: 'in Telessar are preserved specimens of the highest attainments the world knew in ancient days. They tell me that in many things your modern world is yet in its infancy' (551).

The most advanced technologies in Telessar include communication devices that allow users to access the truth of the past and present. These devices inform Reuel that Dianthe still lives and that Aubrey has deceived him. When Reuel first encounters these artefacts, he deems them 'magical!', to which Ai replies, 'No, no, Ergamenes, this is a secret of nature' (575). The phrase 'secret of nature' evokes contemporary discourses about electricity,[9] and it frames the fantastic elements of this story in terms of early twentieth-century technical and scientific advancement.

While Reuel learns some truth through fantastical, technological means, Dianthe learns even more: she meets Aunt Hannah, the emancipated slave who still lives in her cabin near the Livingston plantation. Aunt Hannah reveals that Dianthe, Reuel and Aubrey are siblings. Aubrey, Sr, was aware that he was Reuel and Dianthe's father by Mira, but he believed that Aubrey, Jr, was his and his wife's true heir. But Aunt Hannah confesses that her owner's baby died shortly after childbirth, and she swapped the deceased child with Mira's living baby; Aubrey, Jr, was Mira's son, too (606). Aunt Hannah's slave cabin becomes a crucial site of information exchange that complements Telessar. Hopkins elevates the humble cabin to the level of the hidden utopian city to suggest that Black elders can serve as conduits for the exchange of information that compensates for the intentional erasure of Black pasts and sabotage of Black futures within existing American infrastructures. Unlike Gilman, who continues to invest in narratives of control and advancement, Hopkins flies in the face of the dominant technological narrative by claiming that Black history – from Ethiopian archaeological sites to slave quarters – is the true locus of modernity.

* * *

In 1980, Langdon Winner asked if artefacts have politics, initiating an enduring conversation within the history of technology. Gilman and Hopkins asked resonant questions, and their narratives can help us to expand the conversations that Winner began. They both explore how assumptions about gender or race are manifested in the human-constructed world. Hopkins identifies some value in real and fictional infrastructures. Her *Primer of Facts* celebrates the remnants of historical structures, alongside developments in language and culture, as evidence of the greatness of ancient Ethiopian civilisation. *Of One Blood* imagines what an indigenous African modernity would look like, if a single city in Africa were allowed to thrive, untouched by colonialism. But, even in her speculative fiction, Hopkins does not invest in what we would now consider technological solutionism. She repeatedly demonstrates how physical infrastructures like roads or post offices could create misleading and even damaging information flows. More importantly, she locates the legacy of Black history and the promise of a Black modernity in bodies rather than the built environment. Aunt Hannah's embodied knowledge is just as precious as Telessar's most fantastical devices; the spirituals that Dianthe sings convey more information about the history of slavery than any communication system possibly could (454). As in her conclusion to 'The New York Subway', Hopkins encourages readers not to be distracted by innovations when racism demands immediate attention.

Like Hopkins, Gilman recognised the inextricability of ideas and material systems. In her fiction and non-fiction, she proposed a different way that social life could be organised – a feminist architecture that could transform the American white woman from a 'domestic servant' into a citizen. Although Gilman promoted structural change in the form of different home and city designs, she adapted dominant discourses in her attempts to make her designs seem rational and efficient. For that reason, neither her treatises nor her utopias quite rise to the level of a counter-narrative.

The difference between alternative- and counter-narratives can be felt in the afterlives of Gilman and Hopkins's ideas. General Electric co-opted Gilmanian language about gender equality in its promotional materials only a few years after she published 'Bee Wise'. The most conspicuous example of this appropriation appears in an advertisement called 'The suffrage and the switch', which juxtaposes an image of a woman pressing an electric button alongside a woman's hand dropping a ballot into the ballot box.[10] The text that accompanies the ad underscores this purported parallel: 'Woman suffrage made the American woman the political equal of her man. The little switch which commands the great servant Electricity is making her workshop the equal of her man's.' This advertisement invokes the language of women's rights, but it distorts its allusion by equating the consumption of electric power in the private sphere with women's admission to the public sphere. A Hopkins-esque vision of Black history and ingenuity could never be co-opted by American corporations in the same way.

Although neither Gilman nor Hopkins succeeded in changing the built environment with their words, their narratives have enduring value as we seek to understand the social meanings of technological systems or the assumptions we build into our own infrastructures, today. They invite us to pay attention to the systems we have learned not to notice and to ask what else we might be missing when we, in Edwards's words, do little beyond 'paying our monthly bills'.

In 2020, readers around the world learned to question their heretofore invisible infrastructures and social mores as we first confronted the novel coronavirus, Covid-19. The pandemic, like historical disasters, intensified inequities that were already built into our systems. It exacerbated the gendered divisions in labour that Gilman addressed, as schools closed and left women with a disproportionate caretaking burden.[11] At the same time, Ed Pilkington reported in *The Guardian* that 'Black Americans [are] dying of Covid-19 at three times the rate of white people' (2020: n.p.), signalling the extent to which American social, economic and infrastructural systems disproportionately put People of Colour – and especially Black people – at risk. The problems that Hopkins and Gilman identified in our infrastructures are enduring. As we seek to build new systems, especially in the wake of this recent humanitarian disaster, returning to these texts can help us learn from the past to imagine a more equitable future.

Notes

1. Narrative is not the only strategy that marginalised people have used to push against the technologies that contribute to their marginalisation. See Eglash, Croissant and Fouché (2004); Eglash (2019: 227–51); and Gaskins (2019: 252–74).

2. While my page numbers refer to the reprint from the Pauline Hopkins Society website, Hathi Trust Digital Library has the entire 1904 *Voice of the Negro* available for readers interested in analysing the images that attend her article and the teasers that advertised the piece when it was forthcoming. Available at: <https://babel.hathitrust.org/cgi/pt?id=uva.x000372425&view=1up&seq=7> (last accessed 27 January 2022).
3. See Lieberman (2017: 7-12, 91-128).
4. See Lieberman (2017: 18–21).
5. For more on Hopkins's biblical literalism, see Williams (2018: 148-54).
6. On Hopkins's often uncredited use of sources in *Of One Blood*, see Sanborn (2015: 67–87) and Dworkin (2018: e14–e20).
7. On the relationship between plantations and medical laboratories, see Rusert (2019: 25–49).
8. Hopkins oscillates between specific descriptions of Ethiopia and invocations of the continent of Africa as a whole. Her slippage between country and continent allows the former to stand for the latter. The discovery of modern conveniences in Ethiopia undermines the myth of Africa's lack of development, for example.
9. On electricity as a secret of nature, see Lieberman and Kline (2017: 1–27).
10. For a reproduction of this image and a further discussion of its significance, see Einav Rabinovitch-Fox's chapter on 'Advertising', in this volume.
11. See 'The Impact of COVID-19 on Women', United Nations Policy Brief, 9 April 2020, available at: <https://www.un.org/sexualvialenceinconflict/wp-content/uploads/2020/06/report/policy-brief-the-impact-of-covid-19-on-women/policy-brief-the-impact-of-covid-19-on-women-en-1.pdf> (last accessed 4 March 2022).

Works Cited

Allen, Polly Wyn (1988), *Building Domestic Liberty: Charlotte Perkins Gilman's Architectural Feminism*. Amherst: University of Massachusetts Press.

Bijker, Wiebe E. (2007), 'Dikes and Dams, Thick with Politics', *ISIS*, 98: 1, pp. 109–23.

Castells, Manuel (2010), *The Rise of the Network Society. The Information Age: Economy, Society, and Culture, Vol. 1*, 2nd edn. Oxford: Wiley Blackwell.

Dworkin, Ira (2018), 'Black Livingstone: Pauline Hopkins, *Of One Blood*, and the Archives of Colonialism', *American Literary History*, 30: 4, pp. e14-e20.

Edwards, Paul N. (2003), 'Infrastructure and Modernity: Force, Time, and Social Organization in the History of Sociotechnical Systems', in *Modernity and Technology*, ed. Thomas J. Misa, Philip Brey and Andrew Feenberg. Cambridge, MA: MIT Press, pp. 185–225.

Eglash, Ron (2019), 'Anti-Racist Technoscience: A Generative Tradition', in *Captivating Technology: Race, Carceral Technoscience, and Liberatory Imagination in Everyday Life*, ed. Ruhan Benjamin. Durham, NC: Duke University Press, pp. 227–51.

Eglash, Ron, Jennifer L. Croissant and Rayvon Fouché, eds (2004), *Appropriating Technology: Vernacular Science and Social Power*. Minneapolis: University of Minnesota Press.

Gaskins, Nettrice R. (2019), 'Techno-Vernacular Creativity and Innovation across the African Diaspora and Global South', in *Captivating Technology: Race, Carceral Technoscience, and Liberatory Imagination in Everyday Life*, ed. Ruhan Benjamin. Durham, NC: Duke University Press, pp. 252–74.

Gilman, Charlotte Perkins (1900), *Concerning Children*. Boston: Small, Maynard, & Co.

Gilman, Charlotte Perkins (1904), *Human Work*. New York: McClure, Phillips, & Co.

Gilman, Charlotte Perkins (1995 [1913]), 'Bee Wise', reprinted in *The Yellow Wall-Paper and Other Stories*. Oxford: Oxford University Press, pp. 226–34.

Hopkins, Pauline E. (1904), 'The New York Subway', *The Voice of the Negro*, 1: 12, pp. 605, 608–12, <http://www.paulinehopkinssociety.org/bibliography/prose/> (last accessed 27 January 2022).

Hopkins, Pauline E. (2007 [1905a]), 'The Dark Races of the Twentieth Century VI: The North American Indian – Conclusion', *The Voice of the Negro*, 2: 5, reprinted in *Daughter of the Revolution: The Major Nonfiction Works of Pauline E. Hopkins*, ed. Ira Dworkin. New Brunswick, NJ: Rutgers University Press, pp. 327–31.

Hopkins, Pauline E. (1905b), *A Primer of Facts Pertaining to the Early Greatness of the African Race and the Possibility of Restoration by its Descendants – with Epilogue*. Cambridge: P. E. Hopkins & Co., reprinted in *Daughter of the Revolution: The Major Nonfiction Works of Pauline E. Hopkins*, ed. Ira Dworkin. New Brunswick, NJ: Rutgers University Press, pp. 334–52.

Hopkins, Pauline E. (1988), *Of One Blood, or the Hidden Self*, in *The Magazine Novels of Pauline Hopkins*. Oxford: Oxford University Press, pp. 441–621.

Hughes, Thomas P. (2012), 'The Evolution of Large Technological Systems', in *The Social Construction of Technological Systems: New Directions in the Sociology and History of Technology*, ed. Wiebe E. Bijker, Thomas P. Hughes and Trevor Pinch. Cambridge, MA: MIT Press, pp. 45–76.

Kern, Stephen (1983), *The Culture of Time and Space, 1880–1918*. Cambridge, MA: Harvard University Press.

Lieberman, Jennifer L. (2017), *Power Lines: Electricity in American Life and Letters, 1882–1952*. Cambridge, MA: MIT Press.

Lieberman, Jennifer L. and Ronald R. Kline (2017), 'Dream of an Unfettered Electrical Future: Nikola Tesla, the Electrical Utopian Novel, and an Alternative American Sociotechnical Imaginary', *Configurations*, 25: 1, pp. 1–27.

MacDougall, Robert (2014), *The People's Network: The Political Economy of the Telephone in the Gilded Age*. Philadelphia: University of Pennsylvania Press.

Marx, Leo (1997), '*Technology*: The Emergence of a Hazardous Concept', *Social Research*, 64, pp. 965–88.

Mattelart, Armand (1996), *The Invention of Communication*, trans. Susan Emanuel. Minneapolis: University of Minnesota Press.

Nye, David E. (2003), *America as Second Creation: Technology and Narratives of New Beginnings*. Cambridge, MA: MIT Press.

Pilkington, Ed (2020), 'Black Americans Dying of Covid-19 at Three Times the Rate of White People', *The Guardian*, 20 May, <https://www.theguardian.com/world/2020/may/20/black-americans-death-rate-covid-19-coronavirus> (last accessed 27 January 2022).

Rubenstein, Michael (2010), *Public Works: Infrastructure, Irish Modernism, and the Postcolonial*. Notre Dame, IN: University of Notre Dame Press.

Rusert, Britt (2019), 'Naturalizing Coercion: The Tuskegee Experiments and the Laboratory Life of the Plantation', in *Captivating Technology: Race, Carceral Technoscience, and Liberatory Imagination in Everyday Life*, ed. Ruhan Benjamin. Durham, NC: Duke University Press, pp. 25–49.

Sanborn, Geoffrey (2015), 'The Wind of Words: Plagiarism and Intertextuality in *Of One Blood*', *J19*, 3: 1, pp. 67–87.

Schivelbush, Wolfgang (1997), *The Railway Journey: The Industrialization of Time and Space in the Nineteenth Century*. Berkeley: University of California Press.

'The Suffrage and the Switch' (1921), General Electric Advertisement, miSci General Electric Collection.

Webster, Daniel (1858), 'Opening of the Northern Railroad to Lebanon, N.H.', in *The Works of Daniel Webster*, vol. II, 11th edn. Boston: Little, Brown and Company.

Williams, Nathaniel (2018), *Gears and God: Technocratic Fiction, Faith, and Empire in Mark Twain's America*. Tuscaloosa: University of Alabama Press.

Winner, Langdon (1980), 'Do Artifacts Have Politics?', *Daedalus*, 109: 1, pp. 121–36.

24

Paperwork: Atomic Age Bureaucracy in C. P. Snow's *Strangers and Brothers*

Caroline Z. Krzakowski

After the Second World War, as scientists and philosophers on both sides of the Atlantic grappled with the threat of nuclear weapons, C. P. Snow reflected on the national and ethical dimensions of Britain's atomic programme, as well as on nuclear disarmament, in the novels *The New Men* (1954) and *Corridors of Power* (1964). Set amidst the context of the Cold War, the novels represent how civil servants wield power as they circulate files and deal in paperwork to manage the risks of the nuclear age. In the decades when Britain was falling behind the United States in the development of new defence technologies, Snow's works represent the Civil Service as a stable and traditional institution. In these novels, a twentieth-century technology – atomic weapons – collides with the Civil Service, a Victorian institution which nonetheless provides the administrative framework for the use of nuclear weapons by the state.

In this chapter, I examine the function of paperwork in two novels from Snow's ten-volume *Strangers and Brothers* (1940–70) series: *The New Men*, which looks back on the years between 1939 and 1947, and *Corridors of Power*, which focuses on the period between 1955 and 1959. The *Strangers and Brothers* series as a whole is a retrospective first-person memoir of the novels' central character and narrator, Lewis Eliot, a barrister, civil servant and novelist. *The New Men* looks back on the beginnings of Britain's nuclear programme during the Second World War, when Eliot works as a government representative tasked with recruiting scientists to work on the project. Set during the Cold War and in the wake of the attacks on Hiroshima and Nagasaki, *Corridors of Power* is concerned with the politics of nuclear disarmament. These two novels are joined thematically by their focus on Britain's development of nuclear technologies during the Second World War and the Cold War. Through the series as a whole, Eliot rises through the ranks of the British Civil Service, moving in a vast network of characters – civil servants, politicians, scientists – in settings that shift from Whitehall and Cambridge to London homes and country houses. Along these almost exclusively male circuits, women make only occasional appearances as wives, daughters, secretaries or typists. Women interact with technologies only in supporting roles; they rarely direct the uses of paperwork and atomic energy. A few of the novels offer a brief glimpse of Eliot's personal life, but quickly measure the effect of private events on his career. Time and growth are marked by outward, public action and by Eliot's ascent through a rigid hierarchy. The novels in *Strangers and Brothers*, with their dispassionate and detached accounts of Eliot's career, resemble a personnel file and constitute a kind of paperwork in themselves.

The New Men and *Corridors of Power* were written at a time of modernisation in the British Civil Service, when the British government increasingly sought to place experts in Civil Service positions to advise ministers in all areas of state governance. The Civil Service underwent radical changes during the establishment of the Welfare State, and grew in power and influence in the following decades. As John Turner explains,

> Ministers and civil servants were firmly in control of most of the machinery of government. As the economic role of the state grew, with nationalization of major sectors of industry and the enlargement of the welfare state, Whitehall's control over society increased rather than diminished ... and doubt about the capacity of the civil service to respond to new challenges led Harold Wilson in 1966 to commission the Fulton Report. Fulton recommended that government departments should separate policy advice, given by a cadre of elite civil servants, from the management of functions. (Turner 2009: 45)

Published in 1968, the Fulton Report on the State of the British Civil Service led to reforms that modernised the conservative institution, opening it up to members of the middle classes, as well as to women. The creation of a modern civil service required a mobilisation of the education system as well. Leading the Labour government, Harold Wilson 'claimed he would get the country moving again by wresting control from the public-school amateurs and by putting power in the hands of managers, scientists, and technologists who would be produced in the new universities and technical colleges' (Cannadine 2005: 106).

The revolutionary atmosphere of the 1960s challenged the structure of the Civil Service, which had not changed since its creation a century earlier, during another period of technological and scientific innovation. As Thomas Richards explains, the control of new technologies by the state goes back to the Victorian era:

> Much Victorian thought participated in seeing the state as central to human life, and more, in imagining a kind of complete documentary knowledge of human life that would exist solely for the state. The thread uniting the thought of Bentham and Mill with the thought of Russell and Keynes and C. P. Snow was the idea that knowledge is inconceivable without the state: the question of the state is a question of knowledge, especially scientific knowledge; that the classing of knowledge must be underwritten and directed by the state in its various capacities; that all epistemology became and must remain state epistemology in an economy of controlled information. (1993: 74)

In the 1950s and 1960s, as knowledge of physics became the key to state power and global alliances, the Civil Service went through another period of resurgence and modernisation.

Snow celebrated the modern Civil Service, and drew on his own experience in his fiction. Trained as a chemical physicist, he worked at the Ministry of Labour from 1940 to 1944, and later at the Ministry of Technology from 1964 to 1966. Snow referred to both scientists and civil servants as the 'New Men', or the men of the future. The designation 'New Men' ascribes modernity to both scientific innovation and managerial ability. In 'New Men for a New Era', an article he wrote for *The Sunday Times*, Snow outlines the character of the modern civil servant:

> in any kind of industry and Civil Service, it has become common form to test a man for how well he can get on in a group. This is quite modern . . . to be valuable in this society, a man has to be able to sacrifice some of the external expressions of his personality. Disciplined, unexhibitionistic, capable of subduing their egos . . . these men are coming forward everywhere to answer the social need. They are the 'new men' of our time. (qtd in Weintraub 1963: 55)

The ideal civil servant is unheroic and neutral; he does not insist on his authorial originality in writing an official document. In the Civil Service, documents are unsigned and memos are unattributed; these are understood as the product of collective effort, and thus also protect individual bureaucrats from carrying responsibility for actions which such documents could entail.

Despite his interests in modern science, Snow – along with his contemporaries Kingsley Amis, Doris Lessing and Angus Wilson – was sceptical of modernism. Thus,

> Snow expressed a number of objections to modernist fiction: that it was unreadable; that it alienated ordinary readers; that it was causing the death of the novel; that it provided unsuitable models for younger writers; that it was hostile to science; that it was politically reactionary; that it was mindless; that it was arcane; that it was old-fashioned; that it was not truly experimental; and that it was too much like abstract painting. (Rabinovitch 1994: 904–5)

Snow's novels are instead modelled on nineteenth-century realist fiction, and in particular on Anthony Trollope's serial novels *The Chronicles of Barsetshire* and the *Palliser* series. Both Snow and Trollope use the novel sequence to represent incremental change and political manœuvring in exclusive and close-knit social communities. Trollope, like Snow, worked as a civil servant, spending his career in the British Postal Service. In his biography of Trollope, Snow praises Trollope's efforts to build and expand the British Postal Service, the first of its kind in the world. In Trollope's time, the Civil Service was 'administratively primitive', writes Snow, because the Victorians were

> groping their way into an entirely different administrative world. Their structures emerged from the eighteenth century, for which even then they were barely adequate, and had to fit themselves for a society needing to be far more articulated, to an extent which no one alive then completely understood . . . the country was having to create what is now called an infrastructure. (Snow 1975: 45)

Snow's analysis of Victorian administration in this passage sheds light on his novelistic practice. His fictions of the modern Civil Service represent the growth and transformation of state infrastructure in response to historical change. The etymology of the term 'articulated', which Snow uses to designate the function of administration, is derived from the Latin for 'joining of structures' (*Oxford English Dictionry*). 'Articulation' also refers to clear or articulate speech or communication. Snow understands the role of the Civil Service as articulating, or joining together, structures of society into an organisation. Snow's novels, by making visible the motivations of civil servants and the details of their work, further articulate or communicate the hidden work of the Civil Service, as well as civil servants' motivations. In *The New Men*, the development of nuclear weapons and the bombing of Hiroshima, 'events too big for men', are narrated and articulated as distinct administrative events, each materialised by a document. To render comprehensible the scale of such significant events, Snow's narrative breaks down their proportions into a series of representable administrative tasks.

Snow's fiction centres on the workings of the British government from within, and reflects on the social significance of civil servants' bureaucratic paperwork. Elected parliamentary representatives are supported by a vast system of civil servants who report to the secretaries of various ministries. Civil servants manage the state and influence political decisions through the technologies of paper documents and writing. Paperwork formalises a process of consensus-building and policy-making that steers the new atomic science and its resultant technologies in a direction and for a purpose overseen by the state. The ethical dilemmas atomic scientists and civil servants face are mediated through a series of documents that break down large-scale decisions into a documented series of incremental decisions, each materialised by a paper trail.

Recent theories of paper and of bureaucracy can help us to shed light on the relationship between paperwork, institutions and the fictional civil servants in Snow's novels. In *The Demon of Writing: Powers and Failures of Paperwork*, Ben Kafka defines paperwork as 'those documents produced in response to a demand – real or imagined – by the state', and argues that 'modern political thought was founded and confounded by its encounters with paperwork' (Kafka 2012: 10). Civil servants' agency and responsibility are mediated through paperwork in Snow's novel series. As paper documents are invented to mark discrete steps in the political process, they in turn determine and frame which kinds of political questions can be posed. The political process itself – consulting experts on a given policy and documenting these discussions – is shaped by civil servants' paperwork. Lisa Gitelman's analysis of paper in *Paper Knowledge: Toward a Media History of Documents* emphasises the different kinds of work that paper does. She writes that '[t]he word document descends from the Latin root *docer*, to teach or show, which suggests that the document exists in order to document' (2014: 1). As Gitelman goes on to explain, the document is connected to specific settings and contexts (4). Governmental and ministerial paperwork is conditioned by the rhetorical practices of the Civil Service, as well as by its contributors and users. My chapter builds on Gitelman's theory by showing how in fictions of the Civil Service, paperwork is social, collaborative and processive.

The work of civil servants in Snow's novels centres on files, each of which corresponds to a particular government or ministerial project. Files are not public documents; they are created for an audience of a few specialised readers who commit the content of secret files to memory. Only members of particular committees can access the information in a file, and small groups of civil servants garner power and authority through their knowledge of the original documents. The most important files are read by the smallest number of civil servants. In *The New Men*, Lewis Eliot is tasked by his superior, Thomas Bevill, with recruiting scientists for the secret nuclear weapons development centre in Barford. During their preliminary meeting, Bevill invites Eliot 'into his confidential files' (Snow 2000a: 13), and insists that he read the information once and thereafter remember it. Secret documents are not circulated or copied; they must be memorised so as to limit leaks. Eliot recalls that on that day,

> Bevill showed us his private dossier of the uranium project. We must not refer to it again by that name, he said: as with all other projects of high secrecy, he copied out the 'appreciations' in his own hand, keeping no copies: the documents were then mounted in a loose-leaf cover, on which he printed a pet name . . . He turned over the cover, and we saw, painted in bold capitals, the words: 'Mr. Toad'. (16)

The appreciation, a bureaucratic genre *par excellence*, refers to information contained in a file that is rewritten and reframed to suit the needs of a specific ministry or subcommittee in Whitehall. The appreciation turns information into future government proposals, policies, bills or laws. The committee members working on 'Mr. Toad' each create a particular version of the file in their 'appreciations' to suit their purpose. The civil servants are, to quote Ben Kafka, powerful by virtue of their 'communion with paper' (2012: 11); the individual power of civil servants rests in their ability to edit the contents of a file and to present information suitable to a given audience. Eliot recalls that civil servants like the high-ranking Thomas Bevill fulfil a role for their government:

> by 1939 he had become such a link as all governments needed, particularly at the beginning of a war, before the forms of administration had settled down: they needed a man like Thomas Bevill as the chairman of confidential committees, the man to be kept informed of what was going on, the supreme post office. (12)

Like a postal system, Bevill knows the provenance of information, determines its destination and keeps track of its route. His epistemological power surpasses that of a postal system, since he also knows the content of all communications. Individual civil servants have access to certain files in circulation; the most powerful among them know of all the files.

Writing is central to the work of civil servants. They master a range of genres in administrative writing: memoranda, précis, white papers and parliamentary speeches. Some, like the précis, are private, and only for the use of a minister. Others, like the draft of a speech, are intended for the public and are crafted as such. Different genres of government paperwork correspond to the function and the work that a document performs in the context of the state management. Writing about British colonial administration, Matthew Hull argues in *Government of Paper* that administrative systems are created by their approach to paper documents:

> In the late nineteenth century, the bureaucracy of the East India Company formalized all of its written practices: British colonial administration . . . was not an organization simply employing various written genres (reports, records, and manuals) but rather an organization whose overall structure and practices were constituted in large measure by this 'genre system.' (Hull 2012: 10)

Snow's fictionalised British Civil Service is similarly constituted by the genres of documents it uses. Every interaction between a ministry and its staff of civil servants is mediated by paper and structured by the protocols of paperwork. In *Corridors of Power*, Eliot works for Roger Quaife, a cabinet minister who champions nuclear disarmament, and helps him win support for his proposal. Eliot reflects on the laboriousness of writing a parliamentary speech for Quaife:

> In the middle of July, Roger was making his first ministerial speech. I did not need reminding, having drafted enough of them, how much speeches mattered – to parliamentary bosses, to any kind of tycoon. Draft after draft: the search for the supreme, the impossible, the more than Flaubertian perfection: the scrutiny for any phrase that said more than it ought to say, so that each speech at the end was bound by the law of official inexplicitness, to be more porridge-like than when it started out in its first draft. (Snow 2000b: 22)

Snow's representation of Eliot's concern for finding 'le mot juste' suggests that linguistic artfulness is central to Eliot's administrative work as well as to Snow's novel-writing. Eliot's years of experience with the genre of the speech leads him to sacrifice literary craft to ensure political success. Quaife's speech avoids alienating supporters or making too many promises. Snow's representation of civil servants celebrates, rather than satirises, their attention to detail. Snow's novels suggest that bureaucrats' linguistic ability and literary craft also constitute a skill possessed by novelists.

Civil servants and scientists cooperate and clash in *The New Men* and *Corridors of Power*. Whereas the scientists take risks in the pursuit of technological innovation, civil servants seem like vestiges of nineteenth-century bureaucracy, upholding traditions and following protocols. Snow's civil servants take a long view of history and political change; they worry about the unforeseen consequences of atomic weapons. Governments, political parties and prime ministers are elected and replaced; civil servants remain in their positions for decades. Thomas Bevill remains ambivalent about physicists, even as he organises the committees overseeing nuclear research. He confides to Eliot his mistrust of the physicists: '[o]ur fellows can't make much of a difference to the world, and those chaps can. Do you think it will be a better world when they've finished with it?' (2000a: 63). Bevill's use of 'finished' here has apocalyptic undertones: he fears that the scientists' atomic pursuits could be too successful, and thus cause global annihilation. His response is to stave off an apocalypse by controlling the use of scientific research. Paradoxically, by not 'making a difference' the way that scientists do and by controlling the uses of science, civil servants like Bevill protect the future from destruction.

With the revelation of the leak of a secret document detailing the possible fallout from a nuclear bombing, the tension between scientists and civil servants reaches a crescendo. Eliot, who is tasked with finding the source of the leak, recalls that:

> One of the security branches had begun asking questions. They had some evidence (so it seemed, through the muffled hints) that there might have been a leakage . . . None of us knew what the evidence was, and the only hints we received were not dramatic, merely that a Barford paper had 'got loose.' We were not told where and the paper itself was unimportant. It was nothing but a 1943 estimate of the destructive power of the nuclear bomb. I looked it up in our secret files; it was signed by a refugee called Pavia, by Nora Luke and other mathematicians, and was called

Appreciation of the Effects of Nuclear Fission. The typescript was faded, in the margin were some corrections in a high Italian hand. Much of the argument was in mathematical symbols, but after twenty pages of calculation, some conclusions were set out in double spacing, in the military jargon of the day, with phrases like 'casualization,' 'ground zero,' 'severe destruction.' (113–14)

Although the leaked document confirms that the British government and scientists are well aware of the scale of the destruction and loss of life that the use of an atomic weapon would cause, Eliot minimises the importance of the leak. The administration of war has put him in contact with such predictions, and he confines his responsibility to his work in the institution. During meetings with other civil servants at Whitehall, he notices that, even when national security is threatened, their 'faces were impassive, the shut faces of committee men' (2000b: 82). The leaked paper momentarily forces him to reflect on his own role in the predicted violence that a nuclear weapon would cause, but he quickly concludes that he has limited influence:

Anyone who worked on the inside of scientific war saw such documents. And most men took it as part of the day-by-day routine, without emotion . . . most men did not need to justify themselves, but just performed their duty to society, made the calculations they were asked to make, and passed the paper on. (2000a: 114)

Eliot's response to the leak is to follow institutional protocol and fall back on his minor role. The reader learns nothing of Eliot's thoughts about the leak and its possible effects. Faced with a crisis in British security, the Civil Service documents it and sends the paperwork to the archives. Eliot is aware of the ethical quandary that documenting catastrophe poses, remembering that

[o]nce, alone in my office in the middle of the war, it occurred to me: there must exist memoranda about concentration camps: people must be writing their views on the effects of a reduction of rations, comparing the death rate this year with last. (114)

He imagines the atrocities of the Holocaust from the point of view of a Nazi civil servant who documents and archives the unspeakable. Faced with this chilling and momentary comparison, Eliot remains confident in his country's moral superiority, and therefore in the value of his bureaucratic work. Alan Sinfield, who writes about Snow's novels in the context of the post-war political context, rejects Eliot's complacency, arguing that, in *The New Men* and *Corridors of Power*, Snow fails to represent successfully the crises of treason and of nuclear war at the centre of the novels. Instead, Sinfield argues, Snow's British characters show a

servile adoption of the US interpretation of the Cold War, and a consequent collapse of any serious political ethics. In this light, the civilized anxieties of the characters appear as the maunderings of a superseded power elite that has lost confidence in itself. (Sinfield 2004: 110)

Paradoxically, even as they follow the lead of the Americans, the British bureaucrats continue to champion and defend institutional traditions in their everyday work.

To help find the source of the leak, Eliot searches through the meticulous personnel files created and kept for each of the scientists recruited for Barford. Since the beginning of the war, he has kept information about their background and education, as well as their political convictions and affiliations. By combing through these records, he finds that Eric Sawbridge, one of the most eminent and idealistic physicists working on 'Mr. Toad', had left-leaning tendencies as a student in the 1930s, and is not surprised when Sawbridge is found guilty of leaking the document. Eliot's navigation of documents reveals that, as Lisa Gitelman argues, paperwork is unpredictable, as paper documents are both stable and ephemeral (2014: 3). In *The New Men*, paperwork is similarly paradoxical: it is vulnerable – subject to leaks, loss or enemy eyes – as in the case of the secret document. However, paperwork can also be reliable, as are Eliot's personnel files, and tell the story of an individual's motives. In the end, Eliot's mastery of paperwork ensures his control of scientists' treachery.

With the revelation of Eric Sawbridge's treason, Eliot reflects on the ideological differences between the engineers and the physicists working at Barford and distinguishes between each group's approach to technological advancements:

> [The] physicists, whose intellectual life was spent in seeking new truths, found it uncongenial to stop seeking when they had a look at society. They were rebellious, questioning, protestant, curious for the future and unable to resist shaping it. The engineers buckled to their jobs and gave no trouble, in America, in Russia, in Germany; it was not from them, but from the scientists, that came heretics, forerunners, martyrs, traitors. (2000a: 158–9)

Eliot's language suggests that the role of the Civil Service is to control scientists' curiosity, even as they use new findings to promote the national agenda. While the scientists pursue their research, it falls to the civil servants to think about the social dimensions of new advancements such as nuclear technology.

In the last year of the Second World War, as British physicists continue to develop their methods for extracting plutonium and cooperate with American scientists, they learn that the United States has begun testing its weapon. Eliot recalls that,

> by the end of June, not only the Whitehall Committee, but the top men at Barford all knew that completed bombs were in existence: that the trial was fixed for the end of July: that there was a proposal, if the trial went according to plan, to use a bomb on a Japanese town. (150)

The news is received with a mixture of wonder, fear, envy and outrage. Even as the British scientists at Barford cooperated with the United States to develop a nuclear weapon, they hoped to outpace the Americans. The civil servants and politicians dream of the power that Britain would derive from being the first state to have such a weapon in its arsenal, and imagine relying on a nuclear weapon as a deterrent to enemy attack. Then, in August 1945, when they hear of the nuclear bombing of Hiroshima, Eliot and the Whitehall committee convene to discuss their position. Some scientists and civil servants are absolute in their opposition to using a nuclear weapon on account of the death and destruction it would cause. As the committee deliberates, others give 'a conditional no with much the same feeling behind it; but if there were *no other way* of saving the war against Hitler, they would be prepared to drop the bomb' (160–1). The British civil servants work with a realist political approach, believing that violence is central to the power of the state. Eliot and the committees accept the state's use of violence as a means to power. Although their work is not public, they nonetheless legitimate the British use of violence. The day after the bombing of Hiroshima, Eliot wrestles with his sense of lost agency and confides in his brother that 'It's happened now . . . there's nothing to do' (171). His brother, a physicist, disagrees. Eliot eventually returns to his paperwork, reconciled with taking a long view of its meaning in a larger context.

The New Men examines the nature of power – for individuals, civil servants and scientists. Civil servants' power is not directly visible to constituents. Drafting white papers and memoranda, men like Lewis Eliot must serve their ministers, regardless of their political affiliations. Eliot's narration of the *Strangers and Brothers* series mirrors his professionalism as a civil servant: he is detached from political events and intimate with the practice of state administration. The central importance of his work pushes other areas of his life to the margins. As Ben Kafka points out, '[h]aving a lot to do does not always mean having a lot of power, but having a lot of power always means having a lot to do, and in the modern era, at least, most of what it has to do is paperwork' (2012: 17). Eliot's neutrality might be mistaken for a lack of political conviction, or even of political responsibility. By following bureaucratic protocol, he ensures the correctness of government administration, regardless of its ends.

Working away from the political limelight and expected to maintain professional neutrality, civil servants like Eliot worry about their responsibility for political events. Citing the eighteenth-century French bureaucrat Louis-Sébastien Mercier, Ben Kafka writes that civil servants are 'all the more powerful with their pens because their actions are never visible' (Kafka 2012: 80). Eliot would agree. In *Strangers and Brothers*, state papers, particularly secret in wartime, conceal the state's intentions and actions. This approach to administration stands in contrast with the ideals imagined by the architects of the French Revolution, who were meticulous about including clauses in their new documents which ensured that French society could surveil the records of its administrators. Ben Kafka draws attention to the distinction that these writers drew between the terms 'accountability' and 'responsibility':

> The choice of the word 'accountability' over the word 'responsibility' was a choice for paperwork, since the former term, unlike the latter, carried with it the connotation of records, accounts, registers, and receipts. Every action or transaction undertaken by any person with or on behalf of the state had to be documented in certain anticipation of an eventual accounting. (Kafka 2012: 44)

The term 'accountability' does not occur in *The New Men*; civil servants do not account for their work or the decisions they produce, nor does their paperwork leave a clear trail. Snow's novels, however, offer a deferred, retrospective accounting as narratives; they make visible the work of fictional civil servants.

A broader commitment to national and global responsibility animates Snow's *Corridors of Power*. Written during the Cold War, the novel engages with the fear of global nuclear proliferation and concerns about national security. Compared to the other novels in the series, *Corridors of Power* is concerned with the collaboration between civil servants and politicians. Lewis Eliot makes an unusual decision to support the Conservative Minister of Defence, Roger Quaife, who is a champion of nuclear disarmament. Ultimately, Eliot's overt political alignment effectively ends his career in the Civil Service. The novel exposes the motivations that drive the civil servants, scientists and politicians who debate nuclear disarmament. Concerned with the future and its protection, Eliot reflects on the visibility and invisibility of civil servants' motives. He wonders:

> Once or twice during the next few months, I found myself wondering whether Roger and his associates would qualify for a footnote in history. If so, what would the professionals make of them? I did not envy the historians of the job. Of course there would be documents. A good many of them I wrote myself. There would be memoranda, minutes of meetings, official files, 'appreciations,' notes of verbal discussions. None of these was faked ... And yet they gave no idea, in many respects were actually misleading, of what had really been done, and, even more, of what had really been intended. I supposed that a few historians might make a strong guess as to what Roger was like. But how was a historian going to reach the motives of people who were just names on a file? (2000b: 79)

Eliot looks back on his present from an undated future. He is less anxious about the possibility of total annihilation in the aftermath of a nuclear war than he is about the limited ability of government documents to explain individual motivations. He imagines the work of paper going on after his death, when he will not be able to correct historians. He worries that even the existence of a documented paper trail will not clarify the motivations of the individuals involved in the deliberations. The genre of administrative paperwork represents the stages in a bureaucratic process, but omits information about individual civil servants and their motivations.

In *Corridors of Power*, Eliot's concerns about a distant historical future mingle with worries about Britain's political standing in a time of change. During a speech in Parliament, co-written with Eliot, Quaife argues that Britain should embrace nuclear disarmament and its own reduced importance in world politics:

> All choices involve risks. In our world, all the serious choices involve grave ones. But there are two kinds of risk. One is to go on mindlessly, as though our world were the old world. I believe, as completely as I believe anything, that if this country and all countries go on making these bombs, testing these bombs – just as though they were so many battleships – then before too long a time, the worst will happen ... This country can't be a super-power any longer ... The future is firmly poised. Our influence upon it is finite, but it exists. (2000b: 343)

The novel's immediate concerns, and Quaife's comments, are played out against the backdrop of the Suez Crisis. Britain's failed attempt to take control of the Suez Canal in 1957, and its rejection of an intervention by the United Nations, exposed its weakened geopolitical power. One faction of politicians and civil servants in *Corridors of Power* views Britain's possible nuclear disarmament as a further weakening of influence, whereas others argue for a new alignment of British foreign policy with other NATO powers. In Quaife's and now Eliot's view, Britain's nuclear policy should correspond to its limited post-war global influence. Quaife hopes to convince Parliament and the public that Britain's Cold War strategy should include abandoning imperial ambitions and cooperating with the United States and Europe.

Corridors of Power represents discussions about disarmament as bureaucratic procedures conducted by government committees. The novel also explores the consequences of scientists' use of open, public platforms to voice their objections to state policy. Among opponents of Quaife's project is Dr Brodzinski, a Polish refugee and a physicist who worked at Barford during the war. Having been a victim of Soviet persecution in the 1930s, he is adamant about the need for deterrent weapons to protect the West against Soviet aggression. Unable to win the support of scientists and politicians at home, he looks beyond Whitehall to influence the course of events. In a series of public lectures on modern physics Brodzinski delivers in the United States, he informs the American public that Britain is questioning the ethics of nuclear weapons, and therefore its commitment to the Cold War. Eliot learns of Brodzinski's US lectures while studying British newspapers' reactions to Quaife's latest parliamentary speech. Eliot gauges the response from newspapers ranging in political affiliations:

> The headlines, on the morning after the dinner in Fishmongers' Hall, had a simple but pleasing eloquence. ARMED SERVICES ALL-IMPORTANT: then, in smaller letters, 'No substitute for Fighting Men. Minister's Strong Speech,' said the *Daily Telegraph* (Conservative) . . . SPREAD OF ATOMIC WEAPONS, 'How many Countries Will Possess the Bomb?' said the *Manchester Guardian* (centre) . . . In the same week, I noticed a tiny news item, as obscure as a *fait divers*, in the 'Telegrams in Brief' column of *The Times*. 'Los Angeles. Dr. Brodzinski, British Physicist, in a speech here tonight, attacked "New Look" in British defence policy as defeatist and calculated to play into hands of Moscow.' (2000b: 190)

Similarly to Eric Sawbridge, who leaks the document about nuclear fallout in *The New Men*, Dr Brodzinski is also a minor character in the series who disseminates secret information beyond Whitehall and British national borders. Eliot uses the trusted means of ministerial paperwork to confirm and contain Brodzinski's betrayal. He hunts for evidence in the files of the minister's office and comes across a file of press cuttings that some junior ministers have been keeping.

> With a curious sense of déjà vu, mixed up with incredulity and a feeling that all this had happened time out of mind, I began to read them. Brodzinski's lecture at UCLA: SCIENCE AND THE COMMUNIST THREAT: Danger, danger, danger: Infiltration: Softening, Conscious, Unconscious, as bad or worse in his own country (UK) as in the US: People in high positions, scientific and non-scientific, betraying defence; best defence ideas sabotaged; security risks . . . (2000b: 192)

Stylistically, this passage represents how paperwork functions as the technology of the Civil Service. Written in what I will call a 'précis style', the language, punctuation and capitalisations document Eliot's simultaneous reading and translation of the file into his own administrative 'appreciation'. The précis style shows how information contained in a file circulates among civil servants and is recontextualised, iteratively, with each reading. The junior ministers' notes and appreciations on the newspaper article contextualise the significance of Brodzinski's lecture for the Ministry of Defence; Eliot's reading, in turn, highlights significant terms. Each retelling of the event (Brodzinski's lecture) is framed by another layer of commentary. Presumably, the file will go on to other readers before a response is crafted. In this process, the individual names of writers and commentators are obscured, and writing is forcibly collaborative.

Eliot learns, first through the public medium of the newspaper, and later in files circulated only among civil servants, that Brodzinski used the platform of the public lecture to cast doubt on Britain's commitment to the Cold War, thereby threatening the 'special relationship' between Britain and the United States. The scientist may have divulged compromising information to the Americans, but the novel reasserts the civil servant's power. The ministerial files documenting the effect of the lecture on US–British relations also serve to prepare and control a response to the event. Knowing the content of files is one of the means by which civil servants show their power. When it is revealed that Eliot helped Quaife draft white papers and parliamentary speeches in favour of disarmament, he is questioned about his political beliefs by Monteith, a fellow civil servant and member of the security services. Monteith relies only on his memory of Eliot's personnel file to interrogate him. Resentful of the interview, Eliot nonetheless admires his colleague's skill, observing that

> [h]e had not laid out a single note on the desk, much less produced a file. Throughout the next three hours, he worked from nothing but memory. In his own office, there must have been a dossier a good many inches high . . . [a]ll this material he had stored in his head and deployed with precision. It was an administrator's trick . . . .(250–1)

By committing the content of the personnel file to memory, the interviewer can temporarily inhabit the life of his subject and scrutinise that person's motivations. When used by the secret services, paperwork is rendered invisible by memorisation so that it becomes the interviewer's weapon. Paperwork becomes a concept; the content of files can exist abstractly and in the absence of material artefacts.

The concern with leaked scientific secrets in *Corridors of Power* and *The New Men* is a recurring theme in Cold War literature more broadly. It also speaks to the reorganisation of knowledge along national lines that occurred during this period. As Sandrine Kott explains, the secrecy of the Cold War paradoxically led to greater information exchange internationally: 'the Cold war, like other wars, was a time when each belligerent observed its enemies in order to learn from their experiences and innovations, which in turn promoted the circulation of knowledge and expertise and prompted a process of productive learning' (Kott 2017: 341). Such an acceleration of information exchange poses the risk of leaks. The British physicists developing a fission bomb for the secret 'Mr. Toad' project in *The New Men* – Martin Eliot, Eric Sawbridge and Walter Luke – maintain that 'pure science was not national' (160). In contrast, Thomas Bevill and the civil servants worry that the physicists are more committed to the international open scientific exchange than they are to national interests, even in wartime. Snow's contemporary Rebecca West feared the use of atomic weapons by Britain's enemies more than she feared atomic science itself. In a series of articles collected as *The New Meaning of Treason* (1964), West removes any veneer of heroism from her portraits of traitors – the atomic scientists Alan Nunn May, Karl Emil Fuchs and Bruno Pontecorvo, who divulged secrets to the Soviet Union – and details the threat of their treasonous acts to Britain, as well as the judicial proceedings which find the scientists guilty. In her analysis of treasonous scientists, she echoes Snow's conclusion that the professional sharing of information among scientists, rather than Communist sympathies, is at the root of their treachery. Writing about Alan Nunn May, West contends that:

> Although the scientists involved asserted that Dr. Alan Nunn May had been right in giving away the secrets of atomic energy to the Soviet Union on the ground that all scientific discoveries should be shared, at the same time they asserted that the surrender of these secrets was of no consequence, since science was universal, and therefore the Soviet scientists were bound to discover all that we knew about atomic energy through their own researches, and the only thing to be said against Dr. Nunn May was that he had taken unnecessary trouble. (West 1964: 159)

For West, the response to scientific treason lies in judicial proceedings; for Snow, rather, it lies in managerial prevention. Both writers would agree that in times of war, science should be contained by national boundaries. Fictional scientists like Eric Sawbridge and Dr Brodzinski seek to share information internationally, whereas civil servants safeguard national nuclear programmes because their allegiance to the nation is taken for granted.

Snow's post-war fiction repurposes nineteenth-century realism to reveal the daily work of secretive branches of government. The novelistic structure of *The New Men* and *Corridors of Power* contrasts the pace and rhythm of work in two technologised government roles: science and administration. The work of scientists and civil servants also proceeds along different timelines. In *The New Men*, a physicist explains that in science: '[t]he days of crisis were few . . . it was only after long periods of preparation, measured in months, not days, that they came to a "result" – one day of excitement, and afterward another period of building, routine, long-drawn-out suspense' (2000a: 37). For scientists, the process of discovery and the development of new technologies is cumulative and marked by a sudden discovery or advancement which brings innovation. In contrast, the Civil Service moves at a deliberately constant slower pace as it follows its procedures and processes of documentation. As Snow remarks in his biography of Trollope, the Civil Service creates infrastructures for a changing context only belatedly, once the changes have taken place. Scientists' innovations precede the state's creation of administrative structures in which they will be held. The structure of Snow's novel series adopts the slow pace of bureaucratic work, rather than the rapid and sudden advancements of nuclear science. Eliot's denotative narration, devoid of sudden epiphanies, contrasts with the speed of scientific discovery in this period. By looking at events on a global scale retrospectively, *Strangers and Brothers* affords a longer view of change over time. Snow seems to suggest that it is only by looking back – as though reviewing the contents of a file – that change can be made visible. Snow's novels revel in detailing the work of this hidden political class behind the scenes. By articulating the events that materialised in paperwork and by showing individual characters' motivations, *The New Men* and *Corridors of Power* fill a gap left by paperwork. Giving a fuller view of state administration, the novels function as a 'supreme Post Office', to echo Thomas Bevill's term for the Civil Service, a novelistic and omniscient civil servant through which all communications pass.

Works Cited

Cannadine, David (2005), 'C. P. Snow, the Two Cultures, and The Corridors of Power', *Yet More Adventures with Britannia: Personalities, Politics and Culture in Britain*, ed. William Roger Louis. London and New York: I. B. Tauris.

Gitelman, Lisa (2014), *Paper Knowledge: Toward a Media History of Documents*. Durham, NC: Duke University Press.

Hull, Matthew S. (2012), *Government of Paper: The Materiality of Bureaucracy in Urban Pakistan*. Oakland: University of California Press.

Kafka, Ben (2012), *The Demon of Writing: Powers and Failures of Paperwork*. New York: Zone Books.

Kott, Sandrine (2017), 'Cold War Internationalism', in *Internationalisms: A Twentieth-Century History*, ed. Glenda Sluga and Patricia Clavin. Cambridge: Cambridge University Press, pp. 340–62.

Rabinovitz, Rubin (1994), 'The Reaction Against Modernism: Amis, Snow, Wilson', in *The Columbia History of the British Novel*, ed. John Richetti. New York: Columbia University Press, pp. 895–917.

Richards, Thomas (1993), *The Imperial Archive: Knowledge and the Fantasy of Empire*. New York: Verso.

Sinfield, Alan (2004), *Literature, Politics, and Culture in Postwar Britain*. London: Continuum.

Snow, C. P. (2000a [1954]), *The New Men*. Looe: Stratus.

Snow, C. P. (2000b [1964]), *Corridors of Power*. Looe: Stratus.

Snow, C. P. (1975), *Trollope: A Biography*. New York: Scribner's.

Turner, John (2009), 'Governors, Governance, and Governed: British Politics since 1945', in *The British Isles Since 1945*, ed. K. Burk. Oxford: Oxford University Press, pp. 1–62.

Weintraub, Stanley (1963), *C. P. Snow: A Spectrum*. New York: Scribner.

West, Rebecca (1964), *The New Meaning of Treason*. London: Viking.

25

INFORMATION: LITERATURE AND KNOWLEDGE IN THE AGE OF BRADSHAW AND BAEDEKER

James Purdon

IN SYLVIA TOWNSEND Warner's *Lolly Willowes* (1926), the protagonist Laura, having swapped the bustle of London for the peace and quiet of the Chiltern Hills, decides to spend some of her new-found leisure time reading. Having brought no books of her own, she borrows a couple of volumes from her landlady:

> From Mrs Leak's library she chose *Mehalah*, by the Rev. Sabine Baring-Gould, and an anonymous work of information called *Enquire Within Upon Everything*. The next morning was fine and sunny. She spent it by the parlour fire, reading. When she read bits of *Mehalah* she thought how romantic it would be to live in the Essex marshes. From *Enquire Within Upon Everything* she learned how gentlemen's hats if plunged in a bath of logwood will come out with a dash of respectability, and that ruins are best constructed of cork. During the afternoon she learned other valuable facts like these, and fell asleep. (Warner 2020: 75)

Like many modern readers, Laura finds herself dividing her attention between the escapist pleasures of literary romance and the valuable facts to be gleaned from a work of information. In this case, however, these two forms of reading also suggest the two worlds between which Laura herself is beginning to transition. The practical if soporific advice retailed by *Enquire Within* (1856) – the Chartist editor Robert Kemp Philp's most successful contribution to the Victorian craze for self-improvement – recalls the bourgeois domesticity of daily life in her late brother's London household. Meanwhile, the popular gothic novel *Mehalah* (1880), by the eminent nineteenth-century folklorist Sabine Baring-Gould, feeds the fascination for the supernatural and the weird that will ultimately carry Laura into a new life as a *bona fide* modern-day witch.

Laura Willowes's reading preferences might seem to have little to do with questions of modernism and technology. Yet this marginal moment in a middlebrow novella of the 1920s serves to demonstrate both the evident popularity of informational reading in the early twentieth century and the sharp contrast many writers had begun to draw between such reading and its literary alternatives or complements. It also gives a good sense of what 'information' most readily suggested to a typical reader of the 1920s: an organised but discontinuous collection of facts, figures, measurements, recipes, instructions and the like, which might (or might not) turn out to be of practical use. As I shall argue, the ascendancy of this kind of informational reading came to be widely understood as a threat to the practice of literature itself. How many readers might be tempted, like Laura, to exchange the pleasures of the imagination for practical advice on hat-revival and model-making? Fearing the worst, writers such as Ford Madox Ford, Virginia Woolf, E. M. Forster and Aldous Huxley would emphasise what they saw as an antagonism between informational and literary reading: an antagonism exacerbated by the many new technical and social transformations of the modernist period. Many of these writers' most characteristic works, I suggest, are marked by a double movement: by representing scenes of informational reading, they acknowledge the new social power of such reading; at the same time, they work hard to re-establish literature as that form of writing which cannot be reduced to information – to 'valuable facts'.

In a way, they were right to be concerned: of the two volumes chosen by Laura to pass the time it is the work of information rather than the literary romance that has the stronger claim to enduring cultural influence. For according to the computer scientist Tim Berners-Lee, it was *Enquire Within Upon Everything* – a book remembered from his childhood – that suggested the name for 'ENQUIRE', one of his earliest projects in digital information management and an early step in the development of the World Wide Web (Gillies & Cailliau 2000: 168–71). Thanks largely to Berners-Lee and other digital innovators, contemporary readers have grown used to thinking of information as sheer content stored in binary codes and recuperable in various formats for various purposes. Before the computer revolution, however, information was more readily understood as a set of genres, and the conventions associated with those genres. John Guillory, for instance, has singled out the bureaucratic memorandum as the paradigmatic instance of such 'information genres': those classes of document, central to modern commerce and statecraft, whose formal features are determined primarily by their core functions of recording and transmitting information (Guillory 2004).

Certainly, for many late nineteenth- and early twentieth-century writers, especially those with professional administrative experience, 'information' readily suggested the innumerable memos and vast compendiums of official data – the so-called 'blue books' – which weighed upon the minds and groaning desks of overworked bureaucrats. A growing body of recent scholarship has traced connections between such forms of institutional information-work and modernist literary practice (Wollaeger 2008; Kafka 2012; Purdon 2016). But, as *Lolly Willowes* reminds us, not all information genres were intended for official use. 'Information' could refer to a wide field of written material, from the stark numerical columns of railway timetables to the terse prose of tourist guidebooks. The daily newspaper was understood as a source of information; so too was a list of London clubs or cricket scores. For most people, most of the time, 'information' was less likely to evoke dusty parliamentary archives or densely-ruled office ledgers than newspapers and magazines, guidebooks and gazetteers, timetables and city directories. Such demotic forms represented the public, everyday dimension of information and they reached vast numbers of readers: more than any government memo or blue book; more, certainly, than any new novel or volume of poetry.

Furthermore, these information genres were thoroughly hybrid. Newspapers carried paid advertising, society circulars, lists of financial and economic data, meteorological reports, accounts of sporting fixtures, and much more besides. A railway guide might include not just timetables, but advertisements, announcements, maps and telephone numbers, as well as lists of local hotels and even schools. In this chapter I bring these varied kinds of informational writing together not in order to reify the category of 'information', but because this was what the majority of the period's writers meant when they used the term. Of course, they used the information, too: they read newspapers, checked train times, looked up addresses, pored over maps. Information, in this context, was not a problem; it became a problem only when considered in the abstract, as a general repository for other deep-seated anxieties. Rendered abstract, information could be made to stand for a kind of instrumental, ephemeral form of writing and reading in opposition to which the distinctive value of literature could be defined and defended. In *Lolly Willowes*, Warner glances ironically at the encroachment of informational reading on the space of literature: so stimulating are the 'valuable facts' purveyed by *Enquire Within* that Laura promptly dozes off. But the novella also articulates what some writers had come to see as a real problem for literature at a moment when its displacement by information seemed all too likely.

* * *

Information, at the beginning of the twentieth century, was not quite so obviously technological a concept as it would later become. Techniques and mechanisms for gathering, reproducing, storing and circulating information have a long history. Alphabetisation, paper, the codex, double-entry book-keeping, the printing press, the index-card, punched tape: the history of such innovations, dating back millennia, constitute a history of 'information technology' *avant la lettre*. The *lettre* itself only became available a decade or so after the end of the Second World War, when management scientists began to recognise the potential of new digital electronic computers for storing and processing large volumes of corporate data (Leavitt and Whisler 1958: 42). By that point, the term 'information' had acquired a new technological currency through its association with the emerging field of cybernetics, and in particular the work of 'information theory' pioneers like Claude Shannon.

Communications engineers like Shannon used the term 'information' to stand for a measurable quantity: the mathematical improbability of receiving a particular signal or observing the outcome of a particular event. The more improbable the signal or outcome, the more 'information' it could be said to contain, irrespective of its content. 'Frequently the messages have meaning;' Shannon explained, 'that is they refer to or are correlated according to some system with certain physical or conceptual entities. These semantic aspects of communication are irrelevant to the engineering problem' (Shannon 1948: 379). Yet such ways of thinking about information, even today, remain largely orthogonal to ordinary usage. When we complain about corporations or hackers playing fast and loose with our information, we are generally thinking not about a mathematical quantity, but precisely about interpretable content which 'refer[s] to [. . .] certain physical or conceptual entities'. Names, addresses, photographs, bank account numbers: this is the kind of information we worry about. And when we say we are seeking information about a particular topic, we still turn, as our great-grandparents did, to encyclopaedias, handbooks and similar works of reference, even if we consult online editions more often than bound volumes. The advent of information theory in fact did little to affect the everyday sense of information, so that a time-travelling Victorian arriving in the twenty-first century would have little difficulty in understanding contemporary concerns about its use and misuse, or about its relentless proliferation.

Modernism did not have an information theory: not in the cyberneticians' sense of the term. What it did have, in unprecedented abundance, was a wide and proliferating range of technologies and genres dedicated to the acquisition, organisation and dissemination of information. The modernist wave of cultural renewal followed a remarkable half-century or more of accelerating innovation in this respect. New methods of communication (the electric telegraph, the telephone), representation (photography, phonography, cinematography), reproduction (offset printing, lithography, hot metal typesetting) and distribution (the railways, steam-ships, motor haulage) had enabled and encouraged a rapid rise in the availability of all kinds of informational material, as well as the speed at which it travelled. To this established ecology of informational media, the first few decades of the twentieth century would add further new examples: teletype, radio broadcasting, the newsreel, television.

At the same time, technological development was accompanied by a series of social and administrative changes that amplified the effects of those new technologies. In Britain, the growing influence and prestige of administrative and managerial occupations, both in the gradually reforming Civil Service and in private sector organisations, had placed information-work at the centre of professional and political life (Perkin 1989). The educational reforms of the 1870s and 1880s, by introducing compulsory elementary schooling, had contributed to rising national levels of literacy (Lawson and Silver 2007). And the mid-nineteenth-century repeal of the so-called 'taxes on knowledge' – comprising the advertisement tax, newspaper stamp duty and tax on paper – had established the economic conditions for a mass-market periodical press (Hewitt 2014). A mass press had already existed in the more fiscally lenient United States, but there too the demand for up-to-date information on a national scale was boosted by the growth of commerce, the westward expansion of the nation and its communications infrastructures, and the Civil War.

One result of these technological and administrative changes was a massive increase in the production and circulation of informational writing, especially in the pages of the burgeoning periodical press which aimed its products at a growing mass market of time- and concentration-poor readers eager to be entertained, surprised and informed. The most famous of these, *Tit-Bits*, founded in 1881 by the canny publishing impresario George Newnes, carried jokes on its cover, brief articles inside on subjects historical and contemporary, and 'Tit-Bits of Information' on the back page ('It takes about 3,000 worms to spin silk enough to make a lady's dress'). From its first issue onwards, *Tit-Bits* pitched itself as a solution to the problem of information management even as it added to the flood of facts and figures to which readers were daily exposed:

> It is impossible for any man in the busy times of the present to even glance at any large number of the immense variety of books and papers which have gone on accumulating, until now their number is fabulous. It will be the business of the conductors of *Tit-Bits* to find out from this immense field of literature the best things that have ever been said or written, and weekly to place them before the public for one penny. ('Tit-Bits' 1881: 1)

Mixing information and literature – and sealing the bargain with a shameless allusion to Matthew Arnold ('the best that has been thought and said') – *Tit-Bits* became synonymous with a new kind of ephemeral, informational reading that had found a wide audience not only among the literate lower classes, but at nearly every level of society. Joseph Conrad and Virginia Woolf both unsuccessfully submitted stories. So did James Joyce, who took his revenge in *Ulysses* (1922), in which Leopold Bloom grabs an old copy to read on the toilet and subsequently to wipe himself with. By 1904 – the year in which Joyce's novel is set – the magazine was enjoying a stable circulation of well above half a million weekly copies. If, as Bloom's sanitary use of his *Tit-Bits* suggests, the vast new mass of cheap information was widely disparaged as disposable, nonetheless, it sold.

In a 1901 essay, part of a series on popular writing, G. K. Chesterton took the measure of this 'Literature of Information':

> The really extraordinary thing is that the most appalling fictions are not actually so popular as that literature which deals with the most indisputed and depressing facts; men are not apparently so interested in murder and love-making as they are in the number of different forms of latchkey which exist in London, or the time that it would take a grasshopper to jump from Cairo to the Cape. (Chesterton 1901: 493)

Chesterton found the 'widespread madness of information for information's sake' to be, counterintuitively, a sign of social progress rather than mental degeneration. While reassuring his readers that '[w]e can no more think of amusing ourselves with it than of reading whole pages of a Surbiton local directory', he nonetheless suggested that the new appetite for trivia which inflated the circulation of magazines like *Tit-Bits* should be seen as reflecting the 'babyish and indiscriminate curiosity' of the newly educated, or half-educated, lower classes (Chesterton 1901: 493–4). Chesterton imagined the typical consumer of this 'literature of information' as the sort of half-educated reader who would otherwise have spent their leisure time devouring lowbrow fiction. And Newnes himself had defended *Tit-Bits* on the basis that it provided 'superficial readers' with a wholesome alternative to the 'so-called sporting papers' (Pound 1966: 25). But the appetite for information was not restricted to newly literate members of the lower classes; nor were popular magazines of the *Tit-Bits* type the only focus of cultural anxiety. If *Tit-Bits* represented the 'literature of information' at its most lowbrow, some commentators found reason to worry that more respectable forms of information might exert a similarly malign influence on the minds of readers. Writing in 1911, Ford Madox Ford blamed the introduction of an organised 'telegraphic Press' in Britain – an innovation he dated to the period of the Boer War (1899–1902) – for a decline in literary reading:

> Before that time, though this tendency was gradually dying, the public was accustomed to accept with equanimity news that was a day or two old – to accept it with equanimity and to ponder over it for some small length of time. But nowadays, even in remote country districts, the Englishman is overwhelmed every morning with a white spray of facts – facts more or less new, more or less important, more or less veracious. And the commercial man who in the old days read his Browning or his Ruskin as a duty now equally as a duty plays his round of golf to increase his physical well-being, since this perusal of facts will have stilled that position of his mind that craves for the printed page (Ford 1911: 125).

There was, no doubt, an element of nostalgia in Ford's criticism. (A cynic might wonder just how many Victorian men of commerce regularly returned from the office to spend their evenings relaxing with *Modern Painters* or *The Ring and the Book*.) But his concern was genuine: the reader who depended solely on the daily paper was, as he saw it, no longer the heir and custodian of a cultural tradition, but the passive recipient of a standard (and standardising) diet of constantly-changing facts. Whether imagined as the fragmentary trivia of *Tit-Bits*, or the newspapers' digest of current events, this continuous stream of information threatened to displace traditional forms of humanistic cultural formation. It was not just 'the Englishman' who risked being overwhelmed by a technologically-channelled torrent of information, but English literature itself.

* * *

The figure of the unliterary reader, who satisfies his craving for print with information, haunts the margins of early twentieth-century fiction. As an example, take the solicitor Mr Davis in Leonard Woolf's autobiographical novel *The Wise Virgins* (1914), who, like Ford's 'commercial man', divides his occasional off-hours between the golf links and the consumption of information:

> He read the *Times* steadily through breakfast, and at dinner and in the evening contributed sparingly facts, figures, and statements to the conversation. He was one of those persons who seem to give nothing to and to receive nothing from the atmosphere of the circle in which they find themselves, whose work in life is to make arrangements for other people, and to keep them right on matters of general information. As he had a habit of reading Bradshaw, the A. B. C., and Whitaker's Almanack, when another person would find relaxation in a novel, his arrangements and information were usually excellent, being based upon a firm foundation of knowledge. (Woolf 2007: 229)

If the mass-circulation newspaper was instrumental in producing the impression of a unified national public life, connecting breakfasters in remote country districts with the centres of power, then other informational genres may be said to have performed similar operations. The densely tabulated columns of *Bradshaw's Railway Guide*, for instance, presented a vision of a nation bound together not by news but by steel and steam, representing and facilitating the operation of a unified transport network choreographed down to the minute in a newly synchronised, nation-wide time-zone. The exhaustive *Whitaker's Almanack*, meanwhile, not only provided catalogues of social, meteorological, commercial and geopolitical data, but in doing so established a standard national (and imperial) frame of reference. To browse its catalogues of information is to enter the mind of Ford's 'commercial man'; it is to know what men like Mr Davis considered important, from the ranks of British peers, to the import-export balance of Kenya, to the number of salmon caught annually in the River Tay.

To some modernist writers, this new emphasis on a standardised public world in which informational writing takes precedence – in which the only reality of consequence is that empirical reality which can be expressed in the form of facts, figures and statistics – had been responsible for a corresponding devaluation of the inner life of daily consciousness. Virginia Woolf, for instance, in an essay celebrating the prose writing of Thomas De Quincey, explicitly linked the dominance of public, informational forms of reading and writing to what she judged to be the modern novel's neglect of private experience:

> [O]f all writers the novelist has his hands fullest of facts. Smith gets up, shaves, has his breakfast, taps an egg, reads *The Times*. [. . .] And therefore all that side of the mind which is exposed in solitude they ignore. They ignore its thoughts, its rhapsodies, its dreams, with the result that the people of fiction bursting with energy on one side are atrophied on the other; while prose itself, so long in service to this drastic master, has suffered the same deformity, and will be fit, after another hundred years of such discipline, to write nothing but the immortal works of Bradshaw and Baedeker. (Woolf 1926: 601)

Subjected to the information-minded 'discipline' of literary realism, Woolf argues, English prose (and the novel in particular) is continually at risk of being reduced to the kind of writing that merely transmits information: the kind of writing represented here by *The Times*, *Bradshaw* and the travel guides of Karl Baedeker. Just as Ford's 'commercial man' had felt the effects of information overload in his diminished capacity for reading, Woolf's imaginary novelist, equating truth with transcription and verisimilitude with verifiable fact, suffers from the same complaint in his writing. Information pushes out interiority; fact takes the place of feeling; reality is reduced to the close shave, the boiled egg and the published certainties of the daily paper.

Informational writing repeatedly plays an important role in Woolf's own fiction, where it tends to be associated with a dissonance or divergence between a public, patriarchal reality, composed of empirical facts, and the no less real, but less valued, experience of 'that side of the mind which is exposed in solitude'. One way of understanding this dissonance or divergence is as a critique of literary realism's insistence on external, material realities: the kind of critique Woolf offers in the essay 'Mr Bennett and Mrs Brown', when she censures her Edwardian elders for writing novels in which 'character' disappears under the weight of 'information' and 'facts' about social and economic circumstances (Woolf 1924). Woolf's fiction, however, is never so unequivocal, or so polemical, as her literary criticism. If, in the latter, she frequently invokes forms of informational writing as representative genres of a public reality from which the claims of interiority and subjectivity have been excluded, her fiction does not reverse that process by excluding the claims of information. Rather, it is precisely when Woolf's characters are obliged to recognise the authority and objectivity of informational writing that they assert most forcefully the counterclaims of their own subjective experience.

In the early short story 'The Mark on the Wall' (1917), Woolf experiments with a style of writing designed to shift the attention of her narrative voice away from the plain external reality of the titular mark ('a small round mark, black upon the white wall') to the loose concatenation of vividly colourful mental images it provokes in the observer. The story amounts to a series of interruptions. While reading a book after tea, the narrator glances up at the coals burning in the fireplace, her mind wandering to childhood fantasy – 'that old fancy of the crimson flag flapping from the castle tower'; 'the cavalcade of red knights riding up the side of the black rock' – when 'the sight of the mark interrupt[s]' the imaginary scene (Woolf 1921: 79). Her musing mind then drifts to the previous occupants of the house, then back once again to the mark, and so on in a repeated pattern of meditative digression followed by return to empirical reality. Throughout the story, Woolf insists on the reality of the imagination as a proper subject for fiction while asserting that, far from being solidly grounded in empirical fact, the very notion of a public, shared 'reality' depends upon a contingent and mutable set of social conventions disseminated through informational writing:

> How shocking, and yet how wonderful it was to discover that these real things, Sunday luncheons, Sunday walks, country houses, and tablecloths were not entirely real, were indeed half phantoms, and the damnation which visited the disbeliever in them was only a sense of illegitimate freedom. What now takes the place of those things I wonder, those real standard things? Men perhaps, should you be a woman; the masculine point of view which governs our lives, which sets the standard, which establishes Whitaker's Table of Precedency, which has become, I suppose, since the war half a phantom to many men and women ... (85)

What is newly explicit here in Woolf (though it had already been tacitly present in Ford's 'commercial man') is the degree to which informational discourse both refers to and reinforces a hierarchy in which the masculine-coded public world of standardised information is valued more highly than the private world of individual perception and imagination, which Woolf codes as feminine. And not only values it more highly: insists that it is more *real*. In her reference to Whitaker's Table of Precedency – the section of *Whitaker's Almanack* which catalogues the British nobility – Woolf invokes not merely one popular information genre, but the whole social organisation of patriarchal power whose structures and conventions are codified in such standard works of reference: 'The Archbishop of Canterbury is followed by the Lord High Chancellor; the Lord High Chancellor is followed by the Archbishop of York. Everybody follows somebody, such is the philosophy of Whitaker; and the great thing is to know who follows whom.' (88–9).

Later, in *Three Guineas* (1938), Woolf will return to 'the impeccable *Whitaker*' as a source for her facts and figures regarding women's employment and salaries (Woolf 1938: 68). In 'The Mark on the Wall', however, *Whitaker's Almanack* prefigures Bradshaw and Baedeker as the chief exemplar of that masculine world of information that claims the right to determine what counts; and the order in which it is to be counted. It is the pervasive power of that world, represented by *Whitaker's*, that Woolf blames for the alienation of the thinking, feeling subject from its own experience:

> How peaceful it is down here, rooted in the centre of the world and gazing up through the grey waters, with their sudden gleams of light, and their reflections – if it were not for Whitaker's Almanack – if it were not for the Table of Precedency! (88)

But there is an irony to account for here. For it is precisely in her dissent from 'the philosophy of Whitaker' – her rejection of an informational understanding of reality – that the narrator of 'The Mark on the Wall' comes to be constituted *as* a subject. Woolf's insistence on the possibility of an alternative mode of organising experience, in which the mind of the subject herself is located at the 'centre of the world' rather than at its margins, is prompted by the recognition that Whitaker and his Table of Precedency seem to have nothing whatever to do with her own private experience. And it is through that very recognition that this version of a modernist subject asserts its own existence.

As if to clinch the point, at the very end of 'The Mark on the Wall' a second form of informational writing is introduced when the observer's silent companion (her husband, it is strongly implied) rises from his chair to go and buy a newspaper – even though, as he says, 'it's no good buying newspapers. . . . Nothing ever happens. Curse this war; God damn this war!' (91). It is he who brings the story to an end, in three linked ways: first, by positively identifying the mark on the wall as a snail, collapsing the myriad possibilities offered by lyrical meditation into a single verified fact; secondly, by turning to the outside world, specifically in the form of the newspaper, with its standardising sense of the significant and the insignificant; and, thirdly, by invoking the war. With its new forms of propaganda and censorship, the war was to change the way readers understood and consumed information: it is 'no good buying newspapers' not only because the war has squeezed out all other news, but because press reports cannot be trusted to represent the progress of the conflict itself accurately (Redley 2007).

* * *

Woolf's passing jibe, in the De Quincey essay, at the 'immortal works of Bradshaw and Baedeker', yokes together two of the more immediately recognisable representatives of early twentieth-century information culture. An essential vademecum for British travellers since the end of the 1830s, *Bradshaw's Railway Guide* was information in its purest form. As the railways had grown, so too had the notoriously complicated *Bradshaw's*, from thirty pages in the first edition to nearly a thousand by the end of the century, filled not only with times of arriving and departing trains, but tide tables and steam-ship schedules, advertisements for hotels and outfitters, and much else besides. The guide did not merely describe the transportation network, but actively facilitated its smooth operation. It constituted the written manifestation of the railway's ordering logic of efficiency, organisation and precision, familiarising readers with the protocols according to which the system operated. *Bradshaw's* thus became a byword for the impersonal world of pure information. When, in *The Valley of Fear* (1915), Sherlock Holmes suggests to Dr Watson that the key to a cipher might be found among 'standardized books which anyone may be supposed to possess', Watson's first thought is: 'Bradshaw!' (Doyle 1959, 13).

As well as providing railway travellers with accurate timetables, *Bradshaw's* also published a series of travel guides for tourists. Its main competitors in this market were the firm of John Murray (which had been publishing travel guides since 1836) and the German firm of Karl Baedeker, whose guides began appearing in English from 1861. While Bradshaw became the generic name for any collection of railway timetables, Baedeker held the same position among tourist guidebooks. Like the railway timetable, mass-market tourist guides were the product of a new technological era of mass transportation and mass tourism: the age of steam. But they also played a key role in publicising and facilitating those developments, enabling travellers to plan itineraries, to book passage and to arrive on time. Above all, they provided information of a kind that enabled their readers to understand tourist travel as a series of standardised itineraries. If *Whitaker's Almanack* could be relied upon to tell British travellers everything that was worth knowing, the guidebooks of Bradshaw, Murray and Baedeker would tell them everything that was worth seeing, and how to get there.

Like the railways whose routes they traced, however, these informational companions were sometimes regarded as having dispelled the romance of travel. Travelling through Italy with his mother in 1901, E. M. Forster noted with disappointment that the experience had been diminished by his enthusiastic preparatory reading: 'It strikes me so forcibly about Italy that I know it all already. I have got it up so well that nothing comes across as a surprise' (qtd in Heath 2008: 531). Forster's early fiction is filled with characters who suffer from the same problem, mistaking information for experience and relying on their Baedekers to interpret the world beyond England. In *Where Angels Fear to Tread* (1905), Forster even mocks up a purported guidebook entry for the fictional Tuscan town where much of the book's action takes place. Learning that her widowed daughter-in-law Lilia has contracted an engagement to an unsuitable Italian, Mrs Herriton consults her son Philip's Baedeker for information about the place where the calamity has occurred:

> *Monteriano* (pop. 4800). Hotels: Stella d'Italia, moderate only; Globo, dirty. *Caffe Garibaldi. Post and Telegraph office in Corso Vittorio Emmanuele, next to theatre. [. . .] A walk round the Walls should on no account be omitted. The view from the Rocca (small gratuity) is finest at sunset. [. . .]
>
> Mrs. Herriton [. . .] was not one to detect the hidden charms of Baedeker. Some of the information seemed to her unnecessary, all of it was dull. Whereas Philip could never read 'The view from the Rocca (small gratuity) is finest at sunset' without a catching at the heart. (Forster 1905: 24–5)

Forster's irony neatly suggests both Mrs Herriton's imperviousness to the pleasures of foreign travel and Philip's rather conventional, Baedeker-guided pretensions to cosmopolitanism. Meanwhile, the promise of aesthetic fulfilment, interrupted by the bracketed advisory – '(small gratuity)' – replicates the way that the ubiquitous handbook itself continually impinges upon the experience of travel, impairing its readers' capacity for unmediated connection both with their surroundings and with their fellow-travellers.

To Forster, over-reliance on such informational writing – a sin to which his English characters are particularly inclined – is always at odds with a fully conscious experience of the world. In *A Room With a View* (1908), Lucy Honeychurch arrives in Florence clutching a copy of *Baedeker's Handbook to Northern Italy*. It is only once Lucy has been 'emancipated' from the book by the self-styled cosmopolitan novelist Miss Lavish (who absent-mindedly disappears with it into the streets surrounding Santa Croce) that she is able to experience Florence without regarding the city as an object of study: 'Then the pernicious charm of Italy worked on her and, instead of acquiring information, she began to be happy' (Forster 1908: 30). Lucy spends most of the novel learning how to be happy by emancipating herself not only from her Baedeker, but from the world of petty information, middle-class sightseeing and standardised travel that it represents. Later, when it looks as if Lucy will miss her chance to marry the free-thinking George Emerson, with whom she is in love, and will instead go to Greece with the dull, elderly Alan sisters, Forster makes it clear that she is at risk of falling back into that conventional world: her preparations for the trip include researching the names of the Greek gods and goddesses in a 'mythological dictionary', contemplating a tour of the British Museum's collection of classical sculpture and – inevitably – purchasing a new Baedeker (295). But Forster has other plans for his heroine. In the end, Lucy does marry George, and the two return to Florence, where we leave them basking in the songs of Italian coachmen and the sound of the flowing Arno, without a Baedeker in sight.

The Baedeker, for Forster, was a symbol of disenchantment: of the world's mystery and romance demystified and distilled into a set of facts and itineraries. But it was also a symptom of the growing dominance of an informational world-view which his novels continually reject and resist, none more so than *A Passage to India* (1924). There are no Baedeker guides in *A Passage to India*. And Adela Quested, the young English schoolteacher who insists that she wants to see 'the real India', is no Lucy Honeychurch. But the informational spirit of the travel guide makes itself powerfully felt in the novel, beginning with the Baedeker-red cloth binding of the first edition, and continuing in Forster's touristic opening description of his fictional setting: 'Except for the Marabar Caves – and they are twenty miles off – the city of Chandrapore presents nothing extraordinary . . .' (Forster 1924: 5). This is India as it might be described, if not by Baedeker – since Baedeker's *Indien* (1914) was published only in German – then by Murray or Bradshaw. Uniquely among Forster's novels, which tend to open in the midst of conversations or correspondence, *A Passage to India* begins by inviting the reader to imagine a place mapped and catalogued in the totalising language and syntax of information, before going on to show how 'the real India' everywhere eludes the explanatory systems imposed by colonial authorities.

By the time he came to write *A Passage to India*, Forster no longer thought of information as merely a crutch for bewildered tourists. Instead, he had come to understand it as the dominant ideology of the British administrative class, thoroughly internalised and embodied in the figure of the government-school headmaster, Fielding. The central event of *A Passage to India* is Miss Quested's accusation that the Indian Dr Aziz has assaulted her in the course of a group sightseeing expedition to the Marabar Hills. When Aziz is arrested, Fielding finds himself caught between his friendship with Aziz, whom he believes to be innocent, and the expectation among the European community that he should support Miss Quested. After a heated altercation at the English club, Fielding gazes at the hills, contemplating the unanswered questions that surround the alleged assault:

> What miscreant lurked in them, presently to be detected by the activities of the law? Who was the guide, and had he been found yet? What was the 'echo' of which the girl complained? He did not know, but presently he would know. Great is information, and she shall prevail. It was the last moment of the light, and as he gazed at the Marabar Hills they seemed to move graciously towards him like a queen, and their charm became the sky's. At the moment they vanished they were everywhere, the cool benediction of the night descended, the stars sparkled, and the whole universe was a hill. Lovely, exquisite moment – but passing the Englishman with averted face and on swift wings. (191)

'Great is information, and she shall prevail': Fielding's rationalist credo adapts a well-known proverb ('*Magna est veritas et praevalet*') originating in the apocryphal 1 Esdras. But where the Biblical text speaks of the all-conquering power of *truth* ('*veritas*'), Fielding relies on the rather more contemporary intervention of information. For Fielding, information is no longer simply a collection of facts or statistics; it has become an abstract principle. What he does not see – and what Forster enables the reader to see, in his lengthening, lyrically descriptive sentences – is how thoroughly his own immersion in that principle has limited his capacity for direct experience of those aspects of the world which cannot readily be brought to informational order.

In the novel, of course, information does not prevail. Fielding never does learn what, if anything, happened between Aziz and Miss Quested. The trial of Aziz breaks down not because the facts of the matter emerge, but because Miss Quested begins to doubt her own interpretation of events, and withdraws her accusation. Moreover, Forster takes great pains to ensure that the matter is, in the final analysis, undecidable: 'I will it to remain a blur,' he would later write, 'and to be uncertain, as I am of many facts in daily life' (Forster 1985: 125). The ideology of information, which gains its power from the idea that the world consists of objective facts which can be clearly and unambiguously communicated, proves incapable of resolving human problems of misunderstanding and miscommunication that instead require acts of interpretation and imaginative sympathy. Indeed, *A Passage to India* is, among other things, Forster's ironic demolition of the clarifying and civilising virtues of information.

* * *

In 1901, G. K. Chesterton had depicted 'the literature of information' as trivial both in content and in cultural significance, a diversion for readers who lacked the time and education for literary indulgence. By 1936, as the following passage from an essay of Aldous Huxley's suggests, things had changed:

> The subject-matter of the literature of information has been enormously increased and has become more disquietingly significant than ever before. At the same time improvements in the technique of supplying information have created a demand for information. Our tendency is to attach an ever-increasing importance to news and to that quality of last-minute contemporaneity which invests even certain works of art, even certain scientific hypotheses and philosophical speculations, with the glamour of a political assassination or a Derby result. Accustomed as we are to devouring information, we make a habit of reading a great deal very rapidly. There must be many people who, once having escaped from school or the university, never read anything with concentration or more than once. They have no verbal props to shore against their ruins. (Huxley 1947: 44).

Huxley's complaint echoes Ford Madox Ford's nostalgia, a quarter of a century earlier, for the old days, before the 'telegraphic press', when Victorian gentlemen were allegedly united through their dutiful reading of Ruskin and Browning. Like Ford, Huxley takes the view that the modern mind's capacity for concentration has been attenuated by an unrelenting diet of easily-assimilated, technologically-mediated information. It is this accelerated, continually updated, ephemeral, virtual world of information that now takes the place of an older cultural tradition in creating the shared mental life of modern societies, so that even art, science and philosophy have been subdued by the informational imperatives of novelty and surprise.

Yet here, a few years before the long-dreaded outbreak of the Second World War, it is to literary allusion that Huxley turns for an antidote to the onslaught of technologically-mediated information. T. S. Eliot's line – 'These fragments I have shored against my ruins' – condenses post-First World War despair at the catastrophe of European civilisation. In drawing on *The Waste Land*, as so many writers of his generation did throughout the 1920s and 1930s, Huxley turns Eliot's poem itself into a fragment for his own use, insisting on literature's capacity to provide a renewed cultural and moral framework outside ephemeral cycles of information. In this, Huxley can be seen as a late representative of those writers who, throughout the first half of the twentieth century, invoked information as a mode of discourse in direct opposition to literary culture, a standardised and instrumental body of mere data associated variously with the relentless ephemeral output of the mass newspaper press, and the dull functionality of statistics and timetables. Yet even as they warned against the rise of information as a mode of relation to the world and its objects, modernist writers found uses for it. Writing about the cultural dominance of information, in its various forms, became a way of writing about mass literacy, about the impact of new technologies, about the standardisation and democratisation of education, about the perceived philistinism of the clerkly and commercial classes, about the effects of new media, advertising and propaganda. Resistance to the informational principles of simplicity, clarity and transparent communicability produced new experiments in style and a new attentiveness to hidden, subjective realities which could not be represented in the forms or formats associated with informational writing. As information was transformed from a term denoting a mass of inchoate fact into an abstract principle of modern life, it not only shaped the styles and objects of modern literature, but enabled modernist writers to think in new ways about the distinctiveness, and the distinctive value, of literature itself.

Works Cited

Chesterton, G. K. (1901), 'The Truth About Popular Literature. / V. / The Literature of Information', *The Speaker*, 3 August, pp. 493–4.
Conan Doyle, Arthur (1959 [1915]), *The Valley of Fear*. London: John Murray.
Ford, Ford Madox (1911), *The Critical Attitude*. London: Duckworth.
Forster, E. M. (1905), *Where Angels Fear to Tread*. Edinburgh and London: William Blackwood and Sons.
Forster, E. M. (1908), *A Room with a View*. London: Edward Arnold.
Forster, E. M. (1924), *A Passage to India*. London: Edward Arnold.
Forster, E. M. (1985), Letter to Goldsworthy Lowes Dickinson (26 June 1924), *Selected Letters of E. M. Forster*, vol. 2, ed. Mary Lago and P. N. Furbank. London: Collins.
Gillies, James, and Robert Cailliau (2000). *How the Web was Born: The Story of the World Wide Web*. Oxford: Oxford University Press.
Guillory, John (2004), 'The Memo and Modernity', *Critical Inquiry*, 31: 1 (Autumn), pp. 108–32.
Heath, Jeffrey M., ed. (2008), *The Creator as Critic: And Other Writings by E. M. Forster*. Toronto: Dundurn.

Hewitt, Martin (2014), *The Dawn of the Cheap Press in Victorian Britain: The End of the 'Taxes on Knowledge', 1849–1869*. London: Bloomsbury.
Huxley, Aldous (1947 [1936]), 'Writers and Readers', in *The Olive Tree*. London: Chatto and Windus.
Kafka, Ben (2012), *The Demon of Writing: Powers and Failures of Paperwork*. Cambridge, MA: MIT Press.
Lawson, John and Harold Silver (2007), *A Social History of Education in England*. Abingdon: Routledge.
Leavitt, Harold J. and Thomas L. Whisler (1958), 'Management in the 1980s', *Harvard Business Review*, 36: 6 (November–December), pp. 41–8.
Perkin, Harold (1989), *The Rise of Professional Society: England Since 1880*. Abingdon: Routledge.
Pound, Reginald (1966), *The Strand Magazine 1891–1950*. London: Heinemann.
Purdon, James (2016), *Modernist Informatics: Literature, Information, and the State*. Oxford: Oxford University Press.
Redley, Michael (2007), 'Origins of the Problem of Trust: Propaganda During the First World War', in *Communication in the Age of Suspicion: Trust and the Media*, ed. Vian Bakir and David M. Barlow. London: Palgrave Macmillan, pp. 27–38.
Shannon, Claude (1948), 'A Mathematical Theory of Communication', *Bell System Technical Journal*, 27: 3 (July), pp. 379–423.
'Tit-Bits' (1881), *Tit-Bits*, 1 (22 October), p. 1.
Warner, Sylvia Townsend (2020). *Lolly Willowes: or The Loving Huntsman*. London: Penguin.
Wollaeger, Mark (2008), *Modernism, Media, and Propaganda: British Narrative from 1900 to 1945*. Princeton, NJ: Princeton University Press.
Woolf, Leonard (2007 [1914]), *The Wise Virgins*. New Haven, CT: Yale University Press.
Woolf, Virginia (1921), 'The Mark on the Wall', in *Monday or Tuesday*. London: Hogarth Press, pp. 79–91.
Woolf, Virginia (1924), *Mr. Bennett and Mrs. Brown*. London: Hogarth Press.
Woolf, Virginia (1926), 'Impassioned Prose', *Times Literary Supplement*, 1285 (16 September), pp. 601–2.
Woolf, Virginia (1938), *Three Guineas*. New York: Harcourt Brace.

26

Computation: The Work of Calculation Between Human and Mechanism

Andrew Pilsch

This chapter concerns computation during the modernist period. Reading this in the twenty-first century, you may conclude that this will be a chapter about computers: the devices we use daily to interact with the Internet, to stream film and music, to chat with distant relations or to do most of our shopping. It will partly be about that but, more broadly, this chapter considers computation, the general process digital computers (and their analogue and human precursors) were created to perform.

Despite using computers on a day-to-day basis – especially when we consider that most mobile phones, TVs and smart home devices are all digital computers – most people probably could not offer a definition of computation. *Wikipedia* offers an easily accessible definition: 'any type of calculation that includes both arithmetical and non-arithmetical steps and follows a well-defined model' ('Computation' 2019: n.p.). Mathematician Robert I. Soare offers a more technical definition, drawn from computability theory (the branch of mathematics that models the underlying logic of computation outside the instantiation in particular machines):

> A *computation* is a process whereby we proceed from initially given objects, called *inputs*, according to a fixed set of rules, called a *program*, *procedure*, or *algorithm*, through a series of *steps* and arrive at the end of these steps with a final result, called the *output*. (Soare 1999: 6)

This merely formalises the earlier definition: a computation follows a series of repeatable steps to transform given inputs (which could be something you shout at Siri, as much as a differential equation you need solved) into desired output. This focus on step-by-step procedure is why computer science studies and creates algorithms.

The *Oxford English Dictionary* defines an algorithm as 'a procedure or set of rules used in calculation and problem-solving' ('Algorithm' n.d.: n.p.). So, while there are other models possible for describing it, computation, in its present digital incarnation, often involves a series of calculations performed in service of a series of steps designed to produce some more complex project. Computation becomes particularly important to mathematics after the invention of calculus, when mathematics begins to require increasingly complex calculations. To manage these labour-intensive tasks, mathematicians devised computers, which were rooms of people performing calculations by hand or machine, both analogue and digital, that could compute the results of a particular equation or problem. Much of the development of computers, in their human as well as their machinic incarnation, happened during the modernist period.

Jeremy Gray glosses the role of computation in mathematics in *Plato's Ghost*, an account of mathematics' 'modernist transformation' at the dawn of the twentieth century. Addressing the difference between thought and computation (and the growing realisation that computation is *not* thought), he offers the following explanation of computing:

> Consider just one of the questions [. . .] a machine [. . .] could answer: find sin(1°). It is unlikely that anyone not trained in mathematics would know how to do this, and many a mathematics student today would stumble their way toward the answer. To be sure, it is partly because [. . .] all users of mathematics simply ask their nearest computer for the answer without even wondering how the machine on their desk actually finds it. [. . .] [O]nce the theory is worked out, the calculation is entirely routine. The hard work of thinking goes into finding routines that are quick and work uniformly for a large range of inputs. The actual computation is so little evidence of thought that exactly this task was delegated by the mathematician de Prony during the French Revolution to a team of unemployed hairdressers. (Gray 2008: 431)

Computation is the labour of mathematics as a day-to-day enterprise, in contrast to the more demanding work of initially deriving a solution to a problem. Once the algorithm is known, it is mechanical routine to figure out the sine for any angle. In the time before computing machines, the work was performed by humans, employees with a status equivalent to de Prony's unemployed hairdressers. While it takes years to acquire the training necessary to work out how to compute sine for the first time, the calculation of sine requires comparatively little skill.

While we may assume that our digital computers today – that tell us the weather or give us a recipe for pancakes or let me write these words – are not still involved in this day-to-day labour of calculation, the solving of mathematical questions is still at the core of all digital computing: the Bézier curves of this typeface, percentile screen dimming as the light in this coffee shop shifts, calculating the arc of my finger as I move my mouse.

If we assume computation to be about digital computers, modernism and computation might be a brief chapter indeed. Colossus, the series of digital computers built at Bletchley Park to assist efforts to break the Nazi's Enigma code, was constructed in secret during the Second World War. John van Neumann's *First Draft of a Report on the EDVAC*, which detailed the architecture of the classified ENIAC and EDVAC computers and formalised the modern architecture of all subsequent digital computers, was published in 1945. These foundational moments – the first digital computer and the formalisation of shared-memory architecture – lie outside the accepted bounds of the high modernist period.

However, as I detail in this chapter, the digital computer was invented as a by-product of Alan Turing's work to prove that the *Entscheidungsproblem* – the 'decision problem', a major open question in mathematics posed and refined by mathematician David Hilbert between 1900 and 1928 – was unsolvable. Turing's proof culminates three decades of intense work on the question of computability: whether it can be known in advance if a solution to a particular problem can be found using an algorithm. Turing's solution imagined a mechanism that could automate the tedious work of computation, which was still at this point done by humans. Automating thought by mechanising calculation is an important figure for many in the modernist avant-garde. While these operations – automatic writing or Tristan Tzara's instructions for writing a Dada poem – can be connected to a critique of industrialisation's automation of the body, I argue here, when considered alongside the stunning innovations that made digital computation possible in the late 1930s, these routinisations of the body equally anticipate a coming automation of the mind. The modernist period marks the emergence of the theoretical basis for contemporary computer culture and, in certain avant-garde formations that should be considered as algorithmic, the first artistic responses to these new cultural and economic forms.

The Mathematical Origins of the Digital Computer: 1900–35

Alongside modernist innovations in music, literature and the visual arts, Gray's *Plato's Ghost* makes the case for a similar transformation in the domain of mathematics. Gray argues that, around 1900, mathematics shifted from conceiving of itself as a tool in service of physics and astronomy to a self-contained and autonomous theory that dealt with its own specific questions. This transition was brought on by professional pressures to formalise mathematics as a discipline distinct within the modern university, but also by a series of profoundly unsettling discoveries.

For Gray, mathematical modernism emerges due to the simultaneous realisation, in geometry and algebra, that the fundamental units of analysis – namely, the point and the number – are poorly defined (Gray 2008: 20–1). Previous generations of mathematicians simply assumed that everyone knew what these were and that it was unnecessary to define them rigorously. However, with the invention of certain advanced topics, such as topology in geometry and set theory in algebra, inconsistencies and paradoxes emerged in established mathematical discourse. Several of these hinged on the lack of foundational, axiomatic definitions of these basic units. The interest in mathematics on the part of logic and language philosophy, best exemplified by Edmund Husserl and Bertrand Russell, raised further issues for this crisis of faith: was mathematics real? Was it true (Gray 2008: 27)? The quest to establish this truth and reground mathematics was the impetus for modernisation.

In *Modernism, Fiction, and Mathematics*, Nina Engelhardt makes a compelling case for the importance of this modernisation to literature, offering readings of mathematical modernism in Hermann Broch's *The Sleepwalkers* trilogy (1931) and Robert Musil's *The Man Without Qualities* (written from 1921 to 1943), while also tracing the centrality of this turn in Thomas Pynchon's *Gravity's Rainbow* (1973) and *Against the Day* (2006). Engelhardt suggests that, while 'scholarship on modernism is surprisingly underrepresented in literature and science studies', mathematics, which is often more difficult for humanists to understand than the more narrative and empirical nature of the hard sciences, is more central to modernist art, as mathematics becomes in modernism 'a formal science that works with abstract concepts and not with the empirical methods of the natural sciences' (Engelhardt 2018: 3–4). Engelhardt's analysis shows the importance of understanding this other formalism in the context of artistic and literary modernism.

The chief figure in mathematical modernism, someone whose career was defined by an effort to create a consistent and provable base for mathematics, was David Hilbert. As Gray characterises,

> For Hilbert, the way forward was into a reformulation of mathematics and logic [...] He was a free spirit, optimistic that every problem can be solved, he saw no limitations on the human mind when it came to mathematics .... (Gray 2008: 415)

Hilbert thus engaged in a programme of axiomatisation, enumerating the basic assumptions that could structure a provably true system for all mathematics. Additionally, as well respected as he was as a problem solver, Hilbert was famed as a problem poser: the twenty-three so-called Hilbert Problems, first enumerated at a mathematical conference in 1900, structured much of the work in mathematics during the twentieth century. He additionally posed a number of other famous problems, including the decision problem, which emerged when

> [i]n 1928 at the International Congress in Bologna [Hilbert] spelled out three problems: Was mathematics complete – can every properly formulated statement be proved or disproved? Is it consistent – is it impossible to prove a false statement or derive a contradiction? And is mathematics decidable? [...] Given a correctly formulated sentence, can it be decided if the sentence is provable? (Gray 2008: 433)

This last question is the decision problem. Initially, Hilbert was confident all three questions would be answered positively; however, this confidence was shattered by an up-and-coming young mathematician.

At a 1930 conference honouring his life and achievement – 'the day before Hilbert was scheduled to speak [...] and to be made an honorary citizen of his native city' – Kurt Gödel delivered the paper outlining the first incompleteness theorem, which says that it is impossible to prove every statement to be true in the terms of a system complex enough to contain arithmetic, thus invalidating Hilbert's entire project (Gray 2008: 429). While incompleteness had answered Hilbert's first question from 1928 in the negative and suggested pathways to answering the second also in the negative, by the mid-1930s, the third question, the decision problem, was still open. In 1936, however, several solutions to the problem, proving it was in fact not possible, were simultaneously published. While all of them are important to the emergence of the digital computer, Alan Turing's solution was most important in establishing the impossibility of computing truth. His simple solution imagined a machine that could perform the work of a human computer.

The Work of Computation

Turing's solution, as I discuss below, utilised a particular mechanisation of the human mind to imagine the impossibility of solving Hilbert's decision problem. Specifically, Turing abstracted the by-hand calculations that were already a major part of most scientific work and became increasingly important to many emerging industries during Turing's life. To understand Turing's proof and what computation meant in the modernist period better, I outline what human computation looked like around the turn of the twentieth century.

David Alan Grier, in *When Computers Were Human*, calls the work of the human computer 'blue-collar science', referring to the 'hard work of processing data or deriving predictions from scientific theories' (Grier 2007: 5). In contrast to the purely intellectual work of deriving a theory, computation consists of rote, often boring work. It was uncreative but still relied on a degree of technical sophistication.

Grier traces the origins of human computers to two factors: the discovery of calculus and the Industrial Revolution. Calculus, which studied the mathematics of motion, required a large number of complex calculations to solve problems and soon computers – sequestered labourers – were organised to complete this drudgery on behalf of scientists. Alexis-Claude Clairaut's eighteenth-century use of several friends to do the bulk mathematical verification of Halley's prediction of his comet's return marks, in Grier's account, one of the first times the bulk processing of data was sequestered from the work of scientific theorising (Grier 2007: 15).

While calculus provided a need, the Industrial Revolution provided a form for computation, which Grier traces to Adam Smith's discussion in *The Wealth of Nations* of the need to apply the division of labour to scientific research (Grier 2007: 26–45). Specifically, computation laboratories, as the rooms where computers did their work were called, borrowed 'the division of labor, the idea of mass production, and the development of professional managers' from capitalist theories of labour over the roughly 200 years during which human computers were an integral part of the scientific and technical process (Grier 2007: 6).

In the modernist period, Grier articulates several major changes in computing, including shifting domains from astronomy to electrical and ordnance engineering and seeing the introduction of 'mass-produced adding and calculating machines' which 'had a greater impact in the fields of economics and social statistics' (Grier 2007: 7). Francis Galton, who coined the term 'eugenics', used human computers to study population genetics in an attempt to prove natural selection, leading to the founding of biometrics as a field of research (Grier 2007: 102–13). The First World War was a boon for computers working on ballistics calculations used to develop new and more effective artillery (Grier 2007: 126–44). After the War, military computers began to work in industry, which increased the efforts to standardise computation (Grier 2007: 145–74).

Megan Faragher offers an account of computation's role in the emerging field of market research and the consequences for H. G. Wells's fiction. She discusses *The Home Market: A Handbook of Statistics*, a 1936 book that 'collected, for the first time, demographic data about the British public in one volume that was well organized and easily understood', in the context of the emergence of tabulated population data (Faragher 2019: 55–74). These early data visualisation techniques connect, Faragher argues, to the emerging idea of a universal visual language, discussed in both Otto Neurath's work and in Wells's *The Shape of Things to Come* (1933). While Neurath imagined universal language as a 'ground up' process created 'collectively through informed, data-literate citizens', Wells's novel imagines a world governed literally from above by the Air Dictatorship, a 'committee of linguists who delineate the parameters of a universal global English' (Faragher 2019: 70).

Faragher's discussion of *The Home Market* and 'the new data-driven sociology' it represents (which is itself reliant on the tabulating power of human computers) reveals a central concern surrounding computers in this period. The data-driven sociology in *The Shape of Things to Come* shows Wells's view of 'demography [. . .] as a cudgel with which to drive communities into order and then study the success of that ordering via quantitative analysis' (Faragher 2019: 71). Order imposed from above is foundational to the work of computing. While technical and, as Grier points out throughout *When Computers Were Human*, one of the few avenues of employment for mathematically minded women, it is fundamentally industrial labour in which cognition is directed from elsewhere. As much as the modernist period saw the mechanisation of human computing laboratories and the application of computation to population demographics, the way in which the computer came to be a figure for externally directed human cognition becomes extremely important for thinking through modernism's artistic engagements with computation.

On or About 1936

While many readers are no doubt familiar with the effort, led by Alan Turing, to create Colossus at Bletchley Park during the Second World War, it is less widely known that Turing was part of a generation of mathematicians who defined the problem of computability before the war. The vision to create the first general-purpose digital computer was implied by this original mathematical research, but only as a side effect of it. Initially, as I suggested above, a group of logicians were working independently on a proof of the impossibility of Hilbert's decision problem. As shown by Turing's work on Colossus, and the subsequent turn to computer science by many logicians after the war, all of these proofs provide models for general-purpose computing. So while it is impossible to compute the truth value of a sentence, in the process of proving this impossibility Turing specifically generated a simple and elegant description of the general work of computation – a description that was sufficiently abstract to make it possible to imagine making a machine that could solve any problem that was computable (which is quite a few problems).

In 1936 a number of related models for computation appear: Alonzo Church's lambda calculus, Emil Post's finite combinatory processes, and, most famously, the Turing Machine. All of these models attempt to solve the question of decidability posed by Hilbert by exploring a class of numbers that came to be called computable: numbers such as π (the ratio of a circle's circumference to its diameter) that can, using a variety of formulas, be defined to a desired number of decimal points.

While Church's lambda calculus first proved the impossibility of computing truth, the mathematical ground of his theory is extremely complex. In contrast to this baroque system, Alan Turing later claimed to have invented his solution while 'lying in Grantchester meadows in the summer of 1935' (Gandy 1992: 82). As mathematician Robert Soare explains, 'as a boy, Turing had been fascinated by his mother's typewriter' and, in thinking about the decision problem on a series of summer days, he began to imagine 'a kind of idealized typewriter with a reading head moving over a fixed unbound tape [. . .] on which the head writes' (Soare 2016: 235). At the time, it was widely known in mathematics that computable numbers are computable because they can be generated by an algorithm, a mechanical process. So, as M. H. A. Newman explained in his 1955 obituary for Turing, 'to the question "what is a mechanical process?" Turing returned the characteristic answer "Something that can be done by a machine,"' which, in contrast to the complexity of Church's solution, had a refreshing simplicity (qtd in Gandy 1992. 80).

Thus, in 'On Computable Numbers' (1936), Turing defines a machine to compute real numbers:

> The machine is supplied with a 'tape' [. . .] running through it, and divided into sections (called 'squares') each capable of bearing a 'symbol'. At any moment there is just one square [. . .] which is 'in the machine'. We may call this square the 'scanned square'. The symbol on the scanned square may be called the 'scanned symbol'. The 'scanned symbol' is the only one of which the machine is, so to speak, 'directly aware'. However, by altering its m-configuration the machine can effectively remember some of the symbols which it has 'seen' (scanned) previously. (Turing 1936: 231)

By manipulating these symbols (reading, writing and erasing), the head can be made to move along the tape and perform a variety of mathematical operations, including, as Turing shows, the computation of real numbers.

However, it is not simply a matter of Turing having imagined a machine to solve the problem of decidability. Turing's machine was based specifically on the calculating work already being done by human computers in laboratories all over the world. Before explaining the operation of the machine's tape, quoted above, Turing briefly notes '[w]e may compare a man in the process of computing a real number to a machine which is only capable of a finite number of conditions' (Turing 1936: 231). While a brief mention in Turing's paper, this comparison is crucial to the success of Turing's proof. Soare explains:

> Turing's paper was distinguished because: (1) Turing analyzed an idealized *human* computing agent [. . .] which brought together the intuitive conceptions of a 'function produced by a mechanical procedure' that had been evolving for more than two millennia [. . .] (2) Turing specified a remarkably simple formal device (*Turing Machine*) and demonstrated the equivalence of (1) and (2). (Soare 2016: 235)

Turing's solution was, then, to combine the understanding that an algorithm mechanises human thought with an actual mechanism: taking the automated cognition required of human computers, he described an actual machine that could do the same. He operationalised a particular routine understanding of human thought.

Turing's analysis was more convincing than Church's, despite both being proved mathematically equivalent in 1937, because of this human connection. By mapping from the work of humans to a then theoretical machine that could do the same work, Turing took an 'intuitive notion' of the mental labour of calculation and showed that it actually contained 'a unique meaning which can be stated with complete precision' (Gandy 1992: 86). Turing's proof further offers a concrete example of the way in which certain aspects of human cognition are, in fact, mechanical in the strictest sense: they can be reproduced by machines. Though Turing's later work on artificial intelligence has yet to result in a general model of machine intelligence akin to human thought, the mental execution of an algorithm is clearly mechanical. The question remains: how did this mechanisation of thought function in modernist art?

Automatic Writing

Turing's proof of the impossibility of solving the decision problem was revolutionary for mathematics in how it idealised the mechanisation of human thought. While mechanising the human is quite familiar in discussions of the avant-garde, it is often discussed in terms of the labouring body. Michael Szalay observes in *New Deal Modernism* that automatic writing is a means of 'insisting that writing made most sense as a form of labour' to the radical left (Szalay 2000: 76). Meanwhile, Tim Armstrong, in *Modernism, Technology, and the Body*, situates automatic writing in relation 'to the dialectic of *attention* and *distraction* central to turn-of-the-century psychology' (Armstrong 1998: 187). Armstrong traces a refinement of the method in modernist art from notions of a 'second self' that emerge from spiritualist practice to a focus on 'modes of production' (Armstrong 1998: 187). Both scholars situate automatic writing in the context of industrialisation and the automation of the body. However, in this section I situate modernist interest in automatic writing not as a response to the already established norms of industrialisation but, instead, as a co-participant in the emergent discourses of computability and computation. As I show here, Armstrong's focus on production, coupled with debates in modernist writing surrounding the psychic origins of automatic writing (in the unconscious, in the ego, in the distracted mechanism of the body itself), mirrors the split between intellectual work and the rote labour of computation. Modernist authors in the avant-garde turn to automatic writing as a way of machining the psyche and, as Turing does in his proof of the impossibility of computing certain problems, rendering idealised and dehumanised the operations of the writer, making writing into a computable procedure.

In 'Manifesto of Surrealism' André Breton defines the movement as 'Psychic automatism in its pure state, by which one proposes to express [. . .] the actual functioning of thought' (Breton 1969: 26). For Breton and the Surrealists, the act of automatic writing becomes a procedure for creating art 'in the absence of any control exercised by reason' (Breton 1969: 26). The purpose of the artist in modernity, for Breton, is to escape 'the reign of logic' because 'in this day and age logical methods are applicable only to solving problems of secondary interest' (Breton 1969: 9). As these practices developed, Surrealists increasingly scrutinised the non-logical character of automatic writing, questioning where their writing comes from. Both questions, of the non-logical nature of procedure and the location of thought, are also present in human computation, as discussed previously.

In the Manifesto section titled 'Secrets of the Magical Surrealist Art', Breton outlines the procedure for writing automatically in the Surrealist manner. '[Settle] yourself in a place as favorable as possible to the concentration of your mind upon itself,' suggests Breton. 'Have writing materials brought to you [. . .] the first sentence will come spontaneously' once you '[f]orget about your genius, your talents, and the talents of everyone else' (Breton 1969: 29–30). This manual for automatic writing documents an algorithm: follow these steps to produce non-rational thought. This raises the question of how resistant to 'logical methods' Surrealist automatic writing actually is. Laurent Jenny, in 'The Adventures of Automatism', suggests that Breton is, at least by 1935, well aware of this contradiction. Criticism from within and without the Surrealist movement caused all Surrealist writing to be seen in the context of 'disruptive traces of "magical dictation"' and these magical utterances thus become subject to a 'rhetorical dimension' that is 'the trace of a figure of intention' because of Breton's first account of automatic writing (Jenny 1989: 106). As Jenny shows, Breton's writing during the mid-1930s is increasingly haunted by the realisation that automatic writing, far from liberating the unconscious to speak freely, is haunted by a strong rhetorical intent and, more damningly, by the spectre of deliberate style.

Jenny reads the technical section of the first manifesto in terms of the rhetorical canon of invention, those sets of heuristics that have constituted the basis of all public speaking since the ancient Greeks. He observes that 'Anyone can apply the technique: passivity, speed, tips to avoid stalling . . . So that this "magical art" of discourse is also the most profane, the most shareable, the most reproducible – in short the most rhetorical' (Jenny 1989: 107). Within recent rhetorical theory, heuristic invention has been re-evaluated specifically for its procedural characteristics. James J. Brown, Jr, argues that the obsessive invention heuristics offered in Desiderius Erasmus's *De Copia* (1512) represent an attempt to embrace specifically the 'machinic' aspects of rhetorical eloquence. Erasmus's introductory textbook for students of rhetoric advocates an abundant style 'to enlarge and enrich your expression [. . .] so nothing is redundant' (Erasmus 1978: 300). In this quest for abundance, Erasmus famously offers, as an example of copiousness, a chapter composed of 195 variations of the sentence 'Your letter pleased me greatly' (Erasmus 1978: 348–54). This obsessive cataloguing of variation is meant to turn the rhetoric student into 'someone who has it at his fingertips to turn one idea into more shapes than Proteus himself is supposed to have turned into' (Erasmus 1978: 302).

In Brown's reading of Erasmus, the ability to vary copiously comes from a series of automatic mental machines; Brown traces how translations from Erasmus's Latin original draw out an understanding of eloquence as the result of 'a mechanism that will act on its own' (Brown 2014: 501). The eloquent rhetorician is one who automatically produces endless linguistic variation. Brown then connects these machines to the computing programs, such as the robots that maintain automatic data on *Wikipedia*, that write 'alongside us' (Brown 2014: 501).

Like Erasmus's interest in mental machines, Breton's automatism shifts in response to the growing influence of Salvador Dalí's 'paranoiac-critical "method"', which substituted deliberate mental processes for the free rein of the distracted unconscious (Jenny 1989: 110). In *The History of Surrealism*, Maurice Nadeau explains that Dalí's method became more central when Surrealists began to wonder if 'rather than to trust to chance, which was not always so munificent, would it be possible to *fabricate* "surrealist objects" which would best express the force of the unconscious' (Nadeau 1967: 187). Dalí grounded his method in emerging psychological research which defined paranoia as a 'delirious interpretation of the world' that 'molds it according to [. . .] desire' (Nadeau 1967: 183–4). For Dalí, the Surrealist could use the external world, as much as the internal world of the unconscious, as a catalyst for the production of art by cultivating an egoic stance toward the world.

The shifting account of automatism in Surrealism represents the growing influence of Dalí's more active stance. For instance, Breton, in *Introduction au discours sur le peu de réalité* (1927), relates a trip to a flea market in which a mask is found to be particularly suggestive. Eventually, it is purchased and incorporated into a sculpture Alberto Giacometti is working on that lacked a face. Breton explains that the mask completed Giacometti's unconscious desire for the sculpture and explains that 'the *found object* performs the same function as the dream, in the sense that it liberates the individual from paralyzing affective scruples' (qtd in Nadeau 1967: 187). Dalí's interest in paranoiac methods further led to the theory of 'objects of symbolic function'. Dalí argued that Surrealist practice, once sufficiently paranoiac, could produce, and not just merely find, objects designed to produce these liberations in viewers.

The term 'automatic' has shifted here. Where Breton's earliest accounts suggest a freeing of the imagination to roam wildly, under Dalí's influence 'automatic' comes to mean the careful and studied translation of dream images. Nadeau explains that Dalí saw automatic work as having 'not a grain of imagination', instead offering 'the automatic translation of a text already read' (Nadeau 1967: 187). Rather than a passivity, Dalí's method is an active cultivation of a stance toward the world, not unlike Erasmus's account of the copious style: to appear automatic is the result of careful consideration and planning. Work in rhetorical scholarship accounts for Erasmus's reprogramming in terms of computation, as a transformation of the mind into an algorithm. We find a similar shift, from a passive automatism to an active one, in Surrealism: the machining of thought into a particular algorithm for capturing recalled dream visions in art. However, as we shall see, Surrealism merely reproduces the power dynamic of computation in this shift: there is still an intellectual vision, however unconscious, directing the rote production of art.

Gertrude Stein's work on automatic writing as an undergraduate at Radford College with Leon Solomons in the Harvard Psychology Laboratory suggests the possibility for a modernist critique of this dynamic, however. In their 1896 account of various experiments they performed on one another studying 'normal motor automatism', they find that the process of automatic writing is not, in fact, dictated by the unconscious but by some other factor, as 'the subject was absolutely unable to recall a single word written, but nevertheless felt quite certain that he had been writing, and that he had been conscious of every word as he wrote it' (Solomons and Stein 1896: 501). In their experiments, the researchers made a planchette consisting of 'a glass plate mounted on metal balls, with a metal arm holding a pencil. The subject placed one hand firmly on this and then proceeded to get himself as deeply interested in a novel as possible' (Solomons and Stein 1896: 494). As the subject read a novel, the experiment's operator would slightly move the planchette, 'after which [the arm] will continue of itself if not deliberately checked by the will of the subject' (Solomons and Stein 1896: 494). From this initial motion study, Solomons and Stein created a range of experiments with planchette and novel-reading to study aspects of normal motor automatism.

Solomons and Stein find automatic writing to be an 'extra-personal' phenomenon, rather than an unconscious one: 'Where he is conscious of the movements of his arm, however, they appear to him to be *extra personal*. It is not he but his arm that moves' (Solomons and Stein 1896: 494). They conclude that, while conscious, normal motor automatism displays a degree of independence from the rational, logical control of the higher brain: 'the feeling that the writing is our writing seems to disappear with the motor impulse' (Solomons and Stein 1896: 498). Their self-experimentation shows that the concept of authorship flickers when conscious, rational attention is diverted. Rather than emerging from the unconscious, as Breton theorised, Solomons and Stein instead imagine automatic writing is the production of a rudderless mechanism: what the arm would write when the brain is away. The divide they find mirrors the split between mechanism and intellect in computing understood as division of labour:

mathematicians perform the intellectual work of designing the computation while computers (human or otherwise) perform the dreary work of computation.

Rather than reproduce Breton's early views of an unconscious given free rein, Solomons and Stein's conclusions seem to mirror more accurately the view of automatism developed under the paranoiac-critical method of Dalí: the recording, with 'not a grain of imagination', of a pre-existing dream text (Nadeau 1967: 187). As Tim Armstrong outlines, Solomons and Stein's work was supervised at Harvard by Hugo Münsterberg, who championed a 'physiological explanation' for automatism, going so far as to expose 'a famous medium in 1909' (Armstrong 1998: 197). Given this context, Solomons and Stein's findings are perhaps even more radical for removing the idea of an original, whether spiritual or unconscious.

Armstrong notes that Solomons and Stein's research suggests that 'automatic writing is not produced by the delivery of a message from within (or elsewhere) but by a disconnection of the link between utterance and intention' (Armstrong 1998: 198). This disconnect mirrors the decoupling of calculation from intellect that structures human computing before the digital era, a process idealized in the machine Turing imagined to prove the impossibility of solving the decision problem. Considered in light of the shift to a paranoiac-critical method in Surrealism, these related insights into automatic writing during the modernist period highlight connections to computation: divided in terms of labour and also subject to procedural thought, both computation as a human activity and automatic writing seek to automate the mind, much as industrialism automated the body.

The modernist debate surrounding the author–computer comes full circle in a recent discussion of distant reading in interpreting Gertrude Stein's lengthy *The Making of Americans*. In a 2008 article, Tanya E. Clement argues that 'the complicated patterns of repetition in *The Making of Americans* mirror those a reader might face attempting to read a large collection of like texts at once without getting lost' (Clement 2008: 361). Clement argues that, while 'impossible' to read linearly, *The Making of Americans* reveals under distant reading – the method common in digital humanities in which scholars 'read' a large number of related texts to analyse pattern, structure and word choice – a complex and deliberate construction.[1]

In the extreme repetition of a limited vocabulary and without a consistent use of proper names, Stein's novel has, as Clement traces, been labelled with various synonyms of 'unreadable' for much of its existence. As seemingly random repetitions of texts proliferate, the meaning of the novel, and perhaps the entire process of meaning-making, are subverted. However, by treating the novel as data, Clement shows that the novel 'is structured as a determinate object that progresses with its two distinct halves as interdependent forces' that interact along deliberate patterns (Clement 2008: 373). In this analysis, Clement suggests that the novel emerges from a time when 'Stein was very interested in the notion of art as the composed or constructed object', but one that also 'necessarily entails an element of indeterminacy as a compositional part' (Clement 2008: 374). The interaction of these two halves would seem to admit the idea of an author–computer emerging in modernist avant-garde practices.

Responding to Clement, Natalie Cecire, in 'Ways of Not Reading Gertrude Stein', reminds us that, despite the recent vogue for distant reading, 'the possibility of machinic, outsourced, or otherwise cognitively displaced reading was a site of intense investigation in industry, the arts, and media' during Stein's period, the period that is the birth of computation as a pre-machinic theory (Cecire 2015: 283). Cecire traces the circulation of 'a rose is a rose is a rose', from the poem 'Sacred Emily,' as a decontextualised signifier for all the work of not reading Stein while noting that 'Sacred Emily' is itself a poem about '*oikonomia* . . . the repetitive work in the home that is often construed as non-work' (Cecire 2015: 286–7). As seen earlier, and as Cecire draws out in connecting *oikonomia* to the work of computation, computers were often women whose work was ignored or made transparent on the quest for some particular mathematical truth in the history of mathematics.

Cecire concludes that not reading Stein, like not reading a huge corpus of novels, 'always amounts to a judgment about the kind of labour that would go into reading it: a suggestion that that reading would be drudgery, a kind of worthless work, unrewarding or unremunerable or both' (Cecire 2015: 304). Instead, she argues that Stein is 'continually aligning her writing with housework and with information work' as a means of challenging the traditional narratives of economics and writing (Cecire 2015: 304). Most interestingly, Cecire shows that 'the perpetual question of whether it "pays" to read Stein's unreadable writing anticipates contemporary disciplinary questions about whether "distant readings" [. . .] constitute "worthwhile" scholarship' (Cecire 2015: 303).

Cecire highlights how the continued use of computation to separate labour between intellectual work and drudgery serves as a means of erasing the messy and mind-numbing aspects of creative work. For Stein, text was, most importantly, the result of 'mechanical productions' (Armstrong 1998: 199). To explain that all texts can be read this way, if the reader acquires a method that Armstrong labels 'atomized reading', Stein imagines reading during a haircut, with your glasses off: 'you use your glasses as a magnifying glass and so read word by word making the writing that is not anything be something' (qtd in Armstrong 1998: 199). Stein suggests here that the labour itself is the point and, as Cecire shows, not to read *Making of Americans* is to miss that point. Stein's novel, built on a foundation of automatic writing but expanding far beyond it, recovers the labour lost to computation and centres it as artistic practice in a way that critiques the computational division of labour. She shows that modernist art was already resisting this division and could surface the invisible labour of computation.

The history of computation during modernism is one in which algorithmic calculation oscillated between human and mechanism in both the sciences and the arts. On the one hand, computation was carried out by human computers until Turing's famous proof imagined an idealised mechanical model of this very human process of calculation, which in turn led to the creation of the first digital computers during and immediately after the Second World War. On the other, in the realm of avant-garde art, a number of figures experimented with the same idea: of rendering the artist's mind as calculating mechanism for the purpose of automating the process of artistic production. In both cases, while computation in modernism might seem anachronistic due to the invention of digital computers *after* most agreed-upon ends of the period, in fact the revolutionary implications of modernist thought in both mathematics and art laid the pathways for the invention of the digital computer and the dawn of the information age

Note

1. For more on distant reading, see Jockers (2013). For more on digital humanities in modernism, see Ross and Sayers (2014), Ross and O'Sullivan (2016), and Shawna Ross (2018a; 2018b).

Works Cited

Armstrong, Tim (1998), *Modernism, Technology and the Body: A Cultural Study*. Cambridge and New York: Cambridge University Press.

Breton, André (1969), *Manifestoes of Surrealism*. Ann Arbor: University of Michigan Press.

Brown, Jr, James J. (2014), 'The Machine That Therefore I Am', *Philosophy and Rhetoric*, 47: 4, pp. 494–514, <https://muse.jhu.edu/journals/philosophy_and_rhetoric/v047/47.4.brown.html> (last accessed 28 January 2022).

Cecire, Natalia (2015), 'Ways of Not Reading Gertrude Stein', *ELH*, 82: 1, pp. 281–312, <https://doi.org/10.1353/elh.2015.0005> (last accessed 28 January 2022).

Clement, Tanya E. (2008). '"A Thing Not Beginning and Not Ending": Using Digital Tools to Distant-Read Gertrude Stein's *The Making of Americans*', *Literary and Linguistic Computing*, 23: 3, pp. 361–81, <https://doi.org/10.1093/llc/fqn020> (last accessed 28 January 2022).

'Computation' (2019), *Wikipedia*, <https://en.wikipedia.org/w/index.php?title=Computation&oldid=931621505> (last accessed 28 January 2022).

Engelhardt, Nina (2018), *Modernism, Fiction and Mathematics*. Edinburgh: Edinburgh University Press.

Erasmus, Desiderius (1978), 'Copia: Foundations of the Abundant Style', in *Collected Works of Erasmus*, vol. 24, Toronto: University of Toronto Press, pp. 349–660.

Faragher, Megan (2019), 'Big Data and Universal Design in the Home Market: Are There Market Researchers in Utopia?', in *Humans at Work in the Digital Age: Forms of Digital Textual Labor*, ed. Shawna Ross and Andrew Pilsch. New York: Routledge, pp. 55–74.

Gandy, Robin (1992), 'The Confluence of Ideas in 1936', in *The Universal Turing Machine: A Half-Century Survey*, ed. Rolf Herken. Oxford: Oxford University Press, pp. 55–111.

Gray, Jeremy (2008), *Plato's Ghost: The Modernist Transformation of Mathematics*. Princeton, NJ: Princeton University Press.

Grier, David Alan (2007), *When Computers Were Human*. Princeton, NJ: Princeton University Press.

Jenny, Laurent (1989), 'From Breton to Dali: The Adventures of Automatism', trans. Thomas Trezise, *October*, 51, pp. 105–14.

Jockers, Matthew L. (2013), *Macroanalysis: Digital Methods and Literary History*. Urbana: University of Illinois Press.

Nadeau, Maurice (1967), *The History of Surrealism*, trans. Richard Howard. New York: Collier.

Ross, Shawna (2018a), 'From Practice to Theory: A Forum on the Future of Modernist Digital Humanities', *Modernism/Modernity Print Plus*, 3: 2 (7 August). Available at: <https://doi.org/10.26597/mod.0053> (last accessed 4 March 2022).

Ross, Shawna (2018b), 'Toward a Feminist Modernist Digital Humanities', *Feminist Modernist Studies*, 1: 3 (2 September 2): 211–29. Available at: <https://doi.org/10.1080/24692921.2018.1505821> (last accessed 4 March 2022).

Ross, Shawna and James O'Sullivan, eds (2016), *Reading Modernism with Machines: Digital Humanities and Modernist Literature*. London: Palgrave Macmillan.

Ross, Stephen and Jentery Sayers (2014), 'Modernism Meets Digital Humanities', *Literature Compass*, 11: 9, pp. 625–33.

Soare, Robert I. (1999), 'Chapter 1 - The History and Concept of Computability', in *Studies in Logic and the Foundations of Mathematics*, vol. 140, *Handbook of Computability Theory*, ed. Edward R. Griffor. Amsterdam: Elsevier, pp. 3–36.

Soare, Robert I. (2016), *Turing Computability: Theory and Applications*. Berlin: Springer.

Solomons, Leon M. and Gertrude Stein (1896), 'Normal Motor Automatism', *Psychological Review*, 3: 5, pp. 492–512.

Szalay, Michael (2000), *New Deal Modernism: American Literature and the Invention of the Welfare State*. Durham, NC: Duke University Press.

Turing, Alan M. (1936), 'On Computable Numbers, with an Application to the Entscheidungsproblem', *Proceedings of the London Mathematical Society*, s2–42: 1, pp. 230–65.

27

NETWORKS: MODERNISM IN CIRCULATION, 1920–2020

Shawna Ross

WITHIN MODERNIST SCHOLARSHIP, the term 'network' tends to lend its powerful connotation of complex connectivity to two interpretive contexts: first, in definitions of modernism as a far-flung set of constellations of people, publications and institutions across space and time, and second, in excursions into network analysis that use software to explore and visualise relationships among modernists or their texts. In the former case, the term 'network' crystallises what would be an amorphous cloud of movements into a discrete entity that seems definite but is flexible enough to support the new modernist studies' transnational and transhistorical expansions of what counts as modernism. In the latter case, the term 'network' refers to the computational methods adapted by digital humanities scholars to craft visually compelling graphics and queryable datasets related to a particular text, genre or group of authors, often on a large scale. In both cases, the named entities comprising modernism are related but not conflated, allowing the scholar's argument to overcome the slippery recalcitrance of its subject material while retaining its complexity.

Recent examples of arguments that deploy networks as a figure for modernism's groups of mutual influence include Helen Southworth's *Leonard and Virginia Woolf, the Hogarth Press and the Networks of Modernism* (2010) and *London Art Worlds: Mobile, Contingent, and Ephemeral Networks, 1960–1980* (Applin et al. 2017). For others, studying a single point in the mesh reframes the whole modernist network; Willa Cather does so for Janis P. Stout (2015), H. D. for Georgina Taylor (2001), D. H. Lawrence for Julianne Newmark (2016) and Taxco for A. Joan Saab (2011). By contrast, triangulating many points might redraw the network on a continental scale, as in Patricia Novillo-Corvalán's *Modernism and Latin America Transnational Networks of Literary Exchange* (2017) and Wesley Beal's *Networks of Modernism* (2015). Tracing a network is a political act that can recover occluded radical modernisms, as Wai Chee Dimock does by exploring representations of Native Americans in 'Weak Network: Faulkner's Transpacific Reparations' (2018) and James Gifford does by redrawing lines of influence away from Marxism in *Personal Modernisms: Anarchist Networks and the Later Avant-Gardes* (2014). Clearly, the network – as a model for conceiving of artists and texts as agents whose most salient feature is that they interact with one another in complex ways – offers considerable explanatory power. This power is mobilised for reconstruction, the essentially historical task of uncovering relations that pre-existed critical analysis but had simply escaped recognition. If a reader comes away believing that the network had always existed, then the critic has succeeded.

For digital humanities scholars who collect and clean modernist data to produce a network graph, the novelty of the visualisation justifies the work it requires. An aesthetically pleasing graphic, it boldly halts the march of black lines textually executing the argument. Consumed in the mode of a scholarly sublime, a network diagram – distinct from the argument developing linearly through parallel black lines of text, its comparative immediacy situates it as a given – belies the enormous labour of constructing the dataset underpinning the graphic. In 'Social Network Analysis and the Scale of Modernist Fiction', Sam Alexander (2019) unfolds a series of increasingly sophisticated network graphs, each one pitched at a larger scale by incorporating a greater number of characters or texts. The elegant simplicity of Alexander's diagram of *Mrs Dalloway* (Figure 27.1) illustrates the centrality of the titular character, whereas his visualisation of John Dos Passos's *U.S.A.* (Figure 27.2) mirrors the trilogy's decentralised plethora of connections. A similar sense of expanding efforts imbues the work of Kathryn Holland and Jana Smith Elford (2014), who recovered powerful networks of women at Cambridge by converting the digital resource *Orlando* into a textbase for network analysis. Martialling a large team at the Chicago Text Lab, Richard Jean So and Hoyt Long (2016) assembled a textbase of over 50,000 modernist texts for a multiyear network analysis. Yet, despite all this labour, these digital humanists share the hope of their non-digital counterparts: that they prove the empirical existence of networks that were merely awaiting detection.

But can we prove that these modernist networks truly existed? Some theorists would deem such figurations anachronistic. Patrick Jagoda has argued that network-based analyses like these take part in the ubiquitous 'network imaginary' that emerged at the end of the twentieth century (2016: 3). This discourse identifies many 'objective

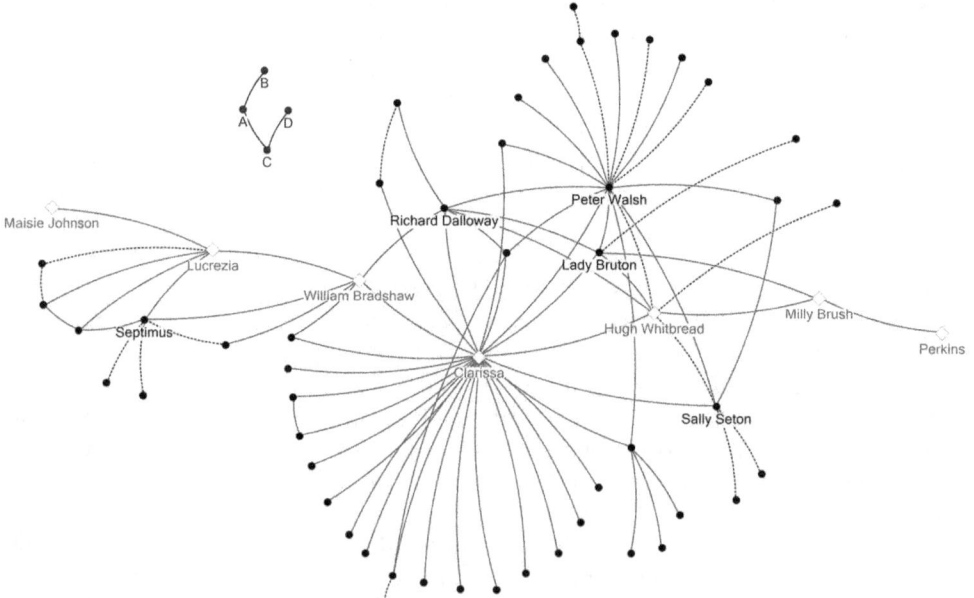

Figure 27.1 Network graph of Virginia Woolf's *Mrs Dalloway*. © Samuel Alexander. Reproduced with permission.

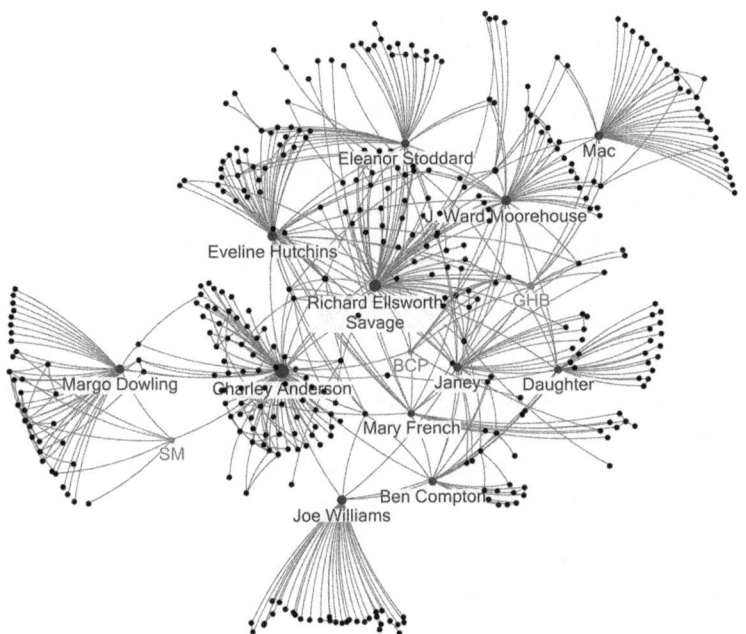

Figure 27.2 Network graph of Jon Dos Passos's *USA*. © Samuel Alexander. Reproduced with permission.

things in the world – natural structures or infrastructural technologies' as networks 'to capture emergent qualities of interconnection in our time', making 'network' so universally applicable that it 'has come to influence disciplines that include biology, economics, epidemiology, informatics, neurology, and sociology' (4). A product of the Internet, globalisation and post-industrial capital, this network imaginary matured in the 1990s, Jagoda concludes. Perhaps the study of 'modernist networks' does draw its aura of excitement anachronistically from visions of networked computers connected laterally by cables and vertically by particles whizzing high in the air and metals mined deep in the earth. But it would be myopic to ignore the history of networks, without which the term would lack its centripetal force. To apply it responsibly, we must consider which usages reflect traits of modernity and modernism that existed before networked computers became the default meaning.

Five centuries of English usage steadily broadened the conceptual territory available for description as a 'network'. As the *Oxford English Dictionary* recounts, this peripatetic term originated in the sixteenth century as a designation for light cloth woven of threads or wires intersecting in a grid-like manner. By the eighteenth century, any physical object constructed of criss-crossing linear components could be referred to as a network – including any organic material or creature possessing a net-like system of veins, nerves or alveoli. In the nineteenth century, writers like Samuel Taylor Coleridge and Ralph Waldo Emerson used it as a conceptual figure composed of causal connections binding immaterial and material agents. In his lay sermon 'Blessed Are Ye That Sow', Coleridge praises Great Britain's infrastructures, social habits and legal protections, particularly 'the arterial or nerve like network of property' protecting individuals' possessions (1817: xi). By 1900, atoms of metal or silicon were described as being composed of microscopic networks, businesses with multiple branches or trade partners were networks, and transportation infrastructures embedded urban territories with intersecting streets, trenches, train tracks, underground railway lines and shipping lanes referred to as networks. It was observed that telecommunications companies were laying networks of wires to connect citizens. By the First World War, physicists and engineers used networks to describe flows of power, whether at the atomic scale of individual electrons or the urban scale of streets criss-crossed by electrical flows routed for domestic utilities. By the Second World War, new forms of cultural content were transmitted through the broadcasting networks of radio and television, and social organisations that conferred cultural capital upon their members were called networks.

Within computer science, the contemporary denotation – a series of microcomputers linked by channels for communicative exchange defined by sending and receiving packets of information – emerged in the 1960s and 1970s. While this usage obviously borrows from earlier technologies that electrically transmitted messages through net-like configurations of machines and cables, it also borrows from graph theory, which dates from the eighteenth century. A branch of mathematics, graph theory provides a formal definition of 'network' and a means of visually representing these essentially abstract entities. Specifically, a network consists of one or more entities called nodes (alternatively, vertices or points), each of which is connected to one or more other nodes through relationships referred to as edges (alternatively, lines or links). A network may be visualised by a graph drawing (or network graph), with the crucial proviso that the resulting graphic is not the network itself, but merely one possible representation of it. The 'nodes and edges' vocabulary that predominates in the digital humanities ultimately derives from this centuries-old branch of mathematics. This retroactive adoption of an older vocabulary shows the persistence of meanings that pre-date the Internet. Like T. S. Eliot's account of a new author whose work reconfigures the canon in 'Tradition and the Individual Talent' (1920), the normalisation of computer networks has radically altered the meaning of the word 'network' but is responsible neither for developing the term's full range of meanings nor for inaugurating the hermeneutic possibilities of network analysis.

The rich history of 'network' clarifies modernism's role in the gradual unfolding of Jagoda's network imaginary. As we shall see, prominent appearances of networks in modernist art demonstrated how important networks were culturally and aesthetically. Moreover, the chaotic, many-stranded development of 'network' boasts the precocity of the avant-garde: each notable usage listed in the *OED* peers into a barely imaginable future, deliberately collapses the distance between conceptual models and infrastructural realities, or freely blends meanings from different eras and disciplines. It would be an oversimplification to call 'modernist networks' an anachronism. Most modernism technically pre-dates networked digital information stored in silicon chips, but, as Andrew Pilsch argues in his chapter on computation in this volume, twenty-first-century technologies would have been unthinkable and unimplementable without the conceptual models under development a century earlier. Analysing modernist networks thus serves as a useful bridge spanning two important phases in network history: an earlier period characterised by the installation of communication and transportation networks and the theorisation of atomic, biological and economic networks, and our contemporary moment, with its network imaginary.

Now we may return to the question I opened this chapter with: whether a network exists before, or is produced by, scholarly analyses that describe modernist social networks or produce network visualisations. Broad definitions of modernism as a 'network' may rely on a post-1990s network imaginary, but they are rooted in experiences that were available to modernist artists. Consequently, some network graphs produced by digital humanists visualise phenomena that were vividly real to modernists, while others support arguments that became conceivable when it became possible to process 50,000 texts into a machine-readable corpus. Sometimes the work of art generates a network, but sometimes the method of scholarship does. To posit a network is to describe an action performed by one of many possible agents: an artist who documents, interprets or participates in a material, historically existing network; an artwork that structurally resembles a network or embodies a cognitive model in the form of a network; or a critic who creates a network visualisation or investigates their subject-matter in the manner of traversing a network. I explore this multiplicity by classifying modernist networks in terms of their agential origins: networks as something a culture does (content), something an author does (style), something an artwork does (publication) and something a reader does (reception). This fourfold approach, by revealing how networks inflect a text's content, style, publication and reception, makes space for historically accurate representations of social and technological networks and for arguments that leverage the explanatory power of the contemporary network imaginary.

Content: Network as a Material Subject of Representation

The most literal interpretation of 'modernist networks' would point to the textual sites at which modernists represented historically existing networks – both the boringly routine and the excitingly emergent – including those of the telephone and the telegraph, as well as their wireless and visual counterparts, radio and television. Meanwhile, the proliferation of roads, railways (both above-ground and underground) and shipping lanes supported new mobilities that effected the 'time–space compression' of modernity (Harvey 1990). Friedrich Kittler associates the inauguration of new media, especially phonography, film and typewriting, with a devaluation of oral and manual communications in favour of technologically mediated means that separate the body from information flows. Defining a 'discourse network' as 'the network of technologies and institutions that allow a given culture to select, store, and produce relevant data', Kittler explains how an entire ecology of machines influenced artists' expectations about the relationship between writing and information (1990: 369). Mark Goble examines how the telephone consolidates one such ecology in MGM's 1932 adaptation of Vicki Baum's *Grand Hotel*. Reformulating the luxury hotel as a communication network, Goble observes, 'One does not step inside the spatial and narrative world of *Grand Hotel* by walking through its massive revolving door and crossing its breathtaking lobby; one enters by way of the telephone' (2010: 114). Goble extends this Kittlerian approach to the media-saturated private spaces of modernism. In *The Autobiography of Alice B. Toklas* (1932), Gertrude Stein's interest in metropolises as telecommunications centres focuses on her home, where the telephone connects Toklas to capitalist networks outside, thereby 'making each transmission of mediated language a commercial transaction as well, an accumulation of economic determinants that "gradually" penetrates both home and self, rendering any vestiges of domestic individualism as backward as gaslight' (Goble 2010: 114).

Mark Nunes similarly explores the capitalist motives shaping telecommunications networks, arguing that they provided 'material and conceptual support for economic practices from the late nineteenth century onward' and were increasingly appropriated for government and military uses during the twentieth century (2014: 356). Modernists reacted to these developments by depicting users requesting access to the information or energy passing through economic, bureaucratic and technological networks. Others depicted service workers managing the systems, the physical infrastructures of networks, including the tracks and lines that transmitted signals, people or objects along a prescribed course. Henry James's 1898 novella *In the Cage* does all of these – which explains a new wave of scholarship on it. Previously considered minor in his œuvre, it is now seen as a prescient account of networked sociability (Larsen 2018; Menke 2000). James castigates the callous egotism of rich customers ('that class that wired everything, even their expensive feelings') and sympathises with an overworked telegraphist ('a young person spending, in framed and wired confinement, the life of a guinea-pig or a magpie'), all the while sketching Europe as a claustrophobically intimate space fused by telegraph wires and London as a semiotic web of intersecting meshes of wood, wire, frosted glass and slips of paper (2001: 126, 117). Though James's heroine delights in the intellectual play of extrapolating life stories from telegrams, her active entanglement in the telegraph network ensnares her all more deeply in the class system exploiting her labour.

Around and after the Second World War, when broadcasting networks invisibly delivered a bewildering number of signals, this ambivalence toward networked communication shaded into pointed critique. In *The Ordeal of Gilbert Pinfold* (1957), Evelyn Waugh fictionalises his own drug-induced hallucinations of BBC presenters penetrating his cabin during a tropical cruise. In this metafictional novel, the transnational wireless network empowers brutal reviewers to pursue Pinfield across global networks of leisure (Waugh 2012). Andrew Gaedtke argues that *Pinfold* and 'other novels of late-modernist mental illness', including Mina Loy's *Insel* and Muriel Spark's *The Comforters*, feature characters 'plagued by the uncertain ontological status' of the world they inhabit (2017: 95). Their delusions, Gaedtke explains, originate from the characters' confusion over the original sources of the networked communications buzzing around them. In Virginia Woolf's *Between the Acts* (1941), the phonograph that soundtracks the titular pageant, filling it with chattering, chuffing and ticking, also invites unwelcome thoughts. Carefully hidden from the audience by a screen of leaves, the phonograph sometimes unifies them but at other times atomises them as it chants, '*Dispersed are we, dispersed are we*' (2008: 66–7, 132–4; emphasis in original). Some listeners are annoyed by its noise pollution (120–1), some feel that it unmasks their lives as merely 'marking time' (57, 118–19) and some believe it lulls patriotic listeners into a passive obeisance to fascist authorities (132–4).

Woolf's linking of fascism with machine-enabled public communications lend credence to Alexander Galloway's argument that in networked cultures, 'interactivity is one of the core instruments of control and organization' because 'organisms must communicate whether they want to or not' (2010: 291). Others are summarily excluded from communicating, leading Galloway to enquire, 'What price must be paid for exclusion? What *larger* price must be paid for inclusion?' (293). One answer can be found in James Purdon's argument that modernist texts 'offer not only a record of precedents but a frame of reference' for 'the peculiar anxieties' that arise when ubiquitous data collection enables government and corporate surveillance (2015: 189). Purdon singles out the fieldwork of Mass Observation, a 'network of operators' that rendered Britain itself 'a text in the process of being written'; as a result, a peculiar 'form of pathology ... emerges from the attempt to turn the entirety of the world's information into meaning' (93, 108). Although some modernists 'suggest the possibility of more authentic social connectivity', Elizabeth Bowen demonstrated that the Second World War foreclosed this progressive option: in *The Heat of the Day* (1948), the beleaguered heroine's attempts to recover incriminating documents dramatise the 'troubling effects of interference between private narratives of everyday life, narratives of public information, and occluded networks of state textuality' (Purdon 2015: 111, 185). As Bowen dramatises, considering modernity's networks requires careful attention to the dystopian possibilities of constant connectivity. Though modernists could travel to restful locales suitable for writing in or dash off messages to publishers or collaborators, knowing they would arrive quickly, these useful infrastructures were equally available to authorities capable of curtailing their freedom of movement or speech.

Style: Network as a Method of Composition

On the level of style, both liberating and claustrophobic connectivities could inspire avant-garde experimentation. The tangentially related fragments that comprise John Dos Passos's *Manhattan Transfer* are nodes of people and events connected by edges of narration that reproduce the tangled transit network alluded to in the title. A particularly dense network diagram is constructed by the highly ordered six-speaker community of Woolf's *The Waves*, with each completed round of speech retracing the same connections and suggesting that the friends' intimacy is as stifling as it is supportive. Such stylistic experiments bear traces of the author's experiences of networked communication. Juan A. Suárez maintains that though T. S. Eliot was 'uneasily entangled in gadgets, circuits, media networks, and technologies of textual production and reproduction', he cannily used them 'to situate *The Waste Land* within a discourse network that brings together the electronic media, language automatism, psychotherapy and the discourse of the unconscious, and the idiom of popular culture' (2001: 748, 747). Lawrence Rainey's reconstruction of the poem's composition reveals how the material traces left by the three typewriters Eliot used testify to the poem's indebtedness to the modern discourse network. On the other hand, the utopian affordances of writing technologies are undercut by Eliot's treatment of typists under his supervision at Lloyds and his troubling depiction of a put-upon typist who 'smoothes her hair with automatic hand, / And puts a record on the gramophone' after a demeaning sexual encounter (Rainey 2005; Eliot 1974: 141). The poem's machines explicitly ground it in the historical shift from a 'kind of writing ... no longer based on *inventio*, imagination', but instead 'fashioned after the automatic receptivity of the electronic media' (Suárez 2001: 758). The poem's polyphonic fragmentation adapts traits of Kittler's network – particularly the piecemeal delivery and interrupted reception of simultaneous streams of information – and disseminates powerful images of the networked technologies that shaped modern daily life.

Other modernist artworks are stylistically informed by the very networks they critique. For Jessica Pressman, contemporary electronic literature adapts modernist stylistic innovations to capitalise on the affordances of particular software packages while unmasking the social injustices endemic to networked computing. Influential works of born-digital art 'remediate specific formal techniques of modernism' (Pressman 2014: 2). In these works, the political problems that troubled modernist experiments reappear. Critiquing Ezra Pound's appropriation of the Chinese ideogram to theorise Imagism, Pressman reveals that his misguided, racist fixation on universal communication is present in 'the central precept of networked computing' because 'the underlying vision of a global network supporting the digital global village' depends on the 'belief in a programmable universal language' (148). This belief that computer code is a universal language – despite being based on English and originally expressed through a limited Roman character set – amounts to 'linguistic totalitarianism' (156). Yet the stylistic experiments made in the name of this dubious pursuit enable exposés of this politically bankrupt belief. Pressman cites Young-hae Chang Heavy Industries's *Nippon*, whose disorienting juxtaposition of Japanese and English streams of text forces the reader to recognise the incommensurability of different languages and the failure of the Internet to respect it (Pressman 2014: 151–4).

Other modernists expose the disunities lingering inside networks. Despite their high connectivity, networks cannot neutralise asymmetries of power, which is why their use as a formal device can unearth political tensions. For John K. Young, miscategorisations of Jean Toomer's *Cane* elide important heterogeneities within modernism, for it is paradoxically misconstrued as both 'a hallmark work of the Harlem Renaissance despite Toomer's uneasy relationship with that movement' and 'in dialogue with a modernist avant-garde typically perceived as if outside the racialist cultural systems circulating in the USA' (Young 2014: 171). Wesley Beal argues that glossing over gaps in literary networks weakens readings of Toomer's style: haphazardly identified as a short-story cycle, *Cane* is instead 'best understood as a network of forms' organised by 'a logic of patterning and repetition that endows its several texts with nodal relationships to each other' (Beal 2015: 54–5). Toomer epitomises Beal's thesis that accounting for the 'tension between totality and fragment, the two most basic tendencies of high modernism' requires us to regard stylistic experiments as attempts to create a 'distributed network' capable of 'negotiating the competing visions of dispersal and unity into a system that accommodates both through its nodal, interconnective configuration' (Beal 2015: 7). In this manner, *Nippon* and *Cane* use network stylistics to connect agents and events without collapsing them and show how some networks sanction or implement systemic practices of exclusion. Though readers may respond with aesthetic appreciation, these pyrotechnics are applied for political purposes, making it crucial to attend to theorists who do not celebrate the emergence of a globe fully connected by networked computers. Galloway argues that networks are 'specific technologies of power, organization, and control' (2010: 282). Less starkly, Nunes acknowledges, 'networking supports both the dominant, oppressive power structures of informational capitalism and the potential for marginalized groups (from the left and right alike) to reroute and mobilize this global space of flows toward their own ends' (2014: 357). Searching for networks' progressive potential in modernism's '-isms' therefore yields more promising results.

Publication: Network as a Site for Sharing Ideas and Resources

Indeed, one of the most persistent strands of criticism explores how modernists collaborated to develop, publish and promote their works. During at-homes, country-house weekends and evenings at cafés and clubs, and by running magazines, presses, bookstores and galleries, modernists forged alliances that comprise 'networks' because of their number, complexity and reciprocity. Although these connections are generally taken to be social – network diagrams conveniently illustrate which artists were friends or lovers – they are also lines of intellectual influence. These exchanges of information link modernism to computer networking, for the essence of computer networking is packet switching: the process that breaks down information into smaller bundles of data, packages these bits of bytes by associating each one with identifying metadata, sends those packets over a distributed network and then reconstitutes the original information at its destination. Modernist networks operated by sending and receiving messages, particularly works of art and ideas about art. Their gatekeeping practices maintained security, with firewalls of negative reviews, rejections, snobbery and blackballing and with whitelists of protégés, patrons, contracts and invitations. The social practices that knit together modernist networks were information practices, ones that communicated aesthetic data. Before the advent of Internet service providers, the traffic of modernist networks was routed through telegraph wires, city streets and publishers' lists, but these infrastructural differences do not render this comparison figurative. Quite literally, the ties uniting artists and publishers regulated the information economy of modernism by weakening or amplifying the signal strength of individual transmissions.

Demonstrating the transformative potential of signal regulation, Taylor (2001) argues that the dynamic network that circulated around H. D. was a hive of feminist activism, while Jo Applin and her co-authors argue that London artists established networks 'beyond the established coordinates of the institutional art world' so that 'artworks that foregrounded political issues connected to constructions of gender, sexuality, race, and nationality became increasingly visible' (2017: 8). Periodicals furnished another rich set of networks. As Faye Hammill and Mark Hussey summarise, 'In scholarship on modernism's print cultures, the idea and image of a network have replaced earlier, more hierarchical notions of structure in explaining and figuring the complex social and professional relationships from which literary modernism arose' (2016: 93). For Jeffrey Drouin, 'a magazine can be understood as a network bound together by conceptual, political, and personal ties frozen in a historical moment' (2014: 115). In some contexts, these constellations are liberatory because they amplify neglected voices. For Southworth, little magazines created 'a lively counterpublic sphere' where 'established authors encountered first-time authors and where old ideas met new ... free from the constraints of commercial publishing' (2010: 16, 14). In other contexts, these opportunities masked omissions. J. Stephen Murphy and Mark Gaipa, for instance, stress how influential magazines like *The Egoist* overdetermined the modernist canon because it promoted 'a tight network of well-connected, recirculating authors' (2014: 56).

Not all networks were as insular as Dora Marsden's *Egoist*. Modernist social networks with more diverse memberships are recovered in Saab's account of networks in Taxco (2011), Stout's of Cather's networks in New Mexico (2015) and Gifford's account of the Personalists who travelled throughout Greece, Egypt and North America (2014). Other scholars creatively reconfigure familiar networks to recover neglected intellectual cross-currents. Consider the Bloomsbury Group, perhaps the most conspicuous modernist network (Laurence 2003; Medd 2012). Holly Henry (2000) shows that Woolf's figures of telescopy positioned her within academic networks of astronomy, and Anna Snaith (2018) restores the place of Indian revolutionaries among the Irish and Russian ones already connected with Bloomsbury. Another radical approach regards modernist networks as systems for enabling resource-sharing – resources of all kinds, including ideas, expertise, money, in-kind donations or manual labour. In attending to 'vast publishers' archives, which contain tremendous quantities of useful and surprising material', such as contracts and sales figures, Claire Battershill treats presses as networks of material resources and advises that scholars mimic this 'DIY, collaborative ethos' (2018: 177; see also Hammond 2018). Jennifer J. Sorensen embraces this ethos in her 'multiplied network reading of . . . the material texts of modernism', which anatomises the visual and tactile networks erected by intermedial 'book-objects' (2016: 4). In particular, the 'handmade bibliographic codes' of the Hogarth Press were fabricated through onerous acts of typesetting, pressing, folding, stapling, gluing and mailing (209).

Focusing on the material aspects of publishing reframes coteries as crafting collectives and hearkens back to the oldest sense of 'network' – a form of sewing in which a grid-like pattern, despite its loose, open appearance, strengthens the fabric and renders it infinitely extensible and mendable. Images of the fibre arts abound beyond Woolf stitching book spines, from *Insel*'s Mrs Jones sewing up her manuscripts into a corpse-shaped sack to fishers repairing nets in Irish plays like John Millington Synge's *Riders to the Sea* and W. B. Yeats's *Deirdre*. It is telling that fishing nets on the modernist stage are always in the process of being repaired, for stitching scenes dramatise how 'network' is a verb in addition to a noun. Though network diagrams render nodes (typically proper names, such as writers, presses or texts) larger and more visually interesting than edges (the connecting lines), 'network' signals an action as much as an object. As Galloway and Thacker stress, '*if there is one truism to the study of networks, it is that networks are only networks when they are "live", when they are enacted, embodied, or rendered operational*' (2007: 62, emphasis in original). Unceasing 'movements of exchange, distribution, accumulation, disaggregation, swarming, and clustering' make networks 'capable of radically heterogeneous transformation and reconfiguration' (61). Every network is 'a multiplicity', capable of ingesting infinitely more agents (60). A modernist network is therefore neither single nor stable. Indeed, if modernism is plural – the new modernist studies, always preferring the term 'modernisms' to 'modernism', asserts it is – modernism is a network *of* networks.

Reception: Network as an Abstract Model

The dynamism and multiplicity of networks are evident in the evolving interpretations of successive generations of readers. Leisure reading and scholarly interpretation, which I join under the umbrella of 'reception', invoke the network as an abstract model whose adaptability makes it capable of encompassing an array of artist collectives, simplifying the complexities of avant-garde texts and visualising the arguments of their interpreters. Bonnie Kime Scott's diagram 'A Tangled Mesh of Modernists'

(1990: 10), with its spiky, bird-nest appearance anticipating the shape of software-produced network graphs created by digital humanists, was created to challenge normative accounts that privileged figures like Eliot, Pound and James Joyce and marginalised female artists. Other uses of networks for reception exemplify Jagoda's network imaginary, such as adaptations of Bruno Latour's Actor-Network Theory. Brad Evans (2015) applies it to Henry James, while Dimock uses it to theorise a school of criticism shaped like 'a multiplayer and multivariable input network' (Dimock 2018: 587). For Modernist Networks, an online scholarly community, the network provides a conceptual model for its 'federation of digital projects', and, more literally, the Internet enables its work. Networked scholarship is necessary because modernism is 'becoming increasingly interdisciplinary, transmedial, and geographically decentered', which means that no single editor, institution or methodology could adequately represent modernism ('What is ModNets').

Among the networks created for reception, network analysis probably springs first to mind. A digital humanities practice deriving from network science and graph theory, network analysis uses software to automate the detection and/or representation of a network. Users may pre-define relationships by providing structured data, automating only the production of a visual rendering (a network diagram), or may employ machine learning (artificial intelligence) to isolate significant actors and relations from unstructured data. This resulting visualisation is usually a two-dimensional polygon composed of an irregular grid of lines (see Figs 27.1 and 27.2). At the intersections and termini of the lines are actors (nodes). Out of each bristling node radiate lines (edges) that, as they move toward other nodes, denote relationships between actors. Two nodes joined by the same edge are referred to as endpoints. A diagram said to be of large size possesses many edges; one of a large order possesses many nodes. The number of edges associated with a node determines the node's degree. A node of a high degree is a 'hub', preferentially positioned centrally in the diagram, while a node of low degree is a 'leaf', typically positioned at the periphery. A diagram with few or no hubs is a distributed graph, whereas a centralised graph possesses many hubs, its edges evenly distributed among them. To create the diagram, a scholar must prepare a dataset, such as a set of plain-text files representing thousands of texts or a relatively compact series of structured entries that predefine actors and their relations. Then, the scholar applies their expertise in modernism and literary criticism methodologies to interpret the diagram in a way that it is useful for other scholars. For instance, a community whose diagram is distributed might be interpreted as more democratic than originally conceived, while nodes representing neglected artists that are of an unexpectedly high degree might be reinterpreted as central to modernism. *Visualizing Periodical Networks*, a special issue of the *Journal of Modern Periodical Studies*, hosts a variety of such interpretations. Chatham Ewing argues that his network diagram of the little magazine *Perspective* works to 'effectively subdivide what critics tend to see as a monolithic group of literary quarterlies' (2014: 16). Drouin reveals how 'a hybrid of human markup and automated analysis' improves research and pedagogy because it allows 'students to do real and valuable groundwork in laying bare the networks of modernism' (2014: 115). These essays support editor J. Stephen Murphy's bold claims that network analysis 'discovers order in what might otherwise look too large and chaotic even to be considered a system' and that 'literary modernism existed before the term was applied to literature and the arts, but as a network phenomenon, produced and perceived within a system of interactions' (2014: vii, xi).

What might give some critics pause is that any network diagram is merely one static interpretation of the network, which is abstract and fluid. This 'static snapshot view' not only elides the 'inherently dynamic, process-based' nature of the network it purports to represent (Galloway and Thacker 2007: 61) but also, if its underlying dataset relies on mass-digitised collections, reproduces the collections' flaws, including transcription errors, flawed metadata and gaps in their holdings. As Katherine Bode argues, 'network analysis inhibits effective engagement with historical evidence' and limits important considerations of 'how a literary system actually cohered and operated' because its 'focus on visualization impedes scholars' understanding of the evidence available to construct and interpret network models' (2018: 125). To ameliorate these flaws, we cannot take a network visualisation as a given – as a complete or objective representation of real relationships. A network graph does not, in fact, pre-exist analysis. We must also apply other forms of analysis (historical, biographical, aesthetic, logical) and critically analyse the datasets and software we employ. For instance, the Modernist Archives Publishing Project team reflected that one network graph 'would not do justice to the theories animating our project about the multifaceted networks of people, businesses, and materials behind modernist literary production', so they developed a prosopographical module to catalogue multiple types of relations between a single pair of endpoints (Battershill et al. 2017: 83). Gabriel Hankins, too, models a layered approach, moving slowly from a 'naïve reading' produced from simple tools by progressively applying more sophisticated tools (2014: 74).

If we keep in mind the rich plurality of modernist networks, of whose many registers I have surveyed only four, we risk no such flatness. Consider Joyce's *Ulysses*. In terms of content, Leopold Bloom's inner monologue and geographical wanderings record information about early twentieth-century Dublin's transportation and communication networks. In terms of style, Joyce's stream-of-consciousness technique reveals that associative patterns structure Bloom's lively mind, effectively reversing the node-privileging of typical network diagrams in order to emphasise connections. In terms of publishing, Joyce relied upon his proximity to modernist hubs, particularly *The Little Review* and Sylvia Beach, to ensure that his sex- and expletive-laced novel could be circulated at all. And in terms of reception, visualisations began to help readers since 1921, when Joyce himself created a table to help a friend keep track of *Ulysses*' many nodes and edges. In 1972, Leo Knuth mused that the novel's 'elements are inextricably interrelated in a kind of web or network, which is more easily depicted in a diagram than described in a discursive report' (1972: 405), foreshadowing digital humanities projects that use network diagrams or networked communications to understand *Ulysses* (Cavender et al. 2016; Hunt et al. 2009; Reyes-Garcia 2017; Visconti 2016). These network reimaginings of the novel are not only for scholars: a piece in *The New York Times* catalogued digital aids and visualisations for the casual *Ulysses* reader (Biersdorfer 2016).

The complexity of *Ulysses*' networks (of content, of style, of publication) necessitates these many interpretive aids produced in the process of reception. Famously, Joyce, writing on the Continent, needed an aid to produce the text in the first place: a map of Dublin. Imagining Joyce huddled over the map, planning Bloom's rambles, recalls the mathematical problem that inaugurated graph theory. The Seven Bridges of Königsberg Problem challenged mathematicians to trace a path through Königsberg by crossing, exactly once, each of the city's bridges over the River Pregel. Proved unsolvable by Leonhard Euler in the eighteenth century, the problem reappeared in 1930, with advances in theoretical computing science, when the Travelling Salesman Problem solicited an algorithm capable of determining the most efficient route between cities. Graph traversability remained incalculable – each optimal path must be determined separately – but the fact that Euler's negation resulted in the invention of the network graph shows how thoughtful practitioners of network analysis respond to problems of complexity not by obliterating or camouflaging it but by generating new modes of representation. *Ulysses* created one such new mode. As a graph traversal of Dublin, it revels gloriously in its multiple, redundant, overlapping and incomplete traversals. Its characters' halting, inefficient perambulations could form a dataset for creating provocatively surreal network graphs, but more importantly, Joyce's ingenious novel demonstrates in itself how, like Euler, modernists responded to the provocations of networks with experimentation. What was incalculable for mathematicians became, for modernists, a material subject to investigate, an abstract form to emulate, a collaborative method to harness and an interpretive future to await.

Works Cited

Alexander, Sam (2019), 'Social Network Analysis and the Scale of Modernist Fiction', *Modernism/modernity*, Print Plus 3: 4, <http://modernismmodernity.org/forums/posts/social-network-analysis> (last accessed 28 January 2022).
Applin, Jo, Catherine Spencer and Amy Tobin (2017), *London Art Worlds: Mobile, Contingent, and Ephemeral Networks, 1960–1980*. State College: Pennsylvania State University Press.
Battershill, Claire (2018), *Modernist Lives*. London: Bloomsbury.
Battershill, Claire, Helen Southworth, Alice Staveley, Michael Widner, Elizabeth Willson Gordon and Nicola Wilson (2017), *Scholarly Adventures in Digital Humanities*. New York: Palgrave Macmillan.
Beal, Wesley (2015), *Networks of Modernism*. Iowa City: University of Iowa Press.
Biersdorfer, J. D. (2016), 'Can't Get Through *Ulysses*? Digital Help Is on the Way', 13 July, <https://www.nytimes.com/2016/07/17/books/review/cant-get-through-ulysses-digital-help-is-on-the-way.html> (last accessed 28 January 2022).
Bode, Katherine (2018), *A World of Fiction*. Ann Arbor: University of Michigan Press.
Cavender, Kurt, Jamey E Graham, Robert P. Fox, Jr, Richard Flynn and Kenyon Cavender (2016), 'Body Language: Toward an Affective Formalism of Ulysses', in *Reading Modernism with Machines*, ed. Shawna Ross and James O'Sullivan. Basingstoke: Palgrave Macmillan, pp. 223–42.
Coleridge, S. T. (1817), *Blessed Are Ye That Sow*. London: Gale and Fenner.
Dimock, Wai Chee (2018), 'Weak Network: Faulkner's Transpacific Reparations', *Modernism/modernity*, 25: 3, pp. 587–601.
Drouin, Jeffrey (2014), 'Close- and Distant-Reading Modernism: Network Analysis, Text Mining, and Teaching the *Little Review*', *The Journal of Modern Periodical Studies*, 5: 1, pp. 110–35.
Eliot, T. S. (1920), 'Tradition and the Individual Talent', in *The Sacred Wood*. London: Methuen, pp. 42–53.
Eliot, T. S. (1974), *The Waste Land*. New York: Harcourt Brace Jovanovich.
Evans, Brad (2015), 'Relating in Henry James (The Artwork of Networks)', *The Henry James Review*, 36: 1, pp. 1–23.
Ewing, Chatham (2014), 'Perspective: Social Networks and Historical Contexts', *The Journal of Modern Periodical Studies*, 5: 1, pp. 1–26.

Gaedtke, Andrew (2017), *Modernism and the Machinery of Madness*. Cambridge: Cambridge University Press.

Galloway, Alexander R. (2010), 'Network', in *Critical Terms for Media Studies*, ed. W. J. T. Mitchell and Mark Hansen. Chicago: University of Chicago Press, pp. 280–96.

Galloway, Alexander R. and Eugene Thacker (2007), *The Exploit: A Theory of Networks*. Minneapolis: University of Minnesota Press.

Gifford, James (2014), *Personal Modernisms: Anarchist Networks and the Later Avant-Gardes*. Edmonton: University of Alberta Press.

Goble, Mark (2010), *Beautiful Circuits*. New York: Columbia University Press.

Hammill, Faye and Mark Hussey (2016), *Modernism's Print Cultures*. London: Bloomsbury.

Hammond, Adam (2018), 'From Modernism to moDernIYsm', *Modernism/modernity*, Print Plus 3: 2 (Summer).

Hankins, Gabriel (2014), 'Visualizing Modernist Magazines with Geographic Information Systems (GIS)', *The Journal of Modern Periodical Studies*, 5: 1, pp. 69–93.

Harvey, David (1990), *The Condition of Postmodernity*. Cambridge, MA: Blackwell.

Henry, Holly (2000), 'From Edwin Hubble's Telescope to Virginia Woolf's "Searchlight"', in *Virginia Woolf in the Age of Mechanical Reproduction*, ed. Pamela Caughie. New York: Garland, pp. 135–58.

Holland, Kathryn and Jana Smith Elford (2014), 'Textbase as Machine', in *Reading Modernism with Machines*, ed. Shawna Ross and James O'Sullivan. Basingstoke: Palgrave Macmillan, pp. 109–34.

Hunt, John et al. (2009), *The Joyce Project*, <http://joyceproject.com> (last accessed 28 January 2022).

Jagoda, Patrick (2016), *Network Aesthetics*. Chicago: University of Chicago Press.

James, Henry (2001), *The Turn of the Screw & In the Cage*. New York: Random House.

Kittler, Friedrich (1990), *Discourse Networks, 1800/1900*, transl. Michael Metteer. Stanford, CA: Stanford University Press.

Knuth, Leo (1972), 'A Bathymetric Reading of Joyce's *Ulysses*, Chapter X', *James Joyce Quarterly*, 9: 4, pp. 405–22.

Larsen, Haley (2018), '"The Spirit of Electricity": Henry James's *In the Cage* and Electric Female Imagination at the Turn of the Century', *Configurations*, 26: 4, pp. 357–87.

Laurence, Patricia (2003), *Julian Bell, the Violent Pacifist*. London: Cecil Woolf.

Marcuse, Herbert (2004), *Technology, War and Fascism: Collected Papers of Herbert Marcuse, Volume 1*. London: Routledge.

Medd, Jodie (2012), *Lesbian Scandal and the Culture of Modernism*. Cambridge: Cambridge University Press.

Menke, Richard (2000), 'Telegraphic Realism: Henry James's *In the Cage*', *PMLA*, 115: 5, pp. 975–90.

Murphy, J. Stephen (2014), 'Visualizing Periodical Networks', *The Journal of Modern Periodical Studies*, 5: 1, pp. iii–xv.

Murphy, J. Stephen and Mark Gaipa (2014), 'You Might Also Like . . .: Magazine Networks and Modernist Tastemaking in the Dora Marsden Magazines', *The Journal of Modern Periodical Studies*, 5: 1, pp. 27–68.

'network, n. and adj', *OED Online*, Oxford University Press, <https://www.oed.com/view/Entry/126342> (last accessed 28 January 2022).

Newmark, Julianne (2016), 'DH Lawrence and Networks of American Literary Criticism', *The D. H. Lawrence Review*, 41: 1, pp. 63–88.

Novillo-Corvalán, Patricia (2017), *Modernism and Latin America Transnational Networks of Literary Exchange*. London: Routledge.

Nunes, Mark (2014), 'Networking', in *The Johns Hopkins Guide to Digital Media*, ed. Marie-Laure Ryan, Lori Emerson and Benjamin J. Robertson. Baltimore: Johns Hopkins University Press.

Pressman, Jessica (2014), *Digital Modernism*. Oxford: Oxford University Press.
Purdon, James (2015), *Modernist Informatics*. Oxford: Oxford University Press.
Rainey, Lawrence (2005), 'Eliot Among the Typists', *Modernism/modernity*, 12: 1, pp. 27–84.
Reyes-Garcia, Everardo (2017), *The Image-Interface*. London: Wiley.
Saab, A. Joan (2011), 'Modernist Networks: Taxco, 1931', *Modernism/modernity*, 18: 2, pp. 289–307.
Scott, Bonnie Kime, ed. (1990), *The Gender of Modernism*. Bloomington: Indiana University Press.
Snaith, Anna (2018), 'Case Study: Race, Empire, and Performative Activism in Late Edwardian Bloomsbury', in *The Handbook to the Bloomsbury Group*, ed. Derek Ryan and Stephen Ross. London: Bloomsbury, pp. 94–108.
So, Richard Jean and Hoyt Long (2016), 'Network Analysis and the Sociology of Modernism', *boundary 2*, 40: 2, pp. 147–82.
Sorenson, Jennifer J. (2016), *Modernist Experiments in Genre, Media, and Transatlantic Print Culture*. London: Routledge.
Southworth, Helen (2010), *Leonard and Virginia Woolf, the Hogarth Press and the Networks of Modernism*. Edinburgh: Edinburgh University Press.
Stout, Janis P. (2015), 'Modernist by Association: Willa Cather's New York/New Mexico Circle', *American Literary Realism*, 47: 2, pp. 117–35.
Suárez, Juan Antonio (2001), 'TS Eliot's The Waste Land, the Gramophone, and the Modernist Discourse Network', *New Literary History*, 32: 3, pp. 747–68.
Taylor, Georgina (2001), *HD and the Public Sphere of Modernist Women Writers, 1913–1946: Talking Women*. Oxford: Oxford University Press.
Visconti, Amanda (2016), *Infinite Ulysses*, <http://infiniteulysses.com/> (last accessed 28 January 2022).
Waugh, Evelyn (2012), *The Ordeal of Gilbert Pinfold*. New York: Back Bay Books.
'What is ModNets', *Modernist Networks*, <https://modnets.org/about/what-is-modnets/> (last accessed 28 January 2022).
Woolf, Virginia (2008), *Between the Acts*. New York: Harcourt.
Young, John K. (2014), 'The Roots of Cane: Jean Toomer in The Double Dealer and Modernist Networks', in *Race, Ethnicity and Publishing in America*, ed. Cécile Cottenet. London: Palgrave Macmillan, pp. 171–92.

28

War: Modernism in Camouflage, Strategic Fantasy and the Technological Sublime

Patrick Deer

WAR FORCED MODERNISM'S uneasy romance with technology into crisis. Now rivals, now critics, now technophiles and technophobes, modernists confronted and embraced from the start the expansionist energies of technology. War would bring an aesthetic, political and ethical reckoning that disturbed and fractured this intimate relationship between modernism and technology. For their part, the more avant-garde writers and artists actively engaged and exacerbated the contradictions in technology revealed by the First World War. The technologies of war, like artillery, the machine gun, high explosive shells, poison gas, aeroplanes, camouflaged Dazzle Ships and the tank, seemed to be the violent double of modernist and avant-garde artistic experimentation. Like T. S. Eliot's *'mon semblable, mon frère'* in *The Waste Land* (1922), these technologies brought 'the shock of the new' to battlefields from late nineteenth-century 'Little Colonial Wars' to the First World War and beyond. Famously celebrated and aestheticised in Filippo Marinetti's Futurist Manifestos, they seemed to offer objective correlatives or even causal mechanisms for avant-garde shock tactics.

Yet the technologies that modernised warfare from 1914 to 1945 shattered the utopian, imperious promise of modern industrial power and communications, revealing and demystifying a dystopian drive towards colonialism and war. This reinforced a modernist sense of irony and epistemological scepticism, which Paul Fussell famously argued in *The Great War and Modern Memory* (1975) marked a descent into a generalised sense of ironic disillusionment after 1914. More disturbing than the epochal violence unleashed by military technology was the revelation for many writers and artists that modern warfare not only impoverished experience, as Walter Benjamin noted in 'The Story Teller', but revealed a more profound transformation of human experience and social relations. Observing famously that 'men returned from the battlefield grown silent – not richer, but poorer in communicable experience', Benjamin argued that this tendency was part of a larger logic of modernisation: 'For never has experience been contradicted more thoroughly than strategic experience by tactical warfare, economic experience by inflation, bodily experience by mechanical warfare, moral experience by those in power' (Benjamin 1969a: 84).

I will argue here that literary modernism offered a powerful lens through which to understand the relationship between technology and modern war not only because of its obsessive ambivalence towards these relations, but because of the intimate relationship between aesthetic experimentation and experimental technologies of violence.

War exposed modernism's internal contradictions. War technology needed culture and narrative to supplement its claims to wage total war, both because of its imperial ambitions – which encompassed combatants and civilian populations alike in a 'war to end all wars' – and because of its vast technical failures, shattering violence and horrifying human costs. Technology claimed to transform and expand the power of armies, navies and air forces, and extend the fighting force of soldiers' minds and bodies. But war technology was lacking; it needed culture and narrative, especially modernist art and literature: to supplement its own 'prosthetic imagination', to use Peter Boxall's immensely helpful term, and to project its strategic fantasies.[1]

In this chapter I will consider several crucial aspects of war technology's wider embedding in modern culture, and its exchanges with experimental forms of modernist culture in particular. I begin with the temporal and historical dimension of modernism's often contradictory exploration of the crises unleashed by war technology. The array of shockingly new aesthetic tactics seemed to augur entry into an epoch remade by total war, but I will argue that many modernists refused technological determinism in favour of representing a contingent social process. Here I consider modernism's implication in the seductive logic by which war technology offered itself as a necessary remedy to the very costly failures it produced, which helped normalise both the national security state and a permanent war economy. Next I explore my argument that war technology needed culture and narrative, especially modernist art and literature, to extend its imperial ambitions and supplement its wartime failures. In response, writers produced a modernism in camouflage that experimented often covertly under the shadow of propaganda, censorship and trauma (Deer 2009: 10–11). Third, I explore the ways that writers and artists responded to the affective disturbances wrought by technology in the war zone, responding to trauma and bodily collapse with an aesthetics of therapeutic narrative and modernist melancholia. By contrast, avant-garde representations of the prosthetic and the machinic allowed both for posthuman critique and a protofascist rearming of the hypermasculine body of the 'New Man'. Fourth, I will trace briefly the ways that experimental writers and artists represented and critiqued the machinic imaginary of a technological sublime, in tropes of imperial air power whose mobility in time and space compensated for the disastrous stasis and deadlock of modern industrialised warfare. I will close by considering the cost of forgetting these lessons about the seductive powers of military technology and war culture.

Distinctions between modernism and the avant-gardes have grown more slippery and less central to recent modernist studies, in part because of the extraordinary proliferation of varieties of modernism anticipated by Peter Nicholls's influential *Modernisms* (1995). But I will argue here that when it come to the relationship between technology and war, the distinctions between modernism and the avant-gardes are extremely helpful in negotiating this tricky field of battle. Modernist writers, both combatants like Ford Madox Ford or Ernest Hemingway and non-combatants like Virginia Woolf, T. S. Eliot, F. Scott Fitzgerald or Djuna Barnes, often shared romantic anti-capitalist attitudes towards technology, treating it with high modernist irony. As Nicholls has argued, they often countered the 'obsession with the new' with 'a counter-tendency during the same period which sought to curb a metaphysics of originality and constant innovation with a modernism preoccupied with its own limits and with the obdurate materiality of a world resistant to aesthetic fantasy' (Nicholls 2020: 427).

By contrast, the avant-gardes, like Futurism, Dada in its New York and Zurich varieties, Expressionism or Surrealism, were often attracted towards a machinic imaginary, assaulting standard notions of the human or projecting ideas of a 'New Man'. In the case of New York Dada, with its Duchampian machines that did not do anything, artists were open to the idea of technology as a kind of parodic, absurd performativity that could reveal the self-sustaining absurdity of war and war culture. One understanding these avant-gardes often have in common is that a narrowly instrumental conception of technology distracts from a more profound social transformation wrought by technology in wartime: viewing war technologies from the vantage point of technology as a social process, as many modernist and avant-garde writers do, yields a more disturbing and broader view.

We Are Making A New World

As a product of the Second Industrial Age, war technology inhabited an unstable temporality which combined the archaic and the futuristic. This naturally resonated with literary modernism's tropes of temporal crisis, of being caught between a dying old order and a new world struggling monstrously to be born. Modernist myths of the First World War as a descent into irony, fragmentation and historic rupture, like the futurist aestheticisations of violence critiqued by Walter Benjamin, have obscured the longer modernist fascination with war as both a machine running out of control and as the engine of civilisation which might produce a 'war to end all wars' or at least a colonising force for social and global order. Avant-gardists often stood disturbingly close to technologies of violence: Marinetti notoriously celebrated the 'hygiene of war' in the 'Futurist Manifesto'; Gertrude Stein and Pablo Picasso in 1915 famously watched a military parade of camouflaged artillery on the Boulevard Raspail in Paris, declaring, 'Nous avons fait ça'; official war artist Paul Nash titled his caustic 1918 painting of the lunar landscape of No Man's Land *We Are Making a New World* (Marinetti 1991: 50; Stein 1990: 84–5). But literary modernism has typically been positioned on the other side of a demystified, ironic modernity, critical of what Benjamin called '[t]his monstrous development of technology' (Benjamin 2019).

Drawing on Ernest Mandel's account of a 'Second Technological Revolution' in *Late Capitalism*, Nicholas Daly has argued of modernism's intimate ties to technological modernisation, '[i]n theoretical terms one could argue that there is no space between the aesthetics of modernism and these technological shifts'. He argues further:

> they are bound together in a common culture. But for practical purposes we can describe a set of relations between the two: modernism incorporated technological change as historical content; it appropriated new representational means for its own artistic practices; and at times it self-consciously drew on the machine world for aesthetic models. The flurry of innovation in mechanical reproduction, that is to say, in technologies of communication and representation, brought the materiality of older media into sharp contrasting focus. (Daly 2016: 404)

War indeed heightened modernism's intimate relationship with technological innovation. But, as I argue here, total war crucially fractured modernism's relationship to technology, introducing intensely political dictates into the formerly binary relations between the aesthetics of modernism and the 'technological shifts' Daly describes. War opened up a space between modernism and technology, as writers and artists were forced to confront the new and relentless demands of official war culture. During the First World War, an official war culture struggled to transform, through propaganda, censorship, official secrecy and surveillance, the permissible limits of representation for modern writers and artists. Thus, literary modernism found itself caught in the unstable and contradictory force field of war, forced to take a position, triangulated between technologies of violence and the struggle to construct an official war culture.

Modernism's uneasy position had the beneficial effect of precluding the technological determinism that too often accompanies accounts of military technology. Embedded within an emerging modern war culture, war technology not only contradicted the experience of soldiers and civilians, as Benjamin had argued, but was part of a larger reorganisation of both individual experience and societies at war. As Herbert Marcuse warned in 1941, technology should be 'taken as a social process in which technics proper (that is, the technical apparatus of industry, transportation, communication) is but a partial factor'. An exile from Nazi Germany, like fellow Frankfurt School intellectuals Adorno and Horkheimer, Marcuse argued against this partial view:

> Technology, as a mode of production, as the totality of instruments, devices and contrivances which characterize the machine age is thus at the same time a mode of organizing and perpetuating (or changing) social relationships, a manifestation of prevalent thought and behavior patterns, an instrument for control and domination. (41–2)

Observing the reach of the Nazi war economy over culture and society, he warned against confusing technology with technics or focusing on its abstract effects on human experience as if they were external to society. To use a medical analogy, by focusing on revolutionary changes and the 'shock of the new' in military technology, on rupture and discontinuity, the symptoms were mistaken for the disease.

Above all, the focus on modern technology in wartime served to normalise war as a 'social process' for civilian populations and 'a mode of organizing and perpetuating (or changing) social relationships', and to habituate the modern sensorium to 'the shock of the new' of violent armed conflict. The power of war technologies blurred the boundaries of war and peace, allowing 'total war' to seem both a totalising and a quintessentially modern condition. This in turn made social and economic preparations for war a seemingly inevitable consequence of modernisation and condition of modernity. Technology helped total war become a self-fulfilling prophecy, and the national security states and the war economies that emerged during the First World War become a permanent feature of modern life. As many writers and theorists since Benjamin have observed, modernism, with its fascinated yet ambivalent relationship to technology, was caught up in exactly this struggle for social transformation.

War Technology, Culture and Modernism in Camouflage

How did modernists or avant-gardists come to occupy such an intimate relationship with technologies of violence? Their obsession with technology during wartime seems especially striking, given that few canonical high modernist writers, artists and intellectuals were combatants or experienced war directly until the area bombing of the Second World War brought war home to civilian populations. Anticipating the kind of fully mobilised and persuasive official war cultures that were constructed during the Second World War, during the First World War art and literature were mobilised in the service of the war effort. Beyond serving the often less subtle aims of propaganda and official war artists schemes, one of their major roles was to supplement and enhance the technologies of war. To take one notable example, modern artists like the Cubists Jacques Villon and Raoul Dufy, and the Vorticists Leon Underwood and Edward Wadsworth, were deployed as *camoufleurs* to produce battlefield camouflage on the Western Front or to use Dazzle Ship naval vessels as their vast floating canvases. Franz Marc, a friend of Klee and Kandinsky, painted huge tarpaulins to hide artillery emplacements from aerial reconnaissance, writing home: 'I am curious what effects the Kandinskys will have at 2,000 metres. The nine tarpaulins chart a development from Manet to Kandinsky' (Deer 2009: 44). As members of both aesthetic and military avant-gardes, experimental artists and writers discovered their disturbing proximity to and complicity with technological experiments in modern industrialised warfare. But by exposing artistic experimentation's uncomfortably intimate relationship with war culture, they could also open up a space for critique.

Despite their imperial claims to wage a thoroughly modern, mobilised and propagandised 'total war', the war planners and strategists of the 1914–18 period lacked the means or the methods to do so. This was where their strategic fantasies about technology harnessed to waging total war came in. The strategists and war machines claimed to have the capacity to command and control technology sufficient to the task, whether it was artillery, high explosive shells or mines, all directed by pre-radio-era communications and reconnaissance over the trenches. Naval ships and submarines connected by telegraph or radio waged naval blockades and a war at sea, rudimentary aeroplanes and dirigibles piloted by 'knights of the air' fought to command air superiority, and, late in the war, the lumbering mechanised armoured vehicles nicknamed 'tanks' helped break the deadlock of static trench warfare. But as became rapidly and notoriously clear in the bloody deadlock of the Western Front, with its low technology of barbed wire, trench fortifications and mud, these many interlocking technologies would founder disastrously. The situation was worsened by the high command's suspicion of their mass conscript armies and colonial troops. On the home front, advances in communication and media were harnessed to propaganda, censorship, surveillance and official secrecy administered by burgeoning national security states in Britain and the US. These advances helped consolidate and reinvigorate imperial vision over both the far-flung battlefields in the colonies and the hundreds of thousands of colonial troops fighting alongside the European mass conscript armies. It would take until 1918 for the armies to develop the modern all-arms tactics that would produce the long-promised war of space and movement on the ground. Combined with faster-moving ground troops and mechanised forces, air power and the bombing of civilians would be deployed after the First World War to suppress the anti-colonial uprisings that produced a 'Crisis of Empire' in 1919–20.

War seemed to offer a systemic fix for the crises of modernity, offering through war culture and militarised technologies the kind of totalising 'cultural tradition' required, as Jürgen Habermas has argued, by the 'incomplete project' of modernity

(Habermas 1983: 11). Could war revolutionise culture and communication 'covering all spheres – cognitive, moral practical and expressive' (11), where the utopian projects of the avant-gardes had failed? When technological realities and military budgets failed to deliver, war culture provided a crucial resource to shore up modern states and their war machines through a promiscuous logic of bricolage and camouflage. Little wonder that the rival claims of modernism as a 'cultural tradition' that could cover 'all spheres' of modern experience and counter 'a rationalised everyday life' drew the attention of the war planners and strategists. In the absence of adequate technology to wage total war, the strategists turned to the resources of culture to mobilise a futuristic imaginary of a war of space and movement. For several different reasons, war technology required cultural representations to complete its workings and to fulfil the strategic fantasies that surrounded it. First, technologies at war produced during Mandel's so-called 'Second Technological Revolution' offered vast and horrifying destructive power. Yet they failed to deliver on their promise of instrumentality or productivity: to produce lethal violence with precision and control or to wage total wars that mobilised entire populations. As historian David Edgerton has argued, war and killing were shaped much more powerfully by the 'shock of the old' of small arms, artillery and barbed wire than by fantasies of innovation (Edgerton 2008: 138–46). If technology functioned as a supplement to thought, as philosophical critiques of Enlightenment rationality since Heidegger have often insisted, then culture was also in a supplementary, prosthetic relation to technology (Bradley 2011: 1–20). In practice, the gaps between destructive power and available communication networks meant that war technology was insufficient to function without being embedded in narratives and representations that could complete its profound lack of signification. Lastly, technologies of violence have a profoundly objectifying and silencing force, as Simone Weil argued after the fall of France in *The Iliad, or the Poem of Force* (1940) (Weil 1965: 6), yet modern total war required that they be part of a much larger struggle to colonise various spheres of experience. War technology needed war culture.

As these strategists increasingly sought to bring modernists into the fold of official war culture, however, modernism's ambivalences and emphasis on subjective experience proved difficult to integrate into official projections. Modernist representations of war powerfully challenge and blur the boundaries so important to official war culture, between frontline and home front, civilians and combatants, perpetrators and victims of violence, heroes and enemies. Furthermore, the vividness or veracity of writers' perspectives on war and technology could vary drastically, depending on their distance from the frontlines, military rank, access to mass media and communications, or their relation to the state in wartime and its powers of censorship, propaganda and official secrecy. Combat experience of trench warfare, artillery bombardments and poison gas in the First World War transformed the poetry of Wilfred Owen, Siegfried Sassoon and Edmund Blunden, creating the hybrid forms, disfigured pastorals and unstable affective range of the 'trench lyric', which ranges from the defiant free verse of Owen's 'Dulce et Decorum est' to brutally satirical sonnets like Sassoon's 'Glory of Women' and the melancholy imagism of Isaac Rosenberg's 'Returning We Hear Larks'. These poetic experiments were produced under duress in a cultural environment dominated by propaganda and censorship, and hostile to the 'cosmopolitan sympathies' of the pre-war avant-gardes, who were branded unpatriotic, queer and obscene. The result was a 'modernism in camouflage', as I have argued elsewhere, in which writers frequently disguised their experiments, operating in multiple genres as they struggled to represent the dislocations of war under the shadow of mass communications, patriotic popular culture and propaganda (Deer 2009; Wollaeger 2006). Rosenberg, for example, a working-class Jewish socialist, considered himself a conventional Georgian poet but corresponded with Ezra Pound.

Wartime produced many such collisions of genres. Robert Graves experimented with scathing irony in his memoir, *Goodbye to All That* (1929), and David Jones produced a Joycean epic of poetry and prose, *In Parenthesis* (1937). Wyndham Lewis and T. E. Hulme served in the artillery, producing starkly different approaches to modernist aesthetics in Lewis's angular machinic Vorticism and Hulme's more conservative classicism. As a young artillery officer in the Austro-Hungarian army, Ludwig Wittgenstein kept notes for his *Tractatus Logico-Philosophicus* (1921), completing the manuscript in an Italian prisoner of war camp. In the plastic arts, Cubist and Vorticist Henri Gaudier-Brzeska's brief but heroic military service produced a sculpture carved out of the butt of a German rifle, a more highbrow instance of the arts and crafts produced in the trenches as a coping mechanism and protest against the dehumanisation of industrialised warfare. The young sculptor's death inspired Lewis's second and final war issue of *Blast!* (1915), which pursued a peculiarly British critique of Italian Futurism tempered by first-hand experience of the war that Marinetti had been glorifying. Ironically, most of the other Futurists would die in battle. Ford Madox Ford's undistinguished military career as a transport officer in logistics and in the official propaganda campaign and his experience of shell shock, as well as his pre-war literary collaborations with Joseph Conrad, provided form and content for his remarkable modernist masterpiece, the *Parade's End* tetralogy (1924–8), and a series of notoriously and deliberately unreliable memoirs of transatlantic modernism. On the other side of No Man's Land, combat experience in the German army produced remarkably different perspectives in Erich Maria Remarque's anti-war bestseller, *All Quiet on the Western Front* (1929), which was burned by the Nazis, Otto Dix's Expressionist satires of war and home front jingoism, and Ernst Jünger's obsessively hypermasculine and resolutely patriotic revisions of his terrifying and exhilarating memoir, *Storm of Steel* (1922).

In the face of technological failures and military crises, culture and narrative were mobilised to shore up the ruins. Despite the disastrous slaughter of the First World War, militarist and futurist representations of technologies of violence – including air power, tanks, artillery, submarines, radio, mass media and propaganda – displayed an uncanny ability to cross the great cultural divides, disturbing and capturing both popular and high literary imaginations. Yet official war cultures overshadowed by censorship and jingoistic propaganda paled in comparison to national war literatures and artistic movements that often protested against the horror and foregrounded what Wilfred Owen called 'the pity of war'. Modernist writers registered the ironic failures of wartime in a more critical and contradictory register, refusing the recuperative logic that made militarism its own remedy.

Traumas of the New

Despite the exhilarating futuristic visions and pleasures promised by technologies of violence, their failures produced an association with psychological trauma and bodily collapse, which threatened the boundaries between the frontline and the home front.

The trauma and bodily collapse produced by artillery barrages, poison gas, bombing raids and machine gun fire proved omnidirectional, producing 'shell shock' and terrible wounding and death on a mass scale. Modern war technologies were thus haunted by their affective power over the minds and bodies of both the enemy they targeted and the troops they were supposed to enhance, encompass and empower prosthetically. The war machine responded by reasserting boundaries and projecting a hypermasculine rear-mouring of the body and a weaponisation of shock. Yet as writers and artists made clear in their exploration of temporality and the spaces of war, modern memory was haunted by the traumatic, racialised and highly gendered effects of technologies of violence on mind and body, unable to exorcise the ghosts and demons of global conflicts.

The avant-garde's willingness to embrace the prosthetic and the posthuman exploration of the machinic produced remarkable protests against the futility of war in Dadaist performances and Expressionist art. But it also could be channelled towards the rear-moured hypermasculinity of the 'New Man' celebrated obsessively in Jünger's *Storm of Steel*. Junger's text can be read as a modern self-help guide to succeeding as a storm-trooper in the fireswept zone. This took its darkest forms in the Freikorps's protofascist, misogynist imaginary of homosocial 'totality armour' that would protect against the feminised flows of revolution explored in Klaus Theweleit's *Male Fantasies* (1987).

Behind the lines, the challenges of working as a nurse caring for terribly injured soldiers, given the rudimentary state of First World War medicine, was powerfully represented by Mary Borden in the often hallucinatory prose narratives of *The Forbidden Zone* (1929) and by Vera Brittain in her remarkable pacifist memoir, *Testament of Youth* (1933). As one of the few sustained explorations of the 1918 influenza pandemic, which wartime propaganda and censorship misrepresented as 'the Spanish 'flu', Katherine Anne Porter's *Pale Horse, Pale Rider* (1939) captures both the febrile atmosphere of popular patriotism in the US, channelled through the mass media, and the traumatic impact of the global influenza outbreak on a young woman journalist. It reads as disturbing and prophetic in the wake of the Covid-19 pandemic.

The traumatic psychological effects of war technology, which are clearly legible in Brittain, Borden and Porter's work, were diagnosed in soldiers during the First World War as 'shell shock', and were assumed to be produced by the effects on mind and body of the blast waves of high explosive shells. This somatic explanation anticipated the recent epidemic of traumatic brain injuries during the US wars in Iraq and Afghanistan. The 'combat fatigue' experienced during and after the Second World War with the psychiatric treatment of Holocaust survivors and Vietnam veterans was redefined as the now ubiquitous diagnosis of post-traumatic stress disorder (PTSD) in 1980 (Shephard 2003). Trained in colonial ethnography, W. H. R. Rivers worked with shell-shocked soldiers during the First World War as a military psychiatrist at Craiglockhart military hospital, producing his remarkable experiment in Freudianism, 'The Repression of War Experience' (1918). Preferring a cathartic form of psychoanalysis to the brutal technology of electric shock treatment espoused by the competing school of shell shock doctors, he treated both Siegfried Sassoon and Wilfred Owen before they were sent 'back up the line to death'. Sassoon survived the cure and the war; Owen did not.

Post-war trauma was powerfully represented in the work of non-combatant modernists like Virginia Woolf, in the silence and indirection of *Jacob's Room* (1922), and the hallucinatory fugue states of shell-shocked First World War veteran Septimus Smith in *Mrs Dalloway* (1925). Similar post-war gendered disturbances haunt the wounded minds and bodies in Eliot's *The Waste Land*, although civilian technologies like the gramophone and motorcar seem to have supplanted wartime objects. Although he served as an officer, F. Scott Fitzgerald never saw foreign service in the First World War; he represents American veterans pursuing a decidedly post-war Jazz Age existence in *The Great Gatsby* (1925) but engages much more powerfully with the psychological disturbances of post-First World War transatlantic society in *Tender is the Night* (1934). In the novel's most ironic evocation of the devastation of the European war, Dick Diver leads his entourage in a mock-heroic exercise in battlefield tourism to the trenches of the former frontline in Northern France, lecturing his alcoholic friend, a US war veteran and failing modernist composer, Abe North, on the Freudian 'love battle' of the Great War. This haunting, devastatingly ironic episode concludes when the tour party meet a young war widow hopelessly hunting for the grave of her husband in amongst the massed headstones of a war cemetery. They advise her to place her wreath symbolically at a randomly chosen gravestone, self-satisfied that they have handled her grief appropriately.

Wounded while serving as a Red Cross ambulance driver on the Italian front, Ernest Hemingway combined his brief experience of combat and six months of recovery in a military hospital with careful military historical research in *A Farewell to Arms* (1929). His famously pared-down representations of military and other kinds of action, and sparse dialogue depicting the silences wrought by war trauma and damaged yet heroicised post-war masculinity, superbly rendered in the short stories of *In Our Time* (1925), read like an extraordinary, ironic literary technology, reproducible up to a point, wearing out with repeated use, and ultimately lethal to those who wield it. The machinic power of the Hemingwayesque continues to exercise an enormous influence, against which the representations of writers like Borden, Brittain and Rivers nursing wounded bodies and treating shattered minds, offer a powerful counter-narrative.

The Technological Sublime and Modernist Critique

To compensate for the disastrous deadlock, stasis and slaughter of trench warfare, the competing militaries sought to project a futuristic war of space and movement at sea, in the air and later in tank warfare. The mud, barbed wire and lunar landscapes of No Man's Land were countered by the machinic imaginary of a technological sublime that celebrated the shocking, exhilarating and often lethal speed and freedom to move in time and space of aeroplanes, tanks and battleships. The aesthetic fascination of war technology to avant-gardists like Marinetti and the Futurists, or the more ambivalent machinic imaginary of Wyndham Lewis and Vorticism, helped shore up and aestheticise the ruinous impact of these killing machines.

War technology presented a rival perspective on conflict to what James Campbell has called the 'combat gnosticism' offered by the 'trench lyrics' of British war poets, like Owen and Sassoon. Campbell diagnoses this as 'the belief that combat represents a qualitatively separate order of experience that is difficult if not impossible to communicate to any who have not undergone an identical experience'. As Campbell has convincingly argued, this elevation of the combat gnosticism of war writing has tended to limit drastically the canon of war literature and 'simultaneously promoted war literature's status as a discrete body of work with almost no relation to non-war writing' (Campbell 1999: 203). Critics of more recent war literature have argued that this

Hemingwayesque legacy continues to embed war writing within imperial perspectives and reinforces a myth of 'the trauma hero' that renders victims of violence invisible (Antoon 2014; Scranton 2015).

War technology, I would argue, thus offered a rival form of combat gnosticism figured in the aesthetic experience of a 'technological sublime'. Crucial to the war machine's vast effort to maintain control was the strategic fantasy of a 'technological sublime' that was unconcerned with literary realism and freed from the mud, squalor and carnage of the 'trench labyrinth', projecting instead a panoramic imperial vision of battle that frequently took flight into the aerial view. As David Nye has argued, war was a crucial proving ground for this modern technological imaginary (Nye 1994: xvi).

Like the war poets' combat gnosticism, war technology also offered an ethical dimension that displaced what Campbell calls the 'passive humanism' of First World War poetry in favour of a passive spectatorship of the spectacle of war (Campbell 1999: 203). However limiting the 'combat gnosticism' in Owen and Sassoon's trench lyrics, there is nevertheless an accusatory ethical stance towards a home front indifferent to the suffering of masculine combatants (213). But war's technological sublime, I would argue, combines the claim of higher knowledge with an ethical indifference, supplying humankind, as Benjamin famously argued of the Futurists' fascist aestheticisation of politics and glorification of war, with 'the artistic gratification of a sense perception that has been changed by technology . . . Its self-alienation has reached such a degree that it can experience its own destruction as an aesthetic pleasure of the first order' (Benjamin 1969b: 242).

This is best understood not as an aestheticisation of violence, which suggests that the aesthetic is both prior to and in an external relation to a violence into which it introduces beauty. Rather, Benjamin's analysis, like that of many of the more sceptical avant-garde writers and artists, in fact suggests that what we are seeing is an ongoing exchange among aesthetics, politics and the technologies of violence. If, as recent environmentalist theorists such as Langdon Winner have suggested, 'technologies are not neutral', and 'political tendencies, whether authoritarian or democratizing, are internalized as part of their architectural design', then their design also includes, I would argue, aesthetic tendencies (Ross 2005: 344; Winner 1986). These are tendencies that writers and artists can help make visible. It would be more accurate to describe these representations as aesthetic engagements with technologies designed to produce violence, engagements that simultaneously glorify war and hide the horrifying evidence of this violence in aestheticised spectacles. In the face of wartime vistas of the technological sublime and the aestheticisation of the politics and political economy of war, modernist writers could offer a critical epistemological scepticism to counter this spectacularly brutal confidence and inhuman indifference.

The technological sublime of the war in the air came to dominate post-1918 representations of military technology, as the heroicised exploits of the 'knights of the air' survived the muddy and bloody stasis of trench warfare. Flying captured the imagination of William Faulkner, who invented the persona of a Royal Air Force officer and explored civilian barnstorming pilots in his novel *Pylon* (1935); W. B. Yeats in 'An Irish Airman Foresees His Death' (1919); and Antoine de Saint-Exupéry, who earned his wings as a pilot serving in the French colonial air force in Morocco. T. E. Lawrence left behind his own Orientalist imperial romance, *Seven Pillars of Wisdom* (1926) which represented his nomadological experiments in guerrilla warfare with

Arab forces in the desert against the Ottoman Empire, to dedicate himself to the cause of imperial air power in the Middle East. He documented the homosocial, brutalist rigours of life as an RAF airman and his love for flight in the stark prose memoir, *The Mint* (1955), only to die speeding on his motorcycle, Boanerges. Air power and the 1930s obsession with 'airmindedness' is represented more ironically in W. H. Auden's *The Orators* (1932), in the surreal decline and fall of a charismatic, fascistic New Man, partly based on Lawrence, who fails to pull off an attempted military coup in 'Letter to a Wound' and 'Journal of an Airman'.

Air power also interrupts the climax of Virginia Woolf's final novel, *Between the Acts* (1941), when a village pageant is interrupted by a menacing flight of planes. This is the most spectacular of a series of often comical Brechtian alienation effects that force the audience in Woolf's narrative to look at its complicity with the imperial power and nationalist energies of Deep England on the eve of a Second World War. Building on the argument of *Three Guineas* (1938), which began with a plea against the violence of aerial bombing against civilians in the Spanish Civil War that also produced Picasso's protest painting, *Guernica* (1937), Woolf also focused an explicitly feminist critique of militarised masculinity on the young pilots trapped overhead in the grip of an 'unconscious Hitlerism', in her extraordinary essay 'Thoughts on Peace in an Air Raid' (1940). Here late modernism collides with a remarkably courageous critique of the mythology of British air power during the Blitz. This subversive anti-fascist critique of the authoritarian tendencies of the technological drive of air power is nowhere more exuberantly and unnervingly explored than in Rex Warner's Kafkaesque satire *The Aerodrome* (1941), which imagines the colonisation of an English village by a totalitarian air force. Like the modernist dislocations of James Hanley's *No Directions* (1943), Henry Green's *Caught* (1943), or Elizabeth Bowen's *The Demon Lover and Other Stories* (1945) or her post-war spy novel, *The Heat of the Day* (1948), the violence of area bombing and the Blitz is shown in *The Aerodrome*, deforming and disfiguring the form and content of wartime writing in ways that cannot be contained by the official war culture of the People's War. George Orwell's *1984* (1949) can also be read as a dystopian satire on wartime technologies of surveillance and the emergence of a permanent war economy during the Second World War, which would come to dominate Cold War culture.

Follow Me: Vision, Blindness and Oversight

Despite the notorious collapses of vision in the 'troglodyte world' of the trench labyrinth of the Western Front and the foundering of strategy and command and control in the fog of war, the war machine drew on military technology, discipline and oversight to consolidate a commanding, imperial vision of war. Although modernist irony and avant-garde experimentation confronted this play of strategic vision with intense scepticism, this combination of the technological sublime with a panoramic spectacle of war persists into the recent high-tech 'Forever War' era. This is a remarkable forgetting of the lessons of modernist scepticism.

I will close by suggesting that this thoroughly traditional wartime logic of the technological sublime can be seen at work in Peter Jackson's acclaimed documentary, *They Shall Not Grow Old*, released to commemorate the centenary of the end of the First World War, when, after twenty-four minutes of black-and-white footage, digital film technology suddenly seems to bring the muddy, populous battlefield of the Great War trenches vividly to life. Yet for all its visceral, transformative power, this moment of digital reanimation stages the seductive, disturbing power of technology's relationship with war. The use of the full arsenal of digital film technology, forensic lipreading, lip synching of actors with regional accents, sound effects of weaponry and the recreated trench soundscape draws attention to the seemingly doubled power of technology: Jackson's technological mastery claims to allow cinema and TV audiences to experience affectively the true power and violence of the technologies of the First World War. Here a panoramic, commanding vision of battle, powered by a newly digitised technological sublime, allows us to participate in a strategic fantasy of unmediated access to war's horror. But the more subtle and problematic force of *They Shall Not Grow Old*, with its disturbingly forceful title, commands us through the immediacy of digital culture, and seeks to interpellate us, into worlds not of our making. The ironic distance between the trenches and the present is seemingly abolished through a digital sublime, and the violence of the First World War is suddenly normalised, forcing us to inhabit a posthuman world of permanent warfare.

Revealingly, as the frame slowly extends and the silent footage bleeds into colour and sound, the first reconstructed dialogue has a British officer declaring, 'Follow me,' as he leads a single file of soldiers through a muddy trench landscape. The moment interrupts the voiceover recollections of unnamed First World War veterans recalling their journey to the front line:

> We went through towns villages that were absolutely derelict, so we never knew where we were except that we were in Belgium.
> The devastation was something I never could have imagined. The whole place gave one a most eerie sensation.
> There was stunted trees torn to shreds with shellfire, and there was shell holes all over the place.
> We were relieving men of the 28th Division, and as they passed us, we would say, 'What's it like up there?', and the reply invariably came back, 'Bloody awful mate.'
> The old sweats coming back got their tails up alright, but I didn't know what to expect, just hadn't a clue.
> It was deadly warfare. You were facing the Germans.
> *Follow me.* (24' 13')

With the officer's declaration, 'follow me,' Jackson's high-tech digital restoration allows total war to become a total environment which overwhelms the historical and affective distance of jerky black-and-white silent documentary footage and absorbs the dignified outrage and ironic self-reflection so audible in the voiceover narration by First World War veterans interviewed half a century later and incorporated into the film from the oral histories archive at the Imperial War Museum. Through this seamlessly seductive mediation, the film both fulfils the promise of the title of Paul Nash's painting *We Are Making a New World*, and drains it of its irony. The voiceover continues:

> You got the order, 'Load.' You put nine in your magazine, and you put one up the spout. And you put the safety catch on, and you always went up the line prepared to use your rifle immediately.

> That's when you got rigid orders. No talking whatsoever, keep your head down. Single file. No smoking. The Captain would then direct you right to the front trenches.
> When a man goes up the trenches, he usually carries rolled up barbed wire or a bag of bombs, besides his own equipment. That's how they get the stuff up to the front line.
> Now a guide would always be sent out.

The voiceover's reference to 'rigid orders ... direct you ... a guide would always be sent out' is a reminder of how we are being commanded through this newly vivid spectacle. Again, appropriately, the forensically restored dialogue declares:

> *Extend this part of the trench over there. That's it.*
> The trenches in France were a maze. If you didn't have a guide, you could very soon get lost.

The restoration embeds the voiceover recollection about being lost in the maze and needing a guide within the reanimated direct address, '*Extend this part of the trench . . .*' (here in italics). These commands seem to address both the troops slogging through the trenches and command us as audience a century later:

> *Smile. So your mother thinks I'm looking after you.*
> *Up you go, double up double up.*

Unlike modernist irony or the satire of Sassoon, this jokiness feels coercive and urges us to 'double up' by marching on the double. Rather than defamiliarisation and shock, Jackson's film produces an illusion of singularly unironic intimacy and inevitability. This 'false immediacy', to use Adorno's phrase, simultaneously distances, colonising our lived experience, compartmentalising and dividing, and trains us to follow its cues and disciplinary logic.

War technology offered the capacity to survey and discipline massed bodies of troops, to order and control time and space, to bring the shock and lethality of the new weaponry and to harness the vast logistical might of industrial production. The seeming triumph of the Maxim machine gun in colonial Little Wars, or the power of high explosive shells and technology against fortifications, like bombing, naval and armoured warfare, gave rise to strategic fantasies of unlimited technological power that seemed to match the technical achievements of successive industrial revolutions or the expansionist logic of the New Imperialism. As the material realisation of instrumental reason, technologies of violence not only offered new tools for waging war, but also profoundly mediated the relationship of the modern sensorium. Viewed from the vantage point of a century dominated by total war, and through the ironic lens of modernist culture, these technological fantasies would seem to have been radically demystified. Yet the power of war technology persists intact, emerging from the fog and chaos of two World Wars into the present, alongside our fascination with a literary modernism that seems to be its uncanny double.

Note

1. Peter Boxall's rich discussion of modernism and the 'prosthetic imagination' does address some war writing (Boxall 2020: 225–57), and builds powerfully on Tim Armstrong's discussion of 'prosthetic modernism' and war in *Modernism, Technology and the Body: A Cultural Study* (Armstrong 2008; see especially pp. 95–8). On strategic fantasy, see Deer (2009: 4–5).

Works Cited

Antoon, Sinan (2014), 'Embedded Poetry: Iraq; Through a Soldier's Binoculars', *Jadaliyya*, 11 June, n.p.
Armstrong, Tim (2008), *Modernism, Technology and the Body: A Cultural Study*. Cambridge: Cambridge University Press.
Benjamin, Walter (2019), 'The Poverty of Experience', in *The Storyteller Essays*, trans. Tess Lewis, ed. Samuel Titan. New York: NYRB, pp. 42–7.
Benjamin, Walter (1969a), 'The Storyteller', in *Illuminations: Essay and Reflections*, trans. Harry Zohn. New York: Shocken, pp. 83–109.
Benjamin, Walter (1969b), 'The Work of Art in the Age of Mechanical Reproduction', in *Illuminations: Essay and Reflections*, trans. Harry Zohn. New York: Shocken, pp. 217–51.
Boxall, Peter (2020), *The Prosthetic Imagination: A History of the Novel as Artificial Life*. Cambridge: Cambridge University Press.
Bradley, A. (2011), *Originary Technicity: The Theory of Technology from Marx to Derrida*. New York: Palgrave Macmillan.
Campbell, James (1999). 'Combat Gnosticism: The Ideology of First World War Poetry Criticism', *New Literary History*, 30: 1, pp. 203–15.
Daly, Nicholas (2016), 'Art and Its Others 1: The Aesthetics of Technology', in *The Cambridge History of Modernism*, ed. Vincent Sherry. Cambridge: Cambridge University Press, pp. 404–21.
Deer, Patrick (2009), *Culture in Camouflage: War, Empire and Modern British Literature*. Oxford: Oxford University Press.
Edgerton, David (2008), *The Shock of the Old: Technology and Global History Since 1900*. Oxford: Oxford University Press.
Habermas, Jürgen (1983), 'Modernity – An Incomplete Project', trans. Seyla Ben-Habib in *The Anti-Aesthetic: Essays on Postmodern Culture*, ed. Hal Foster. Winnipeg: Bay Press, pp. 3–15.
Marcuse, Herbert (1998), 'Some Social Implications of Modern Technology', in *Technology, War and Fascism, Collected Papers of Herbert Marcuse Vol. One*, ed. Douglas Kellner. New York: Routledge, pp. 41-65.
Marinetti, F. T. (1991), 'The Founding and Manifesto of Futurism', in *Let's Murder the Moonshine: Selected Writings*, ed. R. W. Flint. Los Angeles: Sun and Moon Press, pp. 47–52.
Nicholls, Peter (2020), 'Mud and Metaphysics: The Matter of Modernism', *Forum for Modern Language Studies*, 56: 4 (October), pp. 427–44.
Nye, David (1994), *American Technological Sublime*. Cambridge, MA: MIT Press.
Ross, A. (2005), 'Technology', in *New Keywords: A Revised Vocabulary of Culture and Society*, ed. Tony Bennett, Lawrence Grossberg and Meaghan Morris. Malden, MA: Blackwell, pp. 342–4.
Scranton, Roy (2015), 'The Trauma Hero: From Wilfred Owen to "Redeployment" and "American Sniper"', *Los Angeles Review of Books*, 25 January, n.p.
Shephard, Ben (2003), *A War of Nerves: Soldiers and Psychiatrists in the Twentieth Century*. Cambridge, MA: Harvard University Press.

Stein, Gertrude (1990), *The Autobiography of Alice B. Toklas*, in *Selected Writings of Gertrude Stein*. New York: Vintage, pp. 1–238.
They Shall Not Grow Old (2018), film, directed by Peter Jackson, New Zealand; Great Britain: Wingnut Films.
Weil, Simone (1965), 'The Iliad, or the Poem of Force', *Chicago Review*, 18: 2, pp. 5–30.
Winner, Langdon (1986), *The Whale and the Reactor: A Search for Limits in an Age of High Technology*. Chicago: University of Chicago Press.
Wollaeger, Mark (2006), *Modernism, Media, and Propaganda: British Narrative from 1900 to 1945*. Princeton, NJ: Princeton University Press.

Notes on Contributors

Alix Beeston is Senior Lecturer in English at Cardiff University. She is the author of *In and Out of Sight: Modernist Writing and the Photographic Unseen* (2018) and the editor of the Visualities forum at *Modernism/modernity* Print Plus.

Emily Bloom is a Mellon Public Humanities Fellow at Sarah Lawrence College. She is the author of *The Wireless Past: Anglo-Irish Writers and the BBC, 1931-1968* (2016), which was awarded the First Book Prize by the Modernist Studies Association. Her current work explores disability, media, technology, gender and literature.

Patrick Deer is Associate Professor of English at NYU. He is author of *Culture in Camouflage: War, Empire and Modern British Literature* (2009; paperback edn 2016). His current book project is *We Are All Embedded: America's War Culture Since 9/11*, and his articles on modernism, contemporary literature and war culture have appeared in *Modern Fiction Studies*, *College Literature* and *Modernism/modernity* online.

Enda Duffy is Professor of English at the University of California, Santa Barbara. He is the author of *The Subaltern Ulysses* (1994) and of *The Speed Handbook: Velocity, Pleasure, Modernism* (2009), which won the Modernist Studies Association Book Award in 2010. Professor Duffy is co-editor of *Joyce, Benjamin and Magical Urbanism* (2011), and *Katherine Mansfield's* Bliss and Other Stories (2021). He is editor of an edition of *Ulysses* and of Katherine Mansfield's short stories, and author of numerous articles on Joyce, modern Irish literature, and aspects of modernist literature and culture. He is working on two projects, one on emigration and Irish literary history, the other on energy in modern culture.

Josh Epstein is Associate Professor of English at Portland State University, where he teaches Anglophone modernism, film and media studies, and critical theory. In addition to a range of articles, he has authored one book, *Sublime Noise: Musical Culture and the Modernist Writer* (2014). His current research interests include the 1951 Festival of Britain, the BBC Third Programme and the filmmaker and polymath Humphrey Jennings.

Jana Funke is Associate Professor of English and Sexuality Studies in the Department of English and Film at the University of Exeter. Her research and publications focus on modernist literature, the history of sexuality and sexual science, and feminism and queer theory.

Felicity Gee is Senior Lecturer in Modernism and World Cinema at the University of Exeter. She is the author of *Magic Realism: World Cinema and the Avant-Garde* (2021), and has published widely on Surrealist literature, affect theory and avant-garde film, most recently on Claude Cahun, Leonora Carrington and Abe Kōbō. Felicity's research straddles film, art history and literary studies. Her current research project focuses on the poetry and collage of Surrealist artist Valentine Penrose within the wider context of the international voyage and modernist women's writing.

Alex Goody is Professor of Twentieth-Century Literature and Culture at Oxford Brookes University. Her publications include *Modernist Articulations: A Cultural Study of Djuna Barnes, Mina Loy and Gertrude Stein* (2007), *Technology, Literature and Culture* (2011) and *Modernist Poetry, Gender and Leisure Technologies: Machine Amusements* (2019). She is currently co-editing the volume *Beastly Modernisms: The Figure of the Animal in Modernist Literature and Culture*.

Janice Ho is Associate Professor of English at the University of British Columbia, Vancouver. She has research and teaching interests in modernist, contemporary and postcolonial literatures. Her monograph, *Nation and Citizenship in the Twentieth-Century British Novel*, appeared in 2015, and she is currently working on a book project on colonial development during the mid-twentieth century.

Damien Keane is Associate Professor of English at the State University of New York at Buffalo. He is the author of *Ireland and the Problem of Information*, which was awarded the Robert Rhodes Prize from the American Conference for Irish Studies, as well as articles on radio broadcasting and literary recordings. His current project centres on media, morale and evidence.

Caroline Zoe Krzakowski is Associate Professor of English at Northern Michigan University, where she teaches modern and contemporary British literature. Her first book, *Diplomacy in Modern British Literature and Culture*, is forthcoming.

Joshua Lam is Assistant Professor of English at Michigan State University. His research focuses on race, science and technology in US literature. His current book project examines racialised automatons in American modernism; a second project focuses on racial objectification in contemporary Black poetics. His essays have appeared in the *Journal of Modern Literature*, *College Literature*, *Callaloo* and *boundary 2*.

Jennifer L. Lieberman is Associate Professor of English at the University of North Florida (UNF) and author of *Power Lines: Electricity in American Life and Letters, 1882-1952* (2017), as well as over a dozen articles on technology, literature and American culture. She teaches conventional and incarcerated students on various subjects in these areas, including gender studies and science and technology studies.

Maebh Long is a Senior Lecturer in the English Programme at the University of Waikato. She is the author of *Assembling Flann O'Brien* (2014) and *The Collected Letters of Flann O'Brien* (2018). Maebh is co-editor, with Matthew Hayward, of *New Oceania: Modernisms and Modernities in the Pacific* (2019) and is co-authoring a monograph on Pacific literature, Pacific universities and modernism with him. She is currently working on a project, funded by the Royal Society of New Zealand, which examines concepts of immunity within modernism.

Laura E. Ludtke is a Non-Stipendiary Lecturer in English Literature at Merton College, Oxford, co-host of *LitSciPod: The Literature and Science Podcast*, and Secretary of the British Society for Literature and Science executive committee. Her research and teaching focuses on intersections between modernity, technology, gender and aesthetics in the city in late nineteenth- and early twentieth-century literature.

Leo Mellor is the Roma Gill Fellow in English at Murray Edwards College, University of Cambridge. He is author of *Reading the Ruins: Modernism, Bombsites and British Culture* (2011) and is currently writing about night trains and the European imagination.

Emilie Morin is Professor of Modern Literature at the University of York. Her research and teaching interests revolve around transnational modernism, forms of political writing, literatures of exile and migration, and the intersections between literature and technology. She is currently completing *Early Radio: An Anthology of European Texts and Translations* (forthcoming).

Andrew Pilsch is Associate Professor of English at Texas A&M University, where he specialises in rhetoric and the digital humanities. Pilsch's first book, *Transhumanism: Evolutionary Futurism and the Human Technologies of Utopia*, released in 2017, won the Science Fiction and Technoculture Studies Book Prize. His research appears in *Amodern*, *Philosophy & Rhetoric* and *Science Fiction Studies*.

James Purdon teaches English at the University of St Andrews. His publications include *Modernist Informatics: Literature, Information, and the State* (2016), *British Literature in Transition 1900-1920: A New Age?* (2021) and *The Art of Identification: Forensics, Surveillance, Identity* (with Rex Ferguson and Melissa M. Littlefield, 2021).

Einav Rabinovitch-Fox teaches history at Case Western Reserve University in Cleveland, Ohio. Her research examines the intersections between culture, gender, politics and modernity. Her book, *Dressed for Freedom: The Fashionable Politics of American Feminism* (2021), explores how women used fashion to claim freedoms and promote feminist agendas during the twentieth century. She has published on advertising, fashion and social movements in both scholarly and popular venues, among them *The Washington Post*, *The Conversation* and *Public Seminar*.

Shawna Ross is an Associate Professor in the English Department at Texas A&M, where she specialises in Victorian literature, transatlantic modernism and the digital humanities. Her publications include *Charlotte Brontë at the Anthropocene*, the co-written book, *Using Digital Humanities in the Classroom*, and the co-edited essay collections *Humans at Work in the Digital Age* and *Reading Modernism with Machines*.

Katherine Shingler is an Honorary Research Fellow in Modern Languages and Cultures at the University of Nottingham, and coordinator of the EUniverCities Network at the University of Exeter. Her research interests focus on early twentieth-century literary and visual cultures in France. Her book, *The French Art Novel, 1900–1930*, was published in 2016.

Tom Slevin is a Senior Lecturer in the School of Art, Design and Fashion at Solent University, Southampton. He has published numerous works on modern visual culture, the European artistic avant-garde, photography, critical theory and bodily representation. His current research is concerned with the relationship between technology and visual culture.

Anna Snaith is Professor of Twentieth-Century Literature at King's College. Her publications include *Virginia Woolf: Public and Private Negotiations* (2000) and *Modernist Voyages: Colonial Women Writers in London 1890-1945* (2014). She has edited *The Years* for the *Cambridge Edition of the Works of Virginia Woolf* (2012), *A Room of One's Own and Three Guineas* for Oxford World's Classics (2015) and *Sound and Literature* (2020). She is currently working on a monograph on interwar literary modernism and noise.

Jennifer Sorensen is an Associate Professor of English and Co-Coordinator of Women's, Gender, and Sexuality Studies at Texas A&M-Corpus Christi. Her first book, *Modernist Experiments in Genre, Media, and Transatlantic Print Culture* (2017) and her second book-project-in-progress, *Printing Women: Materializing Gender, Race, and Embodiment in the Modernist Marketplace*, analyse the intersections of gender, race, form and print culture.

Sunny Stalter-Pace is Hargis Associate Professor of American Literature at Auburn University. Her first monograph, *Underground Movements: Modern Culture on the New York City Subway*, was published in 2013. Her recent books have focused on transnational popular performance. *Imitation Artist: Gertrude Hoffmann's Life in Vaudeville and Dance* (2020) is her first biography. She is currently writing a cultural history of the New York Hippodrome.

David Trotter is an Emeritus Professor at the University of Cambridge and co-editor of the Open Humanities Press series Technographies. His most recent books are *The Literature of Connection: Signal, Medium, Interface, 1850-1950* and *Brute Meaning: Essays in Materialist Criticism from Dickens to Hitchcock* (both 2020).

Charles M. Tung is Professor of English at Seattle University, where he teaches courses on twentieth- and twenty-first-century literature, temporal scale, and representations of racial anachronism. He is the author of *Modernism and Time Machines* (2019). His recent work on time and modernity has appeared in *Timescales: Ecological Temporalities Across Disciplines*, *Time and Literature* and *Modernism and the Anthropocene*. His current book project is on big clocks and ethnofuturist timescales.

Jeff Wallace is Professor Emeritus at Cardiff Metropolitan University. His publications include *D. H. Lawrence, Science and the Posthuman* (2005) and *Beginning Modernism* (2011); *Abstraction in Modernism and Modernity: Human and Inhuman* is forthcoming. His research interests are in modernism, science and literature, and literature and philosophy, and he co-edits the Routledge series *New Literary Theory*.

Ian Whittington is Associate Professor of English at the University of Mississippi. He is the author of *Writing the Radio War: Literature, Politics and the BBC, 1939-1945* (2018) and is currently working on a new edition of James Joyce's *Dubliners* (forthcoming 2023) and *The Selected Wartime Broadcasts of Louis MacNeice* (forthcoming 2024).

Index

291 (magazine), 108, 114, 116
6:30 Collection (1934), 352–4, 355

acousmatic sound, 214, 235, 339
Actor-Network Theory, 9, 72, 427
Adorno, Theodor, 5–6, 84, 229, 238, 289
advertising, 67, 70–2, 82, 113, 138–154, 163–4, 167, 264, 265, 267, 346, 373, 402
    and race, 149–51
    and whiteness, 152
    and women's suffrage, 145–6, 373
aeroplane, 91–102, 280, 286, 316, 329, 432, 440
airmindedness, 92, 442
Aldington, Richard, 67–8
    'In the Tube', 67
algorithm, 404–6, 410, 413, 429
allochronism, 45
amplification, 236, 257–70, 328, 425
Anand, Mulk Raj
    Untouchable, 320
anarchism, 38, 321, 418
Anderson, Benedict, 346–7
Anger, Kenneth, 262, 268n
Antheil, George, 14, 226, 228–9, 245; *see also Ballet mécanique*
Anthropocene, 4, 12, 48, 305; *see also* nuclear weapons
anthropocentrism, 3, 6, 11, 194, 208; *see also* humanism
Anti Noise League *see* noise
anti-Semitism, 290, 321; *see also* Nazi Germany

Apollinaire, Guillaume, 107, 117–19, 184, 187, 228
architecture, 4, 45, 128, 131, 319, 369, 373
arc lamp, 25, 28, 30
Armstrong, Tim, 14–15, 52, 274, 276, 277–8, 301, 411, 414, 415
Arnheim, Rudolf, 214
artificial light, 24–31, 102
    arc lamp, 25, 28, 30
    candlelight, 24, 29
    electric light, 28–33, 294–5, 307, 365
    gas light, 25, 28
    incandescent lightbulb, 31; *see also* light-bulb
    neon light, 25, 96
    stage lights, 245, 247
Atherton, Gertrude, 278
atomic science *see* nuclear science
atomic weapons *see* nuclear weapons
Auden, W. H., 91–2, 230, 348
    'The Journal of an Airman', 91
    Letter to Lord Byron, 345, 350–1
    The Orators, 442
    'Poem XXX', 91
automatic writing, 406, 411–15
automatism, 293, 306, 411–14
automaton, 106–7, 109, 245, 295, 296, 297, 307
automobile, 42, 78–90, 117, 147–8, 151, 251, 286, 287, 288, 290, 291, 440
    rear-view mirror, 81, 82
    windscreen, 78, 81, 83, 84, 85, 87
    see also Ford, Henry; Fordism

avant-garde, 27, 31, 32, 64, 85, 106, 109, 117, 126, 134, 183–4, 330, 432–4, 436–7, 439
  and cinema, 192–211
  modernism, distinction from, 433–4
  and music, 226–9
  and performance, 243–56
  and writing, 406, 411–15, 423, 424
  see also Bauhaus; Constructivism; Cubism; Dada; Expressionism; Futurism; Surrealism; Vorticism

Babington Smith, Constance, 102
  Evidence in Camera: The Story of Photographic Intelligence in World War II, 102
Back to the Future (1985), 42, 43
Baedeker (*Baedeker's Handbook*), 396, 397, 398–401
Ball, Hugo, 243
Balla, Giacomo, 29–31, 83, 86, 185
  Printing Press (Macchina Tipografica), 249
  The Street Lamp (Lampada ad Arco), 29–30
  The Worker's Day, 29
Ballard, J. G., *Crash*, 78, 80
ballet, 228, 230, 244, 245, 250, 253, 337
  ballet dancer, 178
  Ballets Russes, 228, 244, 354
  Ballets Suédois, 244
  film ballet, 195, 196
Ballet mécanique (1924), 195, 226, 228–9, 245, 250
Barnes, Djuna, 433
Barthes, Roland, 168, 170–1
  Camera Lucida, 160, 170
Baudelaire, Charles, 26, 28, 207
Bauhaus, 207, 243, 245–8, 250, 252–4
BBC, 214, 216, 217, 219, 220, 221, 231, 232, 237, 330, 346, 422
  The Country of the Blind, 216
  In Touch, 221
  Music While You Work, 231, 235–7, 239, 330, 338, 340n
  Under Milk Wood, 217–19

BBC: The Voice of Britain (1936), 226–7, 230, 233–4
Beckett, Samuel, 2, 11, 214, 320, 324
Beethoven, Ludwig van, 226, 230 232, 234
Belloc, Hilaire
  'The Microbe', 317
  'Newdigate Poem', 23
Bely, Andrei, 66, 72
Benjamin, Walter, 6, 26, 84, 322, 434
  Arcades Project, 69, 70
  'The Destructive Character', 128
  'The Storyteller', 432
  'The Work of Art in the Age of its Technological Reproducibility', 5, 134, 160–1, 234, 441
Bennett, Jane, 10
Berghaus, Günter, 252
Bergson, Henri, 39–40, 85–6, 184
  Creative Evolution, 201
  durée, 40
  Matter and Memory, 85
Berlin Tempelhof, 98
Berlin U-Bahn, 65, 73
Bernays, Edward, 6–7
Berners-Lee, Tim, 391
biopolitics, 329, 335
birth control, 273–4, 280–2
Blast, 27–8, 107, 301, 438
Bletchley Park, 405, 409
blindness *see* disability
Blitz, the, 74, 230, 442
Bloomsbury Group, 426
Blunden, Edmund, 437
Boccioni, Umberto, 29–30, 31, 184–6
  'Against Passéist Venice', 30
  The City Rises, 29
  Development of a Bottle in Space, 185
  Table + Bottle + House, 185–6
  'Technical Manifesto: Futurist Painting', 30, 184
  'Technical Manifesto of Futurist Sculpture', 185
  Unique Forms of Continuity in Space, 184
Bookchin, Murray, 6

Borden, Mary
  The Forbidden Zone, 439, 440
Boult, Sir Adrian, 231, 234
Bowen, Elizabeth, 97–8, 338
  The Demon Lover and Other Stories, 442
  'Hand in Glove', 134
  The Heat of the Day, 423, 442
  To The North, 97–8
Bradshaw (*Bradshaw's Railway Guide*), 79, 395, 396, 397, 398, 399, 400
Bragaglia, Anton Giulio, 186, 187, 204
Bragg, William, 127, 131
Braidotti, Rosi, 10, 106
Braque, Georges, 184, 244
Breton, André, 203, 204, 205, 411–12, 413, 414
  Introduction au discours sur le peu de réalité, 412–13
  'Manifesto of Surrealism', 203, 411
Brierley, Walter
  Means Test Man, 335
British Wireless for the Blind Fund, 219–20
Brittain, Vera
  Testament of Youth, 439, 440
Britten, Benjamin, 230, 348
Briusov, Valery, 247
broadcasting *see* radio; television
Buenos Aires, 65
Buenos Aires Subte, 65
Bungei Nihon, 203
bureaucracy *see* Civil Service (UK); paperwork
Butts, Mary
  'With and Without Buttons', 134–5

Calendar of the Year (1936), 351, 354
Callon, Michael, 9
Camera Work, 161, 162
camouflage *see* war
Campbell Soup, 145–6
Cannon Towels, 141, 142
Canudo, Ricciotto, 245
Čapek, Karel, *R.U.R. (Rossum's Universal Robots)*, 105, 250

capitalism, 6, 37, 39, 40, 42, 45, 52, 72, 94, 96, 98, 131–32, 138, 229, 336, 408, 421–2
  late capitalism, 6, 308–10, 419, 434
  racial capitalism, 290, 297
car *see* automobile
Carrà, Carlo, 'Against Passéist Venice', 30
Caudwell, Christopher, *Death of an Airman*, 94
Cavalcanti, Alberto, 226, 230, 346, 348, 351
Cendrars, Blaise, 107, 245, 250
Central Intelligence Agency (CIA), 257–8, 259, 265, 267–8; *see also* Office of Strategic Services
Chaplin, Charlie
  City Lights, 226
  Modern Times, 290, 296
Cheese Mites (1903), 317
Chesterton, G. K., 'Literature of Information', 394, 401
cigarettes, 139, 140, 147
cinema, 4, 9, 84, 178, 188, 192–208, 227, 230, 245, 247, 275, 286, 331, 353
  avant-garde, 193, 194, 196, 207, 228
  documentary, 99, 193, 230–9, 337, 338, 346, 348–58, 442–4
  Duchamp, Marcel and, 188
  Edison, Thomas and, 177
  Hollywood, 78, 193, 262
  montage technique, 193, 194, 198, 199–200, 201, 204, 208n, 230, 235, 348, 352
  and race, 193
  Stein, Gertrude and, 197–8
  and surrealism, 199, 202–4
  and time, 199, 201
  and war, 443
  Woolf, Virginia and, 96, 182–3
  see also Gunning, Tom; film; Lumière brothers; Third Cinema movement
Civil Service (UK), 376–89
  19th century roots of, 377, 378, 380
  and information management, 393
  modernisation of, 377
  as 'supreme Post Office', 380, 388

Clair, René, *Entr'acte*, 245
class
 and education, 300–1, 310–11
 middle, 14, 139, 143, 149, 151–2, 155, 165, 309, 331, 333, 377, 399
 upper, 23, 79, 99, 281, 289, 333
 working, 74, 119, 204, 231, 301, 328–39, 352–3, 438
 see also elitism; highbrow art; middlebrow; popular culture
Claudel, Paul, *L'homme et son désir*, 244–5
climate change *see* Anthropocene
clock, 36–48
 and national synchronisation, 346–7, 395, 398–9
Clock of the Long Now, 46
clockwork, 36, 38, 48
Close-Up, 193, 197–8
Cocteau, Jean, 227, 228, 250, 277
 Le Boeuf sur le toit, 248
 Les Mariés de la Tour Eiffel, 244
 Parade, 244
Cold War, 102, 376, 382, 386, 442
colonialism, 45, 47, 73, 135, 182, 183, 290, 296, 371, 400, 423, 436
 settler colonialism, 45, 47, 296
 see also imperialism
Columbia Records, 7, 257, 258, 267
The Coming of the Dial (1933), 351–2, 352–3
computation, 404–16
 algorithmic, 404–6, 409–11, 413, 415, 429
 automatic writing and, 411–15
 Colossus (Bletchley Park), 405, 209
 Enigma code, 405
 human computation, 404–5, 407–9
 machine computation, 404–6, 409–10
Conan Doyle, Arthur *see* Doyle, Arthur Conan
Conrad, Joseph, 183, 394, 438
 Chance, 131–2
 Heart of Darkness, 181–2
 Nigger of the 'Narcissus', 316–17
 Nostromo, 131
 The Secret Agent, 38

Constructivism, 243, 244, 250, 251
Corelli, Marie, 278, 279
Cournos, John, *Babel*, 24
Covid-19, 1, 314, 373, 374n, 439
Craig, Edward Gordon, 247
crash
 car crash, 79, 82
 aeroplane crash, 93, 99, 101
Crisis, The, 54
Crown Film Unit *see* General Post Office (GPO) Film Unit
Cubism, 27, 117, 184, 187, 188, 200, 248, 324, 436, 438
Curtis, Edward, 45–6
 'In a Piegan Lodge', 46, 47
 The North American Indian, 45
cyborg, 9–10, 11, 36, 111; *see also* robot

Dada, 14, 71, 195, 229, 243, 248, 250, 251, 252, 315, 406, 434, 439; *see also* New York Dada
Dalí, Salvador, 204, 412–13, 414
Danius, Sara, 15, 52, 88n, 228
data-mining, 102
deafness *see* disability
de Chirico, Giorgio, 245
decision problem *see* Entscheidungsproblem
Delaunay, Sonia, 108, 184
Deleuze, Gilles, 86, 87, 201
Deleuze, Gilles and Félix Guattari, 304, 306
de Maré, Rolf, 244
Depero, Fortunato 244, 248–9, 250
De Quincey, Thomas, 396, 398
de Saint-Exupéry, Antoine, 441
De Stijl, 243, 250
de Zayas, Marius, 109, 119
 'Elle', 116–17
Diaghilev, Sergei, 244, 249
Dickens, Charles, 330
 Hard Times, 37, 330
Dietrich, Marlene, 257–70
 Marlene Dietrich Overseas 257–8, 259, 263–8
digital humanities, 4, 16n, 414, 415, 417–31

digital technology, 4, 106, 309, 404, 405
disability, 52, 212–21
    blindness, 212–21
    British Wireless for the Blind Fund, 219–20
    and eugenics, 213, 289
    hearing loss, 212, 220, 222n, 328–9, 332–7
    speech impairment, 220–1
disability studies, 4, 52, 212–13, 215, 216
discourse network, 11, 421, 423
Disney, 45
Dix, Otto, 438
documentary film *see* cinema
domesticity
    in advertising, 143, 147–8, 149
    in cinema, 194, 226
    clocks and, 45
    electric light and, 23
    in Gilman, 367–9
    and health, 315, 319
    and listening, 233, 234, 257, 266–7
    photography and, 155, 161, 167–8
    as refuge from modernisation, 107, 354
    technology and domestic labour, 4, 105, 294, 304, 315, 329, 367–9
    in Stein, 414–15
domestic space, 45, 161, 168, 257, 319, 357
Doomsday Clock, 38, 43–4, 47
Dos Passos, John, 2
    Manhattan Transfer, 423
    USA Trilogy, 418, 419
Doyle, Arthur Conan
    'The Adventure of the Dying Detective', 322
    The Valley of Fear, 398
Dresden International Photography Exhibition, 163
Du Bois, W. E. B., 281, 287, 297n
    'The Princess Steel', 287
Duchamp, Marcel, 108, 109–12, 115, 117, 119, 187, 188, 434
    Fountain, 320
    The Large Glass (Bride Stripped Bare by her Bachelors, Even), 106, 109, 111–12

Mariée (Bride), 110
Nu descendant un escalier, no. 2, 188–9
Passage de la vierge à la mariée (Passage from Virgin to Bride), 111
Dulac, Germaine, 192–208
    Arabesques, 195, 196, 197
    La Coquille et le clergyman, 193, 201–2
    and Debussy, 195, 197, 201
    and female gaze, 208
    and female temporality, 202
    Gossette, 196
    and Impressionism, 197
    and non-anthropocentrism, 208
    and rhythm, 195–6, 199
    La Souriante Madame Beudet, 201
    and surrealism, 199, 202
    Thèmes et variations, 205–6

Edison, Thomas, 106, 177, 181, 297
education, 145, 167, 300–13
    health, 317–18
    industrial, 290–1, 293
    and literacy, 393, 401–2
Egoist, The, 67, 129, 425
Eiffel Tower, 66, 74, 228, 244
Einstein, Albert, 40–1, 47, 182
    Relativity: The Special and General Theory, 40
Elbe, Lili, 278–9
electricity, 23–33
    age of, 25–6, 32
    domestication of, 23
    electric light *see* artificial light
    electric shock treatment, 295, 439
    nature of, 26
    see also infrastructure
Eliot, T. S., 32, 53, 134
    The Idea of a Christian Society, 301–2
    'Rhapsody on a Windy Night', 28–9
    'Tradition and the Individual Talent', 420
    'The Waste Land', 227, 319–20, 402, 423, 433, 439–40
elitism, 3, 5, 167, 172n, 311n, 353–4
    and education, 300–1
    see also class; highbrow art; middlebrow; popular culture

Ellis, Havelock, 275, 276, 277
Ellison, Ralph, *Invisible Man*, 287, 288, 290, 293–5, 297
Ellul, Jacques, 8
energy, 26–7, 32, 56, 186, 187, 199, 277, 278, 307, 334, 366, 388, 396, 422
Enquire Within Upon Everything (1856), 390–1, 392
ether, 27
ethics, technology and, 10, 310, 376, 379, 382, 441
eugenics, 273, 274, 277–8, 279, 280–1, 408
  and education, 301–2
  and disability, 213, 289
  and germ theory, 320–1
  and race 288–90
Expressionism, 251, 322, 323, 434, 438, 439

factory, 6, 39, 235, 237, 239, 244, 252
  Industrial Health Research Board (Industrial Fatigue Research Bureau), 333–5, 338, 340n
  noise of, 328–39
  racialisation of, 288–90, 291, 292, 293, 294–5, 296, 297
fascism, 5, 290, 422, 233, 239, 441, 442; *see also* Nazi Germany; Second World War
Faulkner, William, 441
  Pylon, 441
  The Sound and the Fury, 42
Fauset, Jessie Redmon, 54
Federal Bureau of Investigation (FBI), 258–64
Feininger, T. Luxe, 252–3
feminism, 145, 213, 369
film, 11, 87, 108, 134, 178, 213, 226, 227, 230, 231, 232, 235, 245, 251, 252, 317, 318, 322, 421, 443–4
  car chase film, 82, 84
  digital film, 404, 443
  documentary film, 99, 237, 238, 252, 337, 338, 346–55
  film criticism, 193, 197
  psychoanalytic film theory, 200, 205
  silent film, 70, 207, 226
  sound film, 230, 331
  see also cinema; *Close-Up*; General Post Office (GPO) Film Unit
fin de siècle, 1, 79, 91, 347
First World War, 24, 103, 105, 402
  aeroplanes in, 93
  and the avant-garde, 243, 432, 434–5, 436
  and blindness, 219
  in film, 442–4
  and gender, 145, 357
  and hearing loss, 332, 333–4
  and infrastructure, 345, 420
  nursing and health, 148, 277–8, 311, 439–40
  trench warfare, 100, 311, 436, 437–8, 440–4
Fitzgerald, F. Scott, 433, 440
flâneur, 28, 83, 88n
flapper, 94, 105, 147, 149, 151
Flusser, Vilém, 11–12, 16n
Ford, Ford Maddox, 391, 394–5, 401, 433, 438
Ford, Henry, 286, 287–8, 290, 295, 296
  My Life and Work, 289–90
Fordism, 286–90, 292
Ford Motor Company, 144, 147, 287, 290, 292
Foregger, Nikolai, 245, 249
Forel, Auguste, 275
Forster, E. M., 399–400, 401
  Howards End, 24, 232
  'The Machine Stops', 1, 4
  Maurice, 276–7
  Passage to India, 324, 400–1
  A Room with a View, 399–400
  Where Angels Fear to Tread, 399
Foucault, Michel, 291, 292, 295
  biopolitics, 329, 335
  Discipline and Punish, 237, 292
  History of Sexuality, 274
  'Of Other Spaces', 41
Frazier, E. Franklin, 281
Fremlin, Celia, *War Factory: A Report*, 330, 338

Freud, Sigmund, 86, 106, 155, 277, 318
  and cinema, 205
  and hypnosis, 275
  Studies on Hysteria, 190
  and war trauma, 439–40
Fülöp-Miller, René, 249
Fulton Report (1968), 377
Future's in the Air, The (1937), 99
Futurism, 40, 64, 88
  in film, 204
  Italian, 27, 29–31, 32, 78, 82, 83, 86, 96, 108–9, 117, 184–8, 204, 251, 286, 330, 438
  in music, 228, 229
  in performance, 243–52
  Russian, 247
  and war, 432, 434, 438, 440, 441

Gaskell, Elizabeth, *North and South*, 330–1
Gaudier-Brzeska, Henri, 438
Gayton, Bertram, 279
gender, 24, 31, 51, 78, 105–9, 111, 115, 119, 139, 140, 141, 145, 147, 148, 149, 178, 221, 275, 277, 294, 318, 338, 372, 373, 425, 439; *see also* transgender
General Electric, 145–6, 373
General Post Office, Dublin, 356
General Post Office (GPO) Film Unit 226, 230–9, 337, 345–6, 348–56, 358, 359n
  Crown Film Unit, 346
  see also 6:30 Collection; *BBC: The Voice of Britain*; *Calendar of the Year*; *The Coming of the Dial*; Jennings, Humphrey; *Listen to Britain*; *Night Mail*; Watt, Harry
General Post Office (UK postal system), 345, 378
germs, 314–27
  cholera, 316, 321
  influenza, 314, 317, 319, 320, 323, 439
  tuberculosis, 316, 317, 319, 320
  see also health
ghosts, 133–5

Gilman, Charlotte Perkins, 364, 365, 366, 367–72, 373
  'Bee Wise' 368–9
  Concerning Children, 367–8
  on domesticity, 367–9
  Human Work, 367
Gitelman, Lisa, 9, 11, 379, 383
glass, 4, 24, 31, 32, 66, 78, 81, 82, 95, 126, 128–30, 422
global warming *see* Anthropocene
Gödel, Kurt, 407
Goldschmidt, Richard, 279–80
Good Housekeeping, 138, 315
GPO *see* General Post Office (GPO) Film Unit
Graham, Kenneth, *The Wind in the Willows*, 79
gramophone, 227, 228, 232, 330, 338, 340n, 423, 440; *see also* phonograph; sound recording
Gramsci, Antonio, 247, 287–8
Grand Hotel (1932), 421
Graves, Robert
  Goodbye to All That, 438
Great War *see* First World War
Green, Henry, 143
  Living, 133
Greenberg, Clement, 16, 324
Greene, Graham, 98–9, 320
  The Bear Fell Free, 93
  England Made Me, 98
Greenwood, Walter, *Love on the Dole* 331–2, 335–6
Grierson, John, 230, 237, 346, 351, 359n
Gropius, Walter, 243, 246, 248, 251, 252
Grosz, George, 250
Guattari, Félix and Gilles Deleuze, 304, 306
Guillory, John, 13, 391
Gunning, Tom, 178, 200
Gwynn-Browne, Arthur. *FSP*, 99

H. D., 134, 197, 198, 208, 417, 425
Habermas, Jürgen, 436–7
Haeckel, Ernst, 41–2
Hall, Radclyffe, 276, 278, 280
Halpern, Moyshe-Leyb, 74

Halstead, Ivor, *Post Haste*, 345
Hanley, James, 'The Machines Stop', 335–6
Haraway, Donna, 9–10, 120; see also cyborg
Haviland, Paul, 108, 109, 114
Hayles, N. Katherine, 10, 309
health
  birth control, 273–4, 280–2
  hearing loss, 212, 220, 222n, 328–9, 332–7
  Industrial Health Research Board (Industrial Fatigue Research Bureau), 333–5, 338, 340n
  nausea, 94, 135, 332
  nursing, 439–40
  pregnancy, 281–2
  trauma, 93, 229, 238, 332, 433, 438–41
  vasectomy, 277
  see also disability; germs; sex; sexuality
Heidegger, Martin, 'The Question Concerning Technology', 6, 302, 305
Hemingway, Ernest, 2, 433, 440, 441
  A Farewell to Arms, 440
heterochrony, 41–2
highbrow art, 83, 199, 229, 238, 438; see also popular culture; middlebrow
Hilbert, David, 405, 406–7, 409
Hillary, Richard, *The Last Enemy*, 99–100
Hiroshima see nuclear weapons
Hirschfeld, Magnus, 275, 277
history, 44–8, 370
  Black history, 372, 373, 381
Hobbes, Thomas, *Leviathan*, 351
Hoffman, E. T. A., 245–6, 308
Hogarth Press, 51, 52, 53, 54, 426
Holden, Inez, *Night Shift*, 338
Holt, William, 336
Honegger, Arthur, 228, 244–5
  Pacific 231, 245
Hoover, J. Edgar, 259–60, 262, 263
Hopkins, Pauline E., 364, 365, 369–73

'The New York Subway', 363–4, 367, 369
Of One Blood, 366, 370–3
Horkheimer, Max, 5–6, 84, 435
hormones, 273–4, 277–80
Hulme, T. E., 438
humanism, 3, 5, 11, 36, 38–9, 41, 251, 294–5, 305, 307, 312n, 395, 441; see also anthropocentrism; posthumanism
Hurston, Zora Neale, 287
Husserl, Edmund, 406
Huszár, Vilmos 245, 248, 250
Huxley, Aldous, 322–3, 329, 391, 401–2
  After Many a Summer, 279
  Antic Hay, 24
  Brave New World, 279, 288–90, 292, 302, 315
  'Education', 302
hypnosis, 203, 275–7
  mesmerism, 370

Image, as Vorticist concept, 27–8
Imagism, 27, 324, 424, 437
Imperial Airways, 99
imperialism, 37, 40, 46, 73, 88, 119, 157, 182, 204, 232, 234, 235, 320, 336, 357, 386, 433, 436, 441, 442, 444; see also colonialism
Impressionism, 81, 197
Industrial Health Research Board see factory
influenza see germs
information, 390–403, 408–9, 422–3
  19th and 20th century proliferation, 393
  as genre, 390–2
  storage of, 392
  see also Bradshaw, Baedeker; *Tit-Bits*; *Whitaker's Almanack*
infrastructure, 38, 40
  electrical, 294–5, 330, 348, 364–5
  as large technological system, 365–6, 368
  and nation-state, 345–61
  scales of, 366

intermediality, 176, 178, 188–90, 227–8, 230–2, 239n, 248; *see also* remediation
International, The, 29
Ireland
    Easter Rising, 356–7, 358
    Irish Republican Army, 355
    Shannon Scheme, 25
Irish Homestead, The, 319
iron, 13, 118, 126, 130–3, 248

J. Walter Thompson Company, 264–5
Jackson, Peter, 442–4
James, Henry, 427
    In the Cage, 422
Jameson, Frederic, 85, 287
Jarry, Alfred, 248, 252
jazz, 227, 229, 334
Jennings, Humphrey, 227, 230–1, 235–6, 237–9, 337; *see also* Listen to Britain
Jones, David, *In Parenthesis*, 438
Jouet, Jacques, 'Metro Poems', 74–5
Joyce, James, 7, 10, 38
    'After the Race', 79–80, 82
    Ulysses, 10, 38, 83, 132–3, 296, 319, 324, 394, 428–9
Jünger, Ernst, *Storm of Steel*, 438, 439

Kafka, Franz, 322, 324, 442
Kandinsky, Wassily, 230, 246–7, 251, 322, 436
Käsebier, Gertrude, 156–71
    'Blessed Art Thou among Women', 155, 158
    and commercialism, 157, 163, 165, 170
    and family, 156, 161, 165, 167, 168, 170, 171
    and Lakota people, 157
    'Lollipops', 155, 156, 157, 160, 168, 171
    'The Manger (Ideal Motherhood)', 155, 159, 162
    and motherhood, 155, 157, 160, 170
    and pictorialism, 162, 164
    and portraiture, 155, 164, 167, 168
    'Real Motherhood', 168
    and Stieglitz, 157, 160, 161, 162, 163
    studio, 160, 161, 164, 168
    and whiteness, 157, 162
    'Yoked and Muzzled (Marriage)', 167
Kiesler, Friedrich, 250
Kilmer, Joyce, 68
Kinugasa, Teinosuke, *A Page of madness (Kurata ippeiji)*, 203–4
Kipling, Rudyard, 'Wireless', 319
Kittler, Friedrich, 11, 421, 423
Kodak, 163–4, 165, 167
    Kodak girl, 164, 167
Kotex, 148
Kracauer, Siegfried, 207
    The Mass Ornament, 6
    Theory of Film, 199
Kupka, František, 187
    The Dream, 188
    Panes by Colours, Large Nude, 188
Kyrou, Ado (Adonis), 199–200, 204, 206

labour *see* class; factory
Ladies' Home Journal, 138, 140, 315
Lamarr, Hedy, 229
Lang, Fritz, *Metropolis*, 106, 109, 226
Larsen, Nella, *Quicksand*, 281
Latour, Bruno, 9, 72, 427
Law, John, 9
Lawrence, D. H., 10, 40, 300–13
    'Education of the People', 300, 303, 304, 307–11
    'Fantasia of the Unconscious', 300, 302, 303, 307, 310, 311, 315
    Lady Chatterley's Lover, 126, 281–2
    'What Is a Man to Do?', 131
Lawrence, T. E.
    The Mint, 442
    Seven Pillars of Wisdom, 441–2
Le Corbusier, 319
Léger, Fernand, 108, 184, 226, 244, 245, 250; *see also* Ballet mécanique
Legg, Stuart, 226, 227, 230–1, 232–3, 234, 351; *see also* BBC: The Voice of Britain; The Coming of the Dial
Lempicka, Tamara de, 'Self Portrait in the Green Bugatti', 86
Lewis, Cecil, *Sagittarius Rising*, 100

Lewis, Wyndham, 26–8, 301, 438, 440
  The Art of Being Ruled, 301
  Blast Manifesto, 107–8
  'A Review of Contemporary Art', 27
  see also Blast
library, 55, 258, 314–5
Life (magazine), 179, 180
light-bulb, 113; *see also* artificial light
Lippmann, Walter, 7, 289
Lissitsky, El, 243, 247, 250
Listener, The, 231
Listen to Britain (1942), 227, 230, 231, 235, 337
Little Review, The, 108, 428
Loew, Heinz, 245, 248
lollipop, 154
London, 23, 25, 28–9, 38, 42, 63, 64, 68, 69, 73, 96, 97, 99, 100, 129 132, 230, 263, 289, 317, 336, 350, 352, 357, 390, 422
London Underground, 69, 73
Loy, Mina, 29–32
  'Café du Néant', 29
  Insel, 276, 422, 426
  lampshade designs, 31–2
  rue du Colisée shop, 32
  Two Plays, 247
  verrovoile, invention of, 32
Lukács, Georg, *History and Class Consciousness*, 39
Lumière brothers, 175, 190

McCutcheon, Wallace, *The X-Ray Mirror*, 178
McKay, Claude, 287
  'Subway Wind', 74
McLuhan, Marshall, 2, 7–8, 15
  The Gutenberg Galaxy, 2
  The Medium is the Massage, 7–8
  Understanding Media, 2, 8
MacNeice, Louis, *Alexander Nevsky*, 216
magazines *see* periodicals
Malevich, Kasimir, 244, 248
manifesto, 16n, 207, 228, 248, 249, 330, 411, 432
  Blast Manifesto, 107–8
  Futurist Manifesto ('The Founding and Manifesto of Futurism'), 30, 78, 82, 248, 432, 434
  'Manifesto of Futurist Dance', 249
  'Manifesto of Surrealism', 203, 411
  'Technical Manifesto: Futurist Painting', 30, 184
  'Technical Manifesto of Futurist Sculpture', 185
Mann, Thomas, 182, 319
Mansfield, Katherine
  'Revelations', 132
  'The Wrong House', 132
Marcuse, Herbert, 5, 435
Marey, Étienne-Jules, 186, 188, 205
Mariën, Marcel, 200, 202–3, 204
Marinetti, F. T., 30, 31, 108, 113, 186, 248–9, 250, 286, 434, 438, 440
  'Against Passéist Venice', 30
  'The Founding and Manifesto of Futurism', 30, 78, 82, 248, 432
  'Let's Murder the Moonlight', 9, 31
  Poupées électrique, 108–9
  Zang Zang Tumb, 228
Marlene Dietrich Overseas (1951)
  see Dietrich, Marlene
Marshall, Paule, *Brown Girl, Brownstones*, 294
Marson, Una, 54
Marx, Karl, 82, 84
  Capital, 82, 84–5, 330
  The Poverty of Philosophy, 39
Marx, Leo, 2, 364
Massine, Léonide, 244, 249
Mass Observation, 100, 235
  People in Production, 330, 340n
  War Factory: A Report, 330, 338
mathematics
  algorithms in, 404–6, 409–11, 413, 415
  calculus, 406, 408, 409
  computability theory, 405, 409–411
  Entscheidungsproblem (decision problem), 405–6
  graph theory, 420
  in literature, 406
  modernist autonomy of, 406

Seven Bridges of Königsberg problem, 428
Matisse, Henri, 215
  'The Windshield, On the Road to Villacoublay', 81–2, 87
Maule, Francis, 145
Mayakovsky, Vladimir, 73–4
mechanomorph, 106, 111, 114, 117, 118, 187
media archaeology, 11, 16n, 38, 48
Méliès, Georges, *Les Rayons Röntgen*, 178
menstruation, 148
Mesmer, Franz Anton, 275; *see also* hypnosis
Metzl, Lothar, 265–6
Meyerhold, Vsevolod, 243, 250, 251
microphone *see* sound recording
microscope, 178, 207, 315, 317–18, 320, 322–4
microwave oven, 9
middlebrow, 68, 90, 391; *see also* class; elitism; highbrow art; popular culture
middle class *see* class; elitism; middlebrow
Milhaud, Darius 244–5
  Machines agricoles, 245
Miller, Mitch, 258, 266, 267
Mirrlees, Hope, *Paris*, 69, 70–1, 73
modern woman, the, 139, 140, 160
Moholy-Nagy, László, 207, 243, 245, 246, 248, 250–1, 252
Moll, Albert, 275
moonlight, 29, 30–1
Moscow, 74
Moscow Metro, 65, 73
motherhood, 141, 155, 158, 157, 160, 162, 169
movie *see* cinema
movie camera, 84, 87
Mozart, Wolfgang Amadeus, 231, 237–8, 246
Mumford, Lewis, 6, 39
  The City in History, 63
  The Pentagon of Power, 8
  Technics and Civilization, 39
  Technics and Human Development, 6
Murnau, F. W., *Nosferatu, eine Symphonie des Grauens*, 207
music, 226–42
  'classical', 230–4, 237–8, 246
  dance music, 227, 232
  Dietrich, Marlene, 257–8, 263–8
  folk, 227, 231
  jazz, 227, 229, 334
  opera 227, 230, 239n, 246, 247
Music While You Work, 231, 235–7, 239, 330, 338, 340n
Muybridge, Eadweard, 79, 188
Muzak Corporation, 265

Naether, Carl, 141
Nash, Paul, 101–2
  'Aerial Flowers', 101
  'The Personality of Planes', 101
  Totes Meer (Dead Sea), 101–2
  We Are Making a New World, 434, 443
nation, 345–61
  infrastructural model, 346–8
National Grid (Great Britain, 1926–46), 25
Native Americans, 47–8, 369, 417
  Blackfoot, 45–7
  Lakota, 157
Nazi Germany, 5, 102, 239n, 260, 261, 267, 287, 290, 295, 382, 405, 435, 438
  anti-Semitism, 287, 321
  Enigma code, 405
  Holocaust, 382, 439
  see also fascism; Second World War
network, 43, 97, 99, 417–31
  computer, 420
  discourse, 11, 421, 423
  modernist depictions of, 421–3
  and modernist style, 423–4
  network analysis, 417, 418–19, 426–9
  network imaginary, 418–19, 421
  publication, 54, 425–6
  reception, 426–9
  social, 419–20
  telecommunication, 39, 42, 420, 421–2
  textile, 419, 426

network (*cont.*)
  utility 25
  visualisations, 418–19, 427–8
  see also computation; information; infrastructure
new modernist studies, 2, 51, 213, 287, 417, 426
newspaper, 68, 71, 73, 249, 386–7
  as information source, 391–2, 395, 398
  and national community, 346–7, 395
  The New York Times, 66, 428
  The Times (London), 127, 395, 396
  see also periodicals
New Woman, the, 105, 113, 116, 117, 118, 119
New York, 24, 31, 42, 65, 74, 147, 157, 161, 163, 228, 265
New York Dada, 106, 107, 434
New York (City) Subway, 65, 70, 71, 367, 369, 373
Night Mail (1936), 230, 337, 348, 349, 350, 352, 355, 359n
Nijinska, Bronislava, 245, 249
Nin, Anaïs, 51–9
  The Diary of Anaïs Nin, 54, 55, 56, 57, 58
  and Gonzalo More, 55, 57
  and letterpress printing, 54, 55, 57, 58, 59
  and the novel, 58
  and print marketplace, 55–6, 57, 59
  and Second World War, 55
  'The Story of My Printing Press', 58–9
  and trauma, 58, 59
  Winter of Artifice, 54, 58, 59
noise
  abatement, 239n, 328–30, 332, 333
  in avant-garde performance, 243, 245, 247, 248, 252
  and hearing loss, 328–9, 332–7
  industrial, 328–41
  Industrial Health Research Board (Industrial Fatigue Research Bureau), 333–5, 338, 340n
  of iron, 131–3
  measurement of, 328–9
  in music, 228–32, 234, 235, 237, 238, 239n, 355
  Noise Abatement League (Anti Noise League), 329, 330, 332, 333, 335
Noise Abatement League *see* noise
nuclear science, 43–4, 379, 381, 387–8
  UK nuclear energy programme, 376
nuclear weapons, 102, 376, 377, 379, 381–2, 385, 386, 387
  disarmament, 381, 385–6
  Hiroshima, 379, 383–4
nuclear war, 43

obscenity, 275, 276, 280, 323, 438
Odle, E. V., *The Clockwork Man*, 36
Office of Strategic Services (OSS), 257–8, 259
  Morale Operations Division, 258, 264–5
  Muzac Project, 265–6
  see also Central Intelligence Agency
Orphism, 187
Orwell, George
  'England, Your England', 345
  Nineteen Eighty-Four, 442
Out of Chaos (1944), 101
Owen, Wilfred, 437–8, 439, 440, 441

Paladini, Vinicio, 245, 246, 249, 250
Pankhurst, Sylvia, 357; *see also* suffragette/suffragist
Pannaggi, Ivo 245, 246, 249, 250
paperwork, 376–89
  documents, 258–62, 379–83, 385, 391
  FBI record-keeping, 257–63
  précis style of, 386–7
Paris, 29, 32, 64, 97, 69, 72, 74, 244, 263, 434
Paris Métro, 66, 69
performance, 243–56
  dance, 178, 195, 204, 205–6, 244–6, 247, 249, 250–4; *see also* ballet
  musical, 231–4, 257, 265–6; *see also* music
  theatrical, 177–8, 243, 244, 245, 247–8, 250, 251–4

periodicals
  291 (magazine), 108, 114, 116
  advertisements, 138–52, 167
  Blast, 27–8, 107, 301, 438
  Bungei Nihon, 203
  Camera Work, 161, 162
  Close-Up, 193, 197–8
  Crisis, The, 54
  De Stijl, 243, 250
  Egoist, The, 67, 129, 425
  Good Housekeeping, 138, 315
  International, The, 29
  Irish Homestead, The, 319
  Ladies' Home Journal, 138, 140, 315
  Life, 179, 180
  Listener, The, 231
  Little Review, The, 108, 428
  magazines, modernist, 51, 138, 198, 250
  as network, 425
  Perspective, 427
  Poetry, 67
  Printer's Ink, 143
  Radio Times, 219, 220, 231, 232
  Suffragette, The, 357
  Tit-Bits, 393–4, 395
  Vogue, 101, 140
  Voice of the Negro, The, 363, 369
  see also newspapers
Perspective, 427
Perspex, 133
pharmakon, 302–3, 308–11
phatic communication, 260, 263, 268n
phonograph, 108, 229, 244, 247, 297n, 329, 393, 421, 422
  long-playing record (LP), 257–8, 266–8
  see also gramophone; sound recording
photography, 9, 45, 52, 79, 86, 102, 134, 140, 155, 182, 185, 186, 190, 207, 251, 393
  Camera Lucida (Roland Barthes), 160, 170–1, 175
  Towards a Philosophy of Photography (Vilém Flusser), 11
  x-ray photography, 176, 178, 179, 181, 183

see also, Käsebier, Gertrude; Stieglitz, Alfred; Marey, Étienne-Jules; Muybridge, Eadweard; Schatz, Howard
photo-journalism, 291
Picabia, Francis, 106, 108, 109, 113–17, 118, 119, 120n, 184, 188, 243
  Américaine, 111, 113
  Fille née sans mère, 114–15
  Mechanical Expression Seen Through Our Own Mechanical Expression, 187
  Portrait d'une jeune fille américaine dans l'état de nudité, 111, 113
  Relâche, 245, 246
  Voilà ELLE, 115–16
Picasso, Pablo, 33n, 244, 184, 244, 250, 434
  Guernica, 31, 442
Pictorialism, 162, 164
Pirandello, Luigi, 245
plastic, 125, 133, 257
Poetry, 67
Political Warfare Executive (UK), 264
popular culture, 198, 394; see also highbrow art; middlebrow; elitism
Porter, Katherine Anne, *Pale Horse, Pale Rider*, 439
postal system, 347, 351, 356, 358, 378, 380; see also General Post Office (UK); US Postal Service
postcolonialism, 48
posthumanism, 3, 9–11, 12, 15, 106, 120, 287, 307, 439, 443; see also Actor-Network Theory; cyborg
Poulenc, Francis, 227–8, 232
  La Voix humaine, 227
Pound, Ezra, 7, 27, 32, 424, 438
  'A Few Don'ts by an Imagiste', 324
  'In a Station of the Metro', 67
  'The Series Artist', 26
Prampolini, Enrico, 248, 250
print, 51–62; see also newspaper; periodicals
Printer's Ink, 143
Progessive Era, 157, 296

propaganda, 6–7, 257–70, 321, 346, 357, 398, 402, 433, 435–6, 437–8, 439
prosthesis, technology as, 14–15, 16, 56, 83, 88, 222n, 274, 433, 437, 439, 445n
public relations, 6–7
public sphere, 167, 187, 235, 239, 354, 367–8, 373
Publish It Yourself Handbook, The, 54
puppetry, 226, 235, 244, 245, 247–8, 250
Puteaux group, 184, 187, 188

race, 286–99, 363–4, 369–73
   and advertising, 139, 149
   and architecture, 4
   and cinema, 193–4
   and eugenics, 280–1, 289–90
   and Fordism, 287–8
   and health policy, 321, 373
   Jim Crow segregation, 287, 291–2
   and print technology, 51–2
   see also eugenics; Native Americans; racial capitalism; whiteness
Rachilde, *Monsieur Vénus*, 107
radar, 9, 238
radio, 4, 9, 25, 134, 212–21, 227, 230, 231, 232, 276, 319, 329, 330, 331, 337, 338
   amateur radio, 221
   and blindness, 212–21
   broadcasting, 357, 393, 420
   feature, 217–18
   intimacy, 216, 217, 220
   listener, 214–15, 216, 217, 218, 219, 220, 222, 234
   and war, 436, 438
radio drama, 215, 216, 217–19, 227
'radio modernism', 212–13, 214, 222n
radio play, 212
Radio Times, 219, 220, 231, 232
railway, 64, 65, 66, 67, 72, 95, 96, 97, 134, 279, 348, 349, 362, 364, 393, 398, 421
   railway timetables, 391; see also Bradshaw

Rancière, Jacques, 311n
Ray, Man, 193, 198
Remarque, Erich Maria, *All Quiet on the Western Front*, 438
remediation, 8, 167, 228, 229, 231; see also intermediality
reverberes, 28
Rhys, Jean, 59, 320
   Voyage in the Dark, 52
Richardson, Dorothy, 129
   The Tunnel, 24
   Pilgrimage, 24, 129
Richter, Hans, 252
robot, 105, 106, 107, 108, 109, 114, 115, 117, 119, 120, 246, 305
Röntgen, Anne Berthe, 175, 181, 190
Röntgen, Wilhelm, 175, 190
Rosenberg, Isaac, 437–8
Rosenhain, Walter, 127, 128
Royal Air Force, 92, 237, 441
rubber, 24, 107, 125, 126
Ruskin, John, 131, 401
Russell, Bertrand, 377, 406
Russolo, Luigi, 30, 185, 243
   'Against Passéist Venice', 30
   The Art of Noise, 228, 330
Ruttman, Walter
   Berlin: Symphony of a Metropolis (*Berlin: Die Sinfonie der Großstadt*), 226, 230, 355, 359n

Sassoon, Siegfried, 437–8, 439, 440, 441, 444
Satie, Erik
   Parade, 228, 244
   Relâche, 245, 246
Schafer, R. Murray, 239n, 330, 333, 336
Schatz, Howard, *Homeless: Portraits of Americans in Hard Times*, 215
Schawinsky, Xanti, 246, 250, 253
Schlemmer, Oskar, 244, 245, 246, 247, 250, 251
   Dance of Forms, 252–3
   Dance of Gestures, 246, 252–3
   The Figural Cabinet, 245, 246
Schmidt, Joost, 245

Schmidt, Kurt 245, 249–50, 252–4
  The Man at the Control Panel, 245
  Mechanical Ballet, 245, 250, 252–4
Schuyler, George, *Black No More*, 287
Schwitters, Kurt 250, 251
  Above and Below, 247
  'Rrrrummmm!!!!', 243
  'Subway Poem', 71
  Ursonate, 252
Second World War, 43, 55, 92, 99, 101, 102, 131, 294, 338, 423, 436, 439, 442
  and broadcasting, 420, 422
  and computation, 392, 405, 409
  Entertainment National Service Association (UK), 330, 338
  factory work in, 235–7, 294, 330, 336, 337–8, 340n
  and nuclear technology, 376, 383; *see also* nuclear weapons
  and sound recording, 257–8, 263–8
  see also fascism; Nazi Germany; Office of Strategic Services; war
Sewell, Anna, *Black Beauty*, 79
sex, 273–85
  biological, 273–4
  pregnancy, 281–2
  vasectomy, 277
  see also birth control; gender; menstruation; motherhood; sexuality
sexuality, 106, 115, 262, 274–7
  machinic, 109, 113–14
  see also gender; sex
Shannon, Claude, 392
Shannon Scheme (Ireland, 1929), 25
Shaw, George Bernard, 234, 316
Simmel, Georg, 'Metropolis and Mental Life', 84
Simondon, Gilbert, 11–12, 16n, 300–13
Sinclair, May, 129–30, 134
  A Defence of Idealism, 129
  Mary Oliver: A Life, 129
Sinclair, Upton, *The Flivver King*, 296
Les Six (The Six), 228, 244; *see also* Honegger, Arthur; Milhaud, Darius; Poulenc, Francis

slavery, 181, 370, 371–2
  factory work likened to, 335–7
  machines as 'slaves', 36, 363
  in USA, 149, 152n, 290, 296, 329
Smith, George Albert, *The X-Rays (The X-Ray Fiend)*, 178
Snow, C. P.
  Corridors of Power, 376–7, 381–2, 384–8
  'New Men' (concept), 377–8
  New Men (novel), 376, 377, 379, 381–4, 386–8
  see also Civil Service (UK); nuclear energy; nuclear weapons; paperwork
soap
  Cadum, 72
  Lifebuoy, 71
  Palmolive, 146, 149
  Woodbury, 146–7
Solomons, Leon, 413–14
Somerville, E. Œ. (Edith Œnone) and Martin Ross (Violet Martin), *Some Experiences of an Irish R.M.*, 79
Sommerfield, John
  May Day, 96–7, 100, 336–7
  The Survivors, 100
sound poetry, 228, 251
sound recording, 217–8, 227, 229, 252, 257–8, 263–8, 286, 287, 329
  high-fidelity recording, 257–8, 266
  magnetic tape, 257, 266
  microphone, 217, 234, 257, 258, 265–6
  see also gramophone; phonograph
Spanish Civil War, 94, 100, 442
Spark, Muriel, *The Comforters*, 422
spark plug, 113
spiritualism, 187, 411
Starling, Ernest 273–4, 279
Stein, Gertrude, 97, 197–8, 200, 206, 208, 413–15, 434
  The Autobiography of Alice B. Toklas, 421
  and automatic writing, 413–15
  The Making of Americans, 414, 415
  'Mrs Emerson', 198

Steinach, Eugen, 277–8
Stevens, Nettie 274
Stevenson, Robert Louis, 'A Plea for Gas Lamps', 23
Stiegler, Bernard 302–3, 308–12
Stieglitz, Alfred, 157, 160, 161, 162, 163, 164, 167, 171
  291 (magazine), 108
  Camera Work, 161, 162
  Photo-Secession, 157, 161, 162, 163, 165
Stoker, Bram, *Dracula*, 316–7, 320
Stopes, Marie 273, 275, 280, 282; *see also* birth control
Stravinsky, Igor, 229, 231
stream of consciousness, 13, 83, 87, 93, 129, 428
Stuckenschmidt, Hans, 250, 253–4
subway, 63–75, 330, 347, 363, 364, 367; *see also* Berlin U-Bahn, Buenos Aires Subte, London Underground, Moscow Metro, Paris Métro
Suez Crisis, 385–6
'Suffrage and the Switch, The' (1923), 145–6, 373
Suffragette, The (newspaper), 357
suffragette/suffragist, 24, 143, 145, 357, 358
Surrealism, 101, 276, 434
  and automatic writing, 411–14
  and cinema, 193, 195, 199–200, 201–4, 205, 208n
  and GPO, 230, 235, 237
Symbolism, 29, 66, 72, 107, 168, 194, 247

Tatlin, Vladimir, 248, 252
Taylor, F. W. *see* Taylorism
Taylorism, 2, 6, 287, 296, 329, 334
technē, 3
technics 6, 8, 15, 38, 39, 301–13, 435
technography, 3, 38
technological determinism, 7–8, 9, 11, 12, 85, 433, 435
telegraph, 25, 26, 39, 42, 52, 78, 83, 91, 95, 131, 175, 319, 345, 348–9, 354, 357, 362, 393–4, 399, 401, 421, 422, 425, 436
telepathy 275, 276
telephone, 9, 25, 52, 85, 97, 227, 329, 351–2, 354, 357, 393 421
television, 7, 8, 9, 58, 134, 213, 346, 393, 420, 421
Teltscher, Georg, 245, 249, 250
  Mechanical Ballet, 245, 250, 252–4
Tennessee Valley Authority (United States, 1933–9), 25
Theater der Klänge, 252
They Shall Not Grow Old (2018), 442–4
Third Cinema movement, 193
Third Programme (BBC), 214
Thomas, Dylan, *Under Milk Wood*, 217–9
time, 25, 36–48
  settler time, 47
Time Machine, The (1960), 42, 43
The Times (London), 127, 395, 396
Tit-Bits, 393–4, 395
Toomer, Jean, 59, 287
  Cane, 52, 424
train *see* railway
transgender, 278–9
transit literature, 97
True Woman, the, 160
tuberculosis *see* germs
Turing, Alan, 405, 407, 409–10, 411, 415
Turner, Hermine, 155, 157, 163, 167, 168
Turner, Mason, 163, 164
Turner, Mina, 155, 157, 160, 163, 164, 166, 167, 168
typesetting, 53, 54, 55, 56, 57, 58, 249, 393, 426
typewriter, 11, 55, 286, 409, 423
Tzara, Tristan, 242, 315, 406

Unclean World, The (1903), 317–18
Union of Soviet Socialist Republics (USSR), 353, 386, 387–8

United Service Organizations (USO), 260, 262
US Post Office, 45, 46, 261, 296–7, 298n

van Neumann, John, 405
vasectomy, 277; see also Steinach, Eugen
Vertov, Dziga, *Man with a Movie Camera*, 226, 230
Villiers de l'Isle-Adam, *L'Ève future*, 106, 111
Vogue, 101, 140
Voice of America, 265
Voice of the Negro, The, 363, 369
Von Freytag-Loringhoven, Baroness Elsa, 'Subjoyride', 71
Von Kleist, Heinrich, 247
Von Schrenk-Notzing, Albert, 275
Von Sternberg, Joseph, 262, 268n
Voronoff, Serge, 277
vortex theory (Helmholtz's), 26
Vorticism, 26, 27, 28, 29, 436, 438, 440

war, 24, 27, 96, 99–102, 332, 398, 432–44
 camouflage, 432, 433, 434–7
 and the 'technological sublime', 433, 440–3
 total war, 237, 258, 433, 434–5, 436–7, 443, 444
 trauma, 93, 229, 238, 332, 433, 438–41
 see also Cold War; First World War; nuclear war; Second World War; Spanish Civil War
Warner, Rex, *The Aerodrome*, 442
Warner, Sylvia Townsend, *Lolly Willowes*, 391–2
Watt, Harry (R. H.), 230, 348, 351, 355; see also Night Mail
Waugh, Evelyn, 87, 93–4
 The Ordeal of Gilbert Pinfold, 422
 Vile Bodies, 93–4
Webster, Daniel, 362, 363–364
Weil, Simone, *The Iliad, or the Poem of Force*, 437
Weiniger, Andor, 245

Wells, H. G., 23, 190, 216–17, 234
 The Time Machine, 190
 'The Country of the Blind' story, 216–17
 'The Country of the Blind' radio adaptations, 217
 The Shape of Things to Come, 408–9
 'The Sleeper Awakes', 23
 'The Stolen Bacillus', 321
 The War of the Worlds, 321
West, Rebecca, *The New Meaning of Treason*, 387–8
West Indies, 74, 294, 297
Whitaker's Almanack, 395, 397–8, 399
whiteness, 149, 151, 157, 162, 280, 291–2, 293–5, 297, 369
 of modernist studies, 287
Wilde, Oscar, 276
Williams, Raymond, 8–9, 239n
Williams, William Carlos, 2, 229, 324
Williams-Ellis, Amabel, *Women in War Factories*, 330, 338
Wilson, Edmund B., 274
wireless see radio
Wittgenstein, Ludwig, *Tractatus Logico-Philosophicus*, 438
Woolf, Leonard, 51, 53
 The Wise Virgins, 395
Woolf, Virginia, 23–4, 37, 42, 96, 98–9, 302
 Between the Acts, 422, 442
 'The Cinema', 96
 'Flying Over London', 98–9
 'Impassioned Prose', 396
 Jacob's Room, 68, 324, 439
 'Kew Gardens', 323
 'The Mark on the Wall' 396–8
 'Modern Fiction', 134, 323
 'Mr Bennett and Mrs Brown', 396
 Mrs Dalloway, 24, 42, 72, 87, 302, 418, 439
 Night and Day, 24
 'On Being Ill', 323
 Orlando, 23, 37, 42, 79, 83, 280, 281, 318

Woolf, Virginia (*cont.*)
   A Room of One's Own, 273, 281, 285, 315
   'Solid Objects', 125, 126
   'Thoughts on Peace in an Air Raid', 442
   Three Guineas, 397, 442
   To The Lighthouse, 183
   The Waves, 423
working class *see* class
Wright, Basil, 348, 359n
Wright, Richard, 287, 288, 290–3, 295, 296–7, 298n
   12 Million Black Voices, 291
   Black Boy, 290–3
   Lawd Today!, 296–7

x-ray, 26, 126–7, 175–91, 207, 278, 286, 295; *see also* photography

Yakulov, Georgi, *Le Pas d'Acier*, 244, 249
Yeats, W. B., 229, 277
   'An Irish Airman Foresees His Death', 98, 441
   On the Boiler, 301
   'The Statues', 357
Yehoash, 74
Young-hae Chang Heavy Industries, *Nippon*, 424

Zola, Émile, *La Bête humaine*, 80

EU representative:
Easy Access System Europe
Mustamäe tee 50, 10621 Tallinn, Estonia
Gpsr.requests@easproject.com

www.ingramcontent.com/pod-product-compliance
Lightning Source LLC
Chambersburg PA
CBHW060333010526
44117CB00017B/2814